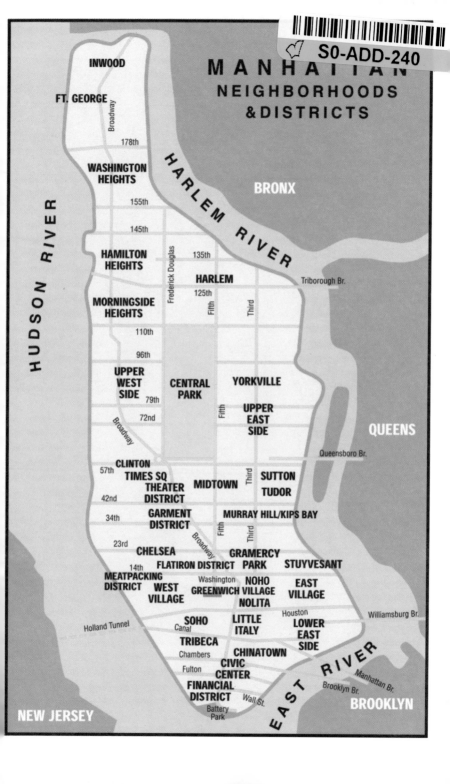

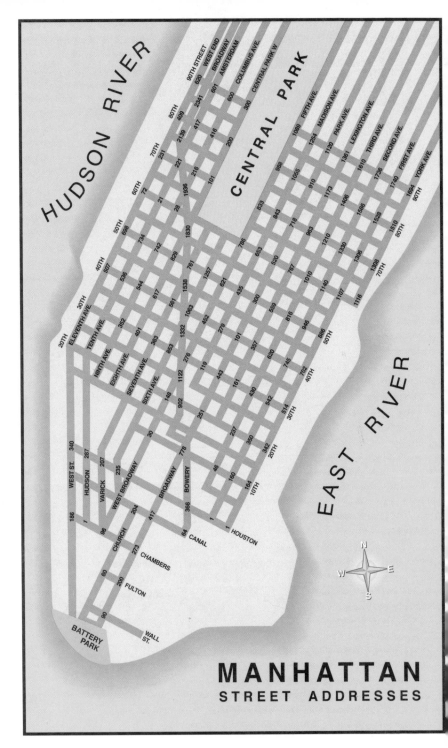

MANHATTAN
STREET ADDRESSES

GERRY FRANK'S

WHERE TO

FIND IT, BUY IT, EAT IT

IN NEW YORK

GERRY FRANK'S
WHERE
TO
FIND IT,
BUY IT,
EAT IT
IN
NEW YORK

GERRY'S FRANKLY SPEAKING, INC.

PO Box 2225
Salem, OR 97308
503/585-8411
800/NYC-BOOK (800/692-2665)
Email: gerry@teleport.com
newyorkcityguidebook.net

Gerry Frank's Where to Find It, Buy It, Eat It in New York
Copyright © 2013
By Gerry Frank

Printed in the United States of America
Library of Congress Catalog Card Number 80-7802

ISBN (13): 978-1879333-24-6

First Edition, 1980
Second Edition, 1981
Third Edition, 1983
Fourth Edition, 1985
Fifth Edition, 1987
Sixth Edition, 1989
Seventh Edition, 1991
Eighth Edition, 1993
Ninth Edition, 1995
Tenth Edition, 1997
Eleventh Edition, 1999
Twelfth Edition, 2001
Thirteenth Edition, 2003
Fourteenth Edition, 2005
Fifteenth Edition, 2007
Sixteenth Edition, 2009
Seventeenth Edition, 2011
Eighteenth Edition, 2013

CONTENTS

Chapter 4
Where to Find It: New York's Best Food Shops

Chapter 5
Where to Find It: New York's Best Services

Chapter 6
Where to Buy It: New York's Best Stores

FROM THE AUTHOR

This 18th edition of **Where to Find It, Buy It, Eat It in New York** is Manhattan's most complete guide. Since the first edition in 1980, I have concentrated on Manhattan (often synonymous with the whole of New York City), which offers residents and tourists a powerful experience. Still in love with my adopted city, I remain insatiably curious about the latest worthwhile retail stores, accommodations, services, restaurants, and museums. Hitting the ground running in search of all these things has been my modus operandi since my soul was first stirred by New York City during childhood visits.

Growing up in a retail family led me to New York and provided me with invaluable training. Through marital liaisons, the Frank family joined with the Meiers to build a major department-store chain that is historic in the annals of retailing history. The first Meier & Frank department store was established in 1857 by my great-grandfather on the banks of the Willamette River in Portland, Oregon. Meier & Frank had its own New York City buying office—an anomaly among retailers and one reason I made so many personal trips to this great city. Today the Meier & Frank stores of old fly under the fine Macy's insignia.

Because the family business was sold, I found myself as a young man without the career I had assumed would be my life's work. So began a second vocation in the political world. I worked for Mark Hatfield, who served Oregon as secretary of state and a two-term governor, and then went on to serve five terms in the U.S. Senate. For 26 years my role was helping with state and federal elections and serving as Hatfield's chief of staff during his lengthy tenure in the Senate. Being in Washington, D.C. with a powerful Senator was stimulating beyond anything I could have imagined. However, for me, the downside to living in our nation's capitol was the round-the-clock clamor, solely focused on politics. I found this confining, if not unhealthy, so I alternated weekends in Oregon and New York.

So began my further accumulation of knowledge about Manhattan, from the familiar to the esoteric. Back in the Senate or at home in Oregon, people would ask me where to go or stay in New York, what to do, and how to find particular items. Finally, they said, "Gerry, you should write a book."

Initially I knew nothing about writing a book but felt confident that I could do the job. Proud of my finished manuscript, I made the rounds of publishing houses in New York. All of them categorically slammed the door in my face. There was no desire for another Manhattan guidebook (especially one written by an Oregonian) or appreciation of my unique expertise. Not to be denied, I decided to self-publish, which left me with several thousand books but no distribution. Off I went, like a door-to-door salesman, to bookstores, hotel gift shops, and anywhere else I thought might benefit from having my book on their shelves.

My efforts have been rewarded through the sale of over 1.1 million copies of **Where to Find It, Buy It, Eat It in New York**. Publishers have since come calling with offers to publish, to which I happily say, "No thanks."

Contemporary New York is much safer and more casual in its expectations and acceptance. New Yorkers were reminded (as we all were) how vulnerable they are with the terrorist attacks of September 11, 2001, but like Americans everywhere they have chosen to rise above the ashes with grace, dignity, and determination. New Yorkers suffered through the dreadful global economic downturn of recent years and the ravages of Hurricane Sandy in 2012. Although many businesses met their demise, life and commerce continues in this bustling metropolis.

Native New Yorkers have told me over the years how much they rely on this book, often referring to it as their Big Apple "bible." One-time tourists and frequent visitors alike also relate how much they depend on it. I hear from readers who ask when the next edition will be published. Nothing pleases me more!

Where to Find It, Buy It, Eat It in New York is a compendium of information and opinions. I mix facts with subjective commentary based on my lifelong interest and expertise in retailing, eating, and travel. No one pays to be listed in my book; these are all my honest choices and appraisals.

I must give credit where credit is due, as I could not have finished the first edition, let alone the 18th, without my team. Cheryl Johnson has been with me since the beginning and capably masters the ins and outs of editorial production. Her husband, Jim, assists Cheryl. Linda Chase relentlessly delves into New York to research my latest finds and make order out of piles of notes and clippings; she is also my very organized executive assistant who keeps my personal life running smoothly. Graphic artist Nancy Chamberlain continues to amaze me with her creative talents. Randy Mishler pulled together all the pieces and presented a fresh look to the format.

It's my honor having you among my readers. Sincerely, I hope you enjoy using ***Where to Find It, Buy It, Eat It in New York*** to help navigate the stimulating streets and eclectic sights of the greatest city in the world.

Gerry Frank

Chapter I

IN AND AROUND THE **WORLD'S GREATEST CITY**

GETTING TO NEW YORK

New York is a popular destination for tourists from around the world. Whether you are a first-time tourist or a regular visitor, you're in for a wonderful treat. Planes, trains, and automobiles bring over 46 million visitors a year to Manhattan.

Three major airports serve New York City, and 110 million passengers annually pass through them on about 100 carriers. **LaGuardia Airport** is most frequently used for domestic flights. **John F. Kennedy International Airport** has both domestic and international flights, as does **Newark Liberty International Airport**, located across the Hudson River in New Jersey. I don't recommend landing at Newark if you are going to the city; it is an expensive hassle.

The most common means of traveling between these airports and Manhattan are by taxicab, shuttle bus, and car or limousine service. Ground transportation representatives at each airport are pros at recommending the best way to reach your destination. Public transportation is usually the least expensive alternative but may take the longest time. Moreover, you will have to load and unload your own luggage and may have to make one or more transfers. Shared-ride vans, such as SuperShuttle, offer door-to-door service, which may make for a lengthy trip into the city. Taxicabs are readily available, and if there are two or more in your party, they can be a good deal. To avoid the chaos of taxicabs and mass transit (but pay a bit more), arrange for a private car or limousine. You'll arrive in style and someone else will schlep your luggage.

Airport Contacts

Keep these contacts handy for information on airport parking, ground transportation, driving directions to the airports, airline information, passenger paging, and lost items.

Kennedy (718/244-4444, panynj.gov/airports/jfk.html)

LaGuardia (718/533-3400, panynj.gov/airports/laguardia.html)

Newark Liberty (973/961-6000, panynj.gov/airports/newark-liberty. html)

Amtrak runs in and out of Pennsylvania Station (commonly referred to as **Penn Station**), a major subway hub located beneath Madison Square Garden between 31st and 33rd streets and Seventh and Eighth avenues. While Amtrak's passenger train service is concentrated between Washington, D.C. and Boston on the Acela Express, long- and short-distance trains from all across the country and some Canadian cities also stop at Penn Station.

The station is open 24/7 and tickets can be purchased anytime from the Quik-Trak machines. Hours for the staffed ticket office and checked baggage are from 5:10 a.m. until 9:50 p.m. An enclosed waiting area for ticketed Amtrak passengers is located in the middle of the main concourse. Be prepared! This is the busiest train station in North America, and you will not want to spend more time here than is necessary. (Call Amtrak at 800/872-7245 or go to amtrak.com for fare and schedule information.)

Metro-North Railroad operates frequent train service in and out of **Grand Central Terminal**, serving 122 stations as far away as Poughkeepsie and Brewster in New York State and New Haven and Waterbury in Connecticut. For schedule information, call 511, go to mta.info/mnr, or stop by a ticket window at Grand Central Terminal, 42nd Street and Park Avenue.

The **Long Island Rail Road** (LIRR) operates frequent train service in and out of Penn Station in Manhattan and Atlantic Terminal in downtown Brooklyn. It serves 124 stations in New York City and throughout the length of Long Island. For schedule information, call 511, go to mta.info/lirr, or stop by a ticket window at Penn Station.

While traveling is expensive, bus travel remains a relative bargain. In addition to Greyhound, several express bus companies operate regularly between New York City and Washington, Boston, Philadelphia, and other cities on the East Coast and beyond. Bus fares remain more economical than air or train fares. Amenities vary by operator. Some offer reserved seats, discounts for frequent riders, Wi-Fi, and TVs, but you're on your own for food and beverage. Be sure to check details carefully.

Many buses depart from **Port Authority Bus Terminal** (between Eighth and Ninth avenues from 40th to 42nd streets), others provide scheduled pickups around town. Among the operators: BoltBus, 877/265-8287, boltbus. com; DC2NY, 202/332-2691, dc2ny.com; Greyhound, 800/231-2222, greyhound. com; Megabus, 877/462-6342, megabus.com; and Peter Pan Bus, 800/343-9999, peterpanbus.com.

If you don't have to drive in New York, then don't! The fact that most New Yorkers don't own cars should tell you something. Traffic congestion, extremely aggressive drivers, unbelievably complicated on-street parking regulations — not to mention pricey towing charges and parking fines — are among the reasons to avoid driving. If you must get behind the wheel, then consult a good map or use a GPS, MapQuest, or some other means to get a clear indication of where you're heading. Don't forget to buckle up!

GETTING AROUND
NEW YORK

Compared to most of the world's large cities, Manhattan is much easier to navigate, mainly because it is confined to an island and is therefore relatively compact. Here are some tips on getting around:

WALKING — Moving under one's own power is still my favorite mode of travel in the city. For one thing, the people watching is great! By walking, you will also feel less guilty about having a meal at one of the eateries along your route. Traveling in a north-south direction, 20 blocks are the equivalent of one mile. Most east-west blocks are much longer. Walking is fast, cheap, and the most interesting way to explore the diverse neighborhoods. If you need directions along the way, duck into a shop or ask one of New York's finest. Many New Yorkers are also willing to aid a perplexed tourist pondering a map, but exercise caution when talking to strangers.

SUBWAY — Millions of people ride the subway every day. It's relatively inexpensive, and it's the fastest way to travel between Upper and Lower Manhattan. With the MetroCard system, you can buy a single ride or a 7- or 30-day unlimited ride card, which is accepted on both the subway and bus systems. Cards can be purchased at subway station booths, many neighborhood merchants, and MetroCard vending machines. All machines accept credit cards and ATM/debit cards, and larger machines also accept currency. Station booths take cash only. Up to three children under 44 inches tall can ride free with a fare-paying adult on buses and subways.

Spend a bit of time familiarizing yourself with the map for subway routes, and don't be afraid to ask where to catch a subway and which train to take. Once in the station, digital displays and audio announcements at many stations will provide the length of time until a train is expected to arrive. The days of unintelligible announcements read by individual conductors are all but over. Visit MTA's TripPlanner (tripplanner.mta.info), an online travel itinerary service for subway, rail, bus, and walking directions.

Manhattan subway stations are nearly all underground, and almost all are on a corner marked by signs with a big "M," "MTA", or an illuminated green globe. Although the subway system operates 24 hours a day, not all station entrances are accessible at all times or have full-time agents. Trains generally run every two to five minutes during rush hours, every five to ten minutes during midday, every five to 15 minutes in the evening, and about every 20 minutes between midnight and 6:30 a.m. (Check the schedule for night service.) As you might guess, subway cars can be very crowded during rush hours.

Once you've passed through the turnstiles and are inside a station, you can transfer between lines or ride for as long as you like. With a MetroCard, you can transfer for free onto a bus within two hours — or anytime you want if you're using an unlimited-ride card. Station names are printed on the walls of the stations and announced inside subway cars. Pay close attention at all times so you don't miss your stop. Subway cars usually have at least one map posted. The newest cars have strip maps that show stops along the line, with a digital readout of the upcoming stop and an announcement of the current and next stations.

The MTA has a full list of Rules of Conduct, and I'd like to add some common-sense suggestions to make your subway journey safe and pleasant:

▦ Don't ride in an empty car. At times of low ridership, move to the car with the conductor — usually in the middle of the train.

▦ Don't wear flashy jewelry or display expensive electronic devices like smartphones, laptops, or tablets.

▦ Don't wander around aimlessly.

▦ Don't stand too close to the tracks; always wait behind the yellow line.

▦ Do watch your wallet or purse, particularly in crowded cars, and don't flash cash when purchasing a MetroCard or at any time.

If you have questions or problems regarding the subway or bus systems, contact the **Metropolitan Transportation Authority (MTA)** at 511 between 6 a.m. and 10 p.m. every day or consult the MTA website (mta.info). You'll find schedules, locate the nearest bus stops or subway stations, be informed of travel advisories, and determine fares. There's also an automated "plan a route" option. Follow the prompts, provide your starting and ending locations, answer a couple of questions, and bus and/or subway lines will be suggested, as well as estimated travel time.

BUSES — Buses operate above ground with bus stops at street corners. Look for a round blue sign with a white bus outline. Many are accompanied by a "Guide-A-Ride" information box with a route map and schedule. Not all stops have bus shelters. As you board a bus, double check the destination and be ready to dip your MetroCard into the fare reader. If you don't have a MetroCard, deposit coins for the fare and ask the driver for a transfer to another bus. Since buses do not accept paper currency, be prepared to carry quarters; otherwise, you might be begging your fellow passengers for change to pay your fare. Follow the route map on the bus or check with the bus operator if you have questions about your destination. You'll have a better opportunity to check out the city on a bus, as they offer a slower ride.

A number of buses run on express routes with limited stops, mainly during weekday rush hours. For safety, late-night and early-morning riders can request a dropoff at non-scheduled bus stops. Many museums, attractions, and major

---

Surrounded by Water

Four waterways surround Manhattan. From its origins in upstate New York, the Hudson River flows along the west side of Manhattan. On the northern tip of the island, the eight-mile long Harlem River empties into the East River. The East and Hudson rivers converge to form Upper New York Bay, also referred to as New York Harbor, near Battery Park.

New York City Taxi and Limousine Commission's Taxi Riders' Bill of Rights

As a taxi rider, you have the right to:

- go to any destination in New York City, Westchester County, Nassau County, or Newark Airport.
- decide the route taken, be it the most direct route or one of your choice.
- a safe and courteous driver who obeys all traffic laws.
- a knowledgeable driver who speaks English and knows city geography.
- air conditioning or heat upon request.
- a noise-free trip without gratuitous horn-honking or radio.
- clean, smoke- and scent-free air.
- working seatbelts for all passengers.
- a taxicab with a clean interior, exterior, and partition.
- accompaniment by a service animal.
- a driver who does not use a cell phone (hand-held or hands-free) while driving.
- decline to tip for poor service.
- Pay by credit or debit card.

stores include the nearest bus stops and subway lines with their address information. Maps are readily available throughout the area. Buses are wheelchair accessible and friendly to those who have problems navigating stairs. The MTA's live bus-tracking service, MTA Bus Time™ (http://bustime.mta.info/) now covers all bus routes in the Bronx and Staten Island, with the rest of the boroughs to come online soon. You can use it to track the current locations of upcoming buses.

TAXIS — All officially licensed medallion taxicabs in New York are yellow, have the words "NYC Taxi" or "NYC" and a big "T" with base information written on the side doors, and post their medallion numbers in a box on the roof. Also, color-coded decals are affixed to the rear passenger window, and the driver's credentials are posted. There are many "cars for hire" (known as gypsy cabs).

The **Taxi and Limousine Commission (TLC)** has mandated that all drivers be required to accept major credit and debit cards and that cabs be equipped to process such transactions. A word of warning: scrutinize your credit card receipt before leaving a taxi. If you want to register a complaint or compliment, or report lost or found items, make note of the driver's name and medallion number and contact the Taxi and Limousine Commission at 33 Beaver Street, New York, NY 10004; 212/NEW-YORK (212/639-9675) or 311 (locally); or nyc.gov/taxi.

Your first encounter with a New York taxi may be at an airport. Legitimate taxi lines form in front of most terminals; follow signs to ground transportation. Cab rides into Manhattan are a flat rate from Kennedy and metered fares from

LaGuardia and Newark. Allow about an hour between Kennedy and anywhere in Manhattan and expect to pay about $45, plus bridge or tunnel toll and tip. A cab ride between LaGuardia and midtown will take about half an hour and cost about $30, plus bridge toll and tip. Allow as long as an hour between Newark and Manhattan and plan to pay more — as much as $70, plus a $15 surcharge and tolls. Cab fares begin at $3 the moment you get in, and then you're charged 40 cents for each additional unit, which is each one-fifth of a mile while traveling or each minute while stopped in traffic or at stoplights. There is also a late-evening and early-morning surcharge and a weekday evening peak-hour surcharge. Standard tipping is 15% to 20% of the price of the trip, and debit and credit cards, as well as cash, are accepted.

Enlist the aid of employees at your hotel, restaurant, or other accommodating businesses to call a cab. If you're on your own, look for the lighted middle number on the roof of the cab, which indicates availability. If the light is off, the cabbie already has a fare or is off-duty. Stand on a corner and raise your arm to flag a taxi. You may observe the creative lengths to which some New Yorkers will go to hail a cab. When giving an address or destination to your driver, it's helpful to also provide the cross street. The familiar yellow taxis operate 24/7 and generally accommodate no more than four passengers. For safety's sake, always enter and exit curbside.

Share a Cab

An innovative website, **CabCorner.com**, matches riders willing to share a taxi and fare. Riders looking to share a trip post their departure location and destination on the website. Also helpful is the estimated shared fare, based on the number of riders and the route. This makes good sense (and cents), and is better for the environment, too!

CAR SERVICES — The countless number of black Lincoln Town Cars and other distinctive black sedans you'll see whizzing through Manhattan are carrying celebrities, politicians, businesspersons, savvy tourists, and folks going out on the town for a special occasion. These cars are not reserved for just the elite; it may be cost-effective to book a stretch limo or passenger van for families (child safety seats available on request) and groups. Unlike yellow taxis, for-hire car services are by reservation only and generally charge by the hour or trip plus tolls and gratuities. Fares are not regulated by the Taxi and Limousine Commission and vary among the many companies. Be sure to agree on a price and method of payment before settling in for a ride.

To forgo the chaos of taxicabs and mass transit, prearrange for a private car or limousine to transport you from the airport. Last-minute reservations can also be made at the ground transportation desks or self-service kiosks, but you might have to wait awhile. Your hotel concierge or bellman will also be able to arrange for a car to drive you around the city for business or pleasure or back to the airport. See the Services section (Chapter V) of this book for my recommendations.

DRIVING — If you're driving in or through New York City, know where

---

Bike It!

For exercise and seeing the sights, biking is a fun mode of transportation. Places to rent bikes, helmets, and accessories are conveniently located.

Champion Bikes (896 Amsterdam Ave, 212/662-2690; championbicycles.com): repair work

Loeb Central Park Boathouse Bike Rental (Central Park, 212/517-2233, thecentralparkboathouse.com): April-November; for use in Central Park only

Pedal Pusher Bike Shop (1306 Second Ave, 212/288-5592, pedalpusherbikeshop.com): largest rental fleet in the city; road racing bikes

Toga Bikes (110 West End Ave, 212/799-9625, togabikes.com) and **Gotham Bikes** (112 West Broadway, 212/732-2453, togabikes.com): New York's oldest bike retailer; two shops

---

you're going and plan an alternate route. Be patient and try to avoid daily rush hours, a city-declared "gridlock day warning," Sunday afternoons, and holidays.

Tune in to an all-news format radio station, such as WINS (1010 AM), for timely traffic updates. Using hand-held mobile devices (talking, texting, or otherwise) while driving is prohibited, and fines are levied on violators. Most streets are one-way, though there are some two-way streets crosstown. Obey directional signs and be aware that streets are often closed for special events or construction. Speaking of signs, pay heed to those mandating no turn on red, no parking, no turning during certain hours, and fire hydrant and crosswalk zones, or you may wind up paying steep fines. Pedestrians do not always confine their crossing to crosswalks, so keep an eye open for jaywalkers and daredevil bike messengers, who often go against the traffic flow.

PARKING — Parking a car in Manhattan can be very costly. Hotel parking fees are sky high, if available, and on-street metered parking spots are rarely empty. Before you claim a spot, look for red-and-white parking signs listing restrictions, which are located on both sides of a street. Be aware of tow-away zones; no parking, no standing, and no stopping signs; and street cleaning rules that ban parking on alternate sides of a street on certain days. Meters accept quarters — lots of them. "Muni-meters" control several parking spots and, in addition to quarters, accept the NYC Parking Card.

Municipal and private parking garages are plentiful, and the rules are confusing. Read the fine print. Also verify rates, afterhours' accessibility, and form of payment before leaving your car or keys. It's possible to search for a parking garage near your destination and compare rates by visiting bestparking.com. Calling 311 or using 311 Online will yield information on public parking and towed vehicles.

BICYCLING — Every day thousands of people ride bicycles to work in New York City. The city has designated bicycle lanes that move in the same direction as traffic. If there is no separate lane, use extreme caution when sharing the roadway with cars and trucks. Bikes are not permitted on city buses, but are permitted on subway trains at all times. However, avoid crowded rush-hour trains and do *not* block doors.

Some buildings provide bike storage, and some employers allow riders to store bikes in their offices. Avoid chaining your bike to anything (sign posts, parking meters, fences, railings, and grates) except bike racks, as you may rack up a fine. Invest in a heavy-duty, theft-deterrent lock, as New York City bike thieves are notoriously quick and nimble. Wear a helmet!

GETTING TO KNOW
NEW YORK

References to New York can mean several different things. New York state is the third most populated state in the country. New York County is the most populated county in New York State. New York City, comprised of five boroughs, is the most populous city in the United States. In this book, New York City, "the city," and Manhattan are used interchangeably and all mean the same thing: the borough of Manhattan. Manhattan is one of four New York City boroughs that are islands. The fifth borough, The Bronx, is attached to the mainland.

A LITTLE HISTORY

Native Americans were the first known inhabitants of this area. Italian explorer Giovanni da Verrazano (for whom the Verrazano Narrows Bridge was named) sailed into New York Harbor in 1524 and discovered Manhattan for his French patron, King Francis I. In 1609, Henry Hudson, a trader for the Dutch East India Company, entered the harbor and navigated the river that now bears his name. The first permanent European settlement in Manhattan, a Dutch trading post called Nieuw Amsterdam, was established at the southern tip of the island, where Battery Park is today.

It's true that the Dutch East India Company bought the area from local Indians for inexpensive beads, cloth, and other trinkets, but the two sides had vastly different understandings of what the agreement meant.

It was renamed New York in 1664 after the British gained control. In the early 1800s, 60,000 New Yorkers lived mainly on the southern tip of Manhattan, with the rest of the island encompassing country estates, fertile farmland, thick forests, and wilderness.

New York's historical museums depict life on the island from the days before skyscrapers, subways, and millions of people.

John Randall, Jr. was instrumental in developing an organizational plan for

---

Dutch Treat

To commemorate the 400th anniversary of the Dutch arrival in Nieuw Amsterdam, the Netherlands government presented New York with a gift of the New Amsterdam Plein & Pavilion, in Battery Park at 1 Peter Minuit Plaza (across from 1 State Street). The white, fiberglass-covered wood structure, shaped like a giant pinwheel, serves as a welcoming oasis for commuters and visitors. It opened to the public in May 2011.

New York City's undeveloped land. The system is referred to as the Randall Plan and encompasses the area from about present-day 14th Street north to 155th Street. Take a look at the map at the front of this book, and you'll see a neatly aligned north-south, east-west grid. Below 14th, many streets take off in different directions — a remnant of Manhattan's rural past. Broadway heads northwest from 14th Street. It was once a footpath and is actually one of our nation's longest streets, reaching all the way to the state capital of Albany, some 160 miles away. Though the Randall Plan proved efficient, one major drawback ultimately cost the city millions of dollars, since little space was set aside for public parks.

KEY TO ADDRESSES

All of Manhattan's east-west streets are numbered, as are many of its north-south avenues. In general, most avenues are one-way and alternately northbound and southbound. Most streets are one-way as well; the even-numbered ones tend to be eastbound, and the odd-numbered ones are westbound. Some major east-west thoroughfares accommodate two-way traffic.

Thanks to the Internet and high-tech information devices and apps, pinpointing an address in Manhattan can be a snap. Phone directories and other publications generally include cross-street information as part of an address listing. If you're stuck finding a location with only the street address, here's a reliable system for figuring it out.

AVENUES — If you have a numerical address on one of the north-south avenues, drop the last number, divide the remainder by two, and add or subtract the number indicated to find the corresponding cross street.

For example, to find 620 Avenue of the Americas:

$62 \div 2 = 31 - 12 = 19$th Street

Avenue A, B, C, or D	Add 3
First Avenue	Add 3
Second Avenue	Add 3
Third Avenue	Add 10
Lexington Avenue	Add 22
Fourth Avenue/Park Avenue South	Add 8
Park Avenue	Add 35
Madison Avenue	Add 26
Fifth Avenue	
addresses up to 200	Add 13
• between 201 and 400	Add 16
• between 401 and 600	Add 18
• between 601 and 774	Add 20
• between 775 and 1288	Subtract 18
• between 1289 and 1500	Add 45
addresses up to 2000	Add 24
Avenue of the Americas/Sixth Avenue	Subtract 12
Lenox Avenue/Malcolm X Boulevard	Add 110
Seventh Avenue	Add 12
Adam Clayton Powell, Jr. Boulevard	Add 20

Broadway
- addresses up to 754 are below 8th Street
- between 755 and 858 . . . . Subtract 29
- between 859 and 958 . . . . Subtract 25
- addresses above 958 . . . . Subtract 31

Eighth Avenue . . . . Add 10
Ninth Avenue . . . . Add 13
Columbus Avenue . . . . Add 60
Tenth Avenue . . . . Add 14
Amsterdam Avenue . . . . Add 60
Eleventh Avenue . . . . Add 15
West End Avenue . . . . Add 60
Convent Avenue . . . . Add 127
St. Nicholas Avenue . . . . Add 110
Manhattan Avenue . . . . Add 100
Edgecombe Avenue . . . . Add 134
Fort Washington Avenue . . . . Add 158

Central Park West and Riverside Drive have formulas of their own. To find the cross street for a building on Central Park West, divide the address by 10 and add 60. To find the cross street for a building on Riverside Drive up to 165th Street, divide the address by 10 and add 72.

Because certain addresses — particularly those on Fifth, Madison, and Park avenues — are thought to be prestigious, many buildings use them even if the entrances are actually on a side street. This is most common in midtown and along Fifth Avenue on the Upper East Side. So if you can't find an address, then look around the corner.

CROSS STREETS — Numbered cross streets run east-west. Addresses on them are easy to find. Allow for a little variation below 23rd Street (because Madison, Eleventh, and Twelfth avenues have yet to begin) and throughout the city wherever Broadway is involved.

EAST SIDE
1 to 49 . . . . . . between Fifth Avenue and Madison Avenue
50 to 99 . . . . . between Madison Avenue and Park Avenue
100 to 149 . . . . between Park Avenue and Lexington Avenue
150 to 199 . . . . between Lexington Avenue and Third Avenue
200 to 299 . . . . between Third Avenue and Second Avenue
300 to 399 . . . . between Second Avenue and First Avenue
400 to 499 . . . . between First Avenue and York Avenue
500 to 599 . . . . between Avenue A and Avenue B

WEST SIDE BELOW 59th STREET
1 to 99 . . . . . . between Fifth Avenue and Avenue of the Americas
100 to 199 . . . . between Avenue of the Americas and Seventh Avenue
200 to 299 . . . . between Seventh Avenue and Eighth Avenue
300 to 399 . . . . between Eighth Avenue and Ninth Avenue
400 to 499 . . . . between Ninth Avenue and Tenth Avenue

500 to 599 . . . . between Tenth Avenue and Eleventh Avenue
600 and up . . . . between Eleventh Avenue and Twelfth Avenue
WEST SIDE ABOVE 59th STREET
1 to 99 . . . . . . between Central Park West and Columbus Avenue
100 to 199 . . . . between Columbus Avenue and Amsterdam Avenue
200 to 299 . . . . between Amsterdam Avenue and West End Avenue
300 and up . . . . between West End Avenue and Riverside Drive

Odd-numbered addresses on east-west streets are on the north (uptown) side, while even-numbered ones are on the south (downtown) side.

NEIGHBORHOODS

Manhattan is composed of many diverse neighborhoods whose names and boundaries change from time to time. There are no hard and fast rules defining neighborhood borders, which are influenced by economics and demographics. Upper Manhattan refers to the area above 59th Street, which runs along the southern border of Central Park. Midtown refers to the area between 34th and 59th streets. The West Side refers to everything west of Fifth Avenue. Likewise, the East Side refers to the area east of Fifth Avenue. Downtown and Lower Manhattan refer to everything below 14th Street. The area between midtown and downtown is made up of roughly ten neighborhoods. (The map at the front of this book is a quick guide to these areas.) I encourage you to visit as many neighborhoods as possible to experience the city's exhilarating sights, sounds, flavors, and people.

Call a Van

New York City's iconic yellow cabs are being replaced with a fleet of Nissan NV200 vans as existing cabs are retired or replaced. The new, more comfortable rides are outfitted with skylights and electronic charging plugs, retractable steps, and low-annoyance horns. A wheelchair accessible model features a fold-flat ramp and a restraint system.

INWOOD AND WASHINGTON HEIGHTS — This racially and ethnically mixed residential neighborhood in northernmost Manhattan is now primarily Dominican. In 1776, this was the site of the last Revolutionary War Battle in New York City, necessitating George Washington's retreat across the Hudson to New Jersey. The Morris-Jumel Mansion, now on 160th Street, served as Washington's headquarters. There are several beautiful parks up here, including Fort Tryon Park (which boasts The Cloisters Museum and Gardens), Inwood Hill Park, and Isham Park. Other points of interest are the Dyckman Farmhouse Museum (the last remaining Dutch Colonial-era farmhouse in Manhattan), Audubon Terrace Historic District, Children's Cultural Center of Native America, USA Track and Field Hall of Fame, and the Little Red Lighthouse (made famous in a 1940s children's book). The Dominican populace is reflected in bodegas, clubs, street vendors, food carts, and ever-audible music. Life in this area was depicted in the Broadway musical *In the Heights*.

Marble Hill is actually the northernmost neighborhood of Manhattan, but it is no longer *on* Manhattan Island, due to the construction of the Harlem River Ship

Channel. For this reason, it is now considered part of The Bronx.

HARLEM — The neighborhoods of Hamilton Heights, Astor Row, Sugar Hill, East Harlem, and Central Harlem all fall within the area known as Harlem. Residents of East Harlem are predominantly Latino, and the remaining population of Harlem is mainly African-American. Harlem is known worldwide as a center of African-American music, politics, and culture. It has experienced a renaissance over time, with much to offer residents and visitors. Because of the neighborhood diversity, there are equally assorted dining, shopping, and entertainment venues. You'll find the City College of New York, Hamilton Grange, St. Nicholas Park, the impressive Museum of the City of New York, the Schomburg Center for Research in Black Culture, the world-famous Apollo Theater, the Classical Theatre of Harlem, and the Dance Theatre of Harlem. Former President Bill Clinton's office is located on West 125th Street. Many notable figures have resided here, including George and Ira Gershwin, F. Scott Fitzgerald, Thurgood Marshall, Kareem Abdul-Jabbar, Harry Houdini, and Adam Clayton Powell, Jr. (for whom a boulevard is named).

MORNINGSIDE HEIGHTS — Since the 1890s, a small and vibrant area along the Hudson River has been known as Morningside Heights. Some people now consider Morningside Heights an extension of the Upper West Side, and a few refer to this area as SoHa (South of Harlem) and incorporate SoHa into their business names. Tom's Restaurant (112th and Broadway) gained notoriety from the popular *Seinfeld* television series. (The exterior was shown as Monk's Cafe.) Colleges and institutions proliferate: Barnard College, Columbia University, the Manhattan School of Music, Cathedral Church of Saint John the Divine, Riverside Church, St. Luke's Roosevelt Hospital, and the Jewish Theological Seminary of America. Riverside Park stretches for four glorious miles along the river and offers abundant recreational opportunities and interesting monuments, the most famous of which is Grant's Tomb. Kids are entertained on the Hippo Playground and the popular winter sledding hill. Check out the variety of convenient neighborhood dining options: Max SoHa (trattoria), Kitchenette Uptown (home cooking), and the Hungarian Pastry Shop (Old World bakery).

UPPER WEST SIDE — This is a largely residential area crowded with families and children. The Upper West Side is ethnically and racially mixed. The apartment buildings facing Central Park have long been considered some of the most desirable in the city for the breathtaking views and coveted location. This area is frequently seen on TV shows and in movies; the magnificent Dakota and Ansonia apartment buildings, as well as the area's unique restaurants and shops, have had recognizable roles.

To say there are lots of quirky and nationally known shops on the Upper West Side is an understatement. Restaurants for every taste, budget, and ethnicity

---

Highbridge Park

Highbridge Park is off the radar, lying along the Harlem River between 155th and Dyckman streets. The gem of this greenspace, the High Bridge (originally the Old Croton Aqueduct), is undergoing renovation to allow pedestrian and bicycle traffic to cross the 130-foot high span into The Bronx. Dating back to 1847, this is New York City's oldest bridge.

Revitalized Harlem

This area is rich in culture, history, architecture, and unique shopping.

Bébénoir (2164 Eighth Ave, 212/828-5775): local designer clothing

The Brownstone (24 E 125th St, 212/996-7980): women's boutique with local designers

Carol's Daughter (24 W 125th St, 212/828-6757): skin-care, hair, and body products

Champs Sports (208 W 125th St, 212/280-0296): sporting goods

Demolition Depot & Irreplaceable Artifacts (216 E 125th St, 212/860-1138): antiques, architectural items

Duke Ellington Circle (110th St at Fifth Ave): a statue of Sir Duke posed beside a grand piano

Grandma's Place (84 W 120th St, 212/360-6776): books and toys

Harlem One Stop (212/658-9160): walking and specialty tours highlighting music, culture, and jazz

Hats by Bunn (2283 Seventh Ave, 212/694-3590): stylish head toppers

Malcolm Shabazz Harlem Market, a.k.a. "**African Market**" (52 W 116th St, 212/987-8131): traditional crafts and textiles; open 365 days a year

The Winery (257 W 116th St, 212/222-4866): wine boutique

abound, some of them open around the clock. Everything is accessible: banks, gyms, cleaners, museums, churches, and schools. Bordering Central Park West is the green expanse of Central Park. Some other notable destinations are Zabar's (among my favorite gourmet shops), ABC Studios, the New-York Historical Society, and the American Museum of Natural History. Lincoln Center encompasses more than a square block and is the cultural gem of this area. Midtown Manhattan and the Upper West Side share Columbus Circle. The Shops at Columbus Circle draw people to the Time Warner Center for upscale shopping and award-winning dining. The huge Whole Foods Market is first-class. The vibrant Museum of Arts and Design is also a magnet.

UPPER EAST SIDE — The Upper East Side is directly east of Central Park. This is a prestigious old-money residential neighborhood with more than its share of sophisticated art museums and galleries, posh boutiques, and fine restaurants and cafes. This area has been home to the Vanderbilts, Rockefellers, Carnegies, and Kennedys, and has rightfully earned such monikers as "Millionaires Row" and the "Silk Stocking District." It is still home to expensive apartment buildings, former mansions, and foreign consulates. The cost of living continues to be among the highest in the United States. Affluent luxury shoppers enjoy superb selections of fine jewelry, multi-carat baubles, furs, and other high-end goods right in their tony backyard. Exclusive private schools reflect the desire for superior education (and status). Weill Cornell Medical College, New York-Presbyterian Hospital, and the Mount Sinai School of Medicine all call this prominent neighborhood home.

Many chic international designers have boutiques in the area. Bloomingdale's and Barneys New York have been fixtures on the retail front for decades. The Upper East Side has the greatest concentration of museums and galleries in the city, including the Cooper-Hewitt, National Design Museum, the Metropolitan Museum of Art, the Solomon R. Guggenheim Museum, the Whitney Museum of American Art, and the Americas Society Gallery. The Asia Society is headquartered here, as is the mayor's official abode, Gracie Mansion. This is an area to stroll for fascinating architecture, celebrity spotting, and colorful window and patio gardens.

MIDTOWN — Many people associate midtown Manhattan with Times Square's convergence of bright lights and towering buildings, but there's much more. The core of midtown comprises theaters, hotels, offices, restaurants, and retailers. Famous names include Tiffany's, F.A.O. Schwarz, Saks Fifth Avenue, Macy's, Lord & Taylor, Bergdorf Goodman, and Niketown New York, which share the avenues with smaller stores and sidewalk vendors. Midtown landmarks worth visiting are Carnegie Hall, Rockefeller Center, St. Patrick's Cathedral, Trump Tower, the Chrysler Building, New York Public Library, Grand Central Terminal, Radio City Music Hall, and bustling Bryant Park. Closer to the East River is Turtle Bay, home to the United Nations and luxurious residences. Well-appointed and spacious environs are constructed in the Sutton Place and Beekman Place areas, with abundant greenspaces and parks. The area is alive with great restaurants, cafes, specialty eateries, and nightclubs.

CLINTON — Some folks still refer to this area as Hell's Kitchen, while others prefer the newer and more descriptive alternative Midtown West. It is no longer the dangerous and violent region of the past, but instead is an upscale neighborhood of diverse residents. Many actors live here because it's close to Broadway theaters. Restaurant Row, on 46th Street, has a profusion of appealing dining options, and Ninth Avenue has attracted quite a number of Thai restaurants. Ethnic grocers, bakers, butchers, and other food shops coexist with offices, car dealerships, horse stables, and myriad small shops. Each day tens of thousands of people pass through the Port Authority Bus Terminal (and past the larger-than-life statue of Jackie Gleason's TV character, bus driver Ralph Kramden) and the Lincoln Tunnel. Passenger ship terminals, Circle Line Cruises, and the Intrepid Sea, Air & Space Museum are on the west side of the Henry Hudson Parkway.

MURRAY HILL AND KIPS BAY — These are primarily residential areas with essential businesses that cater to apartment complexes and institutions. Rents are a bit lower here than in surrounding neighborhoods. Several blocks

---

Did you know?

■ Harlem was named after Haarlem, a city in the Netherlands

■ Morningside Heights was formerly known as Vandewater to honor settler Harmon Vandewater

■ Times Square was previously named Long Acre Square

■ Herald Square, home to Macy's, was named after the New York Herald

■ Washington Heights is named for Fort Washington and Washington Square, named in honor of President George Washington, and was once a cemetery

along the East River are dominated by New York University Medical Center and its associated schools, Bellevue Hospital (the oldest continuously operating public hospital in America) and the Veterans Administration Medical Center. Culturally, The Morgan Library and Museum and Scandinavia House: The Nordic Center in America are of interest.

CHELSEA — Big-box stores have made their mark in this largely residential multicultural neighborhood, which is noted for art galleries, clothing boutiques, small hotels, rocking nightclubs, and extraordinary restaurants. The former noisy, grimy industrial buildings have morphed into luxury lofts mixed with apartment complexes. The Fashion Institute of Technology, the School of Visual Arts, and the High School of Fashion Industries are convenient to the nearby Garment District. The Chelsea Piers development and the Hudson River Park Waterfront Promenade occupy the western border of Chelsea and offer abundant recreational activities; the majority of the elevated High Line Park is in west Chelsea. Foodies are attracted to the Chelsea Market, which has nearly 30 food-related shops. The offices of TV's Food Network are also in this complex. The General Theological Seminary of the Episcopal Church, the Rubin Museum of Art, the Chelsea Art Museum, and the Joyce Theater also call Chelsea home. Madison Square Garden, built atop Penn Station, has been a mainstay for decades and continues to draw thousands to concerts and sporting events.

FLATIRON DISTRICT — The flatiron-shaped building on Fifth Avenue at Broadway is the inspiration for the name of this district. Over the years it has also been referred to as Ladies' Mile, the Photo District, and the Toy District. Notable buildings include the MetLife Tower, the Woolworth Building, and the New York State Supreme Court building. Major retailers with their brightly illuminated storefronts, contemporary residential condominiums, and the Ace and NoMad hotels have changed the face of the neighborhood. In the shadow of the Flatiron Building is Madison Square (not to be confused with Madison Square Garden), a landscaped park with statues. Warm-weather favorites here are the Shake Shack and outdoor concerts.

GRAMERCY — This area has long been one of the city's most elegant, with some streets that are reminiscent of old London. Gramercy Park is a small private park accessible only to key-holding tenants of apartment buildings facing the gated Eden. A few blocks away is the very public Union Square; look for the *Metronome* artwork, which is actually a timepiece. Definitely don't miss the Greenmarket, a favorite farmers market, open seasonally. Stuyvesant Town and Peter Cooper Village are very large private planned communities with multistory residential buildings.

MEATPACKING DISTRICT — This neighborhood incorporates high-end boutiques, romantic restaurants, and fascinating nightlife along its crooked streets where slaughterhouses and meatpacking plants, as well as many illicit activities, once defined this 20-square-block area. West 14th Street has morphed into a destination for high-end designer boutiques and trendy hotels. A former elevated freight railroad has been transformed into High Line Park, which has many varied activities for the entire family.

GREENWICH VILLAGE — Beatniks, jazz clubs, and folk artists in the 1950s and 1960s brought Greenwich Village into the public eye. Coffeehouses, experimental theaters, underground jazz clubs, and comedy clubs are still popular, and now small specialty stores share the buildings. Many middle-class families reside in mid-rise apartments, 19th-century rowhouses, and walkups. Streets are generally named rather than numbered, and the grid layout found throughout the city basically doesn't exist here. Washington Square Park is a well-known gathering spot, and its impressive stone arch and central water fountain are often photographed. It has also been the site of numerous riots and rallies. Families and students from New York University use the park for rest and relaxation and play chess, checkers, or other games. Not surprisingly, the Village has been home to many artists and political figures, such as Edgar Allan Poe, Allen Ginsberg, Bob Dylan, and Abbie Hoffman.

EAST VILLAGE — Within the East Village are Alphabet City, The Bowery, St. Mark's Place, and Loisaida. Similar to Greenwich Village, the East Village proffers offbeat and colorful nightclubs, commerce, and interesting people. Outdoor activities come to life in Tompkins Square, the East River Park (along FDR Drive), and the Toyota Children's Learning Garden. Cooper Union and the Bowery Poetry Club offer a flavor of the neighborhood's past. It's not difficult to imagine Lenny Bruce as a resident. The East Village is also home to some notable off-Broadway productions and boasts the city's highest concentration of bars and taverns.

SOHO — Soho offers energy and charisma. This neighborhood is named for the area South of Houston. The old buildings are embellished with cast-iron works in intricate patterns. Tourists and assertive vendors interact on the sidewalks, haggling over jewelry and souvenir pieces. Other folks patronize the eclectic mix of trendy shops, boutiques, art galleries, and eating places. Businesses stay open late to cater to the weekend and after-work crowds. Buildings are shorter and streets are narrower than uptown.

TRIBECA — Thousands of cars pass through Tribeca each day via the Holland Tunnel. The name of this neighborhood is reflected by its shape — i.e., the Triangle Below Canal Street. It is another trendy residential neighborhood and is a favorite for on-location filming. Enjoy a tranquil respite at Washington Market Park.

Distinct Districts

Crystal District — The five-block stretch of Madison Avenue between 58th and 63rd streets is home to luxury crystal boutiques: Swarovski, Baccarat, Daum, and Lalique.

Diamond District — Dozens of jewelers and gem-cutters are located on 47th Street between Fifth Avenue and Avenue of the Americas.

Financial District — Banks, investment firms, and stock markets are headquartered south of City Hall down to Exchange Place. The heart is the corner of Wall and Broad streets.

Garment District — From Fifth to Ninth avenues between 34th and 42nd streets is the fashion center. Since the early 1900s, this has been the hub of fashion design, production facilities, and fabric and notion suppliers.

Museum Mile — Some of New York's finest museums are strung along Fifth Avenue from 82nd Street to 105th Street.

Theater District — Renowned on- and off-Broadway theaters are scattered from Avenue of the Americas to Tenth Avenue between 42nd and 54th streets.

Worth an honorable mention is the **Flower District**, on Avenue of the Americas between 28th and 29th streets.

> **Where to Hail a Cab**
>
> Some locations are more popular than others for hailing cabs at certain times of day. Penn Station is the best place to flag one down. If you're going in or near the Port Authority or Grand Central terminals, plenty of rides are nearby, too. Above 96th Street, however, taxis are less plentiful. Cabbies hang around Columbus Circle at 59th Street or Broadway (the southwest boundary of Central Park) to accommodate shoppers and visitors to Central Park. Drivers also know that late-night revelers need lifts home, so look for them around nightclubs and hot spots.

The Tribeca Film Center, founded by Robert DeNiro, mixes well with resident artists, local entertainment, and antique stores.

CHINATOWN — The periphery of Chinatown continues to creep into surrounding neighborhoods, including Little Italy, expanding this bustling area. Various dialects of Chinese are spoken freely. Just about any consumer product made in China (and what isn't these days?) is sold here. Prices are noisily negotiated in jam-packed shops along overcrowded Canal Street. Plenty of authentic restaurants and groceries can be found and enjoyed. To learn more about this culture, check out the Museum of Chinese in the Americas. Beware of vendors offering to sell the latest DVDs, brand-name watches, or handbags. This infamous underground economy of copyright-infringed knockoff merchandise attracts both bargain-seeking shoppers and law enforcement.

NOLITA — Short for North of Little Italy, Nolita is one of New York's smaller neighborhoods, sandwiched between Soho, Noho, and Little Italy. Vibrant restaurants, galleries, and boutiques delight residents and visitors. The gilded figure of Puck (Shakespeare's mischievous sprite) keeps watch on the Puck Building, on Lafayette Street. Torisi Italian Specialties and adjacent Parm offer outstanding Italian fare.

LOWER EAST SIDE — This large area encompasses the Cooperative Village and parts of The Bowery and Chinatown. Again, the perimeters change, but there are still vestiges of Jewish heritage, as demonstrated in the Lower East Side Tenement Museum and the Eldridge Street Synagogue. Other worship centers are the Hare Krishna Temple and the Bialystoker Synagogue, which are representative of the varied immigrant populations. Some businesses are closed for Shabbat on Friday afternoon and Saturday, and Sunday remains the primary Jewish shopping day. Visit famous Katz's Delicatessen for a real kosher meal to experience this unique local flavor. The area redevelopment has brought hip nightclubs, a wide range of new restaurants, and ever-changing fashion boutiques. East River Park provides a long, green swath under the Williamsburg Bridge that is host to several ball fields.

LOWER MANHATTAN — The southernmost and oldest part of Manhattan includes the Financial District, the Civic Center, downtown, and Battery Park City — just about everything south of Chambers Street. From the canyons and skyscrapers of Wall Street, this area is hectic. Small family-owned shops are nestled next to major chain stores, along with intimate restaurants. The lineup of imposing structures and museums is impressive: the World Trade Center and National September 11 Memorial and Museum, the beautifully restored and landscaped City Hall, the Federal Reserve Bank, the Vietnam Veterans Memorial, the Skyscraper Museum, the National Museum of the American Indian, Trinity Church, the Federal Hall National Memorial, Fraunces Tavern Museum, and the Museum of American Finance. The South Street Seaport complex extends alongside the East River, just south of the Brooklyn Bridge. If the weather is nice, take a stroll, walk, or bike ride over the bridge. Battery Park City is yet another planned residential area of high-rise apartment buildings whose residents are treated to fabulous views of Battery Park and Castle Clinton National Monument, the Statue of Liberty, Ellis Island, and the Staten Island Ferry.

WHAT TO EXPECT
THE EXPERIENCE

New York is surprisingly clean and safe and much easier to navigate than most people expect. The good news is that it is remarkably livable for its size, and the crime rate has plummeted since the early 1990s. The New York Police Department has a strong 24/7 presence on the streets, on the water, and in the air. Anytime there is a gathering — and there is always something going on in the city — the NYPD is visible. Feel comfortable about approaching officers with questions about directions or anything else. A call to 911 will aid you in an emergency, while 311 is the source for New York City government information and non-emergency issues.

That being said, keep in mind these common sense "don'ts":

- Don't display wads of money or flashy watches, jewelry, or electronics. Leave most of your cash and all of your valuables at home or in the hotel safe.
- Don't use ATMs when no one else is around.
- Don't leave an ATM until you've put your money in a wallet and then put the wallet in your pocket or purse.
- Don't keep your wallet in your back pocket unless it's buttoned. Better yet, carry your wallet in a front pocket, along with keys and other important items.
- Don't wear your purse slung over one shoulder. Instead, put the strap over your head and keep your purse in front of you or to the side.
- Don't doze off on the subway or bus.
- Don't jog in Central Park or anywhere else after dark.
- Don't let yourself believe that staying in "good" neighborhoods protects you from crime. The only time I was ever mugged was on Park Avenue at 62nd Street, and you can't find a better neighborhood than that!
- Don't let anybody in your hotel room, even if they claim to work for the hotel, unless you've specifically asked them to come or have checked with the front desk to verify their authenticity.
- Don't talk to strangers who try to strike up a conversation unless you're sure of their motivation.
- Don't ever leave bags unattended. If you're going to put a bag or backpack on the floor at a restaurant or bathroom stall, put your foot or a leg of your chair through the strap.
- Don't hang your purse or anything else on the back of the door in a public bathroom stall.

Tips for Tipping
AIRPORTS
- Skycap — $1 to $2 a bag (more if the bag is big and/or heavy)
- Taxi drivers — 10% to 15% of the fare

HOTELS
- Doorman — $1 to $2 a bag; $1 to $2 per person for hailing a taxi
- Bellhop — $1 to $2 a bag, depending on size and weight; $1 to $2 for deliveries to your room
- Concierge — $5 to $20 for special services, like securing hard-to-get theater tickets and restaurant reservations
- Housekeeper — $3 to $4 a night; for extra service, an additional $1 to $2
- Room service — 15% to 20% of the bill (before taxes)
- Parking valet — $2 to $5

RESTAURANTS
Check your bill carefully, as a tip may already have been included!
- Coat check — $1 an item
- Maitre d' — $10 to $100 (depending on the occasion, restaurant, and level of service you wish to receive, given before being seated)
- Wait staff — 15% to 20% of the bill before taxes
- Sommelier — 15% of the wine bill
- Bartender/server — $1 to $2 per drink, or 10% to 15% of tab
- Restroom attendant — 50 cents to $1 for handing you a towel or if you use any products or cosmetics
- Buffet server — $1 per person or 10% to 20% of the bill, according to the level of service

- Don't walk around with your mouth open and your camera and map visible while saying things like, "Gee, honey, we sure don't have buildings this tall back home!"
- Don't be afraid to cross the street if a situation doesn't feel right. Shout for help or approach a policeman or store worker if you are being bothered.
- Don't make eye contact with panhandlers, and *never* give them money.
- Move away from unattended packages and immediately report any suspicious items or behavior to authorities.

A final word of warning: watch where you walk. Manhattan has an incredible amount of traffic, and the struggle among cars, taxis, trucks, buses, bicycles, and pedestrians is constant. It may sound silly to repeat a warning from childhood, but look both ways before stepping into the street.

If you're traveling with a group, it's always a good idea to plan a meeting place and contact strategy (be sure to share cell-phone numbers) in case you get separated. If there's an emergency, call 911.

Average temperatures range from highs in the 30s and 40s in December, January, and February (snow is always a possibility) to highs in the 80s and 90s in June, July, and August (when the humidity can be stifling).

TIPPING AND OTHER EXPENSES

No doubt about it: New York can be expensive. Basic hotels start at about $200 a night, while upscale ones often run upwards of twice that. An average dinner at a respectable restaurant will run about $25 (without cocktails or wine). Theater tickets are at least $100. Look for discounts and coupons in publications, on the Internet, and through membership organizations. Elsewhere in this book you'll discover less expensive alternatives and suggestions for free events and activities.

Tipping is expected in many instances. Keep $1 bills handy, as you'll burn through them. You won't be exposing all of your cash if you keep singles separated from larger bills. An easy way to figure out the tip on a restaurant tab is to double the tax, which is 8.875%.

CHECKLISTS

Planning ahead for your trip will help alleviate stress. Read the relevant sections of this book, call ahead, and order tickets well in advance when appropriate. Bear in mind some activities and events are seasonal.

When traveling remember these essentials:
- a government-issued picture ID card
- student ID card, if applicable (to obtain student discounts)
- AARP or similar identification, if you qualify for a senior discount
- emergency contact information
- medications
- tickets for travel and events
- comfortable walking shoes
- umbrella and raincoat (or warm coat, scarf, boots, and gloves)
- opera glasses, if you're heading to the theater
- electronics chargers

Most hotels provide in-room coffeemakers (with coffee), irons, and hairdryers, and they also supply toiletries and mending kits. In-room Internet connections are frequently available (sometimes at a cost), as are in-room safes. Organize your credit cards and cash before leaving the room. Use a secure pocket or money belt. Ladies, be especially mindful of your handbag and do not wear gaudy jewelry. Carry a small bag or tote with these daily essentials:
- mobile phone
- address and phone numbers of places you plan to visit and directions to get there
- maps of the bus and subway systems and an unlimited-use MetroCard
- tissues
- list of public bathrooms in the areas you'll be visiting
- loose change and small bills
- small notepad and pen
- weather-appropriate accessories: sunglasses, sunscreen, water bottle, umbrella, and gloves

Most important of all, *don't forget this book!*

Chapter 2

WHERE TO EAT IT

NEW YORK'S BEST RESTAURANTS

t is possible to get whatever kind of meal you want, at almost any price you want — and often at any hour you want — in this great "eating out" city. Lower Manhattan is no exception with an abundance of interesting and varied eateries.

The restaurant business is making a comeback and because of the recent tough times, owners and chefs are continuing to pay attention to food preparation, reasonable pricing, cleanliness, and, most of all, service. If the restrooms are clean, that is a good sign for general cleanliness through the restaurant.

In my opinion, several areas in the restaurant business need attention. Many chefs have become "celebrities" and some spend more time polishing their image than working and training in the kitchen. Pricing can be outrageous and not always due to rising food costs. Be especially wary of overpriced "daily specials." Some restaurants simply do not oversee the reservation process properly. You may encounter rudeness, incompetence, or unnecessary difficulty getting a table on the day and time you want. Don't let the lack of a reservation deter you from a spot you really want to visit. Walk in and in most cases they will take care of you. It is not acceptable to be told to wait at the bar if the dining room is not full. Another shortcoming is the lack of training and supervision of personnel who greet diners at the door.

Too many are haughty, self-important, and more interested in projecting their personal "style" than greeting diners and setting a proper tone for the dining experience.

Following are some observations that I hope will be helpful:

- Dining hours: Tables are usually available early, up to about 6 p.m. Most restaurants fill up around 8 p.m., especially the more "in" establishments.

- It is very inconsiderate and costly to an establishment if you are a no-show for your reservation. Taking into account Manhattan traffic, most places will give 20 to 30 minutes of leeway to tardy diners. Do not give a credit card number when making reservations, but if you do, be aware of the restaurant's cancellation policy. Try to make a reservation at least a week ahead of time.

- Most restaurants (exceptions noted elsewhere) do not have a strict dress code. Dress neatly and comfortably; business casual is always a safe bet. Unlike the old days, it is rare to see a gentleman in a suit and tie at a nice restaurant or at the theater.

- Some of the best dining spots in New York are the old-time, tried-and-true establishments. They wouldn't be around today if they were not very special. Just because a place is new does not necessarily mean that it is better than those that have taken proper care of patrons for years.

- New York tap water is among the best in the country, so don't waste your dollars on expensive bottled water.

- Study the wine list carefully or enlist a knowledgeable member of your party to do so. Markups on wine can be outrageous.

- Try eating in the bar at some of the pricier establishments. It is quicker and often prices are lower.

- Regarding tipping, a good rule of thumb is to double the tax. If someone gives really special service or attention, a little extra is always appropriate. Before paying your tab, review your bill for unexpected charges; in some instances, especially for parties of six or more, the tip is added to the bill.

In the following pages, you'll find lists of restaurants categorized by neighborhood and specialties. In addition, I've written almost 300 full-length reviews, beginning on page 70. Those restaurants fall into four price ranges, based on the combined cost of an appetizer and entree (not including drinks):

Inexpensive: $19 and under per person

Moderate: $20 to $35 per person

Moderately expensive: $36 to $49 per person

Expensive: $50 and up per person

This book is not a restaurant Yellow Pages. I have selected places where I have personally dined, providing listings in every price range and encompassing almost every type of food. The evaluations are mine alone. No one pays to be listed or receives special favors in a review. Please remember that these write-ups are up to date at the time this volume goes to press, although a given restaurant's situation can change at any time.

If you have a particularly good or bad dining experience, don't hesitate to talk with the owner or manager. Please let me know, too, as your feedback and suggestions are very important. *Bon appétit!*

RESTAURANTS
QUICK REFERENCE GUIDE

Note: Restaurants receiving full write-ups in this chapter are listed by neighborhood in this reference guide. The type of cuisine and the word "Sunday" (if a given restaurant is open that day) follow each address.

CENTRAL PARK AREA
A Voce (Time Warner Center, 10 Columbus Circle, 3rd floor): Italian, Sunday
Jean Georges (Trump International Hotel and Tower, 1 Central Park W): French, Sunday
Landmarc (Time Warner Center, 10 Columbus Circle, 3rd floor): American, Sunday
Luke's Lobster (Plaza Food Hall, 1 W 59th St, lower level): Seafood, Sunday
Nougatine Cafe (Trump International Hotel and Tower, 1 Central Park W): French, Sunday
Plaza Food Hall by Todd English (The Plaza, 1 W 59th St, lower level): Eclectic, Sunday
Sarabeth's (40 Central Park S): American, Sunday

CHELSEA/WEST CHELSEA
The Breslin Bar & Dining Room (Ace Hotel, 16 W 29th St): British/Gastropub, Sunday
Colicchio & Sons (85 Tenth Ave): American, Sunday
Cookshop (156 Tenth Ave): American, Sunday
Da Umberto (107 W 17th St): Italian
Del Posto (85 Tenth Ave): Italian, Sunday
The John Dory Oyster Bar (Ace Hotel, 1196 Broadway): Seafood, Sunday
La Bottega (The Maritime Hotel, 88 Ninth Ave): Italian, Sunday
La Lunchonette (130 Tenth Ave): French, Sunday
Moran's Chelsea (146 Tenth Ave): American, Sunday
Rare Bar & Grill (Hilton New York Fashion District, 152 W 26th St): Burgers, Sunday
Scarpetta (355 W 14th St): Italian, Sunday
Tipsy Parson (156 Ninth Ave): Southern, Sunday
Trestle on Tenth (242 Tenth Ave): American, Sunday

CHINATOWN
Golden Unicorn (18 East Broadway): Chinese, Sunday

EAST SIDE/UPPER EAST SIDE
2nd Ave Deli (1442 First Ave): Deli/Kosher, Sunday

Arabelle (Hotel Plaza Athenee, 37 E 64th St): American/French
Arlington Club Steakhouse (1032 Lexington Ave): Steak, Sunday
Cafe Boulud (20 E 76th St): French, Sunday
Cafe d'Alsace (1695 Second Ave): French, Sunday
Cafe Sabarsky (Neue Galerie New York, 1048 Fifth Ave): Austrian, Sunday
Cucina Vivolo (138 E 74th St): Italian
Daniel (60 E 65th St): French
David Burke Townhouse (133 E 61st St): American, Sunday
Demarchelier (50 E 86th St): French, Sunday
EJ's Luncheonette (1271 Third Ave): American/Diner, Sunday
Elio's (1621 Second Ave): Italian, Sunday
Felidia (243 E 58th St): Italian, Sunday
Fig & Olive (808 Lexington Ave): Mediterranean, Sunday
Fred's at Barneys New York (660 Madison Ave, 9th floor): American, Sunday
Gobo (1426 Third Ave): Vegan/Vegetarian, Sunday
Il Mulino Uptown (37 E 60th St): Italian, Sunday
Il Riccio (152 E 79th St): Italian, Sunday
Il Tesoro Ristorante (1578 First Ave): Italian, Sunday
Il Vagabondo (351 E 62nd St): Italian, Sunday
Jackson Hole Burgers (1270 Madison Ave, 1611 Second Ave, and 232 E
   64th St): Burgers, Sunday
Jacques Brasserie (204-206 E 85th St): French, Sunday
John's Pizzeria (408 E 64th St): Pizza, Sunday
King's Carriage House (251 E 82nd St): American, Sunday
Luke's Lobster (242 E 81st St): Seafood, Sunday
The Mark Restaurant by Jean-Georges (The Mark, 25 E 77th St):
   American, Sunday
Nicola's (146 E 84th St): Italian, Sunday
Our Place (242 E 79th St): Chinese, Sunday
Paola's (Hotel Wales, 1295 Madison Ave): Italian, Sunday
Sarabeth's (1295 Madison Ave): American, Sunday
Serendipity 3 (225 E 60th St): Dessert, Sunday
Sette Mezzo (969 Lexington Ave): Italian, Sunday
Sfoglia (135 E 92nd St): Italian, Sunday
Shake Shack (154 E 86th St): Burgers, Sunday
Sirio Ristorante (The Pierre, 795 Fifth Ave): Italian, Sunday
Sistina (1555 Second Ave): Italian, Sunday
Spigolo (1561 Second Ave): Italian, Sunday
Spring Natural Kitchen (474 Columbus Ave): Health Food, Sunday
Taste (1413 Third Ave): American, Sunday
Vinegar Factory (431 E 91st St): American, Sunday
Vivolo (140 E 74th St): Italian

EAST VILLAGE/NOLITA
Balaboosta (214 Mulberry St): Mediterranean/Mideastern, Sunday
The Beagle (162 Ave A): American, Sunday

DBGB Kitchen & Bar (299 Bowery): French, Sunday
Delicatessen (54 Prince St): American, Sunday
Gyu-Kaku (34 Cooper Sq): Japanese Barbecue, Sunday
Jacques 1534 (20 Prince St): French Gastropub, Sunday
Luke's Lobster (93 E 7th St): Seafood, Sunday
Spring Street Natural (62 Spring St): Health Food, Sunday
Torrisi Italian Specialties (250 Mulberry St): Italian/Deli, Sunday

FLATIRON DISTRICT/GRAMERCY PARK/LOWER BROADWAY/UNION SQUARE

A Voce (41 Madison Ave): Italian
ABC Kitchen (ABC Carpet & Home, 35 E 18th St): American, Sunday
Aldea (31 W 17th St): Mediterranean
Blue Water Grill (31 Union Square W): Seafood, Sunday
City Bakery (3 W 18 St): Bakery/Cafe, Sunday
Craft (43 E 19th St): American, Sunday
Dévi (8 E 18th St): Indian, Sunday
Eleven Madison Park (11 Madison Ave): American/French, Sunday
Gramercy Tavern (42 E 20th St): American, Sunday
Hill Country (30 W 26th St): Barbecue, Sunday
Hill Country Chicken (1123 Broadway): Southern, Sunday
Hurricane Steak & Sushi (360 Park Ave S): Polynesian, Sunday
Maialino (Gramercy Park Hotel, 2 Lexington Ave): Italian, Sunday
Olives New York (W New York Union Square, 201 Park Ave S): Mediterranean, Sunday
Rosa Mexicano (9 E 18th St): Mexican, Sunday
Shake Shack (Madison Square Park, 23rd St bet Madison Ave and Broadway): Burgers, Sunday
Sarabeth's (381 Park Ave S): American, Sunday
Tocqueville Restaurant (1 E 15th St): American
Union Square Cafe (21 E 16th St): American, Sunday
Veritas (43 E 20th St): American, Sunday

GARMENT DISTRICT/MURRAY HILL

2nd Ave Deli (162 E 33rd St): Deli/Kosher, Sunday
Blue Smoke (116 E 27th St): Barbecue, Sunday
Butterfield 8 (5 E 38th St): American, Sunday
Casa Nonna (310 W 38th St): Spanish, Sunday
El Parador Cafe (325 E 34th St): Mexican, Sunday
Jackson Hole Burgers (521 Third Ave): Burgers, Sunday
Keens Steakhouse (72 W 36th St): American, Sunday
Les Halles (411 Park Ave S): French, Sunday
Madangsui (35 W 35th St): Korean Barbecue, Sunday
Marchi's (251 E 31st St): Italian
Millesime (The Carlton Hotel, 92 Madison Ave): French/Seafood, Sunday
The Morgan Dining Room (The Morgan Library & Museum, 225 Madison Ave): American, Sunday

Rare Bar & Grill (Affina Shelburne, 303 Lexington Ave):American, Sunday
Resto (111 E 29th St): Belgian, Sunday
Sarabeth's (Lord & Taylor, 424 Fifth Ave, 5th floor):American, Sunday
Turkish Kitchen (386 Third Ave):Turkish, Sunday
Uncle Jack's Steakhouse (440 Ninth Ave): Steak, Sunday
Wolfgang's Steakhouse (4 Park Ave): Steak, Sunday

GREENWICH VILLAGE/WEST VILLAGE

Babbo (110 Waverly Pl): Italian, Sunday
Blue Hill (75 Washington Pl):American, Sunday
Blue Ribbon Bakery (35 Downing St):American, Sunday
bobo (181 W 10th St): French, Sunday
Buvette (42 Grove St): French, Sunday
Cafe Cluny (284 W 12th St):American/French, Sunday
Camaje (85 MacDougal St): French, Sunday
Chez Jacqueline (72 MacDougal St): French, Sunday
Cowgirl (519 Hudson St): Southwestern, Sunday
Five Points (31 Great Jones St):American/Mediterranean, Sunday
Gobo (401 Ave of the Americas):Vegan/Vegetarian, Sunday
Good (89 Greenwich Ave):American, Sunday
Gotham Bar & Grill (12 E 12th St):American, Sunday
Il Mulino New York (86 W 3rd St): Italian
Jeffrey's Grocery (172 Waverly Pl):American, Sunday
John's Pizzeria (278 Bleecker St): Pizza, Sunday
Joseph Leonard (170 Waverly Pl):American, Sunday
La Ripaille (605 Hudson St): French, Sunday
Le Gigot (18 Cornelia St): French, Sunday
Little Owl (90 Bedford St):American, Sunday
Market Table (54 Carmine St):American, Sunday
Minetta Tavern (113 MacDougal St): French Bistro, Sunday
Miss Lily's Favourite Cakes (132 W Houston St): Caribbean/Diner,
   Sunday
Morandi (211 Waverly Pl): Italian, Sunday
One if by Land, Two if by Sea (17 Barrow St):American, Sunday
Perilla (9 Jones St):American, Sunday
Pó (31 Cornelia St): Italian, Sunday
Recette (328 W 12th St):American, Sunday
Rosemary's Enoteca & Trattoria (18 Greenwich Ave): Italian, Sunday
The Spotted Pig (314 W 11th St): European/Gastropub, Sunday
Strip House (13 E 12th St): Steak, Sunday
Tartine (253 W 11th St): French, Sunday
Wallsé (344 W 11th St):Austrian, Sunday
Waverly Inn (16 Bank St):American, Sunday
Wong (7 Cornelia St):Asian

HARLEM/EAST HARLEM
Corner Social (321 Lenox Ave): American, Sunday
Dinosaur Bar-B-Que (700 W 125th St): Barbecue, Sunday
Rao's (455 E 114th St): Italian
Red Rooster Harlem (310 Lenox Ave): American, Sunday

KOREATOWN
Hanjan (36 W 26th St): Korean/Gastropub

LOWER EAST SIDE
Clinton St. Baking Co. & Restaurant (4 Clinton St): American, Sunday
Freemans (Freeman Alley at Rivington St): American, Sunday
Katz's Delicatessen (205 E Houston St): Deli, Sunday
Schiller's (131 Rivington St): Eclectic, Sunday
Yunan Kitchen (79 Clinton St): Chinese, Sunday

MEATPACKING DISTRICT
Fig & Olive (420 W 13th St): Mediterranean, Sunday
Macelleria (48 Gansevoort St): Italian/Steak, Sunday
Pastis (9 Ninth Ave): French, Sunday
Spice Market (403 W 13th St): Asian, Sunday
The Standard Grill (848 Washington St): American, Sunday
Valbella (421 W 13th St): Italian

MIDTOWN EAST
Aquavit (65 E 55th St): Scandinavian
Artisanal Fromagerie, Bistro and Wine Bar (2 Park Ave): French, Sunday
BLT Steak (106 E 57th St): Steak, Sunday
Bottega del Vino (7 E 59th St): Italian, Sunday
Brasserie (100 E 53rd St): French, Sunday
Café Centro (MetLife Building, 200 Park Ave): Mediterranean
Capital Grille (Chrysler Center, 155 E 42nd St): Steak, Sunday
Casa Lever (390 Park Ave): Italian
Chin Chin (216 E 49th St): Chinese, Sunday
Cucina & Co. (MetLife Building, 200 Park Ave, lobby): Italian
Cucina Vivolo (222 E 58th St): Italian
Docks Oyster Bar and Seafood Grill (633 Third Ave): Seafood, Sunday
Fig & Olive (10 E 52nd St): Mediterranean, Sunday
Four Seasons (99 E 52nd St): American
Fresco by Scotto (34 E 52nd St): Italian
Grand Central Oyster Bar Restaurant (Grand Central Terminal, 42nd St at Vanderbilt Ave, lower level): Seafood
Grifone (244 E 46th St): Italian
Gyu-Kaku (805 Third Ave, 2nd floor): Japanese Barbecue, Sunday
Hatsuhana (17 E 48th St and 237 Park Ave): Japanese

Il Postino (337 E 49th St): Italian, Sunday
La Grenouille (3 E 52nd St): French
Lavo (39 E 58th St): Italian, Sunday
Le Cirque (1 Beacon Court, 151 E 58th St): French
Le Périgord (405 E 52nd St): French, Sunday
Le Relais de Venise (590 Lexington Ave): French/Steak, Sunday
Maloney & Porcelli (37 E 50th St): American, Sunday
Morton's The Steakhouse (551 Fifth Ave): Steak, Sunday
Mr. K's (570 Lexington Ave): Chinese, Sunday
Naples 45 (MetLife Building, 200 Park Ave): Italian
P.J. Clarke's (915 Third Ave): Pub Food, Sunday
The Palm (837 Second Ave and 840 Second Ave): Steak, Sunday (only at 840 Second Ave)
Pershing Square (90 E 42nd St): American, Sunday
Pietro's (232 E 43rd St): Italian
Rosa Mexicano (1063 First Ave): Mexican, Sunday
San Pietro (18 E 54th St): Italian
Shun Lee Palace (155 E 55th St): Chinese, Sunday
Smith & Wollensky (797 Third Ave): Steak, Sunday
Sparks Steak House (210 E 46th St): Steak
Tao (42 E 58th St): Asian, Sunday
Valbella (11 E 53rd St): Italian
Wolfgang's Steakhouse (200 E 54th St): Steak, Sunday

MIDTOWN WEST
Abboccato (136 W 55th St): Italian, Sunday
Ardesia (510 W 52nd St): Eclectic/International, Sunday
Bar Americain (152 W 52nd St): American, Sunday
Benoit (60 W 55th St): French, Sunday
Bond 45 (154 W 45th St): Italian, Sunday
Brasserie 8½ (9 W 57th St): French, Sunday
Brasserie Ruhlmann (45 Rockefeller Plaza): French, Sunday
Brooklyn Diner USA (212 W 57th St): Eclectic/Diner, Sunday
Bryant Park Grill (25 W 40th St): American, Sunday
Capital Grille (Time-Life Building, 120 W 51st St): Steak, Sunday
Carmine's (200 W 44th St): Italian, Sunday
Carnegie Deli (854 Seventh Ave): Deli, Sunday
Circo NYC (120 W 55th St): Italian, Sunday
Del Frisco's Double Eagle Steak House (McGraw-Hill Building, 1221 Ave of the Americas): Steak, Sunday
Del Frisco's Grille (50 Rockefeller Plaza): Steak, Sunday
Ember Room (647 Ninth Ave): Asian Barbecue, Sunday
Il Gattopardo (33 W 54th St): Italian, Sunday
La Silhouette (362 W 53rd St): French, Sunday
Le Bernardin (155 W 51st St): French
Le Rivage (340 W 46th St): French, Sunday

Marea (240 Central Park S): Italian/Seafood, Sunday
McCormick & Schmick's (1285 Ave of the Americas): Seafood, Sunday
Michael's (24 W 55th St): Californian
The Modern (Museum of Modern Art, 9 W 53rd St): American/French
Nobu Fifty Seven (40 W 57th St): Japanese, Sunday
Oceana (McGraw-Hill Building, 120 W 49th St): American/Seafood, Sunday
The Palm (250 W 50th St): Steak, Sunday
Patsy's Italian Restaurant (236 W 56th St): Italian, Sunday
Print (Ink48, 653 Eleventh Ave): American, Sunday
Quality Meats (57 W 58th St): American/Steak, Sunday
Redeye Grill (890 Seventh Ave): American/Seafood, Sunday
Remi (145 W 53rd St): Italian, Sunday
Round Table (Algonquin Hotel, 59 W 44th St, lobby level): American, Sunday
Rue 57 (60 W 57th St): French, Sunday
The Russian Tea Room (150 W 57th St): Continental/Russian, Sunday
The Sea Grill (19 W 49th St): Seafood
Strip House (15 W 44th St): Steak, Sunday
Totto Ramen (366 W 52nd St): Japanese/Noodle Shop, Sunday
Tout va Bien (311 W 51st St): French, Sunday
Trattoria dell'Arte (900 Seventh Ave): Italian, Sunday
Uncle Jack's Steakhouse (44 W 56th St): Steak, Sunday

NOHO/SOHO/LITTLE ITALY
Acme (9 Great Jones St): American, Sunday
Balthazar (80 Spring St): French, Sunday
Barmarche (14 Spring St): American, Sunday
Bistro les Amis (180 Spring St): French, Sunday
Blue Ribbon (97 Sullivan St): Eclectic, Sunday
Butter (415 Lafayette St): American
Cafe Select (212 Lafayette St): Swiss, Sunday
Cupping Room Cafe (359 West Broadway): American, Sunday
David Burke Kitchen (The James Hotel, 23 Grand St): American, Sunday
The Dutch (131 Sullivan St): American, Sunday
Giorgione (307 Spring St): Italian, Sunday
Hundred Acres (38 MacDougal St): American, Sunday
Il Buco Alimentari e Vineria (53 Great Jones St): Italian/Mediterranean, Sunday
Il Cortile (125 Mulberry St): Italian, Sunday
Kittichai (60 Thompson Hotel, 60 Thompson St): Thai, Sunday
Mezzogiorno (195 Spring St): Italian, Sunday
Onieal's Grand Street (174 Grand St): American, Sunday
Osteria Morini (218 Lafayette St): Italian, Sunday
Raoul's (180 Prince St): French, Sunday
Savore (200 Spring St): Italian, Sunday

THEATER DISTRICT/TIMES SQUARE

Barbetta (321 W 46th St): Italian
Brooklyn Diner USA (155 W 43rd St): Eclectic, Sunday
db Bistro Moderne (City Club Hotel, 55 W 44th St): French, Sunday
Ellen's Stardust Diner (1650 Broadway): Diner, Sunday
Gyu-Kaku (321 W 44th St): Japanese Barbecue, Sunday
John's Pizzeria (260 W 44th St): Pizza, Sunday
Orso (322 W 46th St): Italian, Sunday
Ruby Foo's (1626 Broadway): Chinese, Sunday
Shake Shack (691 Eighth Ave): Burgers, Sunday
Wolfgang's Steakhouse (New York Times Building, 250 W 41st St): Steak, Sunday

TRIBECA/DOWNTOWN/FINANCIAL DISTRICT

Acappella (1 Hudson St): Italian
Blaue Gans (139 Duane St): Austrian/German, Sunday
Blue Smoke (255 Vesey St): Barbecue, Sunday
Bouley (163 Duane St): French/American
Bouley Test Kitchen (88 West Broadway, 5th floor): Cooking Classes/Test Kitchen, by appointment
Brushstroke (30 Hudson St): Japanese
Capital Grille (120 Broadway): Steak
Cercle Rouge (241 West Broadway): French, Sunday
Cowgirl Sea-Horse (259 Front St): Southwestern, Sunday
Delmonico's (56 Beaver St): Steak
Duane Park (308 Bowery): American
Il Bagatto (192 E 2nd St): Italian, Sunday
Landmarc (179 West Broadway): American, Sunday
Les Halles (15 John St): French, Sunday
Locanda Verde (The Greenwich Hotel, 377 Greenwich St): Italian, Sunday
Luke's Lobster (26 S William St): Seafood, Sunday
MarkJoseph Steakhouse (261 Water St): Steak, Sunday
Ninja New York (25 Hudson St): Japanese, Sunday
Nobu New York/Nobu Next Door (105 Hudson St): Japanese, Sunday
North End Grill (104 North End Ave): American/Seafood, Sunday
P.J. Clarke's on the Hudson (World Financial Center, Building 4, 250 Vesey St, lobby): Pub Food, Sunday
The Palm (206 West St): Steak, Sunday
Sarabeth's (339 Greenwich St): American, Sunday
Scalini Fedeli (165 Duane St): Italian
Shake Shack (215 Murray St): Burgers, Sunday
Tribeca Grill (375 Greenwich St): American, Sunday
Walker's (16 N Moore St): Pub Food, Sunday
Wolfgang's Steakhouse (409 Greenwich St): Steak, Sunday

WEST SIDE/UPPER WEST SIDE/LINCOLN CENTER
Bar Boulud (1900 Broadway): French, Sunday
Boulud Sud (20 W 64th St): Mediterranean, Sunday
Cafe Lalo (201 W 83rd St): Coffeehouse/Dessert, Sunday
Carmine's (2450 Broadway): Italian, Sunday
'Cesca (164 W 75th St): Italian, Sunday
Ed's Chowder House (Empire Hotel, 44 W 63rd St): Seafood, Sunday
Fairway Cafe & Steakhouse (Fairway Market, 2127 Broadway, upstairs):
    American, Sunday
Gabriel's Bar & Restaurant (11 W 60th St): Italian
Good Enough to Eat (520 Columbus Ave): American, Sunday
Jackson Hole Burgers (517 Columbus Ave): Burgers, Sunday
La Boite en Bois (75 W 68th St): French, Sunday
Land Thai Kitchen (450 Amsterdam Ave): Thai, Sunday
Luke's Lobster (426 Amsterdam Ave): Seafood, Sunday
Ocean Grill (384 Columbus Ave): Seafood, Sunday
Ouest (2315 Broadway): American, Sunday
P.J. Clarke's at Lincoln Square (44 W 63rd St): Pub Food, Sunday
Picholine (35 W 64th St): French/Mediterranean, Sunday
Rosa Mexicano (61 Columbus Ave): Mexican, Sunday
Sarabeth's (423 Amsterdam Ave): American, Sunday
Shake Shack (366 Columbus Ave): Burgers, Sunday
Shun Lee Cafe/Shun Lee West (43 W 65th St): Chinese, Sunday
Telepan (72 W 69th St): American, Sunday

OUTSIDE MANHATTAN
Brooklyn
The Commodore (366 Metropolitan Ave, at Havemeyer St): Southern,
    Sunday
Peter Luger Steak House (178 Broadway, at Driggs Ave): Steak, Sunday

Queens
Park Side (107-01 Corona Ave, at 51st Ave): Italian, Sunday
Uncle Jack's Steakhouse (39-40 Bell Blvd): Steak, Sunday

GERRY'S EXCLUSIVE LIST
THE BEST PLACES TO FIND SPECIFIC FOOD ITEMS AND
SETTINGS IN NEW YORK'S KALEIDOSCOPIC RESTAURANT SCENE

BAGELS
Absolute Bagels (2788 Broadway)
Bagels on the Square (7 Carmine St)
BagelWorks (1229 First Ave)
Barney Greengrass (541 Amsterdam Ave)
Ess-a-Bagel (359 First Ave and 831 Third Ave)
H&H Midtown Bagels East (1551 Second Ave)
Kossar's Bialys (367 Grand St)
Lenny's Bagels (2601 Broadway)
Murray's Bagels (500 Ave of the Americas)

BARBECUE
Big Wong (67 Mott St): Chinese style
Blue Smoke (116 E 27th St and 255 Vesey St)
Bone Lick Park Bar-b-que (75 Greenwich Ave): ribs and pork smoked
  over fruit woods and hickory
Brother Jimmy's BBQ (1485 Second Ave and other locations): ribs,
  sandwiches, good sauce
Daisy May's BBQ USA (623 Eleventh Ave)
Dallas BBQ (1265 Third Ave, 27 W 72nd St, 132 Second Ave, and other
  locations): big and busy
Dinosaur Bar-B-Que (700 W 125th St)
Fatty 'Cue (50 Carmine St): fusion barbecue
Great NY Noodletown (28 Bowery St): Order a whole pig in advance.
Hill Country (30 W 26th St): live music
Kang Suh (1250 Broadway)
Mighty Quinn's Barbecue (103 Second Ave): "Texalina" barbecue
New Kam Man (200 Canal St): Chinese barbecue
Shun Lee Cafe/Shun Lee West (43 W 65th St): classy Chinese
Sylvia's (328 Lenox Ave): reputation better than the food
Virgil's Real Barbecue (152 W 44th St): big, brassy, mass production
Wildwood BBQ (225 Park Ave S): all-natural meats; sports bar

BARS AND PUBS
Alphabet City Beer Co. (96 Avenue C): a.k.a. ABC, small production beer
  and cider
The Bar at Four Seasons Hotel (57 E 57th St)
Baraonda (1439 Second Ave): Italian
Bemelmans Bar at the Carlyle Hotel (35 E 76th St): old-school hotel bar
Birdland (315 W 44th St): jazz

Blarney Rock Pub (137 W 33rd St): Irish all the way

Blue Note (131 W 3rd St): lots of talent

Blue Ribbon Downing Street Bar (34 Downing St): sip and be seen

bobo (181 W 10th St)

Boqueria Soho (171 Spring St) and **Boqueria Flatiron** (53 W 19th St): tapas bar

Bourbon Street Cafe (407 Amsterdam Ave): year-round Mardi Gras

Bourgeois Pig (111 E 7th St): romantic Victorian opulence

Brandy Library (25 N Moore St): fine liquor

Brass Monkey (55 Little W 12th St): Hudson River views from roof deck

Bull & Bear (Waldorf Astoria New York, 301 Park Ave)

Burp Castle (41 E 7th St): 100 international bottles and a dozen taps focusing on Belgian beers

Butterfield 8 (5 E 38th St): unassuming pub and lounge

Camaradas El Barrio (2241 First Ave): Spanish Harlem happy-hour

Campbell Apartment (Grand Central Terminal, 42nd St at Vanderbilt Ave, off West Balcony): unique

Carnegie Club (156 W 56th St): smoking lounge

Cellar Bar (Bryant Park Hotel, 40 W 40th St): hotel bar

Chelsea Brewing Company (Pier 59, West St at 18th St): big place, big steaks

Corner Bistro (331 W 4th St)

d.b.a. (41 First Ave): a relaxed place with an expanded bar list, including 130 single-malt Scotches and 50 tequilas

Dempsey's Pub (61 Second Ave): live Irish music Tuesday evenings

El Quinto Pino (401 W 24th St): tapas bar

Eleven Madison Park (11 Madison Ave)

Employees Only (510 Hudson St): focus on fresh ingredients and rejuvenated classics

Flatiron Lounge (37 W 19th St): plush banquettes, Manhattan's best Manhattans

Freemans (Freeman Alley, off Rivington St bet Bowery and Chrystie St)

Gramercy Tavern (42 E 20th St)

Great Hall Balcony Bar (The Metropolitan Museum of Art, 1000 Fifth Ave): culture

Hudson Bar & Books (636 Hudson St): reading

Jeremy's Ale House (228 Front St): quart-size cups; a favorite of cops

Keens Steakhouse (72 W 36th St)

King Cole Bar (St. Regis New York, 2 E 55th St)

Landmark Tavern (626 Eleventh Ave): 19th-century decor

Little Branch (20 Seventh Ave S): perfectly calibrated cocktails in subterranean venue

Living Room (W New York Times Square, 1567 Broadway): tourists

GERRY'S EXCLUSIVE LIST

Lobby Lounge (Mandarin Oriental New York, 80 Columbus Circle, 35th floor): phenomenal Central Park views
Macao Trading Co. (311 Church St)
McQuaid's Public House (589 Eleventh Ave)
Mercer Kitchen (99 Prince St): celebrity watching
Molly's Pub and Shebeen (287 Third Ave): Irish
Monkey Bar (Hotel Elysée, 60 E 54th St)
Mustang Sally's (324 Seventh Ave): basketball
No Idea (30 E 20th St)
P.J. Clarke's (915 Third Ave, 44 W 63rd St, and 4 World Financial Center)
The Park (118 Tenth Ave): people watching
Peculier Pub (145 Bleecker St): 350 bottles, 27 draft beers!
Pegu Club (77 W Houston St): inventive twists on cocktails
Peter McManus Cafe (152 Seventh Ave)
Pine Tree Lodge (591 First Ave)
Rao's (455 E 114th St)
Rattle N Hum (14 E 33rd St): 40 taps, sizable space
Rock Center Cafe (Rockefeller Plaza, 20 W 50th St): Watch the ice skaters.
Rose Bar (Gramercy Park Hotel, 2 Lexington Ave)
Sakagura (211 E 43rd St): Japanese restaurant bar
Session 73 (1359 First Ave): live music
Silver Lining (75 Murray St): live-jazz, cocktails
Slaughtered Lamb Pub (182 W 4th St): Drink and dine by the fire.
Smoke Jazz and Supper Club (2751 Broadway): best jazz bar
The Spotted Pig (314 W 11th St): gastropub
Stone Street Tavern (52 Stone St): relaxed spot for beers after the market closes
Swift Hibernian Lounge (34 E 4th St): 26 beers on tap
Tonic and the Met Lounge (727 Seventh Ave and 411 Third Ave): boxing
Trailer Park Lounge (271 W 23rd St): turkey burgers
The View (New York Marriott Marquis, 1535 Broadway): rotating rooftop views
Walker's (16 N Moore St): frequented by local firefighters
Waterfront Ale House (540 Second Ave and 155 Atlantic Ave): great Belgian beer, good food
West 79th Street Boat Basin Cafe (79th St at Hudson River, Riverside Park; seasonal): view with a bar
Wollensky's Grill (201 E 49th St)
Zinc Bar (82 W 3rd St): good music

BARS AND PUBS WITH GOOD EATS
Aquagrill (210 Spring St)
Aretsky's Patroon (160 E 46th St)
Babbo (110 Waverly Pl)

The Beagle (162 Ave A)
China Grill (60 W 53rd St)
Cipriani Dolci (Grand Central Terminal, 42nd St at Vanderbilt Ave)
Del Posto (85 Tenth Ave)
Delmonico's (56 Beaver St)
Fanelli's Cafe (94 Prince St)
Five Points (31 Great Jones St)
Gotham Bar & Grill (12 E 12th St)
Gramercy Tavern (42 E 20th St)
Hallo Berlin (626 Tenth Ave)
Hanjan (36 W 26th St): Korean gastropub
Hospoda (321 E 73rd St): Czech gastropub
Keens Steakhouse (72 W 36th St)
Monkey Bar (Hotel Elysée, 60 E 54th St)
Old Town Bar and Restaurant (45 E 18th St)
Picholine (35 W 64th St)
Plaza Food Hall by Todd English (The Plaza, 1 W 59th St., lower level)
Randolph Beer (343 Broome St)
Redeye Grill (890 Seventh Ave)
Stadium Grill (at Bowlmor Lanes in Times Square, 222 W 44th St): food by David Burke
Union Square Cafe (21 E 16th St)
Wollensky's Grill (201 E 49th St)
Yopparai (151 Rivington St): saké bar, plates of yakitori and sashimi
Zutto Japanese American Pub (77 Hudson St)

BARS FOR QUIET CONVERSATION
Bar Pleiades (The Surrey, 20 E 76th St)
Bar Room at the Modern (Museum of Modern Art, 9 W 53rd St)
Bemelmans Bar at the Carlyle Hotel (35 E 76th St)
Blue Bar (Algonquin Hotel, 59 W 44th St)
Burp Castle (41 E 7th St)
Cafe Luxembourg (200 W 70th St)
Carnegie Club (156 W 56th St)
King Cole Bar (St. Regis New York, 2 E 55th St)
Vero (1004 Second Ave and 1483 Second Ave)

BREAKFAST
2nd Ave Deli (162 E 33rd St and 1442 First Ave)
Amy Ruth's (113 W 116th St)
Balthazar (80 Spring St)
Big Wong (67 Mott St): Chinese breakfast
Brasserie (100 E 53rd St)
The Breslin Bar & Dining Room (Ace Hotel, 16 W 29th St)

Brooklyn Diner USA (155 W 43rd St and 212 W 57th St)
Bubby's (120 Hudson St)
Burger Heaven (9 E 53rd St, 20 E 49th St, and 804 Lexington Ave)
Cafe Cluny (284 W 12th St)
Carnegie Deli (854 Seventh Ave)
City Bakery (3 W 18th St)
Cucina & Co. (Macy's, 151 W 34th St; MetLife Building, 200 Park Ave; and 30 Rockefeller Center, concourse level)
Dishes (48 Grand Central Terminal, 42nd St at Vanderbilt Ave, lower level)
E.A.T. (1064 Madison Ave)
EJ's Luncheonette (1271 Third Ave)
El Malecon (764 Amsterdam Ave and 4141 Broadway): Latin American
Ellen's Stardust Diner (1650 Broadway)
Fairway Cafe & Steakhouse (Fairway Market, 2127 Broadway)
The Fitz (Fitzpatrick Manhattan Hotel, 687 Lexington Ave)
Friend of a Farmer (77 Irving Pl)
Grey Dog's Coffee (90 University Pl, 244 Mulberry St, and 242 W 16th St)
Heartbeat (W New York, outside entrance at 149 E 49th St)
Hill Country Chicken (1123 Broadway)
Joseph Leonard (170 Waverly Pl)
Katz's Delicatessen (205 E Houston St)
Kitchenette (156 Chambers St and 1272 Amsterdam Ave)
Locanda Verde (The Greenwich Hotel, 377 Greenwich St): one of the best breakfasts in the city
Maialino (Gramercy Park Hotel, 2 Lexington Ave): a Danny Meyer operation
The Mark Restaurant by Jean-Georges (The Mark, 25 E 77th St): Vongerichten's spacious, chic dining
Mezzanine (Paramount Hotel, 235 W 46th St)
Michael's (24 W 55th St)
Morandi (211 Waverly Pl): Italian breakfast
New York Luncheonette (135 E 50th St)
Nice Matin (201 W 79th St)
Nios (Muse Hotel, 130 W 46th St)
NoHo Star (330 Lafayette St)
Norma's (Le Parker Meridien New York, 118 W 57th St)
Once Upon a Tart (135 Sullivan St)
Pastis (9 Ninth Ave): haven for weekday breakfasts in the Meatpacking District
Peels (325 Bowery): house-cured bacon
Pigalle (790 Eighth Ave)
Popover Cafe (551 Amsterdam Ave)
Pulino's (282 Bowery): breakfast pizza
Rue 57 (60 W 57th St)
Sarabeth's (423 Amsterdam Ave; Hotel Wales, 1295 Madison Ave; 40 Central Park S; 381 Park Ave S; 339 Greenwich St), **Sarabeth's at Lord &**

Taylor (324 Fifth Ave), and **Sarabeth's Bakery** (Chelsea Market, 75 Ninth Ave)

The Standard Grill (848 Washington St)

Sugar Cafe (200 Allen St): open 24/7

Veselka (144 Second Ave)

Viand Coffee Shop (300 E 86th St, 673 Madison Ave, 2130 Broadway, and 1011 Madison Ave): crowded, but great value

Whole Foods Market (270 Greenwich St, 4 Union Square S, 95 E Houston St, 226 E 57th St, 250 Seventh Ave, 808 Columbus Ave, and Time Warner Center, 10 Columbus Circle)

BRUNCH

Acme (9 Great Jones St)

Alias (76 Clinton St)

Aquagrill (210 Spring St)

Aquavit (65 E 55th St): all-you-can-eat Sunday Swedish brunch

Balthazar (80 Spring St)

Barney Greengrass (541 Amsterdam Ave)

Blue Ribbon Bakery (35 Downing St)

Bowery Diner (241 Bowery)

Cafe Gitane (Jane Hotel, 113 Jane St)

Cafe Habana (17 Prince St)

Cafe Lalo (201 W 83rd St)

Candle 79 (154 E 79th St)

Church Lounge (2 Ave of the Americas)

Clinton St. Baking Co. & Restaurant (4 Clinton St)

Colicchio & Sons (85 Tenth Ave)

Cookshop (156 Tenth Ave)

Cupping Room Cafe (359 West Broadway)

David Burke Townhouse (133 E 61st St)

Edi & the Wolf (102 Avenue C)

Eli's Vinegar Factory (431 E 91st St)

Five Points (31 Great Jones St)

Freemans (Freeman Alley, at Rivington St)

Friend of a Farmer (77 Irving Pl)

Good (89 Greenwich Ave)

Good Enough to Eat (520 Columbus Ave)

Hundred Acres (38 MacDougal St)

Isabella's (359 Columbus Ave)

Kittichai (60 Thompson Hotel, 60 Thompson St)

Kutsher's Tribeca (186 Franklin St)

La Ripaille (605 Hudson St)

Minetta Tavern (113 MacDougal St): Keith McNally offers Old World breakfast treats like shirred eggs with black truffles.

Miss Lily's Favourite Cakes (132 W Houston St): Jamaican

Morandi (211 Waverly Pl)
Nice Matin (201 W 79th St)
NoMad (NoMad Hotel, 1170 Broadway)
North End Grill (104 North End Ave): a Danny Meyer production
The Odeon (145 West Broadway)
Olives New York (W New York Union Square, 201 Park Ave S)
Peacock Alley (301 Park Ave)
Petite Abeille (466 Hudson St, 401 E 20th St, 44 W 17th St, and 134 West Broadway)
Pig 'n' Whistle (922 Third Ave and 951 Second Ave): traditional Irish breakfast
Popover Cafe (551 Amsterdam Ave)
Prune (54 E 1st St): inspired weekend brunch
Quantum Leap Natural Food (226 Thompson St)
Rosemary's Enoteca & Trattoria (18 Greenwich Ave)
Sarabeth's (423 Amsterdam Ave, 40 Central Park S, and Hotel Wales, 1295 Madison Ave) and **Sarabeth's at Lord & Taylor** (324 Fifth Ave)
Schiller's Liquor Bar (131 Rivington St)
Spring Street Natural (62 Spring St)
Sylvia's (328 Lenox Ave)
Tartine (253 W 11th St)
Tribeca Grill (375 Greenwich St)
Wallsé (344 W 11th St)
The Wren (344 Bowery): bargain, Irish-style gastropub

BURGERS
5 Napkin Burger (630 Ninth Ave, 2315 Broadway, and 150 E 14th St)
21 Club (21 W 52nd St)
Ai Fiori (400 Fifth Ave)
Bar Six Restaurant (502 Ave of the Americas)
Bill's Bar & Burger (22 Ninth Ave and 16 W 51st St): short-rib blend
Black Iron Burger Shop (540 E 5th St): kitchen open late
Black Market (110 Ave A): excellent house cheeseburger
BLT Burger (470 Ave of the Americas)
Blue Ribbon Bakery (35 Downing St)
Blue Smoke (116 E 27th St)
Brgr (287 Seventh Ave and 1026 Third Ave)
Brindle Room (277 E 10th St)
Burger & Barrel (25 W Houston St): white truffles
Burger Heaven (20 E 49th St, 536 Madison Ave, 9 E 53rd St, 291 Madison Ave, and 804 Lexington Ave)
burger joint at Le Parker Meridien New York (119 W 56th St)
Burgers and Cupcakes (458 Ninth Ave)
Chelsea Grill (675 Ninth Ave)
Coppelia (207 W 14th St): Latin-style

Corner Bistro (331 W 4th St)

db Bistro Moderne (City Club Hotel, 55 W 44th St)

Fanelli's Cafe (94 Prince St)

Five Guys (112 Fulton St, 296 Bleecker St, 316 W 34th St, 36 W 48th St, 690 Third Ave, 43 W 55th St, and 2847 Broadway): worth the calories; a Virginia-based chain

Flip (Bloomingdale's, 1000 Third Ave): choose your own combination

Great Jones Cafe (54 Great Jones St)

Half King (505 W 23rd St): one of the best budget burgers

Hard Rock Cafe (1501 Broadway)

Home Restaurant (20 Cornelia St)

J.G. Melon (1291 Third Ave)

Jackson Hole Burgers (232 E 64th St, 521 Third Ave, 1611 Second Ave, 1270 Madison Ave, and 517 Columbus Ave)

Keens Steakhouse (72 W 36th St)

Knickerbocker Bar and Grill (33 University Pl)

The Lion (62 W 9th St): with pork belly

Little Owl (90 Bedford St): sliders

Mark (33 St. Mark's Pl): lively little burger bar

Market Table (54 Carmine St)

Minetta Tavern (113 MacDougal St): Black Label hamburger

The Odeon (145 West Broadway)

Old Town Bar and Restaurant (45 E 18th St)

P.J. Clarke's (915 Third Ave, 44 W 63rd St, and 4 World Financial Center)

Pastis (9 Ninth Ave)

Patroon (160 E 46th St)

Paul's da Burger Joint (131 Second Ave)

Peels (325 Bowery): steakhouse-style cheeseburger

Pop Burger (60 Ninth Ave and 83 University Pl)

Popover Cafe (551 Amsterdam Ave)

Rare Bar & Grill (Affinia Shelburne, 303 Lexington Ave and Hilton New York Fashion District, 152 W 26th St)

Resto (111 E 29th St)

Rodeo Bar (375 Third Ave)

Royale (157 Ave C)

Rue 57 (60 W 57th St)

Shake Shack (Madison Square Park, Madison Ave at 23rd St; 366 Columbus Ave; 154 E 86th St; 691 Eighth Ave; and 215 Murray St): a New York City experience brought to you by the extraordinary Danny Meyer

Soup Burg (1095 Lexington Ave)

The Spotted Pig (314 W 11th St)

Stand (24 E 12th St)

Steak 'n Shake (1695 Broadway)

Txikito (240 Ninth Ave): Basque-inspired ingredients

GERRY'S EXCLUSIVE LIST

Union Square Cafe (21 E 16th St)
Waverly Inn (16 Bank St)
White Horse Tavern (567 Hudson St)
Whitehall Bar & Kitchen (19 Greenwich Ave)
Whitmans (406 E 9th St): Try the Juicy Lucy!
Wollensky's Grill (201 E 49th St)
Zaitzeff (72 Nassau St and 711 Second Ave): Kobe beef, hormone-free sirloin

CHEAP EATS

107 West (2787 Broadway)
Beyoglu (1431 Third Ave)
BonChon Chicken (207 W 38th St, 104 John St, 325 Fifth Ave, and 957 Second Ave)
Boqueria (171 Spring St)
Bouchon Bakery (1 Rockefeller Center and Time Warner Center, 10 Columbus Circle, 3rd floor)
Buddakan (Chelsea Market, 75 Ninth Ave)
burger joint at Le Parker Meridien New York (119 W 56th St)
Buvette (42 Grove St)
Cafe Lalo (201 W 83rd St)
Carmine's (2450 Broadway and 200 W 44th St)
Cascabel Taqueria (1538 Second Ave)
Chickpea (210 E 14th St, 688 Ave of the Americas, 1413 Madison Ave, and other locations)
City Bakery (3 W 18th St)
Corner Bistro (331 W 4th St)
David Burke at Bloomingdale's (150 E 59th St)
Degustation (239 E 5th St)
Earl's Beer & Cheese (1259 Park Ave)
Frank (88 Second Ave)
Frankie's Spuntino (570 Hudson St and 457 Court St)
Golden Unicorn (18 East Broadway)
Grand Sichuan (15 Seventh Ave, 23 St. Mark's Pl, 368 W 46th St, and other locations)
Gray's Papaya (402 Ave of the Americas and 2090 Broadway)
Il Bagatto (192 E 2nd St)
Ivy's Cafe (154 W 72nd St)
Jean Claude (137 Sullivan St)
John's Pizzeria (278 Bleecker St, 408 E 64th St, and 260 W 44th St)
Katz's Delicatessen (205 E Houston St)
Kitchenette (156 Chambers St and 1272 Amsterdam Ave)
Lil' Frankie's Pizza (19 First Ave)
Mission Chinese Food (154 Orchard St)
Paul's da Burger Joint (131 Second Ave)

Pho Bang (157 Mott St)
Popover Cafe (551 Amsterdam Ave)
The Redhead (349 E 13th St)
Sapporo (152 W 49th St)
The Smith (55 Third Ave, 1900 Broadway, and 956 Second Ave)
Soba-ya (229 E 9th St)
Sosa Borella (832 Eighth Ave)
Spot Dessert Bar (13 St. Mark's Pl and 11 W 32nd St)
Spring Natural Kitchen (474 Columbus Ave)
Spring Street Natural (62 Spring St)
Supper (156 E 2nd St)
Sylvia's (328 Lenox Ave)
Tartine (253 W 11th St)
Tea & Sympathy (108 Greenwich Ave)
Tossed (295 Park Ave S)
Turkish Cuisine (631 Ninth Ave)
Vanessa's Dumpling House (118 Eldridge St, 220 E 14th St, and 310 Bedford St)
Veselka (144 Second Ave)
'wichcraft (555 Fifth Ave and other locations)
Xi'an Famous Foods (81 St. Mark's Pl, 67 Bayard St, and 24 W 45th St)
Yakitori Totto (251 W 55th St)
Zum Schneider (107 Ave C)

CHEESE PLATES
Artisanal Fromagerie, Bistro and Wine Bar (2 Park Ave)
Circo NYC (120 W 55th St)
craftbar (900 Broadway)
Daniel (60 E 65th St)
Eleven Madison Park (11 Madison Ave)
Gramercy Tavern (42 E 20th St)
Jean Georges (Trump International Hotel and Tower, 1 Central Park W)
La Grenouille (3 E 52nd St)
Le Cirque (1 Beacon Court, 151 E 58th St)
The Morgan Dining Room (The Morgan Library and Museum, 225 Madison Ave)
Picholine (35 W 64th St)
Solera (216 E 53rd St)
Telepan (72 W 69th St)
Wallsé (344 W 11th St)

COFFEE BARS
71 Irving Place (71 Irving Pl)
Aroma Espresso Bar (145 Greene St, 161 W 72nd Ave, and 205 E 42nd St)
Bluebird Coffee Shop (72 E 1st St)

GERRY'S EXCLUSIVE LIST

Cafe Grumpy (224 W 20th St and 13 Essex St)
Cafe Lalo (201 W 83rd St)
Caffe Dante (79-81 MacDougal St)
Caffe Roma (385 Broome St)
City Bakery (3 W 18th St)
Cupcake Cafe (545 Ninth Ave)
Cupping Room Cafe (359 West Broadway)
Ferrara Bakery and Cafe (195 Grand St)
French Roast (78 W 11th St and 2340 Broadway)
Hungarian Pastry Shop (1030 Amsterdam Ave)
Irving Farm Coffee Company (56 Seventh Ave)
Jack's Stir Brew Coffee (138 W 10th St and 222 Front St)
Joe The Art of Coffee (141 Waverly Pl, 9 E 13th St, 405 W 23rd St, and other locations)
Kaffe 1668 (275 Greenwich St and 401 Greenwich St)
La Colombe Torrefaction (319 Church St, 270 Lafayette St, and 400 Lafayette St)
Laughing Man Coffee & Tea (184 Duane St): organic brews
Le Pain Quotidien (1131 Madison Ave; ABC Carpet & Home, 38 E 19th St; and other locations)
Once Upon a Tart (135 Sullivan St)
Oren's Daily Roast (1144 Lexington Ave and other locations)
The Roasting Plant (81 Orchard St and 75 Greenwich Ave)
Sarabeth's (Hotel Wales, 1295 Madison Ave; 423 Amsterdam Ave; and 40 Central Park S), **Sarabeth's at Lord & Taylor** (424 Fifth Ave), and **Sarabeth's Bakery** (Chelsea Market, 75 Ninth Ave)
Sensuous Bean (66 W 70th St)
Starbucks (numerous locations)
Stumptown Coffee Roasters (Ace Hotel, 18 W 29th St)
Third Rail Coffee (240 Sullivan St)
Veselka (144 Second Ave)
Zabar's (2245 Broadway)

DELIS AND QUICK LUNCHES
2nd Ave Deli (162 E 33rd St and 1442 First Ave)
Amy's Bread (Chelsea Market, 75 Ninth Ave; 672 Ninth Ave; and 250 Bleecker St)
Artie's Delicatessen (2290 Broadway)
Balthazar (80 Spring St)
Barney Greengrass (541 Amsterdam Ave)
Ben's Kosher Deli (209 W 38th St)
Bread (20 Spring St)
Carnegie Deli (854 Seventh Ave)
Charles St. Food (144 Seventh Ave S)
City Bakery (3 W 18th St)

City Market Cafe (178 Fifth Ave, 551 Madison Ave, and 1100 Madison Ave)
Clinton St. Baking Co. & Restaurant (4 Clinton St)
Crumbcake Cafe (254 Eighth Ave)
Dil-E Punjab (170 Ninth Ave)
Dishes (6 E 45th St; 399 Park Ave; and Grand Central Terminal, 42nd St at Vanderbilt Ave)
E.A.T. (1064 Madison Ave)
Ess-a-Bagel (831 Third Ave and 359 First Ave)
Fine & Schapiro (138 W 72nd St)
Food Exchange (309 Madison Ave, 1400 Broadway, and 120 E 59th St)
Garden of Eden (7 E 14th St, 162 W 23rd St, and 2780 Broadway)
Grace's Marketplace (1237 Third Ave)
Juice Generation (171 W 4th St, 644 Ninth Ave, 117 W 72nd St, and other locations)
Junior's (1515 Broadway; Grand Central Terminal, 42nd St at Vanderbilt Ave, lower level; and West 45th St, Broadway at Eighth Ave)
Just Salad (320 Park Ave, 134 W 37th St, 600 Third Ave, and other locations)
Katz's Delicatessen (205 E Houston St)
Lansky's (235 Columbus Ave)
M&O Market and Deli (124 Thompson St)
Samad's (2867 Broadway)
Sarabeth's (423 Amsterdam Ave; 40 Central Park S; and Hotel Wales, 1295 Madison Ave)
Zabar's (2245 Broadway)

DESSERTS
Acme (9 Great Jones St)
Asiate (Mandarin Oriental New York, 80 Columbus Circle, 35th floor)
BabyCakes (248 Broome St): vegan
Bouley (163 Duane St)
Cafe Lalo (201 W 83rd St)
Cafe Sabarsky (Neue Galerie New York, 1048 Fifth Ave)
Calliope (84 E 4th St)
ChikaLicious (203 E 10th St)
Cupcake Cafe (545 Ninth Ave)
David Burke Townhouse (133 E 61st St)
Ferrara Bakery and Cafe (195 Grand St)
Gramercy Tavern (42 E 20th St)
Hearth (403 E 12th St)
Il Laboratorio del Gelato (88 Ludlow St)
Jacques Torres Chocolate (350 Hudson St, 285 Amsterdam Ave, 30 Rockefeller Plaza, and other locations)
Jean Georges (Trump International Hotel and Tower, 1 Central Park W)
Lady M Cake Boutique (41 E 78th St and Plaza Food Hall by Todd English, 1 W 59th St)

Magnolia Bakery (401 Bleecker St, 200 Columbus Ave, 1240 Ave of the Americas, and other locations)
Once Upon a Tart (135 Sullivan St)
Petrossian Restaurant (182 W 58th St)
Schiller's Liquor Bar (131 Rivington St)
Serendipity 3 (225 E 60th St)
Veniero's (342 E 11th St)
wd-50 (50 Clinton St)
Zabar's Cafe (2245 Broadway)

DIM SUM

The serving of small tea pastries called dim sum originated in Hong Kong and has become a delicious Chinatown institution. Although dim sum is usually eaten for brunch, some restaurants also serve it as an appetizer. Dim sum items are rolled over to your table on carts, and you simply point at whatever looks good. This eliminates the language barrier and encourages experimentation. When you're finished, the accumulated small plates are counted and the bill is calculated accordingly.

Here are some of the most popular dim sum dishes:

Cha Siu Bow (steamed barbecued pork buns)
Cha Siu So (flaky buns)
Chun Guen (spring rolls)
Dai Tze Gau (steamed scallop and shrimp dumplings)
Don Ta (baked custard tarts)
Dow Sah Bow (sweet-bean-paste-filled buns)
Fancy Fans (meat-filled pot sticker triangles)
Four-Color Siu Mai (meat-and-vegetable-filled dumplings)
Gau Choi Gau (pan-browned chive and shrimp dumplings)
Gee Cheung Fun (steamed rice-noodle rolls)
Gee Yoke Go (savory pork triangles)
Ha Gau (shrimp dumplings)
Jow Ha Gok (shrimp turnovers)
Pot Sticker Kou The (meat-filled dumplings)
Satay Gai Tran (chicken satay)
Siu Mai (steamed pork dumplings)
Tzay Ha (fried shrimp ball on sugarcane)

For the most authentic and delicious dim sum in New York, try these places:
Dim Sum Go Go (5 East Broadway)
Golden Unicorn (18 East Broadway): an especially fine selection
Jing Fong (20 Elizabeth St)
New Mandarin Court (61 Mott St)
Oriental Garden (14 Elizabeth St)
Our Place (242 E 79th St)
Ping's Seafood (22 Mott St)
Redfarm (529 Hudson St)

Ruby Foo's (1626 Broadway)
Shun Lee Cafe/Shun Lee West (43 W 65th St)

DINERS
Bowery Diner (241 Bowery)
Brooklyn Diner USA (212 W 57th St and 155 W 43rd St): outstanding
City Diner (2441 Broadway): retro-elegant
The Diner (44 Ninth Ave): Meatpacking District
Ellen's Stardust Diner (1650 Broadway)
Hudson Diner (468 Hudson St)
Miss Lily's Favourite Cakes (132 W Houston St)
Skylight Diner (402 W 34th St)
Tick Tock Diner (481 Eighth Ave): open 24 hours
Westway Diner (614 Ninth Ave)

DINING SOLO
Some of these restaurants have dining counters, while others are tranquil and suitable for single diners.
Aquavit (65 E 55th St)
Babbo (110 Waverly Pl)
Cafe S.F.A. (Saks Fifth Avenue, 611 Fifth Ave, 8th floor)
Carnegie Deli (854 Seventh Ave)
Caviar Russe (538 Madison Ave)
Chez Napoléon (365 W 50th St)
Cupcake Cafe (545 Ninth Ave)
Elephant & Castle (68 Greenwich Ave)
Eleven Madison Park (11 Madison Ave)
Gotham Bar & Grill (12 E 12th St)
Grand Central Oyster Bar Restaurant (Grand Central Terminal, 42nd St at Vanderbilt Ave, lower level)
J.G. Melon (1291 Third Ave)
Jackson Hole Burgers (232 E 64th St, 521 Third Ave, 1611 Second Ave, 517 Columbus Ave, and 1270 Madison Ave)
Joe's Shanghai (9 Pell St and 24 W 56th St)
Joseph Leonard (170 Waverly Pl)
Kitchenette (156 Chambers St and 1272 Amsterdam Ave)
La Bonne Soupe (48 W 55th St)
La Caridad 78 (2199 Broadway)
Locanda Verde (The Greenwich Hotel, 377 Greenwich St)
Naples 45 (MetLife Building, 200 Park Ave)
Pepolino (281 West Broadway)
Raoul's (180 Prince St)
Republic (37 Union Square W)
Sarabeth's (Hotel Wales, 1295 Madison Ave; 423 Amsterdam Ave; and 40 Central Park S), **Sarabeth's at Lord & Taylor** (424 Fifth Ave), and **Sarabeth's Bakery** (Chelsea Market, 75 Ninth Ave)

Trattoria dell'Arte (900 Seventh Ave)
Union Square Cafe (21 E 16th St)
Viand Coffee Shop (673 Madison Ave, 1011 Madison Ave, 300 E 86th St, and 2130 Broadway)

FAMILY-STYLE DINING
Carmine's (2450 Broadway and 200 W 44th St)
China Grill (60 W 53rd St)
Phoenix Garden (242 E 40th St)
Piccolo Angolo (621 Hudson St)
Ruby Foo's (1626 Broadway)
Sambuca (20 W 72nd St)
Tao (42 E 58th St)

FIRESIDE
21 Club (21 W 52nd St): cocktail lounge
Alta (64 W 10th St)
Bouley (163 Duane St)
Cornelia Street Cafe (29 Cornelia St)
The Dutch (131 Sullivan St)
Employees Only (510 Hudson St)
I Trulli (122 E 27th St)
Keens Steakhouse (72 W 36th St)
Lobby Bar (The Bowery Hotel, 335 Bowery)
Locanda Verde (The Greenwich Hotel, 377 Greenwich St)
Molly's Pub and Shebeen (287 Third Ave)
Moran's Chelsea (146 Tenth Ave)
One if by Land, Two if by Sea (17 Barrow St)
Quality Meats (57 W 58th St)
Vivolo (140 E 74th St)
Water's Edge (401 44th Dr at East River, Queens)
Waverly Inn (16 Bank St)
wd-50 (50 Clinton St)

FOREIGN FLAVORS
Some of these commendable ethnic establishments do not have full write-ups in this chapter. Here are the best of the more exotic eateries, arranged by cuisine:

Afghan | **Afghan Kebab House** (1345 Second Ave and 764 Ninth Ave)

African, North | **Nomad** (78 Second Ave)

African, South | **Xai Xai** (369 W 51st St)

Argentinean | **Chimichurri Grill** (609 Ninth Ave) and **Sosa Borella** (832 Eighth Ave)

Asian | **Chopshop** (254 Tenth Ave), **The General** (199 Bowery), **Toy** (Gansevoort Meatpacking NYC, 18 Ninth Ave), and **Wong** (7 Cornelia St)

Australian | **Public** (210 Elizabeth St) and **Tuck Shop** (68 E 1st St; 115 St. Mark's Pl; and Chelsea Market, 75 Ninth Ave)

Austrian | **Cafe Sabarsky** (Neue Galerie New York, 1048 Fifth Ave), **Seäsonal Restaurant & Weinbar** (132 W 58th St), and **Wallsé** (344 W 11th St)

Belgian | **The Cannibal** (113 E 29th St), **Petite Abeille** (466 Hudson St, 401 E 20th St, 44 W 17th St, and 134 West Broadway), and **Resto** (111 E 29th St)

Brazilian | **Churrascaria Plataforma** (Belvedere Hotel, 316 W 49th St), **Churrascaria Tribeca** (221 West Broadway), **Circus** (132 E 61st St), and **Emporium Brazil** (15 W 46th St)

British | **Jones Wood Foundry** (401 E 76th St)

Caribbean/Latin | **Don Pedro's** (1865 Second Ave) and **Negril Village** (70 W 3rd St)

Chilean | **Pomaire** (371 W 46th St)

Chinese | **Big Wong** (67 Mott St), **Bo Ky** (80 Bayard St), **Chin Chin** (216 E 49th St), **China Fun** (246 Columbus Ave), **Flor de Mayo** (484 Amsterdam Ave and 2651 Broadway), **Golden Unicorn** (18 East Broadway), **Grand Sichuan** (229 Ninth Ave, 15 Seventh Ave, 368 W 46th St, and 23 St. Mark's Pl), **Hop Lee** (16 Mott St), **Jing Fong** (20 Elizabeth St), **Joe's Ginger** (25 Pell St), **Joe's Shanghai** (9 Pell St and 24 W 56th St), **Mr. K's** (570 Lexington Ave), **Nice Green Bo** (66 Bayard St), **Oriental Garden** (14 Elizabeth St), **Ping's Seafood** (22 Mott St), **Red Egg** (202 Centre St), **Shanghai Cuisine** (89-91 Bayard St), **Shun Lee Palace** (155 E 55th St), **Shun Lee Cafe/Shun Lee West** (43 W 65th St), **Tang Pavilion** (65 W 55th St), **Wu Liang Ye** (36 W 48th St), and **Yunnan Kitchen** (79 Clinton St)

Cuban | **Cabana** (1022 Third Ave and 89 South St), **Cafecito** (185 Ave C), **Cafe Con Leche** (424 Amsterdam Ave), **Cafe Habana** (17 Prince St), **Coppelia** (207 W 14th St), and **Victor's Cafe** (236 W 52nd St)

East European | **Petrossian Restaurant** (182 W 58th St), **Sammy's Roumanian Steak House** (157 Chrystie St), and **Veselka** (144 Second Ave)

Ethiopian | **Meskerem** (468 W 47th St and 124 MacDougal St) and **Queen of Sheba** (650 Tenth Ave)

French | see restaurant write-ups (beginning on page 70)

German | **Blaue Gans** (139 Duane St), **Hallo Berlin** (626 Tenth Ave), **Heidelberg Restaurant** (1648 Second Ave), **Loreley** (7 Rivington St), and **Zum Schneider** (107 Ave C)

Greek | **Ammos** (52 Vanderbilt Ave), **Avra** (141 E 48th St), **Avra Estiatorio** (141 E 48th St), **Estiatorio Milos** (125 W 55th St), **Ithaka** (308 E 86th St), **Kellari Taverna** (19 W 44th St), **Molyvos** (871 Seventh Ave), **Periyali** (35 W 20th St), **Pylos** (128 E 7th St), **Snack** (105 Thompson St), **Thalassa** (179 Franklin St), and **Uncle Nick's** (747 Ninth Ave)

Indian | **Banjara** (97 First Ave), **Bombay Talkie** (189 Ninth Ave), **Brick Lane Curry House** (306-308 E 6th St), **Bukhara Grill** (217 E 49th St), **Chola** (232 E 58th St), **Darbar** (152 E 46th St), **Dawat** (210 E 58th Ave), **Dévi** (8 E 18th St), **Haandi** (113 Lexington Ave), **Haveli** (100 Second Ave), **Indus Valley** (2636 Broadway), **Minar** (5 W 31st St and 138 W 46th St), **Moti Mahal Delux** (1149 First Ave), **Salaam Bombay** (319

Greenwich St), **Tamarind** (41-43 E 22nd St and 99 Hudson St), **Tulsi** (211 E 46th St), **Utsav** (1185 Ave of the Americas), and **Yuva** (230 E 58th St)

Indonesian | **Bali Nusa Indah** (651 Ninth Ave)

Irish | **Eamonn's Bar & Grill** (9 E 45th St), **The Fitz** (Fitzpatrick Manhattan Hotel, 687 Lexington Ave), and **Molly's Pub and Shebeen** (287 Third Ave)

Italian | see restaurant write-ups (beginning on page 70)

Japanese | **Benihana** (47 W 56th St), **Bond Street** (6 Bond St), **Curry Ya** (214 E 10th St), **Donguri** (309 E 83rd St), **EN Japanese Brasserie** (435 Hudson St), **Hakata Tonton** (61 Grove St), **Hakubai** (The Kitano New York, 66 Park Ave), **Hatsuhana** (237 Park Ave and 17 E 48th St), **Ippudo** (65 Fourth Ave), **Japonica** (100 University Pl), **Jewel Bako** (239 E 5th St), **Kurumazushi** (7 E 47th St), **Kyo Ya** (94 E 7thSt), **Megu** (62 Thomas St and 845 United Nations Plaza), **Minamoto Kitchoan** (608 Fifth Ave), **Nobu Fifty Seven** (40 W 57th St), **Nobu New York** and **Nobu Next Door** (105 Hudson St), **Omen** (113 Thompson St), **Ozu** (566 Amsterdam Ave), **Sakagura** (211 E 43rd St), **Seo** (249 E 49th St), **Soto** (357 Ave of the Americas), **Sugiyama** (251 W 55th St), **SushiSamba** (245 Park Ave S and 87 Seventh Ave S), **Sushi Yasuda** (204 E 43rd St), **Torishin** (1193 First Ave), and **Yakitori Totto** (261 W 55th St)

Korean | **Cho Dang Gol** (55 W 35th St), **Danji** (346 W 52nd St), **Do Hwa** (55 Carmine St), **Dok Suni's** (119 First Ave), **Gahm Mi Oak** (43 W 32nd St), **Gaonnuri** (1250 Broadway, 39th floor), **HanGawi** (12 E 32nd St), **Kang Suh** (1250 Broadway), **Kori** (253 Church St), **Kum Gang San** (49 W 32nd St), **Kunjip** (9 W 32nd St), **New York Kom Tang** (32 W 32nd St), **New WonJo** (23 W 32nd St), and **Seoul Garden** (34 W 32nd St)

Lebanese | **Al Bustan** (319 E 53rd St), **Ilili** (236 Fifth Ave), **Naya** (1057 Second Ave), and **Naya Express** (688 Third Ave)

Malaysian | **Laut** (15 E 17th St) and **New Malaysia Restaurant** (46-48 Bowery)

Mediterranean | **Antique Garage** (41 Mercer St), **August** (359 Bleecker St), **Balaboosta** (214 Mulberry St), **Boulud Sud** (20 W 64th St), **Dervish** (146 W 47th St), and **Il Buco Alimentari e Vineria** (53 Great Jones St)

Mexican | **Cascabel Taqueria** (1538 Second Ave), **Dos Caminos** (825 Third Ave, 373 Park Ave S, and 475 West Broadway), **El Parador Cafe** (325 E 34th St), **Empellón Cocina** (105 First Ave), **Empellón Taqueria** (230 W 4th St), **Fresco Tortillas** (819 Second Ave), **Hecho en Dumbo** (354 Bowery), **Itzocan Cafe** (438 E 9th St), **La Esquina** (106 Kenmare St), **Maya** (1191 First Ave), **Mexicana Mama** (525 Hudson St and 47 E 12th St), **Mexican Radio** (19 Cleveland Pl), **Pampano** (209 E 49th St), **Rosa Mexicano** (1063 First Ave, 9 E 18th St, and 61 Columbus Ave), **Toloache** (251 W 50th St, 166 E 82nd St, and 83 Maiden Lane), and **Tortilla Flats** (767 Washington St)

Middle Eastern | **Balaboosta** (214 Mulberry St), **Cleopatra's Needle** (2485 Broadway), and **Moustache** (90 Bedford St, 265 E 10th St, and 1621 Lexington Ave)

Moroccan | **Cafe Mogador** (101 St. Mark's Pl) and **Zerza** (320 E 6th St)

Persian | **Persepolis** (1407 Second Ave)

Polynesian | **Hurricane Steak & Sushi** (360 Park Ave S)

Portuguese | **Aldea** (31 W 17th St), **Macao Trading Co.** (311 Church St), and **Pao** (322 Spring St)

Puerto Rican | **Cuchifritos** (168 E 116th St) and **La Taza de Oro** (96 Eighth Ave)

Russian | **FireBird** (365 W 46th St),   (41 E 20th St), **Russian Samovar** (256 W 52nd St), and **Uncle Vanya Cafe** (315 W 54th St)

Scandinavian | **Aquavit** (65 E 55th St) and **Smörgås Chef** (Scandinavia House: The Nordic Center in America, 58 Park Ave; 53 Stone St; and 283 W 12th St)

Scottish | **Highlands** (150 W 10th St) and **St. Andrew's** (140 W 46th St)

Southwestern | **Agave** (140 Seventh Ave S)

Spanish and South American | **Alcala** (342 E 46th St), **Boqueria** (171 Spring St and 53 W 19th St), **Cafe Español** (172 Bleecker St and 78 Carmine St), **Cafe Riazor** (245 W 16th St), **La Fonda del Sol** (MetLife Building, 200 Park Ave), **Rayuela** (165 Allen St), **Solera** (216 E 53rd St), **Tio Pepe** (168 W 4th St), and **Toledo** (6 E 36th St)

Thai | **Kin Shop** (469 Ave of the Americas), **Peep** (177 Prince St), **Pongsri Thai** (106 Bayard St, 165 W 23rd St, and 244 W 48th St), **Royal Siam** (240 Eighth Ave), and **Topaz** (127 W 56th St)

Tibetan | **Tsampa** (212 E 9th St)

Turkish | **Ali Baba** (212 E 34th St and 862 Second Ave), **Beyoglu** (1431 Third Ave), **Pasha** (70 W 71st St), **Pera Mediterranean Brasserie** (303 Madison Ave), **Sip Sak** (928 Second Ave), **Turkish Cuisine** (631 Ninth Ave), **Turkish Kitchen** (386 Third Ave), and **Üsküdar** (1405 Second Ave)

Vietnamese | **Le Colonial** (149 E 57th St), **Mekong** (18 King St), **Nha Trang** (87 Baxter St and 148 Centre St), **Omai** (158 Ninth Ave), and **Pho Viet Huong** (73 Mulberry St)

FRENCH BISTROS

Balthazar (80 Spring St)

Cafe Boulud (The Surrey, 20 E 76th St)

Cafe Luxembourg (200 W 70th St)

Flea Market Cafe (131 Ave A)

Jean Claude (137 Sullivan St)

JoJo (160 E 64th St)

Le Gigot (18 Cornelia St)

Pastis (9 Ninth Ave)

Raoul's (180 Prince St)

Rue 57 (60 W 57th St)

GAME

Game is generally offered at these restaurants in winter months or by special request.

Aquavit (65 E 55th St)
Babbo (110 Waverly Pl)
Barbetta (321 W 46th St)
Blue Hill (75 Washington Pl)
Cafe Boulud (The Surrey, 20 E 76th St)
Daniel (60 E 65th St)
Eleven Madison Park (11 Madison Ave)
Felidia (243 E 58th St)
Four Seasons (99 E 52nd St)
Il Mulino New York (86 W 3rd St)
Jean Georges (Trump International Hotel and Tower, 1 Central Park W)
La Grenouille (3 E 52nd St)
Le Périgord (405 E 52nd St)
Ouest (2315 Broadway)
Picholine (35 W 64th St)
Tocqueville Restaurant (1 E 15th St)
Union Square Cafe (21 E 16th St)

HEALTHY FARE

Angelica Kitchen (300 E 12th St): organic and vegan
Calista Superfoods (301 E 49th St and 1217 Lexington Ave): inventive, made from scratch
Candle 79 (154 E 79th St)
Four Seasons (99 E 52nd St): expensive
Gobo (401 Ave of the Americas and 1426 Third Ave)
HanGawi (12 E 32nd St)
Josie's Restaurant (300 Amsterdam Ave)
Popover Cafe (551 Amsterdam Ave)
Pure Food and Wine (54 Irving Pl)
Quantum Leap Natural Food (226 Thompson St)
Spring Street Natural (62 Spring St): your best bet
Zen Palate (663 Ninth Ave and 115 E 18th St)

HOTEL RESTAURANTS AND BARS

Manhattan hotel dining has regained some of its glow of long ago. No longer are on-premises eateries just for the convenience of registered guests. Now they are destinations for those who desire a less trendy scene with an inviting, elegant atmosphere. Noteworthy choices include:

6 Columbus (308 W 58th St): **Blue Ribbon Sushi Bar & Grill**
60 Thompson Hotel (60 Thompson St): **Kittichai** (sophisticated Thai)
Ace Hotel (20 W 29th St): **The Breslin Bar & Dining Room, The John Dory Oyster Bar**, and **Stumptown Coffee Roasters**

Affinia Shelburne (303 Lexington Ave): **Rare Bar & Grill** (elegant burger spot) and **Rare View Rooftop Lounge**

The Algonquin Hotel (59 W 44th St): **Round Table**

Andaz Wall Street (75 Wall St): **Bar Seven Five** (after-hours watering hole)

The Carlton Hotel (92 Madison Ave, 2nd floor): **Millesime** (French treasures from the sea)

Carlyle Hotel (35 E 76th St): **Bemelmans Bar** and **The Carlyle** (overpriced)

Chambers Hotel (15 W 56th St): **Má Pêche** and **Momofuku Milk Bar**

The Chatwal Hotel (132 W 44th St): **The Lambs Club** (upscale American)

City Club Hotel (55 W 44th St): **db Bistro Moderne** (Daniel Boulud's urbane bar-restaurant)

Dylan Hotel (52 E 41st St): **Benjamin Steak House**

Empire Hotel (44 W 63rd St): **Ed's Chowder House** (raw bar and restaurant)

Gansevoort Meatpacking NYC (18 Ninth Ave): **Plunge** (rooftop)

Gramercy Park Hotel (2 Lexington Ave): **Maialino** (Danny Meyer's house)

The Greenwich Hotel (377 Greenwich St): **Locanda Verde**

Hilton Times Square (234 W 42nd St): **Restaurant Above** and **Pinnacle Bar** (breathtaking views, creative American menu with Italian accents)

Hotel Elysée (60 E 54th St): **Monkey Bar** (great history and eclectic menu with Asian touches)

Hotel Plaza Athenee (37 E 64th St): **Arabelle** (dignified)

Hotel Wales (1295 Madison Ave): **Paola's** (Italian) and **Sarabeth's** (delightful)

Ink48 (653 Eleventh Ave): **Print** and **Press Lounge**

Inn at Irving Place (56 Irving Pl): **Cibar Lounge** and **Lady Mendl's Tea Salon** (very proper)

Kimberly Hotel (145 E 50th St): **Upstairs** (rooftop lounge)

The Kitano New York (66 Park Ave): **Hakubai** (Japanese)

Le Parker Meridien New York (118 W 57th St): **burger joint** (lobby) and **Norma's** (breakfast, brunch, and lunch)

Library Hotel (299 Madison Ave): **Madison and Vine** (American bistro and wine bar)

The London NYC (151 W 54th St): **Maze** (casual) and **Gordon Ramsay** (fine dining)

The Lowell (28 E 63rd St): **Pembroke Room**

Mandarin Oriental New York (80 Columbus Circle): **Asiate** (*prix-fixe* only dinner, fabulous views)

The Mark (25 E 77th St): **The Mark Restaurant by Jean-Georges** (lavish brunch menu)

New York Marriott Marquis (1535 Broadway): **The View** (revolving top-floor eatery with New York-centric menu)

The Pierre (2 E 61st St): **Sirio Ristorante** (Italian) and **Two E Bar** (eclectic)

Ritz-Carlton New York, Battery Park (2 West St): **2 West** (modern American)

St. Regis New York (2 E 55th St): **Astor Court** (you can't do better) and **King Cole Bar**

Sheraton New York Times Square Hotel (811 Seventh Ave): **Hudson Market Burger**

Shoreham Hotel (33 W 55th St): **Shoreham Bar and Restaurant** (California cuisine)

Soho Grand Hotel (310 West Broadway): **Grand Bar & Lounge** (upscale bar menu)

The Standard High Line (848 Washington St): **The Biergarten** (German fun) and **The Standard Grill** (American)

The Surrey (20 E 76th St): **Bar Pleiades** (Coco Chanel-inspired decor) and **Cafe Boulud** (French)

Trump International Hotel and Tower (1 Central Park W): **Jean Georges** (The Donald's personal gem) and **Nougatine Cafe** (casual)

Trump Soho New York (246 Spring St): **Koi** (Japanese)

W New York (541 Lexington Ave): **Heartbeat** (especially breakfast)

W New York Times Square (1567 Broadway): **Blue Fin** (seafood)

W New York Union Square (201 Park Ave S): **Olives New York** (Mediterranean; Todd English)

Waldorf Astoria New York (301 Park Ave): **Bull & Bear** (British atmosphere), **Oscar's** (cafeteria), and **Peacock Alley** (sumptuous Sunday brunch)

Washington Square Hotel (103 Waverly Pl): **North Square Restaurant and Lounge** (moderately priced American)

Westin New York Grand Central (212 E 42nd St): **The LCL: Bar & Kitchen** (a.k.a. The Local; casual, seasonal American menu)

KOSHER

Kosher dining experiences in New York City run the gamut from elegant restaurants with celebrity chefs to the falafel stand outside Rockefeller Center and the kosher hot dog stand at Shea Stadium. Especially with kosher dining, phone ahead to make sure restaurants are open.

Abigael's on Broadway (1407 Broadway): largest kosher restaurant

Azuri Cafe (465 W 51st St): Middle Eastern, inexpensive

Cafe K (8 E 48th St): This may be the busiest lunch spot in New York City.

Cafe Roma Pizzeria (854 Amsterdam Ave)

Caravan of Dreams (405 E 6th St): natural, raw, and vegetarian East Village kosher restaurant

Circa (22 W 33rd St): This upscale cafeteria lunch location has everything from sushi to create-your-own salads and hot lasagna—all delicious!

Colbeh (32 W 39th St): Mediterranean

Eden Wok (43 E 34th St): great kosher Chinese restaurant with sushi bar

Estihana (221 W 79th St): closest kosher choice to the Museum of Natural History

Jack's Wife Freda (224 Lafayette St): cozy Soho spot that re-imagines (as in tweaks) Jewish dishes

Jerusalem II (1375 Broadway): Crowds keep coming back to one of the first and best pizza, falafel, and salad-bar emporiums in town.

Le Marais (150 W 46th St): This French steakhouse, which has a butcher store

in the front, sets the kosher standard

Lox at Cafe Weissman (The Jewish Museum, 1109 Fifth Ave): This museum was the old Felix Warburg mansion, and this intimate spot in the basement is a kosher oasis on Museum Row.

Mendy's (875 Third Ave; 61 E 34th St; 30 Rockefeller Plaza; and Grand Central Terminal, 42nd St at Vanderbilt Ave): huge portions, fantastic food, and friendly service

My Most Favorite Food (247 W 72nd St): Expensive pasta, fish, salads, and desserts are all delectable.

Pongal (110 Lexington Ave): all kosher vegetarian

Talia's Steakhouse & Bar (668 Amsterdam Ave): Glatt kosher restaurant

Tevere (155 E 84th St): old family Italian/Jewish recipes and great traditions

Va Bene (1589 Second Ave): superb pastas, Sunday brunch

Yonah Schimmel Knish Bakery (137 E Houston St): Schimmel started serving knishes to immigrants 150 years ago, and is still in business.

LATE HOURS

The city that never sleeps...

69 (69 Bayard St): Chinese

Agozar Cuban Bistro Bar (324 Bowery St)

Balthazar (80 Spring St)

Baraonda (1439 Second Ave)

Bereket (187 E Houston St)

Big Arc Chicken (233 First Ave)

Black Iron Burger Shop (540 E 5th St)

Blue Ribbon (97 Sullivan St)

Blue Ribbon Sushi (119 Sullivan St)

Cafeteria (119 Seventh Ave)

Cafe Lalo (201 W 83rd St)

Carnegie Deli (854 Seventh Ave)

Corner Social (321 Lenox Ave)

Cozy Soup 'n' Burger (739 Broadway)

dell'anima (38 Eighth Ave)

Employees Only (510 Hudson St)

Frank (88 Second Ave)

French Roast (78 W 11th St and 2340 Broadway)

Fuleen Seafood (11 Division St)

Gahm Mi Oak (43 W 32nd St)

Gray's Papaya (2090 Broadway and 402 Ave of the Americas)

Great NY Noodletown (28 Bowery)

Green Kitchen (1477 First Ave)

Han Bat (53 W 35th St)

Kum Gang San (49 W 32nd St)

Landmarc (Time Warner Center, 10 Columbus Circle and 179 West Broadway)

L'Express (249 Park Ave S)
The Lion (62 W 9th St)
Macao Trading Co. (311 Church St)
The Meatball Shop (84 Stanton St)
Momofuku Ssäm Bar (207 Second Ave)
New Wonjo (23 W 32nd St)
Pastis (9 Ninth Ave)
P.J. Clarke's (915 Third Ave, 44 W 63rd St, and 4 World Financial Center)
Raoul's (180 Prince St)
Remedy Diner (245 E Houston St)
The Spotted Pig (314 W 11th St)
Sushi Seki (1143 First Ave)
Terroir Murray Hill (439 Third Ave)
This Little Piggy Had Roast Beef (149 First Ave)
Veselka (144 Second Ave)
Viand Coffee Shop (2130 Broadway and 300 E 86th St)
Wollensky's Grill (201 E 49th St)

MUNCHING AT THE MUSEUMS

Even some of the smallest museums have cafes. Often these are upscale spots where you can rest your feet and get a surprisingly good bite to eat. They are usually quite expensive. Some of the best:

Asia Society and Museum (725 Park Ave): **Garden Court Cafe**

The Jewish Museum (1109 Fifth Ave): **Lox at Cafe Weissman**

The Metropolitan Museum of Art (1000 Fifth Ave): **Cafeteria** (basement) and **Petrie Court Cafe and Wine Bar** (looks onto Central Park)

The Morgan Library and Museum (225 Madison Ave): **The Morgan Cafe** and **The Morgan Dining Room**

Museum of Arts and Design (2 Columbus Circle): **Robert** (9th floor)

Museum of Modern Art (9 W 53rd St): **The Modern**

Neue Galerie New York (1048 Fifth Ave): **Cafe Sabarsky**

New-York Historical Society (170 Central Park W): **Caffe Storico**

Rubin Museum of Art (150 W 17th St): **Cafe at the RMA**

Scandinavia House: The Nordic Center in America (58 Park Ave): **Smörgås Chef**

Solomon R. Guggenheim Museum (1071 Fifth Ave): **The Wright**

Whitney Museum of American Art (945 Madison Ave): **Untitled** (Danny Meyer is in charge)

OLD-TIMERS

1783: **Fraunces Tavern** (54 Pearl St)
1794: **Bridge Cafe** (279 Water St)
1864: **Pete's Tavern** (129 E 18th St)
1868: **Old Homestead** (56 Ninth Ave)
1885: **Keens Steakhouse** (72 W 36th St)
1887: **Peter Luger Steak House** (178 Broadway, Brooklyn)

1888: **Katz's Delicatessen** (205 E Houston St)
1890: **P.J. Clarke's** (915 Third Ave)
1906: **Barbetta** (321 W 46th St)
1913: **Grand Central Oyster Bar Restaurant** (Grand Central Terminal, 42nd St at Vanderbilt Ave, lower level)
1920: **Waverly Inn** (16 Bank St)
1926: **Palm One** (837 Second Ave)
1927: **Minetta Tavern** (113 MacDougal St)
1929: **21 Club** (21 W 52nd St)

OUTDOOR DINING/DRINKS

5 Ninth (5 Ninth Ave)
Aquagrill (210 Spring St)
Barbetta (321 W 46th St): garden
Bello Giardino (71 W 71st St)
The Biergarten (The Standard High Line, 848 Washington St)
Blue Water Grill (31 Union Sq W)
The Boathouse (Central Park at E 72nd St)
Bottino (246 Tenth Ave)
Bryant Park Grill (25 W 40th St)
Bull McCabe's (29 St. Mark's Pl)
Café Centro (MetLife Building, 200 Park Ave)
Caffe Dante (79-81 MacDougal St)
Casimir (103-105 Ave B)
Chelsea Brewing Company (Pier 59, West St at 18th St)
Da Nico (164 Mulberry St)
Da Silvano (260 Ave of the Americas)
Druids (736 Tenth Ave)
Financier Patisserie (3-4 World Financial Center, 1121 Ave of the Americas, 90 Nassau St, and other locations)
Finnegan's Wake (1361 First Ave)
Gigino (Wagner Park, 20 Battery Pl)
Grotto (100 Forsyth St)
Hallo Berlin (626 Tenth Ave)
Home Restaurant (20 Cornelia St)
Hudson Beach Cafe (Riverside Park, Riverside Dr at 105th St)
I Trulli (122 E 27th St)
Il Gattopardo (13-15 W 54th St)
Jackson Hole Burgers (232 E 64th St, 1611 Second Ave, and 517 Columbus Ave)
La Lanterna (129 MacDougal St)
Metro Grill Roof Garden (Hotel Metro, 45 W 35th St)
Mezzogiorno (195 Spring St)
Moda Restaurant (The Flatotel, 135 W 52nd St)
New Leaf Cafe (Fort Tryon Park, 1 Margaret Corbin Dr)

GERRY'S
EXCLUSIVE
LIST

Nice Matin (201 W 79th St)
Nougatine Cafe (Trump International Hotel & Tower, 1 Central Park W)
O'Flaherty's Ale House (334 W 46th St)
Pampano (209 E 49th St, 2nd floor terrace)
Paradou (8 Little West 12th St)
The Park (118 Tenth Ave)
Pastis (9 Ninth Ave)
Patroon (160 E 46th St, 3rd floor)
Pete's Tavern (129 E 18th St)
Pure Food and Wine (54 Irving Pl)
Roc Restaurant (190-A Duane St)
Rock Center Cafe/The Rink Bar (Rockefeller Center, 20 W 50th St)
Ryan's Irish Pub (151 Second Ave)
San Pietro (18 E 54th St)
Shake Shack (Madison Square Park, 23rd St bet Madison Ave and Broadway;
    409 Fulton St; seasonal)
SouthWest NY (225 Liberty St)
Spring Street Natural (62 Spring St)
SushiSamba (87 Seventh Ave S and 245 Park Ave)
Terrace 5 (Museum of Modern Art, 11 W 53rd St)
Trattoria dell'Arte (900 Seventh Ave)
Waverly Inn (16 Bank St)
West 79th Street Boat Basin Cafe (Riverside Park at 79th St; seasonal)
White Horse Tavern (567 Hudson St)
Yaffa Cafe (97 St. Mark's Pl)

PERSONAL FAVORITES
40 Carrots (Bloomingdale's, 1000 Third Ave, 7th floor): nice atmosphere, great
    name, wonderful coffee frozen yogurt
ABC Kitchen (ABC Carpet & Home, 35 E 18th St)
Arlington Club Steakhouse (1032 Lexington Ave)
Babbo (110 Waverly Pl): fabulous food
Balthazar (80 Spring St): really fun atmosphere
Barbetta (321 W 46th St): a classy operation
Blue Ribbon (97 Sullivan St): great value
Bouley (163 Duane St): none better
Brooklyn Diner USA (212 W 57th St and 155 W 43rd St): satisfying meals
    all day
Cucina & Co. (MetLife Building, 200 Park Ave, lobby; Macy's, 151 W 34th St;
    and 30 Rockefeller Center, concourse level): great quick meals
Del Posto (85 Tenth Ave): very classy service
Forty Four (Royalton Hotel, 44 W 44th St): *the* cocktail spot
Golden Unicorn (18 East Broadway): great Chinese platters
Gotham Bar & Grill (12 E 12th St): all is good

Gramercy Tavern (42 E 20th St): quintessential New York
Il Mulino New York (86 W 3rd St): Italian heaven!
Jackson Hole Burgers (232 E 64th St, 521 Third Ave, 1611 Second Ave, 1270 Madison Ave, and 517 Columbus Ave): best burgers
La Grenouille (3 E 52nd St): beautiful
Lavo (39 E 58th St)
Le Périgord (405 E 52nd St): impeccable
Marchi's (251 E 31st St)
McCormick & Schmick's (1285 Ave of the Americas): fresh seafood
The Modern (Museum of Modern Art, 9 W 53rd St): great setting
Nobu New York (105 Hudson St): Japanese food at its best
One if by Land, Two if by Sea (17 Barrow St): romantic
Peter Luger Steak House (178 Broadway, Brooklyn)
Piccolo Angolo (621 Hudson St): like family
Quality Meats (57 W 58th St)
Sfoglia (1402 Lexington Ave): wonderful bread
Shake Shack (Madison Square Park, Madison Ave at 23rd St; 366 Columbus Ave; 154 E 86th St; 691 Eighth Ave; and other locations): delicious shakes
Smith & Wollensky (797 Third Ave): old-time flavor
Spice Market (403 W 13th St)
Tao (42 E 58th St)
Union Square Cafe (21 E 16th St): justly famous

PIZZA
Accademia di Vino (2427 Broadway)
Adrienne's Pizzabar (54 Stone St)
Angelo's Pizzeria (117 W 57th St, 1043 Second Ave, and 1697 Broadway)
apizz (217 Eldridge St): gourmet
Artichoke Basille's Pizza & Brewery (328 E 14th St, 114 Tenth Ave, and 111 MacDougal St): really good
Arturo's Coal Oven Pizza (106 W Houston St)
Bella Vita (211 W 43rd St and 158 W 58th St)
Birdbath Bakery (160 Prince St; 200 Church St; and New Museum, 235 Bowery)
Circo NYC (120 W 55th St)
Co. (230 Ninth Ave): baker Jim Lahey's restaurant debut
Da Ciro (229 Lexington Ave)
Da Nico (164 Mulberry St)
Donatella's (184 Eighth Ave): Neapolitan
Emporio (231 Mott St)
Forcella (334 Bowery)
Fred's at Barneys New York (660 Madison Ave)
Giorgione (307 Spring St)
Grandaisy Bakery (250 West Broadway and 176 W 72nd St)
Il Corallo Trattoria (176 Prince St)

Joe's Pizza (7 Carmine St)
John's Pizzeria (278 Bleecker St, 260 W 44th St, and 408 E 64th St)
Kesté Pizza & Vino (271 Bleecker St): margherita
La Pizza Fresca (31 E 20th St): Neapolitan pizza
Lazzara's Pizza Cafe (221 W 38th St, upstairs and 617 Ninth Ave)
Lil' Frankie's Pizza (19 First Ave)
Lombardi's (32 Spring St)
Luigi's Pizzeria (1701 First Ave)
Luzzo's (211 First Ave)
Mezzogiorno (195 Spring St)
Motorino (349 E 12th St)
Naples 45 (MetLife Building, 200 Park Ave)
Nick & Toni's Cafe (100 W 67th St)
Nick's Pizza (1814 Second Ave)
Olio Pizza e Più (3 Greenwich Ave): Mezzaluna (pizza-calzone hybrid)
Orso (322 W 46th St)
Patsy's Pizzeria (2287 First Ave and other locations)
Pizza Mezzaluna (146 W Houston St)
Pizza 33 (489 Third Ave and 268 W 23rd St): by the slice
PizzArte (69 W 55th St): Neapolitan
Pulino's (282 Bowery): little neck clams
Rubirosa (235 Mulberry St)
Sal's & Carmine's Pizza (2671 Broadway): Neapolitan
Serafina (29 E 61st St; 38 E 58th St; 1022 Madison Ave; Time Hotel, 224 W 49th St; and Dream New York, 210 W 55th St)
Stromboli Pizzeria (112 University Pl): Neapolitan
Trattoria dell'Arte (900 Seventh Ave)
Two Boots (42 Ave A, 74 Bleecker St, and other locations)
Vinny Vincenz Pizza (231 First Ave)

POWER MEALS
21 Club (21 W 52nd St)
Balthazar (80 Spring St)
Cafe Boulud (The Surrey, 20 E 76th St)
The Carlyle (Carlyle Hotel, 35 E 76th St)
Daniel (60 E 65th St)
Da Silvano (260 Ave of the Americas)
Delmonico's (56 Beaver St)
Del Posto (85 Tenth Ave)
Four Seasons (99 E 52nd St)
Gabriel's Bar & Restaurant (11 W 60th St)
Gotham Bar & Grill (12 E 12th St)
Il Mulino New York (86 W 3rd St)
Jean Georges (Trump International Hotel and Tower, 1 Central Park W)
La Grenouille (3 E 52nd St)

Le Bernardin (155 W 51st St)
Maloney & Porcelli (37 E 50th St)
Michael's (24 W 55th St)
Monkey Bar (Hotel Elysée, 60 E 54th St)
Morton's The Steakhouse (551 Fifth Ave)
Nobu Fifty Seven (40 W 57th St)
Nobu New York and **Nobu Next Door** (105 Hudson St)
The Palm (837 Second Ave; 840 Second Ave; 206 West St; and 250 W 50th St)
Rao's (455 E 114th St)
Sette Mezzo (969 Lexington Ave)
Smith & Wollensky (797 Third Ave)

PRE-THEATER

Let your waiter know when you are first seated that you will be attending the theater so that service can be adjusted accordingly. Some restaurants have specially priced pre-theater dinners. If it is raining, allow extra time for getting a taxi.

Aquavit (65 E 55th St)
Barbetta (321 W 46th St)
Becco (355 W 46th St)
Blue Fin (W New York Times Square, 1567 Broadway)
Cafe Un Deux Trois (123 W 44th St)
Carmine's (2450 Broadway and 200 W 44th St)
Chez Josephine (414 W 42nd St)
Dawat (210 E 58th St)
Esca (402 W 43rd St)
FireBird (365 W 46th St)
Four Seasons (99 E 52nd St)
Hearth (403 E 12th St)
Hell's Kitchen (679 Ninth Ave)
Indochine (430 Lafayette St)
La Boite en Bois (75 W 68th St)
Marchi's (251 E 31st St)
Momofuku Noodle Bar (171 First Ave)
Ollie's Noodle Shop and Grill (411 W 42nd St)
Orso (322 W 46th St)
Picholine (35 W 64th St)
Red Cat (227 Tenth Ave)
Spice Market (403 W 13th St)
Telepan (72 W 69th St)
Thalia (828 Eighth Ave)

ROMANTIC
Barbetta (321 W 46th St)
Blue Hill (75 Washington Pl)

GERRY'S
EXCLUSIVE
LIST

Bouley (163 Duane St)
Caffe Reggio (119 MacDougal St)
Caffe Vivaldi (32 Jones St)
Chez Josephine (414 W 42nd St)
Eleven Madison Park (11 Madison Ave)
Erminia (250 E 83rd St)
FireBird (365 W 46th St)
Four Seasons (99 E 52nd St)
I Trulli (122 E 27th St)
Il Buco (47 Bond St)
Il Cortile (125 Mulberry St)
Jean Georges (Trump International Hotel and Tower, 1 Central Park W)
King Cole Bar (St. Regis New York, 2 E 55th St)
Lady Mendl's Tea Salon (Inn at Irving Place, 56 Irving Pl)
La Grenouille (3 E 52nd St)
Le Périgord (405 E 52nd St)
One if by Land, Two if by Sea (17 Barrow St)
Paola's (Hotel Wales, 1295 Madison Ave)
Scalinatella (201 E 61st St)
Spice Market (403 W 13th St)
Water's Edge (401 44th Dr and East River, Queens)

ROOFTOP DRINKS
230 Fifth Garden Bar (230 Fifth Ave): heated
Ava Lounge (Dream New York, 210 W 55th St)
Birreria (Eataly, 200 Fifth Ave)
Bookmarks Lounge (Library Hotel, 299 Madison Ave)
Cantor Roof Garden Cafe (The Metropolitan Museum of Art, 1000 Fifth Ave)
The Delancey (168 Delancey St)
Empire Hotel Bar and Lounge (44 W 63rd St): view of Lincoln Center
Glass Bar (Hotel Indigo, 127 W 28th St)
Gramercy Terrace (Gramercy Park Hotel, 2 Lexington Ave, 18th floor)
Hudson Terrace (621 W 46th St)
La Piscine (Hotel Americano, 518 W 27th St): rooftop pool bar via external glass elevator
mad46 (Roosevelt Hotel, 45 E 45th St)
Plunge (Gansevoort Meatpacking NYC, 18 Ninth Ave)
Press Lounge (Ink48, 653 Eleventh Ave)
Rare View Rooftop Lounge (Affinia Shelburne, 303 Lexington Ave)
Salon de Ning (The Peninsula New York, 700 Fifth Ave)
Sky Room (Fairfield Inn & Suites by Marriott Times Square, 330 W 40th St)
Soaked (Mondrian Soho, 150 Lafayette St); 360 degree views
Sunset Lounge (Hotel on Rivington, 107 Rivington St)
Tonic East (411 Third Ave): year-round

Top of the Strand (The Strand Hotel, 33 W 37th St)
Upstairs (Kimberly Hotel, 145 E 50th St)

SANDWICHES
Alidoro (105 Sullivan St)
Amy's Bread (672 Ninth Ave; 250 Bleecker St; and Chelsea Market, 75 Ninth Ave)
Baoguette (61 Lexington Ave, 120 Christopher St, and 75 Nassau St)
Bread Market Cafe (1290 Ave of the Americas)
Cafe Gitane (242 Mott St and Jane Hotel, 113 Jane St)
Call Cuisine (1032 First Ave)
Carnegie Deli (854 Seventh Ave)
City Bakery (3 W 18th St)
Cosi Sandwich Bar (841 Broadway and other locations)
Cucina & Co. (MetLife Building, 200 Park Ave)
Deb's Catering (200 Varick St)
Defonte's of Brooklyn (261 Third Ave): over-the-top heros
E.A.T. (1064 Madison Ave)
Faicco's Pork Store (260 Bleecker St)
Manganaro's Hero Boy (494 Ninth Ave)
Mile End Sandwich (53 Bond St)
Nicky's Vietnamese Sandwiches (150 E 2nd St)
Once Upon a Tart (135 Sullivan St)
Parm (248 Mulberry St)
Piada (601 Lexington Ave): Italian
Popover Cafe (551 Amsterdam Ave)
Porchetta (110 E 7th St)
Potbelly Sandwich Shop (501 Seventh Ave)
Salumeria Biellese (376-378 Eighth Ave)
San Matteo Panuzzo (121 St. Marks Pl): pizza-dough sandwich
Shopsin's (120 Essex St)
Shorty's (576 Ninth Ave)
Sosa Borella (832 Eighth Ave)
Sullivan Street Bakery (533 W 47th St)
Taboonette (30 E 13th St): hearty flatbread sandwiches
Todaro Bros. (555 Second Ave)
Union Square Cafe (21 E 16th St)
'wichcraft (555 Fifth Ave and other locations)

SEAFOOD
Aquagrill (210 Spring St)
Aquavit (65 E 55th St)
BLT Fish & Fish Shack (21 W 17th St)
Blue Fin (W New York Times Square, 1567 Broadway)
Blue Ribbon (97 Sullivan St): oyster bar

Blue Water Grill (31 Union Square W)
Docks Oyster Bar and Seafood Grill (633 Third Ave)
Ed's Lobster Bar (222 Lafayette St)
Esca (402 W 43rd St)
Estiatorio Milos (125 W 55th St)
Fish Tag (222 W 79th St)
Grand Central Oyster Bar Restaurant (Grand Central Terminal, 42nd St at Vanderbilt Ave, lower level)
The John Dory Oyster Bar (Ace Hotel, 1196 Broadway)
Kurumazushi (7 E 47th St)
Le Bernardin (155 W 51st St)
Lure Fishbar (142 Mercer St)
Marea (240 Central Park S)
Mary's Fish Camp (64 Charles St)
McCormick & Schmick's (1285 Ave of the Americas)
Mermaid Inn (79 MacDougal St, 96 Second Ave, and 568 Amsterdam Ave): oyster bar
Millesime (The Carlton Hotel, 92 Madison Ave)
North End Grill (104 North End Ave)
Ocean Grill (384 Columbus Ave)
Oceana (McGraw-Hill Building, 120 W 49th St)
Oriental Garden (14 Elizabeth St)
Pearl Oyster Bar (18 Cornelia St)
Primola (1226 Second Ave)
Remi (145 W 53rd St)
The Sea Grill (Rockefeller Center, 19 W 49th St)
Westville (210 W 10th St, 173 Ave A, and 246 W 18th St)

SHOPPING BREAKS

To replenish your energy, here are some good places to eat in the major Manhattan stores:

ABC Carpet & Home (888 Broadway, 212/473-3000): **ABC Cocina** (Latin American), **ABC Kitchen** (Jean- Georges Vongerichten's green restaurant), and **Le Pain Quotidien** (bakery and cafe)

Barneys New York (660 Madison Ave, 212/833-2200): **Fred's** (upscale)

Bergdorf Goodman (men's store, 745 Fifth Ave, 212/753-7300): **Bar III**

Bergdorf Goodman (women's store, 754 Fifth Ave, 212/753-7300): **Bar 5F** (7th floor), **BG Restaurant** (7th floor), and **Goodman's** (plaza level)

Bloomingdale's (1000 Third Ave, 212/705-2000): **B Cafe** (6th floor), **David Burke** (1st floor), **Flip** (lower level), **40 Carrots** (7th floor), and **Le Train Bleu** (6th floor)

Lord & Taylor (424 Fifth Ave, 212/391-3344): **Sarabeth's** (5th and 6th floors)

Macy's (151 W 34th St, 212/695-4400): **Au Bon Pain** (street level and 8th floor), **Cucina & Co.** (cellar), **Macy's Cellar Bar and Grill** (cellar), **Starbucks** (3rd floor), and **Stella 34 Trattoria** (6th floor, Italian eatery)

Saks Fifth Avenue (611 Fifth Ave, 212/753-4000): **Cafe S.F.A.** (8th floor, tasty and classy)

SOUTHERN FLAVORS AND SOUL FOOD

107 West (2787 Broadway)
Amy Ruth's (113 W 116th St)
Ashford and Simpson's Sugar Bar (254 W 72nd St): dinner and live entertainment Tuesday to Saturday
Bubby's (120 Hudson St)
Charles' Country Panfried Chicken (2841 Frederick Douglass Blvd)
Great Jones Cafe (54 Great Jones St)
Londel's Supper Club (2620 Frederick Douglass Blvd)
Miss Mamie's Spoonbread Too (366 W 110th St)
Miss Maude's Spoonbread Too (547 Lenox Ave)
Sister's Caribbean Cuisine (47 E 124th St)
Sylvia's (328 Lenox Ave)
Tipsy Parson (156 Ninth Ave)

STEAKS

Arlington Club Steakhouse (1032 Lexington Ave)
Bistro le Steak (1309 Third Ave): inexpensive and good
BLT Steak (106 E 57th St)
Bull & Bear (Waldorf Astoria New York, 301 Park Ave)
Capital Grille (Chrysler Center, 155 E 42nd St; Time-Life Building, 120 W 51st St; and 120 Broadway)
Churrascaria Plataforma (Belvedere Hotel, 316 W 49th St)
Del Frisco's Double Eagle Steak House (1221 Ave of the Americas)
Frankie and Johnnie's (269 W 45th St and 32 W 37th St)
Harry's Cafe & Steak (1 Hanover Sq)
Keens Steakhouse (72 W 36th St)
Le Marais (150 W 46th St): kosher
Maloney & Porcelli (37 E 50th St)
MarkJoseph Steakhouse (261 Water St)
McCormick & Schmick's (1285 Ave of the Americas)
Morton's The Steakhouse (551 Fifth Ave)
The Palm (837 Second Ave; 840 Second Ave; 206 West St; and 250 W 50th St)
Patroon (160 E 46th St): outrageously expensive
Peter Luger Steak House (178 Broadway, Brooklyn): a tradition since 1887
Pietro's (232 E 43rd St)
Quality Meats (57 W 58th St)
Ruth's Chris Steak House (148 W 51st St)
Smith & Wollensky (797 Third Ave)
Sparks Steak House (210 E 46th St)
Strip House (13 E 12th St)

T-Bar Steak & Lounge (1278 Third Ave)
Uncle Jack's Steakhouse (440 Ninth Ave; 44 W 56th St; and 39-40 Bell Blvd, Queens)
Vic & Anthony's Steakhouse (233 Park Ave S)

SUSHI

In the early 1980s, sushi bars became the trendy haute cuisine of the fashionable set. To this day, New Yorkers love to wrap their chopsticks around succulent slivers of raw or cooked seafood on rice. Although many are content to order assortments concocted by the chef, true aficionados prefer to select by the piece. To tailor your next sushi platter to your own taste, here's what you need to know:

Amaebi (sweet shrimp)
Anago (sea eel)
California roll (avocado and crab)
Hamachi (yellowtail)
Hirame (halibut)
Ika (squid)
Ikura (salmon roe)
Kappa maki (cucumber roll)
Maguro (tuna)
Nizakana (cooked fish)
Saba (mackerel)
Sake (salmon)
Tekka maki (tuna roll)
Toro (fatty tuna)
Umeshiso maki (plum roll)
Unagi (freshwater eel)
Uni (sea urchin)

Give any of these a try for sushi:

Aki (181 W 4th St)
Blue Ribbon Sushi (119 Sullivan St)
Bond Street (6 Bond St)
Chez Sardine (183 W 10th St)
Hatsuhana (17 E 48th St and 237 Park Ave)
Japonica (100 University Pl)
Jewel Bako (239 E 5th St)
Kurumazushi (7 E 47th St, 2nd floor)
Kyo Ya (94 E 7th St)
Masa (Time Warner Center, 10 Columbus Circle, 4th floor)
Megu (62 Thomas St and 845 United Nations Plaza)
Neta (61 W 8th St)
Nippon (155 E 52nd St)
Nobu Fifty Seven (40 W 57th St)
Nobu New York and **Nobu Next Door** (105 Hudson St)
Ruby Foo's (1626 Broadway)

Sapporo East (164 First Ave)
Sasabune (401 E 73rd St)
Shabu-Tatsu (216 E 10th St)
Sugiyama (251 W 55th St)
Sushi-Azabu (428 Greenwich St)
Sushi of Gari (347 W 46th St, 370 Columbus Ave, and 402 E 78th St)
Sushi Seki (1143 First Ave)
Sushi Yasuda (204 E 43rd St)
Sushi Zen (108 W 44th St)
Sushiden (19 E 49th St and 123 W 49th St)
SushiSamba (87 Seventh Ave and 245 Park Ave)
Takahachi (85 Ave A and 145 Duane St)
Tomoe Sushi (172 Thompson St)
UshiWakamaru (136 W Houston St)
Yama (38 Carmine St, 122 E 17th St, and 308 E 49th St)

TAKEOUT AND DELIVERY
Balthazar (80 Spring St)
Bread (20 Spring St)
Brick Lane Curry House (306-308 E 6th St)
Bubby's (120 Hudson St)
Cafe Español (172 Bleecker St)
City Market Cafe (551 Madison Ave, 178 Fifth Ave, and 1100 Madison Ave)
City 75 (75 Rockefeller Plaza): buffet by the pound
Cucina Vivolo (138 E 74th St and 222 E 58th St)
Dean & Deluca (560 Broadway and 1150 Madison Ave)
Demarchelier (50 E 86th St)
Food Passion (1200 Lexington Ave)
Henry's (2745 Broadway)
Jacques Brasserie (204-206 E 85th St)
Jubilee (347 E 54th St)
Just Salad (320 Park Ave, 134 W 37th St, 100 Maiden Lane, and other locations)
Kitchenette (156 Chambers St and 1272 Amsterdam Ave)
L'Absinthe (227 E 67th St)
La Caridad 78 (2199 Broadway)
Lorenzo and Maria's Kitchen (1418 Third Ave)
Maria Pia (319 W 51st St)
Molyvos (871 Seventh Ave)
Murray's Cheese Shop (254 Bleecker St and Grand Central Market, Lexington Ave at 43rd St)
Pepe Giallo to Go (253 Tenth Ave)
Sarabeth's Bakery (Chelsea Market, 75 Ninth Ave)
Schiller's Liquor Bar (131 Rivington St)
Sushi Zen (108 W 44th St)

GERRY'S
EXCLUSIVE
LIST

Tea & Sympathy (108 Greenwich Ave)
Tio Pepe (168 W 4th St)
Tossed (295 Park Ave S)
Turkuaz Restaurant (2637 Broadway)
Virgil's Real Barbecue (152 W 44th St)
Westville (173 Ave A, 210 W 10th St, 246 W 18th St, and 333 Hudson St)
'wichcraft (555 Fifth Ave and other locations)

TEATIME
Alice's Tea Cup (102 W 73rd St, 156 E 64th St, and 220 E 81st St)
Astor Court (St. Regis New York, 2 E 55th St)
Bar Seine (Hotel Plaza Athenee, 37 E 64th St)
Cafe S.F.A. (Saks Fifth Avenue, 611 Fifth Ave, 8th floor)
Cha-An (230 E 9th St, 2nd floor): Japanese teahouse
Crosby Bar (Crosby Street Hotel, 79 Crosby St): afternoon tea service
The Gallery (Carlyle Hotel, 35 E 76th St)
Gotham Lounge (The Peninsula New York, 700 Fifth Ave)
Harney & Sons (433 Broome St)
King's Carriage House (251 E 82nd St)
Lady Mendl's Tea Salon (Inn at Irving Place, 56 Irving Pl)
The Morgan Cafe (The Morgan Library and Museum, 225 Madison Ave)
Palm Court (The Plaza, 59th St at Fifth Ave)
Pembroke Room (The Lowell, 28 E 63rd St)
Podunk (231 E 5th St)
Radiance Tea House & Books (158 W 55th St)
The Russian Tea Room (150 W 57th St)
Sant Ambroeus (1000 Madison Ave and 259 W 4th St)
Sarabeth's (Hotel Wales, 1295 Madison Ave; 423 Amsterdam Ave; and 40
    Central Park S)
T Salon (230 Fifth Ave, Suite 1511)
Tea & Sympathy (108 Greenwich Ave)
Teanissimo (90 Rivington St)
Two E Bar (The Pierre, 2 E 61st St)
Ty Lounge (Four Seasons Hotel New York, 57 E 57th St): weekends

TOP-RATED
Aquagrill (210 Spring St)
Babbo (110 Waverly Pl)
Barbetta (321 W 46th St)
Blue Ribbon Sushi (119 Sullivan St)
Bouley (163 Duane St)
Cafe Boulud (The Surrey, 20 E 76th St)
Craft (43 E 19th St)
Daniel (60 E 65th St)
db Bistro Moderne (City Club Hotel, 55 W 44th St)

Del Posto (85 Tenth Ave)
Eleven Madison Park (11 Madison Ave)
Four Seasons (99 E 52nd St)
Gotham Bar & Grill (12 E 12th St)
Gramercy Tavern (42 E 20th St)
Il Mulino New York (86 W 3rd St)
Jean Georges (Trump International Hotel and Tower, 1 Central Park W)
Keens Steakhouse (72 W 36th St)
Kyo Ya (94 E 7th St)
La Grenouille (3 E 52nd St)
Le Bernardin (155 W 51st St)
Le Périgord (405 E 52nd St)
Maialino (Gramercy Park Hotel, 2 Lexington Ave)
The Mark Restaurant by Jean-Georges (The Mark, 25 E 77th St)
Mas (Farmhouse) (39 Downing St)
Masa (Time Warner Center, 10 Columbus Circle, 4th floor)
The Modern (Museum of Modern Art, 9 W 53rd St)
Momofuku Ko (163 First Ave)
Nobu Fifty Seven (40 W 57th St)
Nobu New York and **Nobu Next Door** (105 Hudson St)
Oceana (McGraw-Hill Building, 120 W 49th St)
Pearl Oyster Bar (18 Cornelia St)
per se (Time Warner Center, 10 Columbus Circle, 4th floor)
Peter Luger Steak House (178 Broadway, Brooklyn)
Picholine (35 W 64th St)
Public (210 Elizabeth St)
Sasabune (401 E 73rd St)
Scarpetta (355 W 14th St)
Sugiyama (251 W 55th St)
Sushi of Gari (402 E 78th St, 347 W 46th St, and 370 Columbus Ave)
Sushi Seki (1143 First Ave)
Sushi Yasuda (204 E 43rd St)
Union Square Cafe (21 E 16th St)
Veritas (43 E 20th St)

VEGAN/VEGETARIAN
Angelica Kitchen (300 E 12th St)
Barbetta (321 W 46th St)
Benny's Burritos (113 Greenwich Ave and 93 Avenue A)
Bhojan (102 Lexington Ave)
Blossom (187 Ninth Ave)
Cafe Blossom (466 Columbus Ave and 41 Carmine St)
Candle Cafe (1307 Third Ave and 2427 Broadway)
Caravan of Dreams (405 E 6th St)
Chennai Garden (129 E 27th St)

GERRY'S EXCLUSIVE LIST

Chola (232 E 58th St)
Dévi (8 E 18th St)
Dirt Candy (430 E 9th St)
Dovetail (103 W 77th St)
EN Japanese Brasserie (435 Hudson St)
Gobo (1426 Third Ave and 401 Ave of the Americas)
Green Table (Chelsea Market, 75 Ninth Ave)
HanGawi (12 E 32nd St)
Maoz Vegetarian (59 E 8th St, 558 Seventh Ave, 200 W 40th St, and other locations)
Monte's Trattoria (97 MacDougal St)
Peacefood Cafe (460 Amsterdam Ave)
Pure Food and Wine (54 Irving Pl)
Quantum Leap Natural Food (226 Thompson St and 203 First Ave)
Quintessence (263 E 10th St)
Salute! (270 Madison Ave)
Snack (105 Thompson St)
Soomsoom Vegetarian Bar (166 W 72nd St)
Souen (28 E 13th St, 210 Ave of the Americas, and 326 E 6th St)
Spring Street Natural (62 Spring St)
Two Boots (42 Ave A and other locations)
V-Note (1522 First Ave)
Vatan (409 Third Ave)
Vegetarian's Paradise 2 (144 W 4th St)
Village Natural (46 Greenwich Ave)
Zen Palate (633 Ninth Ave and 115 E 18th St)

VIEW RESTAURANTS

These are restaurants with a view, beyond the bars and lounges listed in "Rooftop Drinks" (see page 60).

A Voce (Time Warner Center, 10 Columbus Circle, 3rd floor): Central Park view
Asiate (Mandarin Oriental New York, Time Warner Center, 80 Columbus Circle, 35th floor)
Bryant Park Grill (25 W 40th St): refreshing view of Bryant Park
Cabana (89 South St): seaport view including outside seating
Gaonnuri (1250 Broadway, 39th floor): stunning high-rise view of cityscape
Gigino at Wagner Park (20 Battery Pl): terrace views of Miss Liberty
The Modern (Museum of Modern Art, 9 W 53rd St): outdoor sculpture garden
per se (Time Warner Center, 10 Columbus Circle, 4th floor): Central Park
Sea Grill (19 W 49th St): Rockefeller Center view
The View (New York Marriott Marquis, 1535 Broadway): lounge; revolves high above Times Square

World Yacht Cruises (Pier 81, 41st St at Hudson River): Manhattan from the water

WINE BARS

Ara (24 Ninth Ave)
Artisanal Fromagerie, Bistro and Wine Bar (2 Park Ave)
Bar Boulud (1900 Broadway)
Blue Ribbon Downing Street Bar (34 Downing St): 300-bottle wine list
Bottega del Vino (7 E 59th St)
Cafe Katja (79 Orchard St): Austrian wines and nibbles
Casellula Cheese & Wine Cafe (401 W 52nd St): extensive cheeses and superb tasting menu
Drunken Horse (225 Tenth Ave): international selection
Epistrophy (200 Mott St): romantic
I Tre Merli (463 West Broadway)
I Trulli (122 E 27th St)
Il Buco Alimentari e Vineria (53 Great Jones St)
Il Posto Accanto (190 E 2nd St)
Jadis (42 Rivington St)
Lelabar (422 Hudson St): artsy wine room with good, affordable vino
Morrell Wine Bar & Cafe (1 Rockefeller Plaza)
Paradou (8 Little West 12th St)
Pata Negra (345 E 12th St): Spanish hams and cheeses
Tangled Vine Wine Bar & Kitchen (434 Amsterdam Ave): ecofriendly
Ten Degrees (121 St. Mark's Pl)
Terroir (413 E 12th St): 50 wines by the glass
Terroir Tribeca (24 Harrison St): a roomier version of Terroir
Turks and Frogs (323 W 11th St and 458 Greenwich St)
Veritas (43 E 20th St)
Wined Up (913 Broadway, 2nd floor)
Xicala Wine & Tapas Bar (151-B Elizabeth St)

Higher-end Burgers

All three locations of **5 Napkin Burger** (630 Ninth Ave, 212/757-2277; 150 E 14th St, 212/228-5500; and 2315 Broadway, 212/333-4488) are packed all the time with society matrons, blue collar Joes on their lunch hours, and hordes of yuppies and their pals. There are sushi and tempura, Hell's Kitchen wings, lobster rolls, fish and chips, and kobe beef hot dogs, but the main attraction is the huge burger...and I mean big! With all the trimmings it is so thick you'll have a hard time getting it in your mouth! Make no mistake, it is a really good burger, and it should be for $15.95! With the deadening noise level it is impossible to have a private conversation; the ambiance is zero. But, oh those burgers!

WHAT TO EXPECT
THE BEST IN EVERY PRICE CATEGORY

2ND AVE DELI

1442 First Ave (at 75th St)	212/737-1700
Daily: 9 a.m.-midnight	

162 E 33rd St (bet Lexington and Third Ave)	212/689-9000
Daily: 6 a.m.-midnight (Fri, Sat till 4 a.m.)	2ndavedeli.com

Moderate

Both locations of this famous kosher deli and restaurant continue to draw crowds who love the gigantic portions and quality plates. The rather nondescript settings seem unimportant when there's a menu offering up favorite Jewish deli dishes. A plate of delicious crisp dill pickles is placed in front of you at the start. Appetizers include chopped liver, meatballs, franks, and chicken wings. Soups include the favorite matzoh ball. There are also blintzes, potato pancakes, challah French toast, knishes, kugels, cole slaw, huge open (and closed) sandwiches, burgers, deli platters, and many beef entrees. Don't forget the chicken, fish, and steaks. I rate these places as among the best delis in the city — or anywhere, for that matter.

A VOCE

Time Warner Center

10 Columbus Circle (at Eighth Ave), 3rd floor	212/823-2523
Lunch: Mon-Sat; Dinner: Daily; Brunch: Sun	

41 Madison Ave (at 26th St)	212/545-8555
Lunch: Mon-Fri; Dinner: Mon-Sat	avocerestaurant.com

Moderately expensive

A Voce offers guests an excellent ingredient-driven contemporary Italian menu. Both locations are well-appointed. The newest locale, at Columbus Circle, has a stunning Central Park view for those lucky enough to sit by the window. Patrons of the Madison Avenue restaurant are treated to an outside dining piazza in nice weather. Menus change frequently, but highlights include Mediterranean sea bass, rosemary and lemon marinated chicken, and excellent pasta dishes including linguine with sea urchin. Save room for some really good desserts. My favorites are chocolate-caramel tart with sorbetto and Tuscan doughnuts (*bomboloni* a la Toscana) with bittersweet chocolate.

ABBOCCATO

136 W 55th St (bet Ave of the Americas and Seventh Ave)	212/265-4000
Breakfast: Daily; Lunch: Mon-Sat; Dinner: Daily	abboccato.com

Moderately expensive

The Livanos family, known and respected on the New York restaurant scene, own this elegant Italian dining spot, which serves some traditional (as if you are really in Italy) plates, so expect big things — especially if you like rather fussy Italian dishes. Personally, I prefer a simpler approach, so I have found some items

---

Grill Time

Seafood enthusiasts can choose from two locations of the **Atlantic Grill** (1341 Third Ave, 212/988-9200 and Lincoln Center, 49 W 64th St, 212/787-4663). Both restaurants share the same upscale casual concept with slightly different menus. Brunch, lunch, and dinner feature fresh treats from the deep that are served raw, breaded and fried, grilled, barbecued, sauteed, or sauced. My favorite presentation is the stunning tower of shellfish — two, three, or four tiers of plates loaded with crab, shrimp, clams, oysters, lobster, and mussels. A hazelnut and banana parfait with salted caramel sauce finishes a perfect meal!

---

here to be a bit overwhelming but nonetheless very good. As either a starter or light meal, a great selection of cicchetti (small plates) tempt the taste buds. Most of the appetizers, especially the pastas, are excellent, and the breadsticks are fabulous! The entrees are noteworthy, especially the veal chops. The $35 *prix-fixe* dinner is a great value. A sizeable dessert menu, including homemade gelati, is a dream. However dreamy the dining experience, the sizable tab will wake you up.

ABC KITCHEN

ABC Carpet & Home
35 E 18th St (at Broadway)   212/475-5829
Lunch: Mon-Fri; Dinner: Daily; Brunch: Sat, Sun   abckitchenyc.com
Moderately expensive to expensive

Super-chef Jean-Georges Vongerichten offers fresh, organic, local ingredients at ABC Carpet & Home. Although many of the items on the full menu are pricey, with careful selection you can do well. The setting is warm and modern, and the front desk personnel and wait staff are exceptionally friendly, informed, and efficient. Seasonal soups and a wonderful apple and pear salad are great starters. The variety of pastas and whole-wheat pizzas is excellent. Vegetable dishes are particularly appealing. Entrees range from $24 (cheeseburger) to $39 for wood-oven-roasted Maine lobster; seafood dishes are the main attraction. The dessert menu is large and varied. A sundae of salted caramel ice cream with candied peanuts and popcorn, whipped cream, and chocolate sauce is almost a meal in itself. ABC offers a one-of-a-kind, noisy, fun atmosphere, good people-watching, and really delicious platters. A fitting description of this place would be a "haute green cuisine" experience.

ACAPPELLA

1 Hudson St (bet West Broadway and Chambers St)   212/240-0163
Lunch: Mon-Fri; Dinner: Mon-Sat   acappella-restaurant.com
Moderately expensive

Acappella, classy and upscale in atmosphere, food, and pricing, provides a very special Tribeca dining experience with a highly professional staff. It's a good place for a romantic interlude, for an important business lunch, or to experiment with some unique Northern Italian dishes. You'll find homemade pastas, risotto, calamari, fish, veal scaloppine, veal chops, Kobe beef, breaded breast of chicken, and prime steak on the menu. For dessert, splurge on the homemade Italian cheesecake or chocolate truffle torte.

ACME

9 Great Jones St (bet Lafayette St and Broadway)	212/203-2121
Dinner: Daily; Brunch: Sat, Sun	acmenyc.com

Moderately expensive

You may be a bit stymied finding Acme's location if you are unfamiliar with NoHo; Great Jones Street is a two block section completing West and East Third streets where odd-numbered addresses are uncharacteristically on the south side of the street. Executive chef Mads Refslund describes the fare as "New Nordic" and divides the menu into raw, cooked, soil, sides, and sea/land categories. Depending on the season, you may find interesting items such as duck in a jar, country toast (with cheese and vegetables), hay-roasted vegetables, Arctic char, chicken and eggs, and much more. This lively place (formerly Acme Bar & Grill), has been overhauled to include dining tables with an eating bar and rail for walk-in customers. A cocktail bar (open Thursday through Saturday, 7 p.m. to 3 a.m.) is downstairs with a limited menu from the restaurant.

ALDEA

31 W 17th St (bet Fifth Ave and Ave of the Americas)	212/675-7223
Lunch: Mon-Fri; Dinner: Mon-Sat	aldearestaurant.com

Moderately expensive

You'll find the best seats at Aldea are at the chef's counter, overlooking the kitchen. Chef George Mendes, in his first solo restaurant venture, orchestrates this sleek, contemporary Portuguese hot spot. Lunch and dinner menus reflect the best of the current season from land and sea. Small bites, charcuterie, sandwiches, and entrees like New Zealand venison or Spanish mackerel pepper the menu.

AQUAVIT

65 E 55th St (bet Park and Madison Ave)	212/307-7311
Lunch: Mon-Fri; Dinner: Mon-Sat	aquavit.org

Moderately expensive

For fresh, yet authentic Scandinavian cuisine, you can't do better than Aquavit. Owner Hakan Swahn has partnered with Chef Marcus Jernmark to create a first-class establishment. The warm, rustic space combines clean lines and natural textures in a natural light-filled space. Hearty lunch appetites will enjoy the Scandinavian bouillabaisse or Swedish meatballs. A four-course *prix-fixe* and seven-course chef's tasting menu are offered at dinner. Early choices include herring, Maine sea urchin, and rabbit confit. Cod, monkfish, squab, and Spanish octopus are main course offerings. My dessert suggestion is the orange crème brûlée with rum moscavado ice cream, caramel truffles, and pistachio brittle.

ARABELLE

Hotel Plaza Athenee

37 E 64th St (bet Madison and Park Ave)	212/606-4647
Breakfast, Lunch, Dinner: Tues-Sat	arabellerestaurant.com

Moderately expensive to expensive

Dining in this attractive room is a civilized experience. It is elegant and charming, and the adjacent lounge is one of the classiest spots in Manhattan. The wait staff is unusually attentive and professional. For starters, try lobster bisque or spring pea soup. Entrees are driven by seasonal fish, seafood, and meats; if available, the Arctic char and veal tenderloin are big winners. Decadent desserts and afternoon tea are sure to please any sweet tooth. Live entertainment is offered Monday (magician) and Tuesday (jazz soloists from Julliard) from 6 p.m. to 8 p.m.

ARDESIA

510 W 52nd St (bet Tenth and Eleventh Ave)   212/247-9191
Dinner: Daily   ardesia-ny.com
Moderate

On a street not known for good restaurants, Ardesia is popular with young folks who like to eat casually while enjoying a beer or glass of wine; nothing fancy, just solid food at a reasonable price, served by waiters who seem to savor the experience as much as the diners. Lots of interesting starters: homemade New York pretzels, lemongrass shrimp skewer, and seared flank steak. A number of tasty sandwiches and salads are worth the relatively tiny prices. Artisanal cheese and charcuterie made in-house are excellent. Save room for s'mores for dessert!

ARLINGTON CLUB STEAKHOUSE

1032 Lexington Ave (near 74th St)   212/249-5700
Dinner: Daily   arlingtonclubny.com
Moderately expensive to expensive

Talented chef Laurent Tourondel is the master commander of this highly successful TAO Group newcomer. Loud and crowded, it is a U.E.S. destination for excellent steaks, exquisitely presented-sushi and sashimi. The trademark basket of piping-hot popovers is fabulous and presented to the table while diners peruse the menu. This steakhouse's offerings include dry-aged prime beef; the 34-ounce cote de boeuf for two is worth the price for very special occasions. You won't go wrong with the house potatoes or truffled gnocchi alongside the rack of lamb (superb) or Dover sole. On-the-job partner Paul Goldstein and his crew run a very professional operation with well-above-standard service. The clubby atmosphere is achieved through the use of warm brick walls and ceilings, curved banquettes bordering the dining room, comfortable high-back benches and chairs surrounding the tables, and arched ceilings drawing the eye up to the mezzanine level. A compelling hum translates into a good time at this sexy hotspot!

ARTISANAL FROMAGERIE, BISTRO AND WINE BAR

2 Park Ave (at 32nd St)   212/725-8585
Lunch: Mon-Fri; Dinner: Daily; Brunch: Sat, Sun   artisanalbistro.com
Moderately expensive to expensive

Imagine a combination of the best aspects of bistro, brasserie, and fromagerie, and you'll have a clear picture of this exciting operation. Being a cheese lover, I found the menu and stylish cheese counter, which doubles as a retail shop, first-rate. I was pleasantly surprised by Artisanal's superior execution of various steaks and signature chicken. A Maine lobster and avocado salad is a great way to start. A seafood platter features littleneck clams, east and west coast oysters, jumbo shrimp, and more. Several fondues are offered, including the Artisanal blend, a classic fusion of three Swiss cheeses and aged Gouda, and Stout. House specialties include delicate Dover sole or a casserole of duck, garlic sausage, and lamb. For dessert, cruise the cheese counter and load your plate from a selection of 100 handcrafted choices, or try Artisanal's renowned cheesecake with buttery pecan-shortbread crust and a plunge of praline and caramel sauce. Seating is comfortable in the spacious art deco room, and service is highly informed and personable. An extensive wine selection, too!

BABBO

110 Waverly Pl (at Washington Square)   212/777-0303
Lunch: Tues-Sat; Dinner: Daily   babbonyc.com
Moderate to moderately expensive

Surely you have heard about Babbo! For many years 110 Waverly Place has been one of my favorite dining addresses. First it was the legendary Coach House, and now it is the magnificent Babbo, which means "daddy" in the native tongue. It has become one of the most respected houses of fine Italian dining in New York, and this is one of the toughest reservations in Manhattan. The townhouse setting is warm and comfortable, the service is highly professional, and an evening at Babbo is one you will savor for a long time! Most everything is good, but I especially recommend sweetbreads, grilled ribeye steak for two, and beef cheek ravioli. Wonderful desserts might include chocolate hazelnut cake, saffron panna cotta, pistachio and chocolate semifreddo, and the ever-popular cheese plate. Best of all is the assortment of homemade gelati and sorbetti.

BALABOOSTA

214 Mulberry St (at Spring St)   212/966-7366
Lunch: Tues-Fri; Dinner: Daily; Brunch: Sat, Sun   balaboostanyc.com
Moderately expensive

Balaboosta is as warm and cozy a place as you'll find in your own neighborhood; understandable since the name is Yiddish for "perfect housewife." The front window is lined with large jars of pickles and preserves and offers a view of the open kitchen where Mediterranean and Middle Eastern cuisine is prepared. Start with the small plates, appetizers, daily ceviche, or a chalkboard special. Lunch options include a goat cheese-stuffed lamburger, Tunisian sandwich, and crusty chicken schnitzel. Later in the day, grilled fish, steaks, chicken, and lamb chops are accompanied by couscous, vegetables and other sides appropriate to the region.

Dining at the Time Warner Center

The exclusive address of the **Time Warner Center** (10 Columbus Circle) is home to upscale shops, markets, and restaurants. As you would expect, the variety is wide and prices are generally expensive. **A Voce** (212/823-2523, Italian), **Bouchon Bakery** (212/823-9366, American/French), and **Landmarc** (212/823-6123, French) are all on the third floor. **Center Bar** (212/823-9482, tapas-style small plates), **Masa** and the more modest **Bar Masa** (212/823-9800, Japanese), **per se** (212/823-9335, American/French), and **Porter House New York** (212/823-9500) have stylish dining facilities on the fourth floor. All are open for dinner, and most serve lunch. Call well in advance for reservations. Also on this floor is **Stone Rose Lounge** (212/823-9769), a prime venue for cocktails and small bites.

Beyond Bacon and Eggs

Forget your usual breakfast of cold cereal and dry toast and try some of these great morning choices:

Bacon: **Jack's Wife Freda** (224 Lafayette St, 212/510-8550): house-cured duck bacon

Belgian waffles: **Le Pain Quotidien** (100 Grand St, 212/625-9009; 1131 Madison Ave, 212/327-4900; and other locations) and **Petite Abeille** (466 Hudson St, 212/741-6479; 134 West Broadway, 212/791-1360; 44 W 17th St, 212/727-2989; and 401 E 20th St, 212/727-1505)

Corned beef hash: **Carnegie Deli** (854 Seventh Ave, 212/757-2245)

English-style breakfast: **The Breslin Bar & Dining Room** (Ace Hotel, 16 W 29th St, 212/679-1939)

Pancakes: **Clinton St. Baking Co. & Restaurant** (4 Clinton St, 646/602-6263), **Friend of a Farmer** (77 Irving Pl, 212/477-2188), and **Veselka** (144 Second Ave, 212/229-9682): raspberry

Roast beef hash and poached eggs: **Wollensky's Grill** (201 E 49th St, 212/753-0444): weekend brunch

---

Some of these items plus Moroccan baked eggs, breakfast pizza, and their rendition of French toast are tempting brunch dishes. The service is attentive, the food is delicious, and the environs are most relaxing.

BALTHAZAR

80 Spring St (at Crosby St)   212/965-1414
Breakfast: Daily; Lunch: Mon-Fri; Dinner: Daily; Brunch: Sat, Sun
Moderate   balthazarny.com

This brasserie is a fun, popular destination at any time of the day (or night, as they serve late). The setting at Balthazar – with old mirrors, ceiling fans, and a yellow tin ceiling – is unique, and the food is quite good, considering the size of the operation. The bustling personnel are well-trained; you will not wait for your water glass to be filled. Excellent bakery items shine at breakfast. Be sure to pick up some tasty bread next door at their bakery on your way out. At lunch and dinner you can enjoy delicious seasonal salads, sandwiches, cheeses, paninis, fabulous French onion soup, brandade, escargots, steak frites, and an abundant seafood selection (including a seafood bar). For dessert the tarte tatin is a must. A separate takeout menu is offered in the bakery, which is open daily until 8.

BAR AMERICAIN

152 W 52nd St (bet Ave of the Americas and Seventh Ave)   212/265-9700
Lunch: Mon-Fri; Dinner: Daily; Brunch: Sat, Sun   baramericain.com
Moderately expensive to expensive

Bar Americain is indeed almost purely American. Perhaps best described as an American brasserie, the setting is large with offbeat decor; chef Bobby Flay has made the room come alive. The food quality and attentive, professional service make this a good bet. The cocktails are numerous and interesting. To start, an eye-catching raw bar is stocked with oysters, clams, lobsters, and more. One could make a meal on the appetizers. Vidalia onion soup with blistered Vermont cheddar cheese is superb. The same holds true for crawfish and Dungeness crab griddle cakes. Among the entrees, cioppino, duck (with dirty wild rice), and rack of pork are definitely worth a try. Five steak dishes are offered. Don't pass up a side of hot potato chips with blue cheese sauce. You'll want to take extra time to study the excellent dessert menu!

BAR BOULUD

1900 Broadway (bet 63rd and 64th St)   212/595-0303
Lunch: Mon-Fri; Dinner: Daily; Brunch: Sat, Sun   barboulud.com/nyc
Moderate

Located just steps from Lincoln Center, the sleek wine-cellar-like dining room features a charcuterie bar and communal tables. The rustic French menu features a number of Daniel Boulud's favorites. You'll find signature terrines and patés, hearty soups, and seasonal French bistro cooking. The croque monsieur with housemade ham, gruyere cheese, and béchamel is delicious. For heartier fare, you'll find coq au vin, steak frites, and seasonal seafood with a distinctive French flavor. Charcuterie specialties are available daily. Bar Boulud features a good showing of cheese, ice creams, sorbets, and rich chocolate treats for dessert. This is an obvious winner for Lincoln Center opera-goers.

BARBETTA

321 W 46th St (bet Eighth and Ninth Ave)   212/246-9171
Lunch, Dinner, Supper: Tues-Sat   barbettarestaurant.com
Moderate to moderately expensive

Barbetta is one of those special places you'll find only in New York! Owner Laura Maioglio is a very special person, as well. This elegant restaurant serves Piemontese cuisine. Piemonte is located in northern Italy, and the cuisine reflects that charming region. You can dine here in European elegance. One of New York's oldest restaurants, Barbetta celebrated its 107th year in 2013. Amazingly, it is still owned by its founding family. A special attraction is dining alfresco in the garden during the summer. The main dining room and private rooms are magnificent! Barbetta offers an extensive a la carte menu at lunch and dinner. Before theater, Barbetta serves a pre-theater *prix-fixe* menu with eight choices at each of its three courses. Service is expeditious so that you can make opening curtain. Among Barbetta's signature dishes are the delicate gnocchetti, light as powder puffs; Bagna Cauda; quail's nest of fonduta; beef braised in Barolo wine; and rack of venison. Tasty fish and seafood dishes abound. Sixteen desserts are prepared daily including an assortment of cakes, tarts, fruits, and one of the best panna cotta in the city.

John Campbell's Historic Watering Hole

Here's a bar that is both an attraction and a thriving watering hole. The story of the **Campbell Apartment**, located off the West Balcony of Grand Central Terminal (42nd St at Vanderbilt Ave, 212/953-0409), is a fascinating one. The space was once the private office of John Campbell, a very wealthy financier. In its heyday, these classy digs had a butler and some of the most expensive furnishings available. Even jaded New Yorkers like to tell stories about this fellow and that room. It is surely worth a visit!

Eat Your Greens

You can count on these places for good salads:

Angelica Kitchen (300 E 12th St, 212/228-2909): organic ingredients

City Bakery (3 W 18th St, 212/366-1414): salad bar

Commerce (50 Commerce St, 212/524-2301): twenty herbs and lettuces

Gotham Bar & Grill (12 E 12th St, 212/620-4020): seafood salad

Michael's (24 W 55th St, 212/767-0555): Tuscan Caesar kale salad

Pastis (9 Ninth Ave, 212/929-4844): mixed greens

Pearl Oyster Bar (18 Cornelia St, 212/691-8211): Caesar salad

The Standard Grill (The Standard High Line, 848 Washington St, 212/645-4100): chef's salad

---

Barbetta's wine list, recipient of many awards, numbers over 1,700 labels.

BARMARCHE

14 Spring St (at Elizabeth St)   212/219-2399
Dinner: Daily; Brunch: Sat, Sun   barmarche.com
Moderate

Spring Street is full of small, cozy, and interesting places to dine. The area is called Nolita (shorthand for "north of Little Italy"). One of the best stops hereabouts is Barmarche, where the folks are very friendly, the food is excellent, the price is right, and the atmosphere is appealing. You'll find bistro fare and small plates (like chilled oysters), along with fresh salads, taquitos, and one of the best burgers in the city. The garlic fries served with the burgers are crisp and delicious. Barmarche is perfect for a date or small group.

THE BEAGLE

162 Ave A (bet 10th and 11th St)   212/228-6900
Dinner: Daily   thebeaglenyc.com
Inexpensive to moderate

Former Oregonian Matt Piacentini is at the helm of this cozy East Village cocktail haven. He's quick to correct erroneous assumptions that the business name pays tribute to the popular canine. Rather, the H.M.S. Beagle provided the inspiration. The Beagle specializes in cocktails – really good cocktails made with top-drawer ingredients – and sherry by the glass. In fact, you'll need to search the island to find a larger offering of sherries by the glass. Food takes a back seat to the aforementioned drinks. Light dinner fare includes bar food staples: sandwiches, burgers, interesting appetizers, and a few nightly specials on the chalkboard. But, if you want a good drink (or if you're an Oregonian and long for a connection with the Beaver State) in a relaxing atmosphere, head to the Beagle – no dogs allowed.

BENOIT

60 W 55th St (bet Fifth Ave and Ave of the Americas)   646/943-7373
Lunch: Mon-Sat; Dinner: Daily; Brunch: Sun   benoitny.com
Expensive

In an attractive room that has seen its share of ups and downs over the years, master foodie Alain Ducasse has designed a charming bistro with special touches only the French can create. One immediately notices the warm greeting, very professional service, and interesting diners. What to eat? It is like going to heaven by way of France! The paté en croute (an 1892 recipe) is fabulous; a charcuterie and paté selection is varied and filling. "Ladies who lunch" will delight in the quenelles de brochet, and the cassoulet is sensational. At lunch, feast on escargots, lobster ravioli, chocolate soufflé, the flawless onion soup, or dishes created with fresh, seasonal ingredients. Portions are huge! Take your time and savor the atmosphere as well as the platters.

BISTRO LES AMIS

180 Spring St (at Thompson St)   212/226-8645
Lunch, Dinner: Daily; Brunch: Sat, Sun   bistrolesamis.com
Moderate

Bistro les Amis is a delightful bistro worth stopping by in the middle of a Soho shopping trip or gallery excursion. In the warmer months, the doors open onto the sidewalk, and the passing parade is almost as inviting as the varied menu. French onion soup with gruyere is a must, and salmon marinated with fresh dill and herbs is just as good. Lunch entrees include sandwiches and fresh salads. In the evening, seafood and steak dishes are available. Steak frites with herb butter is first-class. A *prix-fixe* menu is offered to early diners. There's nothing very fancy about this bistro – just good food with an extra touch of friendly service.

BLAUE GANS

139 Duane St (bet Church St and West Broadway)   ·   212/571-8880
Lunch: Mon-Fri; Dinner: Daily; Brunch: Sat, Sun   kg-ny.com
Moderate to moderately expensive

Chef Kurt Gutenbrunner lives up to his heritage with Austro-German bistro Blaue Gans ("Blue Goose"), which offers delicious platters like red cabbage and salad, smoked trout, beef goulash, wiener schnitzel, käsekrainer (with sauerkraut), blood sausage, and Kavalierspitz (boiled beef shoulder) served with fabulous creamed spinach. Tafelspitz (boiled beef) is considered to be Austria's national dish, and it, too, is available. I am a great lover of Vienna, especially the fabulous Sacher torte, an Austrian tradition. Unfortunately, Blaue Gans' Sacher torte falls far short of fabulous. Instead, go for the Salzburger Nockerl, a warm dessert soufflé that's jazzed up with tart huckleberries. The folks here are delightful, which makes the meal even more memorable.

BLT STEAK

106 E 57th St (bet Park and Lexington Ave)   212/752-7470
Lunch: Mon-Fri; Dinner: Daily   bltsteak.com
Moderately expensive to expensive

Chef Tourondel's considerable talents in the kitchen have made this modern American steakhouse one of the best in Manhattan. The delicious popovers served at the start absolutely melt in your mouth! Most of the pricey salads are big and healthy, but save room for the main show: hanger steak, Wagyu ribeye steak, filet mignon, New York strip steak, and more. You have your choice of eight great sauces to accompany the meat entree. Also on the menu: fish, shellfish, and

---

Celebrity Chefs

New York has many world-class restaurants with world-class chefs. They have not only made their mark in the kitchen, but as television hosts, cookbook authors, and designers of kitchenware and food product lines. Here are some of the big-name personalities:

Mario Batali: Italian empire, Eataly

David Bouley: genius in the kitchen

Daniel Boulud: namesake eateries around town

David Burke: creative

David Chang: Momofuku empire

Tom Colicchio: the man behind Craft

Todd English: Plaza Food Hall

Danny Meyer: Shake Shack (and much more) impresario

Drew Nieporent: Nobu and other unique houses

Marcus Samuelsson: Red Rooster Harlem

Jean-Georges Vongerichten: master of French cuisine

Michael White: Marea and other Italian spots

---

potatoes done six different ways. (I could make an entire meal of BLT's potato choices!) The rack of lamb is superb. Chocolate tart smothered with creamy pistachio ice cream is one of the best desserts in Manhattan (or anywhere).

BLUE HILL

75 Washington Pl (bet Ave of the Americas and MacDougal St)   212/539-1776
Dinner: Daily   bluehillfarm.com
Moderate to moderately expensive

Dramatic it is not. Comfortable it is – barely. Solid it is – in spades. Blue Hill is named for a farm owned and operated by Dan and David Barber, who also own this restaurant. The restaurant reflects the chef's solid upbringing with David Bouley. The limited menu, with only a half dozen appetizers and entrees, includes some spectacular standouts and changes periodically. A Farmers Feast, a five-course tasting menu that changes daily, is a great culinary experience. An extended seven-course tasting menu offers five savory and two sweet choices. Poached duck is a specialty. The crabmeat salad, if available, is top-rate. If your evening plans involve intimate conversation, forget Blue Hill, as eavesdropping is inevitable. The chocolate bread pudding ("chocolate silk") is really the only dessert worth the calories.

BLUE RIBBON

97 Sullivan St (bet Spring and Prince St)   212/274-0404
Daily: 4 p.m.-4 a.m.   blueribbonrestaurants.com
Moderate

Blue Ribbon is one of the most popular spots in Soho, with a bustling bar scene and people lining up for its limited number of tables. Regulars savor the exceptional food in this unpretentious restaurant. There is a raw bar to attract seafood lovers, along with clams, lobster, crab, boiled crawfish, and the house special

"Blue Ribbon Royale" appetizer platter. One can choose from two dozen appetizers, including barbecued ribs, smoked trout, caviar, and chicken wings. Entrees are just as wide-ranging: sweetbreads, catfish, tofu ravioli, fried chicken and mashed potatoes, burgers, and more. How the smallish kitchen can turn out so many dishes is amazing, but they certainly do it well. Don't come for a relaxed evening; this is strictly an all-American culinary experience. Those who experience hunger pangs after midnight will appreciate the late hours. Try the excellent sushi at their nearby **Blue Ribbon Sushi** (119 Sullivan St, 212/343-0404). Then there is the **Blue Ribbon Sushi Bar & Grill** (308 W 58th St, 212/397-0404), in the 6 Columbus hotel. The sushi menu is expanded, with a wide variety of popular cold and hot dishes, all expectedly very good. This location also offers traditional or Asian breakfast and Sunday brunch.

BLUE RIBBON BAKERY

35 Downing St (at Bedford St)   212/337-0404
Lunch, Dinner: Daily; Brunch: Sat, Sun   blueribbonrestaurants.com
Moderate

The rustic breads at this cafe and bakery are excellent, and there is so much more. Downstairs, customers dine in a fantastic brick oven atmosphere, complete with a wine cellar and family dining room, and wonderful fresh-bread aroma. The menu features signature brick oven breads, sandwiches, steaks, seafood, cheeses, seasonal salads, local fish, veggies, and yummy desserts (including profiteroles).

BLUE SMOKE

255 Vesey St (bet North End Ave and West St)   212/889-2005
116 E 27th St (bet Lexington Ave and Park Ave S)   212/447-7733
Lunch, Dinner: Daily; Brunch: Sat, Sun   bluesmoke.com
Moderate

And then there were two! Danny Meyer filled a real void in the Manhattan dining scene with Blue Smoke, satisfying legions of barbecue lovers who found it difficult to get authentic down-home ribs in the Big Apple. Now there are locations in Murray Hill and the Financial District! In addition to ribs, you'll find chili, smoked beef brisket, tasty sandwiches, pit-baked beans, and a combo of ribs, pulled pork, chicken, and sausage. Blue Smoke is not just a barbecue place but a full-fledged scene, with an ultra-busy bar attracting fun-loving trendsetters. A variety of delicious homestyle desserts, from award-winning key lime pie to sticky toffee pudding, rhubarb crisp, and chocolate layer cake served with a glass of cold milk. Call ahead for larger orders or special requests, such as a coconut layer cake with coconut buttercream and Italian meringue.

BLUE WATER GRILL

31 Union Square W (at 16th St)   212/675-9500
Lunch: Mon-Sat; Dinner: Daily; Brunch: Sun   brguestrestaurants.com
Moderate

This seafood restaurant really knows the ocean and all the edible creatures that inhabit it! Blue Water Grill is a highly professional operation. Superbly trained personnel operate in a building that once served as a bank and is now a very bustling restaurant. Wonderful appetizers may include lobster bisque, shrimp and lobster spring rolls, and lump crab cakes. Tuna, salmon, swordfish, and other fish are

---

Restaurants for a Crowd

The Big Apple boasts some big restaurants. Top chefs and restaurateurs keep pumping up the square footage of their newest outposts. Bigger is not necessarily better, but at these operations, size and quality coexist just fine, along with the hum of hundreds of conversations.

Buddakan (Chelsea Market, 75 Ninth Ave, 212/989-6699): Asian hot spot

Del Posto (85 Tenth Ave, 212/497-8090): palatial

Morimoto (88 Tenth Ave, 212/989-8883): modern space

Nobu Fifty Seven (40 W 57th St, 212/757-3000): done with style and grace

Rosa Mexicano (9 E 18th St, 212/533-3350): festive south-of-the-border treats

Spice Market (403 W 13th St, 212/675-2322): family-style Asian street cuisine

Tao (42 E 58th St, 212/888-2288): impressive Asian bistro

---

prepared "simply grilled." Lobsters and oysters (several dozen varieties) are fresh and tasty as are the extensive sushi offerings. For those who want to stick to shore foods, pastas, chicken dishes, and grilled filet mignon are available. A half dozen sensibly priced desserts include molten chocolate tart with cappuccino ice cream.

BOBO

181 W 10th St (at Seventh Ave)   212/488-2626
Dinner: Daily; Brunch: Sat, Sun   bobonyc.com
Moderately expensive

Tucked away in an unassuming building just off Seventh Avenue, bobo is a warm and charming place to dine, but you should insist on eating upstairs. Attentive service, sizeable portions, and quite good food make this a rather romantic dining spot. A glassed-in garden terrace opens in warm months. Menu favorites include Long Island crescent duck duo, pan-seared bass, and steak au poivre. Entrees feature seafood dishes with bass, cod, and skate usually available. Braised short ribs are delicious. Eight cheeses are listed at reasonable prices, or finish with the housemade sorbet and ice cream.

BOND 45

154 W 45th St (bet Ave of the Americas and Seventh Ave)   212/869-4545
Breakfast: Mon-Sat; Lunch, Dinner: Daily; Brunch: Sat, Sun   bond45.com
Moderate to moderately expensive

Busy restaurateur Shelly Fireman has created a huge dining hall in the middle of the Theater District. Billed as an Italian steak and seafood room, Bond 45 is named for the old Bond men's store that used to occupy this site. If it's Italian, Bond 45 has it! The antipasto bar at the entrance makes a mouth-watering beginning. Beyond that, there are salads, mozzarella, carpaccio dishes, cured meats, pastas, steaks, and so on. An abundance of wait personnel ensures prompt service. The dessert selection doesn't live up to the rest of the fare.

BOTTEGA DEL VINO
7 E 59th St (bet Fifth and Madison Ave)   212/223-2724
Breakfast, Lunch, Dinner: Daily   bottegadelvinonyc.com
Moderately expensive

This is a serious restaurant that serves serious food. The midtown location is a replica of the Venice original, pampering guests with Northern Italian cuisine combined with fresh and seasonal ingredients. Service is professional and buoyant. All the dishes are tasty, especially the steaks. If risotto with shrimp and asparagus tips is on the menu, go for it! Grilled Australian lamb chops, veal scaloppini, and Mediterranean sea bass are typical entrees. Desserts are tasty and filling; the cheese selection with sweet marmalades is excellent, and the ambrosia cake is, well, pure ambrosia.

BOULEY
163 Duane St (at Hudson St)   212/964-2525
Lunch, Dinner: Mon-Sat   davidbouley.com
Expensive

BOULEY TEST KITCHEN
88 West Broadway (at Chambers St), 5th floor   212/964-2525
By appointment only   bouleytestkitchen.com

BRUSHSTROKE (a Bouley creation)
30 Hudson St (bet Duane and Reade St)   212/791-3771
Lunch, Dinner: Mon-Sat   brushstrokenyc.com
Expensive

There is no end to the culinary genius of David Bouley, one of the most celebrated chefs in the United States. His flagship Tribeca restaurant, **Bouley**, features a newly remodeled state-of-the-art kitchen and is one of Manhattan's finest dining venues, with superb French fare and service. Offerings include such delights as black cod marinated with pistachio miso, New Zealand venison with black truffle gnocchi, and delicious desserts like pineapple carpaccio. Private dining options include the main dining room, the appropriately named Red Room, the Chef's Pass, and at his other sites. The versatile Red Room can accommodate 50

The Whole Hog!

Go whole hog on a party with your friends! Known for great food and good times, these places will also roast a whole pig, complete with trimmings. Particulars vary by location. Advance reservations are a must, usually several days to a week ahead of time.

Back Forty (190 Ave B, 212/388-1990): porchetta style

The Breslin Bar & Dining Room (Ace Hotel, 16 W 29th St, 212/679-1939): duck-fat potatoes, dessert

DBGB Kitchen & Bar (299 Bowery, 212/933-5300): chili-braised beans, roasted potatoes, and baked Alaska

Nuela (43 W 24th St, 212/929-1200): whole pig; cumin-lime rice, scallion pancakes

seated guests and is reminiscent of the south of France, where eating and drinking are of primary importance. Nestled between the kitchen and main dining room, Chef's Pass is an intimate space, seating up to 13 guests, where Chef Bouley personally familiarizes guests with the ingredients that compose his dishes. Via the interactive element of Skype, guests can be introduced to the artisans who create the products that inspire him. Two blocks away, **Bouley Test Kitchen** is a distinct venue for visiting chefs, interactive demonstrations, a catering special event space, cooking classes, testing ground for professional and home cooks, and the place where recipes are developed for all Bouley entities. Finally, **Brushstroke** moves Kaiseki cuisine (traditional Japanese menus) forward as the Tsuji Cooking Institute chefs combine inspiration with highest quality ingredients sourced both locally and from Japan. Off-premise catering is available through the Bouley Private Dining Team.

BOULUD SUD

20 W 64th St (bet Central Park West and Broadway)   212/595-1313
Lunch: Mon-Fri; Dinner: Daily; Brunch: Sat, Sun   bouludsud.com
Moderately expensive

Daniel Boulud has added another wonder to his Manhattan empire. Boulud Sud is around the corner from popular Bar Boulud and Épicerie Boulud, an eat-in, take-out market. The menu features flavors that travel the entire Mediterranean region from the shores of Southern France to the coast of North Africa and beyond plus the full selection of wines offered at Bar Boulud. There is an emphasis on grilled fish and lamb as well as an abundance of fresh vegetables on menu sections entitled "De La Mer," "Du Jardin," and "De La Ferme." An octopus appetizer with marcona almonds is outstanding, so is the robust main course chicken tagine. Desserts, ice cream, and sorbets are all homemade with grapefruit givré the number one pick. Lincoln Center patrons will appreciate a three-course *prix-fixe* menu before the evening performance. Boulud's corner is a nice addition to the neighborhood.

BRASSERIE

100 E 53rd St (bet Park and Lexington Ave)   212/751-4840
Breakfast, Lunch: Mon-Fri; Dinner: Daily; Brunch: Sat, Sun   patinagroup.com
Moderate

Brasserie is a New York tradition for those who like big, brassy, fun dining spots that serve very good food. What was once a round-the-clock operation now keeps handy late hours (Mon-Thurs till 11 p.m.; Fri, Sat till midnight; Sun till 10 p.m.). The sleek, attractive quarters include a grand staircase fit for a fashion show with sexy lighting and a bar that offers all manner of goodies. Much of the food has a French flair, but there are also well-prepared grill dishes, short ribs, grilled fish, scallops, crab cakes, pot-au-feu, steamed mussels with frites, and daily specials. Favorites include good old-fashioned onion soup gratinée, burgers, and chicken chop chop salad. For dessert, try the chocolate beignets.

BRASSERIE 8½

9 W 57th St (bet Fifth Ave and Ave of the Americas)   212/829-0812
Lunch: Mon-Fri; Dinner: Daily; Brunch: Sun   patinagroup.com
Moderately expensive

Both the interior and the dining are dramatic at Brasserie 8½. Descending a long spiral staircase, you enter a spectacular room filled with comfy chairs, an attractive bar, a wall of Léger stained glass, and a collection of signed Matisse prints. Even the tableware is pleasing. The menu features the best of the season. Veggies, lamb, veal, and fish may be roasted or grilled in appealing combinations, with a French point of view. Specials are offered daily. Great desserts might include chocolate soufflé with malt ice cream. Sunday buffet brunch is worth a visit. A private room is available for special events.

BRASSERIE RUHLMANN

45 Rockefeller Plaza (enter on 50th St, bet Fifth Ave and Ave of the Americas)
Lunch, Dinner: Mon-Sat: Brunch: Sun   212/974-2020
Moderate to moderately expensive   brasserieruhlmann.com

The attraction is the location – right in the heart of the midtown shopping area. The large room (232 seats) at Brasserie Ruhlmann is bold and classy, the service is highly professional, and you are greeted with genuine enthusiasm. Some signature dishes: roasted free-range chicken, steak frites, and shrimp and lobster roll. Top the meal off with a yummy profiterole drizzled in chocolate sauce. You will also appreciate designer Emile-Jacques Ruhlmann's red art-deco interior. Brasserie Ruhlmann closes late.

THE BRESLIN BAR & DINING ROOM

Ace Hotel
16 W 29th St (at Broadway)   212/679-1939
Breakfast, Lunch: Mon-Fri; Dinner: Daily; Brunch: Sat, Sun   thebreslin.com
Moderately expensive

Hot, hot, hot, hot! This area is hot, the hotel is hot, the bar is hot, and the restaurant is especially hot! In an old-time atmosphere, the Breslin is a very comfortable place to dine, with friendly and efficient service. As you might expect in a cool, gastropub atmosphere, the snack choices are unusual: caramel popcorn, pork scratchings, and scrumpets with mint vinegar; all fall in the $5 to $9 range. Terrine boards offer rustic pork, rabbit and prune, and more for $33. The

---

Bargain Slices

What's not to like about pizza? You can drop lots of dough on a gourmet Italian pie at the best pizzerias and Italian restaurants, or you can spend about a buck for a slice to quell the craving for a triangle of melted cheese, tangy tomato sauce, and crunchy crust. Dollar-a-slice specials have been popping up around town. Here's a sampling:

2 Bros. Pizza (32 St. Mark's Place, 212/777-0600)

99 Cent Fresh Pizza (151 E 43rd St, 212/911-0257; 569 Ninth Ave, 212/268-1461; and 388 Ave of the Americas, 212/780-0020)

FDR 99 Cent Slice Pizza (150 E 2nd St, 212/253-5950)

Mamani Pizza (151 Ave A, 212/388-1715)

Papa John's (21 Maiden Lane, 212/608-7272; 2119 First Ave, 212/360-7077; and 703 Lenox Ave, 212/491-4331)

French Fare

Bouillabaisse: French seafood stew

Confit: goose, duck, or pork that has been salted, cooked, and preserved in its own fat

Coulis: a thick, smooth sauce, usually made from vegetables but sometimes from fruit

Croque madame: grilled ham-and-cheese sandwich, topped with a cooked egg

En croute: anything baked in a buttery pastry crust or hollowed-out slice of toast

Foie gras: duck or goose liver, usually made into paté

Tartare: finely chopped and seasoned raw beef, often served as an appetizer

Terrine: finely minced ingredients or paté prepared in a loaf shape

---

chargrilled lamb burger is a bargain at $21, while the pig's foot for two goes for $48. I liked the side of crispy potatoes with house kraut. The bars are cozy and crowded, and the whole experience is unique. Diets are out the window here, so don't forget a great dessert.

BROOKLYN DINER USA

212 W 57th St (bet Broadway and Seventh Ave)	212/977-1957
155 W 43rd St (bet Broadway and Ave of the Americas)	212/265-5400
Breakfast, Lunch, Dinner, Late Supper: Daily	brooklyndiner.com
Moderate	

Brooklyn Diner USA (which is located in Manhattan) is worth a visit. With all-day dining, an expansive menu, pleasant personnel, better-than-average diner food, and reasonable prices, these places are winners. You can find just about anything your heart desires: breakfast fare, chicken soup, sandwiches (the cheeseburger is a must), salads (Chinese chicken salad is a favorite), hearty lunch and dinner plates of comfort food, homemade desserts, and good drinks. Their muffins are moist, flavorful, and outrageously good. Pastrami and corned beef are made on-site and carved to order. A tile floor and comfortable booths add to the authentic diner ambience.

BRYANT PARK GRILL

25 W 40th St (bet Fifth Ave and Ave of the Americas)	212/840-6500
Lunch: Mon-Fri; Dinner: Daily; Brunch: Sat, Sun	bryantparkgrillnyc.com
Moderate	

Bryant Park Grill is one of Manhattan's most charming American grills. It is ideally situated behind the New York Public Library in a space covered and heated in the winter, open in the summer, and festive all year round. Adjacent is the Bryant Park Cafe, which serves small and large plates of wonderfully delicious fare. A handy location in midtown, a refreshing view of Bryant Park, and a sensible, family-friendly menu make this a popular destination. Although the menu changes with the seasons, one can count on a good selection of soups, salads, and steak and seafood items at lunch and dinner. A weekend *prix-fixe* brunch is served alongside the regular lunch menu. Personnel are friendly and child-oriented.

BUTTER

415 Lafayette St (bet 4th St and Astor Pl)   212/253-2828
Dinner: Mon-Sat   butterrestaurant.com
Moderately expensive

Noisy and fun, Butter prides itself on churning out exceptional dishes featuring in-season bounty. The appetizer menu includes cavatappi pasta with spicy lamb sausage, lobster rolls, and fresh salads. For entrees, try any of the seafood dishes and the outstanding grilled organic ribeye, or their popular duck breast with roasted grapes. The raspberry beignets with vanilla dipping sauce will appeal to your sweet tooth. A five-course menu is offered for $90. Pair your meal choices with something from their award-winning, 225 bottles wine list.

BUTTERFIELD 8

5 E 38th St (bet Fifth and Madison Ave)   212/679-0646
Lunch, Dinner: Daily   butterfield8nyc.com
Moderate

Old-time New Yorkers remember Butterfield 8 as a classy telephone prefix. This nostalgic phrase was revived as an attractive, busy retreat serving American fare. The atmosphere is strictly old-time New York, and so is the food: Caesar and chopped Cobb salads, Angus burgers, Atlantic salmon, and pan-roasted chicken. There's even macaroni and cheese. What's for dessert? New York-style cheesecake, of course! A young, attractive wait staff makes visiting here a pleasure.

BUVETTE

42 Grove St (bet Bedford and Bleecker St)   212/255-3590
Breakfast, lunch, dinner: Daily   ilovebuvette.com
Moderate

Here's a find in the West Village: a tiny (50-seat) French gastrothèque which is open until the wee hours. For breakfast, Chef Jody Williams whips up wonderful steamed eggs, fresh pastries and espresso with hot chocolate. In addition to traditional croque monsieur and madame sandwiches for lunch, Buvette serves croque

---

Something for Everyone

These dishes may be delicacies to some and revolting to others. You be the judge!

Ceviche (marinated seafood): **Rosa Mexicano** (1063 First Ave, 212/753-7407; 61 Columbus Ave, 212/977-7700; and 9 E 18th St, 212/533-3350)

Haggis (Scotch pudding made of sheep innards): **St. Andrew's** (140 W 46th St, 212/840-8413)

Tripe (edible parts of the cow stomach): **Locanda Verde** (The Greenwich Hotel, 377 Greenwich St, 212/925-3797)

Sweetbreads (thymus gland of veal): **Casa Mono** (52 Irving Place, 212/253-2773)

forestier, a vegetarian variety containing roasted mushrooms. Cassoulet, coq au vin, octopus salad, charcuterie, and other choices are on the dinner menu along with small plates of tartinettes and cheeses. The ambience is delightful and the outdoor garden is charming, especially with a glass of wine; reservations not required.

CAFE BOULUD

20 E 76th St (at Madison Ave)   212/772-2600
Lunch: Mon-Sat; Dinner: Daily; Brunch: Sun   cafeboulud.com/nyc
Moderately expensive

Cafe Boulud is a famous name in Manhattan food circles. The food is quite good, though the room is rather drab and I sometimes find the attitude haughty. Once seated, however, you'll enjoy the innovative menu. There are always vegetarian selections, world cuisines (every season highlights a different area), traditional French classics and country cooking, and menu items inspired by the "rhythm of the seasons." A three-course *prix-fixe* menu is available at lunch and brunch. Evening prices are higher, but remember this place belongs to *the* Daniel Boulud, one of the nation's best chefs. Unfortunately he isn't in the kitchen at Cafe Boulud, because he is busy doing great things at his flagship restaurant, Daniel, but you can count on the talents of his award-winning chef, Gavin Kaysen.

CAFÉ CENTRO

MetLife Building
200 Park Ave (45th St at Vanderbilt Ave)   212/818-1222
Breakfast, Lunch: Mon-Fri; Dinner: Mon-Sat   patinagroup.com
Moderate

A grand cafe reminiscent of 1930s Paris, New York's Café Centro offers a classic Parisian brasserie menu. Guests are greeted with a gas-fired rotisserie and a beautiful open kitchen that's spotlessly clean and efficient. For starters, crusty French bread is laid out in front of you. Specialties include a hefty seafood platter, excellent steaks and French fries, sea bass, endive salad, and moist, flavorful roast chicken. The pastry chef turns out a variety of changing desserts: apple fritters, beignets, molten chocolate cake, and a sampler plate of cookies and petit fours. Adjoining the dining room is a busy beer bar that serves sandwiches and appetizers.

CAFE CLUNY

284 W 12th St (at 4th St)   212/255-6900
Breakfast, Lunch: Mon-Fri; Dinner: Daily; Brunch: Sat, Sun   cafecluny.com
Moderate to moderately expensive

Located on hard-to-find West 12th Street, Cafe Cluny is worth tracking down. You can drop by anytime and be assured of very good French-American food at sensible prices. Sandwiches and salads are the order of the day at noon. A pricier dinner menu features chicken, beef, and fish entrees. A three-course *prix-fixe* meal is offered for $35. Daily specials are offered for both lunch and dinner at this neighborhood favorite.

CAFE D'ALSACE

1695 Second Ave (at 88th St)   212/722-5133
Lunch: Mon-Fri; Dinner: Daily; Brunch: Sat, Sun   cafedalsace.com
Moderate

If bistro ambience appeals to you, then check out this casual charmer on the Upper East Side. The menu is large and varied: quiches (excellent!), sandwiches, sausages served with sauerkraut, salads, sirloin or lamb burgers, trout, steaks, choucroute (pork, duck, or seafood), and a full brunch selection. Young helpers provide informed service. The chef features several Alsatian specialties, including sugar cookies, chocolate and fruit tarts, and fruit soufflé for dessert. This place stocks over 100 varieties of beer, and a beer sommelier is on hand to help with selections.

CAFE LALO
201 W 83rd St (bet Amsterdam Ave and Broadway)   212/496-6031
Mon-Thurs: 8 a.m.-2 a.m.; Fri: 8 a.m.-4 a.m.; Sat: 9 a.m.-4 a.m.; Sun: 9 a.m-2 a.m.
Moderate   cafelalo.com

This place can be busy, but in my opinion, this is the best dessert shop in town. You will be reminded of a fine European pastry shop as you enjoy delicious desserts with cappuccino, espresso, cordials, or other libations from the well-stocked bar. Cafe Lalo offers more than a hundred decadent choices, including cakes, cheesecakes, tarts, pies, and connoisseur cheese platters. Yogurt and ice cream are also available, and soothing music makes every calorie go down sweetly. Breakfasts and brunches are a treat. Delivery is offered throughout Manhattan.

CAFE SABARSKY
Neue Galerie New York
1048 Fifth Ave (at 86th St)   212/288-0665
Breakfast, Lunch: Wed-Mon; Dinner: Thurs-Sun   cafesabarsky.com
Moderate

Buffet Lines
Savvy New Yorkers line up to fill their plates with items from a number of attractive and well-stocked buffets. The assortment is staggering, with salad bars, breads, hot and cold entrees, and desserts. At the bigger operations there are stations for carving meats, preparing omelets, and ordering pasta dishes. Service is quick, prices are generally reasonable, and you select only what you want to eat.

Bombay Palace (30 W 52nd St, 212/541-7777): Indian lunch

Brasserie 8½ (9 W 57th St, 212/829-0812): Sunday brunch

The Carlyle (Carlyle Hotel, 35 E 76th St, 212/570-7192): Sunday brunch, expensive

Chola (232 E 58th St, 212/688-4619): Indian lunch extravaganza

Dhaba (108 Lexington Ave, 212/679-1284): Indian lunch

Palm Court (The Plaza, 768 Fifth Ave, 212/546-5302): weekend brunch

Taste (1413 Third Ave, 212/717-9798): all-day salad bar in their cafe next door

Turkish Kitchen (386 Third Ave, 212/679-6633): Sunday brunch

Water Club (East River at 30th St, 212/683-3333): Sunday brunch

---

Free Bar Munchies

There may be no such thing as a free lunch, but these establishments provide gratis sustenance for their customers, usually during happy hour. Details vary at each location.

Cupping Room Cafe (359 West Broadway, 212/925-2898): free happy-hour chicken wings

Iron Horse (32 Cliff St, 646/546-5426): free burger or hot dog on Sunday

Keens Steakhouse (72 W 36th St, 212-947-3636): free hard-boiled eggs all day and happy-hour appetizers

Rudy's Bar & Grill (627 Ninth Ave, 646/707-0890): free Hebrew National hot dogs

---

The setting is quaint, the personnel are gracious, the prices are right, and the German-Austrian food is delicious. For breakfast, try Sabarsky Frühstück (Viennese mélange, orange juice, soft-boiled eggs, and Bavarian ham). Lunch and dinner selections include pea soup with mint, paprika sausage salad, crepes with smoked trout, Bavarian sausage, späetzle with mushrooms and peas, and Hungarian beef goulash. Cafe Sabarsky also serves sandwiches, sensational sweets (like Viennese dark chocolate cake and traditional apple strudel), Viennese coffees, and much more. Cafe Sabarsky is crowded, so come early and expect to wait. Music is offered for special events, such as the spring and fall cabaret series. The same lunch and dinner menu is served in the lower level of the Neue Galerie, at **Cafe Fledermaus** (Thursday through Sunday).

CAFE SELECT

212 Lafayette St (bet Broome and Spring St)   212/925-9322
Breakfast, Lunch, Dinner: Daily   cafeselectnyc.com
Moderate

Whether it is breakfast (served until 5 p.m. daily), lunch, or dinner, this casual dining spot offers wholesome food at reasonable prices. For breakfast, fresh croissants, eggs any way you want, fresh fruit, and bircher müesli are all tasty. At lunchtime, a nice assortment of soups and salads is available, as well as cheese tartlets and crepes. The croque monsieur sandwich (prosciutto cotto, gruyere, béchamel, pugliese) is filling and delicious. A turkey and avocado sandwich is available for $8. The menu changes seasonally, and diners will find such satisfying items as veal sausage, breaded chicken breast, and quiche.

CAMAJE

85 MacDougal St (bet Bleecker and Houston St)   212/673-8184
Daily: noon-midnight; Brunch: Sat, Sun   camaje.com
Inexpensive to moderate

In tiny Village quarters with a capacity of about two dozen, this cozy French bistro may evoke memories of some wonderful little place you discovered in Paris. Camaje is one of those New York restaurants relatively few know about, yet those who do, return often. Abigail Hitchcock knows how to cook a great meal. From the moment delicious, crusty bread arrives through the serving of excellent homemade desserts, everything is wholesome and tasty. There's onion soup gratinee, a half-dozen sandwiches, crostini, small plates, meat and fish entrees, and vegetable side dishes. You can create your own three-ingredient crepe. Try one of their crepe sucrées for dessert; my favorite is a chocolate ice-cream crepe with caramel sauce. Another plus is the large selection of quality teas. Cooking classes are offered several times a week. Reservations are recommended.

CAPITAL GRILLE
Time-Life Building
120 W 51st St (at Seventh Ave)   212/246-0154

Chrysler Center, Trylon Towers
155 E 42nd St (bet Lexington and Third Ave)   212/953-2000
Lunch: Mon-Fri; Dinner: Daily

120 Broadway (at Nassau St)   212/374-1811
Lunch: Mon-Fri; Dinner: Mon-Sat   thecapitalgrille.com
Moderately expensive

Hungry for lobster bisque? Start here! With all the top-drawer steakhouses in Manhattan, it's amazing they are all so busy. The Chrysler Center location is stunning, having been designed by Philip Johnson with glass and steel pyramids. The room exudes comfort and congeniality, and this is underscored by a welcoming, efficient, and informed wait staff. Some say this is a "Republican" establishment, but no one asks for political affiliation and I found them to be pleasant to everyone. The midtown location is handy and popular; the Broadway house in the financial district is equally appealing. The menu is full of the usual appetizers, soups, and salads (a good bet for lunch), and the dry-aged steaks, chops, and fresh, creative seafood dishes are fabulous. Desserts are good – I liked the flourless chocolate espresso cake. The bar is popular, which might have something to do with the award-winning wine list.

Soup's On
Not much compares to a bowl of steaming chowder, stew, or soup to stave off the chill of New York's notorious wicked, wet, and cold winters. Here are my recommendations:

Alfanoose (8 Maiden Lane, 212/528-4669): lentil soup

Aquagrill (210 Spring St, 212/274-0505): Manhattan clam chowder

Carnegie Deli (854 Seventh Ave, 212/757-2245): chicken noodle soup

Grand Central Oyster Bar Restaurant (Grand Central Terminal, 42nd St at Vanderbilt Ave, 212/490-6650): oyster stew

Kelley and Ping (127 Greene St, 212/228-1212): duck or chicken broth with noodles

La Bonne Soupe (48 W 55th St, 212/586-7650): French onion soup

Pearl Oyster Bar (18 Cornelia St, 212/691-8211): New England-style clam chowder

Union Square Cafe (21 E 16th St, 212/243-4020): black bean soup (seasonal)

Gastropubs

Head to one of these drinking establishments, which also serve really good pub grub:

The Beagle (162 Ave A, 212/228-6900): cocktail haven

The Breslin Bar & Dining Room (20 W 29th St, 212/679-1939): casual; British

DBGB Kitchen and Bar (299 Bowery, 212/933-5300): a Daniel Boulud operation; over a dozen sausage varieties

The Half Pint (76 W 3rd St, 212/260-1088): over 200 types of beers; build-your-own sandwiches

The Spotted Pig (314 W 11th St, 212/620-0393): NYC's first gastropub

CARMINE'S

2450 Broadway (bet 90th and 91st St)	212/362-2200
200 W 44th St (bet Seventh and Eighth Ave)	212/221-3800
Lunch, Dinner: Daily	carminesnyc.com
Moderate	

Want to treat the gang or the whole family? Call Carmine's for reservations and show up famished. You will find Southern Italian-style family dining with huge portions and zesty seasonings. The platters are delicious and filling. Arrive early if your party numbers less than six, as they will not reserve tables for smaller parties after 7 p.m. Menu choices run the gamut of pastas, chicken, veal, seafood, and tasty Italian appetizers (such as calamari). Wall signs explain the offerings. There is also a delivery menu.

CARNEGIE DELI

854 Seventh Ave (at 55th St)	212/757-2245, 800/334-5606
Breakfast, Lunch, Dinner: Daily (6:30 a.m-4 a.m.)	carnegiedeli.com
Moderate	

There's no city on earth with delis that compare to New York's, and Carnegie Deli is one of the best. With a location in the middle of a busy hotel district it is perfect for midnight snacks. Everything is made on-premises, with free delivery between 6:30 a.m. and 2 a.m. within a five-block radius. Making your food choice is difficult, but I dare say your favorite Jewish mother didn't make chicken soup better than Carnegie's homemade variety. Order it with matzo balls, golden noodles, rice, kreplach, or kasha. Beyond soup, there are great blintzes, and gargantuan sandwiches galore, including a very juicy burger with all the trimmings. You'll find lots of fish entrees, corned beef, pastrami, and rare roast beef. There is an unequaled choice of egg dishes, salads, and numerous side orders of everything from hot baked potatoes to potato pancakes. Desserts cover everything from A to Z – even Jell-O – and outrageous New York cheesecake is served plain or topped with strawberries, blueberries, or cherries.

CASA LEVER

390 Park Ave (at 53rd St)	212/888-2700
Breakfast, Lunch: Mon-Fri; Dinner: Mon-Sat; Brunch: Sat	casalever.com
Expensive	

Milanese-influenced cuisine, Warhol-adorned walls, and space-pod type dining booths describe this Lever Building restaurant – and at a high price. A-list types dine here on classic dishes like veal Milanese, carpaccio, veal shank gremolata, homemade pastas, and a limited raw bar, all prepared with premium ingredients. Italian cheeses are offered on the dessert menu, as are other regional sweets. A peach bellini or mimosa is the perfect accompaniment to the Saturday brunch selection of frittata and egg dishes.

CASA NONNA

310 W 38th St (bet Eighth and Ninth Ave)   212/736-3000
Lunch: Mon-Fri; Dinner: Daily   e2hospitality.com/casa-nonna-new-york
Moderate

Great Italian food comes from the kitchen at Casa Nonna which means "Grandmother's House" in Italian. Executive chef Julio Genao has crafted a menu which includes a long list of antipasti, pizzas baked in a wood-fired oven, paninis served with mixed greens or caponata, salads such as tuna and Tuscan tomato-bread, homemade pasta dishes, and authentic meat and fish entrees. This roomy, attractive Hell's Kitchen restaurant is near Penn Station and is good for a romantic dinner for two, pizza and beer after work, or a family dinner with the kids; take-out and delivery area also available. Casa Nonna is part of ESquared Hospitality which operates other highly-regarded restaurants.

CERCLE ROUGE

241 West Broadway (bet Walker and White St)   212/226-6174
Lunch: Mon-Fri; Dinner: Daily; Brunch: Sat, Sun   cerclerougeresto.com
Moderate

Cercle Rouge offers classic bistro dishes in a true French setting. The house-made paté, the foie gras pasta, duck magret, wild boar, and the cote-de-boeuf for two are among the specialties. Other features include a spacious outdoor terrace and private party facilities. Brunch reservations are a must.

'CESCA

164 W 75th St (at Amsterdam Ave)   212/787-6300
Dinner: Daily; Brunch: Sun   cescanyc.com
Moderate to moderately expensive

You'll love 'Cesca's atmosphere, situated in a former hotel lobby that is both intimate and elegant. The wait staff is highly skilled and accommodating, and the food is deliciously Italian from start to finish. Perennial favorites and seasonal choices like dry aged steaks, slow-roasted duck, braised beef short ribs, or ahi tuna carpaccio and grilled octopus salad, are uniformly well done and delivered from an open kitchen. You'll also find delicious pasta and seafood and lamb offerings. Superb Italian bread adds to the meal. Two private dining rooms accommodate special events.

CHEZ JACQUELINE

72 MacDougal St (bet Bleecker and Houston St)   212/505-0727
Dinner: Daily; Brunch: Sat, Sun   chezjacquelinerestaurant.com
Moderate

It's no wonder that Chez Jacqueline is a very popular neighborhood French

---

Fried Chicken

Crispy fried chicken is one of my all-time favorite foods any time of year – especially if it is dipped in buttermilk, fried golden brown, and served with potato salad and baked beans. These places will satisfy your poultry craving:

Blue Ribbon Sushi Bar & Grill (308 W 58th St, 212/397-0404)

Blue Smoke (116 E 27th St, 212/447-7733): at dinner only

Bobwhite Lunch and Supper Counter (94 Ave C, 212/228-2972)

Charles' Country Panfried Chicken (2841 Frederick Douglass Blvd, 212/281-1800)

Clinton St. Baking Co. & Restaurant (4 Clinton St, 646/602-6263): at dinner only

Georgia's Eastside BBQ (192 Orchard St, 212/253-6280)

Red Rooster Harlem (310 Lenox Ave, 212/792-9001)

The Redhead (349 E 13th St, 212/533-6212)

---

bistro. The atmosphere and service are appealingly relaxed. Whether you are hand-holding lovers or seasoned seniors, everyone has a good time on a special evening here. Popular appetizers are fish soup, escargots, and chicory goat-cheese salad. Roasted loin of lamb and braised pork shoulder are frequent entrees. My favorite is hearty beef stew in red wine, tomato, and carrot sauce. For dessert, try the caramelized apple tart anglaise.

CHIN CHIN

216 E 49th St (bet Second and Third Ave)   212/888-4555
Lunch, Dinner: Daily   chinchinny.com
Moderate to moderately expensive

Chin Chin is a Chinese restaurant with two rooms whose classy ambience and prices reflect a superior cooking style. The soups and barbecued spare ribs are terrific starters. Chin Chin house specialties include Grand Marnier prawns and orange beef. I'd concentrate on the seafood dishes, though you might also try the wonderful Peking duck dinner, with choice of soup, crispy duck skin with pancakes, fried rice, poached spinach, and homemade sorbet and ice cream. The menu is similar at lunch and dinner. A reasonable ($24.07) four-course *prix-fixe* lunch is available.

CIRCO NYC

120 W 55th St (bet Ave of the Americas and Seventh Ave)   212/265-3636
Lunch: Mon-Fri; Dinner: Daily   circonyc.com
Moderately expensive

Were it not for the fact that the owners are the sons of Sirio Maccioni (the legendary restaurateur of Le Cirque fame), this establishment might just be written off as another Italian restaurant. But here we have three brothers — Mario, Marco, and Mauro (and mother Egidiana) — operating a classy establishment with a friendly, circus-themed ambience, deliciously authentic Tuscan menu, and a touch of Le Cirque's magic. The tastiest items include housemade pizzas and pastas, including Mamma Egi's famous ravioli with ricotta, spinach, butter, and sage. Satisfying soups, excellent seafood and veal dishes, and outstanding desserts round out the menu. You'll enjoy an Italian favorite called *bomboloncini:* small vanilla-, chocolate- and marmalade-filled doughnuts. A three-course *prix-fixe* menu ($28 lunch, $48 dinner) as well as pre- and post-theater dinners ($38) make this a real Italian gem in midtown.

CITY BAKERY
3 W 18th St (at Fifth Ave)   212/366-1414
Breakfast, Lunch: Daily; Brunch: Sat, Sun   thecitybakery.com
Moderate

The moment you walk into bustling City Bakery, your taste buds will begin to tingle. It is really not a bakery but a buffet operation. Your eyes and stomach will savor the fresh-looking salad bar, tempting hot entrees, hearty sandwiches, yummy pastries, and much more. Treat yourself to their "so good" hot chocolate, made from melted candy bars, and a sweet and salty pretzel croissant. Or go for something healthier from the juice bar. I am impressed with the well-trained personnel, who keep displays well stocked, tables clean, and checkout counters running efficiently. For a casual, moderately priced meal in plain surroundings, this is a good deal.

CLINTON ST. BAKING CO. & RESTAURANT
4 Clinton St (at Houston St)   646/602-6263
Breakfast, Lunch, Dinner: Daily; Brunch: Sat, Sun   greatbiscuits.com
Moderate

Come here for New York's best pancakes and waffles! Their hot buttered cider is famous, too. Clinton Street may be a bit out of the way — it's on the Lower East Side — but the trip is worth it if you want wholesome food at very reasonable prices. At breakfast you will find homemade granola, French toast, great pancakes, biscuit sandwiches, omelets, and more. For lunch, home-made soups, salads, eggs, and sandwiches are featured. The evening menu includes eclectic twists to the American menu, as well as award-winning fried chicken. Homemade cakes and pastries are available all day. Extra thick shakes, sundaes, and sodas are a feature of their fountain. The atmosphere may be a bit dull, but the food certainly is not. A large takeout menu is available.

COLICCHIO & SONS
85 Tenth Ave (at 15th St)   212/400-6699
Lunch: Mon-Fri; Dinner: daily; Brunch: Sat, Sun (Tap Room);
Dinner: Daily (Dining Room)   colicchioandsons.com
Tap Room: Moderately expensive; Dining Room: Very expensive

Award-winning chef Tom Colicchio's restaurant, Colicchio & Sons, is a "wow" dining destination geared to creating memories. The Tap Room is more affordable, relatively speaking. Take a tip from the Tap Room menu categories and eat this (caramelized onion soup with bacon, raisins, and stinky cheese), maybe this (speck and black-cabbage pizza), then this (beef short rib hoagie, a namesake burger with drunk onions, or quail with braised peanuts). Complete your meal with the daily ice cream and sorbet selection (choose a sampler of one, three, or six flavors). Dinner in the more refined dining room offers meats, seafood, and fish from around the country. Choose from selections like Hudson Valley rabbit and Co-

---

Clarke's Standard

If you crave a juicy hamburger, think of **Clarke's Standard** (636 Lexington Ave, 212/838-6000 and 101 Maiden Lane, 212/797-1700; clarkes-standard.com) where beef is ground according to standards established at the city's classic butcher shops and hot dogs are custom blended. Other choices are limited to turkey and housemade veggie burgers, a couple of chicken sandwiches, and sides of fries, tater tots, and chili. The vibe is retro: sandwiches are served on a tray in paper and cardboard holders and fries are in handy paper cups. Little Clarke's ice cream cups are akin to the orange and vanilla summertime treats of childhood; flavors reflect present-day tastes for salted caramel, mint chip, and more. The midtown locale is small, busy, and frequently has a line out the door.

---

lumbia River sturgeon, all given the Colicchio touch. For a real treat, order dinner from the market or tasting menu. You can spend over $200 apiece if you go all out with wine pairings.

THE COMMODORE

366 Metropolitan Ave (at Havemeyer St), Brooklyn   718/218-7632
Dinner: Daily
Inexpensive to moderate

Yes, this is an ordinary bar outside of the Manhattan mainstay of this guide-book, but the Commodore serves some of the most unordinary bar food around. Leave the kids behind, put on your casual clothes, and order the fried chicken with biscuits. You'll devour every tasty morsel off the bone and add another dab of honey butter to the homemade biscuits. Also try the burgers and sandwich-es with "adult cheese" (spicy poblano), crispy fries, and drinks that really pack a punch.

COOKSHOP

156 Tenth Ave (at 20th St)   212/924-4440
Breakfast, Lunch: Mon-Fri; Dinner: Daily; Brunch: Sat, Sun   cookshopny.com
Moderate to moderately expensive

This place is always packed, and that's no surprise! The Cookshop is one of the most pleasant dining venues on the far West Side, with really great food (fea-turing mainly organic items from local farms), efficient service, and a fun atmo-sphere. Meats, fish, poultry, and seasonal game entrees are prepared on the grill, in the stone oven, or on the rotisserie. Oysters by the piece are also available. There is a nice selection of cheeses, and an interesting seasonal dessert menu.

CORNER SOCIAL

321 Lenox Ave (at 126th St)   212/510-8552
Lunch and dinner: Daily; Brunch: Sat, Sun   cornersocialnyc.com
Moderate to moderately expensive

A lot is happening at this comfy, rustic, corner gathering spot. For starters, it is open until 4 a.m. on weekends with plenty of food, drink, and a DJ pumping out the tunes. The bar-type food is sourced primarily from local vendors. What to eat? Try the cheeseburger spring rolls, rigatoni pasta with braised chicken ragu, or the meatloaf sandwich. Come around on the weekend for brunch and enjoy a complimentary drink with an entree such as buttermilk fried chicken and pancakes or cornflake encrusted French toast. An outdoor seating area is crowded in nice weather and provides a birdseye view of Lenox Avenue. Lastly, local artists' works are featured throughout the space capturing this historic neighborhood.

COWGIRL
519 Hudson St (at 10th St)   212/633-1133
Breakfast, Lunch, Dinner: Daily; Brunch: Sat, Sun

COWGIRL SEA-HORSE
259 Front St (at Dover St)   212/608-7873
Lunch, Dinner: Daily; Brunch: Sat, Sun   cowgirlnyc.com
Inexpensive to moderate

    Cowgirl is Manhattan's version of Texas chuckwagon cuisine. Colorful and busy, the menu is varied, with something for everyone: burgers, fajitas, enchiladas, chilis, chicken, steaks, sausages, catfish, and macaroni and cheese. Kids love the place! Portions are large and quite tasty, the wait staff enters into the fun, and the tab is accommodating, too. The smoked barbeque ribs are a specialty, bathed in a delicious sauce and served with really tasty barbeque beans and slaw. The number-one customer pick is the chopped salad – chicken, bacon, apple, avocado, cheese, nuts, tomatoes, and greens. Ask for the ice cream "baked potato" for dessert: vanilla ice cream shaped like a spud, with heaps of hot fudge, chopped pecans, and a pat of butter (which is really frosting). If that sounds like a bit much, you can opt for a slice of pecan or key lime pie or a Callebaut chocolate brownie (ice cream optional). Just as its name indicates, the South Street Seaport satellite, Cowgirl Sea-Horse, has a seafood focus.

Best Breads

Bread is not only the staff of life, but one of the top criteria when I rate a restaurant. Some of the city's best breads come from these shops:

Amy's Bread (75 Ninth Ave, 212/462-4338; 250 Bleecker St, 212/675-7802; and 672 Ninth Ave, 212/977-2670): baguettes, chocolate cherry rolls, semolina raisin fennel loaves

Dawat (210 E 58th St, 212/355-7555): naan

Moishe's Homemade Kosher Bakery (115 Second Ave, 212/505-8555): cornbread (Sunday and Tuesday afternoons)

Omai (158 Ninth Av, 212/633-0550): banana bread

Orwasher's Bakery (308 E 78th St, 212/288-6569): artisan wine and ale breads; pumpernickel

Silver Moon Bakery (2740 Broadway, 212/866-4717): sourdough *boule*

Zabar's (2245 Broadway, 212/787-2000): Eli's raisin pecan bread

P.S. By the way, in my opinion, good bread should always be served warm.

CRAFT

43 E 19th St (bet Broadway and Park Ave S)   212/780-0880
Dinner: Daily   craftrestaurant.com
Expensive

There are a number of reasons why Craft is utterly unique and worth visiting. The atmosphere is conducive to good eating, and the help is particularly friendly. Even the way you order is unique. Everything is a la carte. The menu is divided into sections: fish and shellfish, meats, pasta, vegetables, mushrooms, potatoes, and grains. You can put together any combination you find appealing, and the classic farm-to-table plates won't overwhelm your appetite. Chef/owner Tom Colicchio came from the Gramercy Tavern, and his expertise shows. The dessert selection includes wonderful cheeses, pastries, chocolate soufflé, fruits, ice creams, and sorbets (with many sauces available). If you're not terribly hungry or there are picky eaters in the group, head to Craft. **craftbar** (900 Broadway, 212/461-4300), its sister operation, is more casual, with a contemporary New American menu and composed dinner plates.

CUCINA & CO.

MetLife Building
200 Park Ave (45th St at Vanderbilt Ave), lobby   212/682-2700
Breakfast, Lunch, Dinner: Mon-Fri   patinagroup.com
Takeout: Mon-Fri (7 a.m.-9 p.m.)
Moderate

This treasure is hidden in the bowels of the huge MetLife Building. The Cucina & Co. takeout counter is one of the best in mid-Manhattan, displaying all sorts of prepared foods, sandwiches, salads, great cookies and cakes, breads, and whatever else you might want to take home or to the office. A bustling, crowded cafe that serves first-class food at reasonable prices for such a prime location adjoins. You will find delicious burgers (served on sesame brioche rolls), baked pastas, quiches, seafood, health-food dishes, and a good selection of dessert items. The service is fast and the personnel highly professional. (They have to be in order to serve so many people during rush hours!) I heartily recommend this place, especially for lunch. Two other Cucina & Co. locations (30 Rockefeller Center, 212/332-7630 and Macy's Cellar, 151 W 34th St, 212/868-2388) occupy similarly prime Manhattan locales and offer the same quality of food and service. Unlike the MetLife location, the other two are also open on weekends.

CUPPING ROOM CAFE

359 West Broadway (bet Broome and Grand St)   212/925-2898
Breakfast, Lunch: Mon-Fri; Dinner: Daily; Brunch: Sat, Sun
Moderate   cuppingroomcafe.com

The Cupping Room Cafe is one of the most popular places in Soho to meet and dine. In a noisy, convivial atmosphere, with a bar where you can drink and/ or eat, all the news of the area is exchanged. The diverse comfort-food offerings at lunch and dinner include pastas, seafood, chicken, steaks, and vegetarian dishes. But breakfast and brunch are where they really shine: freshly baked pastries, fruits and cheese, waffles, pancakes, wonderful French toast, and eggs and omelets. Eggs Benedict can be custom-made at their Benedict bar. For lighter dining, there are soups, sandwiches, burgers, and salads. Ask about daily dessert items; most are delicious, fresh, reasonably priced, and caloric. Live R&B, jazz, or world music is performed Wednesday through Saturday nights (no cover charge).

DA UMBERTO

107 W 17th St (bet Ave of the Americas and Seventh Ave)   212/989-0303
Lunch: Mon-Fri; Dinner: Mon-Sat   daumbertonyc.com
Moderate to moderately expensive

Da Umberto is a Tuscan trattoria appealing to the senses of serious Italian diners. A groaning table of inviting antipasto dishes greets guests. One could easily make an entire meal just from this selection. All of the platters look so fresh and healthy! Owner Vittorio Assante is around much of the time, ensuring that the service is as good as the food. Look into the glass-framed kitchen at the rear to see how the professionals work. You'll see well-prepared pastas, fish, veal, game (in season), and chicken. Your waiter will have many specials to detail. If you have room, chocolate truffle cake and tiramisu are the best of the dessert selections.

DANIEL

60 E 65th St (bet Madison and Park Ave)   212/288-0033
Dinner: Mon-Sat   danielnyc.com
Expensive

Want an "aha" moment? Every detail at Daniel is a work of art, especially the dishes placed in front of you. If you are ready to have an absolutely superb dining experience and money doesn't matter, then join the often long waiting list for a table in this appealing space, which is a treat for the eyes as well as the stomach. Daniel Boulud deserves to feel immensely proud of his strikingly contemporary four-star restaurant. The wait staff is highly professional and knowledgeable. Signature dishes change seasonally on the contemporary French menu. It might be a duo of roasted beef tenderloin and braised short ribs (the best I have ever tasted), suckling pig with leeks, swordfish, or tuna – each dish infused with a dose of comfort. Desserts are works of art, especially the chocolate creations. Don't miss the cheese selection! An a la carte menu is available in the bar and lounge. Every time I visit this restaurant I don't want the meal to end, and I can't think of a higher compliment.

Superb Recommendations

I firmly believe that a meal at one of the classy, elegant Manhattan restaurants can be an exceptional treat. When you consider the quality of the meal, the service received, and the atmosphere, I am convinced that you get more than your money's worth. I have a few strong recommendations for just such an experience. These houses are superb!

Arlington Club Steakhouse (1032 Lexington Ave, 212/249-5700): steakhouse

Barbetta (321 W 46th St, 212/246-9171): Italian

Bouley (163 Duane St, 212/964-2525): French

Le Périgord (405 E 52nd St, 212/755-6244): French

DAVID BURKE KITCHEN
The James Hotel
23 Grand St (bet Ave of the Americas and Thompson St)   212/201-9119
Breakfast: Daily; Lunch: Mon-Fri; Dinner: Daily; Brunch: Sat, Sun
Moderately expensive   davidburkekitchen.com

This David Burke winner serves delicious good ol' American fare, this time in the Soho neighborhood. Whimsy is one of chef Burke's strong points, and this place goes right along. How about "ants on a log?" – bone marrow with garlic and pickled mushrooms. You can sip and snack at the Treehouse Bar or eat in the attractive dining room, complete with a carving station right in the center. Order the duck meatball lasagna for a starter, then grilled branzino with quinoa, roasted carrot, almonds and cumin-citrus glaze. Check the daily specials for buttermilk fried chicken, which I hope will eventually appear on the daily menu.

DAVID BURKE TOWNHOUSE
133 E 61st St (bet Park and Lexington Ave)   212/813-2121
Lunch: Mon-Fri; Dinner: Daily; Brunch: Sat, Sun   davidburketownhouse.com
Moderately expensive

Let's start at the end! To me, this establishment from famed chef David Burke really shines with its desserts. Butterscotch panna cotta, warm "drunken" dough-nuts with three decadent sauces, and petit fours are all created by an excellent pastry chef. Of course, there are other attractions at this spot, which is popular with ladies. Pretty, posh, and meticulous describe this place. Their chicken and shrimp chef's salad is absolutely delicious. I also like the way bread is served at dinner: warm, in a small pan, like a muffin. The menu changes periodically.

DB BISTRO MODERNE
City Club Hotel
55 W 44th St (bet Fifth Ave and Ave of the Americas)   212/391-2400
Breakfast: Daily; Lunch: Mon-Fri; Dinner: Daily; Brunch: Sat, Sun
Moderate to moderately expensive   dbbistro.com/nyc

Renowned restaurant impressario Daniel Boulud's db Bistro Moderne is, for him, a more casual dining experience. Even burgers are served, and they are very good; at $32, they should be! Of course, this is no ordinary hamburger. It is ground sirloin filled with red wine-braised short ribs, foie gras, and black truffle, served on a parmesan bun and accompanied by delicious, light pommes soufflé in a silver cup. Diners have their choice of two rooms with a communal table that is com-fortable for singles. The menu offers several items in each category of fish, char-cuterie, and meats. For dessert, the cheese selection is a real winner, as are any of Daniel's specialties that use berries and other fresh fruit. The location makes db Bistro Moderne ideal for Broadway theatergoers.

DBGB KITCHEN & BAR
299 Bowery (bet 1st and Houston St)   212/933-5300
Lunch: Mon-Fri; Dinner: Daily; Brunch: Sat, Sun   dbgb.com/nyc
Moderate

Daniel Boulud has created a lively winner with DBGB Kitchen & Bar. This is a fun place and noisy, too. Designed with the influence of the Bowery neighbor-hood's restaurant-supply businesses in mind, bottles, gleaming copper pots, and dishes are stored on open shelving in the dining area. The kitchen is also open and part of the ambience. Overlooking the kitchen is the Kitchen Table, the private dining section. The French brasserie menu is varied: sausages, meats, salads, and burgers (order the ménage a trios, a platter of three burgers and trimmings — Yankee, Piggie, and Frenchie). Go whole hog and order the roasted pig feast for up to eight guests (72 hours notice required). Set your sights on a dessert of Baked Alaska for two and plan your meal accordingly.

DEL FRISCO'S DOUBLE EAGLE STEAK HOUSE

McGraw-Hill Building
1221 Ave of the Americas (at 49th St)   212/575-5129
Lunch: Mon-Fri; Dinner: Daily   delfriscos.com
Expensive

DEL FRISCO'S GRILLE

50 Rockefeller Plaza (51st St, bet Fifth Ave and Ave of the Americas) 212/767-0371
Lunch, Dinner: Daily   delfriscosgrille.com
Moderately expensive

   Del Frisco's offers a good meal with accommodating service in two different settings. At the McGraw-Hill location, where corporate types fill the room, both the ceiling and prices are high. Fresh, warm bread is brought to the table as you enjoy a seafood appetizer or great beefsteak tomato and sliced onion salad. Savory steaks, veal dishes, and lobster are all first-rate, with large accompanying side dishes. A $34 *prix-fixe* lunch is a good value here. The location at Rock Plaza has an upscale bar and grill with wood-burning oven and large patio. Here you'll find some of the same steaks and seafood, but the menu is less "fussy" and equally delicious. Beef stroganoff, macaroni and cheese, meatloaf, burgers, and sandwiches are all available. In-house desserts include warm banana bread pudding, crisp chocolate soufflé cake with raspberries, and strawberries Romanoff with vanilla ice cream. All are winners.

DEL POSTO

85 Tenth Ave (bet 15th and 16th St)   212/497-8090
Lunch: Mon-Fri; Dinner: Daily   delposto.com
Expensive

   Del Posto is big and bold! No question about it, this is an "occasion" restaurant. Mario Batali has shown what can be done with good taste. Afterward, diners may notice that their wallets have become a bit thinner, but they will long remember the experience of dining here. The room is warm and opulent, with adequate space between tables, a huge staff, informed service, and beautiful china. Some dishes are prepared tableside. Bread baskets are superb. Soothing piano music will calm those who arrive after a harried day. All of these touches speak to this class operation. What to order? Try veal agnolotti with parsnips and espresso or garganelli verdi al ragu Bolognese (butterscotch semifreddo). There is a five-course *prix-fixe* dinner for $115. Should you feel a bit self-indulgent, order the eight-course tasting menu ($165); the highlight is chef Mark Ladner's 100-layer lasagna. Leave room for the fine selection of complimentary after-dinner cookies. Private party spaces on the balcony level provide an enchanting view of the scene below.

Storm Casualties

In October 2012, Hurricane Sandy's storm surge flooded streets, tunnels, and subway lines in New York City, knocking the city to her knees for days. Businesses in Lower Manhattan and along the rivers were particularly hard hit. While the majority of restaurants have reopened, a few remain temporarily closed as of this writing, including **Bridge Cafe** (bridgecafenyc.com) and **Capsouto Frères** (capsoutofreres.com).

Happily, I have learned that two of my favorite houses, Brooklyn's **River Cafe** (rivercafe.com) and the **Water Club** (thewaterclub.com), are once again open for business.

DELICATESSEN

54 Prince St (at Lafayette St)   212/226-0211
Breakfast: Mon-Fri; Lunch, Dinner: Daily; Brunch: Sat, Sun   delicatessennyc.com
Moderate

Don't be confused by the name of this busy downtown restaurant. Chef Michael Ferraro's Delicatessen is a full-fledged restaurant which serves international comfort food for breakfast, lunch, and dinner. There's always a wide variety of seasonal specials alongside signature dishes like tuna tartare to cheeseburger spring rolls. Breakfast dishes, stuffed brioche French toast, burrata omelet with roasted tomatoes, and smoked salmon plate, are offered all day. For dessert, a refined take on comfort food classics such as s'mores in a jar and seasonal cobblers finish off a meal on a sweet note. On the plus side, the glass-ceilinged courtyard doubles as a lounge and private event room, and there is outside seating; on the down side, service could be better.

DELMONICO'S

56 Beaver St (at William St)   212/509-1144
Lunch: Mon-Fri; Dinner: Mon-Sat   delmonicosny.com
Moderately expensive

You've heard and read about Manhattan's Financial District, but if you really want a feel for the area and the people who make it tick, have a meal at Delmonico's. It is truly a New York institution dating from 1837. The atmosphere is old-time New York, but with a very appropriate renovated flair. As you might imagine, service is highly professional. The wine cellar is filled with a huge selection of the world's best vintages. Private dining is also offered. The Delmonico steak (a boneless ribeye that originated here) and other prime meat cuts are house specialties, with accompaniments like famous Delmonico potatoes (the recipe was created here many years ago). Delmonico steaks may be served elsewhere, but the authentic item is found only at the namesake restaurant. Don't be afraid to try chicken, duck, eggs Benedict, lobster Newberg, rack of lamb, or tuna here; all are made from tried and true recipes. The adjoining Grill Room offers more casual dining, including a less costly bar menu. By all means try Baked Alaska, the signature dessert; the cheese selection is superb. After over a century of presenting gourmet plates, Delmonico's is still on top! **Delmonico's Kitchen** (207 W 36th St, 212/695-5220) is a recent addition offering an updated twist on Delmonico's original menu.

DEMARCHELIER

50 E 86th St (at Madison Ave)   212/249-6300
Lunch, Dinner: Daily; Brunch: Sun   demarchelierrestaurant.com
Moderate

For years diners have come to this French bistro for two reasons: good food and no pretense. If you like solid French fare like artichokes and asparagus in season, crusty bread, paté de campagne, and salad niçoise, you will love Demarchelier. Drop in on Friday for delicious bouillabaisse. Steak dishes are also a specialty. Service is extremely efficient and prompt – ideal if you are in a lunch rush. Takeout dishes are available, too.

DÉVI

8 E 18th St (bet Broadway and Fifth Ave)   212/691-1300
Lunch: Mon-Fri; Dinner: Daily   devinyc.com
Moderate to moderately expensive

You can't do better than Dévi for Indian food. The setting is attractive – colorful, yet understated, and small enough to be inviting. The excellent food lives up to the setting. A full vegetarian selection is offered. Seafood, poultry, and meat dishes are featured. Lamb apricot sausage kabob is a tasty entrée. For those who really know Indian food, the side dishes are very special (like crispy okra salad, spiced spinach sauce with mushrooms, and wonderful Indian bread). A full menu of unusual desserts is presented: Indian ice cream, crispy saffron bread pudding, and much more. The staff is attentive, polite, and helpful.

DINOSAUR BAR-B-QUE

700 W 125th St (at 12th St)   212/694-1777
Lunch, Dinner: Daily   dinosaurbarbque.com
Moderate

Dinosaur ribs are not on the menu! Instead, it's dry-rubbed and slow pit-smoked pork, beef, and chicken entrees – plus the obligatory fried catfish – that sate hungry carnivores. Choose from freshly made beans, greens, salads, chili, deviled eggs, fried green tomatoes, and more as side dishes. Combination platters are a convenient solution to the ordering dilemma. Sandwiches include the aforementioned meats, or you can choose a ground beef, turkey, or portobello mushroom burger. There are good times to be had at this bustling ribs-and-more joint. Reservations are accepted. Order the party package to go if you're hosting that big game party.

DOCKS OYSTER BAR AND SEAFOOD GRILL

633 Third Ave (at 40th St)   212/986-8080
Lunch: Mon-Fri; Dinner: Daily; Brunch: Sat, Sun   docksoysterbar.com
Moderate

Fresh seafood is just waiting for you at Docks Oyster Bar and Seafood Grill. You'll find swordfish, lobster, tuna, Norwegian salmon, red snapper, and other seafood specials that change with the season. Crab cakes are outstanding. At dinner the raw bar offers oyster and clam selections. For a lighter meal, try steamers in beer broth or mussels in tomato and garlic. Delicious smoked sturgeon and whitefish are available, as are great beef entrees. Docks has a special New England clambake on Sunday and Monday nights. The atmosphere and waiters are congenial.

Isn't it Romantic!

These places are especially conducive for a romantic dinner:

Barbetta (321 W 46th St, 212/246-9171): Italian; incredible garden

Blaue Gans (139 Duane St, 212/571-8880): Austrian

Bouley (163 Duane St, 212/964-2525): French; opulent

Daniel (60 E 65th St, 212/288-0033): French

Eleven Madison Park (11 Madison Ave, 212/889-0905): French; stunning

Il Buco (47 Bond St, 212/533-1932): Mediterranean; antique-filled ambience

Le Bernardin (155 W 51st St, 212/489-1515): French; seafood

Le Périgord (405 E 52nd St, 212/755-6244): French

The Modern (Museum of Modern Art, 9 W 53rd St, 212/333-1220): French-American

One if by Land, Two if by Sea (17 Barrow St, 212/228-0822): American

Trattoria dell'Arte (900 Seventh Ave, 212/245-9800): Italian

DUANE PARK

308 Bowery (bet Houston and Bleecker St)　　　212/732-5555
Dinner: Tues-Sat　　　duaneparknyc.com
Moderately expensive

Simply entertaining! At Duane Park the added attraction to dinner is a burlesque show on Friday and Saturday evenings; singers, magicians, and musicians perform on other nights. Now located in the Bowery, the 70-seat restaurant is elegant, with white tablecloths, stately columns, and gleaming chandeliers. The seasonal menu features such items as roasted organic chicken, rack of lamb, pork tenderloin, and other beef and fish items — grilled, roasted, or sauteed. Various side dishes like charred leeks, macaroni and cheese, creole fries, and cheese grits further spice things up. Rhubarb crisp with ginger custard sauce is a tasty finisher.

THE DUTCH

131 Sullivan St (at Prince St)　　　212/677-6200
Lunch: Mon-Fri; Dinner: Daily; Brunch: Sat, Sun　　　thedutchnyc.com
Moderate to moderately expensive

At the corner of Prince and Sullivan is The Dutch, chef Andrew Carmellini's joint venture with Locanda Verde restaurateurs Josh Pickard and Luke Ostrom. This attractive corner location is welcoming and tastefully appointed. The menu is regional American; for lunch or dinner starters and late night, the Oyster Room offers Louisiana crawfish, American caviar, and tantalizing seafood platters. Salads or assorted vegetable appetizers are good alternatives. The lunch menu features sandwiches and fried chicken, and snacks and a short list of entrees satisfy the late night crowd. About a dozen dinner selections include dry-aged meats, fresh fish, and seasonal game dishes. The 40-ounce beef ribeye dinner for two is excellent. For dessert, I recommend the freshly made pies (cherry-buttermilk or caramel apple — a la mode, of course) or the devil's food cake with black pepper boiled icing. Linger over brunch with the Dutch's version of iced tea (a boozy concoction of gin, Pimm's, curacao, and iced tea) and select from savory egg dishes made with local organic eggs, housemade bologna sandwiches, muffins and scones, steak tartare, and aforementioned seafood.

ED'S CHOWDER HOUSE

Empire Hotel
44 W 63rd St (bet Broadway and Columbus Ave)   212/956-1288
Breakfast, Lunch, Dinner: Daily   chinagrillmgt.com
Moderate to moderately expensive

To show your out-of-town guests what Manhattan life is really like, then a stop at the Empire Hotel (near Lincoln Center) should be on the schedule. First, move to the rooftop bar for a pre-dinner drink. The place is literally jumping, noisy, crowded, and full of folks making all kinds of deals. Besides a complete array of drinks (including really unique cocktails), a bar menu of tasty items like crudités, crispy calamari, quesadillas and sliders are available. When your ears begin to ache, it's time to go downstairs to Ed's Chowder House for a peek at the New England atmosphere and a vast array of delicacies from the deep. Chowders? Four or five of them, from clam to crab. Raw bar? Atlantic oysters, littleneck clams, and lobster. Shellfish platters? Whatever you want, from $49 to $119. The main bill of fare presents a wide variety of seafood to choose from: tuna, skate, salmon, sea bass, scallops, cod, you name it. Non-seafood diners will find chicken paillard and filet mignon. For dessert, try apple cobbler a la mode.

EJ'S LUNCHEONETTE

1271 Third Ave (bet 73rd and 74th St)   212/472-0600
Breakfast, Lunch, Dinner: Daily   ejsluncheonette.com
Inexpensive to moderate

The line forms in all types of weather for breakfast, lunch, and dinner at this Upper East Side destination. You'll find great flapjacks, waffles, omelets, sandwiches, burgers, baked items, salads, and a good deal more including daily lunch and dinner blue plate specials. Shakes and malts are offered in a variety of flavors such as orange creamsicle and chocolate covered bacon. In addition to a huge menu, especially at breakfast, you'll enjoy the very reasonable prices. Free delivery, too!

EL PARADOR CAFE

325 E 34th St (bet First and Second Ave)   212/679-6812
Lunch, Dinner: Daily   elparadorcafe.com
Moderate

El Parador is the granddaddy of New York's Mexican restaurants, having been in business since 1959. Delicious Mexican food is served in a fun atmosphere at down-to-earth prices. Moreover, these are some of the nicest folks in the city. Warm tortilla chips arrive at your table while you study the list of specialties. There are quesadillas, Spanish sausages, ceviche, and black bean soup to start; delicious shrimp and chicken dishes follow. Create your own tacos and fajitas, or try stuffed jalapenos. El Parador has over 50 brands of premium tequila, and they concoct what many consider the best margaritas in New York.

From the Sea

Attention, mussel lovers! Set your sights on **Flex Mussels** (174 E 82nd St, 212/717-7772 and 154 W 13th St, 212/229-0222) for fresh Prince Edward Island mussels prepared the classic way with white wine, herbs, and garlic. There are other variations on the bivalves. Ingredients such as Indian curry, lobster, chorizo sausage, and Kalamata olives are added to create tasty, foreign-influenced dishes. Although the emphasis is on mussels, Flex also serves crab cakes, greens, fish and chips, lobster rolls, and chicken.

ELEVEN MADISON PARK

11 Madison Ave (at 24th St)   212/889-0905
Lunch: Thurs-Sat; Dinner: Daily   elevenmadisonpark.com
Expensive

Swiss chef Daniel Humm and general manager Will Guidara purchased Eleven Madison Park from restaurateur Danny Meyer in 2011. The most noticeable change is the menu: a tasting menu of 14 to 16 courses for lunch or dinner will set you back $195; wine pairing is an additional $145. Don't expect to rush through your meal, instead, plan about three hours for this dining experience. There will be plenty of time to appreciate the classy environs on the main floor or in the two private balcony suites.

ELIO'S

1621 Second Ave (at 84th St)   212/772-2242
Dinner: Daily
Moderate to moderately expensive

For years Elio's has been the classic clubby Upper East Side dining room for those who are recognizable, as well as those who aspire to be. In not so fancy surroundings, with waiters who greet regulars as if they are part of the family, tasty platters of beef carpaccio, clams, mussels, stuffed mushrooms, and minestrone are offered as starters. Lots of spaghetti and risotto dishes follow, along with seafood (their specialty), liver, scaloppine, and more of the usual Italian assortment. For dessert, try the delicious sorbets. Although half the fun is watching the not-so-subtle eye contact among diners, the food is excellent, and it is easy to see why Elio's remains a neighborhood favorite.

ELLEN'S STARDUST DINER

1650 Broadway (at 51st St)   212/956-5151
Breakfast, Lunch, Dinner: Daily   ellensstardustdiner.com
Inexpensive to moderate

With its singing wait staff, Ellen's fits right into the theater neighborhood. This 50s diner is a fun and noisy spot that serves satisfying food the traditional American way. The breakfast menu includes bagels and muffins, along with tasty buttermilk pancakes, French toast, and omelets. For the rest of the day, comfort foods are in order: salads and sandwiches, burgers, chicken pot pie, chili, meatloaf, Norman Rockwell's turkey dinner, and Gene Kelly's beef stew. Don't forget the egg creams, shakes, malts, and a nice selection of caloric desserts, and be sure to ask that your shake be made "thick!" Delivery is available.

EMBER ROOM

647 Ninth Ave (bet 45th and 46th St)   212/245-8880
Dinner: Daily; Brunch: Sat, Sun   emberroom.com
Moderately expensive

Todd English's Asian fusion barbecue restaurant is a Hell's Kitchen hot spot that will satisfy the taste and olfactory senses. Feast on progressive Thai comfort food including dim sum appetizers, sandwiches, and smoky and saucy entrees like green curry lasagna or chocolate baby back ribs. The setting is eye-appealing as well. Four thousand soothing Thai temple bells cover the ceiling of this space. Peek into the open kitchen with its six-foot wood-burning oven.

FAIRWAY CAFE & STEAKHOUSE

Fairway Market
2127 Broadway (at 74th St), upstairs   212/994-9555
Breakfast and Lunch: Daily (as Fairway Cafe); Dinner: Daily (after 5:30 p.m., as
    Fairway Steakhouse)   fairwaymarket.com
Moderate

Fairway is known to most folks as a busy market. Take the stairway by the entrance, however, and you'll find a rather bare-bones room that serves unbelievably good food – much of it of the comfort variety – at comfortable prices. Breakfasts include eggs, pancakes, omelets, smoked salmon, and the like. The luncheon soups, salads, and sandwiches are extremely good values for the quality offered. Evening brings a modestly priced steakhouse, with complete steak dinners – choice cuts, plus salad, soup, and vegetables – for under $45. The seasonal menu brings chops, rack of lamb, short ribs, fish, chef Mitchel's famous roasted chicken, and even pasta, burgers, and pizza. All desserts are only $7. Yes, those fantastic cupcakes, too.

FELIDIA

243 E 58th St (bet Second and Third Ave)   212/758-1479
Lunch: Mon-Fri; Dinner: Daily   felidia-nyc.com
Expensive

Chef/owner Lidia Bastianich has made her mark in New York's Italian food circles. She's a well-respected restaurateur, cookbook author, TV chef, purveyor of her own line of sauces and tabletop items, and wine producer. Since 1981 Lidia has greeted diners at Felidia, her warm and cozy Upper East Side townhouse. Choices are either a la carte or from the chef's tasting menus, including a vegetar-

---

Gotham's Famous Egg Cream

A New York invention, the egg cream is generally credited to Louis Auster, a Jewish immigrant who owned a candy store at Stanton and Cannon streets in the early 20th century. Mostly to amuse himself, he started mixing carbonated water, sugar, and cocoa until he concocted a drink he liked. It was such a hit that Schraft's reportedly offered him $20,000 for the recipe. Auster wouldn't sell and secretly continued making his own syrup in the back room of his store. When he died, his recipe went with him. Some years later, Herman Fox created another chocolate syrup, which he called Fox's U-Bet. To this day Fox's brand is regarded as the definitive egg cream syrup.

Good Eating at JFK

There is something to satisfy every palate and wallet at Kennedy Airport. There are plenty of places for a quick bite on the run, as well as full-service restaurants where you can enjoy a nice meal. Some of Manhattan's better restaurants have set up satellite kitchens at JFK.

Au Bon Pain: Terminals 4, 8

Balducci's: Terminals 2, 3, 7

The Palm Bar & Grille: Terminal 4

Todd English's Bonfire Bar and Bonfire Steakhouse:
   Terminals 2, 7

ian option. Offerings include at least a half dozen fresh pastas with a tantalizing combination of seasonal ingredients, as well as entrees of bass, veal tenderloin, calves liver, tripe, and other delectables from land and sea. The roasted pears and grapes are remarkable and refreshing.

FIG & OLIVE

808 Lexington Ave (bet 62nd and 63rd St)	212/207-4555
10 E 52nd St (bet Fifth and Madison Ave)	212/319-2002
420 W 13th St (bet Ninth Ave and Washington St)	212/924-1200
Lunch: Mon-Fri; Dinner: Daily; Brunch: Sat, Sun	figandolive.com
Moderately expensive	

Fig & Olive is about passion for the best olive oils, flavors, and cuisine from the Riviera and coastal regions of the south of France, Italy, and Spain. This Mediterranean cuisine is enhanced with delicate or robust flavors which are derived from a variety of extra virgin olive oils which are selected to be the perfect match with each dish. For example: the appetizer truffle mushroom croquette is served with truffle olive oil aioli and a salad of figs, apples, cheeses, and walnuts is tossed with a fig balsamic and aromatic arbequina olive oil dressing. Similarly, rosemary garlic olive oil and fresh herbs are a delicious addition to the grilled lamb chops. For dessert, crème brûlée cheesecake and chocolate *pot de crème* are outstanding choices. The large variety of extra virgin olive oils are offered for tasting at the beginning of each meal and sold in a retail display at each location.

FIVE POINTS

31 Great Jones St (bet Lafayette St and Bowery)	212/253-5700
Lunch: Mon-Fri; Dinner: Daily; Brunch: Sat, Sun	fivepointsrestaurant.com
Moderate	

In a charming, busy, and inviting space, Five Points serves some of the best food in New York at prices that won't make you squirm! For years this has deservedly been one of the most popular rooms in downtown Manhattan. The changing menu offers a wonderful choice of appetizers: oysters, marinated olives, spicy fried squid, beet salad, and many more. For the main course, a number of pastas are featured, along with seafood dishes (octopus and shrimp). If you're lucky enough to visit on "Lobster Monday" you can feast on a whole lobster dinner with all the trimmings for $24. Order the decadent blackout cake, if offered.

Sunday brunch features homemade biscuits, egg dishes from the wood oven, plus melt-in-your-mouth pancakes. Five Points has one of the most diverse brunch menus in the city. No wonder they are always packed!

FOUR SEASONS

99 E 52nd St (bet Park and Lexington Ave)   212/754-9494
Lunch: Mon-Fri; Dinner: Mon-Sat   fourseasonsrestaurant.com
Expensive

The elegant Four Seasons is awe-inspiring in its simplicity and charm. Two separate dining areas — the Grill Room and the Pool Room — have different menus and appeal. *Prix-fixe* and a la carte menus are available in both rooms. The dark suits (translation: business and media heavy hitters) congregate at noon in the Grill Room, where the waiters know them by name and menu preferences like great salads, a wonderful duck entree, steak tartare, and burgers. The Pool Room is more romantic and feminine; tables surround a bubbling marble pool. Society mavens and couples who want to dine with the stars are made to feel at home with superb service. The dessert menu can only be described as obscene; individual soufflés are a splendid treat. Patrons are invited for a peek into the magical kitchen; request a tour. Enjoy live music on Wednesday evenings.

FRED'S AT BARNEYS NEW YORK

660 Madison Ave (at 60th St), 9th floor   212/833-2200
Lunch, Dinner: Daily; Brunch: Sat, Sun   barneys.com
Moderate to moderately expensive

It would be a tossup as to which is better at Fred's — the food or the people watching – where the "beautiful" people definitely like to see and be seen. You'll find the dishes ample and delicious (and they should be, at the prices charged). Selections include beef, chicken, and lamb entrees, seafood dishes, pastas, salads, pizzas, and sandwiches. Tasty French fries are served Belgian-style. There's no shortage of selections or calories on the dessert menu. I just wonder if all those skinny model-types really finish their meals!

FREEMANS

Freeman Alley (at Rivington St)   212/420-0012
Lunch: Mon-Fri; Dinner: Daily; Brunch: Sat, Sun   freemansrestaurant.com
Moderate

You don't want to miss Freemans – even though it is almost impossible to locate. It used to be a halfway house. Freemans is crowded, noisy, and unpretentious. It has a nice kitchen, extra-friendly service personnel, clean restrooms, and a great

---

Druze Cuisine

Gazala Place (380 Columbus Ave, 212/873-8880 and 709 Ninth Ave, 212/245-0709) is the only place in Manhattan to enjoy Druze cuisine. The Druze are a mixed-race religious community originating in Israel, Jordan, Lebanon, and Syria. Hospitality is a hallmark here. The tasty fare is Middle Eastern, influenced by those regions with an emphasis on hummus, falafel, wraps, and kabobs.

No Ordinary Pizza

Are you feeling adventuresome when it comes to pizza? Forgo pepperoni and try one of these toppings on your Italian pie:

Artichoke Basille's Pizza & Brewery (114 Tenth Ave, 212/792-9200): burnt anchovies (intentional)

Balaboosta (214 Mulberry St, 212/966-7366): fresh carrot puree

The Mark Restaurant by Jean-Georges (The Mark, 25 E 77th St, 212/744-4300): black truffles

Pulino's (282 Bowery, 212/226-1966): beef meatballs and pickled chiles

bar and bartender. Try Freemans signature cocktail, made with pomegranate molasses. But most of all, it has really delicious food. You must start with "Devils on Horseback": Stilton-stuffed prunes wrapped in bacon and served piping hot. Then there is a delicious hot artichoke dip with crisp bread; all the breads are excellent. If on the menu, the roasted pork loin and seared filet mignon are outstanding. Hunter's stew (elk, venison, and wild boar meat) with potato dumplings is unusual and filling. Desserts are just okay, but a visit here is so unique you can overlook your sweet tooth! Reservations can only be made for parties of six or more.

FRESCO BY SCOTTO

34 E 52nd St (bet Madison and Park Ave)　　　　　　　212/935-3434
Lunch: Mon-Fri; Dinner: Mon-Sat　　　　　　　　　　frescobyscotto.com
Moderate to moderately expensive

For the past several decades, Fresco by Scotto has become a midtown Manhattan tradition for lunch and dinner. Owned and operated by the hospitable Scotto family, the restaurant is often referred to as the "NBC Commissary." Potato and zucchini chips with gorgonzola cheese, chicken meat balls, and pappardelle with duck and wild mushroom ragu are menu items worth noting. Fresco offers countless meat and fish dishes, scrumptious pastas, and homemade bomboloni for dessert. Executive chef Beau Houck, former chef de cuisine at Five Points and Sign of the Dove, and graduate of the Culinary Institute of America, is ingredient-driven and inspired by the changing seasons. **Fresco on the Go** (40 E 52nd St, 212/754-2700; Mon-Fri: 6 a.m.-8 p.m.) offers homemade muffins and pancakes, sticky buns, and eggs-to-order for breakfast. At noon, delicious sandwiches, pizzas, soups, salads, and homemade pastas are available.

GABRIEL'S BAR & RESTAURANT

11 W 60th St (bet Broadway and Columbus Ave)　　　　212/956-4600
Lunch, Dinner: Mon-Sat　　　　　　　　　　　　gabrielsbarandrest.com
Moderate

For dining in the Lincoln Center area, Gabriel's is a winner. You are greeted by Gabriel Aiello, an extremely friendly host. And what good food and drink! Delicious bread. Fresh peach or blueberry bellinis. A fine assortment of Italian appetizers. Then it's on to first-class pastas (like tagliatelle with peppers), chicken, steaks, wood-grilled seafood dishes, and a daily risotto special. The in-house gelati creations are among New York's best, as is the flourless chocolate torte. Gabriel doesn't have to blow his own horn; his satisfied customers are happy to do it for him! Party facilities are available.

GIORGIONE

307 Spring St (bet Greenwich and Hudson St)   212/352-2269
Lunch: Mon-Fri; Dinner: Daily   giorgionenyc.com
Moderate

When the name Deluca (as in Dean & Deluca) is involved, you know it is a quality operation. Giorgio Deluca is one of the partners in this attractive, high-tech establishment, which features shiny metal-top tables and an inviting pizza oven that turns out remarkable pies. This is a very personal restaurant, with Italian dishes like you'd find in mother's kitchen in the Old Country: carpaccio, prosciutto, ravioli, risotto, and linguine. The minestrone is as good as I have ever tasted. Pizzas come in eight presentations. A raw bar is also available. Finish with a platter of tasty Italian cheeses or pick from the appealing desserts.

GOBO

401 Ave of the Americas (at 8th St)   212/255-3902, 212/255-3242 (delivery)
Lunch, Dinner: Daily
1426 Third Ave (at 81st St)   212/288-5099, 212/288-5099 (delivery)
Lunch, Dinner: Daily; Brunch: Sun   goborestaurant.com
Moderate

Gobo's claim to fame is "food for the five senses." Vegans and vegetarians give high marks to the variety of appetizing meals. Bean curd, tofu, seaweed, protein nuggets, and seitan are interestingly prepared with other organic ingredients to create Asian-style entrees, salads, and sides. Also popular are organic fruit and veggie smoothies, organic teas, and vegan chocolate cake.

GOLDEN UNICORN

18 East Broadway (at Catherine St)   212/941-0911
Lunch, Dinner, Dim Sum: Daily; Dim Sum Breakfast: Sat, Sun
Inexpensive to moderate   goldenunicornrestaurant.com

Golden Unicorn prepares the best dim sum outside of Peking! This bustling, two-floor, Hong Kong-style Chinese restaurant serves delicious dim sum every day of the week (until 4 p.m.; 5 p.m. on the weekend). Besides delicacies from the rolling carts, diners may choose from a wide variety of Cantonese dishes off the regular menu. Pan-fried noodle dishes, rice noodles, and noodles in soup are house specialties. Despite the size of the establishment (they can accommodate over 500 diners), you will be amazed at the fast service, cleanliness, and prices. This is one of the best values in Chinatown.

GOOD

89 Greenwich Ave (bet Bank and 12th St)   212/691-8080
Lunch: Tues-Fri; Dinner: Daily; Brunch: Sat, Sun   goodrestaurantnyc.com
Moderate

This popular destination for locals is a casual, take-your-time establishment. The solid, contemporary American fare is served by friendly personnel. The brunch menu highlight is the "Good Breakfast": a heaping plate of eggs with a choice of pancakes, home fries, and bacon or sausage. Burgers and green-chile macaroni and

Brooklyn's Best Restaurants

Brooklyn has successfully made a mark on the dining scene with a large number of great dining options. Restaurants in all categories have received top ratings by critics and are now drawing customers from the city. Previously only a handful of choices were worth the trip across the East River; now, times have changed, and patrons have even more possibilities to the age old question: "Where shall we go for dinner?"

Bar Corvo (Prospect Heights): Italian
Buttermilk Channel (Carrol Gardens): American
Colonie (Brooklyn Heights): American
Di Fara (Midwood): Pizza
Five Leaves (Greenpoint): American
The Grocery Restaurant (Carrol Gardens): American
Gwynnett Street (Williamsburg): Modern American
Locanda Vini e Olii (Clinton Hill): Italian
Mimi's Hummus (Ditmas Park): Mideastern
Momo Sushi Shack (Bushwick): Sushi
Pete Zaaz (Crown Heights): Pizza
Peter Luger Steak House (Williamsburg): Steak
Saraghina (Bedford-Stuyvesant): Pizza
Saul (Boerum Hill): American
Tanoreen (Bay Ridge): Mediterranean/Mideastern

cheese are tasty, and overnight roasted pork is a good bet for dinner.

GOOD ENOUGH TO EAT

520 Columbus Ave (at 85th St)   212/496-0163
Breakfast: Daily; Lunch: Mon-Fri; Dinner: Daily; Brunch: Sat, Sun
Inexpensive to moderate   goodenoughtoeat.com

New York is a weekend breakfast and brunch town, and you cannot do better than Good Enough to Eat in both categories. Savor the apple pancakes, four-grain pancakes with walnuts and fresh bananas, and chocolate chip and coconut pancakes. Additional offerings: French toast, waffles, a dozen kinds of omelets, scrambled-egg dishes, corned beef hash, real Irish oatmeal, fresh-squeezed orange juice, and homemade sausage. Lunches feature inexpensive and delicious salads, burgers (juicy and delicious), pizzas, and sandwiches. More of the same is served for dinner, plus meatloaf, turkey, pork chops, fish, and roast chicken plates. A children's menu is available for lunch and dinner. This is comfort food at its finest, all the way through wonderful homemade pies, cakes, and ice creams.

GOTHAM BAR & GRILL

12 E 12th St (bet Fifth Ave and University Pl)   212/620-4020
Lunch: Mon-Fri; Dinner: Daily   gothambarandgrill.com
Moderately expensive

The Gotham is a must! Since 1984 it has been recognized as one of New York's best. Dining here can be summed up in one word: exciting! It is not inexpensive, but every meal I have had has been worth the tab – and there is a really good *prix-fixe* lunch deal. You may also eat at the bar. Alfred Portale is one of the most talented chefs in the city and his menu is devoted to seasonality. The modern, high-ceilinged space is broken by direct spot lighting on the tables. Fresh plants and floral arrangements lend a bit of color. For starters try the seafood salad or striped bass ceviche, excellent free-range chicken, and superior dry aged New York steak. Each entree is well seasoned and attractively presented. Rack of lamb is one of the tastiest in town. For dessert try the s'mores sundae or the excellent artisanal cheese selection.

GRAMERCY TAVERN

42 E 20th St (bet Park Ave S and Broadway)   212/477-0777
Lunch, Dinner: Daily (Tavern)   gramercytavern.com
Lunch: Mon-Fri; Dinner: Daily (Dining Room)
Moderate (Tavern)
Expensive (Dining Room)

   Gramercy Tavern continues as a comfort touchstone. Every detail has been honed to perfection, and the public has responded. This is a very busy place, both in the rustic tavern (where meals are prepared on a wood-burning grill) and the fine dining area in the back. The space is unusually attractive, the servers are highly trained, and the food is excellent. The ceiling is a work of art, the private party room is magnificent, and there is not a bad seat in the house. Chef Michael Anthony's seasonal American cuisine can be sampled with both regular and vegetarian tasting menus. You'll enjoy a superior offering of cheeses, sorbets, and ice creams for dessert. This New York institution is a great place for a party!

GRAND CENTRAL OYSTER BAR RESTAURANT

Grand Central Terminal (42nd St at Vanderbilt Ave), lower level   212/490-6650
Lunch, Dinner: Mon-Sat   oysterbarny.com
Moderate

   Native New Yorkers are familiar with the nearly century-old institution that is the Oyster Bar at Grand Central. This midtown destination is popular with commuters and residents alike. They serve over 2,000 folks a day! The young help are

---

Modern Japanese

If you have a yen for modern Japanese cuisine, **Haru Sushi**, has plenty to offer. Of course you'll find sushi and sashimi on the menu plus appetizers, lunch boxes, entrees, sushi rolls, hand rolls, and special rolls. Attractive locations are conveniently located around town and they also provide pickup and delivery services. Please note that the Saké Bar serves the same menu and is the only locale with a full bar.

- 205 W 43rd St, 212/398-9810: Lunch, Dinner: Daily
- 433 Amsterdam Ave, 212/579-5655: Lunch: Sat, Sun; Dinner: Daily
- 220 Park Ave S, 646/428-0989: Lunch: Mon-Fri; Dinner: Daily
- 1 Wall Street Court, 212/785-6850: Lunch: Mon-Fri; Dinner: Daily
- 1329 Third Ave, 212/452-2230: Dinner: Daily
- Saké Bar: 1327 Third Ave, 212/452-1028: Lunch, Dinner: Daily (full bar)

Healthy Choices

If you've ever doubted the delectability of "health foods," then check out the highly popular **Just Salad** (320 Park Ave, 30 Rockefeller Plaza (level 6), 600 Third Ave, 134 W 37th St, 100 Maiden Lane, and other locations; 212/244-1111,justsalad.com). A dozen salads and wraps are made to order as you watch. All are fresh and well priced. You'll also find a selection of tasty soups. Delivery is available.

accommodating, and the drain on the pocketbook is minimal. The menu boasts more than 72 seafood items (with special daily entrees), about 30 varieties of oysters, a superb oyster stew, clam chowder (Manhattan and New England styles), oyster pan roast, bouillabaisse, coquille St. Jacques, Maryland crab cakes, Maine lobsters, 75 wines by the glass, and marvelous homemade desserts.

GRIFONE

244 E 46th St (bet Second and Third Ave) 212/490-7275
Lunch: Mon-Fri; Dinner: Mon-Sat grifonenyc.com
Moderately expensive

New Yorkers get so hyped up about trendy new places that they tend to forget about old-timers that quietly continue doing a good job. Grifone is one of those. If you are looking for an attractive, comfortable, and cozy place to dine — one with impeccable service and great food — then try Grifone. The long menu is Northern Italian, and the many daily specials include a good selection of pasta, chicken, veal, fish, and beef dishes. A takeout menu is available as well. Quality never goes out of style. Just ask the neighborhood regulars who flock here year after year.

GYU-KAKU

805 Third Ave (bet 49th and 50th St), 2nd floor 212/702-8816
321 W 44th St (bet Eighth and Ninth Ave) 646/692-9115
34 Cooper Square (bet 5th and 6th St) 212/475-2989
Lunch: Mon-Fri; Dinner: Daily; Brunch: Sat, Sun gyu-kaku.com
Moderate to moderately expensive

These Japanese barbecue restaurants are best described as a fun experience with very tasty food. After a gracious greeting, you are seated at tables with a burner in the center. Then you choose from a lengthy menu (which varies slightly by location) of appetizers, salads, soups, beef tongue, kalbi (short ribs), harami (outside skirt), yaki shabu (belly), ribeye, filet mignon, intestines, vegetables, rice, noodles, and more. Accommodating servers will give instructions on how to cook the various items. The Kobe beef slices are marvelous, as are the lamb and seafood dishes. Tender pieces of lobster tail are a treat. Japanese restaurants are generally not great for desserts, but it's worth getting your hands and face gooey with the s'mores dish at Gyu-Kaku.

HANJAN

36 W 26th St (bet Broadway and Avenue of the Americas) 212/206-7226
Dinner: Mon-Sat hanjan26.com
Moderate to moderately expensive

Hanjan is a Korean gastropub. That being said, expect to order several small items from the traditional, modern, and skewer categories for your meal. Popular selections include scallion pancakes (with or without squid), braised pig trotters, pork belly skewers, and fried chicken skin, gizzards, and hearts. Ramen (nowhere near the college-student staple) is served after 10 p.m. The drink choices are nearly global: saké and soju, Asian beers, cocktails with Korean flavors, wines from around the world, and champagne. The atmosphere is relaxed and a long, communal table in the center of the room, which divides the bar from individual tables, encourages guests to intermingle.

HATSUHANA

17 E 48th St (bet Fifth and Madison Ave)	212/355-3345
237 Park Ave (at 46th St)	212/661-3400
Lunch, Dinner: Mon-Fri (Dinner on Sat at the 48th St location)	hatsuhana.com

Moderate

Hatsuhana has a longstanding reputation as one of the best sushi houses in Manhattan. One can sit at a table or the sushi bar and get equal attention from the informed help. There are several dozen appetizers, including broiled eel in cucumber wrap. Next try salmon or chicken teriyaki or any number of sushi dishes. Forget about desserts and concentrate on the exotic appetizer and main-dish offerings.

HILL COUNTRY

30 W 26th St (bet Broadway and Ave of the Americas)	212/255-4544
Lunch, Dinner: Daily	hillcountryny.com

Moderate

Hill Country is an unusual spot, modeled after the old-fashioned meat markets of Central Texas. Its ambience and aroma will bring joy to barbecue fans. Informal dining is available at tables scattered around the premises. Separate stations offer meat dishes (like brisket, pork spare ribs, whole chicken, and Texas sausage), beans, macaroni and cheese, corn pudding, and salads. PB&J cupcakes, banana cream pudding, and seasonal crisps are popular desserts. Live music is featured Wednesday through Saturday. Delivery service is offered, and party platters are arranged for office parties. New York is not a great barbecue town, but this place does its best to bring Texas flavors to the Big Apple.

Lambs Club

Named for a long-gone social organization, **The Lambs Club** (The Chatwal Hotel, 132 W 44th St, 212/997-5262) beckons diners seeking an experience found a half-century ago. Leather banquettes, a luxe bar and grill in an art-deco setting, fireplace, impeccable linens, attentive service, no-nonsense food, and superior cocktails (with hand-cut ice) are the standard. To accommodate hotel guests, breakfast, lunch, dinner, and weekend brunch are served. Pre- and post-theater goers will enjoy the *prix-fixe* offerings by chef Geoffrey Zakarian. Lamb is frequently on the dinner menu. The bar serves a late menu of snacks, beef tartare, and small offerings.

Thai Eatery

Thai cuisine is hot in more ways than one, and several notable new eateries have opened to satisfy diners' desire for this spicy Asian food. Among them is **Kin Shop** (469 Ave of the Americas, 212/675-4295), which offers contemporary Thai cuisine. Plenty of interesting salads, soups, veggies, noodles, curries, and other items are on the menu. Northern Thai noodles with braised goat is a popular selection. A Thai-influenced cocktail is a delicious and relaxing way to while away the wait. Reservations are accepted for lunch and dinner.

HILL COUNTRY CHICKEN

1123 Broadway (at 25th St)   212/257-6446
Lunch, Dinner: Daily; Breakfast: Sat, Sun   hillcountrychicken.com
Inexpensive to moderate

It is easy to see why Hill Country Chicken is so busy with both sit-down customers and takeout orders. The all-natural, hormone-free chicken is moist, flavorful, and very fresh. Pick out your favorites: breasts, thighs, legs, or wings; all priced by the piece. As a crispy fried chicken fan, I was in seventh heaven. Also available are Texas tenders, sandwiches, salads, fries, cheesy fried mashed potatoes, cole slaw, pies, and homemade ice cream. I found the biscuits disappointing, but the pies excellent.

HUNDRED ACRES

38 MacDougal St (Prince and Houston St)   212/475-7500
Lunch: Mon-Fri; Dinner: Daily; Brunch: Sat, Sun   hundredacresnyc.com
Moderately expensive

The weekend brunch crowd likes to linger at this convivial Soho eating place, especially on a warm day when the expansive front French doors are opened wide. It doesn't hurt, either, that brunch cocktails and bloody marys are available both by the glass and by the pitcher. The ever-changing menu focuses on local and all-natural foods; there are sweets, savories, egg dishes, sandwiches, and other kitchen inspirations for brunch. Similarly, the dinner menu is market driven, changes frequently, and encompasses small nibbles, sharable plates, and heartier choices. For lunch, the three-course market menu offers three appetizer and entree choices, plus dessert; a good deal at $24. Hundred Acres has a notable selection of American whiskeys and house cocktails; make it a party and order a pitcher of one of these house favorites: jezebel or sparkling acres.

HURRICANE STEAK & SUSHI

360 Park Ave S (at 26th St)   212/951-7111
Dinner: Daily   hurricanenyc.com
Moderately expensive to expensive

The New York Times gave this expansive restaurant just one star, but I strongly disagree with that evaluation. I found the house very attractive physically, the wait staff unfailingly polite and helpful, and the platters filling and delicious. For those who loved Trader Vic's, this spot will bring back great memories. (I was a Trader Vic's fan.) Michael Stillman, who comes from a noted New York restaurant family, is the proprietor. He has created an atmosphere that is as much a nightclub as an eating house. With accommodations for over 300, the noise level is high, but the service is quick and efficient. What to have? Pupu platters with Peking duck sandwiches, dumplings, spring rolls, salads to share, wings, sushi, and steaks. The menu goes on and on. You can splurge on filet mignon, chicken, mahi-mahi, or several signature sushi rolls. Dieting diners will enjoy the fresh-fruit dessert while the rest of us dig into devil's food cake and Thai coffee ice cream. Drinks are big, pricey, and tasty.

IL BAGATTO

192 E 2nd St (bet Ave A and B)   212/228-0977, 212/228-3703 (delivery)
Dinner: Tues-Sun (closed Aug)   ilbagattonyc.com
Inexpensive to moderate

Il Bagatto is one of Manhattan's best bargains, and the place to come if you're feeling adventurous. Housed in tiny digs in an area you would hardly call compelling, this is an extremely popular Italian trattoria. The owners have discovered the rules of success: be on the job and ensure that every dish tastes just like it came out of mama's kitchen. About a dozen tables upstairs and in the lounge are always filled, so it's best to call ahead for reservations. There's delicious spaghetti, homemade gnocchi with spinach, tortellini with meat sauce (made from a secret recipe), and wonderful tagliolini with seafood in a light tomato sauce. Other menu offerings include chicken, carpaccio, salads, and a few daily specials. They deliver, too. The adjacent wine bar, **Il Posto Accanto** (Lunch, Dinner: Tues-Sat; Brunch: Sat, Sun), serves both food and drink.

IL BUCO ALIMENTARI E VINERIA

53 Great Jones St (bet Bowery and Lafayette St)   212/837-2622
Breakfast, Lunch, Dinner: Daily   ilbucovineria.com
Moderately expensive

One of the most fun places I have visited in a long time has a long name to remember: Il Buco Alimentari e Vineria, located on busy Great Jones Street in downtown Manhattan. This is a market restaurant, with a dry goods section along with a very appetizing butcher case with all manner of cured meats tempting you as you come in or leave. You may look into the open kitchen, but the fun is just to sit back and enjoy some of the best Italian pastas you can imagine. Get started with a super bread basket; I almost ate so much that I didn't have room for the spit-roasted short ribs! What a dish! There is much more: seared Vermont quail, grilled chicken, roasted lamb ribs and on and on to Italian heaven. The cured meats are all spectacular. The curing equipment is located in the basement of the restaurant. There are lots of good choices for dessert including polenta orange

Lincoln Ristorante

Dinner at the very expensive Italian fine-dining hot spot **Lincoln Ristorante at Lincoln Center** (142 W 65th St, 212/359-6500) offers more than just the impressive modern Italian cuisine of chef Jonathan Benno. The Hearst Plaza setting is spectacular. A reflecting pool is viewed through soaring windows, and a pedestrian-friendly grass-covered geometric roof envelops the restaurant. There is much to enjoy at Lincoln Ristorante, although your pocketbook will take a beating.

Carter's Find in the West Village

Restaurateur Graydon Carter saw good bones in the derelict **Beatrice Inn** (285 W 12th St, 646/896-1804) in the West Village. Building on that framework, he restored the cozy restaurant and bar to a neighborhood steak and chophouse. The somewhat pricey menu is not large and the house is still determining what works best. That being said, Carter's following and New York's elite have found the place and made it their local seen-and-be-seen spot.

cake, panna cotta, and first-rate gelati and sorbets. For a lunch or evening of true Italian joy, I would highly recommend this establishment.

IL CORTILE

125 Mulberry St (bet Canal and Hester St)   212/226-6060
Lunch, Dinner: Daily   ilcortile.com
Moderate

Here is a good reason to visit Little Italy! While the area is more for tourists than serious diners, there are some exceptions. Il Cortile is an oasis of tasty Italian fare in an attractive and romantic setting. A bright, airy garden area in the rear is the most pleasant part of the restaurant. The menu is typically Italian, with main listings that include fish, chicken, and veal dishes, plus excellent spaghetti, fettuccine, and ravioli. Sauteed vegetables like bitter broccoli, hot peppers, mushrooms, spinach, and green beans are specialties of the house. Service is excellent and expeditious, and the waiters zip around like they are on roller skates. If you can fight through the gawking visitors, you will find Il Cortile worth the effort!

IL GATTOPARDO

33 W 54th St (bet Fifth Ave and Ave of the Americas)   212/246-0412
Lunch, Dinner: Daily   ilgattopardonyc.com
Expensive

Set in a simple and elegant Manhattan townhouse with an indoor garden, this place appeals to serious gourmets. The interesting and varying appetizers may include beef and veal meatballs wrapped in cabbage, scallops, Parmigiana of zucchini with smoked mozzarella, and braised octopus. Among the many pastas, homemade scialatielli is delicious. Main-course highlights include Neapolitan meatloaf, herb-crusted rack of lamb, fish and shellfish stew, and much more. If your favorite dish is not on the menu, then ask in advance and they'll make it for you. For dessert, warm chocolate cake with artisanal gelati, and tableside *zabaglione* are sinfully good.

IL MULINO NEW YORK

86 W 3rd St (bet Sullivan and Thompson St)   212/673-3783
Lunch: Mon-Fri; Dinner: Mon-Sat
Moderately expensive

IL MULINO UPTOWN

37 E 60th St (bet Madison and Park Ave)   212/750-3270
Lunch: Mon-Sat; Dinner: Daily   ilmulino.com
Moderately expensive

For three decades, Il Mulino New York has produced the authentic cuisine of the Abruzzo coastal region of Italy. Known for turning fresh, simple ingredients into sumptuous feasts, you'll taste the vibrant, Italian flavors in the fresh home-made pastas (center cut tuna with cream mustard sauce or artichoke hearts and bacon in butter sauce), chicken braised in wine, sea bass, and scallops wrapped in pancetta, to name a few. Finish with a luscious dessert like oranges marinated in grand marnier with seasonal berries, prepared tableside. Exemplary service, one-of-a-kind fare, and a stunning atmosphere combine to make this an exceptional experience!

IL POSTINO

337 E 49th St (bet First and Second Ave)   212/688-0033
Lunch: Mon-Sat; Dinner: Daily   ilpostinony.com
Expensive

It is nice to splurge on occasion, if what you get is worth the extra bucks. Il Pos-tino does have rather hefty prices, but the offerings rival the best in Manhattan! The setting is comfortable and not showy. You'll be impressed by the captains, who can recite a lengthy list of specials without hesitation. You have your choice of ground-level tables or a slightly raised balcony; the latter feels more comfortable to me. An extraordinarily tasty bread dish and assorted small appetizer plates get things off to a good start. Pastas like linguine with three kinds of clams or the signature pasta dish, Agnolotti, pasta stuffed with ricotta cheese and spinach in a light cream sauce are sensational. Chicken in a baked crust is very satisfying, and roasted loin of veal for two is also top-grade. Authentic Italian sorbets finish a memorable gourmet experience. Incidentally, lunch is equally tasty and easier on the wallet.

IL RICCIO

152 E 79th St (bet Third and Lexington Ave)   212/639-9111
Lunch, Dinner: Daily
Moderate

There's nothing fancy here – just good Italian fare. Il Riccio is consistent, so you can count on leaving satisfied and well fed. Spaghetti with crabmeat and fresh tomato is one of my favorites. So is thinly sliced beef with truffled pecorino cheese

---

Bars for Smoking

Nowadays, you will get the boot in most New York bars if you try to have a smoke. However, there are a few places left where you can legally light up, toss back a drink, and grab a meal.

Carnegie Club (156 W 56th St, 212/957-9676): cigar bar and jazz

Circa Tabac (32 Watts St, 212/941-1781): over 70 brands of cigarettes; cigars

Club Macanudo (26 E 63rd St, 212/752-8200): private humidors

Hudson Bar & Books (636 Hudson St, 212/229-2642): Monday is ladies' night.

Lexington Bar & Books (1020 Lexington Ave, 212/717-3902): collars required, jackets preferred

Favorite Chocolate Desserts

Bar Room at The Modern (Museum of Modern Art, 9 W 53rd St, 212/333-1220): chocolate and hazelnut dacquoise

Bouley (163 Duane St, 212/964-2525): the Chocolate Frivolous

Cafe Lalo (201 W 83rd St, 212/496-6031): Chocolate Madness

Craft (43 E 19th St, 212/780-0880): chocolate soufflé

Jean Georges (Trump International Hotel and Tower, 1 Central Park W, 212/299-3900): warm, soft chocolate cake

La Grenouille (3 E 52nd St, 212/752-1495): chocolate soufflé

The Spotted Pig (314 W 11th St, 212/620-0393): flourless chocolate cake

and breaded rack of veal. Particularly popular at Il Riccio is the fish, including sea bass, tuna, swordfish, snapper, and halibut. Fruit tarts are homemade and delicious, and a dish of marinated peaches (when available) is the signature dessert. The garden room is a comfortable place to dine in nice weather and accommodates parties up to 25. Service is unfailingly pleasant.

IL TESORO RISTORANTE
1578 First Ave (at 82nd St)   212/861-9620
Dinner: Daily   iltesoro.net
Moderately expensive

When you walk into the latest incarnation of Il Tesoro, the bones of Primavera shine anew with rich wooden panels, elegant marble, and subtle lighting. Centuries-old iron gates cover racks of wine bottles in the private party space in the basement. Chef AJ Black focuses on new classic style Italian cuisine with appetizers such as carpaccio di salmone e tonno, antipasto del giorno, and scallops antica. Delicious secondis include rigatoni bolognese made with pulled, braised beef in a succulent tomato sauce, lamb osso buco, scaloppini favola, and duck braciole. White chocolate crème brûlée and tiramisu, which incorporates chef Black's special liquor blend, are two of the standouts from a rotating array of desserts. An outdoor patio provides a warm weather alfresco dining venue.

IL VAGABONDO
351 E 62nd St (bet First and Second Ave)   212/832-9221
Lunch: Mon-Fri; Dinner: Daily   ilvagabondo.com
Moderate

Il Vagabondo is a good spot to recommend to your visiting friends, and many folks consider it their favorite restaurant! This bustling house has been popular with New Yorkers in the know since 1965. The atmosphere is strictly old-time, complete with white tablecloths, four busy rooms, and an even busier bar. Spaghetti, ravioli, and absolutely marvelous veal, chicken, and eggplant parmigiana are popular dishes. There is no pretense at this place, which is a terrific spot for office parties. You will see happy faces, compliments of a delicious meal and reasonable bill. Save room for the bocce ball dessert (tartufo). Il Vagabondo is the only restaurant in New York with an indoor bocce court!

JACKSON HOLE BURGERS

232 E 64th St (bet Second and Third Ave)	212/371-7187
521 Third Ave (at 35th St)	212/679-3264
1611 Second Ave (at 84th St)	212/737-8788
1270 Madison Ave (at 91st St)	212/427-2820
517 Columbus Ave (at 85th St)	212/362-5177
Breakfast, Brunch, Lunch, Dinner: Daily	jacksonholeburgers.com
Inexpensive	

Jackson Hole is my favorite burger destination! You might think that a burger is a burger. But having tried hamburgers all over the city, I can attest that this chain has some of the best. Each one weighs at least seven juicy, delicious ounces. You can get all kind of burgers: pizza, English, or the Baldouni burger (mushrooms, fried onions, and American cheese), including chicken, turkey, and vegetable options. They have omelets, Mexican items, salads, soup, sandwiches, and wraps, too. The atmosphere isn't fancy, but once you sink your teeth into a Jackson Hole burger, accompanied by great onion rings or French fries and a homemade dessert, you'll see why I'm so enthusiastic. Breakfast or brunch is also served. Check with each location, as service hours vary. Free delivery and catering are available.

JACQUES 1534

20 Prince St (bet Mott and Elizabeth St)	212/966-8888
Lunch, Dinner: Daily; Brunch: Sat, Sun	jacques1534.com
Moderate	

Just steps from the bustling streets of Nolita is Jacques 1534, one part French gastropub and one part sexy underground cocktail lounge. Jacques 1534 brings a fresh and creative approach to the traditional French fare with a locally sourced menu and expertly crafted cocktails. The a la carte menu is basically the same for lunch, dinner, and brunch. A three-course *prix-fixe* menu is also offered for lunch plus a couple of sandwich choices.   Same can be said about the brunch menu with the addition of egg dishes and the bottomless brunch special with unlimited (within two hours) mimosas, bellinis, or bloody marys. The downstairs lounge, which features, cocktails from the colonial settlements, encourages mingling, laughter, and imbibing; after all, it is the reason you're there. Two sister restaurants, **Jacques Brasserie** and **The Pitch & Fork**, are uptown.

Italian Treats

Bruschetta: slices of crispy garlic bread, usually topped with tomatoes and basil

Carpaccio: thin shavings of raw beef topped with olive oil and lemon juice or mayonnaise

Risotto: creamy, rice-like pasta, often mixed with shellfish and/or vegetables

Saltimbocca: Thin slices of veal topped with prosciutto and sage are sauteed in butter and slow-simmered in white wine. The name means "jumps in your mouth."

Zabaglione: dessert sauce or custard made with egg yolks, marsala, and sugar. It is called sabayon in France.

Save on Dining Dollars

- Eat out at lunchtime rather than dinner ... or eat a Sunday brunch.
- Dine at the bar, where the menu is less expensive.
- Order a few appetizers rather than a main entree.
- Don't order bottled water.
- Don't go for the expensive wines. Some less expensive bottles are just as good!
- Don't go for the entree specials, which are often overpriced.
- Don't feel that you must have a dessert.
- The first main dish listed on a menu is usually the most profitable.
- Be sure to "check your check." Watch for included gratuities.

JACQUES BRASSERIE

204-206 E 85th St (bet Second and Third Ave)   212/327-2272
Lunch, Dinner: Daily; Brunch: Sat, Sun   jacquesbrasserie.com
Moderate

There are just so many reasons why this bistro is so popular with folks in the neighborhood. It is cozy, friendly, and moderately priced, and they serve great food. In addition, Jacques himself is one of the friendliest proprietors in town. All of the classic French dishes are available: onion soup, steak au poivre, crème brûlée, cheeses, and a wonderful chocolate soufflé with Tahitian vanilla ice cream. There also are outstanding seafood dishes, including mussels, prepared six ways. Moreover, this bistro is intimate, making it a great place for private parties.

JEAN GEORGES

Trump International Hotel and Tower
1 Central Park W (bet 60th and 61st St)   212/299-3900
Lunch, Dinner: Daily
Very expensive

NOUGATINE CAFE

Front room at Jean Georges
Breakfast, Dinner: Daily; Lunch: Mon-Sat; Brunch: Sun   Moderately expensive
jean-georgesrestaurant.com

Jean-Georges Vongerichten is the master of the cool, calm, formal, and très French dining hall that bears his name. The understated elegance of the room and uninterrupted service set the tone for a fine dining experience. Lunch and dinner are *prix-fixe*; at $38, lunch is a bargain. Dinner starts at $118 for three courses; tasting menus are $198. The more casual cafe, **Nougatine**, offers some of the same menu items (and many more) at a slightly lower price and serves both a la carte and *prix-fixe*. Where to start? The foie gras brûlée with sour cherries, pistachios, and port gelée gets my vote. The menu changes seasonally. Rack of lamb is outstanding, as are the fish dishes. The chocolate dessert tasting, especially if it includes the decadent chocolate cake, is wonderful. You can't do better than Jean Georges, especially if price is unimportant!

JEFFREY'S GROCERY

172 Waverly Pl (at Christopher St)   646/398-7630
Lunch: Mon-Fri; Dinner: Daily; Brunch: Sat, Sun   jeffreysgrocery.com
Moderate to moderately expensive

Jeffrey's may seem like a vintage 1930s mom-and-pop grocery, but the menu and tantalizing aromas tell otherwise. Cozy seating, a communal table, and bar stools accommodate about 40 folks. Don't be surprised if you're asked to scoot down a seat to make room for another diner. Fans of traditional soups, salads, and sandwiches will discover intriguing contemporary twists on Jeffrey's menu. The braised brisket sandwich is tender and satisfying. Dinner plates feature fresh local seafood, meats, and vegetables. You could make a meal out of the cheese, charcuterie, or raw bar offerings. It's a "feel good" kind of place!

THE JOHN DORY OYSTER BAR

Ace Hotel
1196 Broadway (at 29th St)   212/792-9000
Lunch, Dinner: Daily   thejohndory.com
Moderate

The John Dory at the Ace Hotel is one of the city's hot spots. The corner space is light and bright, thanks to spacious floor-to-ceiling windows. A raw bar and small plates dominate the menu. A separate bar serves over a dozen signature cocktails. Be prepared to wait for a table and just relax and enjoy the scene. This is Friedman and Bloomfield territory, which translates into a no-reservations policy. It's very casual, with bar tables and stools (no white-cloth draped tables). You can also join the crowd standing at the bar late into the night.

JOHN'S PIZZERIA

278 Bleecker St (bet Ave of the Americas and Seventh Ave)   212/243-1680
                                              johnsbrickovenpizza.com
260 W 44th St (bet Eighth Ave and Broadway)   212/391-7560
408 E 64th St (bet First and York Ave)   212/935-2895
Daily: 11:30 to 11:30   johnspizzerianyc.com
Moderate

Manhattan's three John's Pizzerias have one thing in common: some of the best coal-fired brick-oven handmade pizzas in the city. Mouthwatering thin-crust

---

Superb Breakfast

Head straight to **Norma's** (Le Parker Meridien New York, 119 W 57th St, 212/708-7460) for Manhattan's best breakfast. Any day will be a little brighter with beautifully presented blueberry or buttermilk pancakes, breakfast dumplings, barbecue pulled pork hash, breakfast pizza, Norma's granola with fruits and nuts, a gooey four-cheese omelet, or chocolate blintz crepes. Enjoy the newspaper while sipping a fresh smoothie, orange juice, or French-press coffee or tea. For a big splash, start the morning with the "Zillion Dollar" lobster frittata ($1,000), with a generous serving of sevruga caviar! Just as tasty for lunch, this menu is offered until Norma's 3 p.m. closing. Possible star-spotting as well!

Indian Cuisine

Junoon (27 W 24th St, 212/490-2100) is a relatively new Indian restaurant near the Flatiron Building. The main dining room is well-appointed with statues and antique carvings. The private and semiprivate dining rooms have similarly sumptuous appointments. Food is prepared in five elements of Indian cuisine: clay oven, open fire pit, curry, cast-iron cooking, and stone cooking. The Five Elements Menu is a special five-course tasting dinner for $75. An intriguing part of the restaurant is the remarkable spice room, which is visible to guests. Roasted and ground daily, the spices are incorporated into exotic dishes and cocktails. Warm and delicious breads are also made on-site. Attentive service, an enticing menu, and moderate prices make this a popular spot for lunch or dinner.

varieties include cheese and tomatoes to a gut-busting extravaganza of cheese, tomatoes, anchovies, sausage, peppers, meatballs, onions, and mushrooms. John's does appetizers, salads, sandwiches, and cheese ravioli well, too. Interestingly, the enormous 44th Street pizzeria occupies the former Gospel Tabernacle Church in Times Square, seats about 400 people, and can handle groups of any size in a New York minute.

JOSEPH LEONARD

170 Waverly Pl (at Grove St)   646/429-8383
Breakfast, Lunch: Tues-Fri; Dinner: Daily; Brunch: Sat, Sun   josephleonard.com
Moderate to moderately expensive

Chef Jim McDuffee has a winner! Just one bit of advice before venturing to this place for dinner – come early. Joseph Leonard is a small, rustic place with an exceedingly busy small bar and a no-reservations policy that can mean quite a wait later in the evening. Wait or not, the New York strip steak is worth a visit in itself. Feast upon soups, salads, and paté. If they have the butternut squash soup, go for it. Fish, shellfish, chicken, and lamb shank make great main courses. Just don't come here if you want a slow, quiet meal!

KATZ'S DELICATESSEN

205 E Houston St (at Ludlow St)   212/254-2246
Mon-Wed: 8 a.m.-10:45 p.m.; Thurs: 8 a.m.-2:45 a.m.; Fri: 8 a.m. - all night;
   Sat: all day; Sun: till 10:45 p.m.   katzdelicatessen.com
Inexpensive to moderate

Going strong since 1888, Katz's Delicatessen is the oldest and largest deli in Manhattan. If you're experiencing hunger pangs on the Lower East Side, then try Katz's hand-carved and overstuffed sandwiches, which are among the best in town. Mainstays include pastrami, hot dogs, corned beef, and potato pancakes. Prices are reasonable. Go right up to the counter and order — it is fun watching the no-nonsense operators slicing and fixing — or sit at a table where a seasoned waiter will take care of you. Try dill pickles and sauerkraut with your sandwich. Incidentally, Katz's is a perfect place to sample the unique (and disappearing) lowbrow "charm" of the Lower East Side. While you wait for a table or discover that the salt and pepper containers are empty and the catsup is missing, you'll know what I mean. Catering (at attractive rates) and private party facilities are available. Their "Send a Salami to Your Boy in the Army" promotion started during World War II and is still going strong.

KEENS STEAKHOUSE

72 W 36th St (bet Fifth Ave and Ave of the Americas)   212/947-3636
Lunch: Mon-Fri; Dinner: Daily   keens.com
Moderate

Keens Steakhouse is one of the most reliable longtime Manhattan restaurants; a truly unique New York institution. I can remember coming here decades ago, when those in the garment trade made Keens their lunch headquarters. This has not changed; Keens still has the same attractions: the bar reeks of atmosphere, and there are great party facilities and fine food to match. Keens has been a fixture in the Herald Square area since 1885. For some time it was for "gentlemen only," and although it still has a masculine atmosphere, ladies are made to feel comfortable and welcome. The famous mutton chop with mint is the house specialty, but other delicious dishes include steak, lamb, fish, and lobster. They do single-malt Scotch tastings from fall through spring and stock one of the largest collections in New York. If you have a meat-and-potato lover in your party, this is the place to come. Save room for the fantastic key lime pie.

KING'S CARRIAGE HOUSE

251 E 82nd St (bet Second and Third Ave)   212/734-5490
Lunch: Mon-Sat; Dinner: Tues-Sat; Tea: Daily (at 3 p.m.); Brunch: Sun
Moderately expensive   kingscarriagehouse.com

Even some folks in the immediate neighborhood are unaware of this sleeper. King's is indeed an old carriage house, remade into a charming two-story dining salon that your mother-in-law would love. The ambience is Irish manor house. In a quaint setting with real wooden floors, you dine by candlelight in a very civilized atmosphere. The luncheon menu stays the same: salads, sandwiches, and lighter fare. Afternoon tea is a treat. The continental menu changes nightly and may feature grilled items (like loin of lamb). On Sundays, it is a roast dinner (leg of lamb, loin of pork, chicken, or tenderloin of beef). The $49 *prix-fixe* menu is a really good value. I found the Stilton cheese with a nightcap of ruby port absolutely perfect for dessert. Chocolate truffle cake and rhubarb tart are excellent, too.

KITTICHAI

60 Thompson Hotel
60 Thompson St (at Broome St)   212/219-2000
Dinner: Daily; Brunch: Sat, Sun   kittichairestaurant.com
Moderately expensive

Kittichai serves real Thai food! In this aesthetically opulent setting, one's eyes will rest as much on the tableware, the black-draped service personnel, and the fish tank as on the food. As is true of most Thai restaurants, seafood is high on the list. Don't overlook the baby back ribs in tamarind glaze. For entrees, crispy whole sea bass and grilled Arctic char in tamarind coconut broth are winners. Kittichai's curries are exceptional. Omelets, pancakes, and other brunch classics are prepared with Thai influences. Honestly, I found this place a bit much both in attitude and dishes, but you do get a peek at the mystique of Thailand.

LA BOITE EN BOIS

75 W 68th St (at Columbus Ave)   212/874-2705
Lunch: Mon-Sat; Dinner: Daily; Brunch: Sun   laboitenyc.com
Moderate

La Boite en Bois is ideal for pre-theater diners. You don't have to pronounce the name of this French restaurant properly to have a good time. It packs them in every evening for obvious reasons: delicious food, personal service, and moderate prices. Salads are unusual, and the country paté is a great beginner. For an entree, I recommend filet of snapper, roast chicken with herbs, or *pot-au-feu*. The atmosphere is intimate, and all the niceties of service are operative from start to finish. The French toast at brunch is a treat. Desserts are made in-house; try one of their sorbets. La Boite en Bois is small and popular, so call ahead for reservations.

LA BOTTEGA

The Maritime Hotel
88 Ninth Ave (at 17th St)   212/243-8400
Breakfast: Daily; Lunch: Mon-Fri; Dinner: Daily; Brunch: Sat, Sun
Moderate   themaritimehotel.com

In nice weather, outside dining at La Bottega is very pleasant. At other times, the inside restaurant seating at this downtown hotel offers a relaxing setting for business meetings and gatherings with friends. The food is regional Italian, moderately priced, with no surprises. Pizzas, pastas, and salads are the main offerings. The burrata caprese (salad with burrata cheese) is one of the best light dishes. Several flavors of gelato are on the dessert menu.

LA GRENOUILLE

3 E 52nd St (bet Fifth and Madison Ave)   212/752-1495
Lunch, Dinner: Tues-Sat   la-grenouille.com
Expensive

Congratulations are in order for a 50-year anniversary! Put on your finest clothes to dine at La Grenouille, a special place that must be seen to be believed. Beautiful fresh-cut flowers herald a unique, not-to-be-forgotten dining experience. The food is as great as the atmosphere, and although prices are high, La Grenouille is worth every penny. Celebrity-watching adds to the fun. You'll see most of the famous faces at the front of the room. The professional staff serves a complete French menu. Be sure to try the cold hors d'oeuvres, which are a specialty of the house, as are the lobster dishes, sea bass, and poached chicken. Nowhere in New York are sauces any better. The dessert soufflés are superb. The tables are close together, but what difference does it make when the people at your elbows are so interesting?

LA LUNCHONETTE

130 Tenth Ave (at 18th St)   212/675-0342
Lunch, Dinner: Daily
Inexpensive to moderate

La Lunchonette proves that you don't have to be fancy to succeed, as long as you serve good food. In an unlikely location, this popular spot offers some of the tastiest French dishes around: snails, sauteed portobello mushrooms, and lobster bisque to start, and omelets, grilled lamb sausage, sauteed calves liver, and more for entrees. On Sunday evening, live accordion music is a feature. You'll be pleasantly surprised when the bill comes!

LA RIPAILLE
605 Hudson St (bet 12th and Bethune St)   212/255-4406
Lunch, Dinner: Daily; Brunch: Sat, Sun   laripailleny.com
Moderate

Since 1980 this small, bright, Parisian-style bistro in the West Village (complete with fireplace) makes a cozy spot for an informal, intimate meal. You might want to enjoy a cocktail on the lovely outdoor terrace. The chef puts his heart into every dish. Entrees are done to perfection. The seafood is always fresh, and they do an excellent job with lamb and duck magret. Desserts are classic French and delicious.

LA SILHOUETTE
362 W 53rd St (bet Eighth and Ninth Ave)   212/581-2400
Lunch: Mon-Fri; Dinner: Daily   la-silhouettenyc.com
Moderately expensive

La Silhouette's menu is decidedly French. Diners have several menu options: a la carte, *prix-fixe* (lunch and dinner) and a five-course dinner menu with or without wine pairing. More often than not an appetizer featuring a poached heirloom egg is offered, perhaps with mascarpone polenta or as part of a savory leek tart. Other choices include versions of endive salads, paté, and foie gras. There are a limited number of main course meat and seafood selections; however, if you like duck, then you may want to order the seasonal preparation. An interesting, and delicious dessert is the popcorn crème brûlée made with apples, salted caramel ice cream, and caramel popcorn. This contemporary restaurant with sunken dining room is apropos for date night or pre-theater dining and the six-seat bar is a delightful perch while you're waiting for your dinner party.

LAND THAI KITCHEN
450 Amsterdam Ave (at 82nd St)   212/501-8121
Lunch, Dinner: Daily   landthaikitchen.com
Moderate

Land Thai Kitchen has become a neighborhood favorite with its well-prepared and -presented Thai food at good prices. The menu offers about a dozen noodle and rice dishes and combinations from the wok. Other main offerings are fish, steak, and chicken, all served with jasmine rice. Appetizers, salads, and side dishes round out the menu. The chef is known for spicy sauces; ask your server to have the heat of the dish turned up or down to suit your taste. Delivery and takeout are available.

LANDMARC
Time Warner Center
10 Columbus Circle (at 60th St), 3rd floor   212/823-6123
Breakfast, Lunch, Dinner, Late Night: Daily (7 a.m.-2 a.m.)

179 West Broadway (bet Leonard and Worth St)   212/343-3883
Lunch, Dinner: Daily; Brunch: Sat, Sun   landmarc-restaurant.com
Moderate

Restaurants Near Carnegie Hall

Just as there are a wide variety of performances staged at Carnegie Hall, there are varied opportunities to indulge the appetite. Here are some great choices in the neighborhood.

Brasserie 8½ (9 W 57th St, 212/829-0812): French brasserie

burger joint at Le Parker Meridien New York (118 W 57th St, 212/708-7414): burgers, shakes

Great American Health Bar (35 W 57th St, 212/355-5177): breakfast, lunch, dinner

Le Pain Quotidien (922 Seventh Ave, 212/757-0775): European; breakfast, lunch, dinner

Mangia (50 W 57th St, 212/582-5882): breakfast and lunch; pizza, salads, sandwiches, entrees, sweets

Nobu Fifty Seven (40 W 57th St, 212/757-3000): Japanese; celebrities

The Russian Tea Room (150 W 57th St, 212/581-7100): The well-known name says it all!

Trattoria dell'Arte (900 Seventh Ave, 212/245-9800): Italian; celebrities

---

Landmarc offers a big menu, very tasty food and accommodating staff — what more could you want? Seafood entrees include roasted branzino, grilled salmon, and tuna. Lamb chops, roasted chicken, and burgers are excellent. Daily pasta specials are available, and steaks with French fries are a specialty. Delicious fresh salads like the niçoise are a lunch favorite. Looking for a novel dish? Try the crispy sweetbreads or the popular mussels with a selection of sauces like rosemary and bacon or pesto and tomato. Both locations are crowded and offer high-energy dining.

LAVO

39 E 58th St (bet Park and Madison Ave)   212/750-5588
Lunch: Mon-Fri; Dinner: Daily; Brunch: Sun; Nightclub: Thurs-Sat   lavony.com
Moderately expensive

Talk about a scene! New York's noteworthy young set have descended on the place. A bar, restaurant, and nightclub make up the operation; it is noisy but amazingly efficient for such a mob scene, and the Italian fare is delicious! The menu is full of good dishes: sensational Kobe beef meatballs, Caesar salad, and raw bar items. Steaks and chops, pizzas and pastas are popular dishes for the throngs, who seem to enjoy an atmosphere that is not conducive for people with hearing problems! The Oreo zeppole (deep-fried oreos served with a vanilla milkshake chaser) completes a rather unique experience.

LE BERNARDIN

155 W 51st St (bet Ave of the Americas and Seventh Ave)   212/554-1515
Lunch: Mon-Fri; Dinner: Mon-Sat   le-barnardin.com
Expensive

Surely you have heard of this seafood palace! There has to be one restaurant that tops every list, and for seafood Le Bernardin holds that spot. Co-owner Maguy LeCoze and executive chef Eric Ripert make this house extremely attractive to the eye and very satisfying to the stomach. The old-world service is seamless. Wonderfully fresh oysters and clams make a great start. Whatever your heart desires from the ocean is represented on the menu. What distinguishes La Bernardin is presentation. Signature dishes change seasonally and might include yellowfin tuna (appetizer), monkfish, halibut, and skate. Duck, lamb, and short ribs are available on request. *Prix-fixe* lunch is $72; dinner is $127; tasting menu is $147. The dessert menu usually includes a cheese assortment, superb chocolate dishes, and unusual flavors of ice cream and sorbet.

LE CIRQUE

1 Beacon Court
151 E 58th St (bet Lexington and Third Ave)   212/644-0202
Lunch: Mon-Fri; Dinner: Mon-Sat   lecirque.com
Expensive

It's all about Sirio Maccioni! Probably no one on the Manhattan restaurant scene has more devoted followers than this charming gentleman. His difficult-to-find retreat is frequented by fans looking for quenelle of artichoke, morel risotto, rack of lamb, and duck breast and foie gras. Finish with the signature chocolate passion mousse or pistachio soufflé. Most of all, diners want to be seen by the upper echelon "swells" and get a kiss from Sirio himself. The food is absolutely superb. The atmosphere is what you would expect (classy, subdued, jackets required), as are the prices (expensive). If you want the same great food in a more relaxed setting, head to the cafe and wine lounge. Private facilities are also available. I love watching Sirio, who is the epitome of what a restaurateur should be.

LE GIGOT

18 Cornelia St (bet Bleecker and 4th St)   212/627-3737
Lunch, Dinner: Tues-Sun; Brunch: Sat, Sun   legigotrestaurant.com
Moderate

Le Gigot is a charming, romantic 28-seat bistro in the bowels of the Village. Most taxi drivers have never heard of Cornelia Street, so allow extra time if you come by cab. Once you're here, the cozy atmosphere and warm hospitality of the gentlemen who greet and serve combines with hearty dishes that will please the most discerning diner. My suggestion for a memorable meal: bouillabaisse or, in winter, le boeuf Bourguignon (beef stew in red wine with shallots, bacon, carrots, mushrooms, and potatoes). Snails and patés make delicious starters. Tasty desserts like upside-down apple tart and flambé bananas with cognac are offered. Brunches are a specialty. Le Gigot is a lot less expensive than its counterpart in Paris, but just as appealing. Only cash and American Express are accepted.

LE PÉRIGORD

405 E 52nd St (bet First Ave and East River)   212/755-6244
Lunch: Mon-Fri; Dinner: Daily   leperigord.com
Expensive

Superb! I love this place, which has been charming diners for nearly half a century. Civilized is the word to describe Le Périgord. It is like dining in one of the great rooms of Manhattan in the "good old days," but with a distinctively modern presence. From gracious host Georges Briguet to the talented chef, everything is class personified. Gentlemen should wear jackets. Every captain and waiter

Jacket Required

The more exclusive restaurants still impose a "business casual" dress code that requires men to wear jackets. If you show up without one, don't be surprised if they discreetly loan one to you.

21 Club: jacket required; no jeans or sneakers

Bouley: jacket requested, no sneakers

Daniel: jacket required, no sneakers

Four Seasons: jacket preferred

Jean Georges: jacket required, tie optional; no jeans, sneakers, and T-shirts

La Grenouille: jacket required

Le Bernardin: jacket required, no sneakers

Le Cirque: jacket required; no shorts and open-toe shoes

Le Périgord: jacket preferred

Picholine: jacket preferred; no jeans or sneakers

---

has been trained to perfection. Fresh roses and Limoges dinner plates adorn each table. But this is just half the pleasure of the experience. Every dish – from the magnificent cold appetizer buffet that greets guests to the spectacular pastry trolley – is tasty and memorable. You may order a la carte, of course. Soups are outstanding. Dover sole melts in your mouth. A fine selection of game is available in winter. Roasted free-range chicken, served with the best potato dish I have ever tasted (bleu de gex potato gratin), is spectacular. Finish your meal with a selection of cheeses. The luxurious setting of Le Périgord makes one appreciate what gracious dining on a special night out is all about.

LE RELAIS DE VENISE

590 Lexington Ave (at 52nd St)   212/758-3989
Lunch, Dinner: Daily   relaisdevenise.com
Moderate

Direct from Paris, and really packing them in, Le Relais is a straightforward French steakhouse. The simple menu offers trimmed midwestern sirloin steak, a tasty sauce that is a closely guarded family recipe, French fries, and green salad with walnuts for $26.95. The steak and fries arrive in two servings. Young people love this place because of the comfortable price and the noisy, over-the-top energy. This is truly one of the better bargains in Manhattan. What they lose in big checks, they make up for in volume! Desserts include delicious in-house profiteroles, crème brulée, meringues, and a seasonal fruit selection. Service is pleasant and quick, but this is not a place for a leisurely meal.

LE RIVAGE

340 W 46th St (bet Eighth and Ninth Ave)   212/765-7374
Lunch, Dinner: Daily   lerivagenyc.com
Moderate

A great choice for pre-theater dinner, Le Rivage is one of the survivors along the highly competitive "restaurant row" of 46th Street. They continue to please by serving French food that's well prepared and reasonably priced. Escargots, onion soup, coq au vin rouge, and peach melba are all delectable and well-presented. The atmosphere and pleasant attitude of the servers will put you in the proper frame of mind to enjoy an after-dinner Broadway show.

LES HALLES
411 Park Ave S (bet 28th and 29th St)   212/679-4111
15 John St (at Broadway)   212/285-8585
Daily: 7 a.m. to midnight   leshalles.net
Moderate

Come here anytime you are hungry! These popular brasseries provide tasty food in an appealing atmosphere at reasonable prices. Specialties like blood sausage with apples, choucrote garnie (sauerkraut with sausage and pork), and filet of beef are served in hefty portions with fresh salad and delicious French fries. Harried waiters try their best to be polite and helpful, but they are not always successful, as tables turn over rapidly. If a week in Paris is more of a dream than a reality, then you might settle for mussels, snails, onion soup, and classic cassoulet at this busy establishment. About a dozen dessert items include chocolate-banana cake with chocolate sauce and crepes Suzette, prepared tableside. Les Halles' butcher shop, by the front door, is open daily.

LITTLE OWL
90 Bedford St (at Grove St)   212/741-4695
Lunch: Mon-Fri; Dinner: Daily; Brunch: Sat, Sun   thelittleowlnyc.com
Moderate

With tiny tables and a capacity of only 30 diners, this corner establishment is a very personal place with a wait staff that is warm and eager to please. Every seasonal Mediterranean-influenced dish I've tasted is excellent and reasonably priced. They are famous for their signature gravy meatball sliders and pork chops that are a juicy, fat cut served with creamy butterbeans. Or try the lobster ravioli or seafood fritters – all good. The brunch menu is particularly attractive, with dishes like whole-wheat pancakes, surf and turf tacos, and a bacon cheeseburger with spiced fries. Just one drawback: Little Owl is very popular, so reservations are a must.

LOCANDA VERDE
The Greenwich Hotel
377 Greenwich St (at N Moore St)   212/925-3797
Breakfast, Dinner: Daily; Lunch: Mon-Fri; Brunch: Sat, Sun locandaverdenyc.com
Moderate

Comfortable, energetic, and Italian — that describes this Greenwich Hotel taverna. The chefs have brought their experience from other top Manhattan restaurants to create enticing menus. Start the day with a combination of pomegranate, blood-orange, and Valencia-orange juices; a whole grain waffle with strawberries and mascarpone cream; and Chef Karen DeMasco's fresh pastries. It's hard to pass up the lunch and dinner pasta dishes with duck sausage, and the wood-burning oven turns out flavorful, succulent leg of lamb and other entrees. Desserts such as mango crostada with coconut caramel or the chocolate budino with hot fudge pose real dietary dilemmas. Though cozy inside, the casual dining atmosphere extends to the outdoors in summer.

The Biergarten

Tucked under the High Line is The Standard High Line hotel's **The Biergarten** (848 Washington St, 212/645-4646). Traditional German sausages and pretzels, along with famous mugs of German beer, are served in a great atmosphere. It's an excellent spot for an after-work drink or a fun evening. Biergarten is open until midnight on weekdays and 1 a.m. on weekends. Zum Wohl!

LUKE'S LOBSTER

93 E 7th St (at First Ave)	212/387-8487
242 E 81st St (at Second Ave)	212/249-4241
426 Amsterdam Ave (bet 80th and 81st St)	212/877-8800
26 S William St (at Stone St)	212/747-1700
Plaza Food Hall, 1 W 59th St (at Fifth Ave), lower level	646/755-3227
Sun-Thurs: 11-10; Fri, Sat: 11-11	lukeslobster.com
Moderate	

A trip to Luke's Lobster is reminiscent of a summer visit to Maine. Tasty lobster rolls are piled high with fresh lobster (which is the main attraction), and mayo is optional. Crab and shrimp rolls, soups, and sodas, also sourced from the Pine Tree state, round out the menu. Since seating is limited, the interesting collection of Maine fishing-village kitsch will keep you occupied as you wait; or simply take your order to go.

MACELLERIA

48 Gansevoort St (at Greenwich St)   212/741-2555
Lunch: Mon-Fri; Dinner: Daily; Brunch: Sat, Sun   macelleria.com
Moderately expensive

Macelleria (Italian for butcher shop) is a bright spot in the Meatpacking District, and is essentially a Northern Italian steakhouse with added attractions. The setting is what you might expect: masculine and unpretentious, with outside tables for nice-weather dining. Friendly and welcoming help make an excellent first impression. The menu is traditional, with some pleasant additions: fresh and filling salads, a number of pastas, chicken, seafood, chops, and veal. Prime, dry-aged steaks are the primary draw. I highly recommend this spot for dinner with business partners after consummating a big deal. For private events, try the wine cellar or the chef's table — located in the meat locker!

MADANGSUI

35 W 35th St (bet Fifth Ave and Ave of the Americas)   212/564-9333
Lunch: Mon-Fri; Dinner: Daily   madangsui.com
Moderate

I got hooked on Korean barbecue while in South Korea, so it was only natural that I've been trying out various places in Manhattan that duplicate those authentic tastes. Madangsui surely qualifies. The menu literally covers over a hundred dishes, with combinations sure to please. The place is usually crowded with Korean folks and their families — an indication that Madangsui knows what it is doing! Personally, I get a big kick out of fixing my own dishes on the hot plate in the middle of the table. The fresh, butterflied short rib is absolutely first-rate. You'll also find an extensive array of rice, chowder, and vegetarian dishes.

MAIALINO
Gramercy Park Hotel
2 Lexington Ave (at 21st St)   212/777-2410
Breakfast, Lunch: Mon-Fri; Dinner: Daily; Brunch: Sat, Sun   maialinonyc.com
Moderately expensive

I have the utmost respect for Danny Meyer. This gentleman knows what pleases the American diner, and his operations exude this in spades. It is a fully Italian concept, topped with the Meyer heritage of superb service. If only every dining house in the city could train its people like Danny does! This trattoria is bright and cheery, with food stations placed between the bar and crowded dining room. Come early if you want a table. The menu is as big in size as it is in variety. Perhaps start with fried artichokes and anchovy sauce. Move on to an assorted plate of salami and then an Italian delight like suckling pig ragu. If you can, save room for pork and pecorino sausage and, of course, dessert. My favorite Italian dessert is tartufo (frozen chocolate truffle and brandied cherries), but you might also try one of the delicious tarts or bread pudding with chocolate and hazelnuts. What a feast! And what a special experience to dine in such class. Bravo (again), Danny!

MALONEY & PORCELLI
37 E 50th St (bet Park and Madison Ave)   212/750-2233
Lunch: Mon-Fri; Dinner: Daily   maloneyandporcelli.com
Expensive

This midtown Alan and Michael Stillman establishment has a brand new look and vibe. Father and son have reenergized this gem in their Fourth Wall Restaurant portfolio. While some of the menu favorites remain unchanged, customers will find new entries reflecting culinary trends, new cocktails, new ambience (music, artwork, lighting, etc.), and updated uniforms for the servers. But the meat dishes — fabulous steaks from beef butchered on premises and pork, veal, or lamb shank

---

Diner Lingo

Small restaurants, diners, and delis are usually colorful places to take a meal. Since the quarters are generally quite close, it's inevitable to eavesdrop on the staff's dialogue. They seem to have a language all their own. Here are some examples, along with their meanings:

Axle grease: butter

Bossy in a bowl: beef stew

Bullets: baked beans

In the alley: served as a side dish

Italian perfume: garlic

On the hoof: meat cooked rare

Vermont: maple syrup

Wreck 'em: scramble the eggs

Masa Reservations

Dinner at **Masa** (Time Warner Center, 10 Columbus Circle, 4th floor, 212/823-9800), Chef Masa's incredible 26-seat zen-like Japanese dining experience, requires advance reservations and a lot of yen. The *prix-fixe* meals start at $400 and include nearly 30 courses, five of which are appetizers. Don't blow off your reservation, though. Failure to appear may translate into a $200 per person charge to your credit card, which must be used to guarantee a reservation. A cancellation or decrease in the number in your party must be made 48 hours prior to the reservation. Groups of five or more must deposit half the total charge one week ahead of their reservation. That being said, kampai!

— are wonderful. Lobster dishes are another specialty. It is tempting to fill up on the great bread basket, but leave room for first-rate appetizers like fire-grilled pizzas, crab cakes, and tuna and avocado tartare. A tempting dessert selection is also available. A weekend wine dinner is offered on Friday and Saturday after 8 p.m. Inviting private dining rooms would make a special event indeed special.

MARCHI'S

251 E 31st St (at Second Ave)   212/679-2494
Dinner: Mon-Sat   marchirestaurant.com
Moderate

Come to Marchi's for a unique, leisurely meal and an evening you will long remember. Marchi's has been a New York fixture since 1930, when it was established by the Marchi family in an attractive brownstone townhouse. Three sons are on hand, lending a homey flavor to the restaurant's three dining rooms and garden patio (a great spot for a private dinner). It's almost like eating at your; favorite Italian family's home, especially since there are no menus. Bring a hearty appetite to take full advantage of a superb feast. The first course is a platter of antipasto — including radishes, finocchio, and Genoa salami — plus a salad of tuna, olives, and red cabbage. The second is an absolutely delicious homemade lasagna. The third is crispy deep-fried fish, light and tempting, served with beets and string beans. The entree is delicious roast chicken and veal served with fresh mushrooms and tossed salad. Dessert consists of fresh fruit, cheese, lemon fritters, and sensational crostoli (crisp fried twists sprinkled with powdered sugar). The tab is reasonable. You'll experience a little taste of Italy in Marchi's garden, with the Empire State Building as your centerpiece. Unbelievable!

MAREA

240 Central Park S (bet Broadway and Seventh Ave)   212/582-5100
Lunch: Mon-Sat; Dinner: Daily; Brunch: Sun   marea-nyc.com
Expensive

Dinner at this regional Italian seafood restaurant will soothe frazzled nerves. Flawless service, a sleek and classy contemporary setting, and beautifully presented food from chef Michael White add to the contentment. Fresh seafood dominates the menu, but a couple of meat or poultry selections are also offered. Lunch and brunch have a *prix-fixe* menu only. A la carte and tasting menus are offered at dinner. Especially notable are the caviar, handmade pasta, and strati di cioccolato dessert (dark chocolate cream, salted caramel mousse, coffee crumble, and gelato). Bring along a gold credit card!

THE MARK RESTAURANT BY JEAN-GEORGES

The Mark
25 E 77th St (at Madison Ave)   212/606-3030
Breakfast, Lunch, Dinner: Daily; Brunch: Sat, Sun   themarkrestaurantnyc.com
Moderately expensive

Jean-Georges Vongerichten is a busy chef with operations all over the world. He chose a good location at the Mark, as the neighborhood is wanting for good eating spots. And just as you would expect in this classy hotel, you get a very classy restaurant with the added bonus of great people-watching. The ladies who lunch. The big-time power brokers. The couples from the society lists. All of them (and you, too) will be enjoying the excellent food: wonderful pea soup, shrimp salad with avocado, veal Milanese, and roasted lobster. You will even find a superb burger and a fantastic black-truffle pizza! Save room for the Grand Marnier souf-flé. I found the folks who serve to be down to earth, with none of the attitude you might expect at a place like this.

MARKET TABLE

54 Carmine St (at Bedford St)   212/255-2100
Lunch: Mon-Fri; Dinner: Daily; Brunch: Sat, Sun   markettablenyc.com
Moderate

This place is always packed, and it is easy to see why. The food is excellent, the personnel polite and helpful, the prices moderate, and the atmosphere invit-ing. It's all about comfort food: crisp salads, crispy chicken cutlet, Angus strip loin, and more. The hamburgers alone are worth a visit — huge, juicy, and served with delicious fries. Spiced Long Island duck breast with rhubarb and cashew puree is perfectly done. An inventive brunch menu includes spring pea soup and eggs benedict with prosciutto and buttermilk biscuits. With great food, good value, and a friendly neighborhood location, Market Table is a winner.

MARKJOSEPH STEAKHOUSE

261 Water St (at Peck Slip)   212/277-0020
Lunch: Mon-Fri; Dinner: Daily   markjosephsteakhouse.com
Moderately expensive to expensive

If the trendy uptown steakhouses turn you off, then head downtown — with good directions, as Water Street turns into Pearl Street near this location. This comfortable, homey neighborhood room is high on quality meat (USDA prime dry-aged) and low on attitude. The room is filled with folks in casual garb who are more intent on delving into huge, juicy steaks than wondering who's at the next table. If you're dining with a group, the hot seafood platter (lobster, shrimp, clams, calamari, and mussels) is a great place to start. Porterhouse steak and filet mignon are highly recommended. Baked and hash brown potatoes are great side dishes. At lunch, the burgers are big and wonderful, as is the signature steak sandwich. If there's still room for dessert, opt for tartufo or the MarkJoseph special. You'll be surprised at its contents! A private area for larger parties requires reservations.

Dining with a Water View

If a romantic dinner with a water view is on your agenda, make reservations at one of these restaurants.

Battery Gardens (Battery Park at State St, 212/809-5508): New York Harbor view

The Boathouse (Central Park Lake, 212/517-2233): picturesque lake view

Bridge Cafe (279 Water St, 212/227-3344): beneath the Brooklyn Bridge; closed for storm repairs at printing

Cabana (South Street Seaport, 89 South St, 212/406-1155): Pier 17; Nuevo Latino

Gigino (Wagner Park, 20 Battery Pl, 212/528-2228): Statue of Liberty scene

Riverpark (450 E 29th St, 212/729-9790): East River views; alfresco dining

River Cafe (1 Water St, Brooklyn, 718/522-5200): great views of the Lower Manhattan skyline and East River

Water Club (500 E 30th St, 212/683-3333): Long Island City landscape

---

MCCORMICK & SCHMICK'S

1285 Ave of the Americas (at 52nd St)   212/459-1222
Lunch: Mon-Sat; Dinner: Daily   mccormickandschmick.com
Moderate to moderately expensive

This is a winner! Since I live on the Pacific coast, I can recognize a great seafood house. The Oregon-founded McCormick & Schmick's restaurant chain has an operation in Manhattan, and it is a dandy. The fresh seafood sheet (printed every morning) lists over ten seafood species from the world's waterways, all prepared with imagination and care. And the prices, unlike those at some of the so-called class seafood houses in Manhattan, are very much within reach of the average pocketbook – 15 lunch items under $20. What's good and special: oysters on the half-shell, cedar plank salmon, and Idaho rainbow trout. There are also ample choices for non-seafood diners. Be sure to check out the in-house desserts: upside-down apple pie with caramel sauce and the signature Chocolate Bag (a bag made of chocolate and filled with white chocolate mousse and fresh berries).

MEZZOGIORNO

195 Spring St (at Sullivan St)   212/334-2112
Lunch, Dinner: Daily   mezzogiorno.com
Moderate

Mezzogiorno has long been considered the meeting and greeting place for downtown art and fashion trendies. The place is busy and noisy, and tables are close together, so you might want to opt for an outside table in nice weather. The decor is best described as "modern Florence." Enticing recipes are simple and authentic Italian. The salad selection is outstanding, and their lasagna is one of Manhattan's best. Mezzogiorno is also famous for pizza, with over a dozen choices.

You'll find all the ingredients for a wonderful make-believe evening in Tuscany right here in the heart of Manhattan.

MICHAEL'S
24 W 55th St (bet Fifth Ave and Ave of the Americas)   212/767-0555
Breakfast, Lunch: Mon-Fri; Dinner: Mon-Sat   michaelsnewyork.com
Moderately expensive to expensive

Located conveniently for shoppers, business types, hotel visitors, and the like, this very attractive restaurant would best be described as "a midtown scene." Its several rooms are filled with modern art treasures and fresh flowers. Service is professional and attentive. You'll see some familiar media faces, society types, important-looking business execs, and ordinary fat-walleted gawkers. While items can be pricey, there is no question about the quality or presentation. Appetizers and small plates include clams, oysters, duck confit sliders, and Korean steak tacos. Ravioli, sweet potato noodles, and crab pizza are tasty offerings. Perhaps the real treat is the fabulous Cobb salad, one of the best in New York. Prepare to splurge!

MILLESIME
The Carlton Hotel
92 Madison Ave (bet 28th and 29th St)   212/889-7100
Breakfast: Daily; Lunch: Mon-Fri; Dinner: Mon-Sat; Brunch: Sun
Moderately expensive   millesimerestaurant.com

Millesime is a charming, beautiful brasserie with tile floors, soaring walls, and a Tiffany skylight dome. This French seafood restaurant offers the old and the new — like wonderful fresh bread, a really good Caesar salad, and the almost forgotten quenelles (a seasoned dumpling of fish, meat, and poultry) with rich lobster sauce. Expertly prepared shellfish platters for two, four, or eight people will certainly satisfy. Finger bowls bring back the days of class dining, apt for a restaurant whose name literally means "vintage." Breakfasts will appease American and French palates alike, with cold cereal, eggs en cocotte, and many other choices.

MINETTA TAVERN
113 MacDougal St (at Bleecker St)   212/475-3850
Dinner: Daily; Brunch: Sat, Sun   minettatavernny.com
Moderate

Keith McNally and his team run this longtime Greenwich Village favorite. "Parisian steakhouse meets classic New York City tavern" best describes this house. Minetta's ambience: vintage wall mural, red-leather banquettes, photo gallery, and a long mahogany bar up front have been preserved. Located where Minetta Brook wandered through Manhattan in the early days, this tavern was made famous by Eddie "Minetta" Sieveri, a friend of many sports and stage stars of yesteryear.

Pork Anyone?
If you are craving a great pork dinner, then a trip to tiny **Porchetta** (110 E 7th St, 212/777-2151) is a must. They also have great roast potatoes and a vegetarian dish. The ambience and delicious aromas will delight you. Whether you eat in or take out, you won't leave Porchetta hungry, sorry, or broke.

Food Trucks

Not that long ago the only trucks roaming the streets with things to eat were the summertime ice-cream vendors. Times have changed! Contemporary New York food trucks are large, artfully decorated, and outfitted with kitchens to prepare and serve pastries, sandwiches, soups, full meals, even freshly cooked French fries. Some have become so successful that they have led to bricks-and-mortar restaurants. The bottom line is that food trucks now offer an easy option for a quick snack anywhere in the city. There are websites to help you choose a truck by location and cuisine (findnycfoodtrucks.com).

Comfort dishes like great burgers, pastas, and meat and potatoes are featured. Everyone is made to feel comfortable here. Night owls will appreciate the supper menu, offered from midnight to 1 a.m.

MISS LILY'S FAVOURITE CAKES

132 W Houston St (near Sullivan St)   646/588-5375
Lunch: Mon-Fri; Dinner: Daily; Brunch: Sat, Sun   misslilysnyc.com
Moderate

A lot is happening at Miss Lily's Caribbean-isle diner. The sound of Jamaican music throbs throughout the rooms which are decorated with vintage record albums and unpretentious (read: plastic and Formica) furnishings. Authentic jerk chicken is offered as an entree with salad, rice, and peas as well as one of three main ingredient choices for jaquitos (the house version of mini tacos). A couple of menu standouts, corn on the cob (grilled with jerk spices and finished with toasted coconut) and festivals (cornmeal fritters), should be a part of any meal. There are other tasty mains and, of course, a favorite cake of the day. Miss Lily's Bake Shop and Melvin's Juice Box is a more casual outpost next door for fresh juices, shakes, sandwiches, salads, and Caribbean classics (open daily for eat-in or take-out).

THE MODERN

Museum of Modern Art
9 W 53rd St (bet Fifth Ave and Ave of the Americas)   212/333-1220
Lunch: Mon-Fri; Dinner: Mon-Sat (Dining room)   themodernnyc.com
Lunch, Dinner: Daily (Bar Room)
Museum hours (Cafe 2 and Terrace 5)
Moderate to moderately expensive (The Modern and Bar Room)

Both the Museum of Modern Art and its dining venues are special New York treats. Under the expert eye of restaurateur Danny Meyer, the museum features four unique dining venues. The Modern's stunning and elegant **Dining Room** features a grand view of the outdoor sculpture garden and offers *prix-fixe* menus of chef Gabriel Kreuther's exquisite, contemporary French-American cuisine. Sturgeon and sauerkraut tart and rabbit-truffle Alsatian dumplings are tasty offerings. Next door, the more casual and vibrant **Bar Room** offers small plates of Alsatian-inspired cuisine. The tarte flambé is worth a visit in itself. **Cafe 2** and **Terrace 5** are located within the museum on the upper floors and are accessible to museum visitors only, with some dishes aimed at quick service and kids.

MORANDI

211 Waverly Pl (at Seventh Ave S)   212/627-7575
Breakfast, Lunch: Mon-Fri; Dinner: Daily; Brunch: Sat, Sun   morandiny.com
Moderate

For the Italian food lover who wants authentic dishes without a huge tab, Morandi is the ultimate. The setting is comfortable and inviting, the service prompt, and the menu unbelievably complete. You'll find every antipasti, salad, and primi and secondi piatti you could imagine. The paninis and pastas are delicious. Daily specials are anticipated by regular customers. I recommend meatballs with pine nuts and raisins or dry-aged porterhouse with rosemary for two. You can even come for a hearty Italian breakfast served with Morandi's delicious bread. The homemade gelati is excellent.

MORAN'S CHELSEA

146 Tenth Ave (at 19th St)   212/627-3030
Lunch, Dinner: Daily; Brunch: Sat, Sun   moranschelsea.com
Moderate

The years have been kind to this exceptionally charming tavern, complete with fireplaces in every room, hardwood paneling, large and attractive party facilities, and a cozy bar that survived Prohibition days. There is copper everywhere you look. The old tin ceiling adds a special dimension. A traditional and contemporary American menu offers fresh seafood, aged chops, lobster, crab cakes, steaks, lamb, salmon, scallops, prime rib, and shepherd's pie. You'll also find excellent burgers, fresh salads, and a few pastas. If you are looking for a unique venue for a group of up to 200, I strongly suggest checking out Moran's. The personnel are friendly and accommodating.

THE MORGAN DINING ROOM

The Morgan Library and Museum
225 Madison Ave (bet 36th and 37th St)   212/683-2130
Lunch: Tues-Fri; Brunch: Sat, Sun   themorgan.org
Moderate

The Morgan Library and Museum is a grand place to visit, and you can extend the experience by eating in the cozy dining room where J.P. Morgan himself broke bread. It is a great place to meet friends, and the tab is surprisingly friendly. First courses include salads, soups, and seasonal gravlax. Among the tasty entrees are large salads, wild white shrimp, and grilled poussin. Director Patricia Japngie has assembled a friendly staff.

MORTON'S THE STEAKHOUSE

551 Fifth Ave (at 45th St)   212/972-3315
Lunch: Mon-Fri; Dinner: Daily   mortons.com
Moderately expensive to expensive

A recent makeover at Morton's uptown location gives both the dining room and bar a sleek, modern design. Not only is the decor inviting, but every member of the highly efficient staff at this high-end franchised steakhouse has been trained in the Morton's manner — personalized service! Appetizers are heavy in the seafood department. Shrimp, oysters, smoked salmon, sea scallops, and salads are attractive and appetizing. The steaks and lamb chops are so tender you can cut

> **Theme Restaurants**
>
> Check out these splashy operations, which are good, kid-friendly party venues.
>
> **Barking Dog Luncheonette** (1678 Third Ave, 212/831-1800 and other locations): canine themed; dogs welcome
>
> **Hard Rock Cafe** (1501 Broadway, 212/489-6565): Elvis has not left the building.
>
> **Jekyll and Hyde** (91 Seventh Ave S, 212/989-7701): haunted!
>
> **Ninja New York** (25 Hudson St, 212/274-8500): subterranean, secret paths
>
> **Planet Hollywood** (1540 Broadway, 212/333-7827): memorabilia galore

them with a fork, and they arrive promptly, too. (Not the case in many steakhouses.) There are several potato choices, including wonderful hash browns. Sauteed spinach with mushrooms and steamed broccoli and asparagus are fresh and tasty. Top it all off with a delicious soufflé — chocolate, Grand Marnier, lemon, or raspberry — that's large enough for two. The busy bar offers Bar Bites, a menu of tasty small plates of salads, sandwiches, pizza, seafood, and various other appetizers. Morton's will have an upcoming Freedom Tower location for late 2013.

MR. K'S

570 Lexington Ave (at 51st St)   212/583-1668
Lunch, Dinner: Daily   mrksny.com
Moderately expensive to expensive

Mr. K's is an elegant, art deco Chinese dining room where high-powered politicos and famous celebrities come to dine. Whet your appetite with Shanghai spring rolls, dumplings, and a delicious seafood dish of sauteed lobster, shrimp, and scallops. Of course, there is chicken and corn chowder; in my opinion, no Chinese dinner is complete without it. Share an assortment of plates with your table partners: lemon chicken, Peking duck, honey-braised pork ribs, baked Chilean sea bass, and sesame prawns with shiitake mushrooms. If you like spicy dishes, try the firecracker prawns with Szechuan sauce!

NAPLES 45

MetLife Building
200 Park Ave (45th St at Vanderbilt Ave)   212/972-7001
Breakfast, Lunch, Dinner: Mon-Fri   patinagroup.com
Moderate

Naples 45 may well be the best pizza house in Manhattan! Absolutely delicious, authentic Neapolitan pizzas are made with caputo flour (imported from Southern Italy) and other tasty ingredients. Cooked in an oak-burning oven, the pizzas are a sight to behold and taste. You have your choice of individual ten-inch pizzas or their "Mezzo Metro," large enough to feed three or four persons. Other offerings include small dishes (like veal meatballs and baked eggplant), pizza-oven sandwiches, soups, seafood, pastas, and salads. Takeout and delivery are available, as is patio dining in nice weather. The place can be jammed!

NICOLA'S

146 E 84th St (bet Lexington and Third Ave)   212/249-9850
Dinner: Daily   nicolasnyc.com
Moderately expensive

Upper-crust New Yorkers who like a clubby atmosphere and good food — which are not often found together — love this place! At times the noise level rivals that of a Broadway opening. In a setting of rich wood with familiar framed faces on the walls, no-nonsense waiters serve delicious platters of pasta, veal, chicken, and fish. The emphasis is Italian, and there are inviting daily specials in every category.

NINJA NEW YORK

25 Hudson St (bet Duane and Reade St)   212/274-8500
Lunch: Sat, Sun (in summer); Dinner: Daily   ninjanewyork.com
Moderately expensive

Be prepared for loads of fun and the unexpected as you enter a ninja village re-creation — fire, chants, screams, swords, hand signals, and costumed ninja servers — all while enjoying a Japanese-style dinner. This is a perfect spot to celebrate with friends in either the Village or Rock Garden dining rooms. Dine on sushi, sashimi, appetizers, a variety of main courses, and desserts, many of which are prepared and served with special effects. The signature dish, Katana, is angus steak with fried risotto and Alaska king crab with tomato mango sauce. Kids will get a kick out of the ninja antics; there's even a special menu for guests under 12. Beware of ninjas dropping in from the ceiling or appearing out of nowhere.

NOBU FIFTY SEVEN

40 W 57th St (bet Fifth Ave and Ave of the Americas)   212/757-3000
Lunch: Mon-Sat; Dinner: Daily

NOBU NEW YORK

105 Hudson St (at Franklin St)   212/219-0500
Lunch: Mon-Fri; Dinner: Daily

NOBU NEXT DOOR

105 Hudson St (at Franklin St)   212/334-4445
Dinner: Daily   noburestaurants.com
Expensive

Nobu Matsuhisa and partners have put together spectacular venues for those who love sushi and great Japanese food that's not too complex and unfailingly tasty. Yes, these places are busy and expensive, but they are worth every penny and any frustrating wait for reservations. Because I like salty dishes, this menu appeals to me. The Nobu eateries are classy and crowded, with an unmistakable party atmosphere. Sitting at the sushi bar allows you to watch the well-trained staff perform like a symphony orchestra. A wood-burning oven adds to the splendid array of dishes. The black cod is a standout. Dozens of sushi and

---

Raw Bars

Connoisseurs of raw-bar delicacies will find these spots to be some of the best in the city. The assortment depends on market availability.

Aquagrill (210 Spring St, 212/274-0505)

Atlantic Grill (1341 Third Ave, 212/988-9200 and 49 W 64th St, 212/787-4663)

Balthazar (80 Spring St, 212/965-1414)

Blue Ribbon (97 Sullivan St, 212/274-0404)

Grand Central Oyster Bar Restaurant (Grand Central Terminal, 42nd St at Vanderbilt Ave, lower level, 212/490-6650)

Marea (240 Central Park S, 212/582-5100)

The Mark Restaurant by Jean-Georges (The Mark, 25 E 77th St, 212/606-3030)

Momofuku Ssäm Bar (207 Second Ave, 212/254-3500)

Ocean Grill (384 Columbus Ave, 212/579-2300)

Oceana (McGraw-Hill Building, 120 W 49th St, 212/759-5941)

Pearl Oyster Bar (18 Cornelia St, 212/691-8211)

---

sashimi selections are available. The chef's choice multicourse *omakase* dinner is an excellent pick. Fresh, delicious salads abound. Leave room for the Bento Box dessert: warm chocolate soufflé cake with green-tea ice cream. You're going to pay well for all these treats — especially if you have the Wagyu beef — but you'll leave relishing a very special dining experience. **Nobu to Go** (105 Hudson St) is available for takeout orders every evening.

NORTH END GRILL

104 North End Ave (bet Murray and Vesey St) 646/747-1600
Lunch: Mon-Fri; Dinner: Daily; Brunch: Sat, Sun northendgrillnyc.com
Moderately expensive

Nowadays you can find one of Danny Meyer's restaurants seemingly anywhere in Manhattan; he has used his magic touch to bring us some of the city's best eating places. One of his newer establishments is way downtown at Battery Park City; the location is next to a new Conrad Hotel. The North End Grill puts out very good food. Typically, the service is prompt and informative, and the buzz is definitely present. You may enjoy eating at a bar (open for drinks all day) looking into the open kitchen or in the more formal dining room. The market-driven menu is seafood-centric and emphasizes a variety of grilling techniques. For starters, you'll find oysters on the half shell, or a unique grilled clam pizza. On to a number of egg dishes, then a fine selection of salads. I loved the charcoal-grilled albacore with green lentils, olives, and linguica sausage. The pork chop or whole wood-fire-grilled branzino are delicious entrees; try a side of super thrice-fried spiced fries. For dessert, the winner is the butterscotch pot de crème with chocolate streusel and "single maltmallows." Genial General Manager Kevin Richer keeps the place going in typical professional Meyer style.

OCEAN GRILL

384 Columbus Ave (at 78th St)   212/579-2300
Lunch: Mon-Sat; Dinner: Daily; Brunch: Sun   oceangrill.com
Moderate to moderately expensive

Ocean Grill is one of the few good seafood restaurants on the Upper West Side. Watching the passing parade from an outside table is fun. Popular with young professionals, the place is quite noisy. To start, the raw bar offers a selection of oysters and sushi. Ocean Grill's feature is the rotating menu of simply grilled fish — salmon, tuna, mahi-mahi, wild striped bass, and more — prepared with your choice of marinades and sauces. For a party, chilled shellfish towers offer a selection of lobster, clams, crab, oysters, shrimp, and more. Other attractions include crab cakes, lobster bisque, and seafood Cobb salad, as well as three-course *prix-fixe* options at lunch and dinner. For brunch, various omelets and benedicts, as well as blueberry and buttermilk pancakes, are good bets.

OCEANA

McGraw-Hill Building
120 W 49th St (bet Ave of the Americas and Seventh Ave)   212/759-5941
Lunch: Mon-Fri; Dinner: Daily   oceanarestaurant.com
Expensive

For the freshest seafood meal, you'll want to dine at Oceana. The location is spot-on. So is the 50-foot-long Italian marble bar, featuring nightly specials and interesting potent drink concoctions. It's all here — cafe and raw bar, private dining, and small bites — each item outstandingly prepared to capture the best flavor of the fresh catch. Check the menu for seafood towers (appropriately named the Radio City, the Rock, and the Oceana), herb-crusted halibut, potato gnocchi, and carrot waffle with toasted coriander ice cream. Oceana is an ideal choice for pre- and post-theater functions.

OLIVES NEW YORK

W New York Union Square
201 Park Ave S (at 17th St)   212/353-8345
Breakfast, Lunch: Mon-Fri; Dinner: Daily; Brunch: Sat, Sun   olivesnewyork.com
Moderate

For foodies, this is the place! The trendy crowd seems to like the modern Mediterranean influence of Todd English's open-kitchen charmer. A spirited atmosphere with a modern and sexy new design combines with superbly trained personnel and great food to make a pleasant dining experience. Portions are big, with delicious handcrafted pastas high on the list. If your tastes are not too fancy, the burgers are good and the whole wheat banana waffles with caramelized bananas, toasted coconut, and fondue are "to die for."

ONE IF BY LAND, TWO IF BY SEA

17 Barrow St (bet Seventh Ave and 4th St)   212/255-8649
Dinner: Daily; Brunch: Sun   oneifbyland.com
Expensive

One if by Land, Two if by Sea is housed in an 18th-century carriage house once owned by Aaron Burr. Allow extra time to find this place, as Barrow Street (one of the West Village's most charming) is generally unknown to taxi drivers,

Rosanjin Tribeca

For a serene, intimate, and very expensive Japanese dining experience, head down to **Rosanjin Tribeca** (141 Duane St, 212/346-0664). Dishes are served a la carte or as a several-course kaiseki dinner ($80 to $200). Service to the nine tables is impeccable. Major ingredients are imported from Japan, while seasonal produce and fish are sourced locally. Saké is served by the carafe or bottle, with pairings for the multicourse dinners. Japanese beer is also available.

and there's no sign out front! Candlelight, flowers, a fireplace, and background piano music all add to the ambience of this romantic room. Tables at the front of the balcony are particularly appealing. Individual beef Wellington, poached lobster, and lamb chop cassoulet are excellent choices on the three-course *prix-fixe* menu. A chef's tasting menu is also available. Strawberry brioche French toast served at brunch is quite tasty.

ONIEAL'S GRAND STREET

174 Grand St (bet Lafayette and Mulberry St) 212/941-9119
Dinner, Late Night Menu, Brunch: Daily onieals.com
Moderate

This legendary and historic former speakeasy, with its secret tunnel to the old police headquarters, evokes memories of days long past. Housed beneath a 150-year-old hand-carved mahogany ceiling, this bar, lounge, and restaurant achieved latter-day celebrity as a backdrop on HBO's *Sex and the City*. You'll find marinated grilled yellowfin tuna, Cobb salad, hanger steak au poivre, shitake risotto, and one of the best burgers in town. For dessert, try the Four Devils chocolate cake (named after the four devils intricately carved into the ceiling). Service at Onieal's is friendly and efficient.

ORSO

322 W 46th St (bet Eighth and Ninth Ave) 212/489-7212
Lunch, Dinner: Daily; Brunch: Sun orsorestaurant.com
Moderate

The same menu is featured all day long at this cozy midtown trattoria, which is great for theatergoers or others with unusual dining hours. Orso is one of the most popular places on "restaurant row," so if you're planning to dine here, be sure to make reservations. The intimate room is watched over by a portrait of Orso, a Venetian street dog who served as the restaurant's inspiration. The ever-changing menu offers many good salads, appetizers, and small plates, as well as a variety of pizzas and pasta dishes. Venetian-style sauteed calves liver and oven roasted quail with faro and sausage are two popular regional favorites. .The apple crostate with vanilla gelato, one of many homemade desserts, will finish off a great meal. A special Sunday brunch menu is available.

OSTERIA MORINI

218 Lafayette St (bet Kenmare and Spring St) 212/965-8777
Lunch: Mon-Fri; Dinner: Daily; Brunch: Sat, Sun osteriamorini.com
Moderate to moderately expensive

This is not just another Italian restaurant! Osteria Morini, under the capable direction of chef Michael White, is a superb Northern Italian house. Calorie-counting is out and great taste is the order of each meal. Diners will find a bit of Old World decor, a lot of noise, and waiters who can't do enough for their patrons. The handmade pastas, like tortellini zingara (meat filled with peas, red peppers, and cream) or the gnocchi (ricotta dumplings) will please any discerning palate. A number of veal, Cornish hen, and fish dishes (like grilled sea bass), plus pork chops and succulent braised beef short ribs round out the delicious menu. Chef White is the consummate host, delighting in personally visiting with his guests. I would hope that he is cooking the night you are there.

OUEST

2315 Broadway (at 84th St)   212/580-8700
Dinner: Daily; Brunch: Sun   ouestny.com
Moderate

Ouest continues to be overflowing with happy locals enjoying one of the best rooms in the city. The comfortable booths, open kitchen, cozy (if dark and noisy) balcony, and pleasant serving staff combine to make Thomas Valenti's jewel first-class. This is not surprising with Valenti's vast experience. The bistro menu is inviting, with appetizer choices like oyster "pan roast," goat-cheese ravioli, and several fresh salads. Crispy duck breast and medallions of lamb melt in your mouth. Nightly specials include meatloaf on Sunday. From delicious warm bread at the start to rich chocolate cake for dessert, the experience at Ouest is pure pleasure.

OUR PLACE

242 E 79th St (bet Second and Third Ave)   212/288-4888
Lunch: Mon-Fri; Dinner: Daily; Brunch: Sat, Sun   ourplace79.com
Moderate

Our Place is not a typical Chinese restaurant. Classy service, moderate prices, and delicious food have been its trademarks for more than 23 years. Appreciative Upper East Siders keep its two bright and spacious dining rooms filled for nearly every meal. Many favorite traditional Chinese dishes are on the menu — enjoy moo shu pork, tangerine beef, Szechuan chicken, duck-wrapped lettuce with pine nuts, home-style chicken casserole, and Peking duck, plus dim sum on weekends. Free delivery is offered in a wide area. Prices are as comfortable as the chairs.

P.J. CLARKE'S

915 Third Ave (at 55th St)   212/317-1616

P.J. CLARKE'S AT LINCOLN SQUARE

44 W 63rd St (at Columbus Ave)   212/957-9700

P.J. CLARKE'S ON THE HUDSON

World Financial Center, Building 4, lobby
250 Vesey St (bet West St and North End Ave)   212/285-1500
Lunch, Dinner: Daily   pjclarkes.com
Moderate

Beginning in 1884 as a saloon, P.J. Clarke's can rightfully be called a Manhattan institution. Every day at lunch and dinner, regulars are joined by hordes of visitors

Dining in Harlem

Harlem has a growing share of respectable dining options.

Amy Ruth's (113 W 116th St, 212/280-8779): soul food; excellent chicken and waffles

Dinosaur Bar-B-Que (700 W 125th St, 212/694-1777): affordable roadhouse barbecue

Melba's (300 W 114th St, 212/864-7777): down south comfort food; live music Tuesdays

Miss Maude's Spoonbread Too (547 Lenox Ave, 212/690-3100): pork chops and spoonbread, of course

Patsy's Pizzeria (2287-2291 First Ave, 212/534-9783): since 1933

Rao's (455 E 114th St, 212/722-6709): famous Italian landmark

Red Rooster Harlem (310 Lenox Ave, 212/792-9001): affordable comfort food

Settepani (196 Lenox Ave, 917/492-4806): Italian; breakfast, too

Sylvia's (328 Lenox Ave, 212/996-0660): soul food and Sunday entertainment

guzzling at the liquor bar, eyeing the raw bar, or fighting for a table. No one is disappointed with the sizable platters, great burgers, and fresh seafood. Check out the daily blackboard specials and numerous tasty sides. Service is highly professional, and the price is right. Upstairs at the Third Avenue location, you'll be taken with the decor at **The Sidecar** (212/317-2044), which has its own kitchen and entrance. All patrons at P.J. Clarke's on the Hudson have a stunning view of New York Harbor and the Statue of Liberty. A seasonal cafe alongside the marina is great for leisurely dining. The 63rd Street locale is a stellar place before or after a performance at Lincoln Center.

THE PALM

837 Second Ave (at 44th St)	212/687-2953
Lunch: Mon-Fri; Dinner: Mon-Sat	
840 Second Ave (at 44th St)	212/697-5198
Lunch: Mon-Fri; Dinner: Daily	
206 West St (at Warren St)	646/395-6393
Lunch: Mon-Fri; Dinner: Daily	
250 W 50th St (bet Eighth Ave and Broadway)	212/333-7256
Lunch: Mon-Sat; Dinner: Daily	thepalm.com
Expensive	

Steak and lobster lovers still have a special place in their hearts for the Palm (a.k.a. Palm One), even with the glut of steakhouses in Manhattan. The original location started on Second Avenue as a speakeasy in 1926. Now there are three more locations with much the same atmosphere – masculine and earthy – so don't get too dressed up. The newest (Palm Tribeca, on West St) is steps from the Financial District and Battery Park. They're noted for huge, delicious steaks, chops, and jumbo Nova Scotia lobster. Don't miss the terrific "half and half" (cottage fries and onion rings). Daily specials vary among the Palm locations. Unfortunately, indolent waiters may be a part of the scene.

PAOLA'S

Hotel Wales
1295 Madison Ave (at 92nd St)   212/794-1890
Lunch, Dinner: Daily; Brunch: Sat, Sun   paolasrestaurant.com
Moderately expensive

For a romantic evening, Paola's is a wonderful and welcoming place in the Hotel Wales! The Italian home cooking is first-class, with matriarch Paola overseeing the kitchen. Great filled pastas (like squash ravioli and sausage) and superb veal dishes are served with tasty hot vegetables. Top it all off with a slice of rich ricotta cheesecake or lemon tart. Casual sidewalk dining is offered in summer months.

PARK SIDE

107-01 Corona Ave (51st Ave at 108th St), Queens   718/271-9274
Lunch, Dinner: Daily   parksiderestaurantny.com
Moderate to moderately expensive

I've included this landmark Italian restaurant because it is exceptional, even though it is outside of Manhattan. Visit Park Side, in Queens, if you want to show someone who claims to know everything about New York a place he or she likely hasn't heard about. Or eat here on your way to or from LaGuardia or Kennedy Airport. This first-class, spotlessly clean restaurant serves large portions of wonderful Italian food at affordable prices. Start with garlic bread and then choose from over 20 kinds of pasta and an opulent array of fish, steak, veal, and poultry dishes. The meat is all prime-cut and fresh — nothing frozen. Finish with a choice from the extensive dessert menu. You'll find polite, knowledgeable waiters in an informal atmosphere. Get a table in the Garden Room or the Marilyn Monroe Room upstairs. Eat to your heart's content, and be pleasantly surprised at the tab.

PASTIS

9 Ninth Ave (at Little West 12th St)   212/929-4844
Breakfast, Lunch: Mon-Fri; Dinner: Daily; Brunch: Sat, Sun   pastisny.com
Moderately expensive

Keith McNally, who knows how to present a restaurant, turned this Meatpacking District warehouse into one of the highest energy rooms in Manhattan. The communal table is a nice touch in the center of the dining space for singles and others who do not want to wait in the reservation line. Note: Pastis will be on temporary hiatus beginning in January 2014 for about nine months due to building construction.

PATSY'S ITALIAN RESTAURANT

236 W 56th St (bet Broadway and Eighth Ave)   212/247-3491
Lunch, Dinner: Daily   patsys.com
Moderate to moderately expensive

The Scognamillo family has operated this popular eatery since 1944, specializing in Neapolitan cuisine. At present, Patsy and Concetta's son, Joe, and grandson, Frank, are taking care of the front of the house, while another grandson, chef Sal,

David Chang's Empire

What is momofuku? It translates into "lucky peach," but in the dining arena it is the domain of chef David Chang. His original **Momofuku Noodle Bar** (171 First Ave, 212/475- 7899) is open daily for lunch and dinner. You'll find noodles, small dishes, and a large variety of small plates, with items changing by the season, plus heritage pork and shellfish offerings.

Momofuku Ssäm Bar (207 Second Ave, 212/254-3500) is open daily for lunch and dinner. This noisy place first offers a choice of ssäm (a kind of wrap) or bowl, pork shoulder steak, roasted scallops, shanghai noodles and cranberry beans. You won't go away hungry. Best description: earthy, Asian-accented New American. Reserve ahead for their feast!

Momofuku Milk Bar (251 E 13th St, 15 W 56th St, and 561 Columbus Ave; 347/577-9504 for all locations) does justice to pies, cakes, breads, cookies, and croissants. Many are their own concoctions, with names like dream girl pie and compost cookie. But where's the peach?

Inside Chambers Hotel, **Má Pêche** (15 W 56th St, 212/757-5878; online reservations only) presents a New American menu of small plates like trout Sichuan, shrimpballs, and pork buns. Changing entrees include tasty roasted lamb brisket or fried rice with duck and sweet potato. Delicious bakery goods from the Momofuku Milk Bar delight the neighborhood crowd.

The 12-seat **Momofuku Ko** (163 First Ave) is one of the hardest restaurants in town to score a lunch or dinner reservation. Prices hover around $125 to $175 per plate for the multicourse, three-hour meal. This is superb eclectic dining, if you have the patience to wait for a seat. There are no walk-ins, and reservations are accepted only online (momofuku. com) seven days in advance. Good luck!

is following the family tradition in the kitchen. "Patsy" was an immigrant gentleman chef whose nickname graces this bilevel restaurant. Each floor has its own cozy atmosphere and convenient kitchen. The family makes sure that every party is treated with courtesy and concern, as if they are in a private home. A full Italian menu includes a special soup and seafood entree each day. If you can't find what you like among the more than a dozen pasta choices and the many signature dishes — chicken cacciatore, veal chop *siciliano*, or stuffed calamari — you are in deep trouble! There are also *prix-fixe* lunch and dinner (pre-theater) menus, which are convenient if you are headed to Lincoln Center, Carnegie Hall, or the Theater District.

PERILLA

9 Jones St (bet Bleecker and 4th St)   212/929-6868
Dinner: Daily; Brunch: Sat, Sun   perillanyc.com
Moderate to moderately expensive

For a leisurely weekend brunch in the Village, Perilla is a good bet. With equal quality in both food and service, this neighborhood hideaway offers an ever-changing New American menu of satisfying flavors. For brunch, creamy white grits, vanilla scented doughnuts, and French toast are tasty choices. Of course there are nightly dinners, too. Try spicy duck meatballs or the Monday night bourbon barbecue tasting. I found the dessert offerings to be particularly appealing. The cheese selection is excellent and reasonably priced. The milk chocolate malted cake or vanilla panna cotta with grapefruit sorbet are interesting choices. Perilla really packs a lot into a compact, informal space of 18 tables and ten bar seats.

PERSHING SQUARE
90 E 42nd St (at Park Ave)   212/286-9600
Breakfast: Daily; Lunch: Mon-Fri; Dinner: Daily; Brunch: Sat, Sun
Moderate   pershingsquare.com

Pershing Square serves throngs of hungry local and traveling New Yorkers in a space opposite Grand Central Terminal. The odd-shaped room is full of energy and conversation, much of it relating to the broad variety of menu offerings. For those who missed breakfast before boarding their train, Pershing Square offers Irish oatmeal, eggs Benedict, brioche French toast, and great buttermilk or whole-wheat pancakes. Omelets are a specialty. Lunch and dinner items include seafood dishes, boneless beef short ribs, roast chicken, steaks, and pastas. The grilled ham-burger with a choice of cheese or crispy fries is a winner any time of day. Seafood dishes — like seared yellowfin tuna, seared sea scallops over angel hair pasta, and grilled Atlantic salmon — are popular for dinner. Try coconut cream for dessert. A friendly wait staff and an attractive bar are pluses.

PETER LUGER STEAK HOUSE
178 Broadway (at Driggs Ave), Brooklyn   718/387-7400
Lunch, Dinner: Daily   peterluger.com
Expensive

If it's steak you want, you simply can't do better than Peter Luger Steak House. Their reputation is sometimes larger than the restaurant itself! Folks don't come to this bustling spot for the ambience or service. The menu makes it simple: your choices are steak for one, two, three, or four. The creamed spinach and steak sauce (which they sell by the bottle) are out of this world. Daily luncheon specials include pot roast, roast prime rib, and chopped steak. Peter Luger is only a stone's throw from Manhattan (take the first right off the Williamsburg Bridge), and the staff is accustomed to ordering cabs. Making reservations well in advance is suggested.

PICHOLINE
35 W 64th St (bet Broadway and Central Park W)   212/724-8585
Dinner: Daily   picholinenyc.com
Moderately expensive to expensive

Terrance Brennan showcases his culinary expertise in this attractive restau-rant near Lincoln Center. The warm atmosphere is achieved through the use of dusky lavender, shades of purple, and crystal chandeliers; a perfect backdrop for the seasonal, Mediterranean-inspired plates. The many positives include outstand-ing service, perfectly done fish dishes, superbly prepared game, and daily classic cuisine specials. There are two private dining options: the intimate wine room (seats four to eight) is lined with 2,500 wine bottles and features a cheese cave; the elegant L'Olivier Room seats up to 22 guests. I always look forward to the

Update on Post House Dining

The **Post House** restaurant in The Lowell hotel on the Upper East Side is closing in August 2013 for a six-month renovation. This is according to the Department of Labor. It is yet to be determined if this tiny steakhouse will return or be replaced with another restaurant in the magnificent lobby setting.

magnificent cheese dessert cart, with more than 60 artisanal cheeses. Jackets are preferred for gentlemen. There is also a separate wine and cheese bar.

PIETRO'S

232 E 43rd St (bet Second and Third Ave)   212/682-9760
Lunch: Mon-Fri; Dinner: Mon-Sat (closed Sat in summer)   pietros.com
Moderately expensive to expensive

Pietro's is a steakhouse featuring Northern Italian cuisine. Everything is cooked to order. Tell your companions not to bother dressing up. Bring an appetite, however, because portions are huge. Although they're best known for delicious steaks, you will also find abundant chicken and veal selections (marsala, cacciatore, scaloppine, piccata, francaise, etc.), seafood, chops, pasta, and nine potato dishes. Prices border on expensive, but you'll certainly get your money's worth. By the way, Pietro's is very child-friendly.

PLAZA FOOD HALL BY TODD ENGLISH

The Plaza
1 W 59th St (at Fifth Ave), lower level   212/986-9260
Daily: 11:30-10   toddenglish.com
Varying price ranges

The concourse of the famed Plaza Hotel is alive with tantalizing aromas, beautiful foods, and the bustle of diners and shoppers enjoying an eclectic array of edible (and nonedible) choices by Chef Todd English. There is something for everyone at the inviting food stations, whether you choose to sit at the counter areas or take out. The offerings include a bakery, sushi bar, cheese and charcuterie, fresh seafood and raw bar, grill (sliders, salads, and burgers), dumpling bar, brick-oven pizza, wine bar, and seasonal marketplace. A demo kitchen features cooking classes, wine tastings, and other events. Fresh, local ingredients are widely used. A discerning selection of gift baskets, cookware, and home goods adds to the appeal of this destination.

PÓ

31 Cornelia St (bet Bleecker and 4th St)   212/645-2189
Lunch: Wed-Sun; Dinner: Daily   porestaurant.com
Moderate to moderately expensive

Steven Crane has found the formula for a successful eating establishment. The small space is always busy! The service is family-friendly, informed, and quick. The food is hearty, imaginative, and exceptionally tasty. The prices are right. As I have noted before, if the bread is good, chances are what follows will be also. Pó has crusty, fresh Italian bread. The creative pasta dishes — tagliatelle, fettuccine, linguine, and a special or two — are huge. Other entrees (like grilled salmon or veal picatta) are available, along with lunch paninis like grilled portobello with roasted peppers. Affogato, an unusual and satisfying dessert, consists of coffee gelato in chilled cappuccino with chocolate caramel sauce.

PRINT

Ink48
653 Eleventh Ave (at 48th St)   212/757-2224
Breakfast, Lunch: Mon-Fri; Dinner: Daily; Brunch: Sat, Sun   printrestaurant.com
Moderate

On the far reaches of the West side, this attractive dining spot is located off the hotel lobby of Ink48. The mood is modern and comfortable, with pleasant personnel serving farm-to-table dishes that are uniformly tasty. Chef Charles Rodriguez is in the kitchen serving up fresh salads, chicken, soups, steak, and whatever else makes a traveler happy. The crab salad with roasted beets and avocado is delicious, and the braised short ribs and grilled pork chops are first-class. The extensive brunch menu features steamed mussels, a yogurt parfait, and an excellent burger with exceptional French fries piled high. On a clear day be sure to visit the rooftop lounge, Press, for fantastic views of the city.

QUALITY MEATS

57 W 58th St (bet Fifth Ave and Ave of the Americas)   212/371-7777
Lunch: Mon-Fri; Dinner: Daily   qualitymeatsnyc.com
Moderately expensive to expensive

Michael Stillman — son of Smith & Wollensky boss Alan Stillman — operates a quasi-steakhouse that's become popular with younger meat lovers. It has a butcher-shop look on several levels. Outstanding chef Craig Koketsu is in the kitchen, and the wait staff really know what they are doing. Quality Meats has all

James Beard House

167 W 12th St (bet Ave of the Americas and Seventh Ave) 212/675-4984
jamesbeard.org

Attention, foodies! The legendary James Beard had roots in Oregon, so anything to do with his life is of special interest to this author. He was a familiar personality on the Oregon coast, where he delighted in serving the superb seafood for which the region is famous. When Beard died in 1985, his Greenwich Village brownstone was put on the market and purchased by a group headed by the late Julia Child. Now the home is run by the nonprofit James Beard Foundation and features continuing education and kids' programs, as well as tastings, readings, and tours. Notable chefs show off their substantial talents here. This is a great opportunity for a one-on-one with some really interesting folks as an observer or volunteer. Call or check the website for scheduled events. The foundation's private boardroom is a unique, elegant dining space for a special gathering. Schedule a multicourse tasting with a renowned chef (up to 12 guests) for an exceptional epicurean experience!

Traditional Italian

Italian restaurants are on both sides of Little Italy's Mulberry Street. At one time, this was the seat of superb Italian cuisine, but times have changed. **Pellegrino's** (138 Mulberry St, 212/226-3177) is one of the best for traditional Italian lunches and dinners. Most of the pastas are homemade and linguine alla Sinatra with lobster, shrimp, and clams in a light red clam sauce is over the top. To experience the sights and aromas of the neighborhood, take a table outside but avoid coming in September during the Feast of San Gennaro — it's a mob scene.

---

of the basics soundly covered. They have lots of oyster selections, ample salads, and tasty appetizers. Entrees include a number of steaks (the filet is fantastic), rack of lamb, seared scallops, and veal chops. Don't pass up pan-roasted crispy potatoes, gnocchi and cheese, sauteed spinach, and grilled asparagus. For dessert, the homemade ice creams are a treat (especially the "coffee and doughnuts") as are the red velvet cake, warm apple-plum tart, and coconut flan. The **Charcuterie Bar** offers individual items and a sampler plate as well. And check out the very unique restrooms!

RAO'S

455 E 114th St (at First Ave)	212/722-6709
Dinner: Mon-Fri	raos.com
Expensive	

If you want to go to Rao's — an intimate, old-time (1896) Italian restaurant — you will need to plan a bit in advance — like a year ahead! The place is crowded all the time for several reasons: the Neapolitan cuisine is great, celebrity-watching is fantastic, and there are only ten tables and one seating. If you're lucky enough to score a "rez," don't walk or take a car; hail a taxi and step out in front of the Spanish Harlem restaurant. When you're ready to leave, they will call a cab. Frankie Pellegrino is a gregarious and charming host who makes guests feel right at home and will even sit at your table while you order. Be prepared for leisurely dining. While you're waiting, enjoy the excellent bread and warm atmosphere. Believe it or not, besides the luscious, award-winning pasta, the Southern fried chicken (Rao's style) is absolutely superb and would be my number-one choice. No credit cards.

RAOUL'S

180 Prince St (bet Sullivan and Thompson St)	212/966-3518
Dinner: Daily	raouls.com
Moderately expensive	

There are dozens of good places to eat in Soho, and Raoul's is certainly one to visit. This long, narrow restaurant used to be an old saloon. Gone are the once paper tablecloths and funky walls covered with a mishmash of posters, pictures, and calendars. With good reviews the bistro is now more "art gallery" with white tablecloths, yet it remains neighborly, friendly, and intimate. House favorites include steak au poivre and paté maison. Raoul's is a natural for those whose days begin when the rest of us are ready to hit the sack.

RARE BAR & GRILL
Affinia Shelburne
303 Lexington Ave (at 37th St)   212/481-1999
Hilton New York Fashion District
152 W 26th St (bet Ave of the Americas and Seventh Ave)   212/807-7273
Breakfast, Lunch, Dinner: Daily; Brunch: Sat, Sun   rarebarandgrill.com
Moderate

If noise is your thing, you will be right at home at Rare. At the Lexington Avenue location, tables are filled with yuppies and button-down business types, and this restaurant literally vibrates with energy. The food is almost secondary to the scene, but the burgers are fabulous. You can get a classic burger or order one of their more exotic types: Mexican, T-bone, filet mignon, lobster, lamb, and vegetable. They also serve a tasting basket of French fries (cottage, shoestring, sweet potato and parmesan truffle with three dipping sauces), salads, and soups. The more recent Fashion District location is in the hotel lobby. There are some differences in menu offerings, so if you have a favorite item in mind, you might call ahead. Check out the panoramic view from the seasonal rooftop lounge, Rare View.

RECETTE
328 W 12th St (at Greenwich St)   212/414-3000
Dinner: Daily; Brunch: Sun   recettenyc.com
Very expensive

Enter the white-paned doors and you will find yourself ensconced in this casual yet sophisticated Greenwich Village establishment. Recette is known for its menu of playful American snacks and small plates with dynamic flavors. Chef Jesse Schenker has pulled together his best recipes for a memorable five-, seven-, or ten-course tasting menu. Seasonal vegetables, fruits, seafood, and meats such as Peekytoe crab, veal cheeks, sweetbreads, and duck are combined in tantalizing and unique combinations. Decadent desserts are prepared by pastry chef Christina Lee, formerly with per se.

RED ROOSTER HARLEM
310 Lenox Ave (bet 125th and 126th St)   212/792-9001
Lunch: Mon-Fri; Dinner: Daily; Brunch: Sat, Sun   redroosterharlem.com
Moderate

In chef Marc Samuelsson's crowded, boisterous house, you will see both old-time and modern Harlem touches. Dirty rice and shrimp, fried yard bird (chicken),

---

A Second Helping of Diner Lingo (used by waiters)
Burn the British: a toasted English muffin
Cackleberries: eggs
Flop two: two fried eggs over easy
Heart attack on a rack: biscuits and gravy
Houseboat: banana split
Nervous pudding: jelly
Sinkers and suds: doughnuts and coffee

No Nonsense Italian

Pepe Rosso to Go (149 Sullivan St, 212/677-4555) is a no-nonsense Italian restaurant. The bill of fare lists pastas, paninis, salads, and antipasti, all at very reasonable prices. Delivery and takeout (within a 10-block radius) are the biggest part of Pepe's business. There is beer, wine, and limited seating on-site

---

superb uptown steak frites, and Helga's meatballs are all worth crowing about. Additional items: gingered carrot soup as an appetizer, sweet potato doughnuts and pie, and Momma Sandy's whoopi pies. Head to Red Rooster for mid-America comfort cooking at its best, but be sure to make a reservation. Upstairs, **Ginny's Supper Club** (212/421-3821) offers live jazz and blues performances most evenings as well as a special gospel brunch on Sunday.

REDEYE GRILL

890 Seventh Ave (at 56th St)   212/541-9000
Lunch: Mon-Fri; Dinner: Daily; Brunch: Sat, Sun   redeyegrill.com
Moderately expensive

Redeye Grill is a busy, bustling place. Owner Sheldon Fireman created an eye-appealing, sophisticated mega room across from Carnegie Hall. Specialties of the house include all shapes and sizes of shrimp, a huge seafood appetizer platter, grilled fish, and pastas. Steaks, burgers, egg dishes, sushi, and their famous lobster Cobb salad round out the menu. The personnel are hip and helpful, but the scene is the major attraction. Live music is featured nightly, and outdoor terrace dining is available during spring, summer, and fall.

REMI

145 W 53rd St (bet Ave of the Americas and Seventh Ave)   212/581-4242
Lunch: Mon-Fri; Dinner: Daily   remi-ny.com
Moderate

Remi operates in a spectacular space in midtown, handy to hotels and theaters. In an unusually long room dominated by a dramatic 120-foot Venetian wall painting by Paulin Paris, the food soars as high as the setting. In warm weather, the doors open up and diners can enjoy sitting at tables in the adjoining atrium. Waiters' attire, chairs, and wall fabrics all match in attractive stripes. Antipasto like baked eggplant and mozzarella gratinée will get you off to a delicious start. Come here for the best seafood risotto in town! The spaghetti, taglioni, and ravioli can match any house in Venice. Of course, there are fish and meat dishes for more mainstream appetites. The chocolate-raspberry mousse cake is superb. Paddle on down (Remi means "oars") for a first-class experience. Takeout and delivery are available.

RESTO

111 E 29th St (bet Lexington and Park Ave)   212/685-5585
Lunch, Dinner: Daily; Brunch: Sat, Sun   restonyc.com
Moderate

This Belgian gastropub offers much more than the delicious burgers for which they have become famous. With an emphasis on seasonal, farm-fresh ingredients, you will find small plates (like deviled eggs with pork toast, charred octopus with potatoes and fennel, and Tuscan kale salad) and a collection of house charcuterie. The housemade sausage is exceptional. Resto's extensive list of Belgian beers adds to the attraction at this popular spot.

ROSA MEXICANO
1063 First Ave (at 58th St)   212/753-7407
Dinner: Daily; Brunch: Sat, Sun

61 Columbus Ave (at 62nd St)   212/977-7700
9 E 18th St (bet Fifth Ave and Broadway)   212/533-3350
Lunch: Mon-Fri; Dinner: Daily; Brunch: Sat, Sun   rosamexicano.com
Moderate to moderately expensive

Rosa Mexicano offers authentic Mexican cuisine in a fun, festive atmosphere. Start with the signature table-side guacamole or a pomegranate margarita. There are also great fresh salads, handmade tacos, sandwiches (at lunch), and many chicken, beef, and seafood entrees. Try corn masa crab turnover or multi-layered, pulled duck tortilla pie. Delicious vanilla flan with espresso is a good finisher. The atmosphere at these three locations is friendly, the energy level high, and the food is definitely worth the tab.

ROSEMARY'S ENOTECA & TRATTORIA
18 Greenwich Ave (at 10th St)   212/647-1818
Breakfast: Daily; Lunch: Mon-Fri; Dinner: Daily; Brunch: Sat, Sun   rosemarysnyc.com
Moderate

Much of the seasonal produce and many of the herbs are fresh from the rooftop garden at this Greenwich Village Italian newcomer across from Jefferson Market Garden. The housemade pastas, foccacia, and mozzarella are equally fresh and delicious on their own or in salads, main dishes, or panini sandwiches. The menu includes weekly specials for lunch and dinner, cheeses, salumis, and dinners-for-two. Rosemary's is a casual, very attractive open space with a wine bar serving proseco on tap. It is a good choice for weekend brunch, date night, or just because; reservations accepted for groups of eight or more.

ROUND TABLE
The Algonquin Hotel
59 W 44th St (bet Fifth Ave and Ave of the Americas), lobby level   212/840-6800
Breakfast, Lunch, Dinner: Daily; Brunch: Sat, Sun   algonquinhotel.com
Moderate to moderately expensive

This room has seen a lot of history! In yesteryear, the Algonquin's famous Round Table served all manner of famous personalities in the arts, business, and

---

For Saké Lovers!
Sakagura (211 E 43rd, 212/953-7253) is a very popular destination for saké (over 200 choices) and Japanese small plates. This basement hangout, with the ambience of Tokyo, is known as one of the top saké bars in the U.S. Most small plates are priced well under $10. Sakagura is open weekdays for lunch and daily for dinner.

politics who met to exchange stories and repartee. It is still alive and kicking! The Round Table reeks of days past, but the food is very good and the servers will shower you with loving care. Don't expect anything fancy; just relax in the manner of the good old days, but with an updated touch. A $39 pre-theater menu is offered.

RUBY FOO'S

1626 Broadway (at 49th St)   212/489-5600
Lunch, Dinner: Daily   rubyfoos.com
Moderate

Mega Pan-Asian house! Busy Ruby Foo's is billed as a dim sum and sushi palace, with the best dishes being in the latter category. However, if you and your tablemates share the roasted Peking duck, you will go home happy. There is a large (changing) selection of maki rolls: spicy tuna, fresh crabmeat, tempura shrimp, and California (crab and avocado). Sushi platters are well-selected and great for a party. Dim sum, hand rolls, soups, salads, and rice dishes are also featured. The crowd is hip, the noise level high, the food very good, and the value outstanding. Takeout and delivery are offered in the Times Square area.

RUE 57

60 W 57th St (at Ave of the Americas)   212/307-5656
Breakfast, Lunch, Dinner: Daily; Brunch: Sat, Sun   rue57.com
Moderate (lunch) to moderately expensive (dinner)

This Parisian-style brasserie is one busy place due to its extremely convenient location, friendly service, and pleasant atmosphere. The menu encompasses soups and salads, sandwiches, oysters and clams, steaks, varied other entrees (like salmon, chicken, and miso bass) and daily specials. The young ones will enjoy the great burgers. Lovers of Japanese cuisine will find sushi, sashimi, and Japanese platters to share. Don't pass up the beefsteak-tomato salad with charred onions and Roquefort!

THE RUSSIAN TEA ROOM

150 W 57th St (bet Ave of the Americas and Seventh St)   212/581-7100
Breakfast, Lunch, Dinner: Daily   russiantearoomnyc.com
Expensive

For a bit of nostalgia and perhaps a taste of caviar, venison, borscht, chicken Kiev, or beef Stroganoff, try this legendary icon. The ambience is A+ and dining is opulent in the dining room and elsewhere. But the Bear Lounge is magical; a 15-foot tall revolving polar bear aquarium and a golden tree with Venetian glass eggs are as famous as the A-listers who are frequent patrons. Traditional fare is served for breakfast, lunch, dinner, and their famous afternoon teas; the vodka menu is ostensibly the best in the city.

SAN PIETRO

18 E 54th St (bet Fifth and Madison Ave)   212/753-9015
Lunch, Dinner: Mon-Sat   sanpietrorestaurant.us
Expensive

The Bruno brothers have brought the joys and bounty of Southern Italy to their upscale (and pricey) restaurant. Salads with fresh fruits and vegetables are legendary, as is linguine with anchovies. Spaghetti dishes and scialatielli are special, too. Fish, veal, and chicken dishes are well crafted. Desserts include tiramisu, crème brûlée, and gelato. If you want to enjoy tasty Italian dishes while seeing how the other half lives, San Pietro is the ticket!

SARABETH'S

1295 Madison Ave (at 92nd St)	212/410-7335
423 Amsterdam Ave (at 80th St)	212/496-6280
40 Central Park S (bet Fifth Ave and Ave of the Americas)	212/826-5959
381 Park Ave South (at 27th St)	212/335-0093
339 Greenwich St (at Jay St)	212/966-0421

Breakfast, Lunch, Dinner: Daily; Brunch: Sat, Sun

Lord & Taylor
424 Fifth Ave (at 39th St), 5th floor   212/827-5068
Lunch: Mon-Fri; Brunch: Sat, Sun
Moderate   sarabeth.com

A visit to one of Sarabeth's locations reminds me of the better English tearooms. Swinging it is not. Reliable it is. The big draw is the homemade quality of the dishes, including the baked items and excellent desserts. They also make gourmet preserves and sell them nationally, along with their cakes, cookies, and soups. Menu choices include excellent omelets, porridge, and fresh fruit for breakfast; a fine assortment of light items for lunch; and large salads, burgers, seafood sandwiches, chicken pot pies, and fish, game, and meat dishes for dinner. The chocolate mousse cake, chocolate soufflé, warm berry bread pudding, and homemade ice cream are splendid desserts. Service is rapid and courteous. Look in on **Sarabeth's Bakery** (75 Ninth Ave, 212/989-2424), at the Chelsea Market.

SAVORE

200 Spring St (at Sullivan St)   212/431-1212
Lunch, Dinner: Daily   savorenyc.com
Moderate

Soho has no shortage of restaurants, some of them with a snooty attitude that's in keeping with the area. Savore has none of this. You come here for good, fresh Florentine food served in a casual and friendly atmosphere. It is a particularly attractive destination in nice weather, when tables are placed outside. The menu offers a large selection of pastas, like asparagus tagliatelle with crabmeat and potato dumplings with veal ragu. In true Tuscan fashion, salads are served after the main course.

SCALINI FEDELI

165 Duane St (bet Greenwich and Hudson St)   212/528-0400
Dinner: Mon-Sat   scalinifedeli.com
Expensive

Head to this upscale Italian restaurant for a truly classy and classic meal. Michael Cetrulo's offerings are exotic: chive and champagne crabmeat napoleon, soft egg-yolk ravioli with ricotta and spinach . . . and that's just to start! Then it's on to delicious braised short ribs of beef, slow-roasted duck breast crusted with almonds, and wonderful roasted rack of lamb. Desserts are equally fabulous, like almond *semifreddo* with orange-honey sauce and caramelized peaches or warm caramelized apple tart in a baked phyllo crust. Luncheons are a bit lighter. A $70 *prix-fixe* dinner menus and a $100 tasting menu are the order of the day. A private room in the wine cellar is available for parties.

SCARPETTA
355 W 14th St (at Ninth Ave)   212/691-0555
Dinner: Daily   scarpettanyc.com
Moderately expensive to expensive

Chef Scott Conant has created a neighborhood venue that attracts folks from all over the city. At the edge of the Meatpacking District, Scarpetta's townhouse setting is most appealing, with a retractable roof, high rafters, a very busy bar, and rows of light bulbs suspended in unique boxes. What you really come here for, though, is true Italian cooking, and that is exactly what you get. The breads are good enough for an entire meal. In fact, scarpetta refers to the Italian tradition of sopping up great sauces with bread. Pastas are the chef's trademark; his spaghetti is especially marvelous. Other sure bets are black cod and melt-in-your-mouth braised short ribs of beef. Top it all off with wonderful chocolate cake served with salted caramel gelato and chocolate butterscotch. (P.S. I defy you to find the almost hidden outdoor sign!)

SCHILLER'S
131 Rivington St (at Norfolk St)   212/260-4555
Lunch: Mon-Fri; Dinner: Daily (open late Mon-Sat); Brunch: Sat, Sun
Moderate   schillersny.com

There is simply no place quite like Schiller's in Manhattan. Keith McNally has created an unusual, fun, and deservedly popular munching and drinking spot in an area not renowned for exciting places. Schiller's Liquor Bar (that's the full name) joins a group of busy brasseries run by McNally. The casual atmosphere is rather Parisian and the service is informal. Tasty comfort food includes excellent salads, burgers, fish and chips, beef Stroganoff, lamb meatballs, chicken pot pie, and daily specials. Sticky toffee pudding and key lime pie are two of the better desserts. Takeout and delivery are also offered.

THE SEA GRILL
19 W 49th St (bet Fifth Ave and Ave of the Americas)   212/332-7610
Lunch: Mon-Fri; Dinner: Mon-Sat   theseagrillnyc.com
Moderately expensive

At this Rockefeller Center seafood house, which overlooks ice skaters in winter and features open-air dining in nice weather, you'll pay for the setting as well as the food. Take advantage of the well-stocked raw seafood bar to start. Well-prepared main courses include tasty crab cakes, salmon, and delicious sides of roasted cauliflower with pine nuts and Portobello fries. I love the desserts, which might include warm chocolate steamed pudding and warm apple tart. The Sea Grill is one of Rockefeller Center's gems. Now if they could just lighten up on the prices!

SERENDIPITY 3
225 E 60th St (bet Second and Third Ave)   212/838-3531
Daily: 11:30 a.m.-midnight (Fri, Sat till 1 a.m.)   serendipity3.com
Moderate

The young and young-at-heart rate Serendipity 3 numero uno on their list of "in" places, as it has been for a half century. In an atmosphere of nostalgia set in a quaint two-floor brownstone, this full-service restaurant offers a complete selection of delicious entrees, crepes, sandwiches, soups, salads, burgers, and pastas. The real treats are the fabulous desserts, including favorites like hot fudge sundaes and frozen hot chocolate (which can also be purchased in mix form to take home). The "Forbidden Broadway" ice cream sundae is awesome. If you are planning a special gathering for the "kids" in your family, make Serendipity 3 the destination!

SETTE MEZZO

969 Lexington Ave (bet 70th and 71st St)   212/472-0400
Lunch, Dinner: Daily
Moderate to moderately expensive

This spot is a well-kept secret among Manhattan's elite business world. Sette Mezzo is small, professional, and busy, and it makes a great place for people-watching. There are no affectations in decor, service, or food preparation. Don't worry about dressing up, as most diners come casually attired. All of the grilled items are excellent. For some marvelous combinations, ask about the special pasta dishes. For more traditional Italian plates, try veal paillard, stuffed baked chicken, or fried calamari and shrimp. Homemade desserts include several caloric cakes, cheesecakes, and lemon tarts. Cash only.

SFOGLIA

135 E 92nd St (at Lexington Ave)   212/831-1402
Lunch: Tues-Sat; Dinner: Daily   sfogliarestaurant.com
Moderate

Most folks would probably never notice this unassuming little trattoria on the Upper East Side, but believe me, you don't want to miss it! Pronounced SFOG-lea, the restaurant name means uncut sheet of pasta. How appropriate for this rustic Italian eatery. The place is rather bare-bones, with several large farmhouse tables where you might be seated with folks unknown. No problem! The food is so good you will quickly become best friends with the strangers at your elbows as you exchange bites. The staff couldn't be friendlier. Delicious warm bread arrives at the start. The menu changes every few weeks, but you will always find something good: fish, pappardelle, meat, gnocchi, chicken, and more. You'll enjoy just gazing upon the bowls of fruit and vegetables and fresh flowers on the tables.

SHAKE SHACK

Madison Square Park (23rd St bet Madison Ave and Broadway)   212/889-6600
154 E 86th (bet Lexington and Third Ave)   646/237-5035
366 Columbus Ave (at 77th St)   646/747-8770
691 Eighth Ave (at 44th St)   646/435-0135
215 Murray St (bet West St and North End Ave)   646/545-4600
Lunch, Dinner: Daily   shakeshack.com
Inexpensive

This is quite a success story! Danny Meyer's Shake Shack started out as a popular seasonal hot dog cart in Madison Square Park. The lines were long and customers clamored for more of the burgers, fries, hot dogs, frozen custards,

---

Signs That a Restaurant May Be in Trouble

■ The usual one- or two-week vacation closure extends to "still on vacation" three months later.

■ An upscale dinner house turns into a burger joint or lounge.

■ Your reservation is suddenly canceled, allegedly due to a private party taking over the restaurant. A peek in the window reveals a darkened dining room and no customers in sight.

■ Realtors are showing the property to prospective buyers.

■ Coupons with really large discounts.

---

shakes, floats, beer, wine, and such. Each Shack has its own frozen concrete concoctions. I'll have a ShackBurger, cheese fries, and chocolate-truffle cookie-dough concrete — to go, please! Danny has expanded outside the Big Apple with a location in Brooklyn as well (409 Fulton St, Brooklyn; 718/307-7590).

SHUN LEE CAFE
43 W 65th St (at Broadway)   212/595-8895
Lunch: Sat, Sun; Dinner: Daily
Moderate

SHUN LEE WEST
Lunch, Dinner: Daily
Moderately expensive   shunleewest.com

Dim sum and street-food combinations are served in an informal setting at Shun Lee Cafe. It's a fun place where you can try some unusual and delicious Chinese dishes. Service is prompt and offers an excellent choice pre-Lincoln Center. A good-natured waiter comes to your table with a rolling cart and describes the various goodies. The offerings vary, but don't miss stuffed crab claws if they are available. Go on to the street-food items: delicious barbecued spare ribs, a large selection of noodle and rice dishes and soups, and a menu full of mild and spicy entrees. Crispy prawns with ginger and braised duck with seasonal vegetables are great choices. For heartier appetites, Shun Lee West — the excellent Chinese restaurant that adjoins Shun Lee Cafe — is equally good in its more elegant setting. Some of the best Chinese food in Manhattan is served here: tingling curry chicken, lobster Szechuan style, and baby eggplant with ginger, garlic, and scallions. If you come with a crowd, family-style dining is available. Prices are a bit higher at the restaurant than in the cafe.

SHUN LEE PALACE
155 E 55th St (bet Lexington and Third Ave)   212/371-8844
Lunch, Dinner: Daily   shunleepalace.com
Moderate to moderately expensive

All manner of Chinese restaurants can be found in Manhattan. The colorful Chinatown variety. The mom-and-pop corner operations. The overly Americanized establishments. The grand Chinese dining rooms. Shun Lee Palace belongs in the last category, possessing a very classy, refined look. Michael Tong offers a deli-

---

Iconic Dining

The iconic **21 Club** (21 W 52nd St, 212/582-7200; 21club.com) has been around since the 1920s, with a reputation as a place to see and be seen. I can remember fascinating lunches here with my uncle, who was a daily diner. Many celebrities, politicians, and moguls have laid claim to their usual table in the Bar Room and the seating chart may read like an A-list of who's who. The atmosphere is still quite special. At one time, patrons dressed to the nines for an evening at the 21 Club. Yes, there is still a gentleman at the door to give you the once-over and men's jackets are required (no jeans or sneakers) in the Bar Room and restaurant. The Bar Room is open for lunch Tuesday through Friday and dinner Monday through Saturday; take note of the ceiling which holds an astounding collection of sports memorabilia and corporate logo items. The more relaxed Bar 21 and Lounge serves lunch Tuesday through Friday and is a watering hole during evening hours. For elegant dining (Tuesday through Saturday) reserve a table in Upstairs at 21, a romantic spot for marriage proposals, anniversaries, birthdays, and other memorable special occasions. Oh the secrets this former speakeasy holds!

---

cious journey into the best of this historic cuisine. You can dine rather reasonably at lunch; a $20 three-course *prix-fixe* experience is available. Ordering from the menu (or through your captain) can be a bit pricier, but the platters are worth it. Specialties include beggar's chicken (24 hours advance notice required), casserole specials, curried prawns, Beijing duck, and veal, lamb, beef, and pork entrees. Yes, this is just about the closest thing Manhattan has to a real Chinese palace.

SIRIO RISTORANTE
The Pierre
795 Fifth Ave (at 61st St)   212/940-8195
Breakfast, Lunch, Dinner: Daily; Brunch: Sat, Sun   siriony.com
Moderately expensive

The swanky Pierre hotel is home to Sirio Maccioni's latest Manhattan dining venue. This is a homecoming of sorts for the restaurant impresario who at one time served as maitre d' at the hotel's fine dining establishment. Fast forward to the present where Maccioni's culinary team focuses its talents on contemporary versions of traditional Italian dishes. The superb quality and excellent service are on par with sister properties Circo NYC and Le Cirque. The cocktail menu lists inventive selections and wines which are produced in Italy especially for this restaurant. Breakfasts are a treat; especially the frittatas and Sirio's high energy juice (apple, carrot, spinach, celery, red beet, and ginger). Maybe the juice is the octogenarian's secret to always being at the top of his game?

SISTINA
1555 Second Ave (at 80th St)   212/861-7660
Lunch: Mon-Sat; Dinner: Daily
Moderately expensive to expensive

This cheery dining space, with whimsical decor and white tablecloths, has much to offer. Sistina's seasonal Italian menu emphasizes fresh herbs and vegetables. Executive chef Giuseppe Bruno's plates might include braised rabbit with wine and herbs, housemade pappardelle with wild mushrooms, or wild striped bass with blue crab and fresh corn. Daily specials are offered on the pricey menu. A monumental wine list of 65,000 bottles is equally impressive.

SMITH & WOLLENSKY

797 Third Ave (at 49th St)   212/753-1530
Lunch, Dinner: Daily   smithandwollenskynyc.com
Moderate to moderately expensive

For visitors to the Big Apple wanting a taste of what this great city is all about, Smith & Wollensky is a great choice. There is an abundance of space (two floors) and talented, helpful personnel. I always grade a place on the quality of their bread, and Smith & Wollensky's is excellent. The lobster cocktail is one of the best in the city. Featured entrees include wonderful steaks (USDA prime, dry-aged and hand-butchered), prime rib, fresh seafood, and lamb chops. Every man in the family will love the place, and the ladies will appreciate the special attention paid to them. Come here when you and your guests are really hungry.

SPARKS STEAK HOUSE

210 E 46th St (bet Second and Third Ave)   212/687-4855
Lunch: Mon-Fri; Dinner: Mon-Sat   sparkssteakhouse.com
Moderately expensive to expensive

You come to Sparks Steak House to eat, period. This well-seasoned and popular beef restaurant is very traditional with its dark wood paneling. For years, businessmen have made an evening at Sparks a must, and the house has not let time erode its reputation. You can choose from veal and lamb chops, beef scaloppine, and medallions of beef. There are a half-dozen steak items, like steak fromage (with Roquefort), prime sirloin, sliced steak with fresh mushrooms, and top-of-the-line filet mignon. Seafood dishes are another specialty. Rainbow trout, tuna steak, and halibut steak are as good as you'll find in most seafood houses. The lobsters are enormous, delicious, and expensive. Skip the appetizers and desserts, and concentrate on the main dish. An extensive, award-winning wine list and private party rooms are available.

SPICE MARKET

403 W 13th St (at Ninth Ave)   212/675-2322
Lunch, Dinner: Daily   spicemarketnewyork.com
Moderate

This Jean-Georges Vongerichten operation is one of the city's hot dining spots for atmosphere and tasty upscale Asian street food. Located in the trendy Meatpacking District, Spice Market is a charming space with tables surrounding an open area that leads to an inviting downstairs bar. The decor is tasteful, while the food is different and exciting. The Vietnamese spring rolls are yummy, the salads are unusual and good, and the chicken skewer with lime dipping sauce is outstanding. Other wonderful dishes: striped bass or cod with Malaysian chili sauce; onion- and chili-crusted short ribs that melt in your mouth; and a large selection of vegetables, noodles, and rice. Desserts are even better. Thai jewels and fruits with fresh coconut ice — one of the most famous street desserts in Thailand — is a must. Other sweet selections: a fabulous Ovaltine kulfi and mango upside-down cake.

SPIGOLO

1561 Second Ave (at 81st St)   212/744-1100
Lunch: Sat, Sun; Dinner: Daily   spigolonyc.com
Moderately expensive

Some Upper East Siders swear by Executive Chef Joseph D'Angelo's dinner house where contemporary American meets traditional Italian fare. The menu is inspired by seasonal bounty from the land and sea; seafood dishes are quite flavorful, including clams, oysters, and bass or monkfish. Pasta dishes are prepared with market-fresh ingredients in delicious combinations laced with cheese, garlic, and sauces; entrees are hearty and satisfying. Sweet finishes include a half dozen or so Italian desserts and an array of dessert wines and liquors.

THE SPOTTED PIG

314 W 11th St (at Greenwich St)   212/620-0393
Lunch, Dinner: Daily; Brunch: Sat, Sun   thespottedpig.com
Moderate

April Bloomfield and Ken Friedman are the driving forces behind this Manhattan gastropub, which has pig statues and porcine likenesses throughout the boisterous scene. The seasonal British and Italian menu is really good. Start with snacks like deviled eggs or a pot of pickles, then move on to lunch staples of delicious burgers and shoestring potatoes, soup or chowder, and salads. Dinner is served until 2 a.m. Creative beef, lamb, poultry, fish, seafood, and (of course) pork preparations are offered. Vegetarians can make a meal of five side dishes for $24. Beer choices include cask-conditioned ale. This place hops! And in proper gastropub fashion, no reservations are accepted.

SPRING NATURAL KITCHEN

474 Columbus Ave (at 83rd St)   646/596-7434
Lunch: Mon-Fri: Dinner: Daily; Brunch: Sat, Sun   springnaturalkitchen.com

SPRING STREET NATURAL

62 Spring St (at Lafayette St)   212/966-0290
Breakfast: Mon-Fri; Lunch, Dinner: Daily; Brunch: Sat, Sun springstreetnatural.com
Moderate

Spring Street Natural was a leader in offering healthy cuisine. That tradition continues (since 1973), and now at a satellite location on Columbus Avenue in Spring Natural Kitchen. From attractive and unfussy surroundings, the kitchen provides seasonal meals prepared with fresh, unprocessed foods, and most everything is cooked to order. Neighborhood residents are regular customers, so you know the food is top-quality. Specials are offered every day, with a wide variety of natural and flavorful fresh-squeezed juices, organic salads, pastas, vegetarian meals, free-range poultry, and fresh fish and seafood. Try wonderful roasted salmon with cucumber salad and red potatoes. Spring Street also produces great desserts, like warm banana-caramel bread pudding and fresh fruit salad with sorbet.

THE STANDARD GRILL

848 Washington St (at 13th St)   212/645-4100
Breakfast, Lunch, Dinner: Daily; Brunch: Sat, Sun   thestandardgrill.com
Moderate to moderately expensive

The Standard Grill, a bustling Meatpacking District eatery, is a real winner. Not only does the place literally rock, but it also offers first-class American food in every category. The wait staff is superbly trained, friendly, and competent. The house seats hundreds of guests at both an outside patio and an indoor room; a fun beer garden is attached, too. Reservations are strongly suggested. The bread selection is great, and refreshing radishes are a complimentary touch. Menu specialties include patés, oysters, a number of appetizers, and delicious soups. Memorable (sometimes seasonal) entrees include lobster thermidor, steaks, and moist "Million Dollar" chicken. A warm chocolate brownie with toasted marshmallows will hit the spot for dessert. A bowl of bittersweet chocolate mousse (for two) is rightfully named "The Deal Closer."

STRIP HOUSE

15 W 44th St (bet Fifth Ave and Ave of the Americas)	212/336-5454
Lunch: Mon-Fri; Dinner: Daily	
13 E 12th St (bet Fifth Ave and University Pl)	212/328-0000
Dinner: Daily	striphouse.com
Moderately expensive	

The Strip House offers a modern twist to the traditional steakhouse experience. Rich leather, plush fabrics, and dark red walls lined with photographs of sultry 1920s burlesque stars all create a seductive atmosphere. The innovative menu features signature prime cuts of beef, all charred to perfection with house seasoning. Flavorful sides like black-truffle creamed spinach, goose-fat potatoes, and garlic herbed fries complement the entrees. Decadent desserts include 24-layer chocolate cake and vanilla crème brûlée with brandied cherries. **Strip House Next Door** (11 E 12th St, downstairs, 212/838-9197) offers simpler fare, plus items from the original 12th Street menu.

TAO

42 E 58th St (bet Park and Madison Ave)	212/888-2288
Lunch: Mon-Sat; Dinner: Daily; Brunch: Sun	taorestaurant.com
Moderate to moderately expensive	

There's no place quite like this! Tao is billed as an Asian bistro, but it is much more than that. In a huge space that was once a stable, this dramatic dining setting features a huge Buddha looking down as you enjoy wonderful food at reasonable prices. Hordes of diners can be accommodated on two levels of this Asian temple; a sushi bar and several regular bars are also available. Reservations are strongly recommended, as thirtysomethings make Tao their hangout. A number of small plates are available to start, including lobster wontons and squab lettuce wraps. Save room for delicious dragon-tail spare ribs or a marvelous wok-seared New York sirloin with shiitake mushrooms that melts in your mouth. A $27 *prix-fixe* lunch is offered daily.

TARTINE

253 W 11th St (at 4th St)	212/229-2611
Lunch: Mon-Fri; Dinner: Daily; Brunch: Daily	tartinecafenyc.com
Moderate	

This tiny cafe/bakery/French bistro (about 20 chairs) serves some of the tastiest dishes in the Village. There are soups, salads, quiches, and omelets, plus chicken, meat, fish entrees, and daily specials at pleasing prices. French fries are a treat. Desserts and pastries are baked on-premises. For about half the price of what you would pay uptown, you can finish your meal with splendid custard-filled tarts, meringues, fabulous almond-covered chocolate ganache, or warm, thinly sliced cinnamon apples on puff pastry with ice cream. There is always a wait at dinner and brunch — a good sign, since neighborhood folks know the best spots. If you want wine, you are encouraged to bring your own. Cash only.

TASTE

1413 Third Ave (at 80th St)   212/717-9798
Dinner: Daily; Brunch: Sat, Sun   elizabar.com
Moderate (Taste Cafe) to moderately expensive (Taste)

When it comes to quality food (with prices to match), there is no equal in Manhattan to Eli Zabar. Taste has all the pluses and minuses you've come to expect from this gentleman. Weekend brunch items range from pancakes and salmon-slathered bagels to meatloaf on an onion roll. Dinners change seasonally and feature such winners as squash risotto, onion soup, Coho salmon, lamb shank, and Scottish partridge. A wine bar serves good wines that aren't too expensive by the glass. With Zabar's market next door, Taste is obviously offering really fresh food. As you would expect from a Zabar operation, the breads are superb. On weekdays the space operates as the informal, self-service. **Taste Cafe**, with breakfast and lunch offerings of soups, sandwiches, salads, and pastries.

TELEPAN

72 W 69th St (at Columbus Ave)   212/580-4300
Lunch: Wed-Fri; Dinner: Daily; Brunch: Sat, Sun   telepan-ny.com
Moderate to moderately expensive

After you have overloaded on the flashy dining scene, step back and be Bill Telepan's guest. Everything about this place — surroundings, menu, and service — reflects the laid-back personality of chef/owner Telepan. It is a quiet and reliable restaurant enhancing the Upper West Side for more mature diners. Local ingredients are featured on the changing menu. Order the spring vegetables bread soup if it's on the menu; it could easily make an entire meal. There are worthy egg dishes, scallop and sea urchin stew, roasted chicken, and house smoked brook trout. A four-course tasting menu is offered for $69.

TIPSY PARSON

156 Ninth Ave (bet 19th and 20th St)   212/620-4545
Lunch: Mon-Fri; Dinner: Daily; Brunch: Sat, Sun   tipsyparson.com
Moderately expensive

When someone mentions Southern food, I think of warm hospitality and big helpings of grits, hushpuppies, and catfish. All that and more can be found at Tipsy Parson in various delicious combinations. Try grits solo or with shrimp, a pimento cheeseburger, a catfish po' boy sandwich, fried green tomatoes, grilled flank steak with mushrooms and onions, and roasted half-chicken with grilled ramps. Plan a return visit for weekend brunch and indulge in pulled pork spoonbread, biscuits and gravy, or oysters and eggs. Incidentally, the homey restaurant is named for a dessert of brandy-soaked almond cake, custard, fruits, and nuts (also on the menu) – not a tippling Southern minister.

And the Blue Ribbon Goes to...

The Bromberg brothers operate several winning restaurants (blueribbonrestaurants.com). With the Blue Ribbon name attached, you know the food will be first-class. Here is the Blue Ribbon roster:

Blue Ribbon (97 Sullivan St, 212/274-0404)

Blue Ribbon Bakery (35 Downing St, 212/337-0404)

Blue Ribbon Bakery Market (14 Bedford St, 212/647-0408)

Blue Ribbon Sushi (119 Sullivan St, 212/343-0404)

Blue Ribbon Sushi Bar & Grill (308 W 58th St, 212/397-0404)

Blue Ribbon Sushi Izakaya (Thompson LES Hotel, 187 Orchard St, 212/466-0404)

Blue Ribbon Downing Street Bar (34 Downing St, 212/691-0404): right across the street from Blue Ribbon Bakery.

All locations are open daily; hours vary.

TOCQUEVILLE RESTAURANT

1 E 15th St (bet Union Square W and Fifth Ave)   212/647-1515
Lunch, Dinner: Mon-Sat   tocquevillerestaurant.com
Moderately expensive

Husband and wife team Marco Moreira and Jo-Ann Makovitzky operate their pride-and-joy posh restaurant in a Flatiron location. Innovative dishes are featured on a constantly changing American-French menu. At lunchtime, a *prix-fixe* menu is offered. Seasonal ingredients from the Union Square Greenmarket are featured. You will enjoy an absolutely fabulous meal made all the more pleasant by a well-trained and accommodating staff. Homemade brioche, rosemary, and French rolls are so good you must be careful not to ruin your appetite. At dinner a four-course tasting menu ($85) might include cheddar salad, truffled creamy parmesan grits, seared scallops and foie gras, with chocolate soufflé to finish. The locale affords room for private dining (up to 25 people) and a bar area where you can enjoy drinks and snacks or order from the full menu. This talented pair also operates **Catering by Tocqueville**, a service accessible via the restaurant's phone number. Personal food delivery is a given, but they can also take care of location selection, decor, rental items, photographers, and professional service staff.

TORRISI ITALIAN SPECIALTIES

250 Mulberry St (bet Spring and Prince St)   212/965-0955
Lunch: Fri-Sun; Dinner: Daily   torrisinyc.com
Inexpensive (lunch) to expensive (dinner)

You'll be happy to know that reservations are now offered at this popular spot with only 18 seats. Rich Torrisi and Mario Carbone's four-course *prix-fixe* dinner ($75) lists a lineup of four antipasti, two pasta, two entrees, and two desserts which is different and exciting each night. You will see things like leeks brûlée, quail cacciatore, and lemon cake. On days when lunch is not offered, sandwiches, baked ziti, and other lunch items are available at their next-door operation, **Parm**.

TOTTO RAMEN

366 W 52nd St (bet Eighth and Ninth Ave)   212/582-0052
Lunch: Mon-Sat; Dinner: Daily   tottoramen.com
Inexpensive

For quick Japanese comfort food, try Totto Ramen's delicious homemade ramen (noodles) and toppings. The noodles are served al dente, are MSG-free, and
vary in spiciness by the addition of sesame oil. Combinations of chicken or pork
and vegetables create different flavors along with more than a dozen toppings. The
propane torch-crisped pork slices are most interesting. Saké and a few appetizers
round out the menu at this small, casual, very busy space. Note that there is no
takeout or delivery.

TOUT VA BIEN

311 W 51st St (bet Eighth and Ninth Ave)   212/265-0190
Lunch, Dinner: Daily   letoutvabien.com
Moderate to moderately expensive

Since 1948, Tout Va Bien has been consistently preparing old school French
food at reasonable prices. The place is hopping every night — there is so much
noise, hilarity, and crowding that I wonder what would happen if there were an
emergency! This French bistro serves all the things you would expect for hors
d'oeuvres: scallops, escargots, prosciutto, fromage, and other French traditions.
Popular items include boeuf bourguignon (beef stew), veal scaloppini, bouillabaisse
(weekends only), and frog legs. Come to this vibrant spot to celebrate or when
you need cheering up.

TRATTORIA DELL'ARTE

900 Seventh Ave (at 57th St)   212/245-9800
Lunch, Dinner: Daily; Brunch: Sun   trattoriadellarte.com
Moderate to moderately expensive

Native New Yorkers keep Trattoria dell'Arte bursting at the seams every evening. A casual cafe is at the front, seats are available at the antipasto bar in the
center, and the dining room is in the rear. One would be hard-pressed to name a
place at any price with tastier Italian food. The antipasto selection is large, fresh,
and inviting; you can choose a platter with various accompaniments. There are
daily specials, superb pasta dishes, grilled fish and meats, and salads. Wonderful pizzas are available every day. The atmosphere and personnel are warm and pleasant.
I recommend this place without reservation — although you'd better have one
if you want to sit in the dining room. An outdoor sidewalk cafe provides seating
in warmer months.

TRESTLE ON TENTH

242 Tenth Ave (at 24th St)   212/645-5659
Breakfast, Lunch, Dinner: Daily; Brunch: Sat, Sun   trestleontenth.com
Moderate

Employing a restrained Swiss accent, this house does well with a seasonal
menu of farm fresh American entrees. There are chicken and salmon dishes, pork
garlic sausage, seared scallops, a superb crépinette (pulled pork shoulder), and delicious sides. I always enjoy a light and tasty butter-lettuce salad to start. Here it is
made with crispy bacon and delicious buttermilk dressing. Cured meats and aged

Essex Street Eatery

Shopsin's (120 Essex St; shopsins.com) is a small, very casual 20-seat eatery in the Essex Street Market open Wednesday through Sunday for breakfast and lunch. Kenny Shopsin and crew are a bit irreverent, highly opinionated, and a tad quirky which makes this a unique New York City food experience. Reading the staggering menu may cause you to readjust your eyeglasses, although alphabetical entries of pancakes, burgers, and breakfast dishes bring a sense of order to the listings. Where else can you order a pig newton (eggs, grits, pork, and fig gravy sandwich), Capt J (fried chicken, eggs, two mac 'n jack pancakes), or other politically incorrect-named dishes?

cheeses and sandwiches are featured at lunch. A roasted, stuffed whole pig feast, family style, can be requested 72 hours in advance. These folks are down-to-earth and the atmosphere is unpretentious. For more private dining try the garden in the back.

TRIBECA GRILL

375 Greenwich St (at Franklin St)   212/941-3900
Lunch: Mon-Fri; Dinner: Daily; Brunch: Sun   tribecagrill.com
Moderate to moderately expensive

Since 1990, Tribeca Grill has been a fine dining destination, helping to put Tribeca's neighborhood on the map. The setting is a huge old coffee-roasting house that also houses the Tribeca Film Center on the floors above. The bar comes from the historic Jack Dempsey and Maxwell Plum restaurants. The kitchen is first-class. The genius is savvy Drew Nieporent, with actor Robert De Niro as co-owner. Put it all together, and you have a winner. No wonder the people-watching is so good here! Guests enjoy a spacious bar and dining area, an engaging collection of paintings by De Niro's father, ample banquet facilities for private parties, plus a fabulous private screening room upstairs. The food is stylish and wholesome. Chef Kamal Rose's signature dishes include seared sea scallops with butternut squash and mushroom and bacon risotto, and herb roasted chicken with caramelized carrots and haricots verts. The desserts, including the signature banana torte and the Tribeca chocolate cake, also rate with the best. Their world-class wine list (1,900 selections) perennially wins the Grand Award from *Wine Spectator*. Please note the address is Greenwich Street, not Avenue.

TURKISH KITCHEN

386 Third Ave (bet 27th and 28th St)   212/679-6633
Lunch: Mon-Fri; Dinner: Daily; Brunch: Sun   turkishkitchen.com
Moderate

This family-run Turkish delight in Murray Hill has great food and is absolutely spotless. Moreover, the staff exudes charm. There are all kinds of tasty Turkish specialties, like zucchini pancakes, islim kebab (baked lamb shanks wrapped with eggplant slices), hummus, and baked, skewered and grilled chicken and fish dishes. You can wash it all down with sour cherry juice from Turkey or cacik, a home-made yogurt. Locals rave that the "all-you-can-eat brunch" is a great value.

UNCLE JACK'S STEAKHOUSE

440 Ninth Ave (at 34th St)	212/244-0005
44 W 56th St (bet Fifth Ave and Ave of the Americas)	212/245-1550
39-40 Bell Blvd (at 40th St), Queens	718/229-1100
Lunch, Dinner: Daily	unclejacks.com

Moderate (lunch) to expensive (dinner)

Stepping into Uncle Jack's Steakhouse is like going back decades in time. The hand-carved mahogany bar, the antique light fixtures, the blackboard menu, and the private Library Room (Ninth Avenue location) make the place masculine and comfortable. You will be well taken care of, as the wait staff and captains are right on the job. Vegetables and herbs are grown locally and seafood is fresh, local, and imported. Uncle Jack's specializes in Kobe beef aged 28 to 35 days and cooked to perfection; you can expect an equally grand price tag. Seasonal specials and a $24.95 *prix-fixe* lunch offer more comfortably-priced options at this landmark steakhouse.

UNION SQUARE CAFE

21 E 16th St (bet Fifth Ave and Union Square W)	212/243-4020
Lunch, Dinner: Daily; Brunch: Sat, Sun	unionsquarecafe.com

Moderate to moderately expensive

Danny Meyer's stylish Union Square Cafe is a very popular American restaurant (albeit with an Italian soul). The clientele is as varied as the food. The menu is creative, the staff unusually down-to-earth, and the prices very much within reason. For lunch, try the yellowfin tuna burger with ginger-mustard glaze or one of the great pastas. Chef Carmen Quagliata offers such specialties as Fritto Misto and wonderful sunchoke soup. Dinner entrees from the grill are always delicious (lamb chops, shell steak, and veal). I come just for the warm banana tart with honey-vanilla ice cream and macadamia brittle!

VALBELLA

11 E 53rd St (bet Madison and Fifth Ave)	212/888-8955
	valbellamidtown.com
421 W 13th St (bet Ninth Ave and Washington St)	212/645-7777
Lunch: Mon-Fri; Dinner: Mon-Sat	valbellanyc.com

Moderate to moderately expensive

Service is key in today's highly competitive marketplace. At Valbella, it is top-notch. Wait staff are in constant motion and obviously well-trained at both of these elegant locations. The Northern Italian fare is first-rate, featuring a decent selection of typical dishes. The pastas caught my eye: penne alla vodka, cavatelli, linguine, and risotto with lobster tails and pumpkin cream; lamb and veal dishes are also worth trying. Private dining rooms are available at each house.

VERITAS

43 E 20th St (at Park Ave S)	212/353-3700
Dinner: Daily	veritas-nyc.com

Moderately expensive to expensive

You'll like the intimate setting of this Flatiron space which is complemented by an excellent staff. Chef Sam Hazen guides the kitchen at Veritas through a revitalized contemporary American menu. The appetizer selection boasts beef in

Introducing Stella

There's one more reason to visit Macy's at Herald Square. **Stella 34 Trattoria** (212/967-9251), an Italian eatery, is a lunch and dinner destination that comes with an eye-popping view of the Empire State Building. The three wood-burning ovens turn out fabulous entrees and pizzas, substantial selections (strip steak and pork chops), and salads of roasted beets or mixed greens. Stella includes a prosecco bar, gelato counter, and comfortable lounge area, and is open until 9:30 p.m. most nights. Use the department store's entrance on 35th Street and Broadway and take an express elevator straight to the sixth floor.

transition (prepared three ways: tartare, peppered sirloin, and short ribs) and unusual salads. Excellent prosciutto wrapped scallops, maple-brined wooly pig, and a farmer's market tasting are dinner standouts. The chocolate mud pie trifle is a knockout. Complementing the great food is a world-renowned selection of over 3,000 wines and more than 75,000 bottles. Wine bottles are everywhere at Veritas!

VINEGAR FACTORY
431 E 91st St (bet York and First Ave)   212/987-0885
Breakfast, Lunch, Dinner: Daily (downstairs cafe); Brunch: Sat, Sun (upstairs)
Moderate   elizabar.com

Savvy Upper East Siders quickly learned that weekend brunch at Eli Zabar's Vinegar Factory (once a working vinegar factory) is unfailingly delicious. Taste buds spring to alert as you wander the packed aisles of the Vinegar Factory (a great gourmet store) on your way upstairs to the cafe for Saturday or Sunday brunch. Don't expect bargain prices; after all, this is a classy Eli Zabar operation. Quality is substantial. Wonderful breads (Eli is famous for them), a fresh salad bar, omelets, pizzas, pancakes, potatoes, blintzes, chicken pot pie, and huge sandwiches are available, many as self-serve items. Your hungry teens will love the massive portions, and you will appreciate the fast, friendly service.

VIVOLO
140 E 74th St (bet Park and Lexington Ave)   212/737-3533
Lunch, Dinner: Mon-Sat
Moderate to moderately expensive

CUCINA VIVOLO
222 E 58th St (bet Second and Third Ave)   212/308-0222
Breakfast: Mon-Fri; Lunch: Mon-Sat
138 E 74th St (at Lexington Ave)   212/717-4700
Lunch, Dinner: Mon-Sat; Brunch: Sat   vivolonyc.com
Moderate

Angelo Vivolo created a neighborhood classic from an old townhouse back in 1977. Since then the charming two-story restaurant, with cozy fireplaces and professional service, expanded to the Cucina Vivolo specialty food shops. There are great things to eat at each place. You can sit down and be pampered, have goodies ready for takeout, or place an order for delivery. In the restaurant proper, there are pastas, chicken, veal dishes, and daily specials like Italian meatloaf. The Cucina menu offers wonderful Italian specialty sandwiches made with all kinds of breads, as well as soups, cheeses, sweets, espresso, and cappuccino. Note that only the Cucina locations serve breakfast. Regardless of which Vivolo eatery you choose, save room for the cannoli alla Vivolo, a tasty version of the Italian classic.

WALKER'S
16 N Moore St (at Varick St)   212/941-0142
Lunch: Mon-Fri; Dinner: Daily; Brunch: Sat, Sun
Inexpensive to moderate

You'll love Walker's if you are looking for a glimpse of old Manhattan. Hearty food is served at agreeable prices in three crowded rooms. The regular menu includes homemade soups, salads, omelets (create your own), sandwiches, and quiches. Burgers are big and satisfying. A dozen or so daily specials include fish and pasta dishes. For those coming from uptown, it is a bit of an undertaking to get here. For those in the neighborhood, it is easy to see why Walker's is a favorite, especially on Sunday jazz nights.

WALLSÉ
344 W 11th St (at Washington St)   212/352-2300
Dinner: Daily; Brunch: Sun   kg-ny.com
Moderate to moderately expensive

Vienna it is not, but Kurt Gutenbrunner brings a refined, modern take on Austrian flavors to the West Village. The two dining rooms are sparse but elegant. The staff is pleasant and helpful, adding to the dining experience. Appetizers like foie gras terrine and späetzle with braised rabbit are classic favorites. Yes, there is wiener schnitzel with potato-cucumber salad. And you can always hope that crispy cod strudel is on the menu. Great pastries for dessert: chef Kurt's famous apple strudel, crepes with Gran Marnier mousse, and Salzburger nockerl. The Austrian cheese selection is first-rate.

WAVERLY INN
16 Bank St (bet 4th and Waverly St)   917/828-1154
Dinner: Daily; Brunch: Sat, Sun   waverlynyc.com
Moderately expensive to expensive

The Waverly Inn is owned by Graydon Carter, publisher and editor of *Vanity Fair*. If you are lucky enough to make a reservation, you won't be disappointed. Once seated, you'll find the service professional and pleasant. The surroundings, with working fireplace, are charming and lively. Small plates include oysters on the half shell, salads, salmon tartare, crab cakes, and more. If it's on the menu, the

---

Tequila Hangout
Patrons descend upon **Barrio Chino** (253 Broome St, 212/228-6710) for superb after work margaritas and *über* affordable Mexican food. The tiny cantina, known for potent margaritas, is packed to the gills most nights. Reservations accepted for groups of 8 to 14 amigos; however, expect to wait for a coveted lunch, dinner, or brunch seat.

Berkshire pork with roasted apple is a sensational entree. You might also choose a Waverly burger, chicken pot pie, macaroni and cheese, or other "comforting" favorite.

WOLFGANG'S STEAKHOUSE

409 Greenwich St (bet Beach and Hubert St)	212/925-0353
4 Park Ave (at 33rd St)	212/889-3369
New York Times Building	
250 W 41 St (bet Seventh and Eighth Ave)	212/921-3720
200 E 54th St (at Third Ave)	212/588-9653
Lunch, Dinner: Daily	wolfgangssteakhouse.net
Expensive	

Wolfgang Zwiener, once a fixture at the great Peter Luger Steak House in Brooklyn, is head of his own upscale steakhouses in Manhattan. The result is what you would expect — quality red meat. Their signature items include Porterhouse, filet mignon, ribeyes, lamb chops, and fresh seafood. Portions are huge and should be shared. The German potatoes are tasty. Service is professional and prompt, which it should be for the price. I can recommend this classic American steakhouse for a quality (not outstanding) experience.

WONG

7 Cornelia St (bet Bleecker and West 4th St)	212/989-3399
Dinner: Mon-Sat	wongnewyork.com
Moderate to moderately expensive	

Probably one of the more unusual desserts in town is the roast duck ice cream served with poached plums and a delicate five-spice cookie at this Asian fusion restaurant. Chef/owner Simpson Wong keeps the surprises coming with the likes of lobster egg foo young. Instead of fried pancake-like disks slathered in glutinous brown gravy, Wong's foo young is half of a poached lobster tail and a claw served with two fried chicken eggs and salted duck egg yolks topped with crumbled dried shrimp. There are other tempting choices; appetizer scallops with duck-tongue meatballs, rice noodle concoctions, and chicken and beef dishes. The veteran chef has assembled a duckavore dinner consisting of half a dozen duck-as-the-main-ingredient dishes capped off with the duck ice cream; 48 hours notice required, minimum four guests. Reservations are suggested as this austere Cornelia Street restaurant with open kitchen seats no more than 30 diners.

YUNNAN KITCHEN

79 Clinton St (bet Delancey and Rivington St)	212/253-2527
Dinner: Daily	yunnankitchen.com
Inexpensive to moderate	

Trendy and cozy with a vintage touch describes Yunnan Kitchen and market-driven, flavorful, and inexpensive describes the small plates offered at this very popular Lower East Side restaurant. Cold selections include braised beef rolls, tea-smoked duck, and beef tartare and stir-fried mushrooms, crispy whole shrimp, and Chinese greens are on the hot menu. If you can't eat Chinese cuisine without rice, there are several rice dishes as well as incredible lamb meatballs and more. Reservations accepted for parties of six or more; takeout is available.

DON'T BOTHER LIST

Dining out should result in a good meal in a comfortable setting at a fair price. Unfortunately, many restaurants don't meet that criteria and are mediocre at best. Some restaurants on the following list may be well-known, but there are better options elsewhere.

B Bar & Grill: uninteresting food and disinterested servers

Bice: very noisy, expensive, unimaginative food

Bigoli: not much to attract the real Italian food lover

BLT Prime: unlike the sister operations, not ready for prime time

Bobby Van's Steakhouse: They better stop the downhill slide before it is too late.

Brother Jimmy's BBQ: Most brothers do better than this with their barbecues.

Bubba Gump: unclassy tourist trap

Cipriani Downtown: customers are more attractive than the prices

City Crab and Seafood Co.: so-so service, lackluster food

Coffee Shop: attractive wait staff with unattractive attitudes

Crispo: rude service and management

Eisenberg's Sandwich Shop: OK in the good old days!

Fraunces Tavern: You come here mainly for the history.

Giorgio's of Gramercy: good if you are in the area, but don't spend the cab fare if you're not

Giovanni VentiCinque: overpriced dinners; affordable *prix-fixe* lunch

Island Burgers & Shakes: soggy fries, cramped quarters

La Mirabelle: decent food and service, but the dining room needs a coat of paint and more

Le Veau d'Or: time-worn French restaurant

Leopard at des Artistes: The only good part of the experience – the murals!

Michael Jordan's The Steak House NYC: no slam dunk here; overrated

Neary's: Nice people, but the Irish trip ends there.

Nello: big prices and skimpy portions

Old Homestead: just okay, not worth the money

Perry Street: Jean-Georges Vongerichten's great touch is missing at his West Village restaurant.

Philippe: inexcusably bad service, expensive Chinese dishes

Rolf's: Save your dollars for a real trip to Germany.

Rothmann's: inconsistent in every way

Shula's Steak House: pass this one up for a real winner

Swifty's: unpleasant greeting, snobby atmosphere

Triomphe: small in size, with spotty service and high prices

Chapter 3

WHERE TO
FIND IT

MUSEUMS, TOURS,
AND MORE

A WEEK IN
NEW YORK

"I'm going to be in New York for a week. What do you recommend that I do?" I've been asked that question thousands of times in the last 50 years, and it's not an easy question to answer. You could spend an entire lifetime in New York and still never see and do everything this fabulous city has to offer. If you're here for a week, you first need to gather information and make choices.

My advice is to pick one or two places you really want to visit each day and build your itinerary around them. Because New York is so big, I suggest limiting your daily itinerary to just one or two neighborhoods. Also check to be sure that places you want to visit will be open on that day before you get too far along in your planning. Many museums and other tourist spots have reduced hours in the winter months. Of course, some activities are seasonal: ice skating in Rockefeller Plaza can be done only in winter, while Shakespeare in the Park is offered only in summer.

Every trip to New York is different, and every writer will have a varying list of favorites. If you have friends who know New York, by all means ask for their recommendations. The following itinerary for a week in New York combines my own favorites with some of the absolute "don't miss" classics. Whether you follow this outline or take a friend's suggestions, remember that part of the pleasure of New York is simply taking it all in at your leisure. Whatever else you do, spend a little time just walking around!

MONDAY | Getting Oriented

▦ Buy the current edition of *Time Out New York*, and read the various sections over coffee. This is especially useful if you have kids in tow.

▦ Stop by **NYC & Company** (810 Seventh Ave, 3rd floor, at 53rd St), the city's main tourist information center, to pick up maps and brochures and ask questions. Several information kiosks and counters are strategically located around town.

▦ Take a **Hop-On Hop-Off** double-decker bus tour of Manhattan (Gray Line New York Visitor Center, 777 Eighth Ave, 212/445-0848, 800/669-0051).

▦ Walk along Madison Avenue in the 60s and 70s, checking out all the big-name boutiques.

▦ Take a walk or carriage ride through Central Park.

▦ Lunch at one of the restaurants at **Time Warner Center** (10 Columbus Circle).

▦ Dinner at **Sfoglia** (1402 Lexington Ave).

TUESDAY | Museum Mile and Upper East Side

▦ Breakfast at **Norma's** at Le Parker Meridien Hotel (118 W 57th St).

▦ **Cooper-Hewitt, National Design Museum** (2 E 91st St).

▦ **Solomon R. Guggenheim Museum** (1071 Fifth Ave) and lunch in **The Wright**.

▦ The **Metropolitan Museum of Art** (1000 Fifth Ave).

▦ Visit the **Apple Store** (767 Fifth Ave).

▦ Dinner at **Arlington Club Steakhouse** (1032 Lexington Ave).

▦ Take in a show on **Broadway** or at a comedy club.

WEDNESDAY | Midtown

▦ Stroll through **Rockefeller Plaza** (Fifth Ave bet 48th and 51st St).

▦ Stop by **St. Patrick's Cathedral** (Fifth Ave at 51st St).

▦ Visit the **United Nations** (First Ave bet 42nd and 47th St).

▦ Lunch at **Stella 34 Trattoria** (Macy's, 35th and Broadway entrance).

▦ Take the 12:30 p.m. tour of **Grand Central Terminal**, offered by the Municipal Art Society.

▦ Visit the **New York Public Library** (Fifth Ave bet 40th and 42nd St).

▦ Spend the afternoon touring the **Museum of Modern Art** (11 W 53rd St).

▦ Dinner at **Eataly** (200 Fifth Ave): eat in at one of the restaurants or order take-out from the food shops.

THURSDAY | Upper West Side

▦ Start the day with a nosh at **Zabar's** (2245 Broadway).

▦ Stop by the **Cathedral Church of Saint John the Divine** (1047 112th St).

▦ Stock up on sweets at **Mondel Chocolates** (2913 Broadway).

- Lunch at **Cafe Lalo** (201 W 83rd St).
- Spend the afternoon at the **American Museum of Natural History** (Central Park W at 79th St).
- Dinner at **Barbetta** (321 W 46th St).

FRIDAY | Lower Manhattan
- Take the first ferry from Battery Park to the **Statue of Liberty** and **Ellis Island**.
- Walk up the **Battery Park Esplanade**.
- Visit the rebuilt **World Trade Center** complex and the **9/11 Tribute Center** (at Greenwich and Albany St).
- Lunch at **Balthazar** (80 Spring St).
- Stop by **St. Paul's Chapel** (209 Broadway).
- Take a leisurely late-afternoon stroll on the **Brooklyn Bridge**.
- Dinner at **Bouley** (163 Duane St).
- See a Broadway show. Get tickets well in advance from **Americana Tickets**, or try your luck at a **TKTS** booth.

SATURDAY | Chelsea and Soho
- Shop at **ABC Carpet & Home** (888 Broadway).
- Browse the **Strand Book Store** (828 Broadway).
- Go gallery hopping in Chelsea (on and around W 22nd St).
- Have a late-morning brunch at **Aquagrill** (210 Spring St).
- Walk along the **High Line** elevated park (Gansevoort St to West 30th St).
- Dinner at **Osteria Morini** (218 Lafayette St).
- Take a late-evening elevator ride up to the observation deck of the **Empire State Building** (Fifth Ave bet 33rd and 34th St).
- Walk along Fifth Avenue.

SUNDAY | Lower East Side and Midtown East
- Lunch at **Katz's Delicatessen** (205 E Houston St).
- Take one of the many scheduled tours at the **Lower East Side Tenement Museum** (108 Orchard St) or an interesting walking tour of the Lower East Side.
- Visit the remarkable **Eldridge Street Synagogue** (12 Eldridge St).
- Dinner at **Le Périgord** (405 E 52nd Ave).

Information on all places listed in these itineraries can be found in other sections of this book. Whatever else you do during your visit, I have two final pieces of advice:

- Get to know the subway system. It is generally safe, reliable, convenient, inexpensive (particularly if you get a seven-day pass), and by far the most efficient way to travel in New York, unless you have mobility issues. If you take cabs everywhere, you'll burn both money and time.

- Slow down. New Yorkers move very fast. It is fun to get into the flow of things, but it is also good to pause and take a look around. Don't get so focused on your destination that you fail to savor the experience of getting where you're going.

TOP 12 PLACES
TO VISIT IN NEW YORK

There are certain places in New York that everyone has on their "must visit" list. I've listed mine here, in alphabetical order, for easy reference.

Following each museum or sight write-up I've noted whether adult admission is free or if the fee charged is nominal ($1 to $5), reasonable ($6 to $19), or expensive ($20 and up). Taxes and add-ons are extra. Be sure to carefully check suggested admission prices.

AMERICAN MUSEUM OF NATURAL HISTORY

Central Park W at 79th St   212/769-5100
Daily: 10-5:45   amnh.org

Founded in 1869, this remarkable museum has taught generations of New York children and out-of-town visitors alike about the remarkable diversity of our planet and the natural world around us. It is hard to overstate the size of this sprawling place: the museum has 45 permanent exhibition halls in 25 interconnected buildings—including the Rose Center for Earth and Space and the Hayden Planetarium—covering almost 20 acres. The museum alone has more than 32 million artifacts and specimens.

Like several other museums of its size in New York, the American Museum of Natural History can seem overwhelming. My advice is to go to the information desk when you first arrive, get a floor plan, and then sit down and think about where you would like to go. If you're planning to see an IMAX movie or the Space Show at the Rose Center, be sure to note the time on your ticket and plan the other parts of your visit accordingly. While the constantly changing special exhibits are often fascinating, be aware that they are also often very crowded. So, too, are some of the permanent exhibits, including the Hall of Biodiversity, the Akeley Hall of African Mammals, the Milstein Hall of Ocean Life, and the Spitzer Hall of Human Origins. However, exhibits on the Northwest Coast and other Native Americans, as well as Asian, African, and Central and South American cultures, are often entirely empty even on busy days and yet full of fascinating items. Between all of the fossils, minerals, skeletons, and insects, there's really something for everyone. Plan to stay for at least a half day.

Four eateries, more gift shops than you can count, and guided tours are available. Admission fee charged (reasonable).

CENTRAL PARK

Bounded by Central Park W and Fifth Ave from 59th to 110th St

This urban gem was designed in 1858 by Frederick Law Olmsted, the same landscape architect who designed the U.S. Capitol grounds in Washington, D.C. Central Park occupies a rectangle in the heart of Manhattan that's bounded by Fifth Avenue on the East Side and Central Park West on the west side. Its 843 acres of grass, rocky outcroppings, ponds, 21,000 trees, and 58 miles of paths stretch from 59th Street to 110th Street. Tennis courts, baseball diamonds, playgrounds, restaurants, ice-skating (in winter), and a castle can all be found inside

---

New York City's Tallest Building

The new **I World Trade Center** (1,776 feet) has surpassed the Empire State Building as the city's tallest building. Skyscraper construction is elevating the Manhattan skyline, pushing the Empire State Building to the sixth tallest (it reigned as the world's tallest for over 40 years).

---

the park. Thanks to the Central Park Conservancy, a nonprofit organization that began managing the park in 1980, it is all clean, safe, and wonderfully accessible to the 40 million people who use it every year.

Regardless of season, the best way to experience Central Park is just to walk in it. (If you ever get lost, it helps to know that the first digits of the number plate on the lampposts correspond to the nearest cross street.) There's so much to see and do in the park that it's almost a city within the city. Just about every New Yorker has a favorite spot. Some of my favorites include the **Conservancy Gardens** (just off Fifth Avenue and 105th Street), **The Loeb Boathouse** (near 72nd Street on the east side), **Central Park Zoo** (just off Fifth Avenue at 64th Street), **Belvedere Castle** (mid-park, near 79th Street), and **Strawberry Fields** (near Central Park West, between 71st and 74th streets). You can get one of those quintessential New York photos standing on the rock outcroppings just inside the park near 59th Street at Avenue of the Americas.

Another great way to experience Central Park is by attending an event there. Particularly in the summer, it's home to free concerts by the New York Philharmonic and the Metropolitan Opera, Shakespeare in the Park performances, and all sorts of other cultural events. For a complete listing of events, walking tours, and other park activities, go to centralparknyc.org.

EMPIRE STATE BUILDING

350 Fifth Ave (bet 33rd and 34th St)   212/736-3100
Daily: 8 a.m.-2 a.m. (last elevator trip at 1:15 a.m.)   esbnyc.com

Often the first image that comes to mind when people think of New York is this 102-story building. Soaring above its neighbors just south of midtown, this skyscraper was built in 1931 and has defined the New York City skyline ever since. (In case you're wondering, there are 1,860 steps from street level to the 102nd floor!)

Tourists from all over the world and fans of movies like *King Kong, An Affair to Remember*, and *Sleepless in Seattle* simply can't come to New York without visiting this landmark and its observation deck on the 86th floor. On a clear day, you can see about 80 miles. It's worth noting that the ticket desk and line to go through security are actually on the second floor at the visitor's center. The newly renovated lobby on the first floor was restored to the original architects' Art Deco vision and is regularly kept clear for all those who work in the Empire State Building. If you really have your heart set on a visit here, consider coming early in the morning or late at night, or buy advance tickets online. Tickets to the 102nd floor observatory cost extra. An ESB Express Pass, although pricey, will put you at the front of all lines. Admission fee charged (reasonable to expensive, depending on tour package).

FIFTH AVENUE

London. Paris. Tokyo. They all have fashionable streets with out-of-sight rents. But nowhere in the world is quite as fashionable or quite as expensive as New York's Fifth Avenue.

Fifth Avenue starts down in Greenwich Village at **Washington Square Park**, and the **Empire State Building** is on Fifth Avenue between 33rd and 34th streets. However, when tourists say they want to visit Fifth Avenue, they generally mean midtown and the Upper East Side.

The stretch of Fifth Avenue between 42nd and 59th Street is the heart of New York. It was once lined with mansions and is still home to some of the grandest and most recognizable buildings in the city. They include the midtown branch of the **New York Public Library** (at 42nd Street), **Rockefeller Center** (between 48th and 51st Street), **Saks Fifth Avenue** (at 50th Street), **St. Patrick's Cathedral** (at 51st Street), **Tiffany & Co.** (at 57th Street), and **The Plaza** (at 59th Street). The presence of swanky retailers affirms what a tourist mecca and pricey shopping district Fifth Avenue has become.

The stretch of Fifth Avenue between 59th Street and 110th Street runs along the east side of Central Park. You'll find the **Neue Galerie New York** (at 86th Street), the **National Academy Museum & School** (between 89th and 90th Street), the **Jewish Museum** (at 92nd Street), and the **Museum of the City of New York** (between 103rd and 104th Street). When it is completed, the **Museum for African Art** will extend Museum Mile all the way to the top of Central Park, at 110th Street.

Like much of New York, the best way to see Fifth Avenue is on foot. The sidewalks along Central Park are a particular pleasure. There's no subway line running on Fifth Avenue, although there are plenty of buses and cabs. Traffic on Fifth Avenue is one-way heading south. One more tip: Under no circumstances should you go into a store on Fifth Avenue in midtown with "Going Out of Business" signs in the windows. They have a habit of going out of business regularly and this is likely just a come-on.`

LINCOLN CENTER

Columbus Ave bet 62nd and 65th St   212/546-2656
                                                                lincolncenter.org

Just as Museum Mile along Fifth Avenue is the most stunning concentration of art anywhere in the world, the 16-acre Lincoln Center campus may be the world's most amazing grouping of performing-arts institutions. The **Julliard School of Music** is housed here, as well as the **New York City Ballet**, the **Chamber**

Math is Cool

A new museum endeavors to persuade patrons (especially kids) that math is cool. **The National Museum of Mathematics** (11 E 26th St; 212/542-0566; momath.org) opened December, 2012. MoMath strives to enhance public understanding and perception of mathematics by illuminating the patterns that abound in our world with interesting hands-on activities. An unusual example is a smooth ride on a square-wheeled tricycle.

Thrilling Speedboat Tours

If you're a thrill seeker and feel the need for speed, check out these options. Tours operate seasonally.

The Beast (Pier 83 at W 42nd St, 212/563-3200, circleline42.com): Boats reach speeds of up to 45 m.p.h. in New York Harbor; plenty of landmark photo ops. Be sure to hang onto your hat!

The Shark (Pier 16 at South Street Seaport, 212/742-1969, circlelinedowntown.com): This is a high-energy ride with lots of exciting wakes and turns. It is definitely not like a carriage ride in Central Park!

Music Society of Lincoln Center, the **New York Philharmonic**, and the **Metropolitan Opera**, among many others. There is also a branch of the **New York Public Library** devoted entirely to the performing arts.

If you want to peek inside some of these concert halls and other spaces, daily tours are available (212/875-5350). You're also welcome to wander around and enjoy the fountains, open terraces, restaurants, and other public spaces. Each of the several stops is well worth your time. If you're interested in seeing one of the hundreds of performances that take place here every year, then visit the website for the latest information. Seeing a production at Lincoln Center is a special only-in-New-York treat!

LOWER EAST SIDE TENEMENT MUSEUM

108 Orchard St (bet Delancey and Broome St) 212/431-0233
Daily: 10-5 tenement.org

Whether or not you're among the countless thousands in this country whose family traces its arrival in this country to the Lower East Side, a visit to this living history museum is another one of my "must-sees" in New York. Building tours start at the visitors center (103 Orchard St) and then go down the block to the tenement building at 97 Orchard Street, where various apartments are frozen in time. Home to as many as 7,000 people from more than 20 nations between 1863 and 1935, this building is a living memorial to the hundreds of thousands who passed through the Lower East Side as immigrants to this country. An interesting guided tour is "The Moores: An Irish Family in America." Depending on the tour, you'll encounter various immigrant families modeled on real people who lived in this building between the 1860s and the 1930s. Walking tours of the Lower East Side are also available on weekends in warmer months. Take time for the excellent 25-minute film about the history of immigration on the Lower East Side, which runs continuously at the visitors center or browse the excellent gift shop. There is no cost to enter the visitors center. Fee charged (reasonable) for tours; reservations strongly suggested.

THE METROPOLITAN MUSEUM OF ART

1000 Fifth Avenue (bet 80th and 84th St) 212/535-7710
Sun-Thurs: 10-5:30; Fri, Sat: 10-9 metmuseum.org

Five thousand years of art. That's how the Metropolitan Museum of Art ("The Met," as it's known to New Yorkers and art fans) describes its holdings. It's all here: Egyptian tombs. Greek sculptures. African masks. European and Japanese arms and armor. Vases from China. Early American furniture. Tiffany windows. Nineteenth-century costumes. Twentieth-century photography. And no matter how many times you visit or how much time you spend here, there's just no way you'll ever see it all. The depth and breadth of The Met's collection is unparalleled.

There are several ways to approach touring The Met. I suggest coming early on a weekday morning, getting a copy of the floor plan at the information desk, and figuring out a couple areas of the museum you want to visit over the course of a day. You can always break for lunch at one of the museum's several restaurants or end your day with a drink at the **Great Hall Balcony Bar**. Another alternative is taking a "Museum Highlights" tour, offered regularly in various languages. My favorite strategy is simply going where everyone else isn't. Crowds can be overwhelming on weekends and whenever there's a special exhibit. Buying advance admission online is a good way to avoid long lines.

For many people, a favorite part of a Met visit is a trip to one of the museum's many stores. Although you can now visit Met gift stores at LaGuardia and Kennedy airports, as well as at Rockefeller Plaza, it's more fun browsing the shops inside The Met itself. Recommended admission fee (expensive) includes same day entry to the main building and to **The Cloisters Museum and Gardens**, located in northern Manhattan's Fort Tryon Park.

MUSEUM OF MODERN ART

11 W 53rd St (bet Fifth Ave and Ave of the Americas)   212/708-9400
Daily: 10:30-5:30 (Fri till 8)   moma.org

This museum is itself a masterpiece, filled with glass and soaring spaces. Located in midtown, MoMA (pronounced MO-ma) is the leading museum in the world dedicated to modern art. Well over 150,000 pieces of art—paintings, prints, photography, sculpture—are housed here, along with a remarkable archive and film library. From Cezanne, van Gogh, Matisse, and Picasso to Jasper Johns, Jeff Koons, Georgia O'Keeffe, and Jackson Pollack, just about any 20th-century artist you can imagine is represented. Indeed, MoMA's sleek galleries are a Who's Who of modern art history.

MoMA's curatorial departments include Architecture and Design, Print and Drawings, Painting, and Sculpture, Photography, Film, and Media and Performance Art. Pieces from each department are always on display in various collection galleries. In addition, MoMA has changing exhibitions and often hosts special travel-

---

In the News

Some celebrities have the misfortune of making headline news for their not-so-good behavior around town. Details of the scandals and locations of the miscreants' transgressions are revisited on a couple of two-hour, tell-all bus tours.

New York Post Headlines Tour (888/652-2695, nypost.com/tour):
  Thursday: 10 a.m., 2 p.m. Straight out of the *Post's* headlines.

TMZ Tour (855/486-9692, tmz.com): Monday-Friday: 10 a.m., 1 p.m.;
  Saturday, Sunday: 1 p.m., 4 p.m. Very entertaining with fun and games;
  videos shown on drop-down television screens.

Lights, Camera, Action!

The **Museum of the Moving Image** (36-01 35th Ave, Astoria, Queens, 718/777-6888, movingimage.us) is this country's only museum dedicated to anything having to do with films (art, technology, technique, and history). Allow several hours to peruse the interesting exhibits and collections (everything from action figures to a zoetrope), fan magazines, TV- and movie-inspired games and products, costumes, and equipment used throughout the decades. Check the schedule for film showings in the theater and screening room. This museum is both educational and entertaining!

---

ing exhibitions. If you have time, I suggest starting on the sixth floor and working your way down. If you want a quick tour of some of the museum's most famous holdings—including van Gogh's Starry Night, Picasso's Guitar, Matisse's Dance (1), and Andy Warhol's Campbell's Soup Cans—stop by the information desk and get a map.

A visit to this amazing place is not complete without a stop at the MoMA Bookstore (just off the foyer on the first floor) and the MoMA Design Store (across the street). Although there is some overlap between the two stores, there are enough differences to make it well worth your time to peruse both, as well as have lunch at either of the two cafes at MoMA or dinner at **The Modern**, a high-end Danny Meyer restaurant. Admission fee charged (expensive); Fri: 4-8, free. Admission to films is free with same-day museum ticket, otherwise film tickets are $12. Admission to MoMA PS 1, an affiliated museum in Long Island City, is free if you show your MoMA ticket stub within 30 days.

SOLOMON R. GUGGENHEIM MUSEUM

1071 Fifth Ave (at 89th St)   212/423-3500
Sun-Wed, Fri: 10-5:45; Sat: 10-7:45   guggenheim.org

The Solomon R. Guggenheim Museum began in 1939 as the Museum of Non-Objective Painting. It was created to house the growing art collection of American industrialist Solomon Guggenheim. His collection included the work of such contemporaries as Vasily Kandinsky, Paul Klee, and Marc Chagall, and many of those original pieces form the backbone of this remarkable museum today. Of course the collection has grown tremendously, since it incorporates work from artists ranging from late 19th-century impressionists to contemporary artists.

Although Guggenheim museums in Venice, Italy and Bilbao, Spain, showcase parts of the collection, the museum on Fifth Avenue is still the Guggenheim. In addition to the works displayed inside, people put this world-famous museum at the top of their itineraries because of its instantly recognizable building. It's an inverted ziggurat that looks a bit like a snail from the outside and allows visitors on the inside to wind their way through the collection rather than roaming in and out of rooms. The Guggenheim was designed by Frank Lloyd Wright and sits at the north end of Museum Mile, right across Fifth Avenue from Central Park. It opened in 1959 and underwent an extensive renovation for its 50th anniversary. Stand across the street to get the best architectural view.

In some ways, the breadth of the Guggenheim's collection rivals that of the

Museum of Modern Art (in midtown) and the Metropolitan Museum of Art (five blocks south on Fifth Avenue). But the great pleasure of the Guggenheim is that it's a bit smaller and more intimate than its famous cousins, giving art lovers time to linger. If 20th-century art is your passion, then there's no place you'll rather spend a day! Admission fee charged (reasonable); Sat: 5:45-7:45, pay what you wish.

STATUE OF LIBERTY

New York Harbor (south of Battery Park)   212/363-3200
Daily: 9-5 (adjusted seasonally)   nps.gov/stli
    They call her Lady Liberty. This 151-foot copper statue of a woman holding a torch was created by Frederic-Auguste Bartholdi and given to the United States as a gift from France in 1886. Standing on Liberty Island in New York Harbor, it's probably the single most iconic sight in all of New York. For generations of immigrants who came through nearby Ellis Island, it was also the first real sight they had of this new land. The words from "The New Colossus," a poem written by Emma Lazarus to help raise money for the completion of the pedestal for this powerful monument, still express basic instincts of our country and symbolism associated with the Statue of Liberty: "Give me your tired, your poor, Your huddled masses yearning to breathe free."
    A trip to the Statue of Liberty National Monument will take the better part of a morning or afternoon, so plan accordingly. Both the Statue of Liberty and Ellis Island are administered by the National Park Service. Visiting either destination requires a trip by boat from Battery Park. Head to Castle Clinton in Battery Park for tickets and detailed information, or buy your tickets in advance at statuecruises.com or by calling 877/LADYTIX. Tickets to the crown and pedestal are sold via Statue Cruises (201/604-2800, statuecruises.com); crown tickets are limited to 365 per day and should be reserved well in advance. Climbing to the crown entails ascending (and descending) 377 steps (the equivalent to climbing 20 stories) without air conditioning; high heat factors may close the Statue from time to time. Even if you have tickets, you'll need to wait in line for the next available boat. My advice: go early on a weekday and bring along lots of patience. Crown reservations: nominal fee; pedestal reservations: free. Ferry ticket (reasonable) is required.
    The Ellis Island Immigration Museum will not be fully operational for some time due to damage from Hurricane Sandy. Check the website (nps.gov/elis) for updates regarding Ellis Island.

TIMES SQUARE

42nd St at Broadway and surrounding area   timessquarenyc.org
    When I first started writing this book, Times Square was synonymous with petty crime, prostitution, and filth. Not anymore. In fact, I find it hard to believe that the Times Square of yesteryear and the Times Square of the 21st century are the same place. Named for the original New York Times building and incorporating the neighborhood around 42nd Street and Broadway, Times Square is now a center of New York's burgeoning tourist industry. It's full of family-friendly restaurants, hotels, and entertainment venues. The new Broadway pedestrian plaza has eased traffic woes and improved pedestrian safety. A TKTS booth is located under the ruby-red steps in Father Duffy Square at Broadway and 47th Street.

When in Harlem

Harlem is a destination in and of itself deserving a bit of exploration either on your own or via a guided tour with professionals.

Harlem Spirituals (212/391-0900 and 800/660-2166, harlemspirituals. com): Guided coach tours to Harlem, Manhattan, Brooklyn, and the Bronx. Stops may include worship services in a local church, gospel concerts, soul food, jazz, and historic sights.

Taste Harlem (212/209-3370, tasteharlem.com): A walking tour with tastings at fine and casual eateries serving flavors of the South, Caribbean, Africa, and more. Experience Harlem's history, architecture, entertainment, and renaissance.

Harlem Heritage Tourism & Cultural Center (212/280-7888; harlemheritage.com): All tours are led by guides who were born, raised, and continue to reside in Harlem. Walking tour options include gospel concerts, history, civil rights multimedia, and jazz nights.

All of those changes do not, however, put Times Square at the top of my "Top Twelve" list of places to visit. The whole area is wildly crowded with out-of-towners. In fact, it's a bit like going to a big mall somewhere in the nondescript suburbs around the winter holidays.

WORLD TRADE CENTER

Bounded by Vesey, Liberty, and Church St. and the West Side Highway   wtc.com

1 World Trade Center rises a symbolic 1,776 feet in height joining 7 World Trade Center in Lower Manhattan. Four other towers will complete the complex on this emotionally-charged site. When the buildings are completed, they will include observation decks, a performing arts center, vibrant retail and office spaces, and again be a transportation hub. The **9/11 Memorial** (911memorial.org) at the northwest corner of Albany and Greenwich streets offers a quiet place to remember and reflect upon the tragic losses of September 11, 2001. Five galleries constitute **9/11 Tribute Center** (120 Liberty St, 212/393-9160, tributewtc. org) and the **Tribute Center 9/11 Memorial Walking Tours** are led by people directly affected by the events of that day. Fee charged for admission and/or tour (reasonable to expensive).

THE BEST
OF THE REST

The previous "Top Twelve" list includes the museums and sights everyone wants to see when they come to New York. Although many of the museums and sights on that list are definite "must-sees," they are by no means all there is to New York. In fact, some of my "must-sees" are less well known, smaller, or a bit off the beaten path. The following list includes what I consider to be among the crown jewels of this remarkable city.

AMERICAN FOLK ART MUSEUM
2 Lincoln Square (Columbus Ave at 66th St)   212/595-9533
Tues-Sat: noon-7:30; Sun: noon-6   folkartmuseum.org

The museum's collection spans three centuries. Traditional folk art and works by self-taught artists are featured in changing exhibitions that come from the museum's collection and other lenders, public and private. The museum is located in a large two-level space with an excellent gift shop. Live music is featured in the galleries Friday evenings. Admission is free.

BROOKLYN BRIDGE
Broadway at City Hall Park in Lower Manhattan

Spanning the East River, this spectacular suspension bridge links Lower Manhattan to Brooklyn. It took 15 years and two generations to build. After its designer, John Roebling, was killed in an accident, his son Washington and daughter-in-law Emily took over the project. Pedestrians and bicyclists share the bridge's historic 1.3 mile-promenade; bicyclists have the north lane, pedestrians the south. To reach the bridge, go to the east side of City Hall Park, just off Broadway, and follow the signs. For the rest of the story you may want to join a tour or download an iPhone app. Sunset and sunrise are particularly beautiful times to take a stroll on the bridge, although it's open 24 hours a day.

CATHEDRAL CHURCH OF SAINT JOHN THE DIVINE
1047 Amsterdam Ave (at 112th St)   212/316-7490
Daily: 7:30-6   stjohndivine.org

Gracing Amsterdam Avenue on the east side of Columbia University, the Cathedral Church of Saint John the Divine is one of the largest Christian houses of worship in the world. And it isn't even finished! Part Gothic, part Romanesque, this magnificent Episcopal cathedral is so enormous that the Statue of Liberty could easily fit inside the main sanctuary. For information about daily tours, call 212/932-7347. Admission is free, but donations are accepted and a minimal fee is charged for tours.

THE CLOISTERS MUSEUM AND GARDENS
Fort Tryon Park (99 Margaret Corbin Dr)   212/923-3700
Sun-Thurs: 10-5:30; Fri, Sat: 10-9   metmuseum.org/cloisters

Perhaps the finest medieval art museum in the world, this branch of The Metropolitan Museum of Art is also one of the quietest and most beautiful places in

---

Orchard Street

Real-estate developers have had their hands in the demise or disfigurement of the Lower East Side tenements ever since immigration slowed in the 1920s. When they haven't been completely replaced by high-rises, drastic renovations have left these vestiges of mass immigration unrecognizable from their previous historical architecture. The National Trust for Historic Preservation has added this area, once one of the most crowded communities on Earth, to its endangered list. What was a colorful shopping area has greatly changed. A Sunday visit to Orchard Street is still an experience, but you will not find the bargains or selections of past years.

---

all of New York. Built at the far north end of the island on land donated by John D. Rockefeller, Jr. in the late 1930s, the museum incorporates large sections of cloisters and other medieval buildings brought from Europe. Tapestries, ivories, paintings, sculptures, and other decorative items are part of the spectacular collection on display. From the outdoor terrace, you can look at the Hudson River and the steep cliffs known as the Palisades beyond, easily forgetting that you're in a 21st-century city. Recommended admission fee charged (expensive) includes same-day admission to The Metropolitan Museum of Art.

COOPER-HEWITT, NATIONAL DESIGN MUSEUM
2 E 91st St (at Fifth Ave)   212/849-8400
                                                           cooperhewitt.org
Founded as the Cooper Union Museum for the Arts of Decoration in 1897, this remarkable institution became part of the Smithsonian Institution in 1967. A complete renovation has temporarily closed this 64-room mansion until late 2014. Exhibitions and public programs continue at various off-site venues around the city.

FRICK COLLECTION
1 E 70th St (at Fifth Ave)   212/288-0700
Tues-Sat: 10-6; Sun: 11-5   frick.org
This elegant mansion takes my breath away! Built by industrialist Henry Clay Frick almost a century ago to house his growing art collection, the Frick Collection is one of the last great mansions on Fifth Avenue and it is definitely on my "must-see" list. Gilbert Stuart's portrait of George Washington is here, as are works by Vermeer, Rembrandt, El Greco, Goya, and masters ranging from the Italian Renaissance to the 19th century. But it isn't just the paintings that dazzle. Frick's collection also includes stunning Oriental rugs, Chinese porcelain, Limoge enamels, and a wide range of decorative arts that must be seen to be believed. Take time to wander and look at everything from the paintings to the light fixtures and rugs, to the serene Garden Court outside. Admission fee charged (reasonable); Sun: 11-1, pay what you wish.

GRAND CENTRAL TERMINAL
42nd St bet Vanderbilt and Lexington Ave   212/340-2345
Daily: 5:30 a.m.-2:00 a.m.   grandcentralterminal.com

New York's past, present, and future come together in this marble palace that was voted "New York's Greatest Building." Opened in 1913, Grand Central is first and foremost a train station, home to hundreds of commuter trains that operate between Manhattan and points north in Westchester County and Connecticut. It also plays host to an upscale food market, dozens of shops featuring everything from unique toys to fine jewelry and cutting edge technology, and a gourmet dining concourse. (Stores and restaurants keep varying hours.) Exciting events and promotions happen daily in historic Vanderbilt Hall and live guided and audio tours are available on the main concourse for a small fee. There's no charge to wander around the terminal and take in its extraordinary century-old beaux-arts architecture.

THE JEWISH MUSEUM

1109 Fifth Ave (at 92nd St)   212/423-3200
Sat-Tues: 11-5:45; Thurs: 11-8; Fri: 11-4   thejewishmuseum.org

The Jewish Museum is housed in yet another grand Fifth Avenue mansion. This one was donated by Felix Warburg's widow in 1945 (Warburg was a Jewish philanthropist). The museum explores 4,000 years of Jewish culture and has the largest collection of Jewish art and Judaica in the United States, 25,000 works. The heart of the museum is "Culture and Continuity: The Jewish Journey" comprised of 800 objects including paintings, drawings, sculptures, ritual art, archaeology, and photography. A visit to the museum's excellent gift shop or Celebrations, a smaller design shop in an adjacent brownstone, is well worth an extra half-hour. Admission fee charged (reasonable); Sat: free; Thurs: 5-8, pay what you wish.

THE MORGAN LIBRARY AND MUSEUM

225 Madison Ave (at 36th St)   212/685-0008
Tues-Thurs: 10:30-5; Fri: 10:30-9; Sat: 10-6; Sun: 11-6   themorgan.org

Designed in the early 20th century to house the astonishing collection of rare items and prized treasures amassed by Pierpont Morgan (an industrialist and financier), the elegant library and study and their contents will transport you to another time and place. Just imagine yourself surrounded by these paintings, sculptures, furniture, books, architectural details, and textiles spanning many centuries and several continents! It's hard to believe anyone ever lived like this. Morgan's collection includes historical, artistic, literary, and musical works. The spaces in the rest of the museum, including an atrium and other galleries, are often crowded. There is a good place to eat, too. Admission fee charged (reasonable); Fri: 7-9, free.

MUSEUM OF JEWISH HERITAGE:
A LIVING MEMORIAL TO THE HOLOCAUST

36 Battery Pl (in Battery Park City)   646/437-4202
Sun-Tues: 10-5:45; Wed: 10-8; Thurs: 10-5:45; Fri: 10-5 (till 3 during EST)
                                                                         mjhnyc.org

This remarkable and sometimes overlooked museum just north of Battery Park in Lower Manhattan manages to be not only a memorial to those who perished in the Holocaust but also a vibrant, life-affirming celebration of Jewish culture and its endurance. Using first-person narratives, a remarkably diverse collection, and special exhibitions, the museum's three-part permanent display tells the unfolding story of Jewish life a century ago, the persecution of Jews and the

Historic Places of Worship

Because New York was a British colony for much of its early history, the city's lower half is full of historic Episcopal churches. They include:

Church of the Transfiguration, also known as "the Little Church Around the Corner" (1 E 29th St)

Grace Church (Broadway between 10th and 11th St)

St. Mark's Church in-the-Bowery, constructed on the site of Peter Stuyvesant's personal chapel in 1799 (10th St at Third Ave)

St. Paul's Chapel, the oldest church building in the city, dating from 1766 (Broadway between Fulton and Vesey St)

Trinity Church (Broadway at Wall St)

Other historic houses of worship in Manhattan include:

Abyssinian Baptist Church (132 Odell Clark Pl)

Bialystoker Synagogue (7-11 Willett St)

Central Synagogue (652 Lexington Ave)

Congregation Shearith Israel, also known as the **Spanish and Portuguese Synagogue** (8 W 70th St)

Marble Collegiate Church (1 W 29th St)

Riverside Church (490 Riverside Dr)

Temple Emanu-El (1 E 65th St)

Holocaust, and modern Jewish life and renewal in the decades since. An audio guide is available at no charge, and a free activity book assists families with young children to explore the first and third floors. Both the cafe, which has amazing views of the Statue of Liberty and New York Harbor, and the museum's gift shop are worthy of a visit. Andy Goldsworthy's Garden of Stones outside the museum is a terrific spot to sit and meditate. Visitors should be prepared to take their time. Admission fee charged (reasonable); children 12 and under, free; Wed: 4-8, free.

MUSEUM OF THE CITY OF NEW YORK

1220 Fifth Ave (bet 103rd and 104th St)   212/534-1672
Daily: 10-6   mcny.org

Housed in a landmark Georgian-style mansion, this museum is dedicated to preserving the history of New York, starting with its earliest European settlement. A $93 million expansion and modernization project added a tri-level state-of-the-art curatorial center and South Wing gallery space. With that has come a new energy for the changing and permanent exhibitions, lectures, classes, programs for city school students, and other events. Admission fee charged (reasonable).

NEW YORK PUBLIC LIBRARY

455 Fifth Ave (bet 40th and 42nd St)   917/275-6975
Mon, Thurs-Sat: 10-6; Tues, Wed: 10-8; Sun: 1-5   nypl.org

This midtown branch of the New York Public Library is a working library and has the largest collection of circulating and reference works in the entire system.

It's also home to a wide range of public programs. But this isn't just any library! Located along Fifth Avenue, it's a "must-see" if you're in midtown. Standing guard out front are two stately lions named Patience and Fortitude by former mayor Fiorello LaGuardia. Inside you'll find marble staircases, an excellent gift shop, the dramatic Rose Main Reading Room on the third floor (nearly two city blocks long and enhanced with Wi-Fi and laptop docking), an amazing map room on the first floor, and various gallery spaces. Stop by the information desk in the breathtaking lobby to find out about frequent tours offered by the Friends of the New York Public Library. Free admission.

ROOSEVELT ISLAND
East River, between Manhattan and Queens

If you're a photographer looking for that perfect shot of the Manhattan skyline, a trip to Roosevelt Island should be at the top of your itinerary. At various times in its history, Roosevelt Island was known as Blackwell's Island and Welfare Island, and it's been home to prisons, hospitals, and asylums. Renwick Ruin, the former Smallpox Hospital, is the only New York City ruin which is also a landmark. Today this two-mile island in the middle of the East River is home to 14,000 residents, many of whom commute into Manhattan each day. Visitors come for the view, particularly from the tram and from the northwest tip of Lighthouse Park. The Franklin D. Roosevelt Four Freedoms Park is named for the freedoms (freedom of speech and expression, freedom of religion, freedom from want, and freedom from fear) which Roosevelt described in his 1941 State of the Union address. The three-minute tram ride from Manhattan leaves from a small station at Second Avenue and 59th Street and runs daily from 6 a.m. to 2 a.m. (Fri and Sat till 3:30 a.m.) for a nominal fare of $2.50 (subway MetroCards also accepted).

ST. PATRICK'S CATHEDRAL
Fifth Ave between 50th and 51st St   212/753-2261
Daily: 6:30 a.m.-8:45 p.m.   saintpatrickscathedral.org

Designed in the middle of the 19th century by famed architect James Renwick, Jr., this Gothic cathedral is a much-loved Fifth Avenue landmark and the largest Neo-Gothic Roman Catholic church in the United States. The main organ has over 9,000 pipes, and the sanctuary can seemingly seat half of Manhattan. Whether you're here for a service or just peeking inside, it's hard to overstate the beauty and elegance of St. Patrick's. Please remember that this is an active church. Mass is said several times each day, eight times on Sunday, and even more on Holy Days. You are welcome to come in and light a candle or just sit in silence. Here's a tip: the cathedral's steps along Fifth Avenue are one of the best places in New York for resting your feet and watching the world go by! Free admission.

STATEN ISLAND FERRY
Whitehall Ferry Terminal (at the foot of Whitehall St)   nyc.gov/dot

On a typical weekday, five ferries make a combined 100+ round trips between Staten Island and the Whitehall Ferry Terminal on Manhattan's southern tip. The trip covers just over five miles in less than 30 minutes. And what a trip it is! The Staten Island ferries offer some of the very best views of Lower Manhattan's skyscrapers, the Statue of Liberty, and Ellis Island with a comfortable place to sit and take them in. Best of all, the Staten Island ferry is free 24/7!

Up In the Air

Some people say the best way to see all of New York City is from the sky. A helicopter tour not only provides a bird's-eye view, but covers more sights in a short timespan than any other means of sightseeing. Each exhilarating tour departs from the Downtown Manhattan Heliport (Pier 6 and the East River). Tour lengths vary from a quick 12-minute journey to a more-inclusive 30-minute buzz around the Big Apple and beyond; inquire about custom, private, and special occasion tours.

Helicopter New York City (212/747-9282, helicopternewyorkcity. com)

Liberty Helicopters (212/967-6464, libertyhelicopters.com)

Manhattan Helicopters (646/783-3606, flymh.com)

Since inclement weather conditions may cause disruptions to scheduled flights, it might be a good idea to plan your flight at the front end of your trip in case you need to reschedule.

TRINITY CHURCH

74 Trinity Pl (Broadway at Wall St)   212/602-0800
Museum: Mon-Fri: 9-5:30; Sat, Sun: 9-3:45   trinitywallstreet.org

In the heart of Lower Manhattan's Financial District, this is the third iteration of Trinity to occupy a site on land that was part of a charter granted by King William III of England in 1697. This building was completed in 1846, although the headstones in the 2.5-acre graveyard date back to the late 17th century. Believe it or not, Trinity Church was the tallest building in Manhattan for most of the 19th century. Today it offers a small museum (closed during 12:05 services), guided tours (Mon-Fri: 2 p.m.), and concerts, in addition to daily worship services. Admission is free, but donations are accepted.

UNITED NATIONS

First Ave bet 42nd and 47th St   212/963-4440 (tours)
Mon-Fri: 10:15-4:45 (tours)   visit.un.org

New York is a great American city, but it is also a great international city hosting the United Nations. The flags of 193 member nations fly along First Avenue in front of the UN Headquarters. Many languages are spoken in this area as staff members and delegates from all over the world come and go. You can visit the beautiful and peaceful grounds of the UN to take a guided tour of the newly renovated Conference Building. Be sure to stop by the UN Bookstore in the new Visitor Centre, as well as the UN's very own post office before or after your guided tour. Access to guided tours permitted only with a ticket pre-purchased online (reasonable); children must be at least five years of age.

WHITNEY MUSEUM OF AMERICAN ART

945 Madison Ave (at 75th St)   212/570-3600
Wed-Thurs, Sat, Sun: 11-6; Fri: 1-9   whitney.org

The artist and art collector Gertrude Vanderbilt Whitney opened this museum in 1931 with her personal collection of 20th-century American art. It has grown in the years since (and moved twice) while remaining true to its mission of collecting and displaying modern and contemporary American art. (Another move is in the works, this time to the Meatpacking District in 2015.) Of course, the Whitney's mission means its remarkable collection now spans more than a century and continues to expand. It includes the world's largest collections of Edward Hopper, Reginald Marsh, and Alexander Calder, as well as sculptures, paintings, drawings, media installations, and other works by established and emerging artists. Admission fee charged (reasonable); Fri: 6-9, pay what you wish. Danny Meyer's lower-level museum cafe, **Untitled**, is a contemporary Manhattan coffee shop serving farm-to-table fare.

SMALLER MUSEUMS
AND SPECIAL SPOTS

AMERICAN NUMISMATIC SOCIETY

75 Varick St (at Canal St), 11th floor   212/571-4470
Mon-Fri: 10-4   numismatics.org

This location is a museum, library, and research institute devoted to the study of coins from all periods and cultures. There are over 800,000 coins, medals, paper currency, and other artifacts in the society's vast collection. A small gallery of revolving exhibits is open to the public and the numismatic library is available by appointment. Free admission.

AMERICAS SOCIETY GALLERY

680 Park Ave (at 68th St)   212/249-8950
Wed-Sat: noon-6   americas-society.org

The Americas Society was founded in 1965 by David Rockefeller with the simple but important goal of furthering understanding between the Americas. The changing exhibitions in its small but elegant gallery space showcase the diverse work of artists from throughout the Americas. Free admission.

ASIA SOCIETY AND MUSEUM

725 Park Ave (at 70th St)   212/288-6400
Tues-Sun: 11-6 (Fri till 9, Sept-June)   asiasociety.org

Drawing upon private collections and its own extensive holdings of art from more than 30 Asia-Pacific nations, the Asia Society mounts changing exhibits of traditional and contemporary art. By all means visit the lovely Garden Court Cafe for lunch and a boutique that stocks items by Asian and Asian-American designers. Admission fee charged (reasonable); Fri: 6-9, free.

BARD GRADUATE CENTER

18 W 86th St (at Central Park W)   212/501-3023
Tues-Sun: 11-5 (Thurs till 8)   bgc.bard.edu

The Bard Graduate School is known around the world for its passionate commitment to the decorative arts, design, and material culture. Its beautiful townhouse gallery on the Upper West Side hosts several changing exhibits each year. Admission fee charged (nominal).

Museum Memberships and Admissions

Check into yearly membership rates if you plan to make multiple visits to your favorite museum. An annual membership may pay for itself in four or five visits. Member perks, such as special or exclusive events and museum-store discounts, are added values. Many institutions list their entry fees as a *suggested* amount. Translation: offer what you would like to pay. That is especially prudent if you plan to be in a museum for only a short time and the admission charge is steep.

If possible, plan your visit to coincide with free admission hours. Many museums offer free or pay-as-you-wish admission to customers one evening a week. However, a possible tradeoff for going on a free night is a thicker crowd.

BRYANT PARK
Ave of the Americas bet 40th and 42nd St   bryantpark.org

This park symbolizes for me the remarkable transformation that has occurred throughout the city in the past 30 or so years. Long a place to be avoided, Bryant Park is now a thriving part of the city's life. Home to the wonderful Le Carrousel, an ice rink in winter, free movies in summer, and chess and backgammon games throughout the year, this urban jewel sits behind the New York Public Library. Have lunch, attend an event, or just wander through the formal French gardens. Free Wi-Fi is provided.

CHINA INSTITUTE GALLERY
125 E 65th St (bet Lexington and Park Ave)   212/744-8181
Daily: 10-5 (Tues, Thurs till 8)   chinainstitute.org

This is the only not-for-profit gallery in New York (other than the Metropolitan Museum of Art) dedicated to showcasing the traditional, modern, and contemporary art of China. Thematic changing exhibits in this beautiful East Side townhouse are of consistent high quality; many works have never been seen previously in this country. Admission fee charged (nominal).

DRAWING CENTER
35 Wooster St (bet Grand and Broome St)   212/219-2166
Wed-Sun: noon-6 (Thurs till 8)   drawingcenter.org

Dedicated exclusively to showcasing contemporary and historical drawings, this Soho institution mounts highly regarded changing exhibitions. Admission fee charged (nominal).

DYCKMAN FARMHOUSE MUSEUM
4881 Broadway (at 204th St)   212/304-9422
Fri-Sun: 11-5   dyckmanfarmhouse.org

This is the last surviving example of the sort of farmhouse built all over New York well into the 19th century. It is a little time machine sitting on what was once Kingsbridge Road (now known as Broadway). There are some particularly good family programs. Admission fee charged (nominal).

FEDERAL HALL NATIONAL MEMORIAL

26 Wall St (bet Broad and William St)   212/825-6888
Mon-Fri: 9-5   nps.gov/feha

Everyone knows that Washington, D.C., is the nation's capital, but it didn't start out that way. In fact, George Washington was inaugurated on this spot in the first Federal Hall (torn down in 1812 and rebuilt in 1842), which served briefly as the U.S. Capitol. After extensive renovations, this National Park Service site hosts a small gallery and an information center featuring the national parks in New York City. Free admission.

FORBES MAGAZINE GALLERIES

62 Fifth Ave (at 12th St)   212/206-5548
Tues-Sat: 10-4   forbesgalleries.com

The Forbes Galleries, located in the heart of Greenwich Village, are tucked within the lobby of Forbes Magazine's headquarters in New York City. Rotating exhibitions are showcased throughout the year in four changing exhibition spaces. Free admission.

FRAUNCES TAVERN MUSEUM

54 Pearl St (at Broad St)   212/425-1778
Daily: noon-5   frauncestavernmuseum.org

Fraunces Tavern was a meeting place for the Sons of Liberty before the Revolutionary War and the site of General George Washington's farewell address to his officers after the war. Its history can be traced back to 1719, and it is the oldest surviving structure in Manhattan. The first floor still operates as a restaurant (call 212/968-1776 for reservations), while the second floor is dedicated to a museum focused largely on the Revolutionary War period. Admission fee charged (nominal).

HISPANIC SOCIETY OF AMERICA

Audubon Terrace
613 W 155th St (Broadway bet 155th and 156th St)   212/926-2234
Tues-Sat: 10-4:30; Sun: 1-4   hispanicsociety.org

The former farm of naturalist John James Audubon is an unlikely place for the Hispanic Society of America, and a man named Archer Milton Huntington sounds like an unlikely benefactor. But North America's most significant collection of paintings, textiles, ceramics, photographs, and other items from the Iberian Peninsula and Latin America sits atop Audubon's farm and was largely assembled

---

Noteworthy Brooklyn Attractions

Brooklyn Botanic Gardens (1000 Washington Ave, 718/623-7200, bbg.org): over a century of gardening

Brooklyn Museum (200 Eastern Parkway, 718/638-5000, brooklynmuseum.org): outstanding Egyptian Collection

New York Transit Museum (Boerum Pl at Schermerhorn St, Brooklyn Heights, 718/694-1600, mta.info/museum): public transportation history.

The Best of The Bronx

Bronx Museum of the Arts (1040 Grand Concourse, 718/681-6000, bronxmuseum.org)

Bronx Zoo (2300 Southern Blvd, 718/367-1010, bronxzoo.org)

New York Botanical Garden (2900 Southern Blvd, 718/817-8700, nygb.org)

Wave Hill (249th St and Independence Ave, 718/549-3200, wavehill. org): a well-known public garden along the Hudson River

---

by Huntington. If you're interested in the subject, a trek up to this out-of-the-way spot will be well worth your time. An exceptional reference library is also housed here. Free admission.

INTERNATIONAL CENTER OF PHOTOGRAPHY

1133 Ave of the Americas (at 43rd St)   212/857-0000
Tues-Sun: 10-6 (Fri till 8)   icp.org

If you like photography, this center for the study, preservation, and exhibition of photographic art is a "must-see." Beautiful gallery spaces and exceptionally well-conceived shows combine to make visiting here a real treat. Admission fee charged (reasonable); Fri: 5-8, pay what you wish.

INTREPID SEA, AIR & SPACE MUSEUM

Pier 86 (Twelfth Ave at 46th St)   212/245-0072, 877/957-7447
Mon-Fri: 10-5; Sat, Sun: 10-6   intrepidmuseum.org

This hugely popular museum complex contains the 900-foot long aircraft carrier Intrepid (incorporating a theater, children's interactive zone, and the anchor-chain room), the submarine Growler, and 27 aircraft (including the Concorde and the A-12 Blackbird spy plane). Collections of uniforms, medals, photos, and all sorts of memorabilia associated with sea, air, and space are on display throughout the bowels of the carrier. Allow plenty of time to take in the interactive exhibits. Admission fee charged (expensive); check for seasonal closures.

JAPAN SOCIETY GALLERY

333 E 47th St (bet First and Second Ave)   212/832-1155
Tues-Thurs: 11-6; Fri: 11-9; Sat, Sun: 11-5   japansociety.org

Founded in 1907, the Japan Society is a remarkable institution dedicated to furthering understanding between the United States and Japan. In addition to language classes, lecture series, films, and other programs, the society has a small but elegant gallery space that presents three exhibitions every year. Admission fee charged (reasonable).

MERCHANT'S HOUSE MUSEUM

29 E 4th St (bet Lafayette St and Bowery)   212/777-1089
Thurs-Mon: noon-5   merchantshouse.org

Step back in time to an era when this part of town was considered the suburbs and New York was the country's leading port city. Built in 1832, this townhouse is a real time capsule, full of the furniture, clothes, and other items used by one of New York's wealthy merchant families. The servant call bells, elegant four-poster beds, and gas chandeliers are just a few of the many period details you'll see as you wander through this beautifully preserved family home (inside and out). This is the only home of its type from this period in New York City, and it is a National Historic Landmark. The backyard is a replica of a 19th-century garden that includes varietals from the era. Check the schedule for museum-hosted events. Admission fee charged (reasonable).

MORRIS-JUMEL MANSION

65 Jumel Terrace (bet 160th and 162nd St)   212/923-8008
Wed-Sun: 10-4   morrisjumel.org

George Washington used this mansion—located on a hill overlooking the Harlem River, Long Island Sound, the Hudson River, and the Palisades—as his headquarters at the beginning of the Revolutionary War. Built in 1765, its commanding views offered an important strategic position, first to Washington and later to the British. When the British finally left, General Washington returned in 1790 for a dinner with some of the country's founding fathers, including John Adams, Thomas Jefferson, and Alexander Hamilton. Several owners and much more history passed through these rooms in subsequent years. Most of the furniture—including a bed said to have belonged to Napoleon—dates from the 19th century. Admission fee charged (nominal).

MOUNT VERNON HOTEL MUSEUM AND GARDEN

421 E 61st St (bet First and York Ave)   212/838-6878
Tues-Sun: 11-4   mvhm.org

Another time machine that's survived into the 21st century, this amazing little spot started life as a carriage house for a large estate. It served as a day hotel in the early 19th century and eventually became a private home. Now owned and lovingly preserved by the Colonial Dames of America, it's full of period pieces reflecting its years as a destination for day-trippers coming out to the country by boat or by carriage from Lower Manhattan. The Mount Vernon Hotel Museum and Garden (formerly known as the Abigail Adams Smith Museum) will transport you back 200 years. Tours are provided on request by wonderfully knowledgeable docents. Admission fee charged (nominal).

MUSEUM AT ELDRIDGE STREET

12 Eldridge St (bet Canal and Division St)   212/219-0302
Sun-Thurs: 10-5; Fri: 10-3   eldridgestreet.org

New York Stock Exchange

Steeped in history, the world's largest stock exchange originated on Wall Street in 1792. Several locations on Wall and Broad streets were home to the New York Stock Exchange until the erection of the current neoclassical structure on Broad Street in 1903. Home to many of America's greatest companies and its globally recognized trading floor, this National Historic Landmark has been shaped by booms, busts, and images of frenetic trading for over 200 years. Alas, as a sign of the times, this iconic temple of trading is no longer open for public tours.

> **Tweed Courthouse**
>
> Built between 1861 and 1881 as the Old New York County Courthouse and fully restored between 1999 and 2001, the **Tweed Courthouse** (52 Chambers St, 212/788-2656; nyc.gov) is one of New York's greatest civic monuments. It is not only the legacy of Tammany Hall boss William M. Tweed, but also a building unparalleled for its interior cast-iron structural and decorative elements that sit beside polychromed brick and richly carved stonework. The architecture is fascinating and so is the story of "Boss" Tweed who served prison time for embezzling millions of dollars from the city's coffers. This courthouse is currently a working office building and school; free tours are available (call or register online).

For decades after opening in 1887, the Eldridge Street Synagogue was a central part of the life of thousands of Eastern European Jewish immigrants on the Lower East Side. Interactive displays, tours, and public programs tell some of the stories that passed through these doors. Admission fee charged for tour (reasonable); Mon: free.

MUSEUM AT FIT

Seventh Ave at 27th St   212/217-4560
Tues-Fri: noon-8; Sat: 10-5   fitnyc.edu/museum

The Fashion Institute of Technology (FIT), a college of the State University of New York, is one of the world's leading fashion schools for career education in art, design, business, and technology. This gem of a museum is the only museum in New York City dedicated solely to the art of fashion. Free admission.

MUSEUM OF AMERICAN FINANCE

48 Wall St (at William St)   212/908-4110
Tues-Sat: 10-4   moaf.org

This museum is appropriately sited in the building that once housed the Bank of New York, which was founded by Alexander Hamilton (who went on to become our nation's first Secretary of the Treasury). The largest exhibit focuses on New York's financial markets, which are located only a block or so away. Visitors explore the routes of check and credit card transactions, differences between financial institutions, and the Federal Reserve System. There's also a piggybank display! Various forms of money are exhibited, from the earliest tender to the latest currency with hidden anti-counterfeiting technology. Special events having to do with current economic issues are often scheduled. Admission fee charged (reasonable).

MUSEUM OF AMERICAN ILLUSTRATION
MUSEUM OF COMIC AND CARTOON ART

128 E 63rd St (bet Park and Lexington Ave)   212/838-2560
Tues-Fri: 10-5; Sat: noon-4   societyillustrators.org

Changing exhibitions, including some from the Society of Illustrators' and the Museum of Comic and Cartoon Art's permanent collection, are housed in an elegant 1853 carriage house that today serves as the society's headquarters. Books, magazines, and posters are among the items for sale in the museum shop. Free admission.

MUSEUM OF ARTS AND DESIGN
2 Columbus Circle (at Eighth Ave)   212/299-7777
Tues-Sun: 10-6 (Thurs, Fri till 9)   madmuseum.org

The museum, also known as MAD, occupies a recently redesigned building located in the revived Columbus Circle. The concave exterior, covered with small, glazed terra-cotta tiles, seemingly glitters at dusk. Collections and exhibitions are comprised of contemporary objects created in clay, glass, wood, metal, and fiber (from the mid-20th century to the present); the permanent collection includes more than 2,000 objects. Elsewhere in the building, an attractive store sells useful and decorative items and a restaurant, **Robert**, serves a Mediterranean menu and has gorgeous Central Park views. Admission fee charged (reasonable); Thurs: 6-9, free.

MUSEUM OF BIBLICAL ART
1865 Broadway (at 61st St)   212/408-1500
Tues-Sun: 10-6 (Thurs till 8)   mobia.org

Art inspired and influenced by the Bible is interpreted through three annual special exhibitions and educational programs. From ecclesiastical art to contemporary secular work, this fascinating museum takes no stand on religion, but offers a unique perspective on how the symbols and narratives of the Hebrew and Christian Bible influence art and are often incorporated into it. Free admission.

MUSEUM OF CHINESE IN THE AMERICAS
215 Centre St (bet Howard and Grand St)   212/619-4785
Tues-Sun: 11-6 (Thurs till 9)   mocanyc.org

This fine museum is dedicated to telling and preserving the stories of Chinese immigrants to this country through its main exhibition which traces over

High Line Park
You won't be disappointed by a walk along the very popular **High Line** (212/206-9922, thehighline.org), a unique public park built on a 1.45-mile-long elevated rail structure with views of New York's magnificent skyline and the Hudson River. The one-mile route runs from Gansevoort Street and continues up to 34th Street where it terminates at the West Side Rail Yards (that project is in the works). The former freight rail line ceased operation in 1980 and after a decade of efforts by Friends of the High Line, with support from the City of New York, it was redesigned to accommodate a water feature, sundeck, gathering areas, and safe walking surfaces. Areas are designated for educational programs, art installations, and performances, but dogs, Frisbees, and playing catch are prohibited. Park hours fluctuate according to the season; snow and ice removal keeps the High Line open even in the dead of winter. Come spring, food vendors set up shop between April and October. There are currently nine accesses to the park, and since High Line Park sits above city streets, elevators are located at four of those entry points providing wheelchair accessibility.

Photo Policy

Some museums and galleries allow visitors to freely snap photos of famous works on display. Others have strict "no photography" policies enforced by security officers. The same prohibition may apply to sketching. Always check the fine print online before you go or ask at the museum or gallery. You may avoid an embarrassing situation.

160 years of Chinese American history, historical exhibits, and walking tours. The sizable collection includes business, family and community artifacts, documents, newspapers, photographs, and oral histories. Admission fee charged (reasonable).

MUSEUM OF SEX
233 Fifth Ave (at 27th St)   212/689-6337
Sun-Thurs: 10-8; Fri, Sat: 10-9   museumofsex.com
    One might call this the most stimulating museum in New York! Changing exhibitions address a wide range of topics relating to sexuality. A bar serves aphrodisiac potions and nibbles for desired effects, while the museum store has all sorts of exciting merchandise. Admission fee charged (expensive).

NATIONAL ACADEMY MUSEUM & SCHOOL
1083 Fifth Ave (bet 89th and 90th St)   212/369-4880
Wed-Sun: 11-6   nationalacademy.org
    The National Academy is the only institution of its kind that integrates a museum, art school, and association of artists and architects dedicated to creating and preserving a living history of American art. The museum houses one of the largest collections of 19th- and 20th-century American art in the country. Admission fee charged (reasonable).

NATIONAL MUSEUM OF THE AMERICAN INDIAN
1 Bowling Green (foot of Broadway)   212/514-3700
Daily: 10-5 (Thurs till 8)   nmai.si.edu
    The National Museum of the American Indian in New York is located with the Alexander Hamilton Customs House. The museum has two other locations in Washington, D.C. and Suitland, MD. Opened in 1994, this branch in Lower Manhattan offers changing exhibitions featuring both contemporary art and historic objects and a stunning permanent exhibition, "Infinity of Nations." Its terrific gift shop is well worth a visit, as is the building itself. Take time to look up at the intricate details in the ceilings, especially in the rotunda and library, and to descend the exquisite staircase. Free admission.

NEUE GALERIE NEW YORK
1048 Fifth Ave (at 86th St)   212/628-6200
Thurs-Mon: 11-6   neuegalerie.org
    Ronald Lauder and his longtime friend, the late Serge Sabarsky, loved German and Austrian art and design from the early 20th century and dreamed of opening a museum to showcase it. In 1994 Lauder purchased this amazing building, once home to Mrs. Cornelius Vanderbilt III, and transformed their dream into this first-

class museum. Public tours are offered at 2 p.m. on Saturday and Sunday. Children under 12 are not admitted, and children from 12 to 16 must be accompanied by an adult. Admission fee charged (reasonable); first Fri of month: 6-8, free.

NEW YORK CITY FIRE MUSEUM
278 Spring St (bet Hudson and Varick St)   212/691-1303
Daily: 10-5   nycfiremuseum.org

In a renovated 1904 firehouse, this fun museum is a "must-see" for anyone interested in firefighting. With hundreds of artifacts dating from the late 18th century, the collection is among the most extensive of its kind in the country. Highlights include leather fire buckets, hand-pumped fire engines, and a FDNY 9/11 memorial. Admission fee charged (reasonable).

NEW YORK CITY POLICE MUSEUM
100 Old Slip (bet Water and South St)   212/480-3100
nycpm.org

The museum sustained major damage from Hurricane Sandy and was undergoing extensive repairs at time of this book's printing; consult the website for re-opening information.

NEW-YORK HISTORICAL SOCIETY
170 Central Park W (bet 76th and 77th St)   212/873-3400
Tues-Sun: 10-6 (Fri till 8)   nyhistory.org

John James Audubon's watercolors for Birds of America, Thomas Cole's The Course of Empire, and more Tiffany lamps than you can imagine are just a few highlights of the New-York Historical Society. A visit to this grande dame—located just south of the American Museum of Natural History—is a great way to glimpse the city's past. The best part of this museum is the Henry Luce III Center for the Study of American Culture, located on the fourth floor. Brimming with thousands of pieces from the museum's vast permanent collection, it's like wandering through the city's attic. The DiMenna Children's History Museum and a permanent exhibition that takes visitors on an interactive journey from Colonial times through the September 11, 2001, attacks were added after a 2011 renovation. Admission fee charged (reasonable).

Kids' Culture

Even though many New York museums and galleries have programs and sections geared toward youngsters, kids may become bored and disruptive in the confines of the hallowed halls of the world-renowned institutions. Two reasonably-priced museums offer classes, exhibitions, and performances specifically geared toward children and families.

Children's Museum of the Arts (103 Charlton St, 212/274-0986, cmany.org): children's art exhibits, artist-in-residence programs, hands-on programs; closed Tuesday

Children's Museum of Manhattan (212 W 83rd St, 212/721-1223, cmom.org): five floors of interactive exhibits, programs, and diverse cultural experiences; closed Monday

Anne Frank Center USA

The **Anne Frank Center USA** (44 Park Place, 212/431-7993, annefrank.com) contains interactive exhibits depicting Anne Frank's life through her diary during the two years she was in hiding with her family during the Nazi occupation of the Netherlands. This small center includes life-sized photography of her bedroom, photos taken by her father, and a bookstore where copies of her diary and other related items are sold.

NICHOLAS ROERICH MUSEUM
319 W 107th St (bet Broadway and Riverside Dr)   212/864-7752
Tues-Fri: noon-5; Sat, Sun: 2-5   roerich.org

The late Nicholas Roerich was Russian, but in many ways he was a citizen of the world. He dedicated much of his life to convincing governments to protect art even in times of conflict. His own paintings, many done in (and of) the Himalayas, are on display at this unassuming townhouse near Columbia University. Free admission; donations suggested.

PALEY CENTER FOR MEDIA
25 W 52nd St (bet Fifth Ave and Ave of the Americas)   212/621-6800
Wed-Sun: noon-6 (Thurs till 8)   paleycenter.org

Is there an episode of The Brady Bunch you've always wanted to show your kids? A segment of The Ed Sullivan Show you're dying to see again? What about the Nixon-Kennedy debates? Or the Mean Joe Greene Coca-Cola commercial? For folks who love television, this place is Nirvana. In addition to scheduled screenings, you can select from the library's more than 120,000 programs—spanning the history of radio and television—for your own viewing and listening. There's no memorabilia here, just thousands of hours of programming and personalized research assistance. Admission fee charged (reasonable).

RADIO CITY MUSIC HALL
1260 Ave of the Americas (at 50th St)   212/247-4777 (tour information)
Tours: Daily: 11-3   800/745-3000 (tickets)
    radiocity.com

Part of Rockefeller Center, this art deco wonder was built in 1932 and seats nearly 6,000. It's home to a world-famous Radio City Christmas Spectacular, complete with live animals, and varied productions throughout the year. Countless entertainers have performed here over the years, and you can soak up some of its storied history by taking the Stage Door Tour. Admission fee charged (reasonable).

ROCKEFELLER CENTER
Bounded by Fifth Ave, Ave of the Americas, 48th St, and 51st St   212/332-6868
Daily: 6:30 a.m.-midnight   rockefellercenter.com

A sprawling 12-acre complex built in the midst of the Great Depression in the 1930s, Rockefeller Center is in some ways the anchor of midtown Manhattan. Tenants, owners, and even technologies have come and gone, as radio gave way to television at NBC Studios, but this amazing complex is one of the few constants in this ever-changing city. In addition to NBC's famous sets, Rockefeller Center is home to Radio City Music Hall, the beautifully manicured Channel Gardens, the world-famous ice-skating rink, a two-floor Metropolitan Museum of Art store, a U. S. Post Office, and seven major subway stops. A hub of commerce, culture and community, world-class shopping is available at over 100 retailers throughout the center. For entertainment, wave to your friends at home outside The Today Show's windows, or enjoy dinner while people watching at one of the numerous restaurant options. Visit the Top of the Rock Observation Deck (topoftherocknyc.com), towering 70 floors above the sidewalks and take in the 360 degree panoramic view atop 30 Rockefeller Plaza. Guided tours of NBC Studios and Rockefeller Center's art and architecture are also available (for schedules and prices call 212/698-2000 or visit rockefeller-center.com/plan-a-trip/). What I like to do at Rockefeller Center, however, is simply walk around. It's like visiting an old friend! Fee charged for tours (reasonable).

ROSE MUSEUM AT CARNEGIE HALL
154 W 57th St (at Seventh Ave)   212/903-9629
Daily: 11-4:30 (closed June-Sept)   carnegiehall.org/museum

If you're interested in the history of music in New York, this little upstairs museum is the place to stop. Its permanent exhibit traces the history of Carnegie Hall from 1891. It's open to the public during the day and to evening concertgoers during intermission. Tours of Carnegie Hall, including the Isaac Stern Auditorium, are offered fall through spring; call or check their website for details. Free admission to museum; admission fee charged for tours (reasonable).

RUBIN MUSEUM OF ART
150 W 17th St (at Seventh Ave)   212/620-5000
Mon: 11-5; Wed: 11-7; Thurs: 11-5; Fri: 11-10; Sat, Sun: 11-6   rmanyc.org

The Rubin Museum creates an immersive environment for experiencing the art and culture of Himilayan Asia and develops programming that enables visitors to make personal connections to their contemporary lives. Exhibitions (including the Tibetan Buddhist Shrine Room), tours, films, concerts, and talks further understanding of this region. Cafe Serai and a shop extend the experience. Admission fee charged (reasonable); Fri: 6-10, free.

SCANDINAVIA HOUSE: THE NORDIC CENTER IN AMERICA
58 Park Ave (at 38th St)   212/779-3587
Mon-Sat: 11-10; Sun: 11-5; Gallery: Tues-Sat: noon-6 (Wed till 7)
                                                    scandinaviahouse.org

Scandinavia House is home to the American-Scandinavian Foundation. Offering a wide range of public programs, Scandinavia House presents contemporary

---

Contemporary Art
The **New Museum of Contemporary Art** (235 Bowery, 212/219-1222, newmuseum.org) is the first art museum constructed in downtown Manhattan. Nestled among restaurant-supply businesses, this contemporary art museum is uniquely built as seven off-axis stacked rectangles. It features the stimulating works of artists from around the globe in all media, including performance and technology art.

> **Science Museums**
> Just outside of the city are two fascinating science museums with interesting interactive exhibits and educational programs.
>
> **Liberty Science Center** (Liberty State Park, 222 Jersey City Blvd, Jersey City, NJ, 201/200-1000, lsc.org): The nation's largest IMAX Dome Theater.
>
> **New York Hall of Science** (47-01 111th St, Queens, NY; 718/699-0005, nyscience.org): Over 450 hands-on science exhibits.

Nordic culture encompassing the visual arts, music, and literature, along with social policy, business, finance, and technology. These programs include art, design, and historical exhibitions as well as films, concerts, readings, lectures, symposia, language courses, and children's programming that illustrate and illuminate the contemporary vitality of the Nordic countries. A small cafe (Smörgås Chef), a beautiful store, and well-designed public spaces make visiting here a real pleasure. Admission fee charged (nominal).

SEAPORT MUSEUM
12 Fulton St (bet Water and South St)   212/748-8786
Call for days and times   seany.org

Two centuries ago, New York was one of the world's most active ports. Even as recently as 1967—when the Seaport Museum was founded—Fulton Street was synonymous with the Fulton Fish Market (which moved to The Bronx in 2005). Little is left today except the history, and that's what you'll find as you explore the print shop (209 Water Street) and ships while wandering around South Street Seaport. With its cobblestone streets, beautiful old boats, and salty breezes, it's easy to imagine that you've been transported to a different era. At publication time, the galleries were closed due to significant damages to the building's electrical system resulting from Hurricane Sandy.

SKYSCRAPER MUSEUM
Ritz-Carlton New York, Battery Park
39 Battery Pl (at West St), 1st floor   212/968-1961
Wed-Sun: noon-6   skyscraper.org

Where better to have a museum dedicated to the history and future of skyscrapers than New York City? Founded in 1996, this ironically small museum offers various programs, lectures, exhibitions, and walking tours feting the towering buildings. Admission fee charged (nominal).

THE STUDIO MUSEUM IN HARLEM
144 W 125th St (bet Malcolm X and Adam Clayton Powell, Jr. Blvd)
Thurs, Fri: noon-9; Sat: 10-6; Sun: noon-6   212/864-4500
                                              studiomuseum.org

Like the Museum of Chinese in the Americas, this wonderful place is both a museum and a vibrant part of the community. Including gallery space and an auditorium, The Studio Museum in Harlem displays the work of black artists from around the block and around the world. An artist-in-residence program, a wide range of programs for families and children, and film screenings are just a few ways The Studio Museum engages its audience and reaches into the community. Suggested admission fee charged (reasonable); Sun: free.

THEODORE ROOSEVELT BIRTHPLACE

28 E 20th St (bet Broadway and Park Ave) 212/260-1616
Tues-Sat: 9-5 nps.gov/thrb

This wonderful brownstone is a reconstruction of Theodore Roosevelt's childhood home. Operated by the National Park Service, it houses a small museum and various period rooms in the living quarters. Guided tours are offered hourly from 10 to 4, except at noon. Free admission.

TIBET HOUSE

22 W 15th St (bet Fifth Ave and Ave of the Americas) 212/807-0563
Mon-Fri: 11-5; Sun: 11-4 tibethouse.org

Founded at the request of the Dalai Lama, Tibet House U.S. is the center of efforts in this country to present and preserve Tibetan culture. It has a permanent display of Tibetan art and artifacts, a gallery space that offers changing exhibits which showcase contemporary and classical Buddhist-inspired art. Free admission; donations welcome.

THE UKRAINIAN MUSEUM

222 E 6th St (bet Second and Third Ave) 212/228-0110
Wed-Sun: 11:30-5 ukrainianmuseum.org

This museum in the heart of the East Village invites visitors to "discover the wonderful heritage of your parents and grandparents." Displaying folk art, a nu-

---

A Chance of a Ghost!

October 31st isn't the only day to look for ghostly apparitions. You may witness spirited occurrences at any time—friendly or otherwise!

■ The headless ghost of actor George Frederick has been spotted at **St. Paul's Chapel** burial ground.

■ **The Palace Theatre** supposedly harbors over 100 ghosts.

■ Aaron Burr reputedly haunts the restaurant **One if by Land, Two if by Sea** (once his carriage house); flying dishes have been observed.

■ The ghost of Bishop Dubois frequents the **Old St. Patrick's Cathedral**.

■ Unexplained noises, voices, and footsteps occur at **Beth Israel Hospital**.

■ The **Hotel Chelsea** gained notoriety from some of its guests and their activities. Eugene O'Neill, Thomas Wolfe, and Sid Vicious are still making the unearthly scene. Beware of the elevator!

■ **Hotel des Artistes'** resident ghost allegedly touches people.

■ Even though she killed herself, a Ziegfeld Follies chorus girl still appears at the **New Amsterdam Theatre**.

Set Sail from Chelsea Piers

Here are a couple of options for getting out on the Hudson River and enjoying the breathtaking Manhattan skyline and surroundings.

Schooner Adirondack (Pier 62 at W 23rd St, 646/336-5270, sail-nyc. com): An 80-foot 1890s-style pilot schooner available for both public cruises and charters from mid-April through October. Classic Harbor Lines operates two other vessels from Pier 62: Yacht Manhattan (80 feet) and Schooner America 2.0 (105 feet) for fun and interesting cruises.

Bateaux New York (Pier 61 at W 23rd St, 866/211-3805, bateauxnewyork.com): This elegant glass-enclosed sightseeing boat operates lunch and dinner cruises all year long.

mismatic collection, fine arts, costumes, paintings, and an amazing seasonal collection of *pysanky* (Ukrainian Easter eggs), this museum is a terrific cultural resource for anyone who wants to learn more about Ukrainian heritage — yours or otherwise. Admission fee charged (reasonable).

UNION SQUARE PARK
Bounded by Broadway, Park Ave S, 14th St, and 17th St

Union Square Park is home to the city's best-known and largest Greenmarket (which is open all year on Monday, Wednesday, Friday, and Saturday). It's full of New Yorkers and tourists enjoying the beautifully renovated pavillion and grounds with statues of Washington and Gandhi. The popular Tot Lot is one area of the well-appointed playground. Nearby, there are dozens and dozens of great restaurants and interesting businesses.

WEST SIDE JEWISH CENTER
347 W 34th Street (bet Eighth and Ninth Ave)   212/502-5291
Mon-Thurs: 9-5   westsidejewishcenter.org

In the early 1900s, New York claimed the largest Jewish population in the world, with immigrants from Germany, Russia, and Eastern Europe. Founded in 1890, the West Side Jewish Center synagogue and social center has been at this location since 1925 where it is adjacent to Pennsylvania Station, Madison Square Garden, and the Jacob Javits Convention Center. People of all ages engage in interesting classes, lectures, and social programs. Services are offered daily, as well as for Shabbat and holidays, and visitors of any denomination are welcome to attend services or visit the synagogue. Sabbath meals can be arranged in advance. It is truly a sanctuary with heart in the heart of the city. Free admission.

YANKEE STADIUM
1 E 161st St (at Jerome Ave)   646/977-8687
                                                       yankees.com

The "House That Ruth Built" — that's Babe Ruth, the baseball legend — has been replaced with the billion-dollar Yankee Stadium. Field dimensions remain the same, seats and legroom are more spacious, there are more eateries and team stores, more luxury and party suites, and the main scoreboard is seven times larger. The classic tour includes visits to the museum, Monument Park, dugouts, and batting cages and clubhouse when the team is on the road. The Party City Birthday Bash and Twilight tours include food and beverages. There are different hours for individual and small and large groups, depending on game-day schedules; therefore it is best to check the website or call for details. Admission fee charged (reasonable to expensive, depending on tour).

YESHIVA UNIVERSITY MUSEUM

15 W 16th St (at Fifth Ave)   212/294-8330
Sun, Tues, Thurs: 11-5; Mon: 5-8; Wed: 11-8; Fri: 11-2   yumuseum.org

Part of the Center for Jewish History, this large and vibrant museum provides a window into Jewish culture around the world and throughout history through its acclaimed multi-disciplinary exhibitions and award-winning publications. By educating audiences of all ages with dynamic interpretations of Jewish life, past and present, along with wide-ranging cultural offerings and programs, the YU Museum attracts young and old, Jewish and non-Jewish audiences. Admission fee charged (reasonable); Mon, Wed: 5-8 and Fri: 11-2:30, free.

GALLERIES

When people think of viewing art, they often think only of museums. While the art museums in New York are exceptional, anyone interested in art ought to visit some commercial galleries, too. Galleries are places where potential buyers and admirers alike can look at the work of contemporary and 20th-century artists at their own pace and without charge. (A few galleries specialize in older works, too.) Let me stress "admirers alike." A lot of people are afraid to go into galleries because they think they'll be expected to buy something or be treated poorly if they don't know everything there is to know about art. That just isn't true, and an afternoon of gallery hopping can be a lot of fun.

First decide what kind of art you want to see. New York has long been considered the center of the contemporary art world, and it follows that the city is home to literally hundreds of galleries of all sizes and styles. In general, the more formal and conventional galleries are on or close to Madison Avenue on the Upper East Side and along 57th Street. (You'll need to look up to find a lot of them, particularly on 57th Street.) Some of the less formal, avant-garde galleries tend to be in Soho: on West Broadway, between Broome and Houston streets;

Specialty Tours

If you want a particular kind of tour, a guide with special skills or areas of expertise, or a tour led by a multilingual guide (Italian, French, Danish, Spanish, Japanese, German, Dutch, Portuguese, Hebrew, and other languages), contact the **Guides Association of New York** (855/574-2692, ganyc.org). The website has information about the city's licensed guides and their specialties, as well as practical details regarding tours and other hospitality services. GANYC is a nonprofit organization whose members are professional licensed guides and independent contractors.

Scott's Pizza Tours

Scott Wiener runs **Scott's Pizza Tours** (212/913-9903, scottspizzatours. com) where he and his enthusiastic pizza compadres conduct fun- and pun-filled guided tours of some of New York's most significant pizzerias. You'll view pizza ovens and kitchens, learn why New York pizza is legendary, and get the skinny on the history, science, technology, and economics of the Italian pies. Walking tours cover Little Italy and Greenwich Village, and a Sunday tour via a big yellow school bus goes to four pizzerias in the outer boroughs. By the way, Scott lives and breathes pizza; he has amassed a private collection of over 500 unique pizza boxes from around the world and has a book about them in the works.

on Greene Street, between Prince and Houston streets; and on Prince Street, between Greene Street and West Broadway. Some of the more offbeat galleries are also found in Tribeca.

As a general rule, artists who have yet to be discovered go where the rents are lower, and then more established artists and galleries follow. Gallery hot spots include the west end of Chelsea, the northwest corner of the West Village (on and around West 14th Street), the Lower East Side (particularly on and around Rivington Street), and several parts of Brooklyn.

If you want to experience the diversity of the New York gallery scene, sample a couple of galleries in each neighborhood. The Art Dealers Association of America (212/488-5550, artdealers.org) is a terrific resource if you have particular artists or areas of interest in mind.

Galleries are typically known for the artists they showcase. If you are interested in the work of just one artist, the *New Yorker* and *New York* magazine each contain listings of gallery shows. Be sure to look at the dates, as shows can change quickly. *Time Out New York* has a list of galleries by neighborhood in its "Art" section, complete with descriptions of current shows. The Friday and Sunday editions of the *New York Times* are also good resources.

TOURS
AND TOUR OPERATORS

Whether you like to walk or ride, be part of a small group or sightsee with a whole herd, New York has a tour for you. While I definitely advocate getting out and exploring on your own, there are lots of interesting tours that will take you places you either won't go or can't go by yourself. If you're looking for a really personalized introduction to New York, then get in touch with **Big Apple Greeter** (212/669-8159, bigapplegreeter.org). This nonprofit volunteer service is designed to hook up visitors with real New Yorkers.

If you're feeling a little overwhelmed by New York and want to see the sights from the safety and anonymity of a tour bus, **Gray Line** (212/445-0848, grayline-newyork.com) is your best bet. The company offers many packages on its double-decker buses, including trips to the Statue of Liberty and the Empire State Building (over 50 stops in all), on the hop-on and hop-off buses. Prices vary, as do tour lengths. Another great way to get a quick and basic orientation is **Circle Line**'s three-hour cruise around the island of Manhattan. The narration tends toward the corny, but you'll learn a lot, get some great photo opportunities, and really acquire a sense of New York as an island. (Call 212/563-3200 or go to circleline42.com for more information.)

If you want a personal orientation tour, try **Our Town New York** (212/754-4500, 866/691-8687, ourtownnewyork.com), an award-winning boutique tour service. The private and customized tours depart from your hotel's front door. The mode of transportation is a comfortable Mercedes Benz SUV, which accommodates up to six guests. Choose from a list of tours or create your own personalized adventure.

Many of the museums and sights listed in this chapter offer tours of their collections or of surrounding neighborhoods. Just about any tour offered by the **Central Park Conservancy** (212/360-2726, centralparknyc.org) is a personal favorite.

MORE HOT SPOTS
IN NEW YORK

Following are places not mentioned in other parts of this book that offer particularly interesting and popular tours.

CITY HALL
Murray St at Broadway   212/788-2656
Tours: Mon-Thurs: 9-5 (reservations necessary)   nyc.gov

Constructed in the early 19th century and continuously used as the city hall of New York, this grand building is open for public tours. In addition to the grand keystone-cantilevered staircase, soaring rotunda, and restored Council Chamber, you'll get to visit the historic Governor's Room, which houses an impressive collection of portraits and fine furnishings. Free admission.

FEDERAL RESERVE BANK
33 Liberty St (bet Nassau and William St)   212/720-6130
Tours: Mon-Fri: 11:15, noon, 12:45, 1:30, 2:15, 3 (reservations necessary)
                                                        newyorkfed.org

Billions of dollars of gold belonging to central banks, foreign governments, and official international organizations is stashed in the New York Fed's vault resting

---

Touring on Two Wheels

The knowledgeable guides at **Bike the Big Apple** (347/878-9809 and 877/865-0078, bikethebigapple.com) put a different spin on seeing the sights. Of course you can cruise through Central Park and trendy nearby neighborhoods, but they'll also lead riders down the trails of high finance and Chinatown; on a journey in quest of brews, chocolates, and great views; across the East River to Queens and Brooklyn for an ethnic tour; or to check out city lights on a twilight pedal across the Brooklyn Bridge after a swing through Lower Manhattan. Prices include bike and helmet rental fees.

South Street Seaport Water Tours

The South Street Seaport offers East River departures for water travel.

New York Water Taxi (Pier 17, 212/742-1969, nywatertaxi.com): This company's distinctive boats are painted to resemble yellow checker cabs. Commuter schedules, sightseeing tours, and charter boats are offered.

The Pioneer (Pier 16, 212/742-1969, southstreetseaportmuseum.org): Set sail on an 1885 schooner around New York Harbor. Offered in summer only, it can accommodate 35 passengers.

---

on the bedrock of Manhattan Island. Daily tours include an overview of the Federal Reserve System, discussion about New York Fed's role in setting monetary policy, and a glimpse into the gold vault. Reservations must be made at least a week in advance. Free admission.

GRACIE MANSION

88th St at East End Ave   212/570-4751 or 311 (in New York)
Tours: Wed: 10, 11, 1, 2 (reservations necessary)   nyc.gov

Thanks to Fiorello LaGuardia and Robert Moses, New York is one of the few cities in the U.S. with an official mayoral residence. Built in 1799, the house is located in Carl Schurz Park and overlooks the East River. Admission fee charged (reasonable).

MADISON SQUARE GARDEN

33rd St at Seventh Ave   212/465-5800
                                                               thegarden.com

"The Garden" is in the midst of a major transformation. Tours will resume when construction of a new state-of-the-art arena is completed in fall 2013.

METROPOLITAN OPERA

Lincoln Center (Columbus Ave at 64th St)   212/769-7028
Tours: Select weekday and Sun afternoons (Oct-May, during opera season)
                                                          metoperafamily.org

Even folks who are not opera enthusiasts will be wowed by this behind-the-scenes look at this country's most famous opera company. Visit the stage area and get an up-close look at some of the costumes and sets. These popular tours are offered by the Metropolitan Opera Guild. Check the calendar on the guild's website and plan well in advance, as tours often sell out. Admission fee charged (reasonable).

NBC STUDIOS

30 Rockefeller Plaza (49th St bet Fifth Ave and Ave of the Americas) 212/664-3700
Tours: Hours vary by season   nbcstudiotour.com

NBC studios are located at Rockefeller Plaza, right in the heart of midtown. If you want to take a look around the sets of The Today Show, Saturday Night Live, Late Night with Jimmy Fallon, or MSNBC, here's your chance. Children under six are not allowed on the tour. Admission fee charged (expensive).

WALKING TOURS

Walking tours are another great way to get to know parts of New York you otherwise might overlook. Here are some tour guides. Note that days and times of tours vary so check in advance for tour times, meeting places, and prices.

BIG APPLE GREETER

1 Centre St (at Chambers St)   212/669-8159
                                                            bigapplegreeter.org

Big Apple Greeter is like having a new friend show you the wonders of the city! Volunteers from all five boroughs meet individuals or groups of up to six to show them New York City through the eyes of a native. On visits lasting from two to four hours, Greeters use public transportation or travel on foot to introduce visitors to neighborhoods and the city's hidden treasures. There are over 300 Greeters, and they speak some 25 languages among them. They are matched with visitors by language, interest, and neighborhoods. This service is free of charge, and while tipping is not permitted, voluntary donations are accepted. At least four weeks advance notice is required.

BIG ONION WALKING TOURS

                                                212/439-1090, 888/606-9255
                                                              bigonion.com

Seth Kamil and his band of guides—most of them graduate students in American history—share their vast knowledge of New York through a wide array of walking tours. There are over two dozen different tours offered seven days a week. The Multi-Ethnic Eating Tour is the most popular followed by tours to Historic Harlem, Brooklyn Bridge and Heights, Historic Lower Manhattan, Greenwich Village, and Chelsea and the High Line. Fee charged: reasonable and up.

More New York Tours

New York's first family of tour guides operates **Levy's Unique New York!** (877/692-5869; levysuniqueny.com). The clan, led by dad Mark, conducts educational and enlightening tours that are thoroughly entertaining and sometimes zany! The half-day City Highlights tour is the most popular. Other excursions are New York by Land and Sea, Bohemians and Beats of Greenwich Village, Graffiti, Ethnic Eats, and a narrated stroll across the Brooklyn Bridge. Tour times and costs vary; custom tours are also available.

Cliff Strome, **Custom and Private New York Tours** (212/222-1441, customandprivate.com), has a passion for New York. Guests are transported in a chauffeured vehicle (sedan, exotic car, limousine, or bus) to locations which target guests' schedules, interests, preferences, and whims. These tours are laced with humor, folklore, historical drama, and tall tales.

Common New York Terms

Many places in America have their own special words and phrases that people from elsewhere don't understand. Here are some terms commonly heard in New York:

Bridge and tunnel crowd: a disparaging term for visitors from New Jersey; also "B&T crowd"

The City: shorthand for New York City

Coffee regular: coffee with milk and sugar

The FDR: Franklin Roosevelt Drive, an expressway running the length of Manhattan's East Side along the East River

Fuhgeddaboudit: "Forget about it," as in "Don't mention it." It can also mean "No way."

The Garden: Madison Square Garden

Houston: a street in lower Manhattan, pronounced *HOUSE-ton*

The Island: Long Island

The Met: the Metropolitan Opera or Metropolitan Museum of Art

Shmeer: a smear of cream cheese, usually on a bagel

Slice: a piece of pizza

Soda: any sweet carbonated beverage; short for "soda pop"

Straphanger: a subway rider, named for the long-gone leather straps that standing passengers held onto in subways cars

JOYCE GOLD HISTORY TOURS OF NEW YORK

212/242-5762
joycegoldhistorytours.com

Nowhere in the United States are past and present so closely quartered as in New York, and few people are better able to convey that simultaneous sense of timelessness and modernity than historian Joyce Gold. Her scheduled tours, which include Crimes of the Fifth Avenue Gold Coast, Grand Central Terminal, High Line Park, and other colorful neighborhoods and topics, are usually given on weekends. Joyce personally leads all of her public tours and is available for private tours as well. Reservations for her scheduled tours are not required. Fee charged (reasonable).

MANHATTAN WALKING TOUR

914/564-0461
manhattanwalkingtour.com

These guides are akin to a good friend showing you around their beloved hometown imparting behind-the-scenes tales of what makes the neighborhood really tick. Walking tours are scheduled or custom-designed and part of the charm is a limit of eight guests per tour. Choose from several destinations highlighting historic areas and food, or a combination of both. Private tours feature the patrons of the arts (and gossip from that era) and better beer and wine bars on the night tour. Don your walking shoes and join a small group!

MUNICIPAL ART SOCIETY OF NEW YORK

212/935-3960
mas.org

This terrific advocacy group offers a wide array of thematic and area-specific walking tours for people interested in the city's architecture and history. Most tours are led by historians. The diverse topics include art deco midtown, Chelsea art galleries, Harlem, and many other interesting areas and neighborhoods and their famous or infamous residents. Allow several hours for your tour. Fee charged (reasonable).

URBAN PARK RANGERS

212/360-2774 or 311 (in New York)
nyc.gov/parks

The city's Department of Parks and Recreation employs Urban Park Rangers, who give wonderful weekend walking tours of Central Park and other parks throughout Manhattan and the outer boroughs. Many are designed for children or families. Go to the department's website and click "Things to Do" and "Urban Park Rangers" to get a full schedule of upcoming tours and other events. Free admission.

WHERE TO
FIND IT

NEW YORK'S
BEST FOOD SHOPS

The greatest collection of fine food shops in the world is in New York City. You can find an unsurpassed assortment of quality provisions and any type of ethnic food by doing a bit of investigating. You'll be amazed at what you can find in some off-the-beaten-path shops, and oftentimes prices are lower than the fancier shops (but be sure to assess the quality before you purchase). Around any corner could be the very best bagels, smoked fish, or whatever your heart (and stomach) may desire.

Meanwhile, the big names remain nothing less than spectacular; they have been in business for a long time for good reason! Zabar's oozes tradition, fine aromas, and great ambience. Grace's Marketplace, a family operation, offers top-quality produce and foodstuffs in every category. Dean & Deluca, one of the greatest food emporiums in the country, tempts customers at every turn. Whole Foods Market at the Time Warner Center (Columbus Circle) is a behemoth with a huge selection. Eataly, a spectacular food complex, specializes in everything Italian.

These places are just a sampling of some of the better-known names. Lastly, don't be afraid to experiment with new types of cuisine!

ASIAN

ASIA MARKET

71½ Mulberry St (bet Canal and Bayard St)   212/962-2020
Daily: 8-7

The main attractions at Asia Market are fresh fruit and vegetables, plus exotic herbs and spices from all over Asia. You'll find items from Thailand, Indonesia, Malaysia, the Philippines, Japan, and China, plus a staff ready to explain how to prepare dishes from these countries. Asia Market provides produce to some of New York's best restaurants.

BAKERY GOODS

AMY'S BREAD

672 Ninth Ave (bet 46th and 47th St)   212/977-2670
75 Ninth Ave (bet 15th and 16th St)   212/462-4338
250 Bleecker St (bet Ave of the Americas and Seventh Ave)   212/675-7802
Hours vary by store   amysbread.com

At Amy's Bread, the aroma of freshly baked bread and sweets lures locals and tourists to line up outside to sample the many treats for sale. These oases are a cross between a Parisian *boulangerie* and a cozy Midwestern kitchen. Of course, you should come for the bread — Amy's signature semolina with golden raisins and fennel, the green-olive *picholine*, or a simple French baguette. Among the goodies are grilled sandwiches, sticky buns, old-fashioned double layer cakes, and decadent brownies. The staff provides consistent, friendly service.

ARON STREIT

150 Rivington St (bet Clinton and Suffolk St)   212/475-7000
Mon-Thurs: 9-4:30   streitsmatzos.com

Matzo is a thin, wafer-like unleavened bread. According to tradition, it came out of Egypt with Moses and the children of Israel when they had to flee so quickly that there was no time to let the bread rise. Through the years, matzo was restricted to the time around Passover, and even when matzo production became automated, business shut down for a good deal of the year; but not today, and not in New York. Streit is the only family-owned and -operated matzo business in America. It produces matzo throughout the year, pausing only on Saturday and Jewish holidays to clean the machines. Streit allows a peek at the production process, which is both mechanized and extremely primitive. Matzo is baked in enormous thin sheets that are later broken up. If you ask for a fresh batch, they might break it right off the production line. They also offer noodles, wafers, canned soups, potato products, Hanukkah items, and Jewish specialty dishes.

BILLY'S BAKERY

Plaza Food Hall by Todd English
Plaza Hotel, 1 W 59th St, concourse   646/755-3237
Sun-Thurs: 11-8; Fri, Sat: 11-9

184 Ninth Ave (bet 21st and 22nd St)   212/647-9956
Mon-Thurs: 8:30 a.m.-11 p.m.; Fri, Sat: 8:30 a.m.-midnight; Sun: 9 a.m.-10 p.m.
75 Franklin St (bet Broadway and Church St)   212/647-9958
Mon-Fri: 7 a.m.-9 p.m.; Sat: 9-9; Sun: 10-5   billysbakerynyc.com

Korean Grocery Stores

For a taste of Korea's cuisine and culture, amble down 32nd Street between Fifth Avenue and Broadway. This colorful area is the heart of the Korean business district, serving as home to restaurants, bakeries, retail shops, and other businesses. The best selection of groceries is at **Han ah Reum** (25 W 32nd St, 212/695-3283). Other Korean grocers around town include **m2m** (55 Third Ave, 212/353-2698) and **New KC Market** (301 Amsterdam Ave, 212/877-2253).

You simply cannot leave this place without some of the delicacies offered: wonderful layer cakes (like red velvet), cheesecakes, icebox pies, cupcakes, bars, cookies, muffins, and much more. Items are made on-premises at this very clean and professional operation. Special cake designs and inscriptions are options.

BIRDBATH

160 Prince St (bet West Broadway and Thompson St)   646/556-7720
Mon-Fri: 7:45-8; Sat: 9-8; Sun: 9-7

200 Church St (bet Thomas and Duane St)   212/309-7555
Mon-Fri: 8-6

35 Third Ave (at 9th St)   212/201-1902
Mon-Wed: 8 a.m.-9 p.m.; Thurs-Sat: 8 a.m.-10 p.m.; Sun: 9-9 birdbathbakery.com
Numerous other locations

Birdbath, the little sister of City Bakery, is described as organic, seasonal, recycled, sustainable, and eco-friendly, with really good food. Customers arriving via bike, scooter, or skateboard receive a discount. Food from the main kitchen is delivered by bicycle-powered rickshaws, and the business is wind-powered. Breakfast and lunch are offered to go (a couple of stools are available onsite). You'll find crescents, muffins, cookies, veggie burgers, mini pizzas, mac 'n cheese, and desserts, as well as specialty drinks. Emphasis is on regional ingredients.

BLACK HOUND NEW YORK

170 Second Ave (bet 10th and 11th St)   212/979-9505
Mon-Thurs: 10 a.m.-10:30 p.m.; Fri, Sat: 10 a.m.-11:30 p.m.; Sun: 11-10
blackhoundny.com

The Black Hound shines when it comes to cakes. Buttercream and ganache prevail as fillings and icings. Their signature Busy Bee cake is chocolate and almond butter cake with chocolate mousse and marzipan, topped with marzipan and almond petal bees. The checkerboard ebony-and-ivory layer cake with chocolate and vanilla buttercream cake, bittersweet chocolate buttercream filling, and chocolate ganache on the sides is equally appealing. There are lemon, hazelnut, poppyseed, and other variations, too. All are rich, dense, and simply elegant! Cookies, truffles, pastries, and other savories are similarly decadent. With a nod to their name, they turn out bone-shaped butter cookies — for humans. An edible chocolate basket filled with yummy goodies makes a special gift.

CAKES 'N SHAPES
466 W 51st St (at Tenth Ave)   212/629-5512
Hours: by appointment   cakesnshapes.com

Talk about personalizing! Furnish owner Edie Connolly with a picture of a person, place, book cover, company logo, or other image, and she'll impose an edible likeness on a shortbread/sugar cookie, cupcake, or cake. Also available for do-it-yourselfers are edible frosting-sheet images to apply to your own cake or cupcakes. Free-form chocolate and vanilla pound cakes are also available. 3D works of edible art include purses and clothing items, sports equipment, bodies, critters, and consumer products. Cookies are shippable and are individually wrapped in a clear bag, tied with a satin ribbon. You can even send out edible Christmas cards! And for those who are allergic, this is a nut-free bakery.

CORRADO BREAD & PASTRY
1361 Lexington Ave (at 90th St)   212/348-8943
1390 Third Ave (at 79th St)   212/288-2300
Hours vary by store   corradobread.com

The aromas are enticing at these good-looking bakeries. There are about 30 kinds of breads, muffins, and rolls, plus yummy desserts, salads, and made-to-order sandwiches. Try a sandwich of smoked turkey on brioche or tuna on Jewish rye. For a sweet treat, perhaps try a decadent chocolate-mousse raspberry tart. Outdoor cafe tables add a nice touch.

CREATIVE CAKES
400 E 74th St (at First Ave)   212/794-9811
Mon-Fri: 8-4:30; Sat: 9 a.m.-11 a.m.   creativecakesny.com

Creative Cakes knows how to have fun using fine ingredients and ingenious patterns. Cake lovers are fans of the fudgy chocolate cake with buttercream icing and sensational designs. Among other things, Bill Schutz has replicated Radio City Music Hall for a celebrity birthday. Prices are reasonable, and these edible creations are sure to be a conversation piece at any party.

CRUMBS BAKE SHOP
655 Ave of the Americas (bet 20th and 21st St)   212/243-6300
1385 Broadway (bet 37th and 38th St)   212/764-7100
420 Lexington Ave (bet 43rd and 44th St)   212/297-0500
880 Third Ave (at 53rd St)   212/355-6500

Life is Like a Box of Caramels
You might like this assortment of chocolate-covered caramels sprinkled with sea salt:

5th Avenue Chocolatiere (693 Third Ave, 212/935-5454)
L'atelier du Chocolat (59 W 22nd St, 212/243-0033)
The Meadow (523 Hudson St, 212/645-4633)
The Sweet Life (63 Hester St, 212/598-0092)

> **Cheesecake!**
>
> New York is famous for great cheesecakes. These are among the best:
>
> **Eileen's Special Cheesecake** (17 Cleveland Pl, 212/966-5585, 800/521-CAKE)
>
> **Junior's** (1515 Broadway, 212/302-2000 and Grand Central Terminal, 42nd St at Vanderbilt Ave, 212/586-4677): The restaurant is on the lower level, and the bakery is on the main concourse, near Track 36.
>
> **Ruthy's Bakery & Cafe** (Chelsea Market, 75 Ninth Ave, 212/463-8800)
>
> **Two Little Red Hens** (1652 Second Ave, 212/452-0476)

Numerous other locations   crumbs.com
Hours vary by store

Crumbs! Just the name evokes visions of decadent little cakes with mounds of frosting and sprinkles or bits of candy on top. The flavor options are unending: S'mores, Black Forest, cotton candy, Butterfinger, Twinkie, and "The Elvis." Each Monday brings a new cupcake of the week. There are also full-size cakes, doughnuts, brownies, Danish, cookies, muffins, and scones. All products are certified kosher. Now, if only they didn't list calories on the menu! If you can't make it to one of their more than two dozen locations, delivery is offered.

D'AIUTO PASTRY
405 Eighth Ave (bet 30th and 31st St)   212/564-7136
Mon-Fri: 4 a.m.-10 p.m.; Sat, Sun: 7-7

Just thinking about D'Aiuto makes me hungry! You'll find famous Baby Watson cheesecakes, plus an amazing variety of other cakes and pies baked fresh each day by three generations of bakers. Also featured are apple fritters, carrot cake, banana bread, cornbread, crumb cakes, cupcakes, cannolis, pecan pies, banana cream pies, apple strudel, cookies, scones, eclairs, opera pastries, chocolate doughnuts, and much more. Being a personal bakery, they will pretty much create and bake whatever your tastebuds desire!

DOMINIQUE ANSEL BAKERY
189 Spring St (bet Sullivan and Thompson St)   212/219-2773
Mon-Sat: 8-7; Sun: 9-7   dominiqueansel.com

Dominique Ansel is an award-winning pastry chef who has a way with croissants. Dominique's Kouign Amann (aka DKA) is a tender, caramelized version made with croissant-like dough. Cronuts are an edible phenom best described as a cross between a croissant and a doughnut. The flaky dough is shaped like a doughnut, fried in grapeseed oil, and finished with a roll in sugar, cream filling, and sweet glaze. Other temptations include miniature meringues, macaroons, cakes, tarts, and French pastries; savories are served for breakfast and lunch. A word to the wise: cronuts sell out early in the morning and DKAs are gone in the afternoon (they are so popular that customers are imposed a limit of two per person).

DOUGHNUT PLANT

379 Grand St (at Norfolk St)   212/505-3700
Daily: 6:30 a.m.-8 p.m.
Hotel Chelsea
220 W 23rd St (bet Seventh and Eighth Ave)   212/675-9100
Mon-Fri: 7 a.m.-10 p.m.; Sat, Sun: 8 a.m.-10 p.m. (until doughnuts are gone)
                                                          doughnutplant.com

Mark Isreal presides over an establishment that is truly unique, concocting fluffy, fresh organic doughnuts made with spring water. He's come a long way since delivering doughnuts on his bicycle. There are more than 35 flavors, including PB&J, blackout, banana with pecans, "Yankee" (blueberry pinstripes), and rosewater (yes, with edible rose petals!). Unusual glazes from pistachios or fresh raspberries cover some cakes. Square jelly doughnuts are available, too. Doughnuts are hand-cut, yeast-raised, and very large. They also serve cinnamon buns and carrot-cake doughnuts, as well as hot chocolate, chai tea, organic coffee, and other beverages.

DOWNTOWN COOKIE CO.   646/486-3585
                                                        downtowncookieco.com

Traditional chocolate-chip cookies. Edgy lavender cookies. November stuffing cookie. These and more flavors are found at Downtown Cookie via phone or internet. All cookies are handmade to order and are delivered by FedEx or messenger around the city and anywhere in the U.S. Many Manhattan coffeehouses sell Downtown Cookies, too. Be sure to try the chocolate chocolate chip! For that matter, be sure to try them all. Minis are good for buying by the pound, and each month there are new flavors to fit the season.

FERRARA BAKERY AND CAFE

195 Grand St (bet Mulberry and Mott St)   212/226-6150
Daily: 8 a.m.-11:30 p.m. (Fri till 12:30 a.m.; Sat till 1 a.m.)   ferraracafe.com

Five generations have tended this store in Little Italy, one of the biggest little *pasticcerias* (pastry shops) in the world. Open since 1892, Ferrara is reputedly America's first espresso bar. The business deals in wholesale imports and other ventures, but their edible goodies could support the whole operation. This efficiently run Italian bakery makes delicious cannoli, cream puffs, fresh fruit tartlets, cheesecake, and more, to couple with your espresso, soda, or other specialty drink. And don't forget about the rainbow cookies!

GLASER'S BAKE SHOP

1670 First Ave (bet 87th and 88th St)   212/289-2562
Tues-Fri: 7-7; Sat: 8-7; Sun: 8-3   glasersbakeshop.com
Closed July and part of Aug

It won't be hard to find Glaser's Bake Shop on a Sunday. The line frequently spills outside as people queue up to buy the Glaser family's fresh cakes and baked goods. One isn't enough of anything here. Customers typically walk out with arms bulging. Since 1902, the Glasers have run their shop as a family business at this same location, and they're justifiably proud of their brownies, cakes, and cookies (try the chocolate chip!).

Custom Cookies

Playfully illustrated cookies are the backbone of **Eleni's** (Chelsea Market, 75 Ninth Ave, 212/255-7990 and 1266 Madison Ave, 212/831-3170; elenis.com). Each sugar cookie is shaped and hand-iced to match dozens of themes, occasions, and holidays. Cookies are sold individually and in attractive gift boxes (easily shipped or delivered in the city). Themed cupcakes with edible images are also available locally. You are sure to please when you give a box of Eleni's beautifully decorated birthday cookies!

KOSSAR'S BIALYS
367 Grand St (at Essex St)   212/473-4810
Sun-Thurs: 6 a.m.-7 p.m.; Fri: 6-2   kossarsbialys.com

The *bialy* derives its name from Bialystok, Poland, where they were first made. Kossar's brought the recipe over from Europe almost a century ago. Their delicious bialys, bagels, bulkas, and pletzels are sold fresh from the oven. The taste is Old World and authentic; prices can't be beat.

LADY M CAKE BOUTIQUE
41 E 78th St (at Madison Ave)   212/452-2222
Mon-Fri: 10-7; Sat: 11-7; Sun: 11-6   ladym.com

For some of the area's most outstanding cakes (and they *should* be, at the prices charged) a visit to this house is a must. You'll find a dazzling selection of over a dozen handmade cakes, which can be enjoyed in the small cafe (salads and sandwiches till 3 p.m.) or taken home. Special gift packaging for whole cakes is also available for an additional fee. Customers can enjoy tea while sampling goodies by the slice.

LE PAIN QUOTIDIEN
1131 Madison Ave (bet 84th and 85th St)   212/327-4900
833 Lexington Ave (bet 63rd and 64th St)   212/755-5810
100 Grand St (at Mercer St)   212/625-9009
Numerous other locations   lepainquotidien.us
Hours vary by store

Le Pain Quotidien traces its roots to Brussels, Belgium. It is a country-style bakery with long communal tables that serves breakfast, lunch, and light afternoon meals. European breads and pastries are sold at the counter. The meals offered are simple and the service refined. You'll find delicious croissants, *pain au chocolate,* brioche, heaping bread baskets, Belgian sugar waffles, an unusual Tuscan platter, crisp salads, and a splendid board of French cheeses. Wonderful tartines (open-faced sandwiches) are the house specialty; try Scottish smoked salmon with dill or Parisian ham with three mustards. Vegan and vegetarian options are available with a nod to organic ingredients whenever possible. Don't pass up the Belgian-chocolate brownies!

LITTLE PIE COMPANY
424 W 43rd St (at Ninth Ave)   212/736-4780
Mon-Fri: 8-8; Sat: 10-8; Sun: 10-6   littlepiecompany.com

Arnold Wilkerson, former actor, started baking apple pastries for private orders in his own kitchen. He now operates a unique shop that makes handmade pies and cakes using fresh seasonal fruits. Although they specialize in apple pie, they also make fresh peach, cherry, blueberry, and other all-American fruit-pie favorites, along with cream, meringue, and crumb pies. Stop by for a hot slice of pie a la mode and a cup of cider. Delicious brownies, bars, muffins, cupcakes, fruit Danishes, applesauce carrot cakes, white coconut cake, chocolate cream pie, and cheesecakes with wild blueberry, cherry, and orange toppings are also available. No preservatives are used!

MAGNOLIA BAKERY

401 Bleecker St (at 11th St)	212/462-2572
Grand Central Terminal (42nd St at Vanderbilt Ave), lower level	212/682-3588
1240 Ave of the Americas (at 49th St)	212/767-1123
Bloomingdales, 1000 Third Ave (at 59th St)	212/265-5320
200 Columbus Ave (at 69th St)	212/724-8101
Hours vary by store	magnoliabakery.com

Magnolia Bakery opened in 1996 on a quiet corner in the heart of Greenwich Village. It has expanded to several locations throughout the City. Fashioned as a cozy, old-fashioned bake shop, people come for coffee and something sweet. With its vintage American desserts (layer cakes, cookies, icebox desserts) and homey decor, walking into Magnolia is like taking a step back in time.

MOISHE'S BAKE SHOP

115 Second Ave (bet 6th and 7th St)   212/505-8555
Sun-Thurs: 7 a.m.-9 p.m.; Fri: 7 to one hour before sunset

Everything is done to perfection at Moishe's Bake Shop where Jewish bakery specialties are legendary. The cornbread is prepared exactly as it was in the Old Country (and as it should be now). The pumpernickel is dark and moist, and the rye and whole wheat are simply scrumptious. The cakes and pies are special, too! The charming owners run one of the best bakeries in the city, with the usual complement of bagels, bialys, cakes, and pastries. By all means try the challah.

Coffee Old and New

America's oldest coffee merchant, **Gillies Coffee Co.** (Brooklyn), has served New Yorkers since 1840. Customers still value a great cup of joe, but now coffee drinks have evolved into a varied and extensive choice of preparations, sizes, and tastes. There are plenty of decisions to be made. Bold, mild, decaf, or half-caf? Hot, iced, or blended? Whole, 2%, skim, soy milk, or half-and-half? Topped with whipped cream? Would you like a flavored syrup, and will that be regular or sugar-free? Size can range from a two-ounce shot of espresso to a "trento" (30-ounce cup). Don't forget the punch card many shops offer for a free cup after ten or so purchases.

Warning: should you order a regular coffee in New York, chances are that your coffee will come with cream and sugar (a.k.a. "coffee regular"). If that's not to your liking, be sure to specify black.

MURRAY'S BAGELS

500 Ave of the Americas (bet 12th and 13th St)　212/462-2830
murraysbagels.com
242 Eighth Ave (bet 22nd and 23rd St)　646/638-1335
Hours vary by store　murraysbagelschelsea.com

More than a dozen varieties of delicious hand-rolled, kettle-boiled, and oven-baked bagels are featured at Murray's. You'll also find smoked fish, spreads and schmears, pastries, breakfast omelets, soups, salads, sandwiches, and deli items for sandwiches. It's all available for eat-in, catering platters, and free local delivery.

ORWASHER'S BAKERY

308 E 78th St (bet First and Second Ave)　212/288-6569
Mon-Sat: 7:30-7; Sun: 9-4　orwasherbakery.com

For nearly a century, Orwasher's Bakery has served Manhattan's Upper East Side. It is New York's original artisan bakery. They bake about 30 varieties of all-natural breads every day. Originally famous for its classic New York breads — rye, cinnamon raisin, and pumpernickel — Orwasher's now offers a complete line of classic European breads, such as Irish soda and ciabatta. Health-conscious customers will enjoy the hearth-baked whole wheat and multigrain breads. A line of artisan wine breads is made with a natural starter created from fermenting wine grapes. Shaped by hand and baked downstairs in an ancient brick oven, these breads have a slightly sour flavor and are extra crusty. They pair perfectly with farmstand vegetables, stews, cured or braised meats, and fine cheeses. The bakery also carries a full line of classic pastries, as well as cupcakes, artisan cheeses, and superb coffee.

> ### Bakers' Supplies
>
> Attention, all bakers and cake decorators! **New York Cake & Baking Supply** (56 W 22nd St, 212/675-CAKE) is a treasure trove of cake and chocolate supplies. You'll find everything in the baking world at reasonable prices. You can browse conveniently at nycake.com and then phone, fax, or order online.

PASTICCERIA ROCCO

243 Bleecker St (bet Carmine and Leroy St)　212/242-6031
Sun-Thurs: 7:30 a.m.-midnight; Fri: 7:30 a.m.-1 a.m.; Sat: 7:30 a.m.-1:30 a.m.
pasticceriarocco.com

Pasticceria Rocco (formerly known as Rocco's Pastry Shop & Espresso Cafe) is a family-owned pastry and espresso cafe now run by Rocco's three children, using the same recipes and offering the same great tastes. Inside are tempting Italian goodies like crispy biscotti, *panettone*, cannoli (cream- and fruit-filled pastries), freshly baked cookies, decadent cakes, pies, cheesecakes (almost a dozen flavors), gelati, ices, and beautiful holiday indulgences. There are choices for any time of the day: pastries for breakfast, lunch, or break treats; dinner or late-night desserts; and gelato for any reason. The paninis are tasty and pressed to perfection. Enjoy your selection with one of the specialty drinks — perhaps a latte or cappuccino — eat-in or takeout.

POSEIDON BAKERY

629 Ninth Ave (bet 44th and 45th St)   212/757-6173
Tues-Sat: 9-7

Founded in 1923 by Greek baker Demetrios Anagnostou, today Poseidon Bakery is run by his great-grandson, Paul, to the same exacting standards. When a customer peers over the counter and asks about something, the response is usually a long description and sometimes an invitation to taste. This tiny bakery serves up savory and sweet creations like homemade baklava, strudel, *kataIf*, *trigona*, *tiropita* (cheese pie), spanakopita, and *saragli*. Poseidon's handmade phyllo is world renowned. They have cocktail-size frozen spinach, cheese, vegetable, and meat pies for home consumption or parties.

SIGMUND PRETZEL SHOP

29 Ave B (bet 2nd and 3rd St)
                                          646/410-0333
Mon-Thurs: 10-8; Fri, Sat: 10-10;
Sun: 10-6   sigmundnyc.com

Soft pretzels are one of my favorite snack foods, and Sigmund's handmade twisted treats are delicious. The warm, salt-encrusted pretzels are exceptional, as is the hot dog on a pretzel bun. Flavor options include cinnamon-raisin, sesame-, poppy-, sunflower-, and pumpkin-seed, and truffle cheddar pretzels, plus sweet and savory dips. Sigmund's also turns out tasty cookies and pretzel sandwiches stuffed with turkey, ham, or salmon. You'll find their convenient pretzel cart in High Line Park.

> **Milk Delivery**
>
> **Manhattan   Milk   Co.** (917/843-0727, manhattanmilk. com) sells fresh bottled milk (chocolate, too!), organic eggs, cases of water, juices, and other products. They'll deliver to your door (if you're home between 4 a.m. and 10 a.m. to accept the order) or leave it with your doorman at any time. These folks bring convenience to a new level. Service is available anywhere in Manhattan.

SILVER MOON BAKERY

2740 Broadway (at 105th St)   212/866-4717
Mon-Fri: 7:30 a.m.-8 p.m.; Sat, Sun: 8-7; open some holidays
                                              silvermoonbakery.com

In a tiny, busy space, Silver Moon presents delicious artisan breads (French, German, and Italian), French pastries and cakes, tarts, macaroons, challah, brioche (fresh fruit, raspberry, raisin, and chocolate chip), muffins, scones, and more. You can also enjoy a sandwich, soup, or quiche and watch the passing parade. Birthday and wedding cakes are made to order, as are special holiday treats.

SULLIVAN STREET BAKERY

533 W 47th St (bet Tenth and Eleventh Ave)   212/265-5580
Mon-Sat: 7:30-7; Sun: 7:30-4   sullivanstreetbakery.com

Come to Sullivan Street bakery for fresh, crusty loaves of French bread. This is also the place for really authentic Italian country bread. Their sourdough is served in a number of high-quality restaurants, so you know it is first-rate. Sullivan Street Bakery carries the only flatbread *pizza bianca romana* (Roman-style white pizza) in Manhattan. Raisin-walnut bread is another specialty. Great panini sandwiches, too. Perhaps their signature item is their Italian doughnut.

SYLVIA WEINSTOCK CAKES
273 Church St (bet Franklin and White St)   212/925-6698
Mon-Fri: 9-5   sylviaweinstock.com

In the special occasion cake business since the 1980s, Sylvia Weinstock knows how to satisfy customers who want the very best. Lifelike floral decorations are her trademark. Although weddings are a specialty (two months notice is suggested), she will produce masterpieces — including hand-molded sugar figures and exquisitely carved cakes — for any occasion.

TAKAHACHI BAKERY
25 Murray St (bet Church St and Broadway)   212/791-5550
Mon-Fri: 7-7; Sat: 8-7; Sun: 9-6   takahachibakery.com

You'll find a mouthwatering assortment of Japanese pastries, desserts, and sweets on the constantly changing menu at Takahachi. Green-tea cookies and cake, yuzu macaroons, red-bean buns, berry mousse, or truffle cake may be among the tasty selections. They also serve soups and salads. The eating area is a nice place to relax with your cup of tea or coffee.

TU-LU'S GLUTEN-FREE BAKERY
338 E 11th St (bet First and Second Ave)   212/777-2227
Sun-Thurs: 10:30-10; Fri, Sat: 10:30-10:30   tu-lusbakery.com

Tully Lewis's personal need for a change in diet resulted in this gluten-free bakery. Cookies, brownies, muffins, and cupcakes are preservative-free and made with rice and tapioca flour, potato starch, and soy ingredients. The coffee cake (regular and mini-size), red velvet cake, and cupcakes with choice of icing (including dairy-free and vegan options) are especially tasty. Enjoy a panini with honey oat or wholegrain sunflower bread, or indulge in one of their delicious quiches.

TWO LITTLE RED HENS
1652 Second Ave (bet 85th and 86th St)   212/452-0476
Mon-Fri: 7:30 a.m.-9 p.m.; Sat: 8 a.m.-9 p.m.; Sun: 8-7   twolittleredhens.com

No counting calories here! The only things you should count at Two Little Red Hens are the number of luscious cake fillings (16) and more than a dozen frostings and icings. Classic or specialty cakes (and cupcakes) can be ordered in advance or made to order (with special-occasion decorations or custom-drawn images) or stop by and choose from their ready-to-eat goodies. These delicious offerings — pies, tarts, cheesecakes, cookies, muffins, and other morning items — are also served at New York's leading restaurants and gourmet markets. Everything is delicious and decadent. My choice is the Brooklyn Blackout cupcake — chocolate cake, chocolate pudding filling, and rich fudge frosting to die for!

VENIERO'S

342 E 11th St (bet First and Second Ave)   212/674-7070
Sun-Thurs: 8 a.m.-midnight; Fri, Sat: 8 a.m.-1 a.m.   venierospastry.com

Since 1894 Veniero's has been serving appealing Italian pastries, cakes, cheesecake, tarts, and gelati to satisfied customers at moderate prices. The cannolis, with their creamy filling and crisp shells dipped in chocolate, are difficult to resist. The cookie trays are filled with crunchy *quaresimali*, *spumenti*, jelly-filled butter cookies, rainbow cookies, and other Italian treats. Wedding cakes are a specialty. Many of the building's original details, including hand-stamped copper ceilings and etched glass doors, have survived in this appealing shop.

YONAH SCHIMMEL KNISH BAKERY

137 E Houston St (bet First and Second Ave)   212/477-2858
Sun-Thurs: 9-7; Fri, Sat: 9-9   knishery.com

In 1910 the namesake founder started out dispensing knishes among the pushcarts of the Lower East Side. A Yonah Schimmel knish is a unique experience. It neither looks nor tastes anything like the mass-produced things sold at supermarkets and lunch stands. Yonah's knishes have a thin, flaky crust — almost like strudel dough — surrounding a hot, moist filling, and they are kosher. The best-selling filling is potato, but kasha (buckwheat), spinach, red cabbage and other mixtures are also terrific. No two knishes come out exactly alike, since each is handmade. You can order online or by fax (212/477-2858) for delivery anywhere in the continental U.S.

BRITISH

MYERS OF KESWICK

634 Hudson St (bet Horatio and Jane St)   212/691-4194
Mon-Fri: 10-7; Sat: 10-6; Sun: noon-5   myersofkeswick.com

Myers of Keswick is your traditional British grocery store, except it is in New York City! The second generation now runs the Big Apple's version of "the village grocer" for imported staples and fresh, home-baked items you'd swear came from a kitchen in Soho — the London neighborhood, that is. Among the tins, a shopper can find Heinz treacle sponge pudding, trifle mix, ribena, mushy peas, steak and kidney pie, Smarties, lemon barley water, chutneys, jams and preserves, and all the major English teas. Fresh goods include sausage rolls, Myers' pork pie, Scotch eggs, British bangers, and Cumberland sausages, all handmade fresh daily. For Anglophiles and expatriates alike, Myers of Keswick is a *luverly* treat.

CANDY

AJI ICHIBAN

37 Mott St (bet Bayard and Pell St)   212/233-7650
Daily: 10-8   ajiichiban.com.hk

Some of Aji Ichiban's more interesting Asian snacks and confections include dried or preserved pork, squid, crabs, and seaweed; gummy candies are always a favorite choice. Shelves are neatly arranged with packages labeled in both Chinese and English and bulk bins hold more delights. Small dishes atop the bins hold samples which encourage tasting the not-so-familiar contents.

Lower East Side Market

Essex Street Market (120 Essex St, at Delancey St; essexstreetmarket. com) has been an historic Lower East Side shopping destination since 1947. You'll find vendors of seafood, meats, ethnic groceries, baked goods, produce, and bulk-food items. The market also features specialty stores dispensing clothing, electronics, household goods, and religious items. No matter what you are looking for, Essex Street Market will deliver a unique shopping experience.

CHOCOLATE BAR

19 Eighth Ave (bet Jane and 12th St)   212/366-1541
Daily: 7:30 a.m.-10 p.m.   chocolatebarnyc.com

Now this is *my* kind of bar! Chocolate in all forms is sold all day long. Their hot chocolate — ground dark chocolate steamed with milk or soy — is superb. A variety of delicious chocolate bars includes milk chocolate, bittersweet, sea salt, dark, molé, salted almond, and spicy. In fact, everything is delicious: brownies of assorted varieties, bonbons, hand-poured chocolate suckers, almond toffee, and salted caramel truffles. Chocolate enrobes such favorites as popcorn, pretzels, s'mores, and nuts. What a great shop!

DYLAN'S CANDY BAR

1011 Third Ave (at 60th St)   646/735-0078
Mon-Thurs: 10-10; Fri, Sat: 10 a.m.-11 p.m.; Sun: 10-9   dylanscandybar.com

Ralph and Ricky Lauren's daughter, Dylan, continues to expand her candy haven. Dylan's Candy Bar is three floors of fun and sweetness. The third-floor cafe has an ice cream parlor that pumps out custom-made ice cream flavors. With over 5,000 candies from around the world, anyone's sweet tooth can be appeased. From Belgian chocolate bars, chocolate-covered pretzels, -popcorn, and -nuts, to nostalgic Necco wafers and Pixy Stix, you'll find virtually every sugar treat, some offered in bulk (or order online). Dylan's Candy Bar is also party central, offering children, adult, and corporate events. There are plenty of items in the non-edible category as well — accessories, jewelry, T-shirts, candy-themed pajamas, and more. Celebrity guests are not a rarity.

ECONOMY CANDY

108 Rivington St (bet Essex and Ludlow St)   212/254-1531
Mon: 10-6; Tues-Fri, Sun: 9-6; Sat: 10-5   economycandy.com

Now the third generation runs this family business, selling everything from penny candies to beautiful gourmet gift baskets. The selection at Economy Candy includes dried fruits, candies, cookies, nuts, and chocolates — even sugar-free goodies! The best part is the price. Those who bake will appreciate the selection of cocoas, baking chocolate, and glazed fruits. Favorite old-time candies include Skybars, Mary Janes, candy buttons, and Ice Cubes. This is a must-stop for holiday candy treats.

JACQUES TORRES CHOCOLATE

350 Hudson St (at King St)	212/414-2462
Chelsea Market, 75 Ninth Ave (bet 15th and 16th St)	212/229-2411
285 Amsterdam Ave (bet 73rd and 74th St)	212/787-3256
30 Rockefeller Plaza, concourse level	212/664-1804
Hours vary by store	mrchocolate.com

Jacques Torres will send the chocoholic in you to heaven. Jacques specializes in fresh, handcrafted chocolates that are free of preservatives and artificial flavors — from bon bons and truffles to chocolate bars and chocolate-covered cheerios. You'll also find ice cream, cookies, pastries, hot chocolate, espresso, and other sweet delights. The shops are beautifully decorated with crystal chandeliers, mahogany wood counters, and mirrored walls. At the 8,000-square-foot Hudson Street store, a state-of-the-art chocolate manufacturing plant lets you view production from start to finish.

LA MAISON DU CHOCOLAT

1018 Madison Ave (bet 78th and 79th St)	212/744-7117
Mon-Sat: 10-7; Sun: noon-6	
30 Rockefeller Plaza (49th St bet Fifth Ave and Ave of the Americas)	
Mon-Fri: 9:30-7; Sat: 10-7; Sun: noon-6	212/265-9404
63 Wall St (bet Pearl and Hanover St)	212/952-1123
Mon-Fri: 9:30-7; Sat: 11-6	
Plaza Food Hall by Todd English (Plaza Hotel, 1 W 59th St)	212/355-3436
Mon-Sat: 11-8; Sun: 11-6	lamaisonduchocolat.com

La Maison du Chocolat is quite a place! Over 40 delicious variations of light and dark chocolates are available under one roof. They carry French truffles, plain or fancy with fine champagne cognac, orangettes, chocolate-covered almonds, caramels, candied chestnuts (seasonal), and fruit paste. There's even a tea salon that serves pastries and drinks. Everything is made in Paris, and Manhattan's branches are the first outside of France. Prices are a cut above the candy-counter norm, but then so are exotic flavors like September raspberries, freshly grated ginger root, raisins flamed in rum, marzipan with pistachio and kirsh, and caramel butter.

LEONIDAS

485 Madison Ave (bet 51st and 52nd St)	212/980-2608
Mon-Fri: 9-7; Sat: 10-7; Sun: noon-6	leonidas-chocolate.com

The famous Leonidas' Belgian confections are sold and shipped at this store. Over a hundred varieties of exquisite sweets — milk, white, and bittersweet chocolate pieces, plus chocolate orange peels, solid chocolate medallions, fabulous fresh-cream fillings, truffle fillings, and marzipan — are flown in fresh every week. Leonidas' pralines are particularly sumptuous. Jacques Bergier, the genial general manager, can make the mouth water just describing this treasure trove. Best of all, prices are reasonable. Speaking of Leonidas, three retail locations of **Manon Cafe** (120 Broadway, 212/766-6100; 3 Hanover Square, 212/422-9600; and 74 Trinity Pl, 212/233-1111) serve Leonidas' Belgian chocolates, as well as coffee, espresso, cappuccino, sandwiches, and salads.

> ## Shop Like a Chef
>
> If you would like to shop where chefs stock up, consider visiting **Trufette** (a.k.a. **S.O.S. Chefs**, 104 Ave B, 212/505-5813). Among the interesting finds are numerous types of preserves, glazes, syrups, oils, chocolates, truffles, mushrooms, foie gras, spices, flavored salts, nuts, vanilla beans, saffron, fennel pollen, and much more. There are drawers full of interesting specialty items at reasonable prices at this high-end discovery center!

LI-LAC CHOCOLATES

40 Eighth Ave (at Jane St)   212/924-2280
Mon-Thurs: 11-8; Fri, Sat: 11-9; Sun: 11-7

Grand Central Market (Lexington Ave at 43rd St)   212/924-2280
Mon-Fri: 7 a.m.-9 p.m.; Sat: 10-7; Sun: 11-6   li-lacchocolates.com

Li-Lac Chocolates is Manhattan's oldest chocolate house. Since 1923 they have been making Old World artisan chocolates in small batches using the founder's original recipes. The time-honored production and fine quality ingredients result in delicious fresh chocolates — more than 140 items. Walnut fudge, pralines, mousses, French rolls, nuts, glacé fruits, and hand-dipped chocolates are but a few of the gourmet treats.

MARIEBELLE NEW YORK

484 Broome St (bet West Broadway and Wooster St)   212/925-6999
Mon-Thurs: 11-7; Fri-Sun: 11-8   mariebelle.com

Forget about the diet and head to MarieBelle. What awaits you is thick, European-style hot chocolate, homemade cookies, and biscuits, all artistically presented. The exotic chocolate flavors are packed with class. What a great gift for chocoholics! Crepes, fondues, sandwiches, salads, and other light fare are available at the Cacao Bar. Small private events are a specialty.

MONDEL CHOCOLATES

2913 Broadway (at 114th St)   212/864-2111
Mon-Sat: 11-7; Sun: 11-4   mondelchocolates.com

Mondel has been a tasty gem in the neighborhood since 1943. Owner Florence Mondel's father founded the store. The aroma is fantastic! The chocolate-covered ginger, orange peel, nut barks, and turtles are especially good. A dietetic chocolate line is offered.

PAPABUBBLE

380 Broome St (bet Mott and Mulberry St)   212/966-2599
Tues-Sat: noon-9; Sun: noon-6   papabubble.com

This candy shop-cum-laboratory produces sweet treats featuring seasonal flavors. These confections are then formed into finger rings, whimsies (toothbrushes, people, and fried eggs), and lollipops of different sizes and shapes. Personalized candies are a specialty at Papabubble. Colorful, tasty gems may include words, designs, and business names and logos. Satisfy cravings for sugary treats by the piece, bag, or jar.

TEUSCHER CHOCOLATES OF SWITZERLAND

25 E 61st St (at Madison Ave)   212/751-8482
Mon-Sat: 10-6

Rockefeller Center
620 Fifth Ave (bet 49th and 50th St)   212/246-4416
Mon-Sat: 10-6 (Thurs till 7); Sun: noon-6   teuscher-newyork.com

The Swiss chocolates at Teuscher are not just chocolates, they are imported works of art. Chocolates are shipped weekly from Switzerland. They are packed into stunning handmade boxes that add to the decor of many a customer's home. The truffles are almost obscenely good. The superb champagne truffle has a tiny dot of champagne cream in the center. The cocoa, nougat, butter-crunch, muscat, orange, and almond truffles all have their own little surprises. Truffles are the stars, but Teuscher's marzipan and praline chocolates are of similar high quality. If there was an award for "most elegant chocolate shop," it would have to go to Teuscher!

CATERING, DELIS, AND FOOD TO GO

ABIGAIL KIRSCH at PIER SIXTY and THE LIGHTHOUSE

Chelsea Piers, 23rd St at Hudson River   212/336-6060
Call for appointment   abigailkirsch.com

Abigail Kirsch's food, service, and venues are of the highest quality. Pricing is also high, but you will get your money's worth if you are hosting a class event, wedding, corporate function, or intimate cocktail party. You will not have to worry about a single detail as their team draws on over four decades of experience.

AGATA & VALENTINA

1505 First Ave (at 79th St)   212/452-0690
Daily: 8 a.m.-9 p.m.

64 University Pl (bet 10th and 11th St)   212/452-0690
Daily: 9 a.m.-10 p.m.   agatavalentina.com

These very classy gourmet shops, including the cappuccino bar, will make you think you're in Sicily. There are good things to eat at every counter, with each one more tempting than the next. The Italian product line, handpicked by Agata and daughter, Valentina, is extraordinary. You'll love the great selection of gourmet dishes, bakery items, appetizers, magnificent fresh vegetables, meats, cheeses, seafood, candies, and gelati. Extra-virgin olive oil is a house specialty. Gift baskets to order for any occasion!

BANGKOK CENTER GROCERY

104 Mosco St (bet Mott and Mulberry St)   212/349-1979
Daily: 10-8 (Tues till 7)   bangkokcentergrocery.com

You'll find a complete selection of Thai ingredients in this amazing, one-stop store, including teas, sticky rice, rice noodles, lemon grass, curry paste, and all manner of Thai herbs and spices. Bangkok Center also has convenient frozen and prepared foods you can take home for dinner. Snacks, candies, beverages, magazines, and Asian cookware also fill this store.

BARNEY GREENGRASS

541 Amsterdam Ave (bet 86th and 87th St)   212/724-4707

Favorite Chocolate Shops of a Serious Chocoholic (Me!)

5th Avenue Chocolatiere (693 Third Ave, 212/935-5454)

Black Hound New York (170 Second Ave, 212/979-9505)

Chocolate Bar (19 Eighth Ave, 212/366-1541)

Chocolat—Michel Cluizel (584 Fifth Ave, 646/415-9126)

Jacques Torres Chocolate (350 Hudson St, 212/414-2462; 285 Amsterdam Ave, 212/787-3256; 30 Rockefeller Plaza, 212/664-1804; and Chelsea Market, 75 Ninth Ave, 212/229-2441)

Kee's Chocolates (80 Thompson St, 212/334-3284; HSBC Bank, 452 Fifth Ave, 212/525-6099; and 315 W 39th St, 212/967-8088)

L.A. Burdick Handmade Chocolates (5 E 20th St, 212/796-0143)

La Bergamote (177 Ninth Ave, 212/627-9010)

La Maison du Chocolat (1018 Madison Ave, 212/744-7117; 30 Rockefeller Plaza, 212/265-9404; and 63 Wall St, 212/952-1123)

L'atelier du Chocolat (59 W 22nd St, 212/243-0033)

Leonidas (485 Madison Ave, 212/980-2608 and at Manon Cafe locations)

MarieBelle New York (484 Broome St, 212/431-1768)

Martine's Chocolates (400 E 82nd St, 212/744-6289)

Max Brenner, Chocolate by the Bald Man (841 Broadway, 212/388-0030)

Neuchatel Chocolates (55 E 52nd St, 212/759-1388)

Teuscher Chocolates of Switzerland (25 E 61st St, 212/751-8482 and 620 Fifth Ave, 212/246-4416)

Varsano's Chocolates (172 W 4th St, 212/352-1171): hand-dipped

Vosges Haut-Chocolat (132 Spring St, 212/625-2929 and 1100 Madison Ave, 212/717-2929)

Tues-Sun: 8-6 (takeout)   barneygreengrass.com
Tues-Fri: 8:30-4; Sat, Sun: 8:30-5 (restaurant)

This family business has occupied the same locale since 1929. Barney Greengrass lays claim to the title of "Sturgeon King," but it also carries other regal smoked-fish delicacies, including Nova Scotia salmon, belly lox, and whitefish. You will also find caviar, pickled herring, pastrami salmon, and kippered-salmon salad. The dairy and deli line — including vegetable cream cheese, great homemade cheese blintzes, homemade salads and borscht, and a smashing Nova Scotia salmon with scrambled eggs and onions — is world-renowned.

BARRAUD CATERERS
405 Broome St (at Centre St)   212/925-1334
Mon-Fri. 10-6   barraudcaterers.com

Chef/owner Rosemary Howe was born in India and grew up British, and is therefore familiar with Indian and Anglo-Indian food. Her training in developing recipes is on the French side. Because she was raised in the tradition of afternoon tea, she knows finger sandwiches and all that goes with them. With this varied background, her menus are unique. All breads are menu-specific, and every meal is customized from a lengthy list. A wine consultant is available, and consultations on table etiquette are given. Dinners focusing on cheese and wine are a specialty. This is a real hands-on operation, with Rosemary taking care of every detail of your brunch, tea, lunch, or dinner. She also features tasting menus paired with wines for each course.

BUTTERFIELD MARKET

1114 Lexington Ave (bet 77th and 78th St)   212/288-7800
Mon-Fri: 7a.m.-8 p.m.; Sat: 7:30-5:30; Sun: 8-5   butterfieldmarket.com

Since 1915 Upper East Siders have enjoyed the goodies at Butterfield. Highlights of this popular market include an excellent prepared-foods section, sandwiches, produce, a good selection of quality specialty items, breads, tasty pastries, charcuterie, attractive gift baskets, a terrific cheese selection, and a diet-busting candy and sweets section. Catering is a feature, and service is personal and informed. Just a few doors down, **Baked by Butterfield** (1102 Lexington Ave, 212/988-0196) bakes over two dozen varieties of doughnuts daily, along with other pastries and coffee.

CHELSEA MARKET

75 Ninth Ave (bet 15th and 16th St)   212/243-6005
Hours vary by store   chelseamarket.com

One of the most unusual marketplaces in the city is housed in a complex of 18 former industrial buildings, including the old National Biscuit Company (Nabisco) of the late 1800s. The 800-foot-long space is innovative, including a waterfall fed by an underground spring. Among the nearly 40 shops, you'll find **Amy's Bread** (big selection, plus a cafe); **Bowery Kitchen Supply** (kitchen buffs will go wild!); **Chelsea Market Baskets**; **Chelsea Wine Vault** (climate-controlled); **Cleaver Company** (catering and event planning); **Cull & Pistol** (seafood and raw bar); **Ronnybrook Dairy** (fresh milk and eggs); **Buon Italia** (great Italian basics); **Friedman's Lunch** (loaded baked potatoes); **Hale & Hearty Soups** (dozens of varieties); **Imports from Marrakesh**; **The Lobster Place** (takeout seafood); **Sarabeth's**; **Manhattan Fruit Exchange** (for buying in bulk); **Chelsea Thai** (wholesale and takeout); **Morimoto** (Japanese fine dining); **Fat Witch Bakery** (brownies, goodies, and gifts); and **Eleni's** (artfully iced sugar cookies, bagels, ice cream, and more). **Ruthy's Bakery & Cafe** is outstanding!

CITARELLA

2135 Broadway (at 75th St)   212/874-0383 (all locations)
1313 Third Ave (at 75th St)
424 Ave of the Americas (at 9th St)
Mon-Sat: 7 a.m.-11 p.m.; Sun: 9-9   citarella.com

Citarella gourmet market has been serving neighborhood customers since 1912. They started out as a fish market and claim to carry the largest selection of fresh domestic and international seafood in the country. The shelves and cases are stocked with everything you need to fill your pantry with fine ingredients or to bring home a fully prepared meal. From the take-away section, choose from an extensive selection of steamed lobster, salads, soups, and delicious entrees or charcuterie, antipasti, and smoked fish from the deli. Citarella also stocks their own brand of housemade pastas, sauces, oils, vinegars, and chocolates. You can count on Citarella for superb customer service and exceptional ingredients for your special meals; or leave the catering to them.

DEAN & DELUCA

560 Broadway (at Prince St)   212/226-6800
Mon-Fri: 7 a.m.-8 p.m.; Sat, Sun: 8-8
1150 Madison Ave (at 85th St)   212/717-0800
Daily: 8-8   deananddeluca.com

Dean & Deluca is one of the most recognizable names on the American epicurean scene. Don't miss it! The flagship store on Prince Street in Soho offers an extraordinary array of local, national, and international culinary selections. Among the many temptations are fresh produce and flowers, fresh-baked breads and pastries, prepared dishes, a good showing of cheeses and charcuterie, and a selection of meats, poultry, and seafood. A bustling espresso bar serves coffee and cappuccino, as well as sweets and savories. This part of the business has been expanded into smaller cafes throughout the city. To complete the gourmet adventure, Dean & Deluca offers an assortment of housewares. They can also cater intimate gatherings and corporate events.

DELMONICO GOURMET FOOD MARKET

55 E 59th St (bet Madison and Park Ave)   212/751-5559
Daily: 24 hours   delmonicogourmetnyc.com

Delmonico Gourmet Food Market has gourmet groceries, fresh produce, pastries, a bakery, a huge selection of cheeses, and much more. This is a good choice if you are planning a small catered event for your office or home. I like the ultra-clean surroundings and accommodating help. Don't miss the charcuterie selection and salad bars. And if you can't make the trip there, order online and request delivery.

EATALY

200 Fifth Ave (bet 23rd and 24th St)   212/229-2560
Daily: market and restaurant hours vary   eataly.com
Moderate (restaurant)

Forget about Little Italy! This is a one-of-a-kind New York experience you will never forget. This 50,000-square-foot operation is part restaurant, part grocery store, part street fair, and part eating circus. Eataly is an inspired venture combining the genius of Mario Batali, Lidia Bastianich, and Joe Bastianich (in New York) and company founder Oscar Farinetti (in Turin, Italy). This complex comprises several restaurants, a fishmonger, butcher, espresso bar, wine store, cheese store, produce stand, cooking school, lunch-dedicated restaurant, gelati stand, kitchenware, and so much more. It is assembled to evoke the atmosphere of a refined country fair, with hundreds of folks shopping, grazing, browsing, and loving every minute of this unique experience. Eataly has excellent, reasonably priced restaurants, an incredible assortment of edibles, good informational signage, and superb eye appeal. The mixture of foodstuffs is part Italian (mostly dry goods) and part high-quality American. There is even a "vegetable butcher," who will help prepare vegetarian purchases in a most attractive manner. The wine selection is awesome, and the pastries are addictive. Downsides are the sometimes lengthy waits for tables and poorly organized checkout stands.

Manzo, **Pranzo**, and **Birreria** are the only restaurants in the complex that take reservations, Birreria being a substantial rooftop brewery and restaurant with a top-quality meat selection. **La Pizza and Pasta** is worth a visit for the delicious ten-inch pizzas. **Il Pesce** has a raw bar and much more in the seafood category.

ELI'S MANHATTAN
1411 Third Ave (at 80th St)   212/717-8100
Daily: 7 a.m.-9 p.m.   elismanhattan.com

You know that quality is foremost whenever Eli Zabar is involved. This is true at Eli's Manhattan, which carries pristine produce, dairy items, pastries and breads, flowers, prepared foods, appetizers, smoked fish, coffee, wine and spirits, as well as one of the most extensive salad bar selections. Catering and gift baskets for order are available. Prices can be high, but so is quality. A self-service cafe called **Taste** (1413 Third Ave, 212/717-9798) offers breakfast and lunch, and then morphs into an elegant full-service dinner house at 5:30 p.m.

ELI'S VINEGAR FACTORY
431 E 91st St (at York Ave)   212/987-0885
Daily: 7 a.m.-9 p.m.; Brunch: Sat, Sun: 8-4   elizabar.com

Located on the site of what used to be a working vinegar factory, this operation of Eli Zabar's offers bearable prices on fresh produce, pizzas, fish, meats, desserts, seafood, cheeses, baked goods (including Eli's great breads), coffee, deli items, paper goods, and housewares. Breakfast and brunch (on weekends) are available on the balcony. Eli's heirloom tomatoes, greens, and herbs are grown in the five rooftop greenhouses. This is one of the most intriguing food factories around!

FAIRWAY MARKET
2127 Broadway (at 74th St)   212/595-1888
240 E 86th St (bet Second and Third Ave)   212/595-1888
2328 Twelfth Ave (at 133rd St)   212/234-3883
Hours vary by store   fairwaymarket.com

A very busy place! The popular institution known as Fairway made its name with an incredible selection of fruits and vegetables. They offer produce in huge quantities at reasonable prices. Each store offers a wonderful array of cheeses,

---

Patisserie Extraordinaire

Financier Patisserie is an excellent patisserie with numerous locations around town (35 Cedar St, 212/952-3838; 3-4 World Financial Center, 212/786-3220; 62 Stone St, 212/344-5600; 983 First Ave, 212/419-0100; and other locations). Feast your eyes on the beautiful pastries and decadent cakes, which taste as good as they look. Soups, salads, sandwiches, paninis, and breakfast items round out the menu. The selection may vary by store.

Market at Grand Central

Celebrating 100 years! Located in the heart of midtown, **Grand Central Market** (Grand Central Terminal, 42nd St at Vanderbilt Ave; grandcentralterminal.com) has some of Manhattan's finest quality food retailers, including Ceriello Fine Foods, Corrado Bread & Pastry, Dishes at Home, Greenwich Produce, Li-Lac Chocolates, Murray's Cheese Shop, Oren's Daily Roast, Penzeys Spices, Pescatore Seafood Company, Wild Edibles, and Zaro's Bread Basket.

bakery items, organically grown produce, expanded fish and meat departments, and a catering service. Fairway operates its own farm on Long Island and has developed relationships with area produce dealers, and all stores offer a full line of organic and natural grocery, health, and beauty items. In-store cafes at both the Broadway and 86th Street locations are convenient and reasonable. As you make your shopping rounds on the Upper East or West Side, you can't go wrong with a Fairway bag on one arm and a Zabar's bag on the other!

FINE & SCHAPIRO
138 W 72nd St (bet Broadway and Columbus Ave)   212/877-2874
Daily: 10-10   fineandschapiro.com
    Ostensibly a kosher delicatessen and restaurant, Fine & Schapiro also offers great dinners for home consumption. Because of the high quality, they term themselves "the Rolls-Royce of delicatessens." Fine & Schapiro dispenses a complete line of cold cuts, hot and cold hors d'oeuvres, catering platters, and magnificent sandwiches — try the pastrami or hot brisket! Everything that issues from Fine & Schapiro is perfectly cooked and artistically arranged. The sandwiches are masterpieces; the aroma and taste are irresistible. Chicken-in-a-pot, cocktail knishes, and stuffed cabbage are among their best items. Dine-in, takeout, or deliver!

GARDEN OF EDEN
162 W 23rd St (bet Ave of the Americas and Seventh Ave)   212/675-6300
7 E 14th St (bet University Pl and Fifth Ave)   212/255-4200
2780 Broadway (bet 106th and 107th St)   212/222-7300
Mon-Sat: 7 a.m.-10 p.m.; Sun: 7 a.m.-9:30 p.m.   edengourmet.com
    These stores are both farmers markets and gourmet shops! The food items are fresh, appetizing, and priced to please. Moreover, the stores are immaculate and well organized, and the personnel are very helpful. You'll find breads and bakery items, cheeses, veggies, meats, seafood, pastas, desserts, paté, breakfast items, and a wide array of imported goods. All manner of catering services are available.

GLORIOUS FOOD
522 E 74th St (bet East River and York Ave)   212/628-2320
Mon-Fri: 9-5 (by appointment)   gloriousfood.com
    When it comes to catering, Glorious Food is at the top of many New Yorkers' lists. They are a full-service outfit, expertly taking care of every detail

of any event. They have met most every challenge since 1972. Give 'em a try!

GOURMET GARAGE

489 Broome St (at Wooster St)	212/941-5850
1245 Park Ave (at 96th St)	212/348-5850
155 W 66th St (bet Broadway and Amsterdam Ave)	212/595-5850
301 E 64th St (at Second Ave)	212/535-6271
117 Seventh Ave S (at 10th St)	212/699-5980
Hours vary by store	gourmetgarage.com

Perhaps the best way to describe Gourmet Garage is a working-class gourmet food shop. These stores carry a good selection of in-demand items, including fruits and veggies, cheeses, breads, pastries, coffees, fresh meats and seafood, and olive oils, at reasonable prices. Organic foods are a specialty. Catering and gift baskets are available, and delivery is offered for a nominal fee. All locations offer prepared foods (hot and cold) and a sushi bar.

GRACE'S MARKETPLACE

1237 Third Ave (at 71st St)	212/737-0600
Mon-Sat: 7 a.m.-8:30 p.m.; Sun: 8-8	gracesmarketplacenyc.com

Grace's Marketplace is one of the city's finest and most popular food emporiums. Founded in 1985 by Grace Balducci Doria and the late Joe Doria, Sr., the Doria family still presides over this operation, and they can be seen helping customers on the floor. Products, service, and ambience are all top of the line. You'll find smoked meats and fish, caviar, cheeses, fresh pastas, homemade sauces, produce, a full range of baked goods, candy, coffee and tea, dried fruit, pastries, gourmet and international groceries, prepared foods, prime meats, sushi, and seafood. Quality gift baskets and catering are specialties. Try their adjoining restaurant, **Grace's Trattoria** (201 E 71st St, 212/452-2323, gracestrattoria. com), for great Italian fare.

GREAT PERFORMANCES

304 Hudson St (at Spring St)	212/727-2424
By appointment	greatperformances.com

Since 1979 Great Performances has been creating spectacular events in the New York area with the help of folks from the city's artistic community. Each division of this full-service catering company has a team of expert staff.

Grocery Delivery

For New Yorkers who don't find grocery shopping a pleasant pastime, there is **FreshDirect** (212/796-8002, freshdirect.com). Over 3,000 organic and prepared food items can be ordered online from an expansive list, and you can even arrange for a delivery time. Dairy, meats, fish, bakery items, produce, beverages — all fresh and local. They also provide recipes and cooking information. Prices are competitive, as they do not have a storefront or deal with middle men. Delivery charges are reasonable. What a great service!

Produce Markets

Another example of New York's reputation as "the city that never sleeps" is a number of produce markets and grocers that are open all day, every day. You'll appreciate the 24/7 convenience and decent prices.

Annie's (1330 Lexington Ave, 212/861-6078): organic choices, general groceries, fresh flowers, delivery

Number 1 Farmers Market (1458 Second Ave, 212/396-2626): fresh produce, cookies, cheese, flowers, staples

They take pride in recruiting the best and brightest the industry has to offer. From intimate dinner parties to galas for thousands, Great Performances is a complete catering and event-planning resource. They produce their own organic line of seasonal ingredients at their upstate Katchkie Farm.

H&H MIDTOWN BAGELS EAST

1551 Second Ave (bet 80th and 81st St)   212/734-7441
Daily: 24 hours   hhmidtownbagels.com

Delicious bagels are made right on the premises, and if you're lucky, you'll get 'em warm! Delicious spreads and smoked fish can be paired with your bagel choice. Also filling the shop are homemade croissants, strudel, muffins, assorted cookies, soups, knishes, cold cuts, sandwiches, salads, jams, and honeys. The emphasis is on carryout, but tables are available for those who can't wait. Catering and shipping are offered as well.

HAN AH REUM

25 W 32nd St (bet Broadway and Fifth Ave)   212/695-3283
Daily: 9 a.m.-midnight

Note the late hours! Korean (also Japanese and Chinese) food items are the specialties at Han ah Reum. This tightly packed ethnic grocery store has everything from Korean pears, Japanese cucumbers, kalbi, sashimi, acorn flour, and rice cakes to a good selection of fresh fish and meat (some pre-marinated). You'll find many brands of items carried at this central supermarket location.

INTERNATIONAL GROCERY

543 Ninth Ave (at 40th St)   212/279-1000
Mon-Fri: 7:30-6:30; Sat: 7:30-6   internationalgrocerynyc.com

Ninth Avenue is a great wholesale market for international cookery. Accordingly, International Grocery is both a spice emporium and an excellent source of staples for adventurous home cooks. Loose herbs, honey, pastas, olives, pitas, and some cooking utensils and pans create a bazaar-like atmosphere. Or opt for one of the housemade Greek platters of baklava, spanikopita, halvah, yogurt, and feta cheese. You will sacrifice frills for some of the best prices and freshest foodstuffs in town in this compact store.

KELLEY AND PING

127 Greene St (at Prince St)   212/228-1212
Daily: 11:30 a.m.-5:p.m.; 5:30 p.m.-11 p.m.   kelleyandping.com

The exotic cuisines of Asia — Thai, Chinese, Vietnamese, Japanese, Malaysian, and Korean — are popular in restaurants and at home. Kelley and Ping specialize in groceries from this part of the world. An on-premises restaurant has become a major part of the operation, serving lunch and dinner, as well as offering catering services. You'll find lunch boxes, noodle soups, curry, wok items, salads, and rolls. Dinner items expand to chicken, fish, and meat entrees along with small Asian dishes and sides like jasmine rice or vegetable dumplings. Delivery is available to nearby neighborhoods. If you have questions about how to prepare Asian dishes, just ask these helpful folks.

NEWMAN & LEVENTHAL

45 W 81st St (bet Central Park W and Columbus Ave)   212/362-9400
By appointment   newmanandleventhal.com

A kosher caterer since 1980, this firm is known for unique menus, beautiful presentation, and top quality in both indoor and outdoor venues. Be prepared to pay well for outstanding food.

RUSS & DAUGHTERS

179 E Houston St (bet Allen and Orchard St)   212/475-4880
Mon-Fri: 8-8; Sat: 8-7; Sun: 8-5:30   russanddaughters.com

Russ & Daughters has been a renowned New York shop for four generations, and that's no wonder with their reputation for serving only the very best. They carry nuts, dried fruits, bagels, rugelach, salads, lake sturgeon, mackerel, salmon, sable, whitefish, herring, lox, and other specialty smoked fish. A dozen varieties of caviar are sold at low prices. Their chocolates are premium quality. Platters of cheese, fish, salad, or sweets are beautiful. They sell wholesale and over the counter, and will ship anywhere. A Lower East Side shopping trip should definitely include a stop here.

SABLE'S SMOKED FISH

1489 Second Ave (bet 77th and 78th St)   212/249-6177
Mon-Fri: 8:30-7; Sat: 7:30-7; Sun: 7:30-5   sablesnyc.com

Kenny and Danny Sze bring their experience and knowledge (learned at Zabar's) to the Upper East Side. The shop offers wonderful smoked salmon, lobster salad, Alaskan crab salad, caviar (good prices), cheeses, coffees, salads, fresh breads, and prepared to-go foods. Sable's catering service can provide platters (smoked fish, cold cuts, and cheese), jumbo sandwiches, and more.

Chutney Choices

This business started in the Hamptons in 1995 and expanded into Manhattan five years later. **Hampton Chutney Co.** (464 Amsterdam Ave, 212/362-5050 and 68 Prince St, 212/226-9996) makes six varieties of the spicy condiment: cilantro, mango, tomato, curry, pumpkin, and peanut. It is sold fresh by the half-pint, pint, and quart. The cafe's menu features chutney in many Indian dishes. Try a dosa or uttapa (crepe or pancake made with fermented rice and lentil batter) filled with ingredients similar to a gourmet omelet.

Hot Dog!

At my restaurant (Gerry Frank's Konditorei, 310 Kearney St, Salem, OR, 503/585-7070, gerryfrankskonditorei.com), we serve OregonGrassFed beef and we call them "Gerry's Franks!" For the best frankfurters in Manhattan try:

2nd Ave Deli (162 E 33rd St, 212/689-9000 and 1442 First Ave, 212/737-1700)

Artie's Delicatessen (2290 Broadway, 212/579-5959)

Asiadog (66 Kenmare St, 212/226-8861)

Brooklyn Diner USA (212 W 57th St, 212/977-2280 and 155 W 43rd St, 212/265-5400)

Crif Dogs (113 St. Mark's Pl, 212/614-2728)

DBGB Kitchen & Bar (229 Bowery, 212/933-5300)

Gray's Papaya (2090 Broadway, 212/799-0243 and 402 Ave of the Americas, 212/260-3532): inexpensive

Hallo Berlin (626 Tenth Ave, 212/977-1944)

Katz's Delicatessen (205 E Houston St, 212/254-2246)

Nathan's Famous Hot Dogs (stands all over Manhattan)

Old Town Bar and Restaurant (45 E 18th St, 212/529-6732)

Papaya King (179 E 86th St, 212/369-0648 and 3 St. Mark's Pl, 646/692-8482)

Shake Shack (Madison Square Park, Madison Ave at 23rd St, 212/889-6600; 366 Columbus Ave, 646/747-8770; 154 E 86th St, 646/237-5035; 691 Eighth Ave, 646/435-1035; and 215 Murray St, 646/545-4600): Madison Square Park location is seasonal.

Sigmund Pretzel Shop (29 Ave B, 646/410-0333)

Westville (210 W 10th St, 212/741-7971; 246 W 18th St, 212/924-2223; and 173 Ave A, 212/677-2033): vegan

Chicken dishes are specialties. Tables for eat-in are available.

SALUMERIA BIELLESE

378 Eighth Ave (at 29th St)   212/736-7376
Mon-Fri: 7-5:45; Sat: 9-4:45   salumeriabiellese.com

In 1925, Ugo Buzzio and Joseph Nello immigrated from the Piedmontese city of Biella. They opened a Chelsea shop a block away from the current one and began producing Italian-style cured meats and delicious fresh sausage. Word spread among the city's chefs that Salumeria Biellese was producing a quality product, and now they supply many fine restaurants in the city. Still a family-run business, Buzzio's son Marc, along with partners Paul and Fouad, are in charge today. Offerings include sausages (pork, game, beef, lamb, and poultry), cured meats, and specialty patés. Deli offerings include delicious sandwiches, prepared foods, and cheese. **Biricchino** (260 W 29th St, 212/695-6690), a restaurant offering Northern Italian cuisine, is located in back.

SONNIER & CASTLE

554 W 48th St (bet Tenth and Eleventh Ave)   212/957-6481
By appointment   sonnier-castle.com

Since 1997, Sonnier & Castle has brought finesse and style to the table for special events of any size. From playful to sophisticated, their creativity, presentation, service, and innovative cooking will transform any gathering into a memorable one.

SPOONBREAD CATERING

Catering at specified sites   212/865-0700

MISS MAMIE'S SPOONBREAD TOO

366 W 110th St (between Columbus and Manhattan Ave)   212/865-6744
Mon-Fri: noon-10; Sat: noon-10:30; Sun: 11-9

MISS MAUDE'S SPOONBREAD TOO

547 Lenox Ave (between 137th and 138th St)   212/690-3100
Mon-Sat: noon-9:30; Sun: 11-7   spoonbreadinc.com

For authentic soul food, go to these Harlem standouts. Pork chops, spoonbread (a pudding-like cornmeal bread eaten with a spoon or fork), chicken (fried, smothered, roasted, and barbecued), fried catfish, and classic sides like collard greens are prepared fresh daily. Plan to splurge on banana pudding, pecan pie, or fruit cobbler with ice cream. These down-South favorites, along with more upscale selections, are offered by the catering arm of the business, Spoonbread Catering. Some of the multi-cultural cuisine exhibits Asian, Italian, and Mexican influences. Try them for wedding receptions, corporate events, or any other occasion and wow your guests.

TODARO BROS.

555 Second Ave (bet 30th and 31st St)   212/532-0633
Mon-Sat: 6:30 a.m.-10 p.m.; Sun: 6:30 a.m.-9 p.m.   todarobros.com

An icon in the Murray Hill area since 1917, Todaro Bros. carries the very best in specialty foods. Great lunch sandwiches, fresh mozzarella, sausages, olives, and prepared foods are offered daily. The fresh fish and meats are of the highest quality. The cheese department offers a huge variety of imported varieties in their compact space. The shelves are well-stocked with artisanal oils, vinegars, pasta, condiments, coffee, fresh produce, and exquisite pastries mostly from the Mediterranean region.

WHOLE FOODS MARKET

808 Columbus Ave (at 97th St)	212/222-6160
Time Warner Center, 10 Columbus Circle	212/823-9600
226 E 57th St (bet Second and Third Ave)	646/497-1222
4 Union Square S	212/673-5388
250 Seventh Ave (at 24th St)	212/924-5969
95 E Houston (at Bowery)	212/420-1320
270 Greenwich St (bet Murray and Warren St)	212/349-6555
Hours vary by store	wholefoodsmarket.com

First-Class Grocery Markets

For grocery shopping, don't overlook **Westside Market NYC** (77 Seventh Ave, 212/807-7771; 2171 Broadway, 212/595-2536; and 2840 Broadway, 212/222-3367). These are first-class operations — immaculately clean and well-priced, with a large stock. Catering, free delivery within a ten-block radius, and wonderful prepared foods are additional features. You will be very pleasantly surprised! Discover tempting Greek recipes on the website (wmarketnyc.com), compliments of the Zoitas family.

Big, beautiful, and busy accurately describes Whole Foods Market! If you can't find a particular food item here, it probably doesn't exist. These grocery superstores (now seven locations in Manhattan) have a huge deli, bakery, produce, and floral sections, as well as sushi, seafood, fresh juices, and all kinds of carryout items. There are over 40 checkout stands at the Time Warner Center location.

ZABAR'S

2245 Broadway (at 80th St)   212/787-2000
Mon-Fri: 8-7:30; Sat: 8-8; Sun: 9-6   zabars.com

No trip to Manhattan is complete without a visit to this fabulous emporium. True New York shoppers swear by this place! You will find enormous selections of bread, smoked fish, coffee, prepared food, cheese, olives, deli items, gift baskets, candy, and much more. All are of the highest quality and affordably priced. A cafe next door provides snacks all day at bargain prices. Their fresh-from-the-oven rye bread is the best in Manhattan. One important reason for Zabar's success is veteran employees; roughly 50 of them have been with the store for 17 years or more. Upstairs is one of the best housewares departments in America, with a huge selection and good prices. (It opens an hour later than the rest of Zabar's every day except Sunday.) Owner Saul Zabar comes from a legendary food family in Manhattan. You will often see him wandering the aisles to make sure everything is top-notch. General Manager Scott Goldshine and Store Manager David Tait provide the extra-special service for which Zabar's is renowned. And some Saturdays you will find your author at Zabar's autographing this book!

CHEESE

ALLEVA DAIRY

188 Grand St (at Mulberry St)   212/226-7990
Mon-Sat: 9-6; Sun: 9-3   allevadairy.com

Founded in 1892, Alleva is the oldest Italian cheese store in America. The Alleva family has operated the business from the start, always maintaining meticulous standards of quality and service. Robert Alleva oversees the production of over 4,000 pounds of fresh cheese a week, including *parmigiano*, *fraschi*, *manteche*, *scamoize*, and *provoleaffumicale*. The ricotta is superb, and the mozzarella tastes like it was made on a side street in Florence. Quality Italian meats, an olive bar, grocery items, and gift baskets are also offered. Online orders are welcome.

DI PALO FINE FOODS

200 Grand St (at Mott St)   212/226-1033
Mon-Sat: 9-7; Sun: 9-5   dipaloselects.com

The cheeses and pastas offered at Di Palo Fine Foods are simply superb. The family-owned business also carries olive oils, meats, and all manner of traditional products from the various regions of Italy. It's worth a trip to Little Italy.

EAST VILLAGE CHEESE

40 Third Ave (bet 9th and 10th St)   212/477-2601
Daily: 8:30-6:30

Value is the name of the game. For years this store has prided itself on selling cheese at some of the lowest prices in town. They claim similar savings for whole-bean coffees, fresh pastas, extra-virgin olive oils, spreads, quiches, patés, and a wide selection of fresh bread. There is also a deli counter and olive bar. Good service including a knowledgeable staff is another reason to shop here. This is a cash-only operation.

IDEAL CHEESE SHOP

942 First Ave (at 52nd St)   212/688-7579
Mon-Fri: 8:30-6; Sat: 8:30-5   idealcheese.com

Ideal Cheese Shop has been in operation since 1954, and many Upper East Siders swear by its quality and service. Hundreds of cheeses from all over the world are sold here, and the owners are constantly looking for new items. They carry gourmet items: olives, olive oils, vinegars, mustards, coffees, biscuits, preserves, specialty meats, pantry items, and a small line of specialty beers. Order online or through their catalog; they will ship anywhere in the U.S.

The Best Natural Foods Emporiums

In my opinion, **Whole Foods Market** is the best place to go for natural foods. The selection of high-quality merchandise is huge (and expensive), the personnel are knowledgeable, customer service is top-notch, and the prepared foods are outstanding. Convenient locations can be found around town.

Additional quality food emporiums include:

Commodities Natural Market (165 First Ave, 212/260-2600): cheeses, good prices

Gary Null's Uptown Whole Foods (2421 Broadway, 212/874-4000): juice bar and kosher items

Health Nuts (2611 Broadway, 212/678-0054; 1208 Second Ave, 212/593-0116; and 835 Second Ave, 212/490-2979): juice bar

Integral Yoga Natural Foods (229 W 13th St, 212/243-2642): organic produce and baked items, vegetarian; yoga classes offered in the same building

LifeThyme Natural Market (410 Ave of the Americas, 212/420-9099): salad bar, produce

MURRAY'S CHEESE SHOP

254 Bleecker St (bet Ave of Americas and Seventh Ave)   212/243-3289
Mon-Sat: 8-8; Sun: 10-7   murrayscheese.com

This place smells good! This is one of the best cheese shops in Manhattan. Founded in 1940, Murray's offers wholesale and retail international and domestic cheeses of every description. There is also a fine selection of cold cuts, prepared foods, antipasti, breads, sandwiches, and specialty items, including party platters and gift baskets. Behind the counter, helpful and knowledgeable servers are known to be accommodating when asked for a cheese sample. Ask to tour the underground cheese-aging caves! Better yet, sign up for an evening cheese course with tastings, pairings, and useful information. An outlet at Grand Central Market (in Grand Central Terminal) is commuter-friendly.

CHINESE

GOLDEN FUNG WONG BAKERY

41 Mott St (at Pell St)   212/267-4037
Daily: 7-7

Golden Fung Wong is the real thing. Pastries, cookies, and baked goods are traditional and delicious. Flavor is not compromised in order to appeal to Western tastes. The bakery features a tremendous variety of baked goods, and it has the distinction of being New York's oldest and largest authentic Chinese bakery.

NEW KAM MAN

200 Canal St (bet Mott and Mulberry St)   212/571-0330
Daily: 9-8:30   newkamman.com

New Kam Man has evolved from an Oriental grocery store into a source for all things Asian. In addition to Chinese foodstuffs, they carry Japanese, Thai, Vietnamese, Malaysian, and Filipino products. Native Asians should feel right at home in this store, where all types of traditional condiments and snacks are available. All of the necessities for the preparation and presentation of Asian foods can be found, from sauces and spices to utensils, cookware, tableware, even gifts. For the health-conscious, New Kam Man stocks teas and Chinese herbal medicines. Prices are reasonable.

TONGIN MART

91 Mulberry St (at Canal St)   212/962-6622
Daily: 9-8

If you are planning a home-cooked Chinese dinner, there's no better source than this store in Chinatown. Tongin Mart boasts that 95% of its business is conducted with the Chinese community. They have an open and friendly attitude, and care is taken to introduce customers to the wide variety of imported Oriental foods, including Japanese, Thai, and Filipino products. Sushi and sashimi are available at reasonable prices.

COFFEE AND TEA

EMPIRE COFFEE & TEA COMPANY

568 Ninth Ave (bet 41st and 42nd St)   212/268-1220
Mon-Fri: 7:30-7; Sat: 9-6:30; Sun: 10-6   empirecoffeetea.com

Empire Coffee & Tea carries an enormous selection of coffee (75 types of beans!), tea, and herbs. Because of the aroma and array of the bins, choosing is almost impossible; you may need to seek assistance from the helpful personnel. Fresh coffee beans and tea leaves are available in bulk; everything is sold loose and can be ground. Empire also carries a wide selection of gourmet items, mugs, and teapots. Gourmet gift baskets, too!

HARNEY & SONS

433 Broome St (bet Broadway and Crosby St)   212/933-4853
Mon-Sat: 10-7; Sun: 11-7   harney.com

There's something comforting about a cup of tea in a cozy environment. Harney & Sons meets that expectation in spades at their Soho tasting room. In addition to having a spot to take a cup of tea and a sweet, they proffer samples of some of their 250+ teas (hot or iced depending on the season). The staff graciously shares their knowledge about the seemingly endless varieties of tea, brewing tips, and tasting. In addition to tea (loose, bags, and sachets) Harney carries a nice selection of teaware, books, treats, and related gifts.

JACK'S STIR BREW COFFEE

425 W 13th St (at Washington St)   212/647-0900

138 W 10th St (bet Greenwich St and Waverly Pl)   212/929-0821

10 Downing St (bet Waverly Pl and 8th St)   212/929-6011

South Street Seaport, 222 Front St (at Beekman St)   212/227-7631
Hours vary by store   jacksstirbrew.com

Jack's Stir Brew Coffee claims to serve the perfect cup of joe. Behind this claim is the stir-brew process, which oxygenates the coffee, eliminating unpleasant bitterness. Check the chalkboard for your favorite preparations. Certified organic and fair-trade coffees are staples, as are organic milk, brown sugar, and granola. Complete your coffee break with an oversized cookie, bagel, or fruit-filled muffin.

JAVA GIRL

348 E 66th St (bet First and Second Ave)   212/737-3490
Mon-Fri: 6:30 a.m.-7 p.m.; Sat, Sun: 8:30-6

The aroma of fresh-ground coffee in this tiny hideout is overwhelming! For fine coffees, teas, pastries, salads, and sandwiches, look no further. Drink-in or take out. Java Girl has creative gift boxes as well.

McNULTY'S TEA & COFFEE COMPANY

109 Christopher St (bet Bleecker and Hudson St)   212/242-5351
Mon-Sat: 10-9 (closed Tues in July, Aug); Sun: 1-7   mcnultys.com

Since 1895 McNulty's has been supplying discerning New Yorkers with coffee and tea. They carry a complete line of quality spiced and herbal teas, coffee blends ground to order, and coffee and tea accessories. Their blends are unique, and the personal service is highly valued. McNulty's maintains an extensive file of customers' special blend choices and has a welcoming atmosphere.

Buying Caviar

Strictly speaking, caviar is the roe of sturgeon from the Caspian and Black seas. It is a delicacy, and a pricey one at that. Look for caviar at raw bars, on appetizer menus at high-end restaurants, and at trusted stores. More and more restaurants have aligned themselves with sources that pledge sustainability; roe is cultivated from farmed sturgeon to reduce the threat to declining wild stocks. The main caviar types are:

Beluga: large, firm, and well-defined roe with a smooth, creamy texture
Osetra: strong with a sweet, fruity flavor
Sevruga: subtle, clean taste with a crunchy texture
Sterlet: intense flavor, small- to-medium-size grains

The best caviar is at these establishments:

Barney Greengrass (541 Amsterdam Ave, 212/724-4707)

Caviar Russe (538 Madison Ave, 212/980-5908): a luxury spot

Dean & Deluca (1150 Madison Ave, 212/717-0800 and 560 Broadway, 212/226-6800)

FireBird (365 W 46th St, 212/586-0244): housed in a re-creation of a prerevolutionary Russian mansion

Murray's Sturgeon (2429 Broadway, 212/724-2650)

Petrossian Restaurant (182 W 58th St, 212/245-2214): Providing ambience befitting the caviar set, this is a spectacular place to dine.

Russ & Daughters (179 E Houston St, 212/475-4880)

Sable's Smoked Fish (1489 Second Ave, 212/249-6177)

Zabar's (2245 Broadway, 212/787-2000): If price is important, then make this your first stop.

PORTO RICO IMPORTING COMPANY

201 Bleecker St (main store)	212/477-5421
40½ St. Mark's Pl (coffee bar)	212/533-1982
Essex Street Market, 120 Essex St (coffee bar)	212/677-1210
Hours vary by store	portorico.com

Peter Longo's family started a small coffee business in the Village in 1907. Primarily importers and wholesalers, they were soon pressured to open a small storefront as well. That operation gained a reputation for the best and freshest coffee available. Since much of the surrounding neighborhood consists of Italians, the Longo family reciprocated their loyalty by specializing in Italian espressos and cappuccinos, as well as health and medicinal teas. Dispensed along with such teas are folk remedies and advice to mend whatever ails you. Peter has added coffee bars, making it possible to sit and sip from a selection of 150 coffees and 225 loose teas while listening to folklore or trying to select the best from the bins. All coffees are roasted daily at Porto Rico's own facility.

SENSUOUS BEAN

66 W 70th St (at Columbus Ave)   212/724-7725
Mon-Fri: 8-6:30; Sat: 8-5:30; Sun: 9:30-5:30   sensuousbean.com

The Sensuous Bean was in business long before the coffee craze started. This legendary coffee and teahouse carries 70 varieties of coffee and 50 teas. The bulk bean coffees and loose teas come from all around the world; teas from England, France, Germany, Ireland, and Taiwan are featured. They carry a large variety of green, white, chai, herbal, rooibos, and blended loose teas, along with many organic and fair-trade coffees. They make lattes, cappuccinos, espressos, and chais; steep loose tea to order; and offer many sweets, biscottis, and chocolates to accompany these beverages. You can sip your savory cup with neighborhood loyals in the small, cluttered space.

> **Kosher Market**
>
> **Holyland Market** (122 St. Mark's Pl, 212/477-4440) is an excellent place for kosher cheeses and hard-to-find imported Israeli foods.

T SALON

230 Fifth Ave (at 27th St), Suite 1511   212/358-0506
Mon-Fri: 10:30-6; Sat, Sun: by appointment   tsalon.com

Miriam Novalle, the guru at T Salon, has brewed up a wonderful selection of tea and tea accessories. She offers more than 450 custom blends of tea for retail and wholesale purchase. There are green teas, oolong teas, and black teas, as well as white and red teas. Tea blending is Miriam's specialty. You will be happy to hear that afternoon tea is still available by appointment.

TEN REN TEA & GINSENG

75 Mott St (at Canal St)   212/349-2286
Daily: 10-8   tenrenusa.com

A tea lover's paradise! Founded in 1953, this Taiwanese company is the largest tea grower and manufacturer in East Asia. They sell green, oolong, jasmine, black, and white teas, plus tea sets and all manner of accessories. Various kinds of ginseng are also available. Ten Ren means "heavenly love," and you will likely fall in love with one of their flavors. Some of the rarer teas go for more than $100 a pound! Stop in next door to **Ten Ren's Tea Time** (212/732-7178), a cozy spot to sample teas.

FOREIGN FOODSTUFFS (the best)

Craving a specific foreign food item? The following shops feature specialty items from various countries. Each shop is given a full write-up within this Food Shops chapter.

ASIAN (CHINESE, KOREAN, MALAYSIAN, TAIWAN, THAI, VIETNAMESE)

Asia Market (71½ Mulberry St)
Bangkok Center Grocery (104 Mosco St)
Golden Fung Wong Bakery (41 Mott St)
Kelley and Ping (127 Greene St)
New Kam Man (200 Canal St)

The Best Frozen Treats in Manhattan

40 Carrots (Bloomingdale's, 1000 Third Ave, 7th floor, 212/705-3085)

Chinatown Ice Cream Factory (65 Bayard St, 212/608-4170)

Ciao Bella Gelato (285 Mott St, 212/431-3591; 2 World Financial Center, 255 Liberty St, 212/786-4707; Grand Central Terminal, 42nd St at Vanderbilt Ave, 212/867-5311; and other locations): gelati and sorbets

Cones, Ice Cream Artisans (272 Bleecker St, 212/414-1795): Try Johnnie Walker Black Label with macerated kumquats!

E.A.T. (1064 Madison Ave, 212/772-0022)

Emack & Bolio's (389 Amsterdam Ave, 212/362-2747; 73 W Houston St, 212/533-5610; and 1564 First Ave, 212/734-0105): vanilla-bean ice cream

Grom (223 Bleecker St, 212/206-1738 and 1796 Broadway, 212/974-3444): real gelato, with branches in Italy

Il Laboratorio del Gelato (188 Ludlow St, 212/343-9922)

L'Arte del Gelato (Chelsea Market, 75 Ninth Ave, 212/366-0570): Rent their party cart for a special event.

La Maison du Chocolat (1018 Madison Ave, 212/744-7117; 63 Wall St, 212/952-1123; and 30 Rockefeller Plaza, 212/265-9404)

Pinkberry (7 W 32nd St, 212/695-9631; 170 Eighth Ave, 212/488-2510; 41 Spring St, 212/274-8883; and other locations)

Popbar (5 Carmine St, 212/255-4874): gelato on a stick, dipped in chocolate

Ronnybrook Milk Bar (Chelsea Market, 75 Ninth Ave, 212/741-6455): great flavors

Sant Ambroeus (259 W 4th St, 212/604-9254 and 1000 Madison Ave, 212/570-2211)

Sundaes & Cones (95 E 10th St, 212/979-9398): great ice-cream cakes, beautifully decorated

---

New KC Market (301 Amsterdam Ave)
Ten Ren Tea & Ginseng (75 Mott St)
Tongin Mart (91 Mulberry St)

BRITISH

Myers of Keswick (634 Hudson St)

GREEK

Poseidon Bakery (629 Ninth Ave)

INDIAN

Foods of India (121 Lexington Ave)
Kalustyan's (123 Lexington Ave)

ITALIAN

Di Palo Fine Foods (200 Grand St)

Eataly (200 Fifth Ave)
Faicco's Pork Store (260 Bleecker St)
Raffetto's (144 W Houston St)
Salumeria Biellese (378 Fifth Ave)

JAPANESE/KOREAN

Han ah Reum (25 W 32nd St)
Katagiri & Company (224 E 59th St)
Sunrise Mart (4 Stuyvesant St and 494 Broome St)
Takahachi Bakery (25 Murray St)

POLISH

Kossar's Bialys (367 Grand St)

SPANISH

Despaña Brand Foods (408 Broome St)

FRUITS AND VEGETABLES
GREENMARKET

51 Chambers St (bet Broadway and Centre St), Room 228   212/788-7476
grownyc.org

Note: The following Greenmarkets are arranged from uptown to downtown.

Inwood (Isham St bet Seaman and Cooper St)
175th St (175th St at Broadway)
Fort Washington (168th St at Fort Washington Ave)
Columbia (114th St at Broadway)
Mount Sinai Hospital (99th St at Madison Ave)
97th St (97th St bet Columbus Ave and Amsterdam)
92nd St (92nd St at First Ave)
82nd St(82nd St bet First and York Ave)
79th St (78th St at Columbus Ave)
Tucker Square (66th St at Columbus Ave)
57th St (57th St at Ninth Ave)
Rockefeller Center (Rockefeller Plaza at 50th St)
Dag Hammarskjöld Plaza (47th St at Second Ave)
West 42nd Street (42nd St bet Eleventh and Twelfth Ave)
NY/NJ Port Authority (42nd St at Eighth Ave; inside bus terminal)
Union Square (17th St at Broadway)
Abingdon Square (12th St at Eighth Ave)
Stuyvesant Town (Stuyvesant Loop at Ave A; in the Oval)
St. Mark's Church (10th St at Second Ave)
Tompkins Square (7th St at Ave A)
Lower East Side YM (Grand St bet Pitt and Abraham Pl)
Tribeca (Greenwich St at Chambers)
City Hall Park (Broadway at Chambers)
Downtown PATH (West Broadway bet Barclay St and Park Pl)
Bowling Green (Broadway at Battery Pl)
Staten Island Ferry/Whitehall (inside South Street Terminal Building)

Interesting Wine Shops

Boutique bottle shops offer limited selections of wines in trendy environs. Most specialize in good values for the price, with a few premium budget-busters for good measure. Look for interesting and non-traditional marketing of their products.

Appellation Wine & Spirits (156 Tenth Ave, 212/741-9474): organic and biodynamic wines

Bottlerocket Wine & Spirit (5 W 19th St, 212/929-2323): fun and shopper-friendly

Chambers Street Wines (148 Chambers St, 212/227-1434): European artisanal wines

Embassy Wines & Spirits (796 Lexington Ave, 212/838-6551): a hundred kosher vintages

Landmark Wine & Sake (167 W 23rd St, 212/242-2323): large saké selection

Pasanella and Son Vintners (115 South St, 212/233-8383): Sunday afternoon tastings

September Wines & Spirits (100 Stanton St, 212/388-0770): artisanal wines

Union Square Wines & Spirits (140 Fourth Ave, 212/675-8100): Samples are poured from an Enomatic automatic wine dispenser.

Starting in 1976 with just one location and 12 farmers, these unique producer-only open-air markets have now sprung up all over town. They are overseen by the nonprofit growNYC. Bypassing the middle man enables Greenmarkets to provide small family farms in the region with a profitable outlet for their produce. All produce (over 600 varieties), baked goods, flowers, meat, poultry, and fish come straight from the sources. Cheeses, herbs, preserves, honey, candy, handmade items (like candles and wreaths), and more. Come early for the best selection. Call the office number or go online to find out the hours and address of the Greenmarket nearest you. Many are open year-round, although some are open seasonally. The usual operating hours are from 8 to 3, although these vary, too.

GIFT BASKETS

CHELSEA MARKET BASKETS

Chelsea Market
75 Ninth Ave (bet 15th and 16th St)
Mon-Sat: 10-8; Sun: 10-7

888/727-7887, ext 5020
chelseamarketbaskets.com

Inside the bustling Chelsea Market, this retail shop is dedicated to the creation of unique gift baskets. Whether it's for a birthday, housewarming, thank you, or special occasion, the helpful staff will assist you in creating a truly one-of-a-kind gift. First choose an interesting container (basket, hamper, or bag) and then select from an assortment of fudge, cheese, candy, nuts, jams, sauces, teas, and other food items. Or fill your basket with toys, books, stationery, or New York- or food-centric items. Delivery is available as well as online ordering.

MANHATTAN FRUITIER

105 E 29th St (bet Park and Lexington Ave)   212/686-0404
Mon-Fri: 9-5; Sat: deliveries only   mfruit.com

Manhattan Fruitier makes tasty, beautiful gift baskets using fresh seasonal and exotic fruits. You can add such treats as hand-rolled cheddar cheese sticks, smoked salmon, biscotti, and individually wrapped chocolates. Locally handmade truffles, fine food hampers, baked goods, fresh flowers, caviar, and organic and kosher products are also available. Expect to pay for the dazzling results!

HEALTH FOODS

COMMODITIES NATURAL MARKET

165 First Ave (bet 10th and 11th St)   212/260-2600
Daily: 9-9   commoditiesnaturalmarket.com

This small East Village health-food store is just like the vitamins and supplements they sell: full of things that are good for you. They are really more like a gourmet marketplace with a wide range of natural and organic meats, cheeses, produce, dairy products, bulk dry goods, canned foods, and even beauty and cleaning products. The helpful staff will answer questions, make suggestions, and offer tasty samples.

GARY NULL'S UPTOWN WHOLE FOODS

2421 Broadway (at 89th St)   212/874-4000
Daily: 8 a.m.-11 p.m.

Lots of interesting items in this tiny space! Gary Null's Uptown Whole Foods is perhaps Manhattan's premier health-food supermarket. Organic produce, fresh juices, discounted vitamins, and a full line of healthy products are featured. They will deliver in Manhattan and ship anywhere in the country. The organic and kosher takeout deli offers rotisserie chicken, vegetarian entrees, and even popcorn. Prices can be high.

HEALTH & HARMONY

470 Hudson St (bet Barrow and Grove St)   212/691-3036
Mon-Fri: 8 a.m.-8:30 p.m.; Sat: 9-7:30; Sun: 9-7

This is a great find for the health-conscious! Health & Harmony stocks organic produce, cheeses, baked items, and plenty of other good things to eat.

Japanese Confections

For a delicious change, try Japanese candies. Whether your sweet tooth leans toward hard, chewy, crunchy, or chocolate, these stores have the Oriental goodies to satisfy your craving.

Katagiri & Company (224 E 59th St, 212/755-3566)

m2m (55 Third Ave, 212/353-2698 and 2935 Broadway, 212/280-4600)

Sunrise Mart (4 Stuyvesant St, 212/598-3040; 494 Broome St, 212/219-0033; and 12 E 41st St, 646/380-9280)

Tongin Mart (91 Mulberry St, 212/962-6622)

Let Them Eat Cake

Visit these bakeries for special occasion cakes or just because you want to satisfy a sweet-craving:

BabyCakes NYC (248 Broome St, 212/677-5047): vegan, dairy-, egg-, and gluten-free cakes and pastries

Billy's Bakery (184 Ninth Ave, 212/647-9956; 75 Franklin St, 212/647-9958; and Plaza Food Hall, 1 W 59th St, 646/755-3237): icebox cake

Black Hound New York (170 Second Ave, 212/979-9505): chocolate busy bee cake

Cafe Lalo (201 W 83rd St, 212/496-6031): impressive selection

Carrot Top Pastries (3931 Broadway, 212/927-4800 and 5025 Broadway, 212/569-1532): carrot cake, of course

Duane Park Patisserie (179 Duane St, 212/274-8447): blackout cake

Lady M Cake Boutique (41 E 78th St, 212/452-2222 and The Plaza Food Hall, 1 W 59th St, 646/755-3225): alternating layers of handmade crepes and pastry cream

Magnolia Bakery (401 Bleecker St, 212/462-2572; 200 Columbus Ave, 212/724-8101; 1240 Ave of the Americas, 212/767-1123, Bloomingdale's, 1000 Third Ave, 212/265-5320; and Grand Central Terminal, 42nd St at Vanderbilt Ave, lower level, 212/682-3588): white coconut and meringue cake

Moishe's Bake Shop (115 Second Ave, 212/505-8555): kosher

Momofuku Milk Bar (251 E 13th St, 212/777-7773; Chambers Hotel, 15 W 56th St, 212/777-7773; and 561 Columbus Ave, 212/777-7773): cake truffles

Two Little Red Hens (1652 Second Ave, 212/452-0476): red velvet cake

Yura on Madison (1292 Madison Ave, 212/860-1598): chocolate cake

Vitamins and herbs, herbal remedies, and all manner of natural grocery items are available. They will also deliver and ship.

INTEGRAL YOGA NATURAL FOODS

229 W 13th St (bet Seventh and Eighth Ave)   212/243-2642
Mon-Fri: 8 a.m.-9:30 p.m.; Sat: 8 a.m.-8:30 p.m.; Sun: 9-8:30

integralyoganaturalfoods.com

With a mantra of "natural food is healthy food," selection and quality abound in this clean, attractive shop. Vegetarian items, packaged groceries, organic produce, bulk foods, and baked items are available at reasonable prices. A juice bar, salad bar, and deli are on-premises. They occupy the same building as a center that offers classes in yoga, meditation, and philosophy. Across the street is **Integral Apothecary** (234 W 13th St, 212/645-3051), a vegetarian, vitamin, and herb shop with a nutritional consultant on staff.

JUICE GENERATION

171 W 4th St (bet Ave of the Americas and Seventh Ave)   212/242-0440
644 Ninth Ave (bet 45th and 46th St)   212/541-5600
117 W 72nd St (bet Broadway and Columbus Ave)   212/579-0400
2730 Broadway (bet 104th and 105th St)   212/531-3111
Numerous other locations   juicegeneration.com
Hours vary by store

Juice Generation is a healthy choice for quick, delicious food and beverage. *Fresh* and *local* are the key concepts here. Whenever possible, area farmers provide fresh fruits and vegetables, wheatgrass, and dairy products for Juice Generation's smoothies, sandwiches, salads, and organic soups — many of which are vegetarian. For added benefit, choose a refreshing drink that will boost energy, immunity, and help promote weight loss. Poultry, fish, and veggie sandwiches are served on whole-grain breads with low-fat condiment options.

LIFETHYME NATURAL MARKET

410 Ave of the Americas (bet 8th and 9th St)   212/420-9099
Daily: 9 a.m.-10 p.m.   lifethymemarket.com

You'll find one of the area's largest selections of organic produce at this busy, natural supermarket. In addition, there is an organic-salad table, health-related books, a deli serving natural foods, a "natural cosmetics" boutique, a complete vegan bakery, and an organic juice bar. Occupying renovated 1839 brownstones in the heart of the Village, LifeThyme also sells discounted vitamins, does catering, and offers custom-baked goods for any dietary needs.

ICE CREAM AND OTHER GOODIES

For more choices in this category, see the box on page 243.

AMORINO

60 University Pl (bet 10th and 11th St)   212/253-5599
Sun-Thurs: 11-11; Fri, Sat: 11 a.m.-midnight   amorino.com

Amorino is the first stateside location of this Italian franchise. Icy, creamy gelato varieties are made with all natural ingredients resulting in a superb product. There are over 20 flavors from which to choose, plus a flavor of the month. Each gelato tray looks like a work of art with seductive swirls of chocolate, fruits, nuts, and other enticing additions. If you order a cone, dippers artistically fill the sugary holders to resemble a flower in bloom and luscious gelato cakes are beautifully formed and embellished as well. Amorino also serves hot drinks, milkshakes, chocolates, and other fabulous treats.

CHINATOWN ICE CREAM FACTORY

65 Bayard St (bet Elizabeth and Mott St)   212/608-4170
Daily: 11-11   chinatownicecreamfactory.com

Since 1978 this family-run ice cream shop has been churning out frozen, creamy goodness. With dozens of regular and exotic ice cream and sorbet flavors to choose from, you may find it hard to decide what to order. Definitely ask for a taste before you order a bowl or cone! The most popular choice is lychee. You might also enjoy red bean, taro, Zen butter, green tea, or longan (an Asian fruit). Of course, there's always chocolate in the freezer!

Soup for You!
At **Original SoupMan** (110 Pearl St, 212/232-0003; 259-A W 55th St, 212/956-0900; 1021 Ave of the Americas, 646/852-6113; and 918 Third Ave, 212/759-4000), owner Al Yeganeh is a stickler for the rules! You may recall a particular *Seinfeld* episode where he declared, "No soup for you." To avoid the same fate, pick the soup you want, have your money ready, and move to the extreme left after ordering. There are about 50 varieties: various vegetables, chilis, bisques, chowders, and cream soups. The selection varies by location and season. Delicious sandwiches, salads, and wraps are great accompaniments to a bowl of one of Al's soups.

CONES, ICE CREAM ARTISANS
272 Bleecker St (at Seventh Ave)   212/414-1795
Sun-Thurs: 1-11; Fri, Sat: 1-1

The D'Aloisio family brought their original Italian ice-cream recipes to Manhattan . . . and boy, are they good! Cones specializes in creamy gelati made with all-natural ingredients (try the coffee mocha chocolate chip). Every day they offer 32 flavors, including fat-free fruit choices; every season they add a couple of new flavors. All are made on-premises and can be packed for takeout. Made-to-order ice-cream cakes are available, too.

INDIAN
FOODS OF INDIA
121 Lexington Ave (at 28th St)   212/683-4419
Mon-Sat: 10-8; Sun: 11-7

Foods of India is the place to stock up on curry leaves, rice, lentils, dried limes, mango chutney, exotic spices, and all kinds of fresh and dried imported Indian foods. Homemade breads and vegetarian items are also available, all at good prices.

KALUSTYAN'S
123 Lexington Ave (bet 28th and 29th St)   212/685-3451
Mon-Sat: 10-8; Sun: 11-7   kalustyans.com

Since 1944 Kalustyan's has operated as an Indian spice store at its present location. After all this time, it is still a great spot. Many items are sold in bins or bales rather than prepackaged containers. The difference in cost, flavor, and freshness is extraordinary. The best indication of freshness and flavor is the store's aroma! Kalustyan's is both an Indian store and an export trading corporation with a specialty in Middle Eastern and Indian items. There is a large selection of dried fruit, nuts, rice, beans, mixes, coffee and tea, and accessories.

ITALIAN
RAFFETTO'S
144 W Houston St (bet Sullivan and MacDougal St)   212/777-1261
Tues-Fri: 9-6:30; Sat: 9-6

Raffetto's has been producing fresh-cut noodles and stuffed pastas since 1906. Though most of the business is wholesale, Raffetto's will sell their noodles, ravioli, tortellini, manicotti, gnocchi, and fettuccine to anyone. Variations include Genoa-style ravioli with meat and spinach, and Naples-style ravioli with cheese. More than ten homemade sauces are personally prepared by Mrs. Raffetto. Daily bread, dry pasta, cheeses, breads, and bargain-priced olive oils and vinegars are also available.

JAPANESE
KATAGIRI & COMPANY
224 E 59th St (bet Second and Third Ave)   212/755-3566
Daily: 10-8   katagiri.com

Visit Katagiri & Company if you want to impress important clients or friends with a Japanese dinner or sushi party. All kinds of Japanese food, sushi ingredients, bento boxes, and utensils are featured. Fresh fish is available every Monday and Thursday. Ask for party ideas from the helpful personnel. Delivery in Manhattan is available.

SUNRISE MART
4 Stuyvesant St (at Third Ave), 2nd floor   212/598-3040
Sun-Thurs: 10 a.m.-11 p.m.; Fri, Sat: 10 a.m.-midnight
494 Broome St (bet West Broadway and Wooster St)   212/219-0033
Daily: 10-9
12 E 41st St (bet Fifth and Madison Ave)   646/380-9280
Sun-Thurs: 8 a.m.-9 p.m.; Fri, Sat: 11-8

These all-purpose Japanese food marts do a bustling business. Japanese is spoken more often than English, and many packages bear nothing but Japanese calligraphy. In addition to snack foods and candy, they sell fruits, vegetables, meats, fish, and other grocery items. They also carry bowls, chopsticks, and items for the home. The Broome Street location stocks hard-to-find Japanese beauty products. A Japanese bake shop, **Panya Bakery** (8 Stuyvesant St, 212/777-1930), is next door to the Stuyvesant Street location.

LIQUOR AND WINE
ACKER, MERRALL & CONDIT
160 W 72nd St (bet Broadway and Columbus Ave)   212/787-1700
Mon-Sat: 9 a.m.-10 p.m.; Sun: noon-8   ackerwines.com

Acker, Merrall & Condit (AMC, for short) is the oldest wine and liquor store in America, having opened in 1820. There are daily in-store wine tastings. Free delivery is available in Manhattan. This service-oriented firm stocks an outstanding and diverse global inventory in every price range. The Wine Workshop (Acker, Merrall & Condit's special-events affiliate) offers wine-tasting classes and luxury dinners, and private events for companies and individuals. AMC is the largest fine-wine auction house in the world; check their website for live and monthly online auctions.

ASTOR WINES & SPIRITS
399 Lafayette St (at 4th St)   212/674-7500
Mon-Sat: 9-9; Sun: noon-6   astorwines.com

Astor has one of the city's largest selections of French and Italian wines. They also carry wines from every other grape-growing region in the world,

---

Raise Your Glass!

However you prefer your beer — bottles, cans, kegs, or on draft — these outfits offer what seems to be an unending assortment of them. Some have regular tastings and other beer-related events.

Flair Beverages, Inc. (3897 Ninth Ave, 212/569-8713): cash only, low prices

Good Beer (422 E 9th St, 212/677-4836): 625 beers; American craft beers; charcuterie and sausages

New Beer Distributors (167 Chrystie St, 212/473-8757): 800-plus brews, domestic and imported

Whole Foods Market Bowery Beer Room (95 E Houston St, 212/420-1320): 1,000 beers; home-brew needs

---

along with numerous sakes, sparkling wines, and hard liquors. Of special interest to oenophiles is the store's unique "cool room," which holds hundreds of delicate, rare, and organic wines at a constant 57 degrees. Inquire about the upstairs **Astor Center** (astorcenternyc.com), where four unique spaces are available for cooking and wine classes, special events, and private functions.

BEST CELLARS

2246 Broadway (bet 80th and 81st St)　　　　　　　　　212/362-8730
Mon-Thurs: 10-9; Fri, Sat: 10-10; Sun: noon-8

1175 Third Ave (bet 68th and 69th St)　　　　　　　　　212/737-0860
Mon-Sat: 9-9; Sun: noon-8　　　　　　　　　　　　　　bestcellars.com

If you're shopping for great-tasting wines at low prices, come to Best Cellars. They offer over 150 values, most of them under $15. The store layout is both eye-appealing and user-friendly; bottles are organized by flavor and body. Helpful personnel will special order wines that are not in stock.

BOTTLEROCKET WINE & SPIRIT

5 W 19th St (at Fifth Ave)　　　　　　　　　　　　　　212/929-2323
Mon-Sat: 11-9; Sun: noon-8　　　　　　　　　　　bottlerocketwine.com

Quite a place! Wines are organized by regions and themes, such as takeout, gifts, seafood, "green," etc. These folks feature classes, special events, a children's play area, a library of food and wine books, and more. A fact sheet with your bottle and friendly, informed service are extra pluses.

BURGUNDY WINE COMPANY

143 W 26th St (bet Ave of the Americas and Seventh Ave)　　212/691-9092
Tues-Fri: 10-7; Sat: 10-6　　　　　　　　　　　　burgundywinecompany.com

Burgundy Wine Company, a compact and attractive store in Chelsea, specializes in fine Burgundies, Rhones, Oregon wines, and small-grower champagnes, all specially selected. With over 2,000 labels to choose from, there are some great treasures in their cellars; just ask the expert personnel. "Wine and Jazz Wednesdays" feature jazz from 5 to 7.

CRUSH WINE & SPIRITS

153 E 57th St (bet Third Ave and Lexington Ave)   212/980-9463
Mon-Sat: noon-9; Sun: noon-8   crushwineco.com

The focus at Crush Wine & Spirits is on small artisanal producers. Boasting 2,500 labels and an elegant space, they offer weekly free tastings, personal wine consultations, and a stock of rare and collectible bottles at reasonable prices.

GARNET WINES & LIQUORS

929 Lexington Ave (bet 68th and 69th St)   212/772-3211
Mon-Sat: 9-9; Sun: noon-6   garnetwine.com

You'll love Garnet's prices, which are among the most competitive in the city for specialty wines. If you're in the market for Champagne, Bordeaux, Burgundy, Italian, or other imported wines, check here first, as selections are impressive — over 6,000 bottles. Prices are good on champagnes, liquors, and other wines as well.

ITALIAN WINE MERCHANTS

108 E 16th St (bet Union Square E and Irving Pl)   212/473-2323
Mon-Sat: 10-7   italianwinemerchants.com

This place is class personified! Bottles are displayed like an art gallery. Italian Wine Merchants is the leading authority for Italian wines, but their cellar has expanded to carry other artisanal international wines, with specialties in cult and tightly allocated wines, many from undiscovered producers. Take advantage of their personal wine-portfolio manager.

K&D FINE WINES AND SPIRITS

1366 Madison Ave (bet 95th and 96th St)   212/289-1818
Mon-Fri: 9-8:30; Sat: 10-8   kdwine.com

K&D is an excellent wine and spirits market on the Upper East Side. Hundreds of top wines and liquors are sold at competitive prices, including discounts on 12-bottle mixed cases. Free delivery is offered within Manhattan with no minimum.

MISTER WRIGHT FINE WINES & SPIRITS

1593 Third Ave (bet 89th and 90th St)   212/722-4564
Mon-Sat: 9 a.m.-9:30 p.m.; Sun: 1-7   misterwrightfinewines.com

Since 1976 this neighborhood store has specialized in the unique and hard-to-find bottle. Mister Wright has a reputation for amazing global vintages at comfortable prices and extra-friendly Aussie service. If you call ahead to place your order, they will bring it out to your car curbside.

MORRELL & COMPANY

1 Rockefeller Plaza (49th St bet Fifth Ave and Ave of the Americas) 212/981-1106
Mon-Sat: 10-7   morrellwine.com

Peter Morrell is the charming wine expert at this small, jam-packed store, which carries all kinds of wine and liquor — 5,000 bottles strong. The Morrell staff will help you find the right bottle of spirits, including brandies, liqueurs, and wine vintages ranging from old and valuable to young and inexpensive.

Sweet as Pie

Apple pie is oft considered the all-American dessert and none may be better than grandma's! If you're away from her home cooking, here are a few sweet and savory suggestions for a pastry-enrobed meal or dessert.

The Breslin Bar & Dining Room (Ace Hotel, 16 W 29th St, 212/679-1939): beef and Stilton pie

Bubby's (120 Hudson St, 212/219-0666): mile-high apple pie

Ceci-Cela (55 Spring St, 212/274-9179): raspberry kiwi tart

E.A.T. (1064 Madison Ave, 212/772-0022): cherry pie

Highlands (150 W 10th St, 212/229-2670): shepherd's pie

Jones Wood Foundry (401 E 76th St, 212/249-2700): steak and kidney pie

Little Pie Co. (424 W 43rd St, 212/736-4780): key lime pie

Pie Face (1407 Broadway, 646/569-6212; 469 Seventh Ave, 212/518-2654, and 507 Third Ave, 646/438-9648): open 24 hours; ganache covered chocolate mousse pie, pear ricotta pie, chunky steak or chicken mushroom pie

Poseidon Bakery (629 Ninth Ave, 212/757-6173): Greek spinach pie

Sarabeth's (423 Amsterdam Ave, 212/496-6280; 1295 Madison Ave, 212/410-7335; 40 Central Park S, 212/826-5959; 381 Park Ave S, 212/335-0093; 339 Greenwich St, 212-966-0421; Lord & Taylor, 424 Fifth Ave, 212/827-5068; and **Sarabeth's Bakery** (Chelsea Market, 75 Ninth Ave, 212/989-2424): banana cream pie

Check out the inviting menu next door at **Morrell Wine Bar & Cafe** (212/262-7700).

QUALITY HOUSE

2 Park Ave (at 33rd St)   212/532-2944
Mon-Fri: 9-6   qualityhousewines.com

Since 1934 Quality House has boasted one of the most extensive stocks of French wine in the city, with equally fine offerings of domestic, Italian, and selections from Germany, Spain, and Portugal. True to their name, this is a quality house, not a bargain spot. Delivery is available and usually free within the city.

SHERRY-LEHMANN

505 Park Ave (at 59th St)   212/838-7500
Mon-Sat: 9-7   sherry-lehmann.com

Sherry-Lehmann is one of New York's best-known wine and liquor shops, boasting an inventory of over 6,500 high-end wines from all over the world. Prices run the gamut from $5 to $20,000 a bottle. A wide selection of glassware and accessories is available. This firm has been in business since 1932 and offers informed service for its customers.

SOHO WINES AND SPIRITS

461 West Broadway (bet Prince and Houston St)   212/777-4332
Mon-Sat: 10-8   sohowines.com

Soho Wines and Spirits is family-run and offers domestic and imported wines and spirits. The shop is lofty. In fact, it looks more like an art gallery than a wine shop. Bottles are tastefully displayed, and classical music plays in the background. Soho Wines also has a large selection of single-malt Scotch whiskeys. Services include party planning and advice on setting up and maintaining a wine cellar.

VINO

121 E 27th St (bet Lexington Ave and Park Ave S)   212/725-6516
Mon-Sat: 11-10; Sun: noon-9   vinosite.com

Come to Vino if you're looking for unusual varietals from around Italy. Small-production vintners are represented, and many offerings are reasonably priced. Other global vintners can also be found. The staff is extra friendly, and you might get a sample tasting. Free delivery is offered within the neighborhood.

WAREHOUSE WINES & SPIRITS

735 Broadway (bet 8th St and Waverly Pl)   212/982-7770
Mon-Thurs: 9-8:45; Fri, Sat: 9 a.m.-9:45 p.m.; Sun: noon-6:45

If you are looking to save on wine and liquor, especially for a party, Warehouse Wines & Spirits is a good place. This large space has "miles and miles" of low-end bottles at appealing prices.

MEAT AND POULTRY

FAICCO'S PORK STORE

260 Bleecker St (at Ave of the Americas)   212/243-1974
Tues-Sat: 8:30-6 (Fri till 7); Sun: 9-2 (not in summer)

Take a number! Step up to the counter at this Italian institution and order delicious sausages (dried, hot, and sweet). They also sell cuts of pork, veal (cutlets, chops, and ground), pork loin, equally good meat cuts for barbecue, and an oven-ready rolled leg of stuffed pork. Pick up excellent olive oils, cheeses, vinegars, housemade sauces, and ingredients for antipasto. If you're into Italian-style deli, try Faicco's first. And if you're pressed for time, take home their heat-and-eat chicken rollettes or other prepared foods including lasagna, baby back ribs, and eggplant parmesan. The best snack in the neighborhood is Faicco's *arancini* — fried balls of risotto. Bet you can't eat just one!

Quality Meat

Retail customers can buy the same fresh meats as New York's top chefs by going online. Iowa pork spare ribs, New York strip steaks, free-range chickens, Long Island Pekin duck, Rocky Mountain lamb, and seasonal meat packs are just a mouse click away at **DeBragga and Spitler** (212/924-1311, debragga.com). Recipes, too! They have been around since the 1920s, supplying legendary restaurants.

FLORENCE PRIME MEAT MARKET

5 Jones St (bet Bleecker and 4th St)   212/242-6531
Tues-Fri: 8:30-6:30; Sat: 8-6

At Florence Prime Meat Market everything is cut to order by hand. Since 1936 Florence has been supplying high-quality meats in a rustic setting. Countermen prepare your order of sausages, poultry, steak, and game at good prices. Their "Newport steak" is so delicious that many folks have it shipped to them overnight!

GIOVANNI ESPOSITO & SONS

500 Ninth Ave (at 38th St)   212/279-3298
Mon-Sat: 8-6:30

Family members still preside over an operation that has been at the same location since 1932. Homemade Italian sausages are a specialty. Every kind you can imagine — breakfast, sage, garlic, smoked, hot dogs — is available. The cold-cuts selection is awesome: bologna, liverwurst, pepperoni, salami, ham, turkey breast, American and Muenster cheese, and much more. Hosting a dinner? You'll find pork roasts, crown roasts, pork chops, spare ribs, slab bacon, tenderloins, sirloin steaks, short ribs, filet mignon, London broil, corned beef brisket, leg of lamb, pheasant, quail, and venison. Free home delivery is available in midtown for modestly minimum orders.

L. SIMCHICK MEAT

988 First Ave (at 54th St)   212/888-2299
Mon-Fri: 8-7; Sat: 8-6   lsimchick.com

This old-fashioned neighborhood butcher shop sells high-end meats. You'll find wild game, prime meats (veal, pork, and lamb), poultry products, wonderful homemade sausage, and a wide selection of prepared foods. Sides, soups, and ready-to-cook entrees will impress your tablemates. Delivery is provided on the East Side.

LOBEL'S PRIME MEATS

1096 Madison Ave (bet 82nd and 83rd St)   212/737-1373
Mon-Sat: 8-6 (closed Sat in July, Aug)   lobels.com

Through five generations of operation and because of their excellent service and reasonable prices, few in Manhattan *haven't* heard of this shop. Lobel's staff has published nine cookbooks, and they are always willing to explain the best uses for each cut. It's hard to go wrong, since Lobel's carries *only* the best quality meats, and they ship all over the country. In addition to prime cuts, you'll find great ready-to-cook hot dogs and hamburgers.

OTTOMANELLI & SONS

285 Bleecker St (bet Seventh Ave and Jones St)   212/675-4217
Mon-Sat: 8:30-6

This four-brother operation gained its reputation by offering full butcher services with a smile. They offer a top-notch selection of prime meats (common and exotic), game (venison and kangaroo), dry-aged beef, and milk-fed veal. The latter is cut into Italian roasts, chops, steaks, and homemade sausages, and the preparation is unique. Best of all, they will sell it by the piece for a quick meal at home.

PARK EAST KOSHER BUTCHERS & FINE FOODS

1623 Second Ave (bet 84th and 85th St)   212/737-9800
Mon-Wed: 8-7:30; Thurs: 7 a.m.-9 p.m.; Fri: 6 a.m. till 2 hours before Sabbath;
Sun: 8-6   parkeastkosher.com

This is a one-stop kosher shop that carries butcher items (meat, poultry, game), packaged meats, cured and smoked fish, bakery goods, candy, sauces and dressings, pickled products, salads and dips, frozen food, and cheeses. Prepared foods include stuffed cabbage, meatballs, potato kugel, salads, and cakes. Park East stocks over 700 items in all! They promise delivery within three hours throughout Manhattan.

SCHALLER & WEBER

1654 Second Ave (bet 85th and 86th St)   212/879-3047
Mon-Fri: 9-6; Sat: 8:30-6   schallerweber.com

Once you've been in this store, the image will linger because of the sheer magnitude of cold cuts on display. There is nary a wall or nook that is not covered with deli meats. Besides offering a complete line of deli items, Schaller & Weber stocks a wide range of wieners, wursts, smoked meats, game, and poultry. Try their sausage and pork items, which they will prepare, bake, smoke, or roll to your preference. Check out their hard-to-find imported items.

SCHATZIE'S PRIME MEATS

555 Amsterdam Ave (at 87th St)   212/410-1555
Mon-Sat: 8-7; Sun: 10-6   schatziethebutcher.com

Fifth-generation butcher Tony Schatz and his crew offer cut-to-order lamb, veal, poultry, game, and prime beef. "Dirty" brisket (with smoky barbecue sauce) is a specialty. Schatzie's carries a great selection of prepared foods, including complete dinners of turkey, meatloaf, pork loin, and more. Plenty of side dishes, too! Check out the array of Italian cheeses and pastas. Call in the morning and they will prepare dinner to your specifications!

PICKLES

PICKLES, OLIVES, ETC.

1647 First Ave (bet 85th and 86th St)   212/717-8966
Daily: 10-8   picklesandolives.com

This one-of-a-kind shop on the Upper East Side is dedicated to pickles and olives. All are sold the old-fashioned way — out of barrels — and in any quantity. You can buy a single pickle or a whole gallon of them. There are ten varieties of pickles (sweet, hot, sour) and 20 types of olives (garlic-stuffed, cheese-stuffed, lemon-stuffed olives) — you get the idea. If you can't make up your mind, ask for a sample before you buy.

SEAFOOD

LEONARD'S MARKET

1437 Second Ave (bet 74th and 75th St)   212/744-2600
Mon-Fri: 8-7; Sat: 8-6; Sun: 11-6   leonardsnyc.com

A family-owned business since 1910, Leonard's is a reliable source for fresh seafood. You'll find oysters, crabs, striped bass, tilapia, halibut, salmon, live lobsters, and squid. Their takeout seafood department sells lobster and crab

> ## Mediterranean Food Merchant
> **O&CO.** (249 Bleecker St, 646/230-8373 and Grand Central Terminal, 42nd St at Vanderbilt Ave, 212/973-1472) dispenses fine Mediterranean olive oils and other products in attractive, aromatic shops. The oils are produced on small estates. Each bottle's location is identified on the label (much like wine). They also sell truffle oils and salts, balsamic vinegar, tapenades and olives, spreads and crackers, chocolate truffles, and flavored honeys. Olive-oil skin-care products, candles, serving pieces, and other items for home and personal use are available. You'll find plenty of gift ideas in good-looking packages here!

cakes; hand-sliced Norwegian, Scottish, and Irish smoked salmon; and some of the tastiest clam chowder in Manhattan. Beyond the seafood, barbecued poultry, cooked and prepared foods, and cut-to-order aged prime meats (beef, lamb, and veal) round out Leonard's selection. Their homemade turkey chili, braised veal, and poached salmon are customer favorites. Beautiful party platters of boiled shrimp, crabmeat, and smoked salmon can be requested. This service-oriented establishment provides fast, free delivery.

THE LOBSTER PLACE
Chelsea Market
75 Ninth Ave (bet 15th and 16th St)   212/255-5672
Mon-Sat: 9:30-9; Sun: 10-8   lobsterplace.com
   Imagine distributing one million pounds of lobster every year! The Lobster Place does just that, and they have a full line of fish, shrimp, and shellfish, too. A selection of prepared foods and sushi are an added bonus to your visit. These folks have a reputation for great service and reasonable prices. Pick up a lobster roll, crab club, or popcorn scallops from the "Shack in the Back."

MURRAY'S STURGEON SHOP
2429 Broadway (bet 89th and 90th St)   212/724-2650
Daily: 8-7 (Sat till 7:30)   murrayssturgeon.com
   Murray's is *the* stop for fancy smoked fish, fine appetizers, and caviar. Choose from sturgeon, Eastern and Scottish salmon, whitefish, kippered salmon, sable, pickled and schmaltz herring, trout, and lox. The quality is excellent, and prices are fair. Murray's also offers kosher soups, salads, cold cuts, dried fruits, and nuts.

WILD EDIBLES SEAFOOD MARKET
35 Third Ave (bet 35th and 36th St)   212/213-8552
Grand Central Market

Lexington Ave at 43rd St   212/687-4255
Hours vary by store   wildedibles.com
   Wild Edibles specializes in fresh, high-quality seafood. Shrimp. Clams. Mussels. Lobster. Crab. Caviar. Smoked fish. Many of the same foods served at Manhattan's top restaurants are sold here. Some of it is unique and imported. Sustainable items and health foods are stocked at this market, which also offers an oyster bar with wine and beer. Delivery is available throughout the city.

SPANISH
DESPAÑA BRAND FOODS
408 Broome St (bet Lafayette St and Cleveland Pl)   212/219-5050
Mon-Fri: 10-7; Sat: 11-7; Sun: 11-6   despanabrandfoods.com

This gourmet boutique is dedicated to bringing you authentic Spanish flavors. Try their *bocadillos* or warm *caldo gallego*. More specialties: serrano ham, blood sausage, chorizo, all-natural game products, cheeses, chestnuts in syrup, chocolate, specialty drinks, cookbooks, and cookware. When you finish shopping, stop at the Tapas Cafe for a delicious sandwich or tapas.

SPECIALTY SHOPS
THE MEADOW
523 Hudson St (bet W 10th and Charles St)   212/645-4633
Sun-Thurs: 11-9; Fri, Sat: 11-10   atthemeadow.com

The Meadow is a place where the beautiful, the delicious, and the unexpected are brought together. They specialize in artisan salt, the world's great chocolate bars, fresh-cut flowers, bitters, and other gourmet items for the bar and kitchen. In addition, they hold a variety of events including finishing salt, chocolate and wine tastings in sometimes unexpected combinations, plus art openings and occasional dinner parties. Please pass the salt!

SPICES AND OILS
SPICE CORNER
135 Lexington Ave (at 29th St)   212/689-5182
Mon-Sat: 10-9; Sun: 10-8   spicecorner29.com

Spice Corner is an Indian food market. Shelves are packed with beans, rice, grains, nuts, chutneys, and spices like masala and curry powders. There is a good selection of reasonably priced specialty foods (fresh and frozen), cookware, and health and beauty items. You'll enter feeling welcome and leave feeling happy about the prices — they are definitely in your "corner."

Chapter
5

Chapter 5

WHERE TO
FIND IT

NEW YORK'S
BEST SERVICES

Because most New Yorkers lead a very busy existence, it may be desirable to get specialized help for such things related to the home, office, or personal life. The businesses listed here have been carefully checked and provide the best help (at the most reasonable prices). Before entering into an agreement, it may be beneficial to check references, online reviews, or with the Better Business Bureau.

The hotel section encompasses hostels, alternative housing, and large and small hotels — a handy reference for visitors and accommodating visiting relatives.

AIR CONDITIONING

AIR-WAVE AIR CONDITIONING COMPANY

2421 Jerome Ave (at Fordham Rd), The Bronx   212/545-1122
Mon-Sat: 8-5   airwaveac.com

Air-Wave has been in business since 1953, and air conditioning is their *only* business. They have sold, serviced, overhauled, installed, and delivered over a million units over the years, including top brands like Friedrich, McQuay, and Frigidaire. They will also deliver, install, and store portable air conditioners.

ANIMAL ADOPTIONS

AMERICAN SOCIETY FOR THE PREVENTION OF CRUELTY TO ANIMALS

424 E 92nd St (bet First and York Ave)   212/876-7700, ext. 4120
Mon-Sat: 11-7; Sun: 11-5   aspca.org

Founded in 1866, this is one of the oldest animal protection organizations in the world, and pet adoptions are taken very seriously. You'll need to fill out an application, go through an interview, and bring two pieces of identification (at least one with a photograph). The whole process sometimes takes longer than you might wish—but then they're sure that you're serious, and you can go home with a good pet that needs a loving home. Adoption fees for dogs and cats start at $75; puppies and kittens are higher. The adoption fee for cats three years and older is waived. The fee includes a veterinarian's exam, vaccinations, microchipping, and spaying or neutering. There is also a $50 mandatory obedience class for puppies. ASPCA enforces animal cruelty laws, and Bergh Memorial Animal Hospital is on-site.

> **House Calls for Pets**
>
> Dr. Amy Attas and her staff at **CityPets** (212/581-7387) make house calls for dogs and cats. Physical exams, treatments, and vaccinations are provided. When necessary, they will also perform euthanasia at a pet's home.

ANIMAL SERVICES

ANIMAL MEDICAL CENTER

510 E 62nd St (bet FDR Dr and York Ave)   212/838-8100,
                                                    212/838-7053 (appointments)
By appointment; 24 hour emergency   amcny.org

If your pet becomes ill, try Animal Medical Center first; 90 veterinarians on staff. This nonprofit organization does all kinds of veterinary work on domestic and even exotic pets, like birds, ferrets, lizards, and snakes. The care is among the best in the city. They suggest calling ahead for an appointment; emergency care costs more.

BISCUITS & BATH

41 W 13th St (at Fifth Ave)   212/419-2500 (for all locations)
1535 First Ave (at 80th St)
1035 Third Ave (bet 61st and 62nd St)
1067 Park Ave (bet 87th and 88th St)   biscuitsandbath.com
Numerous other locations; hours vary

Over 22 years of dog experience here! Biscuits & Bath offers grooming, training, workshops and seminars, vet care, dog walking, day and overnight care, adoption, a retail boutique, transportation services, and a "new parent" program. The place is dog- and pocketbook-friendly.

Taxis for Pets

Arrange a ride for your dog to the vet, groomer, airport, boarding kennel, or a long-distance destination.

Canine Car Pet Transportation (212/353-2271, caninecar.com): comfortable SUVs, with a courteous, caring driver at the wheel.

Pet Taxi New York (718/355-9665, pettaxinewyork.com): minivans; guardians welcome on the ride

CAROLE WILBOURN

Consultation by appointment   212/741-0397
Mon-Sat: 9-6   thecattherapist.com

Carole Wilbourn is an internationally known cat preventive and corrective therapist who has the answers to most cat problems. Carole makes house calls, phone consults, and Skypes from coast to coast. She has also added Reiki to her behavioral program. As a Reiki practitioner, she gives Reiki to cats and their guardians. Carole can take care of many feline issues with just one session and a follow-up phone call. She does international consultations, takes on-site appointments at Westside Veterinary Center, and is available for speaking engagements. Wilbourn is the author of six cat psychology books.

NEW YORK DOG SPA & HOTEL

32 W 25th St (bet Ave of the Americas and Broadway)   212/243-1199
415 E 91st St (bet First and York Ave)   212/410-1755
Daily: 7 a.m.-10 p.m.   dogspa.com

This is a full-service hotel for dogs! They are staffed 24 hours for boarding, and also offer day care, massage, grooming, training, vet services, and other advanced pet care.

ANTIQUE REPAIR AND RESTORATION
CENTER ART STUDIO

307 W 38th St (bet Eighth and Ninth Ave)   212/247-3550
By appointment   centerart.com

Since 1919 the motto here has been "fine art restoration and display design." The word *fine* should really be emphasized, as owners of fine paintings, sculpture, and ceramics have made Center Art Studio *the* place to go for restoration. The house specialty is art conservation. They will clean and restore paintings, lacquer, terra cotta, scagliola, and plaster. Their craftsmen also restore antique furniture and decorative objects and design and install picture frames, display bases, and mounts for sculpture. Among the oldest and most diverse restoration studios in the city, Center Art offers a multitude of special services for the art collector, dealer, and designer.

MICHAEL DOTZEL AND SON

402 E 63rd St (at York Ave)   212/838-2890
Mon-Fri: 8-4

Dotzel specializes in the repair and maintenance of metal antiques and precious heirlooms. They will polish, rewire, replate, and cast your objects of brass, copper, tin, iron, and silver. Close attention to detail is given, and if an antique has lost a part or if you want a duplication, it can be re-created.

ART APPRAISALS

ABIGAIL HARTMANN ASSOCIATES

415 Central Park W (at 101st St), Room 5C   212/316-5406
Mon-Fri: 9-5 (by appointment; also available on weekends)

ahassociates.weebly.com

This respected firm specializes in fine- and decorative-art appraisals whether it be for insurance, donation, damage, tax, or other reasons. Their highly principled and experienced staff does not buy, sell, or receive kickbacks (a common practice with some auction houses, insurance companies, and galleries). Fees are by the hour, and consultations are available. The friendly personnel can also provide restoration, framing, storage, and estate disposition.

Parking in Manhattan

The only thing more difficult than driving in Manhattan is finding a place to park the car. Here's one solution: go online to **nyc.bestparking.com** and follow the prompts to enter your destination. You'll end up with a map listing parking garages and rates in the immediate area. You can also download an app for your smartphone from the website.

ART SERVICES

A.I. FRIEDMAN

44 W 18th St (bet Fifth Ave and Ave of the Americas)   212/243-9000
Mon-Fri: 9-7; Sat: 10-7; Sun: 11-6

aifriedman.com

A.I. Friedman has one of the largest stocks of ready-made frames in the city for those who want to frame it themselves. Nearly all are sold at discount. In addition to fully-assembled frames, they sell do-it-yourself frames that come equipped with glass and/or mats. Custom framing is also available. They are really a department store for creative individuals, providing a large assortment of tools, furniture, paints, easels, books, and other supplies and materials for the graphic artist.

ELI WILNER & COMPANY

1525 York Ave (bet 80th and 81st St)   212/744-6521
Mon-Fri: 9:30-5:30   eliwilner.com

The primary business of Eli Wilner is selling and restoring period frames and mirrors. He keeps thousands of 19th- and early 20th-century American and European frames in stock and can locate any size or style. Wilner can create an exact replica of a frame to your specifications. Over 25 skilled craftsmen do expert restoration and replication of frames; also frame appraisals. Boasting such clients as the Metropolitan Museum of Art and the White House, Wilner's expertise speaks for itself.

J. POCKER & SON

135 E 63rd St (bet Park and Lexington Ave)   212/838-5488
Mon-Fri: 9-5:30; Sat: 10-5:30 (closed Sat in July-Aug)   jpocker.com

Since 1926 the Pocker family has been in the custom framing business, so rest assured that you will receive expert advice from a superbly trained staff. All framing is conservation-quality. Look to them for custom mirrors, decorative prints, custom plaques, gallery rods, and picture lights; they can handle pickup and delivery and will recommend professional installation services.

JULIUS LOWY FRAME AND RESTORING COMPANY

223 E 80th St (bet Second and Third Ave)   212/861-8585
Mon-Fri: 9-5:30   lowyonline.com

Lowy is the nation's oldest, largest, and most highly regarded firm for the conservation and framing of fine art. Serving New York City since 1907, services include painting and paper conservation, professional photography, conservation framing, and curatorial work. They sell antique and authentic reproduction frames, claiming to have the largest inventory and best selection. In addition, Lowy provides mat-making and fitting services. Their client base includes art dealers, private collectors, auction houses, corporations, and museums.

KING DAVID GALLERY

128 W 23rd St (bet Ave of the Americas and Seventh Ave)   212/727-9700
Mon-Fri: 10-8; Sun: 11-6   kingdavidgallery.com

King David Gallery provides very professional service in a number of areas: design consulting and custom framing for fine art and mirrors, canvas stretching, glass cutting, and 24K gold-leaf framing. They can design and build shadow boxes, glass panels for shower doors, and framed TV mirrors to cover a flat-screen TV. Custom glass work is their primary specialty, but they can do almost anything in this field, beginning with designer sketches and measurements and finishing with expert installation.

LEITH RUTHERFURD TALAMO

By appointment   212/396-0399
                                                         leithtalamo.com

Leith Rutherfurd Talamo runs a full-service art restoration business. Whether it be an oil painting, mural, frame, or sculpture, she can restore your art to its original state. Trained in classical restoration techniques, she is well qualified in the cleaning, relining, reframing, re-hanging, and lighting of your artwork, as well as in gilding and polishing of frames — all done with expertise and class.

BABYSITTERS

BABY SITTERS' GUILD

60 E 42nd St (bet Madison and Park Ave), Suite 912   212/682-0227
Daily: 9-9 (office)   babysittersguild.com

The Baby Sitters' Guild has provided TLC for babies and children since 1940. They charge high rates, but their professional reputation commands them. All of their sitters have passed rigorous scrutiny — thorough background checks and fingerprinting. Many have teaching, nursing, or nanny backgrounds, all are CPR certified, and only the most capable are enlisted. A four-hour minimum is enforced and any travel expenses are reimbursed. Sitters are available 24/7 and some have traveled to New Jersey, Connecticut, and even abroad upon request.

BARNARD BABYSITTING AGENCY

Columbia University, Elliott Hall
49 Claremont Ave (at 119th St), 2nd floor   212/854-2035
Call for hours   barnardbabysitting.com

   Barnard Babysitting Agency is a nonprofit organization run by students at the undergraduate women's college affiliated with Columbia University. The service provides affordable child care in the New York metropolitan area. At the same time, it allows students to seek regular or sporadic employment. An hourly wage, cab fare, and food or money for food are required for each job. A minimum registration fee is required to post babysitting requests.

Babysitting Service

At **Not Just Baby Sitters** (917/523-0065,notjustbabysitters.com), owner Zee Miller Smith strives to make sure the person providing child care in your home is a perfect match for you and your family. She imposes a very strict application and interview process for prospective sitters and conducts home interviews with employers to match suitable caregivers with infants, older children, and the elderly. Members pay an annual fee for unlimited use of placements (short- or long-term, or as needed). Rates vary by the number of children, responsibilities, sitter's experience, and qualifications.

BEAUTY SERVICES

BOTOX TREATMENT
Verve Laser and Medical Spa (240 E 60th St, 212/888-3003)

CELLULITE TREATMENT
Wellpath (903 Madison Ave, 212/737-9604): up-to-date equipment

EYEBROW STYLING
Benefit Boutique Soho (454 West Broadway, 212/769-1111): waxing, tinting
Borja Color Studio (118 E 57th St, 212/308-3232)
Ramy Spa (39 E 31st St, 212/684-9500): complimentary makeup consultation; skin-care products
Shobha (594 Broadway, Suite 403, 212/931-8363; 41 E 57th St, Suite 1304, 212/223-2872; 1790 Broadway, 212/977-7771; and 65 Broadway, 212/425-4900): shaping

EYELASHES
Ebenezer Eyelash (32 W 32nd St, 4th floor, 212/947-5503; 474 Seventh Ave, 6th floor, 212/967-1301; and 41 W 35th St, 2nd floor, 212/967-1308): extensions

HAIR CARE | Best in Manhattan, by area

CHELSEA

Antonio Prieto Salon (127 W 20th St, 212/255-3741): popular styling

Chris Chase Salon (182 Ninth Ave,, 212/206-7991): Japanese conditioning treatment

Gemini 14 (135 W 14th St, 212/675-4546): "Opti-Smooth" straightening treatment

Rudy's (Ace Hotel, 14 W 29th St, 212/532-7200): retro

EAST VILLAGE

Astor Place Hairstylists (2 Astor Pl, 212/475-9854): one of the world's largest barber shops; inexpensive

FLATIRON DISTRICT

Sacha and Olivier (6 W 18th St, 212/255-1100): Parisian-inspired salon

Salon 02 (20 W 22nd St, 212/675-7274): Japanese and Brazilian procedures and treatments

GREENWICH VILLAGE

Red Market (13 E 13th St, 212/929-9600): late night, libations

LOWER EAST SIDE

Tease Salon (137 Rivington St, 212/979-8327): color

MIDTOWN

Bumble & Bumble (146 E 56th St, 212/521-6500): no-nonsense establishment

Kenneth Salon (Waldorf Astoria New York, 301 Park Ave, lobby floor, 212/752-1800): full service with an able staff

Oscar Blandi Salon (545 Madison Ave, 212/421-9800): reliable

Ouidad Salon (37 W 57th St, 4th floor, 212/888-3288): curly- and frizzy-hair specialists

Phyto Universe (715 Lexington Ave, 212/308-0270): private treatment cabins

Pierre Michel (135 E 57th St, 3rd floor, 212/593-1460): full service, wedding specialists

Salon Ishi (70 E 55th St, 212/888-4744): shiatsu scalp massages for men and women

Stephen Knoll Salon (625 Madison Ave, 2nd floor, 212/421-0100): highly recommended by celebrities

Vidal Sassoon (7 W 56th St, 212/535-9200): popular with men and women

SOHO

Frederic Fekkai Salon (394 West Broadway, 2nd floor, 212/888-2600): complimentary Wi-Fi and espresso

Ion Studio (41 Wooster St, 212/343-9060): ecologically sound

Laicale Salon (129 Grand St, 212/219-2424): all services, cutting-edge style

Privé (310 West Broadway, 212/274-8888): all hair services, open daily, house calls

Pas de Deux Salon (79 Worth St, 212/274-0079): hair reconstruction

UPPER EAST SIDE

Frederic Fekkai Salon (Henri Bendel, 712 Fifth Ave, 4th floor, 212/753-9500): elegant

Garren New York (Sherry-Netherland Hotel, 781 Fifth Ave, 212/841-9400): stunning salon, illustrious clients

Halcyon Days Salons and Spas at Saks Fifth Avenue (611 Fifth Ave, concourse level, 212/940-4000): top-grade, full-service

John Barrett Salon (Bergdorf Goodman, 754 Fifth Ave, penthouse, 212/872-2700): braids and blond highlights

Julien Farel Salon (605 Madison Ave, 2nd floor, 212/888-8988): upscale, private hair parties

Mark Garrison Salon (108 E 60th St, 212/400-8000): popular

Rita Hazan Salon (720 Fifth Ave): very good

Salon A· K· S (689 Fifth Ave, 10th floor, 212/888-0707)

Serge Normant at John Frieda (30 E 76th St, 212/879-1000): very "in"

Yves Durif (Carlyle Hotel, 35 E 76th St, 212/452-0954): reliable

UPPER WEST SIDE

Salon Above (2641 Broadway, 2nd floor, 212/665-7149)

WEST VILLAGE

Bumble & Bumble (415 W 13th St, 8th floor, 212/521-6500)

Snip 'n Sip (204 Waverly Pl, 212/242-3880): retro soda shop

HAIR COLORING

Borja Color Studio (118 E 57th St, 212/308-3232): ammonia-free color

Louis Licari Salon (693 Fifth Ave, 212/758-2090): full service

Q Hair (19 Bleecker St, 212/614-8729): brunettes

Salon A· K· S (689 Fifth Ave, 10th floor, 212/888-0707)

Warren-Tricomi (The Plaza, 1 W 58th St, 2nd floor, 212/262-8899 and 1117 Madison Ave, 212/262-8899)

HAIR-LOSS TREATMENT

Le Metric Hair Center for Women (124 E 40th St, Suite 601, 212/986-5620)

Philip Kingsley Trichological Clinic (16 E 52nd St, 212/753-9600)

HAIR REMOVAL

J. Sisters Salon (41 W 57th St, 2nd floor, 212/750-2485): Brazilian bikini-wax specialists

Verve Laser and Medical Spa (240 E 60th St, 212/888-3003): other medical treatments

HAIRSTYLING | By specialty

BLOW-STYLING

Amy's Hair Salon (20 Pell St, 212/406-2746): cash only, appointments suggested

Blow, the New York Blow Dry Bar (342 W 14th St, 212/989-6282): cuts, color, and Blow hair-care product line

Encore Beauty Salon (3 Claremont Ave, 212/222-1241): old-school

Jean Louis David (2146 Broadway, 212/873-1850): good work at reasonable prices

Salon A· K· S (689 Fifth Ave, 10th floor, 212/888-0707): Mika Rummo; house calls also

Salon de Tops (76 Elizabeth St, 212/219-0728): Asian

Warren-Tricomi (The Plaza, I W 58th St, 2nd floor, 212/262-8899 and 1117 Madison Ave, 212/262-8899): for work that lasts

DISCOUNT HAIRCUTS

Parlor (102 Ave B, 212/673-5520): check out Apprentice Monday—prices start at $20!

Tease Salon (199 Second Ave, 212/725-7088): $50 for a wash and cut

FAMILY HAIRCUTS

Feature Trim (1108 Lexington Ave, 212/650-9746)

MEN'S HAIRCUTS

Barbiere (246 E 5th St, 646/649-2640): $40 textured scissor cuts, cash only

Blind Barber (339 E 10th St, 212/228-2123): adjacent lounge (open late)

Chelsea Barber (465 W 23rd St, 212/741-2254): inexpensive

Frank's Chop Shop (19 Essex St, 212/228-7442): cuts for clients from bankers to rap artists

Martial Vivot (39 W 54th St, 212/956-2990): stylish, up-to-the-moment cuts from $125

Neighborhood Barbers (439 E 9th St, 212/777-0798): bargain haircuts at $14

Salon A· K· S (689 Fifth Ave, 10th floor, 212/888-0707): hair coloring

3 Aces Barber Shop (664 Ninth Ave, 212/664-9807): inexpensive

HOME (OR OFFICE) SERVICES

Eastside Massage Therapy Center (351 E 78th St, 212/249-2927)

Gotham Glow (646/397-4438): tans

Harper Monroe (347/460-3228): spa services, all five boroughs

Lady Barber (Kathleen Giordano, 212/826-8616): will do office appointments

Mama Manicures (646/801-6262): hair, nails, facials, massages, eyelashes

Miguel Lopez Salon and Spa (458 West Broadway, 2nd floor, 212/343-2643): home, office, or hotel

Nail Gypsy (718/230-3220): organic

Paul Podlucky (25 E 67th St, 14E, 212/717-6622): hair, his place or yours

Primp In-Home (212/217-6038): full-service and wardrobe consultation

Styled by Jen (917/660-3420): hair, makeup

INTEGRATIVE MEDICINE

Continuum Center for Health & Healing (245 Fifth Ave, 2nd floor, 646/935-2220): East Asian treatments

MAKEUP

Kimara Ahnert Makeup Studio (1113 Madison Ave, 212/452-4252): applications, lessons, and products

Three Custom Color Specialists (54 W 22nd St, 3rd floor, 212/730-8828): cosmetics, custom blends, bridal makeup, by appointment only

MANICURES AND PEDICURES

Angel Nails (151 E 71st St, 212/535-5333): nail-wrapping, massages, waxing

Jin Soon Natural Hand & Foot Spa (56 E 4th St, 212/473-2047; 23 Jones St, 212/229-1070; and 421 E 73rd St, 212/249-9144)

Ohm Spa (260 Fifth Ave, 7th floor, 212/845-9812): eco-friendly, organic, vegan

Paul Labrecque Salon and Spa (171 E 65th St, 160 Columbus Ave, and 66 E 55th St, 212/988-7816)

Pierre Michel (135 E 57th St, 3rd floor, 212/593-1460): old-school

Relax Foot Spa (202 Hester St, 212/226-8288 and 193 Centre St, 212/226-5635): reflexology

Spa Martier (1014 Second Ave, 646/781-9758): mesmerizing nail-art

Sweet Lily Natural Nail Spa and Boutique (222 West Broadway, 212/925-5441): seasonal treatments

Touch of East Nail Salon and Spa (11 W 20th St, 212/366-6333)

Townhouse Spa (39 W 56th St, 212/245-8006): enlivening, soothing, and nourishing pedicures and manicures

Valley NYC (198 Elizabeth St, 212/274-8985): nail-art

MASSAGE

Angel Feet (77 Perry St, 212/924-3576): reflexology

Asia Tui-Na Wholeness (37 E 28th St, 8th floor, 212/686-8082): traditional Chinese

Expecting (NYC) (80 E 11th St, Suite 407, 212/475-0709): prenatal and postpartum

Graceful Services (1095 Second Ave, 2nd floor, 212/593-9904): facials, too

Praba Salon (1794 Third Ave, 212/996-1740): scalp massages, Asian-Indian influence

Relax (716 Greenwich St, 212/206-9714): deep tissue

SPA at Andaz Wall Street (75 Wall St, 212/699-1830): hand and arm massages

MEN'S GROOMING

B Braxton (1400 Fifth Ave, 212/289-3200): spa, hair, beards

Bedford Barbers (322 E 59th St, 212/308-0333): bargain-priced cuts and shaves

Ben's Barbers (217 Ave A, 718/644-6701): low-key, inexpensive

Decatur & Sons (Chelsea Market, 75 Ninth Ave, 646/470-7288): drop-ins welcome

Esquires of Wall St (14 Wall St, 212/349-5064): since 1932

Frederic Fekkai Salon (Henri Bendel, 712 Fifth Ave, 4th floor, 212/753-9500): men's lounge, L'Atelier de Frederic

Geno's Barberia (48 Greenwich St, 212/929-9029): immaculate

Hey Man Day Spa (226 W 4th St, 212/929-0838): waxing, massages, nails

John Allan's (95 Trinity Pl, 212/406-3000; 46 E 46th St, 212/922-0361; and 418 Washington St, 212/334-5358): full service

Kiehl's (109 Third Ave, 212/677-3171 and 157 E 64th St, 917/432-2503): toiletries

La Boîte à Coupe (57 W 57th St, 8th floor, 212/246-2097): cuts, color, manicures, pedicures, waxing

Mortal Man (135 W 28th St, 347/752-2907): waxing, manicures, pedicures, facials

Patrick Melville (Equinox, 45 Rockefeller Plaza, 3rd floor, 212/218-8650): pedicures

Paul Labrecque Salon and Spa (171 E 65th St, 160 Columbus Ave, and 66 E 55th St, 212/988-7816): straight-razor shave

Peninsula Spa (The Peninsula New York, 700 Fifth Ave, 21st floor, 212/903-3910): massages created for men

Pierre Michel (135 E 57th St, 3rd floor, 212/593-1460): manicures

Season Spa (165 Hester St, 212/966-7416): aromatherapy

SkinCareLab (568 Broadway, Suite 403, 212/334-3142): full-service for men and women

Spiff for Men (750 Third Ave, 212/983-3240): post-shave facials and hot-oil scalp treatment, Wi-Fi, coffee, and select beverages

Truman's Gentlemen's Groomers (120 E 56th St, 212/759-5015 and 121 Madison Ave, 212/683-9400): upscale men's spa

Yasmine Djerradine (30 E 60th St, 212/588-1771): men and women, spa and medi-spa

York Barber Shop (981 Lexington Ave, 212/988-6136): old-time

SAUNA

Russian and Turkish Baths (268 E 10th St, 212/674-9250): since 1892, sauna and steam rooms, ice-cold pool

SKIN CARE

Advanced Skin Care Day Spa (140 W 57th St, 212/758-8867): full service

Bluemercury (2305 Broadway, 212/799-0500; 131 Third Ave, 212/396-1500; and 865 Broadway, 212/243-8100): makeup, skin care, and facials

Christine Chin Spa (82 Orchard St, 212/353-0503): facials, waxing

Face to Face (20 W 20th St, 6th floor, 212/633-0404): back and chest treatments

Joean Beauty Salon (80 Lafayette St, 212/227-5120): inexpensive

Lia Schorr (686 Lexington Ave, 4th floor, 212/486-9670)

Ling Skin Care Salons (105 W 77th St, 212/877-2883 and 12 E 16th St, 212/989-8833): facials, waxing

Mario Badescu Skin Care Salon (320 E 52nd St, 212/758-1065): European facials

Miano Viel (16 E 52nd St, 2nd floor, 212/980-3222): great facials by Alla Katkov

Oasis Day Spa (1 Park Ave, 212/254-7722 and Affinia Dumont, 150 E 34th St, 212/545-5254): facials a specialty

Paul Labrecque Salon and Spa (171 E 65th St, 160 Columbus Ave, and 66 E 55th St, 212/988-7816): full service

Shizuka New York Day Spa (7 W 51st St, 6th floor, 212/644-7400): anti-aging facial with intense pulsed light

Smooth Synergy (686 Lexington Ave, 3rd floor, 212/397-0111): medi-spa with a resident physician

Tamago Skin Care (236 E 13th St, 212/505-1599): seaweed facial

Tracie Martyn (101 Fifth Ave, 212/206-9333): resculpting facial

SPAS | By neighborhood
(includes day spas with full or limited services, medi-spas, and body treatments)

CHELSEA
Acqua Beauty Bar (7 E 14th St, 212/620-4329): full service, pedicures
Graceful Spa (205 W 14th St, 2nd floor, 212/675-5145): budget-friendly

FINANCIAL DISTRICT
Setai Spa Wall Street (40 Broad St, 3rd floor, 212/792-6193): full service, June Jacobs products

FLATIRON DISTRICT
Completely Bare (103 Fifth Ave, 3rd floor, 212/366-6060): one of the best laser hair-removal treatments in town; dewrinkling facials
Just Calm Down Spa (30 W 18th St, 212/337-0032): full service, "Peelin' Groovy" facials, chocolate treatments

GRAMERCY
Gloria Cabrera Salon and Spa (309 E 23rd St, 212/689-6815): full service

GREENWICH VILLAGE
Completely Bare (25 Bond St, 212/366-6060)
Silk Day Spa (47 W 13th St, 212/255-6457): "Silk Supreme Eastern Indulgence Body Scrub and Polish," skin care, waxing

KIPS BAY
Oasis Day Spa (1 Park Ave, 212/254-7722): full service
Essential Therapy (122 E 25th St, 212/777-2325): spa services with a healing bent, co-ed, massages, facials

LOWER EAST SIDE
Takamichi Hair (263 Bowery, 212/420-7979): stylist Takamichi Saeki

MEATPACKING DISTRICT
Exhale Spa (Gansevoort Meatpacking NYC, 18 Ninth Ave, 212/660-6766): full service

MIDTOWN
Bliss 57 (12 W 57th St, 877/862-5477)
Bloomie Nails (44 W 55th St, 212/664-1662): nails, massages, facials

Dorit Baxter Skin Care, Beauty & Health Spa (47 W 57th St, 3rd floor, 212/371-4542): salt scrub, lymphatic drainage massage

Elizabeth Arden Red Door Salon (663 Fifth Ave, 212/546-0200): full service

Exhale Spa (150 Central Park S, 212/249-3000): full service

Faina European Skin Care Center and Day Spa (330 W 58th St, Suite 402, 212/245-6557): full service

Frederic Fekkai Salon (Henri Bendel, 712 Fifth Ave, 4th floor, 212/753-9500): the ultimate services; waxing, manicures, pedicures, facials

Halcyon Days Salons and Spas at Saks Fifth Avenue (611 Fifth Avenue, concourse level, 212/940-4000; entrance on 50th Street): full service

Ido Holistic Center (22 E 49th St, 212/599-5300): immune-system boost, Japanese massage

Juva Skin and Laser and Plastic Surgery Center (60 E 56th St, 2nd floor, 212/688-5882): microderm abrasion, massages, and facials

Juvenex (25 W 32nd St, 646/733-1330): 24-hour Korean oasis, body scrub

La Prairie at the Ritz-Carlton Spa (50 Central Park S, 2nd floor, 212/521-6135): top-drawer

Lia Schorr (686 Lexington Ave, 4th floor, 212/486-9670): efficient and reasonably priced, hot-stone foot massage

Metamorphosis (127 E 56th St, 5th floor, 212/751-6051): small but good, men and women

Peninsula Spa (The Peninsula New York, 700 Fifth Ave, 21st floor, 212/903-3910)

Remède Spa (St. Regis New York, 2 E 55th St, lower lobby level 212/339-6715): massages, facials, waxing, body treatments

Salon de Tokyo (200 W 57th St, Room 1308, 212/582-2132): shiatsu parlor, massages, sauna, open till midnight

Spa at the Four Seasons Hotel New York (57 E 57th St, 212/350-6420): exclusive

Susan Ciminelli Beauty Clinic (118 E 57th St, 3rd floor, 212/750-4441): full service, men and women

Townhouse Spa (39 W 56th St, 212/245-8006): full service

MURRAY HILL

Elite Day Spa (24 W 39th St, 212/730-2100): "Sugar Daddy" brown-sugar scrub

Hair Party (76 Madison Ave, 212/213-0056): open 24 hours a day

Oasis Day Spa (Affinia Dumont, 150 E 34th St, 212/545-5254): massages, facials, body scrub

Murray Hill Skin Care (567 Third Ave, 2nd floor, 212/661-0777): full service, "backcials"—i.e., a facial for the back

Yi Pak Spa (325 Fifth Ave, 212/594-1025): massages, body scrub

NOHO

Lali Lali Salon (650 Broadway, 212/228-2611)

SOHO

Bliss Soho (568 Broadway, 2nd floor, 877/862-5477): oxygen facials, laser hair removal

Bunya CitiSPA (474 West Broadway, 212/388-1288): full service

Erbe (196 Prince St, 212/966-1445): full service, facials, skin care, waxing, massages, manicures, pedicures

Haven Spa (150 Mercer St, 212/343-3515): full service, calm and refreshing, open weekends

SkinCareLab (568 Broadway, Suite 403, 212/334-3142): full service, body treatments, facials, men welcome

Soho Sanctuary (119 Mercer St, 212/334-5550): full service, facials

TRIBECA

Aire Ancient Baths (88 Franklin St, 212/274-3777): ancient Roman bathing traditions

Euphoria (18 Harrison St, 2nd floor, 212/925-5925): "Fresh Air Facial," laser, waxing, massages

TriBeCa MedSpa (114 Hudson St, 212/925-9500): exfoliation, skin care, laser, facials

Shibui Spa (The Greenwich Hotel, 377 Greenwich St, 212/941-8900): gorgeous, Japanese-style

UPPER EAST SIDE

Ajune (853 Fifth Ave Ave, 212/628-0044): medi-spa, full service, Botox, facials

Bliss 49 (W New York, 541 Lexington Ave, 877/862-5477): full service

Completely Bare (764 Madison Ave, 3rd floor, 212/717-9300): sunspot removal

Equinox Spa (817 Lexington Ave, 212/750-4671): facials, sports massage

Institute Beauté (885 Park Ave, 212/535-0229): foot facial

Paul Labrecque Salon and Spa (171 E 65th St, 212/988-7816): facials

Yasmine Djerradine (30 E 60th St, 212/588-1771): skin care, remodeling facials, eyebrows, men's facials

UPPER WEST SIDE

All Seasons Nails & Spa (2566 Broadway, 212/666-8822): manicures, pedicures, massages, facials

Ettia Holistic Day Spa (239 W 72nd St, 212/362-7109): massages, waxing, facials, men and women

Paul Labrecque Salon and Spa (160 Columbus Ave, 212/988-7816): Thai massage, facials

Prenatal Massage Center of Manhattan (123 W 79th St, 917/359-8176): postpartum, too

Spa at Mandarin Oriental (Time Warner Center, 80 Columbus Circle, 35th floor, 212/805-8880): deep-tissue massage, holistic foot ritual

TANNING

Brazil Bronze Glow Bar (580 Broadway, Suite 501, 212/431-0077): spray body bronzing

City Sun Tanning (50 E 13th St, 212/353-9700): spray, sunbeds

Paul Labrecque Salon and Spa (171 E 65th St, 212/988-7816): exfoliation, self-tanning moisturizing lotion

Spa at Equinox (203 E 85th St, 212/396-9611): body bronzing

Personal Chefs

Personal chefs provide a full menu of services — cooking classes, gourmet dinners, daily meals, and more. You may find the right person for your culinary needs from this list:

New York Metro Personal Chefs (845/418-2433, nypersonalchefs. com): New York/New Jersey metro area

ReMARKable Palate (917/405-0088): Mark Tafoya

United States Personal Chef Association (800/995-2138, uspca. com): listing of personal chefs

CABINETRY

HARMONY WOODWORKING

153 W 27th St (bet Ave of the Americas and Seventh Ave), Room 902

212/366-7221

By appointment   harmonywoodworking.org

With 30 years of experience, expert woodworker Ron Rubin devotes his time to one-of-a-kind custom projects. Kitchens, bookcases, wall units, entertainment centers, desks, and tables are just a few of the handcrafted designs at Harmony Woodworking.

JIM NICKEL

By appointment   718/963-2138

Jim Nickel, who lives in Brooklyn, is an expert at projects that use wood: cabinets, bookcases, wall sculptures, and much more. He prefers small- to medium-sized jobs and can do an entire project — from consultation and design to installation — all by himself. He has decades of experience and is budget conscious. Call in the afternoon or evening for an appointment.

MANHATTAN CABINETRY

Showroom: 227 E 59th St (bet Second and Third Ave)   212/750-9800
Mon-Thurs: 10-7; Fri: 10-6; Sat: 10-5:30; Sun: noon-5:30 manhattancabinetry.com

The motto at Manhattan Cabinetry is "If you can imagine it, we can build it." Do you need a custom piece for a special nook or have a unique design in mind? Visit the showroom to see product samples, from French Deco reproductions to contemporary designs. They will work with you from design to finish to build bars, credenzas, desks, storage, tables, kitchen cabinets, or whatever your particular need. Check their website periodically to view discounted floor samples.

CARPENTRY

NOTJUSTHANDYMEN.COM

981 Dean St, Brooklyn   212/257-2132, 718/857-1381
By appointment   notjusthandymen.com

Everyone needs a guy like Kellam Clark at some time or another. Major renovations, minor handy work, and even last-minute jobs are no problem for him and his friendly, resourceful crew. They'll do carpentry and sheetrock work; air-conditioning installation, cleaning, and storage; bathroom and kitchen repairs and remodeling; wallpapering; window treatments and installation; door and lock replacement and repairs; furniture assembly; painting; and TV mounting. Other services include moving, domestic cleaning, light fixture installation, and tile work. For emergencies, their 24-hour contact number is 917/399-0583. All five boroughs are serviced.

CARPET CLEANING

STEAMPRO CARPET CLEANING

24-hour customer-service line   718/606-0549
                                                              steampronyc.com

Routine carpet cleaning, carpet and upholstery emergencies, fine-textile cleaning — it's all in a day's work for Robert Torres and his gang. Their product line is eco-friendly and green. A typical carpet job starts with an analysis of the problem; then on to pretreatment, agitation and allowing time for the elements to work, neutralization, steam cleaning, post-grooming, and speed drying. Optional finishing services include deodorizing and Scotchgarding. They'll even leave a spot-cleaning bottle for touchups until their next visit.

CARRIAGES

CHATEAU STABLES/CHATEAU WEDDING CARRIAGES

Call for reservations   212/246-0520
                                                            chateaustables.net
                                                     chateauweddingcarriages.com

If you want to arrive at some big event in a horse-drawn carriage, Chateau is the place to call. They have the largest working collection of antique, horse-drawn vehicles in the U.S. — carriages, surreys, wagons, sleighs, and royal coaches are all available. Although they prefer advance notice, requests for weddings, group rides, hayrides, sleigh rides, tours, funerals, movies, and overseas visitors can generally be handled at any time. This family business has been in operation for nearly half a century.

CARS FOR HIRE

AAMCAR CAR RENTALS

315 W 96th St (bet West End Ave and Riverside Dr)   888/500-8460
Mon-Fri: 7:30-7:30; Sat: 8:30-1 (Sun till 3)

506 W 181st St (at Amsterdam Ave)   888/500-8480
Mon-Fri: 7:30-7; Sat: 8:30-2   aamcar.com

This independent car-rental company has a full line of vehicles, including all sizes of sedans, minivans, passenger vans, cargo vans, and SUVs. AAMCAR has been serving Manhattan for 25 years and is one of the few rental companies that actually guarantees your reservation.

ABC NYC LIMO

Daily: 7 a.m. to 11p.m. (customer service)   718/429-5285
                                                            abcnyclimo.com

This limousine service was founded by a group of experienced chauffers in order to offer elegance, dependability, and first-class service at competitive rates. All drivers have excellent city knowledge and extend first class service. ABC will drive you from airport to city, from hotel to theater, but their specialty

---

Carpet Plus

There's nothing like a clean, plush carpet to enhance the beauty of your home or office. The main carpeting problems come from dirt, food, pets, and red-wine spills. Contact **Flat Rate Carpet** (212/777-9277, 866/466-4576, flatratecarpet.com) to clean up a mess or to re-stretch and Scotchgard carpeting. While you're at it, have them clean mattresses, drapes, blinds, and air ducts. Only organic cleaning products are used. Emergency situations can be handled any time of day or night.

---

is guided tours of New York City. They offer top-notch service for shopping trips, corporate clients, and social occasions.

CAREY NEW YORK

Daily: 24 hours   212/599-1122
                                                                                              carey.com

Carey New York is the grandfather of car-for-hire services. They provide chauffeur-driven limousines and sedans and will take clients anywhere, at any time, in almost any kind of weather. Your driver can act as your expert guide and concierge for a New York tour. Last-minute reservations are accepted on an as-available basis. Discuss rates before making a commitment.

CARMEL CAR AND LIMOUSINE SERVICE

2642 Broadway (at 100th St)   212/666-6666
Daily: 24 hours   carmellimo.com

These people are highly commended for quality service and fair prices. Full-size and luxury sedans, minivans, passenger vans, Lincoln Town cars, and limos are available. Prices are by the hour, and set fees apply for airport transportation.

COMPANY II LIMOUSINE SERVICE

Daily: 24 hours   718/430-6482

This is a good choice! Steve Betancourt provides responsible, efficient service at reasonable prices. I can personally vouch that Steve's reputation for reliability is well-earned.

DMC LIMOUSINE

10 Waterside Plaza   212/481-6365
24 hours   dmclimonyc.com

This limousine company houses a fleet of luxury vehicles in Manhattan. Chauffeurs are professional and discreet and trained private security specialists are also available.

CASTING

SCULPTURE HOUSE CASTING

155 W 26th St (bet Ave of the Americas and Seventh Ave)   212/645-9430
Mon-Fri: 8-5; Sat: 10-3   sculpturehousecasting.com

Sculpture House is one of the city's oldest casting firms. It is a full-service casting foundry, specializing in classical plaster reproductions, mold-making, and casting in all mediums and sizes. Ornamental plastering and repair and restoration work are available. Sculpting tools and supplies are sold as well.

CHAIR CANING
VETERAN'S CHAIR CANING AND REPAIR
442 Tenth Ave (bet 34th and 35th St)   212/564-4560
Mon-Thurs: 7:30-4:30; Fri: 7:30-4; Sat: 8-1   veteranscaning.com

Veteran's Chair Caning and Repair has been family-owned and -operated since 1899. The craft of hand- and machine-caning along with wicker repair are still available here. John Bausert, a third-generation chair caner, has written a book about his craft. His prices and craftsmanship are among the best in town. Bausert believes in passing along his knowledge and encourages customers to repair their own chairs, and necessary materials are sold in the shop. If you don't want to try it yourself, Veteran's will repair your chair (cane, wicker, and wooden). For a charge, they'll even pick it up from your home.

CHINA AND GLASSWARE REPAIR
GLASS RESTORATIONS
1597 York Ave (bet 84th and 85th St)   212/517-3287
Mon-Fri: 10:30-6   glassrestorationinc.net

These folks can restore all manner of crystal, including pieces by Baccarat, Daum, and Lalique, as well as antique art glass and china. Glass Restoration is a find, as too few quality restorers are left in the country. Ask for Gus Jochec!

CLOCK AND WATCH REPAIR
FANELLI ANTIQUE TIMEPIECES
790 Madison Ave (bet 66th and 67th St), 2nd floor   212/517-2300
Mon-Fri: 11:30-6 (Sat by appointment)

Cindy Fanelli specializes in the care of high-quality "investment-type" timepieces, especially carriage clocks, in this beautiful clock gallery. Her store has one of the nation's largest collections of rare and unusual Early American grandfather clocks and vintage wristwatches. She does sales and restoration, makes house calls, gives free estimates, rents timepieces, and purchases single pieces or entire collections.

J&P TIMEPIECES
1057 Second Ave (at 56th St)   212/980-1099
Mon-Fri: 10-5   jptimepieces.com

Fine-watch repair is a family tradition in Europe, but this craft is being forgotten in our country. Fortunately for Manhattan, the Fossners have passed down this talent for four generations. You can be confident of their work on any kind of mechanical watch or clock. They guarantee repairs for six months and generally turn around jobs within ten days.

SUTTON CLOCK SHOP
218 E 82nd St (bet Second and Third Ave)   212/758-2260
Tues-Fri: 11-4 (call ahead); Sat by appointment   suttonclocks.com

Training Schools with Discount Services

Inexpensive prices on beauty services are available if you are willing to patronize training schools. Here are some of the better ones:

Dentistry: **New York University College of Dentistry** (345 E 24th St, 212/998-9800) — initial visit and X-rays, all for $95!

Facials: **Christine Valmy International School** (261 Fifth Ave, 24th floor, 212/779-7800) — Facials start at $27 to $38.

Haircut: **Mark Garrison Salon** (108 E 60th St, 212/570-2455) — training price: $45

Hairstyling: **Bumble & Bumble** (415 W 13th St, 212/521-6500, 866/728-6253) — model project

Hairstyling and manicures: **Empire Beauty Schools** (22 W 34th St, 212/695-4555) — an old-fashioned learning institute; reasonable prices

Massage: **The Aveda Institute** (233 Spring St, 212/807-1492) — 90-minute therapeutic facial for $50; **Swedish Institute** (226 W 26th St, 212/924-5900) — 12 one-hour Swedish or shiatsu massages for $360

Sutton's forte is selling and acquiring unusual timepieces, but this father and son operation also maintains and repairs antique clocks. Some of the timepieces they sell, even the contemporary ones, are truly outstanding. They also sell and repair barometers and will make house calls.

TIME PIECES, INC.
115 Greenwich Ave (at 13th St)　　　　　　　　　212/929-8011
Tues-Fri: 10-6; Sat: 11-5　　　　　　　　　　timepiecesrepair.com

Time Pieces, Inc. has been in business on Greenwich Avenue since 1978. Here Grace Szuwala services, restores, repairs, and sells antique timepieces. Her European training has made her a recognized expert. She has a strong sensitivity for pieces that have more sentimental than real value.

CLOTHING REPAIR

FRENCH-AMERICAN REWEAVING COMPANY
119 W 57th St (bet Ave of the Americas and Seventh Ave), Room 1406
Mon-Fri: 10-4; Sat: 11-2 (closed in July and Aug)　　　212/765-4670

Has a tear, burn, or stain ruined a favorite outfit? Head to French-American Reweaving Company where Ronald Moore's team will work wonders on almost any garment in nearly every fabric. Often a repaired item will look just like new!

METRO CUSTOM DYEING
306 W 38th St (at Eighth Ave), 7th floor　　　　　　212/391-1001
Mon-Fri: 9-5:30　　　　　　　　　　　　　　metrodyeing.com

Designers and fashionistas know the merits of custom fabric-dyeing by the experts at Metro Custom Dyeing. You might use them to dye a garment to cover a stain or create a new look. Metro has perfected their system to color a yard of fabric, an entire line of garments, a wedding dress, a jacket, or a favorite pair of jeans. Dyes are organic, and no chemicals are used in the intricate process. Cotton, silk, and nylon fibers are more dye-friendly than other fabrics, each fiber requiring a different formula for best results. Consultation with these experts will identify the chances of a successful result. Their client list reads like a who's who in the fashion industry and boasts numerous celebrities.

COMPUTER SERVICE AND INSTRUCTION

ABC COMPUTER SERVICES
15 E 40th St (bet Fifth and Madison Ave), Suite 903   212/725-3511
Mon-Fri: 9-5   abccomputerservices.com

ABC Computer provides service, sales, and supplies for desktop and laptop computers, as well as all kinds of printers. They'll work on Apple, Microsoft, and Novell-based systems, and they are an authorized Hewlett-Packard service center. They have been around since 1988, which is a good recommendation in itself.

TEKSERVE
119 W 23rd St (bet Ave of the Americas and Seventh Ave)   212/929-3645
Mon-Fri: 9-8; Sat, Sun: noon-6   tekserve.com

TekServe will take good care of you if you are in need of authorized Apple Computer sales and service. They carry a huge inventory of computers and peripherals, and the firm is noted for excellent customer care. A full range of services — including data recovery, in- and out-of-warranty repairs, rentals, and seminars — is available. They also sell iPods and accessories and will replace batteries while you wait.

DELIVERY, COURIER, AND MESSENGER SERVICES

AVANT BUSINESS SERVICES
60 E 42nd St (bet Park and Madison Ave)   212/687-5145
Daily: 24 hours   avantservices.com

Avant Business Services was doing round-the-clock local and long-distance deliveries even before the big shipping companies got in the business. If you have time-sensitive material, give them a call. They'll promptly pick up your item, even in the middle of the night or during a snowstorm.

CLEMENTINE COURIER
Mon-Fri: 9-7   917/681-3936
                                                             clementinecourier.com

The foundation of this delivery service is quick service and cheap rates.

Computer Repair and Rental

Computers — we definitely can't live without them in this day and age. For excellent computer repair or rental, try the following:

Machattan (249 W 34th St, Suite 601, 212/242-9393): Macs only

Business Equipment Rental (250 W 49th St, 212/582-2020): pickup and delivery are available

> ## Gift Baskets and Party Favors
> If you are stymied for a fun gift idea or unique party favors, try **fill-r-up** (197 E 76th St, 212/452-3026), a gift-basket boutique. Baskets and other cute containers are brimming with items for different themes. Where this business really sparkles is with all the bits and pieces for showers (baby or wedding): monogrammed candy jars, place-card holders, edibles, and party favor bags. Browse the shop and you will come away with great ideas.

Base rates start at $8 for an envelope delivered in Lower Manhattan. Charges increase for special handling, time of day, zone, wait time, weight over ten pounds, larger packages, and flights of stairs. In addition to urgent envelopes, Clementine's friendly couriers will deliver lunch or items provided by their personal shopping service. Someone is on duty 24/7 to handle the delivery needs of all five boroughs and surrounding states.

NEED IT NOW
153 W 27th St (bet Ave of the Americas and Seventh Ave), 1st floor
212/989-1919
Daily: 24 hours   needitnowcourier.com
     Need It Now provides any and all courier services via bicycle, motorcycle, vans, and trucks. They can handle everything from a crosstown rush letter (delivery completed within an hour), or a pre-scheduled service, to delivering nearly anything worldwide.

DRY CLEANERS AND LAUNDRIES
CLEANTEX
2335 Twelfth Ave (at 133rd St)   212/283-1200
Mon-Fri: 8-4   cleantexny.com
     In business since 1928, Cleantex specializes in cleaning draperies, upholstered pieces, balloon and Roman shades, vertical blinds, Oriental and area rugs, and wall-to-wall carpeting. They provide free estimates and will pick up and deliver. Museums, restaurants, churches, and rug dealers are among their satisfied clients.

HALLAK CLEANERS
1232 Second Ave (at 65th St)   212/832-0750
Mon-Fri: 7-6:30; Sat: 8-5   hallak.com
     Hallak has been a family business for four decades. All work is done in their state-of-the-art plant. They will clean shirts, linens, suede (including Ugg footwear), leather, draperies, and even dog beds and dog clothing. Their specialties are museum-quality cleaning and preservation of wedding gowns and a unique couture-handbag cleaning service. For those (like your author) who have trouble with stains on ties, Hallak is the place to go. The expanded rug-cleaning facility can handle all area rugs and Oriental carpets. Their skilled work takes time, though rush service is available at no additional cost. Free pickup and delivery is offered in New York City.

MADAME PAULETTE CUSTOM COUTURE CLEANERS

1255 Second Ave (bet 65th and 66th St)   212/838-6827
Mon-Fri: 7:30-7; Sat: 8-5; Sun: 10-3   madamepaulette.com

This full-service establishment has been in business since 1959. And what a clientele! Christian Dior. Vera Wang. Chanel. Givenchy. Saks. Burberry. Madame Paulette does dry cleaning (including knits, suedes, and leathers), tailoring (including reweaving and alterations), laundry, and household and rug cleaning. Additionally, they provide seasonal storage of furs. Taking care of wedding dresses is a specialty, and they do superior hand-cleaning of cashmere, making sure that each item's shape is maintained. Other specialties include expert repair of garments damaged by water, bleach, and fire, and wet cleaning and hand-cleaning of upholstery and tapestry. Madame Paulette offers free pickup and delivery throughout Manhattan; one-day service is available upon request.

MEURICE GARMENT CARE

31 University Pl (bet 8th and 9th St)   212/475-2778
Mon-Fri: 7:30-6; Sat: 9-3; Sun: 10-3

245 E 57th St (bet Second and Third Ave)   212/759-9057
Mon-Fri: 7:30-6; Sat: 9-3   garmentcare.com

Meurice specializes in cleaning and restoring fine garments. Their Eco-Care process is environmentally friendly. They handle each piece individually, taking care of details like loose buttons and tears. Special services include exquisite hand-finishing; expert stain removal; museum-quality preservation, cleaning and restoration of wedding gowns; careful handling of fragile and chemically sensitive garments; on-site leather cleaning and repair; and smoke, fire, and water restoration. Delivery and shipping are available.

TIECRAFTERS

252 W 29th St (bet Seventh and Eighth Ave)   212/629-5800
Mon-Fri: 9-4:45; Sat: 10-2   tiecrafters.com

At Tiecrafters, old ties never fade away, instead they're dyed, widened, narrowed, straightened, and cleaned. For over 60 years this business has acted on the belief that a well-made tie can live forever, and they provide services to make longevity possible. They restore soiled or stained ties and clean and repair

---

Dependable Cleaners

Chris French Cleaners (57 Fourth Ave, 212/475-5444): an East Village favorite

Fashion Award Cleaners (383 Amsterdam Ave, 212/289-5623): full service

G-G Cleaners (46 Grand St, 212/966-9813): legendary among fashion editors and boutique owners

Hallack Cleaners (1232 Second Ave, 212/832-0750): museum-quality cleaning

Jeeves New York (39 E 65th St, 212/570-9130): extra-special care for an extra price

Same-Day Delivery

For quick and inexpensive same-day delivery of documents or small items in Manhattan, call **Elite Couriers** (212/696-4000) to dispatch a bicycle messenger (or motorcycle, van, or truck). Rates are calculated on a base fee and by zone. This company has been in business since 1981 and serves many clients in the fashion and film industries.

all kinds of neckwear. Owner Andy Tarshis will give pointers on tie maintenance. (Hint: if you hang a tie at night, wrinkles will be gone by morning.) Tiecrafters offers several pamphlets on the subject, including one that tells how to remove spots at home. Their cleaning charge is reasonable, and they also make custom neckwear, bow ties, braces, scarves, vests, and cummerbunds.

VILLAGE TAILOR & CLEANERS

125 Sullivan St (at Prince St)   212/925-9667
Mon-Fri: 7-7; Sat: 8-6   villagetailor.com

This Soho dry cleaner has been in business since 1977. They also make custom men's and ladies' apparel, including leather and suede garments, and perform alterations. Tailoring Nicole Miller gowns and designs is a specialty. Wash-and-fold shirt service is also available, as is same-day turnaround.

ELECTRICIANS
ALTMAN ELECTRIC

535 W 46th St (bet Tenth and Eleventh Ave)   212/924-0400
Daily: 24 hours   altmanelectric.com

Family-owned and -operated for two generations, the licensed crew at this reliable outfit is available day and night. Whether you need increased power, showcase lighting, or emergency repairs, they will do small or large jobs at home or office, and rates are reasonable.

ELECTRONICS REPAIR
NYCiPODDOCTOR.COM

By appointment   646/202-3935
       nycipoddoctor.com

Dropped your portable electronic device? Don't toss it out until you check with these doctors. The techs at NYCiPodDoctor.com provide on-site repairs at homes and businesses throughout Manhattan, replacing screens and making repairs to extend the life of your iPod, iPhone, laptop, or other electronic gadget. If you're not in Manhattan, call to arrange for mail-in service. Free diagnostics are offered.

PORTATRONICS

2 W 46th St (at Fifth Ave), 16th floor   646/797-2838 (both locations)
Mon-Sat: 11-7
307 W 38th St (at Eighth Ave), 8th floor
Mon-Fri: 10-7; Sat: 11-7   portatronics.com

Portatronics provides on-the-spot repair of iPods, iPads, iPhones, laptops, smartphones, cameras, GPS, game consoles, and more. Work on portable electronics may be done while a customer waits or the item is returned by mail. You'll find replacement hard drives, LCD screens, motherboards, headphone jacks, and touch panels.

EMBROIDERY

JONATHAN EMBROIDERY PLUS

256 W 38th St (bet Seventh and Eighth Ave)   212/398-3538
Mon-Fri: 8:30-6; Sat: 9-4   jeplus.com

Any kind of custom embroidery work can be done at this classy workshop. Bring a photo or sketch, or just give them an idea, and Jonathan Embroidery Plus will produce a design you can amend or approve. They specialize in fashion embroidery on all types of fabrics, as well as embellishments with sequins, rhinestones, studs, beads, and grommets. All kinds of garment printing (screen, digital, and heat transfer) are also offered at JE Plus.

MONOGRAMS BY EMILY

224 W 30th St (bet Seventh and Eighth Ave), Suite 606   212/924-4486
By appointment only

Emily is one of the few still doing fine, detailed work on a hand-guided monogram machine. With over 30 years of experience, she guarantees that each monogram is stitched to your exact specification on items such as wedding-dress labels, men's shirts, handkerchiefs, and other delicate items. She'll make suggestions on thread color and style to ensure perfect results.

Fire Extinguishers

Every home should have at least one working fire extinguisher for emergency preparedness. **Able Fire Prevention** (241 W 26th St, 212/675-7777) sells new fire extinguishers and recharges old ones. Able offers pickup and delivery, installation, and cabinets and hardware for mounting extinguishers.

EXTERMINATORS

ACME EXTERMINATING

365 W 36th St (at Ninth Ave)
                                                              212/594-9230
Mon-Fri: 7-5

                                                  acmeexterminating.com

Got uninvited guests? Acme provides pest extermination services to homes, offices, stores, museums, and hospitals. They employ state-of-the-art pest-management technology.

FASHION SCHOOLS

FASHION INSTITUTE OF TECHNOLOGY

Seventh Ave at 27th St   212/217-7999
                                                              fitnyc.edu

In operation since 1944, the Fashion Institute of Technology is an internationally renowned college of art, design, fashion, business, and communication. Part of the State University of New York system, FIT blends liberal arts with a real-world curriculum. Its graduates are successful in fashion,

---

Electronics Disposal

Disposal of broken, out-of-date, and unwanted electronic equipment can be a headache. **The 4th Bin** (646/747-5985, 4thbin.com) has come up with a viable solution. For a reasonable fee, this company picks up electronic waste from residences and businesses, and is then able to reuse or recycle the components.

---

design, and business. The college offers associate, bachelor's, and master's degrees in advertising and marketing, fashion merchandising, fine arts, jewelry design, illustration, photography, production management, technical design, textiles, and toy design. Industry leaders such as Jhane Barnes, Calvin Klein, and Norma Kamali are among its distinguished alumni.

FORMAL WEAR

BALDWIN FORMALS

1156 Ave of the Americas (at 45th St), 2nd floor   212/245-8190
Mon-Fri: 9-7; Sat: 10-5   nyctuxedos.com

Going to an event? Baldwin has been taking care of style details since 1946. They rent and sell all types of formal attire: suits, overcoats, top hats, shoes, and more. They will pick up and deliver for free in midtown and for a slight charge to other Manhattan addresses. Same-day service is guaranteed for rental orders received by early afternoon. Prompt alteration service (from two hours to several days) is available for an additional charge.

FUNERAL SERVICE

FRANK E. CAMPBELL THE FUNERAL CHAPEL

1076 Madison Ave (at 81st St)   212/288-3500
Daily: 24 hours   frankecampbell.com

In time of need, it is good to know of a highly professional funeral home. These folks have been providing superior service since 1898.

FURNITURE RENTAL

CHURCHILL CORPORATE SERVICES

44 W 24th St (bet Fifth Ave and Ave of the Americas)   212/686-0444
Mon-Fri: 9:30-5:30 (by appointment)   furnishedhousing.com

Churchill carries a wide range of furnishing styles, from traditional to contemporary. They can furnish any size business or residence, and they offer free interior decorating advice. A customer can select what is needed from stock or borrow from the loaner program until special orders are processed. Churchill also offers a comprehensive package, including housewares and appliances. They specialize in executive relocations and will rent anything from a single chair to furnishings for an entire home. Churchill offers corporate apartments and housing on a short- or long-term basis. Their clients include sports managers, executives on temporary assignment, actors on short-term contracts, and even people in need of housing due to disaster displacement.

CORT FURNITURE RENTAL

140 E 45th St (bet Lexington and Third Ave), 5th floor   212/867-2800
Mon-Fri: 9-6; Sat: 10-4 (by appointment)   cort.com

CORT rents furnishings and accessories for a single room, an apartment, or an entire office. All furnishings (including electronics and housewares) are available for rental with an option to purchase. An apartment-location service is offered, and a multilingual staff is at your service. The stock is large, and delivery and setup can often be done within 48 hours. All styles of furniture are shown in their showroom, located near Grand Central Terminal.

FURNITURE REPAIR

ALL FURNITURE AND RUG SERVICES

Call for service   888/575-6757
Mon-Sat: 9-6   furnitureservices.com

All Furniture will repair, restore, and clean all parts of your furniture, from leather, fabric, and vinyl to wood and metal (including the innermost mechanisms). The same thoroughness holds true for rugs and carpets. Perhaps the most intriguing part of this business is their "take apart" service. If you're trying to move a ten-foot armoire through an eight-foot door frame, these experts will disassemble the oversized piece, transport it to the new spot, and proceed with reassembly. They work with moving companies to tackle the most difficult pieces of furniture. Same-day and 24/7 emergency services are offered.

GARDENING

GROWNYC

51 Chambers St (bet Broadway and Centre St), Room 228   212/788-7935
Mon-Fri: 9-5   grownyc.org

GrowNYC's Grow Truck program lends and delivers garden tools, plants, and horticultural advice to community greening efforts. Schools, community gardens, block associations, and any new garden efforts are eligible to borrow tools. Loans are limited to one week, but the waiting period is not long and the price (nothing!) is right. You can borrow the same tools several times a season. The Grow Truck may also be able to deliver plants, soil, or other garden supplies you have arranged to be donated. This outfit is a huge resource for recycling information, too.

HAIRCUTS

CHILDREN

COZY'S CUTS FOR KIDS

448 Amsterdam Ave (at 81st St)   212/579-2600
1416 Second Ave (at 74th St)   212/585-2699
Mon-Sat: 10-6   cozyscutsforkids.com

Cozy's takes care of kids of all ages, including the offspring of some famous personalities. What an experience: videos and videogames, themed barber chairs, and balloons. They issue a "first-time" diploma with a keepsake lock of hair! Besides providing professional styling services, Cozy's is a toy boutique. "Glamour parties" for girls, makeup and glamour art projects, ear-piercing, and

---

Travel Agencies

If you wish to use a travel agency for assistance with complicated bookings, group tours, or emergencies, here are some established choices:

AAA Travel (1881 Broadway, 212/586-1723): discounted rates on travel bookings with AAA membership

American Express Travel (374 Park Ave, 212/421-8240): several Manhattan locations; provides emergency AmEx card replacement

Liberty Travel (86 Nassau St, 212/608-0073): locations around Manhattan and the outer boroughs

---

mini-manicures are other services. Their own "So Cozy" hair-care products for children are available in-shop and online. Appointments are strongly suggested.

FAMILY

ASTOR PLACE HAIRSTYLISTS

2 Astor Pl (at Broadway)   212/475-9854
Mon: 8-8; Tues-Fri: 8 a.m.-9 p.m.; Sat: 8-8; Sun: 9-6   astorplacehairnyc.com

What started in 1947 as a neighborhood barbershop has become an East Village institution, giving some of New York's trendiest and most far-out haircuts. It all started when the Vezza brothers inherited their father's barbershop at a time when "not even cops were getting haircuts." Now over 25 stylists offer stylish haircuts at affordable prices.

FEATURE TRIM

1108 Lexington Ave (bet 77th and 78th St)   212/650-9746
Mon-Fri: 10:30-7; Sat: 10:30-6   featuretrim.com

Feature Trim specializes in highlights and coloring for men and women, hairstyling for women, and natural haircuts for men. Easy care, reasonable prices, friendly faces, and more than 50 years of experience have helped them maintain an impressive clientele. Appointments are encouraged, but walk-ins are welcome.

NEIGHBORHOOD BARBERS

439 E 9th St (bet First Ave and Ave A)   212/777-0798
Mon-Sat: 8-8; Sun: 10-7   neighborhoodbarbersnyc.com

"Looking good" remains important, even in today's economy. Neighborhood Barbers is a place to keep a clean-cut look while saving some dough. Owner Eric Uvaydov runs this no-frills East Village barbershop with only three chairs. Services include shampoo, shave and haircut, chest-hair trim, back shave, and beard trims. You'll like the old-school prices and treatment. Youngsters are welcome, too.

PAUL MOLE FAMILY BARBERSHOP

1034-A Lexington Ave (bet 73rd and 74th St)   212/535-8461
Mon-Fri: 7:30-8; Sat: 7:30-6; Sun: 9-4   paulmole.com

Just like its name, Paul Mole Family Barbershop is a family business, and they have been around since 1913. This is a true gentlemen's barbershop, but they employ two children's barbers, too. Hours are customer-friendly and prices are affordable. Men can still get a straight-edged razor shave, manicure, and shoeshine. You can even sit in one of the original chairs (refurbished, of course) that such notables as Gen. George Patton or Joseph Pulitzer once occupied. The place is packed after school and on weekends, so appointments are strongly recommended.

HEALTH AND FITNESS CLUBS

Manhattan has many great athletic facilities. If you're considering joining a club, check newspapers or websites for membership enticements. Be sure to investigate a club thoroughly (staff, cleanliness, equipment, price, and policies) before signing on the dotted line.

Visitors may enjoy reciprocal arrangements through their "home" fitness centers, so check before you travel. Otherwise, your hotel may offer some type of exercise equipment; some even have full-fledged facilities with personal trainers.

Clothes conducive for exercising, yoga, and spinning classes may be sold at some of the listed gyms. The better clubs often carry major brands and boutique fashions, as well as body-care products and more.

Bally Sports Club and **Bally Total Fitness** (multiple locations, 800/515-2582, ballyfitness.com)

Clay (25 W 14th St, 212/206-9200): fitness concierge service

Complete Body & Spa (10 Hanover Sq, 212/777-7702; 301 E 57th St, 212/777-7703; and 22 W 19th St, 217/777-7719)

CrossFit NYC (44 W 28th St, 2nd floor, 212/684-2018): intense program

Crunch (multiple locations, 888/310-6011, crunch.com)

David Barton Gym (215 W 23rd St, 212/414-2022; 30 E 85th St, 212/517-7577; and 4 Astor Pl, 212/505-6800, davidbartongym.com)

Dolphin Fitness Club (94 E 4th St, 212/387-9500, dolphinfitnessclubs.com)

Equinox (multiple locations, 212/774-6363, equinox.com)

Hanson Fitness (63 Greene St, 212/431-7682; 795 Broadway, 212/982-2233; and 132 Perry St, 212/741-2000, hansonfitness.com)

Manhattan Plaza Health Club (482 W 43rd St, 212/563-7001)

New York Health & Racquet Club (multiple locations, 800/472-2378, nyhrc.com)

New York Sports Club (multiple locations, 800/666-0808, mysportsclubs.com)

Pablo Fitness (226 E 54th St, 212/308-0077): small classes

Paris Fitness (752 West End Ave, 212/749-3500)

Reebok Sports Club/NY (160 Columbus Ave, 212/362-6800)

Sal Anthony's Movement Salon (190 Third Ave, 212/420-7242): pay by the class or service for pilates, massage, yoga, and one-on-one sessions

Sports Center at Chelsea Piers (Pier 60, Twelfth Ave at Hudson River, 212/336-6000)

The Sports Club/LA (330 E 61st St, 212/355-5100)

24 Hour Fitness (225 Fifth Ave, 212/271-1002; 153 E 53rd St, 212/401-0660; and 136 Crosby St, 212/918-9811, 24hourfitness.com)

CLUBS WITH CHILD CARE

Equinox (multiple locations, 212/774-6363, equinox.com): all locations
New York Health & Racquet Club (800/472-2378, nyhrc.com): some locations
The Sports Club/LA (330 E 61st St, 212/355-5100)

HEALTH AND FITNESS CLUBS | By specialty

BARRE

The Bar Method (155 Spring St, 212/431-5720): ballet-inspired workout
Pure Barre (1841 Broadway, Suite 330, 917/344-9175 and 78 Fifth Ave, 4th floor, 917/675-1528)

BOOT CAMP

Barry's Bootcamp (135 W 20th St, 646/559-2721 and 1 York St, 646/569-5310): cardio and strength training
Circuit of Change (57 W 16th St, 4th floor, 212/255-0053): holistic workout
Warrior Fitness Boot Camp (29 W 35th St, 3rd floor, 212/967-7977): Train like a Marine.

PERSONAL TRAINERS

The Bodysmith Co. (212/249-1824): in-home training for women
FOCUS Integrated Fitness (115 W 27th St, 212/319-3816)
La Palestra Center for Preventative Medicine (11 W 67th St, 212/799-8900)
Madison Square Club (210 Fifth Ave, 212/683-1836)
Mike Creamer (142 Wooster St, 212/353-8834)
Nimble Fitness (42 E 12th St, 212/633-9030): complimentary assessment
Sitaras Fitness (150 E 58th St, 212/702-9700): a dozen personal trainers

PILATES

Power Pilates (20 Third Ave, 6th floor, 855/670-2897)
RE: AB (33 Bleecker St, Suite 2C, 212/420-9111)
Real Pilates, Alycea Ungaro's Studio (177 Duane St, 212/625-0777)
Soho Sanctuary (119 Mercer St, 3rd floor, 212/334-5550): individual sessions

PRENATAL

Maternal Massage and More (73 Spring St, 212/533-3188): pre- and postnatal, during labor, and with baby, too!
Patricia Durbin-Ruiz (349 E 82nd St, 646/643-8369): pre- and postnatal, yoga, and pilates
Physique 57 (24 W 57th St, Suite 805, 212/399-0570 and 161 Ave of the Americas, 212/463-0570): prenatal workout system and more

SPINNING

Flywheel Sports (39 W 21st St, 212/242-9433; 470 Columbus Ave, 212/242-5161; and 201 E 67th St, 212/327-1217)

Pedal NYC (33 West End Ave, 212/561-5435): spinning and more

SoulCycle (103 Warren St, 212/406-1300 and other locations): SoulBands class — spinning plus upper-body-strengthening resistance bands (at select studios)

SWIMMING

Asphalt Green (1750 York Ave, 212/369-8890): 50-meter indoor Olympic-standard swimming pool

Asser Levy Recreation Center (392 Asser Levy Pl, 212/447-2020): year-round indoor and two seasonal outdoor pools

Chelsea Recreation Center Pool (430 W 25th St, 212/255-3705): indoor pool, water-aerobics classes

Manhattan Plaza Health Club (482 W 43rd St, 212/563-7001): atrium pool with retractable roof

YOGA

Atmananda Yoga Sequence (67 Irving Pl, 2nd floor, 212/625-1511)

Bikram Yoga (143 W 72nd St, 212/724-7303; 182 Fifth Ave, 212/206-9400; 797 Eighth Ave, 212/245-2525; and 173 E 83rd St, 212/288-9642): based on hatha yoga postures, heated room

Integral Yoga Institute (227 W 13th St, 212/929-0585): ashram

Integral Yoga Upper West Side (371 Amsterdam Ave, 2nd floor, 212/721-4000): studio

Jivamukti Yoga School (841 Broadway, 2nd floor, 212/353-0214)

Joschi (163 W 23rd St, 5th floor, 212/399-6307)

Kula Yoga Project (28 Warren St, 4th floor, 212/945-4460): Vinyasa classes

Laughing Lotus Yoga Center (59 W 19th St, 3rd floor, 212/414-2903)

Pure Yoga (204 W 77th St, 212/877-2025 and 203 E 86th St, 212/360-1888)

YogaWorks (1319 Third Ave, 2nd floor, 212/650-9642; 138 Fifth Ave, 4th floor, 212/647-9642; 37 W 65th St, 4th floor, 212/769-9642; and 459 Broadway, 212/965-0801)

HOTELS

New hotels have been springing up all over the metropolitan area, particularly in the downtown area. Some offer unique services and features (rooftop bars and swimming pools with views are very popular), while others simply capitalize on the unending stream of New York visitors. Hotel rates can be budget-breaking, particularly during holiday periods. If you are an intrepid traveler, you might try taking your chances by calling the front desk (rather than the toll-free reservation number) before departing. Room rates are usually better on weekends, when there are fewer business travelers. Sign up for loyalty or frequent-traveler programs, as regular guests may get special deals.

We list some hotels with very good accommodations for the money. Remember that you are or ought to be "out on the town" a good deal of the

---

Hotel & Hostel

For young folks, bargain hunters, and groups, **Broadway Hotel & Hostel** (230 W 101st St, 212/865-7710) is a winner. Rates start at about $50 a night in the hostel for a dormitory-style room with shared bath. Private hotel rooms with private baths start at $168 per night. All guests have access to Wi-Fi, a computer kiosk, and daily housekeeping service. The renovated rooms are comfortable, and security is on duty 24/7. There are no curfews or lockouts. Sorry, no New York State residents or pets.

---

time, so rooms need not be fancy! The big things to watch for are cleanliness, security, and service. By all means avoid using in-room telephones and snack bars, because prices are exorbitant!

I have categorized hotels by nightly room tariff (without taxes or surcharges) as follows:

Inexpensive	$199 and under
Moderate:	$200-$399
Expensive	$400-$599
Very expensive	$600 and up

Keep in mind that approximately 15% will be added to your final bill for state and local sales taxes plus a "bed tax."

SPECIAL HOTEL CLASSIFICATIONS

EXTENDED STAYS

If you are planning to be in Manhattan for awhile, check out these extended-stay facilities. Some require a 30-day minimum stay. Amenities may include kitchens, maid service, fitness and laundry facilities, business centers, and planned activities.

59th Street Bridge Suites (351 E 60th St, 212/221-8300)

The Bowery House (220 Bowery, 212/837-2373): rooms with or without windows, shared baths

Bristol Plaza (210 E 65th St, 212/826-9000)

Marmara Manhattan (301 E 94th St, 212/427-3100): single night stays also

Off Soho Suites (11 Rivington St, 212/979-9815): no minimum requirement

Phillips Club (155 W 66th St, 212/835-8800)

Residence Inn New York (Times Square, 1033 Ave of the Americas, 212/768-0007)

Webster Apartments (419 W 34th St, 212/967-9000): women only

HOSTELS

American Dream Hostel (168 E 24th St, 212/260-9779): family-run and owned; private and dormitory rooms ($59 and up)

Big Apple Hostel (119 W 45th St, 212/302-2603): midtown location, dorms and private rooms

Chelsea International Hostel (251 W 20th St, 212/647-0010): private and dormitory rooms; passport required for check-in

Hostelling International New York (891 Amsterdam Ave, 212/932-2300): one of the world's largest; prices start at $54

Belvedere Hotel (319 W 48th St, 212/245-7000)
Carlton Arms (160 E 25th St, 212/679-0680)
Chelsea Savoy Hotel (204 W 23rd St, 212/929-9353)
Chelsea Star Hotel (300 W 30th St, 212/244-7827): $99 and up; single with shared bath
Excelsior Hotel (45 W 81st St, 212/362-9200)
Gershwin Hotel (7 E 27th St, 212/545-8000)
Holiday Inn Express Madison Square Garden (232 W 29th St, 212/695-7200)
Holiday Inn Soho (138 Lafayette St, 212/966-8898)
Hotel 31 (120 E 31st St, 212/685-3060)
Hotel Grand Union (34 E 32nd St, 212/683-5890)
Hotel Metro (45 W 35th St, 212/947-2500)
Hotel Newton (2528 Broadway, 212/678-6500)
Hotel Stanford (43 W 32nd St, 212/563-1500)
Hotel Wolcott (4 W 31st St, 212/268-2900)
Hudson Hotel (356 W 58th St, 212/554-6000)
La Quinta Inn Manhattan Midtown (17 W 32nd St, 212/736-1600)
Larchmont Hotel (27 W 11th St, 212/989-9333)
Manhattan Broadway Hotel (273 W 38th St, 212/921-9791)
Milburn Hotel (242 W 76th St, 212/362-1006)
Park Central New York (870 Seventh Ave, 212/247-8000)
Ramada Inn Eastside (161 Lexington Ave, 212/545-1800)

HOTELS NEAR AIRPORTS

The following hotels are conveniently located to three major airports. Most provide airport transportation and have restaurants, meeting facilities, business centers, and Wi-Fi. Facilities such as fitness rooms and pools may also be offered.

Comfort Inn JFK Airport (144-36 153rd Lane, Jamaica, Queens, NY; 718/977-0001): complimentary breakfast, inexpensive
DoubleTree by Hilton Hotel JFK Airport (135-30 140th St, Jamaica, Queens, NY; 718/322-2300): full-service business center, moderate
Fairfield Inn by Marriott JFK Airport (156-08 Rockaway Blvd, Jamaica, Queens, NY; 718/977-3300): complimentary continental breakfast, inexpensive
Hampton Inn JFK Airport (144-10 135th Ave, Jamaica, Queens, NY; 718/322-7500): complimentary breakfast, inexpensive
Sheraton JFK Airport Hotel (132-26 S Conduit Ave, Jamaica, Queens, NY; 718/322-7190): free Wi-Fi; moderate

Courtyard by Marriott New York LaGuardia Airport (90-10

Ditmars Blvd, East Elmhurst, Queens, NY; 718/446-4800): outdoor pool and sundeck, moderate

Hampton Inn LaGuardia Airport (102-40 Ditmars Blvd, East Elmhurst, Queens, NY; 718/672-6600): complimentary breakfast and all-day beverages, inexpensive

LaGuardia Airport Hotel (100-15 Ditmars Blvd, East Elmhurst, Queens, NY; 718/426-1500): free Wi-Fi

LaGuardia Marriott (102-05 Ditmars Blvd, East Elmhurst, Queens, NY; 718/565-8900): 432 rooms, inexpensive to moderate

LaGuardia Plaza Hotel (104-04 Ditmars Blvd, East Elmhurst, Queens, NY; 718/457-6300): restaurant and lounge, inexpensive

NEWARK LIBERTY INTERNATIONAL AIRPORT

Crowne Plaza Hotel Newark Airport (901 Spring St, Elizabeth, NJ; 908/527-1600): nice indoor pool, inexpensive

DoubleTree by Hilton Newark Airport (128 Frontage Rd, Newark, NJ; 973/690-5500): indoor pool, inexpensive

Hilton Newark Airport (1170 Spring St, Elizabeth, NJ; 908/351-3900): inexpensive

Newark Liberty International Airport Marriott (1 Hotel Rd, Newark, NJ; 973/623-0006): on airport property, inexpensive

Wyndham Garden Hotel Newark Airport (550 U.S. Route 1 and 9 S, Newark, NJ; 973/824-4000): inexpensive

THE BEST HOTELS IN EVERY PRICE CATEGORY

6 COLUMBUS
6 Columbus Circle (58th St bet Eighth and Ninth Ave)   212/204-3000
Moderately expensive   thompsonhotels.com

It may look like you've arrived in the 1960s with the modernist decor, but technology like flat-screen TVs and iPod docking stations is utterly up-to-date. The 88 rooms (including 16 suites) in this extensively renovated 1903 building feature custom linens and furnishings.   Guests have access to nearby Equinox gym and receive a local newspaper daily. Just off the lobby is the popular Japanese restaurant, **Blue Ribbon Sushi Bar & Grill**, or relax at **Above 6**, the indoor/outdoor rooftop lounge. The hotel is pet-friendly.

ACE HOTEL
20 W 29th St (bet Broadway and Fifth Ave)   212/679-2222
Inexpensive to moderate   acehotel.com

Ace Hotel is among the most original of the newer hotels in New York. It has something for everyone: affordable accommodations, fabulous restaurants, travel shops, and nightly music in the lobby. The lowest room category is a bunk-bedded room for two. The next category has queen or full beds and a garment rack in lieu of a closet. Spend a bit more and rooms are larger with more amenities. All rooms have private baths, mini-refrigerators, and minibars. Many rooms feature vintage or repurposed furnishings, turntables and records, and original art from local and international artists. You can't go wrong with the hotel dining options: Michelin-starred **The Breslin Bar & Dining Room** (English-style, with 24/7 room service), **The John Dory Oyster Bar** (seafood), and **Stumptown Coffee Roasters** (from my hometown of Portland, Oregon).

THE ALGONQUIN HOTEL

59 W 44th St (bet Fifth Ave and Ave of the Americas)   212/840-6800
Moderately expensive   algonquinhotel.com

In 1987 the legendary Algonquin was designated a historic landmark by the City of New York. This home of the famous Round Table — where Dorothy Parker, Alexander Woollcott, Harpo Marx, Tallulah Bankhead, Robert Benchley, and other literary wits sparred and dined regularly — exudes the same charm and character as it did in the Roaring Twenties! There are 181 rooms, including 25 suites (some named after well-known personalities), and the atmosphere is intimate and friendly. The remodeled lobby is the best place in the city for people-watching. Added amenities include a 24-hour fitness center, complimentary Wi-Fi, and business center. Enjoy a meal at **Round Table** or rendezvous at **Blue Bar**, the hotel's updated, classic New York watering hole.

THE BENJAMIN

125 E 50th St (at Lexington Ave)   212/715-2500
Moderate   thebenjamin.com

The Benjamin, a restored 1927 building at a super midtown location, is so sure that guests will have a restful night's sleep that they offer a money-back guarantee. For starters, beds are engineered especially for the hotel. Guests are contacted three days before their stay to plan room-service delivery of sleep-inducing foods and to convey the 12 pillow options from the pillow library (anti-snoring, hypoallergenic, feather, etc.). For dogs traveling with their masters, the Dream Dog program provides a special pet bed, bathrobe, food, spa treatments, and a pet psychic. Lullabies are not included (for pets or humans). Chef Geoffrey Zakarian's restaurant, **The National**, serves fresh cafe and bistro classics.

THE BENTLEY HOTEL

500 E 62nd St (at York Ave)   212/644-6000
Inexpensive to moderate   bentleyhotelnyc.com

This 197-room Upper East Side hotel is situated in the shadow of Rockefeller University and affords views of the East River and skyline. Spacious rooms feature Frette linens and on-site parking. Beyond the gleaming façade is the sleek **Lobby Bar and Cafe** and **Prime at the Bentley**, which features a panoramic view and an eclectic, kosher menu. This location is convenient to Central Park, renowned shopping areas, and public transportation.

THE BOWERY HOTEL

335 Bowery (bet 2nd and 3rd St)   212/505-9100
Moderately expensive to very expensive   theboweryhotel.com

The Bowery is a posh and reliable destination with every amenity one would expect at an uptown hostelry. All guest rooms are classically designed for comfort and timeless elegance, with hardwood floors, large windows, upscale

Maximize Your Lodging Dollars

- Rates may go down closer to your stay. Call before your cancellation deadline to see if that is the case, and then book again at the lower rate. Rather than have a glut of empty rooms, many hotels will drastically lower rates. Bargain with the hotel's desk clerk, not with whoever answers the hotel's offsite 800 number.

- What is a high-demand night at one hotel may be a low-demand night at another. Depending on the timing, you may be able to stay in a more luxurious hotel.

- Rates are typically lowest in January, February, late April, and May.

- Try the large chains' more budget-friendly brands, such as Hampton Inn (by Hilton), Fairfield Inn (by Marriott), Four Points (by Sheraton), and Holiday Inn Express. These outfits are significantly less expensive than the upscale names in the chain.

- Stay in less expensive neighborhoods. The subway is likely just a few minutes away and often the money saved is well worth the short trip.

linens and toiletries, Turkish rugs, and marble bathrooms (some of which include tubs with a view). The one-bedroom suites open onto private terraces, as does the **Lobby Bar**. Room service is available 24 hours a day from **Gemma**, the adjoining restaurant; hotel guests may make dinner reservations at this otherwise no-reservations restaurant.

BRYANT PARK HOTEL
40 W 40th St (bet Fifth Ave and Ave of the Americas)   212/869-0100
Moderately expensive   bryantparkhotel.com

Right across the street from Bryant Park, this contemporary hotel is situated in the American Radiator Building. It is favored by hip fashion and media types. Some suites have terraces to enjoy a bird's-eye view of the park, while the upper-floor suites have views of both the park and the Empire State Building. The property boasts a 70-seat private room, which is often used for press conferences and screenings. On-premises is **Koi**, a Japanese fusion restaurant, as well as the **Cellar Bar**. A 24-hour gym is available for guests. The spacious bathrooms are done in marble, have soaking tubs, and feature premium Molton Brown bath products.

THE CARLTON HOTEL
88 Madison Ave (bet 28th and 29th St)   212/532-4100
Moderate to moderately expensive   carltonhotelny.com

Built in 1904 as the Seville Hotel, The Carlton underwent a $60 million facelift a few years back. Its 317 non-smoking rooms and suites — along with a dramatic three-story lobby, a lobby bar, and fine meeting facilities — blend modern comfort with historic preservation. For those doing business in the Madison Park, Gramercy Park, or Murray Hill neighborhoods, the Carlton is conveniently located. Their excellent French restaurant, **Millesime**, is a plus.

CASABLANCA HOTEL

147 W 43rd St (bet Broadway and Ave of the Americas)   212/869-1212
Moderate   casablancahotel.com

The Casablanca Hotel is a hidden gem close to Times Square. It is a boutique hotel with Moroccan glamour and hospitality, small (48 rooms and suites), and family-owned. Free European-style continental breakfasts and evening wine and cheese receptions are served in **Rick's Cafe.** Wi-Fi is available in all guest rooms, and you will pleased with the comfortable rates.

CROSBY STREET HOTEL

79 Crosby St (bet Prince and Spring St)   212/226-6400
Expensive   thecrosbystreethotel.com

This luxury boutique hotel is located on a quiet cobbled street in Soho. High ceilings and full-length windows provide city and courtyard views from 86 rooms, each individually decorated. Linens, technology, and amenities are all top-drawer; the property also offers a state-of-the-art screening room, valet parking, and event space. It is family-friendly with games, menus, toiletries, and necessary items geared to kids; breakfast, lunch, afternoon tea and dinner are served in the **Crosby Bar and Terrace**. The Meadow Suite comes with its own garden to enjoy. It's difficult to imagine that this space was a car park in its previous life.

DREAM NEW YORK

210 W 55th St (bet Broadway and Seventh Ave)   212/247-2000
Moderate   dreamhotels.com

If you're dreaming of a trendy, modern boutique hotel, then the Dream New York is for you. With 220 modern, eclectic guest rooms and suites, it offers all the comforts of home and then some. You'll find luxurious sheets, bathrobes, complimentary overnight shoeshine, and free passes to Crunch (one block away). Their Italian restaurant, **Serafina**, and two lounges are convenient. The hotel is also pet-friendly.

Real Small Hotel Rooms

Just when you thought New York hotel rooms couldn't get any smaller, they have! As you read the following, consider that the average hotel room is 320 square feet.

Ace Hotel (20 W 29th St, 212/679-2222): 140 square feet, twin bunk beds; moderate

The Jane (113 Jane St, 212/924-6700): 50 square feet, bunk-bed cabin with communal bathroom; inexpensive

The Pod Hotel (230 E 51st St, 212/355-0300): 70 square feet, bunk pod with shared bath or 120 square feet with double bed; inexpensive

The Standard High Line (848 Washington St, 212/645-4646): 250 square feet, standard queen; moderately expensive

Yotel (570 Tenth Ave, 646/449-7700): 167 square feet, premium cabin with overhead bunk; moderate

FOUR SEASONS HOTEL NEW YORK

57 E 57th St (bet Madison and Park Ave)　　　212/758-5700
Expensive　　　　　　　　　　　　　　　　fourseasons.com

Fewer hotel names elicit higher praise or win more awards than Four Seasons. Upscale visitors to the Big Apple have an elegant, 52-story Four Seasons designed by I. M. Pei. This palatial establishment provides 368 oversized rooms and suites (some with terraces), several fine eating places, and a lobby lounge for light snacks and tea. There's also a fully equipped business center, with freestanding computer terminals and modem hookups; a 6,000-square-foot fitness center and full-service spa; and numerous meeting rooms. The principal appeal, however, is the size of certain guest rooms, which run to 600 square feet, offer spectacular city views, and feature luxurious marble bathrooms with separate dressing areas. The Ty Warner Penthouse Suite (4,300 square feet) goes for $40,000 a night (plus tax), making it one of the most expensive hotel rooms in the world.

GANSEVOORT MEATPACKING NYC

18 Ninth Ave (at 13th St)　　　　　　　　　212/206-6700
Moderately expensive　　　　　　　gansevoorthotelgroup.com

In the heart of the vibrant Meatpacking District, known for its cool nightclubs, is this luxury full-service resort. Modern rooms and suites are outfitted with the latest electronics, featherbeds, patented steel Gansevoort bathroom sinks, and in-room safes that accommodate laptop computers. What's really impressive is the 45-foot heated rooftop pool with underwater lighting. The area is surrounded in glass for spectacular unrestricted views of the Hudson River. **Plunge**, the rooftop restaurant and bar, shares the same great vantage point.

GRAMERCY PARK HOTEL

2 Lexington Ave (bet 21st and 22nd St)　　　212/920-3300
Expensive　　　　　　　　　　　　gramercyparkhotel.com

This one-of-a-kind, eclectic resting place can best be described as antiestablishment. Each of the 185 rooms, six suites, and penthouse is different; no cookie-cutter decor here! The Bohemian look of the place and its guests combine to make a stay here both fun and unusual. Old World-luxury, accented with contemporary touches, is found everywhere. Set aside time to relax at the unique **Rose Bar**, **Jade Bar**, or **Gramercy Terrace** or to dine at Danny Meyer's Italian trattoria, **Maialino**. Reservations are a must at all of these popular venues. A key to enter private Gramercy Park is part of the package for guests.

THE GREENWICH HOTEL

377 Greenwich St (at N Moore St)　　　　　212/941-8900
Expensive　　　　　　　　　　　　thegreenwichhotel.com

Owner Robert De Niro should be very proud! Each of the unique 88 rooms and suites at the Greenwich is individually decked out with Moroccan tiles, Tibetan rugs, reclaimed wood floors, English-leather settees, Swedish DUX beds, soaking tubs, and small libraries. A lantern-lit swimming pool is the focal point of the exclusive **Shibui Spa**. Services include massages, manicures, and facials. If you really want to splurge, check into the two-level, two-bedroom

N. Moore penthouse suite. At over 2,000 square feet, it is the size of a small house and features a chef's kitchen, wood-burning fireplace, Turkish steam room, and sauna. Two other luxury suites are also available, if your pocketbook can stand the stress. The restaurant **Locanda Verde** brings leisurely all-day dining with an enticing Italian menu. This hotel has deservedly won a "Leading Hotel of the World" designation.

HILTON NEW YORK FASHION DISTRICT
152 W 26th St (bet Ave of the Americas and Seventh Ave)   212/858-5888
Moderate   newyorkfashiondistrict.hilton.com
    With a nod to its Garment District locale, fashion-themed guest rooms feature tailored decor of pinstripe, herringbone, and silk-tie patterns. Furnishings throughout the boutique hotel are evocative of the iconic cutting and sewing rooms. Amenities include 37" flat-screen TVs, laptop-sized safes, Keurig coffeemakers, and plush Frette bedding and towels.   State-of-the-art room-key security codes limit access to the guest's floor and gym, and programmable safes are provided in each room. Known for their burgers, the **Rare Bar & Grill** serves breakfast, lunch, and dinner; the **Rare View Rooftop Bar** offers spectacular views and libations.

HOTEL ON RIVINGTON
107 Rivington St (bet Essex and Ludlow St)   212/475-2600
Moderate   hotelonrivington.com
    The sleek rooms at this upscale 21-story glass tower hotel have floor-to-ceiling glass walls that afford sweeping views of the city and the rivers; some rooms also have balconies. Luxurious furnishings and oversized closets enhance the larger-than-usual rooms. Some bathrooms have steam showers, Japanese soaking tubs, or showers with a skyline view. Try **CO-OP Food & Drink** for American/Japanese offerings or the full bar at **Viktor and Spoils**.

HUDSON NEW YORK
356 W 58th St (bet Eighth and Ninth Ave)   212/554-6000
Inexpensive to moderate   hudsonhotel.com
    Want a cool and stylish hotel? Hudson New York is an affordable hotel in an often unaffordable area. A lushly landscaped courtyard garden is open to the sky. You will find abundant amenities, including walk-in closets and a plush lounging sofa in some rooms. The 800 guest rooms and 13 suites reveal modern decor and furniture, and attractive wood paneling. The scene is the big thing here, especially **Hudson Common**, a popular beer hall and burger joint.

INK48
653 Eleventh Ave (at 48th St   212/757-0088
Expensive   ink48.com
    The unlikely setting for this Kimpton hotel is a former printing house, explaining the names given **PRINT** restaurant, **Press Lounge**, and **InkSpa**. The contemporary loft design of the 222 rooms and suites is accented by colorful accessories and furnishings, and the magnificent city and river views are framed by large windows. Guests are treated to complimentary morning coffee and tea service.   Room service is available any time of the day. Pets are

New York Hotels with Exceptional Swimming Pools

Crowne Plaza Times Square Manhattan (1605 Broadway, 212/977-4000): 15th-floor indoor lap pool in the New York Sports Club

Empire Hotel (44 W 63rd St, 212/265-7400): rooftop pool with Pool Deck menu and spa services (summer only)

Gansevoort Meatpacking NYC (18 Ninth Ave, 212/206-6700): in the Meatpacking District; heated outdoor, year-round pool and great views; awesome "Renewal Day Package"

Holiday Inn Downtown (440 W 57th St, 212/581-8100): unheated pool on the 11th-floor deck; nonguest passes available for minimal charge

Hotel Americano (518 W 27th St, 212/525-0000): outdoor pool on 10th floor with cozy cabanas; adjacent bar and grill

Le Parker Meridien New York (118 W 57th St, 212/245-5000): penthouse year-round pool with sundeck (Central Park views); nonguests may purchase user passes

Mandarin Oriental New York (80 Columbus Circle, 212/805-8800): 75-foot year-round indoor lap pool in a dramatic setting on the 36th floor, with floor-to-ceiling windows

Millennium U.N. Plaza Hotel (1 United Nations Plaza, 212/758-1234): heated indoor pool, plus an indoor tennis court

The Peninsula New York (700 Fifth Ave, 212/956-2888): luxurious glass-enclosed facility with sun deck dining

Skyline Hotel (725 Tenth Ave, 212/586-3400): heated indoor pool

Thompson LES (190 Allen St, 212/460-5300): outdoor rooftop pool with Andy Warhol image

Trump International Hotel and Tower (1 Central Park W, 212/299-1000): 55-foot lap pool

Trump SoHo New York (246 Spring St, 212/842-5500): outdoor pool on 7th floor surrounded by deck chairs and lounge seating

welcome; walking or sitting arrangements for your animal companion may be made through the concierge.

THE JANE

113 Jane St (bet West and Washington St)   212/924-6700
Very inexpensive   thejanenyc.com

Built in 1908, this West Village building was originally a hotel for sailors; it was restored in 2008. Today, for under $100, you can get a standard single room, inspired by a luxury train cabin, with plenty of storage. The bathrooms of smaller rooms (50 square feet) are communal and co-ed. Captain's Cabins are larger (250 square feet) with private baths; river views and terraces come with some rooms. Air conditioning is individually controlled, but heat is not. Each room comes with an iPod-docking clock radio, free Wi-Fi, flat-screen TV with DVD player, and complimentary bottled water.

JW MARRIOTT ESSEX HOUSE NEW YORK

160 Central Park S (bet Ave of the Americas and Seventh Ave)   212/247-0300
Moderately expensive to expensive   marriott.com

You'll love the superb location right on Central Park! The Essex House, now a JW Marriott property, remains one of the prized resting places in Manhattan. The tastefully decorated rooms and suites are very comfortable and equipped with every modern amenity. A very attractive lobby and all-marble bathrooms add a classy flavor. The **Lobby Lounge** is a convenient place for cocktails or traditional afternoon tea, and a health spa and fully equipped club lounge with business center add to the attractions.

KIMBERLY HOTEL

145 E 50th St (bet Lexington and Third Ave)   212/702-1600
Moderate   kimberlyhotel.com

This charming and hospitable boutique hotel offers guests the kind of personal attention that is a rarity in today's world. There are 188 luxury rooms with marble bathrooms and in-room safes. One- and two-bedroom suites are fully equipped with executive kitchenettes, and private terraces come with most suites, some with spectacular Chrysler Building views. The penthouse-level bar and lounge, **Upstairs**, serves breakfast and small plates at night. Access to the New York Health and Racquet Club is complimentary. Ask about the summer Kimberly yacht excursions, at special rates to hotel guests.

> **The Lowdown on the Loews Regency Hotel**
>
> **Loews Regency Hotel** (540 Park Ave, 212/759-4100) was closed for nearly a year for major renovations. The new look includes attractive public areas, renovated guestrooms, new restaurants, a well-equipped fitness center, and the latest technology to accommodate guests' needs. Reopening is slated for late 2013 or early 2014.

THE KITANO NEW YORK

66 Park Ave (at 38th St)
                                                            212/885-7000
Moderate   kitano.com

A tranquil hotel with Zen-like hospitality describes this Japanese-owned hotel in Manhattan. Rooms are clean, comfortable, and uncluttered, with down comforters and spacious, marble bathrooms. Premium television channels and American and Japanese newspapers are complimentary. Many rooms offer views of Grand Central Terminal, the Empire State Building, or Murray Hill. On-premises you can enjoy Japanese cuisine at **Habukai**, then move to **Jazz at Kitano** for a nightcap and world-class jazz.

LANGHAM PLACE, FIFTH AVENUE

400 Fifth Ave (at 36th St)   212/695-4005
Expensive   newyork.langhamplacehotels.com

This contemporary beauty on Fifth Avenue is housed in a soaring 60-story skyscraper. One hundred and fifty seven larger-than-usual guest rooms and 57 suites are impeccably appointed with fresh orchids, Pratesi linens, an espresso maker, and a bathroom mirror which doubles as a television. Guests have 24/7

Hotels with Parade Views

Looking for a room with a view of the **Macy's Thanksgiving Day Parade**? This much-anticipated annual parade serpentines down Central Park West to Columbus Circle, takes a short jaunt on Central Park South before heading down Avenue of the Americas to 34th Street and the famed Macy's department store. Some hotels offer parade packages and specials. Make your reservations well in advance, but before plunking down a deposit, check on cancellation policies and occupancy limits, and make sure your room is positioned to see this great holiday tradition.

6 Columbus (6 Columbus Circle, 212/204-3000)

JW Marriott Essex House New York (160 Central Park S, 212/247-0300)

Mandarin Oriental New York (80 Columbus Circle, 212/805-8800)

New York Hilton (1335 Avenue of the Americas, 212/586-7000)

Residence Inn New York (1033 Ave of the Americas, 212/768-0007): event spaces, too

The Ritz-Carlton New York, Central Park (50 Central Park S, 212/308-9100)

Trump International Hotel & Tower (1 Central Park W, 212/299-1000)

Warwick New York (65 W 54th Street, 212/247-2700)

access to personal assistants and a fitness center. Michael White's rustic Italian restaurant, **Ai Fiori**, is a big hit and serves three meals a day; the **Measure** lobby lounge is open nightly and hosts live jazz performances. Of course, such opulence comes with a price, so expect to pay big bucks for luxury with a view of the Empire State Building.

LE PARKER MERIDIEN NEW YORK

119 W 56th St (bet Ave of the Americas and Seventh Ave)   212/245-5000
Moderate to moderately expensive   starwoodhotels.com/lemeridien

There's a lot going for this large midtown hotel: great location, 721 ergonomically-designed rooms, atrium pool, junior suites with separate sitting areas, and oversized baths and showers. There are several excellent on-site eateries: **Norma's**, one of New York's top breakfast rooms; and one of the best burgers in town at street-level **burger joint**. There is also **Knave**, an elegant espresso bar by day and alcohol bar at night. You can complete your daily workout in the 15,000-square-foot total wellness center. Note: If you are driving, the entrance to Le Parker Meridien New York is on 56th Street.

LIBRARY HOTEL

299 Madison Ave (at 41st St)   212/983-4500
Moderate   libraryhotel.com

Travelers who are avid readers should check out the Library Hotel with its excellent midtown location. Sixty rooms are individually appointed with artwork and books, room numbers are ingeniously based on the Dewey decimal system, and floors are organized by its ten major categories. Guests can enjoy the 14th-floor Poetry Terrace, which houses 6,000 volumes of verse. Continental breakfast and an afternoon wine-and-cheese reception are complimentary. Additionally, you'll find **Madison and Vine** (American bistro and wine bar) and **Bookmarks** (rooftop lounge) on-premises.

THE LONDON NYC

151 W 54th St (bet Ave of the Americas and Seventh Ave)   212/307-5000
Expensive   thelondonnyc.com

This midtown all-suites hotel boasts of being the tallest place to stay in Manhattan, with 54 floors. The 562 rooms and furnishings are first class, offering views of Central Park and the city skyline, and the service is very personal. The luxury hotel offers a 24-hour business center, fitness facility, and complimentary newspapers. **The London Bar** (small bites), **Gordon Ramsay at the London NYC** (fine dining, seasonal French), and **Maze** (casual, French) provide excellent eating facilities and room service.

THE LOWELL

28 E 63rd St (bet Park and Madison Ave)   212/838-1400
Moderately expensive   lowellhotel.com

Like an attractive English townhouse, The Lowell is a well-located boutique hotel featuring 49 suites and 23 deluxe rooms. The personalized service and attention to detail are outstanding. Amenities include a 24-hour multi-lingual concierge service, at least two phones per room, complimentary Wi-Fi, DVRs, marble bathrooms, complimentary shoeshines, and a fitness center. The 33 suites have wood-burning fireplaces, 14 of them have private terraces, and most include a full kitchen. Try the **Pembroke Room** for breakfast, brunch, pre-theater dinner (5 to 7), tea, and cocktails.

MANDARIN ORIENTAL NEW YORK

Time Warner Center
80 Columbus Circle (at 60th St)   212/805-8800
Expensive to very expensive   mandarinoriental.com/newyork

Boasting a superior location at the Time Warner Center, the Mandarin Oriental New York offers great views of Central Park from the 35th floor up. In its usual classy (and pricey) style, the Mandarin Oriental provides New York visitors 244 elegant rooms and suites, all beautifully furnished and equipped with state-of-the-art technology. Magnificent art pieces dot the public spaces. The 35th-floor eateries include **Asiate**, which features contemporary American with an Asian flair and room service, as well as **Mobar**, a popular spot for drinks. A beautiful ballroom is available, and a two-story spa features "holistic rejuvenation." The 75-foot lap pool has a spectacular setting with views of the Hudson River.

THE MARITIME HOTEL

363 W 16th St (at Ninth Ave)   212/242-4300
Moderate   themaritimehotel.com

Located in an area with few modern hotels, The Maritime is making it convenient for those doing business in Chelsea. Amenities include Italian restaurant **La Bottega** and rooftop cocktail lounge **The Cabanas**, a 24-hour fitness center, in-room safes, goose down duvets, and oversized towels. The 126 cabin-inspired rooms and bathrooms are small, but all rooms face the Hudson River and feature five-foot porthole-style windows to enjoy the view.

THE MARK

25 E 77th St (at Madison Ave)   212/744-4300
Very expensive   themarkhotel.com

In a landmark building dating back to 1927, The Mark underwent a stunning renovation in 2009. The beautiful results make this retreat reminiscent of a luxurious 1930s Parisian hotel — with a modern twist. There are 150 rooms and suites, outfitted with advanced technologies and specially designed Italian bed and bath linens. Some studios and suites include custom kitchens. **The Mark Restaurant by Jean-Georges** is an exemplary elegant dining venue. The handcrafted signature cocktails at the **Mark Bar** are similarly superior. Service and personal attention at this exclusive address are top-notch. Additional features are a gym, Frederic Fekkai salon, daily newspaper delivery, and complimentary shoe shine.

MONDRIAN SOHO

9 Crosby St (bet Grand and Howard St)   212/389-1000
Moderate   mondriansoho.com

Mondrian Soho is a charming member of the Morgans Hotel Group. The 270 "sleeping chambers" (guest rooms) are decorated in a romantic blue-and-white color scheme. Benjamin Noriega-Ortiz used *"La Belle et la Bête"* as a theme throughout. Elegant foyers, mirrors, crystal sconces, and jewel-toned doors add sparkle inside the property. Each comfortable room affords a view of Manhattan and is outfitted with an LCD HDTV, iPod docking station, spa bathroom, and chrome desk; optional in-room spa services. Italian restaurant **Isola Trattoria & Crudo Bar** is inspired by the Italian coast and serves breakfast, lunch, and dinner. Rooftop cocktail bar, **Soaked**, is an excellent summer destination offering panoramic views of the city.

MORGANS HOTEL

237 Madison Ave (bet 37th and 38th St)   212/686-0300
Moderately expensive to expensive   morganshotel.com

Exceptional attention, lush amenities, and a fabulous location make this 114-room beauty a welcome stop for discriminating travelers. Andrée Putman designed the signature black, white, and gray interiors of this boutique hotel. Soothing Malin+Goetz toiletries are a luxurious touch. Rooms are equipped with desks, flat-screen HDTV, and Wi-Fi. Continental breakfast is complimentary.

NEW YORK HILTON

1335 Ave of the Americas (bet 53rd and 54th St)   212/586-7000
Moderate to moderately expensive   newyorkhiltonhotel.com

For leisure travelers interested in shopping, theater, Radio City Music Hall, and other midtown attractions, the New York Hilton midtown location is highly desirable. A popular business and convention hotel, the Hilton outfits its rooms with the most up-to-date communications equipment. Special features include an outstanding art collection, upscale executive floors with a private lounge and large luxury suites, dozens of rooms equipped for the disabled, a highly trained international staff, and an 8,000-square-foot state-of-the-art fitness club and spa. The New York Hilton features several eating and drinking spaces, including newly opened **Herb N' Kitchen** (seasonal salads, sandwiches, and pizzas) and **minus5** ice bar. Room service is no longer offered.

NEW YORK MARRIOTT DOWNTOWN

85 West St (at Battery Park)   212/385-4900
Moderate   nymarriottdowntown.com

Close to Lady Liberty! For those doing business in the Wall Street area, this 497-room hotel (490 rooms and 7 suites) is ideal. Contemporary and deluxe rooms offer quality amenities including restful Revive beds with down comforters, marble bathrooms, a great fitness center, and spectacular views of the harbor and Statue of Liberty. The newly renovated concierge lounge offers complimentary breakfast and hors d' oeuvres. Be sure to check out the popular **Bill's Bar & Burger**, now serving up delicious burgers, fries, and shakes.

NEW YORK MARRIOTT MARQUIS

1535 Broadway (bet 45th and 46th St)   212/398-1900
Moderate to moderately expensive   nymarriottmarquis.com

This one puts you in the hustle and bustle of Times Square! The New York Marriott Marquis has nearly 2,000 guest rooms and suites, sizable meeting and convention facilities, and one of the largest hotel atriums in the world. Visitors can enjoy the two-story revolving rooftop restaurant and lounge, **The View**, or visit **Crossroads American Kitchen & Bar** for more casual breakfast, lunch, or dinner. In addition, a legitimate Broadway theater, a fully-equipped health club, and a special concierge level are on the property.

NEW YORK PALACE HOTEL

455 Madison Ave (bet 50th and 51st St)   212/888-7000
Expensive   newyorkpalace.com

Undergoing a $140 million renovation as this book goes to press, New York Palace Hotel anticipates a stunning redesign and improved technology to be completed at the end of summer 2013. Located close to Rockefeller Center, the 899-room New York Palace offers commanding views of the city skyline. The public rooms encompass the 1882 Villard Mansion, a legendary New York landmark. Amenities include The Towers, Tower Club, and a spa and fitness center. A multilingual concierge staff is ready to serve guests, and function space and a business center are offered. The addition of a new dining space is expected at the completion of the remodel. A complimentary shuttle goes to Wall Street and the Theater District.

NH JOLLY MADISON TOWERS

22 E 38th St (at Madison Ave)   212/802-0600
Moderate   jollymadison.com

Smack dab in the middle of Manhattan, this charming European-style hotel

Short-Term Apartment Rentals

Many travelers and families find that staying in an apartment while visiting New York City can save money, since more guests can be accommodated and meals can be prepared there.

Affordable New York City (212/533-4001, affordablenewyorkcity. com): B&Bs and furnished apartments; four-night minimum stay for B&Bs, five nights for apartments

City Sonnet (212/614-3034, citysonnet.com): hosted rooms, apartments, lofts; minimum five-night stay

Radio City Apartments (142 W 49th St, 877/921-9321, radiocityapartments.com): apartment-style lodging; no minimum stay

has 242 tastefully decorated rooms. The **Whaler Bar**, a breakfast room, and meeting rooms are among the amenities. This is a great location, just blocks from the best shopping and attractions. For a minimal fee, small pets (defined as up to 20 pounds) are welcome.

ON THE AVE HOTEL

2178 Broadway (at 77th St)   212/362-1100
Moderate to moderately expensive   ontheave-nyc.com

Refreshed and ready! Rooms at On the Ave Hotel were completely refreshed mid-2013, with completion of the lobby redesign scheduled for fall 2013. On the Upper West Side this is a great place for those who plan to visit the legendary Zabar's, the American Museum of Natural History, Columbus Circle, and other attractions in the area. Among the many amenities: beautiful bed linens and towels, Italian black-marble bathrooms, suites with private balconies, concierge, and business center. Open balconies on the 14th and 16th floors offer super views and comfortable chairs. Great pizzas and pasta can be enjoyed at their rustic Italian restaurant, **Serafina**.

THE PENINSULA NEW YORK

700 Fifth Ave (at 55th St)   212/956-2888
Expensive   newyork.peninsula.com

When the name "Peninsula" is mentioned, the words *quality* and *class* immediately come to mind. The Manhattan property is certainly no exception. This 1905 landmark offers 239 luxurious rooms, including the palatial Peninsula Suite (more than 3,000 square feet at $24,000 per night!). Room features include oversize marble bathrooms with numerous amenities, printers, large work desks, and audiovisual systems with cable. Features of the 21st-floor Peninsula Spa by ESPA include an enclosed pool, sun terrace, modern fitness equipment, and spa services. **Gotham Lounge** provides convenient all day dining as well as afternoon tea. The rooftop hot spot **Salon de Ning** offers Chinese-inspired dishes amid dramatic views from its east and west terraces. According to hotel sources, an exciting new restaurant is anticipated fall 2013.

THE PIERRE

2 E 61st St (at Fifth Ave)   212/838-8000
Very expensive   tajhotels.com

Overlooking Central Park, The Pierre is the Taj Hotels Resort and Palaces' North American flagship property. The 189 elegant guest rooms (49 are suites) are in luxurious residential-style with rich woods, silk and brocade fabrics, and bathrooms that incorporate floor-to-ceiling, glass-walled showers and soaking tubs. The in-room entertainment and electronics are first-class. Function rooms remain a coveted venue for Manhattan's glitziest events. The well-loved Sirio Maccioni offers traditional Italian dishes at **Sirio Ristorante**. Lobby lounge **Two E** is a grand watering hole and an option for light meals and afternoon tea. A 24-hour fitness center and beauty salon are on-site. With a ratio of three staff members per guest, impeccable and attentive service is assured.

THE PLAZA

Central Park S at Fifth Ave   212/759-3000
Expensive to very expensive   theplaza.com

The Plaza has been a focal point for New York residents and visitors for decades as it possesses one of Manhattan's most prized and famous locations. Over the years a series of ownership changes brought with it the conversion of prime rooms to privately-owned residential suites on Fifth Avenue and Central Park South. Currently 282 guestrooms (102 are suites) on the Plaza's back side continue to offer the well-known Plaza address to the public. The **Palm Court** is still an unforgettable choice for breakfast, lunch, and afternoon tea, and the Plaza Food Hall has brought exciting, new eating options under chef Todd English's talents. Still, for those of us who remember the glory days of this *grande dame*, the latest changes to the Plaza traditions have been difficult to accept.

THE RITZ-CARLTON NEW YORK, BATTERY PARK

2 West St (at Battery Park)   212/344-0800
Expensive

THE RITZ-CARLTON NEW YORK, CENTRAL PARK

50 Central Park S (at Ave of the Americas)   212/308-9100
Expensive   ritzcarlton.com

These two properties provide the outstanding service, comfort, and

---

Concierge Services

ABC NYC Concierge (800/429-5285, abcnycconcierge.com) started as a limousine service, and owner Russell Figaredo expanded the offerings over time. Here's a sampling of their services: concierge, personal assistant, personal chef, travel planning, senior care, and the ever-reliable limousine service. Contact this amazing crew when you need assistance with business or domestic errands, pet sitting or care, special-event tickets and restaurant reservations, personalized shopping and returns, a special night on the town, or planning for out-of-town guests. I'd keep this number handy for just about anything!

amenities identified with The Ritz-Carlton name. At both locations you'll find great views, top-grade lobby-level restaurants, gym and spa services, luxurious rooms and bathrooms, and business centers. Club Level guests get special treatment, which may include unpacking and packing services, Wi-Fi, a library of children's DVDs, and an assortment of snacks.

ROYALTON

44 W 44th St (bet Fifth Ave and Ave of the Americas)   212/869-4400
Expensive   royaltonhotel.com

You know you are in for a treat upon stepping into the lobby of the Royalton. Glass, brass, steel, wood, and suede are combined to create a warm, sophisticated environment. The hotel's 168 rooms feature banquette seating, work areas, iPads, and slate and glass showers. Some rooms have fireplaces and soaking tubs, and in-room spa services are just a phone call away. Three luxurious penthouses with private terraces have amazing views. A fitness center and valet parking are also available. For breakfast, lunch, and dinner you'll find consistently good (and expensive) American dishes at **Forty Four**.

ST. REGIS NEW YORK

2 E 55th St (at Fifth Ave)   212/753-4500
Expensive   starwoodhotels.com/stregis

The St. Regis, a historic landmark in the heart of Manhattan, is rightfully one of the crown jewels of the Starwood Hotels group. The hotel's 164 guest rooms and 65 suites provide luxurious accommodations. All rooms have marble baths, in-room refrigerators, Tavish linens, silk wall coverings, and round-the-clock butler service (including free pressing of two garments upon arrival). Outstanding on-site restaurants include **Astor Court** (breakfast, lunch, afternoon tea, dinner, and Sunday brunch) and the **King Cole Bar** (great Bloody Marys) where a renovation is to be completed fall 2013.

SALISBURY HOTEL

123 W 57th St (bet Ave of the Americas and Seventh Ave)   212/246-1300
Moderate   nycsalisbury.com

I highly recommend the Salisbury to price-savvy travelers as one of New York's best hotel deals! Capably run by Edward Oliva, it has nearly 200 rooms and suites with walk-in closets and safes; many rooms are outfitted with butler's pantries and refrigerators. Suites are large, comfortable, and reasonably priced. The thick walls really are soundproof! If you've waited until the last minute for reservations, the Salisbury is less well-known among out-of-towners, and therefore rooms are usually available. You'll be near Carnegie Hall and other midtown attractions. Folks here are exceedingly friendly. A continental breakfast and Wi-Fi are available for a nominal charge; nearby parking is discounted for hotel guests with cars.

SHERATON NEW YORK TIMES SQUARE HOTEL

811 Seventh Ave (at 53rd St)   212/581-1000
Moderate to moderately expensive   starwoodhotels.com/sheraton

With an outstanding location in central Manhattan and following 2012 room renovations, the Sheraton New York Times Square is an excellent choice for tourists and business travelers. Polished, contemporary upgrades include pillowtop mattresses, ergonomic desk chairs, and extra storage. The exclusive **Club Lounge** on the 44th floor provides breathtaking views, complimentary continental breakfast, evening hors d'ouevres and beverages, Wi-Fi, and other privileges. Take advantage of Sheraton Fitness (powered by Core Performance) and the large selection of equipment, classes, trainers, and saunas. Several in-house eateries include **Hudson Market** (breakfast buffet) and **Hudson Market Burger** (casual American cuisine).

THE STANDARD HIGH LINE

848 Washington St (at 13th St)   212/645-4646
Moderately expensive   standardhotels.com/high-line

This ultramodern Meatpacking District hotel straddles the High Line — a defunct elevated freight railway that is now a linear park. Wall-to-wall and floor-to-ceiling windows in the 338 guest rooms and suites provide views of the Hudson River and dramatic skyline. Rooms have see-through bathrooms with soaking tubs and walk-in rain showers, extra-large-sized towels, and cozy robes. Wi-Fi is complimentary and you can work out while taking in the amazing views from the 17th-floor gym. Food and beverage options are plentiful. **The Standard Grill** and **The Biergarten** are under the High Line, and **Top of the Standard** is up on the roof.

THE STRAND HOTEL

33 W 37th St (bet Fifth Ave and Ave of the Americas)   212/448-1024
Moderate   thestrandnyc.com

Located in the Fashion District, The Strand Hotel is stylish, contemporary, and luxurious. The lobby features a two-story water wall and stone- and glass-circular staircase. There are 177 guestrooms on the 21 floors. Vintage photos from the files of *Condé Nast* are prominently displayed. Guest rooms and public areas are accentuated with rich purple furnishings and accessories. A European buffet breakfast, early-morning coffee bar, fitness center, and unlimited Wi-Fi are complimentary. Relax at the cozy **Strand Bistro** for a contemporary meal or enjoy a dynamic view of the Empire State Building from the rooftop lounge, **Top of the Strand**.

THE SURREY

20 E 76th St (bet Madison and Fifth Ave)   212/288-3700
Expensive   thesurrey.com

Built in 1926 as a residence hotel, the original Surrey was home to many celebrities. It is now modernized and yet maintains its classic integrity. Each of the 189 rooms is tastefully appointed and serenely elegant. Salons include handpainted wardrobes; some rooms are enhanced with fireplaces and terraces. Elsewhere on the property is a private, seasonal roof garden for guests and a fitness center that never closes. **Bar Pleiades** and **Cafe Boulud** are delightful cocktail and dining destinations, or you can enjoy their French fare in your room. Pets are welcome and pampered in style.

TRUMP INTERNATIONAL HOTEL AND TOWER

1 Central Park W (at 60th St)   212/299-1000
Expensive   trumphotelcollection.com

Trump International is the only hotel in the city honored with a Forbes five-star, five-diamond rating. It is everything you'd expect from a place with The Donald's name attached — handcrafted chandeliers, gold-leaf mirrors, rich wood, and plush seating in the 176 luxury suites and guestrooms. Rooms have fully-equipped kitchens. There are special amenities (fresh flowers, umbrellas, and garment bags), 24-hour room service, complete office facilities, entertainment centers in every room, a state-of-the-art fitness center, swimming pool, and marble bathrooms. One of Manhattan's best (and more expensive) restaurants, **Jean Georges**, will pamper your taste buds; it has a five-star, five diamond rating as well. Many rooms have wonderful views of Central Park.

TRUMP SOHO NEW YORK
246 Spring St (at Varick St)   212/842-5500
Expensive   trumphotelcollection.com

The legendary Trump hospitality and opulence is now available downtown at Trump SoHo New York. This newer high-rise hotel boasts 391 guest rooms, of which 132 are one-bedroom suites, 11 are penthouse suites, and 3 are spa suites connecting to **The Spa at Trump**. Each luxurious room is custom furnished by Fendi Casa with Bellino bed linens creating serene, contemporary elegance. The TV remote also controls lights, drapes, and room temperature. All rooms include spacious bathrooms with large soaking tubs and separate showers. Nespresso machines, microwaves, and minibars enhance the experience. Privacy is optimized, with only 12 guest rooms per floor. Views of the city from the rooms are exceptional. Try contemporary Japanese cuisine at fabulous **Koi**. The seasonal **Bar d'Eau** is adjacent to the outdoor pool desk.

W NEW YORK
541 Lexington Ave (bet 49th and 50th St)   212/755-1200
Moderately expensive   starwoodhotels.com

Located in midtown, this Starwood property has 688 rooms (including 62 spacious suites), a large ballroom, Bliss49 Spa, Sweat Fitness Center, and 24-hour room service. The look is strictly modern. Dining options include casual American at **Heartbeat** and appetizers or light snacks from **W Cafe/Oasis Bar**. **Whiskey Blue** is an upbeat cocktail lounge with small bites and **The Living Room** is a cozy lounge just off the lobby. Pets (dogs and cats) are pampered with the P.A.W. program (Pets Are Welcome).

W NEW YORK TIMES SQUARE
1567 Broadway (at 47th St)   212/930-7400
Moderately expensive   starwoodhotels.com

This 57-story W flagship features 509 guest rooms and 43 suites in the heart of Times Square. The modern, high-energy space offers a classy retail store, Sweat Fitness Center, 24-hour room service, pillowtop mattresses and feather beds, comfy robes, and other quality amenities. Ask to stay on the highest floor possible, as the views of Times Square and the Hudson River are dramatic. If you just want to stay in, **Blue Fin** restaurant offers savory seafood and **The Living Room** bar is open until the wee hours. The hotel is pet-friendly.

WALDORF ASTORIA NEW YORK

301 Park Ave (at 50th St)   212/355-3000
Moderate to Expensive   waldorfnewyork.com

The Waldorf Astoria New York has been world-renowned for over a century as one of the first "grand hotels" to combine elegance, luxurious amenities, and personal service. The rich, impressive lobby is bedecked with magnificent mahogany wall panels, hand-woven carpets, and a 148,000-tile mosaic floor. The upper floors house the Waldorf Towers, home to celebrities, royalty, and every American president since Herbert Hoover. The more than 1,400 stately guest rooms and select suites are spacious and richly appointed. Forty meeting venues and ballrooms accommodate special events of most any size. The Grand Ballroom is the only two-tiered, four-story ballroom with a full Broadway stage in New York. Guerlain Spa and the hotel's on-site fitness center are available 24/7. The famed Waldorf-Astoria Sunday brunch is served at **Peacock Alley**, just off the elegant lobby. You'll also find **Bull & Bear** (steaks, seafood, and bar) and the more casual **Oscar's Brassierie** (breakfast and lunch).

Long-Term Home Health Care

When it becomes necessary to look into long-term home health care, call **Priority Home Care** (866/263-5074, priorityhomecare.com). Since 1992 they provide professional and courteous live-in aides, respite relief care, and home visits. Employees specialize in Russian, Asian, Spanish, Polish, Portuguese, Italian, Yiddish, and French languages and customs.

WASHINGTON SQUARE HOTEL

103 Waverly Place (at MacDougal St)   212/777-9515
Inexpensive to moderate   washingtonsquarehotel.com

Located in historic Washington Square Park, this hotel offers good value in rooms, a capable staff, and a nice restaurant. The location is handy for those with business at New York University or visitors who want to explore the Village. The 152 guest rooms are done in art-deco style and are comfortably equipped with pillowtop mattresses, Keurig coffeemakers, granite-top vanities, and complimentary Wi-Fi and continental breakfast are available. **North Square Restaurant and Lounge** is a classy on-site venue for cocktails or dining, or visit the **Deco Room** for formal tea service. And for a meal in the park, request a picnic lunchbox.

THE WOLCOTT HOTEL

4 W 31st St (bet Fifth Ave and Broadway)   212/268-2900
Inexpensive   wolcott.com

Perhaps one of Manhattan's better hotel bargains, The Wolcott Hotel offers a good location (just south of midtown) with views of the Empire State Building. The 200 rooms offer private baths, good security, direct-dial phones, TVs with pay movies and videogames, Wi-Fi, in-room safes, iron and ironing boards, clock radios, laundry facilities, and small fitness and business centers. No wonder students, foreign travelers, and savvy business people are regular patrons!

HOUSING ALTERNATIVES

Many travelers and families visiting New York City prefer to stay someplace other than a hotel. In this Alternative Housing section I present options such as apartments, bed and breakfasts, townhouses, and dormitory housing.

ABODE
Mailing address: 520 E 76th St, Suite 3E, New York, NY 10021
Mon-Fri: 9-5   212/472-2000, 800/835-8880 (outside tri-state area)
Moderate to moderately expensive   abodenyc.com

Would you like to stay in a delightful old brownstone? How about a contemporary luxury apartment in the heart of Manhattan? Abode selects apartments with great care, personally inspecting them to ensure the highest standards of cleanliness, attractiveness, and hospitality. All are nicely furnished. Nightly rates begin at $200 for a studio and rise to $550 for a three-bedroom apartment. Extended stays of a month or longer receive discount rates.

AKA CENTRAL PARK
42 W 58th St (bet Fifth Ave and Ave of the Americas)   646/744-3100

AKA SUTTON PLACE
330 E 56th St (bet First and Second Ave)   212/752-8888

AKA TIMES SQUARE
123 W 44th St (bet Ave of the Americas and Broadway)   212/764-5700

AKA UNITED NATIONS
234 E 46th St (bet Second and Third Ave)   646/291-4200
                                                        stayaka.com

Specializing in stays of a week or longer, AKA offers prime locations for business and leisure travelers visiting Manhattan. Each apartment-hotel location offers something different in the way of accommodations. There are studios and suites, some with kitchens. Some offer outdoor dining areas with unsurpassed city views. All offer meticulous housekeeping. The 56th street location offers one- and two-bedroom apartments. AKA is a great option if you're looking for a bit more comfort and privacy than your standard hotel room.

AT HOME IN NEW YORK
P.O. Box 407, New York, NY 10185   212/956-3125 or 800/692-4262
Inexpensive to expensive   athomeny.com

For most people, the words "bed and breakfast" connote quaint country inns, but B&Bs can also be found in Manhattan throughout the city. Accommodations are available in various settings — apartments, co-ops, artists' lofts, and condos — and rates are a fraction of those at higher-priced hotels. At Home in New York carefully screens hosted and unhosted properties to fit every need and budget. In addition to breakfasts, hosts often dish out favorite tips for a true local experience.

CHELSEA PINES INN

317 W 14th St (bet Eighth and Ninth Ave)   212/929-1023
Moderate   chelseapinesinn.com

This isn't your typical inn; it is a 19th-century five-story walk-up with movie-themed guest rooms and common areas. All rooms have private bathrooms, flat-screen TVs, and iPod docks (alas, there's no elevator.) Local calls, Wi-Fi, and continental breakfast are free. As befits the eclectic Chelsea locale, the inn is gay- and lesbian-friendly.

HOSTELLING INTERNATIONAL NEW YORK

891 Amsterdam Ave (at 103rd St)   212/932-2300
Inexpensive   hinewyork.org

Hostelling International New York provides inexpensive overnight accommodations for travelers of all ages. This renovated century-old landmark has over 672 beds. They offer meeting spaces, Wi-Fi, coffee bar, complimentary continental breakfast, self-service kitchens, lockers, a TV and games room, and laundry facilities to individuals and groups. Guests under 18 must be accompanied by a parent, or in groups, a chaperone. There is a strict rule forbidding alcohol on the premises; smoking must be confined to outdoor areas. And, the price is right!

INN NEW YORK CITY

266 W 71st St (bet West End Ave and Broadway)   212/580-1900
Expensive   innnewyorkcity.com

For a secluded, civilized stay! Inn New York City offers four suites behind a discreet exterior in a restored 19th-century townhouse. Depending on the suite chosen, you may find a double Jacuzzi, extensive library, leaded glass skylights, fireplaces, baby grand piano, private terrace, or a fully-equipped kitchen stocked with hearty delights. Additional services include high-speed Internet, cable TV, daily newspapers, maid service, and a 24-hour concierge. Personal laundry is done on request at no additional charge — a real plus.

IVY TERRACE B&B

230 E 58th St (bet Second and Third Ave)   516/662-6862
Moderate   ivyterrace.com

There are six studio apartments in this charming century-old townhouse, two with outdoor terraces. Kitchens are stocked with breakfast goodies. Hardwood floors, ceiling fans, and 15-foot ceilings are very inviting. Innkeeper Vinessa promises special care, including tips of where to eat and explore. There is a three-night minimum, and weekly rates are available. Local calls and Wi-Fi are free.

92Y RESIDENCE

1395 Lexington Ave (at 92nd St)   212/415-5660, 800-858-4692
Moderate   92y.org/residence

The 92Y Residence offers convenient, inexpensive, and secure dormitory housing for students, interns, and working men and women with a minimum age of 18 and older. There are shared bathroom and kitchen facilities. Special discounts for Y health-club memberships and single and double rooms are available. Free Wi-Fi, weekly linen service, and 24/7 security are provided. Stays can range from 30 days to one year. Admission is by application.

Best for Design

Looking for an Architect or Decorator? Here are some of the very best:

Ashley Whittaker Design (191 E 76th St, Suite 5A, 212/650-0024): neotraditionalist

Bella Mancini Design (41 Union Square W, Room 523, 212/741-3380): Bella Zakarian Mancini is mindful of budgets.

Bilhuber and Associates (330 E 59th St, 6th floor, 212/308-4888): Jeffrey Bilhuber has contemporary ideas.

David Anthony Harris Interiors (524 Broadway, Suite 206, 212/675-5863): an eye for detail

Glenn Gissler Design (1123 Broadway, Suite 1100, 212/228-9880): works well with art

Miles Redd (77 Bleecker St, Suite C111, 212/674-0902): color expert

MR Architecture & Decor (245 W 29th St, 10th floor, 212/989-9300): David Mann is very practical.

S.R. Gambrel (55 Grove St, 212/925-3380): You can't beat Steven Gambrel for detailing.

Sara Story Design (54 Thompson St, 212/228-6007): contemporary, eclectic

Shamir Shah Design (10 Greene St, 212/274-7476): interior and architectural design

Specht Harpman Architects (338 W 39th St, 10th floor, 212/239-1150): Scott Specht and Louise Harpman are pocketbook-conscious.

Steven Holl Architects (450 W 31st St, 11th floor, 212/629-7262): residential and commercial, worldwide

PHILLIPS CLUB

Lincoln Square
155 W 66th St (at Broadway)   212/835-8800, 877/644-8900
Moderate to moderately expensive   phillipsclub.com

This 162-unit residential hotel near Lincoln Center is designed for long-term visitors but will also take short-stay customers. Studios and suites come with fully-equipped kitchens, flat-screen TVs, and Bose sound systems. Other features include 24-hour concierge, laundry and valet service, in-room safes, a handy conference room, and preferential access at the nearby Reebok Sports Club/NY.

ROOMS TO LET

83 Horatio St   212/675-5481
Inexpensive to moderate   roomstolet.net

An oasis in the middle of the city! This bed and breakfast is located on a quiet street of Greenwich Village in an 1840s home complete with antiques, paintings, a parlor, and garden. There are four rooms available, including a suite with its own bathroom; smaller rooms have a shared bath. Small private terraces and glimpses of the Hudson River can be enjoyed from some rooms. Booking is completed online and requires a four-night minimum stay. Continental breakfast is included.

SOLDIERS', SAILORS', MARINES', COAST GUARD & AIRMEN'S CLUB

283 Lexington Ave (at 37th St)   212/683-4353, 800/678-8443
Inexpensive   ssmaclub.org

   Since 1919 this organization has been providing friendly, safe, affordable accommodations for our military personnel and their families visiting Manhattan. American and allied servicemen and women — active, retired, veterans, reservists, military cadets, NYFD, NYPD, EMS, and Coast Guard personnel — are welcomed at this convenient Murray Hill location. Proof of eligibility must be shown. Rates are extremely low (with no tax); if you're traveling solo, you may be assigned a roommate. Rooms have two, three, four, and six beds. Communal bathroom facilities are on each floor. There are several lounges, TVs with DVD players, and a lobby canteen with refrigerator, microwave, and coffee. A complimentary continental breakfast is provided each morning.

WEBSTER APARTMENTS

419 W 34th St (at Ninth Ave)   212/967-9000, 800/242-7909
Inexpensive   websterapartments.org

   This is one of the best deals in the city for working women with moderate incomes. The hotel operates on a policy developed by Charles B. Webster, a first cousin of Rowland Macy (of the department-store family). Webster left an endowment to found these apartments, which opened in 1923. Residents include working college students, interns, designers, actresses, secretaries, and other business and professional women. Facilities include dining rooms, recreation areas, a library, and lounges. The Webster has private gardens for guests, and meals can be taken outdoors. Rates are on a sliding scale based on income and range from $305 to $335 per week; this includes two meals a day and maid service. Women visiting New York on business can stay for a daily rate of $85; three-night minimum.

INTERIOR DESIGNERS

AERO STUDIOS

419 Broome St (bet Lafayette and Crosby St)   212/966-4700
Mon-Sat: 11-6   aerostudios.com

   Thomas O'Brien's staff is well equipped to handle everything from a major commercial interior design project to a minor residential one. Be sure to visit his Aero, Ltd. boutique for a collection of home furnishings, decor, and lighting — beautiful items with both meaning and style.

Jewelry Repair

For minor or major jewelry repairs, try these:

Donna Distefano (37 W 20th St, Suite 1106, 212/594-3757): will also replace lost stones; by appointment

Hernandez Jewelry (1427 Ave of the Americas, 212/265-4070): works wonders with repairs, including watches

Murrey's Jewelers (1395 Third Ave, 212/879-3690)

BERCELI INTERIOR REMODELLING
1402 Lexington Ave (bet 92nd and 93rd St)　　　212/722-8811
Mon-Fri: 9-6:30; Sat: 10-6　　　berceli.com

　　Give Berceli a call if you're ready to redo your kitchen or bathroom. For over two decades they have worked with homeowners to bring function and beauty to home interiors. Whether the style is contemporary or traditional, they use only the finest American and European products and appliances. They'll do the whole job (consult, design, install, and finish), or you can choose to do portions of the work in order to save costs. Berceli has earned high marks from co-ops and condominium boards, and they are committed to customer satisfaction.

MARTIN ALBERT INTERIORS
257 W 39th St (bet Seventh and Eighth Ave), 12th floor
　　　212/673-8000, 800/525-4637
Mon-Thurs: 9-5:30; Fri: 9-5　　　martinalbert.com

　　Martin Albert Interiors specializes in custom furniture and custom window treatments. You can choose from thousands of fabric samples for your project. Custom upholstery and slipcovers, a furniture shop (bring a photo and they will re-create the piece), custom draperies, motorized shades, and a large selection of drapery hardware. Martin Albert does it all!

RICHARD'S INTERIOR DESIGN
1390 Lexington Ave (bet 91st and 92nd St)　　　212/831-9000
Mon-Fri: 10-6; Sat: 10:30-3　　　richardsinteriordesign.net

　　Richard's offers interior design services, in-home consultation, and installation. Reupholstery, slipcovers, draperies, top treatments, shades, bedroom ensembles, custom cabinetry, and wall coverings are available. You'll find thousands of imported decorator fabrics, including tapestries, damasks, stripes, plaids, silks, velvets, and floral chintzes; these are all first-quality goods at competitive prices. There is also a selection of carpeting and area rugs.

JEWELRY SERVICES
GEM APPRAISERS & CONSULTANTS
589 Fifth Ave (at 48th St), Suite 1309　　　212/333-3122
By appointment (Mon-Thurs)　　　robaretz.com

　　Robert C. Aretz is a graduate gemologist and a certified member of the Appraisers Association of America. For over 40 years he has provided appraisals for major insurance companies, banks, and jewelry stores through Gem Appraisers & Consultants. His specialty is antique jewelry, gemstones, diamonds, and natural pearls. Aretz also does private appraisals and/or consultations for estate, insurance, tax, equitable distribution, and other purposes. The company offers a broker service for jewelry sales as well.

L AND M WATCH REPAIRS
25 W 47th St (bet Fifth Ave and Ave of the Americas), 2nd floor　　212/398-0490
Mon-Fri: 9:30-5

　　Check out these folks when your timepieces need help — wristwatches, pocketwatches, and other jewelry repairs. L and M Watch will work on all major brands as well as replace batteries and watchbands.

RISSIN'S JEWELRY CLINIC

10 W 47th St (bet Fifth Ave and Ave of the Americas), Suite 902 212/575-1098
Mon, Tues, Thurs: 9:30-5 (closed first two weeks of July)   rissinsjewelryclinic.com

Rissin's is indeed a clinic! The assortment of services is staggering: jewelry repair and design, antique and museum restorations, supplying diamonds and other stones, eyeglass repair, pearl and bead stringing, restringing of old necklaces, stone identification, and appraisals. Joe and Toby Rissin run the place. Joe's father was a master engraver, and the family tradition has been passed along. *Honesty* and *quality* are their bywords. Estimates are gladly given, and all work is guaranteed.

LAMP REPAIR

THE LAMP SURGEON

On location   917/414-0426
Daily: 8:30-8:30   lampsurgeon.com

Roy Schneit brings over 30 years of experience as a lamp surgeon — repairing, restoring, refinishing, and re-wiring at customers' homes, offices, and apartments. Services include work on table and floor lamps, halogen lamps, chandeliers, wall sconces, antiques, and custom lampshades.

LANDSCAPE DESIGN

AMERICAN FOLIAGE & DESIGN GROUP

122 W 22nd St (bet Ave of the Americas and Seventh Ave)   212/741-5555
Mon-Fri: 8-5   americanfoliagedesign.com

Planning a special event? The focus at American Foliage is on concepts and designs for anything to do with gardens and exteriors for theater, film, and corporate or private special events. These folks sell or rent live and artificial plants, props, lighting and special-effects items, and party supplies. Full service is provided, including trucking and installation.

LEATHER REPAIR

FORDHAM REPAIR CENTER

39 W 32nd St (bet Fifth Ave and Broadway), Room 604   212/889-4553
Mon-Fri: 8:30-5:30   fordhamrepair.com

Fordham Repair Center is a business you will want to note. They repair, clean, and refurbish leather luggage, handbags, wallets, briefcases, and totes — even your great-grandmother's old trunk. Ripped stitching and bindings, broken zippers and locks, missing wheels, and damaged handles receive careful attention to bring goods back to useful life.

MODERN LEATHER GOODS

2 W 32nd St (bet Fifth Ave and Broadway), 4th floor   212/279-3263
Mon-Fri: 8:30-4:45; Sat: 8:30-1 (closed Sat in July and August)
                                                         modernleathergoods.com

Modern Leather Goods, a family business since 1939, is the place to go for repairs and reconditioning. Ask for owner Tony Pecorella. They are authorized with all major luggage manufacturers. They also reglaze alligator bags, clean leather and suede, and repair shoes and leather clothing.

SUPERIOR LEATHER RESTORERS

141 Lexington Ave (at 29th St) 212/889-7211
Mon-Thurs: 10-6; Fri: 10-5; Sat: 10-3 (closed Sat in summer)

superiorleathernyc.com

Leather repair is the highlight of the services offered at Superior Leather Restorers. They are experts at cleaning leather (suede, shearling, and reptile) and repairing or replacing zippers on leather items. They can make alterations and even remove ink spots. Superior has the answer to all leather-related problems. Many major stores in the city use this family-owned business for luggage and handbag work. Just ask Gucci, Calvin Klein, Bergdorf Goodman, and Prada!

LOCKSMITHS

AAA ARCHITECTURAL HARDWARE

44 W 46th St (at Ave of the Americas) 212/840-3939
Mon-Thurs: 8-5:30; Fri: 8-5 aaahardware.com

Do *not* call with a flat tire! This "AAA" began as a locksmith business. It has been a family-operation for over 60 years, and that says a lot. Services have expanded to keying systems, designing and installing electronic security, and architectural hardware.

NIGHT AND DAY LOCKSMITH

1335 Lexington Ave (at 89th St) 212/722-1017
Mon-Fri: 9-6; Sat: 9-4 (24 hours for emergencies)   nightanddaylocksmiths.com

Just as the name indicates, Night and Day Locksmith answers its phone 24 hours a day for your locksmith and security needs. Owner, Mena Sofer, keeps up on the latest expertise for on-the-spot service. Posted hours are for the sale and installation of locks, window gates, intercoms, car alarms, safes, and keys. Welding is a specialty.

MARBLE WORKS

PUCCIO MARBLE AND ONYX

661 Driggs Ave, Brooklyn (main office) 718/387-9778, 800/778-2246
Mon-Fri: 8:30-4:30 (appointments recommended) pucciostone.com

Since 1950 the Puccio family's tradition has been "work of the highest quality" in marble, onyx, and granite. The sculpture and furniture designs range from traditional to sleekly modern. Now the third and fourth generations show dining and cocktail tables, chairs, chests of drawers, buffets, desks, consoles, and pedestals. Custom-designed installations include foyer floors, bathrooms, kitchens, bars, staircases, fountains, and fireplaces. Retail orders are accepted. They are the largest distributor and fabricator of onyx in the country.

MEDICAL SERVICES

CENTER FOR HEARING AND COMMUNICATION

50 Broadway (bet Morris St and Exchange Pl), 6th floor 917/305-7700,
917/305-7999 (TTY)
Mon, Wed, Fri: 8-5; Tues, Thurs: 8-7 (by appointment) chchearing.org

These folks come highly recommended. People of all ages with any degree of hearing loss are served by this not-for-profit organization. They test hearing, evaluate and dispense hearing aids, and provide speech and language therapy, as well as mental-health counseling. Support groups are conducted to assist people with hearing loss (and their families) in all aspects of their lives.

DR WALK-IN MEDICAL CARE

1627 Broadway (at 50th St)	888/535-6963
125 E 86th St (at Lexington Ave)	212/828-8060
131 Eighth Ave (at 17th St)	212/675-4800

Hours vary by store
Numerous other locations in Manhattan   drwalkin.com

Take note: if you find yourself ill in New York, these convenient locations inside Duane Reade drugstores may be able to help you feel better. Licensed physicians and medical assistants are on duty to perform basic care and screenings, tend to minor sprains and lacerations, administer vaccinations, write prescriptions, and make referrals to appropriate specialists. (However, you should head for the emergency room for any life-threatening condition or broken bones.) Appointments are not necessary, and they will bill most major insurance companies for you.

Docs 'R Us

The task of finding a good doctor in Manhattan has gotten easier, thanks to **Top Doctors, New York Metro Area**. It identifies over 6,000 primary and specialty doctors. Only the top docs are included in this helpful resource, available at book outlets and online at castleconnolly.com.

N.Y. HOTEL URGENT MEDICAL SERVICES

Urgent Care Center of New York	212/737-1212
Daily: by appointment	travelmd.com

Keep this information handy; this is one of the most valuable services in Manhattan! Dr. Ronald Primas, the CEO and medical director, is tops in his field. This outfit is locally based and has been in operation over 15 years. All manner of health care is available on a 24/7 basis: internists, pediatricians, obstetricians, surgeons, dentists, chiropractors, physicians on call, and more. Doctors will

---

In Case of Illness

New York City's largest hospitals offer world-class treatment by top doctors.

Beth Israel Medical Center (10 Nathan D. Perlman Place, 212/420-2000)

Memorial Sloan-Kettering Cancer Center (1275 York Ave, 212/639-2000)

The Mount Sinai Hospital (1 Gustave L. Levy Place, 212/241-6500)

New York-Presbyterian Hospital/Weill Cornell Medical Center (525 E 68th St, 212/746-5454)

NYU Langone Medical Center (550 First Ave, 212/263-7300)

Medical House Calls

Remember when doctors made house calls? Well, in New York, some of them still do! In addition to office appointments, house calls are routine with **New York House Call Physicians** (20 Park Ave, Suite 1A, 646/957-5444, doctorinthefamily.com). They will cater to patients' schedules and location of choice. The doctor's black bag has been expanded to include mobile medical equipment, allowing them to perform numerous procedures. They carry suture equipment, digital electrocardiogram machines, and ophthalmoscopes.

When necessary, the doctors have admitting privileges at Beth Israel Medical Center. Costs are flat-fee based and include most testing, medication dispensing, and procedures. They do not bill insurance companies, Medicare, or Medicaid, so plan on using a credit card or cash. Available services include family medicine, hospice, pain management, pediatric care, psychotherapy, ultrasound, and addiction treatment. Patients of all ages are welcome to call or visit.

come to your hotel or apartment, arrange for tests, prescribe medications, admit patients to hospitals, and provide nurses. They also give travel immunizations and consultations, and they are an official WHO-designated yellow-fever vaccination site. The urgent-care center is also available around the clock by appointment for patients not requiring a house call. Payment is expected at time of service; credit cards are accepted. All physicians are board-certified and have an exemplary bedside manner.

PASSPORT HEALTH

1001 Ave of the Americas (bet 37th and 38th St), Suite 1215   212/403-2823
By appointment   passporthealthusa.com

Travel to certain overseas destinations may require immunizations and/or vaccinations. Passport Health has competent, professional physicians and nurses with up-to-date health information from the Centers for Disease Control and World Health Organization. Travel-related products and conveniences are also available.

MOVERS

BIG APPLE MOVING & STORAGE

83 Third Ave (bet Bergen and Dean St), Brooklyn 212/505-1861, 718/768-7818
Mon-Fri: 9-5   bigapplemoving.com

Big Apple Moving & Storage has a sterling reputation and receives high marks from satisfied customers. Even though they are located in downtown Brooklyn, they do 80% of their moving business in Manhattan. They are experts with antiques, art, and high-end moves, yet manage to keep rates reasonable. You'll find moving supplies at their "do-it-yourself" moving store where every size of box, container, and wood crate for moving or storage is stocked. They also have bubble pack, plate dividers, custom paper, and "French wraps" for crystal and delicate breakables. For those who need overnight or short-term storage, Big Apple will keep your entire truckload of furniture inside their high-security, heated warehouse. Interstate and international moving is also provided, and every item is fully wrapped and padded before leaving your residence.

THE BOX BUTLER
Daily: Delivery and pick up   888/881-0810
                                                              theboxbutler.com

So where can you store seasonal clothes, sports equipment, suitcases, and Christmas decorations? The Box Butler offers short- or long-term storage options. They deliver empty containers and locks to your residence or business. You box the items and inventory the contents. The containers are then transported to their secure warehouse for storage. When you need your items, contact them for delivery. The monthly rate is based upon the size of your container. The Box Butler is also good for stowing trade-show displays, client records, and furniture and household items during a remodeling job.

BROWNSTONE BROS. MOVING
321 Rider Ave (at 140th St), The Bronx   718/665-5000
Mon-Fri: 9:30-5   brownstonebros.com

Brownstone Bros. has been offering packing, moving and storage services with a very personal touch since 1977. They are highly rated by customers. Here's a good tip from them: to avoid the inconvenience of temporary loss, personally move your medicines, remote-control devices, and other important small items to your next location.

MOVING RIGHT ALONG
101-21 101st St, Ozone Park, NY   718/738-2468
Mon-Fri: 9-5; Sat: 9-1:30   movingrightalong.com

With three decades of service and a top-quality reputation, Moving Right Along is an excellent choice if you have a move ahead of you. Moving, storage, packing, and crating are offered. Their handy home-cleaning and junk-removal service will help get your residence ready for quick occupancy. Be sure to check out their Furniture Depot for pre-owned furniture, antiques, and imports.

WEST SIDE MOVERS
963 Columbus Ave (bet 107th and 108th St)   212/874-3800
Mon-Fri: 8-6; Sat: 9-3; Sun: 10-3   westsidemovers.com

This well-respected moving company is a family-run business that started in the kitchen of a studio apartment back in 1972. From its Upper West Side location, West Side Movers continues to offer dependable residential and

---

Moving Your Treasures
FlatRate Moving (212/988-9292) uses only the most experienced and trained movers to perform "Elite Luxury Moving Services." Special collections, such as wine, necessitate special handling. They take extreme care in packing, padding, and labeling items. Then they inventory, photograph, and transport the goods in secure vans.

office moving, including disassembly and short-term storage. They are expert in the handling of fine art and antiques. Close attention is paid to efficiency, promptness, and courtesy. Packing consultants will help do-it-yourselfers select moving boxes and other supplies; boxes come in a multitude of sizes, including four different options for mirrors alone.

OFFICE SERVICES

PURGATORY PIE PRESS

19 Hudson St (bet Duane and Reade St), Room 403   212/274-8228
Mon-Fri: by appointment   purgatorypiepress.com

Purgatory Pie Press is ideal for small printing jobs. They do graphic design and handset typography, hand letterpress printing, die-cutting, and hand bookbinding. They'll also create envelopes, logos, and other identity designs. They can even design handmade paper with unique watermarks. Specialties include printing and calligraphy for weddings and parties. They also make limited-edition postcards and artists' books. Private lessons and small group classes are offered in letterpress printing.

WORLD-WIDE BUSINESS CENTRES

575 Madison Ave (at 57th St), 10th floor   212/605-0200, 800/296-9922
Mon-Fri: 9-5:30   wwbcn.com

World-Wide Business Centres caters to executives who need more than a hotel room and to companies that need a fully-equipped, furnished, and staffed office in New York on short notice. A full range of well-trained office staff and telecommunication services are available. Desk space, private offices, and conference rooms may be rented on a temporary (hourly, daily, weekly, or monthly) basis.

OPTICIANS

E.B. MEYROWITZ AND DELL OPTICIANS

19 W 44th St (at Fifth Ave)   212/575-1686
Mon-Fri: 9-5:45; Sat: 10-4:30   ebmeyrowitz-dell.com

E.B. Meyrowitz does on-the-spot repair of eyeglasses, and you're welcome to stop by for regular optical needs, too. The large frame selection includes various materials ranging from 18-K gold to buffalo horn to titanium. Just bring your prescription; opticians are ready and waiting.

PAINTING

ALLCITYPAINTING

65 Water St (at Old Slip)   888/896-7950
Mon-Fri: 8 a.m.-9 p.m.; Sat, Sun: 8-5   allcitypainting.com

AllCityPainting will gladly take over when you're sprucing up your residential or commercial environs. They'll paint inside or out, hang wallpaper, perform tile glazing, plaster, refinish hardwood floors, and even remodel an entire kitchen or bathroom. They expertly patch, spackle, and repair damaged areas before getting started. Interior designers and architects are among the clients who appreciate their quick turnaround time and neat, professional workmanship. They are licensed, insured, and EPA-certified.

BERNARD GARVEY PAINTING

By appointment   718/894-8272

Bernard Garvey is a meticulous, reliable painter who can also do plastering and decorative finishes. His team serves residential clients, and customers tout the reasonable prices, positive attitude, and terrific work.

GOTHAM PAINTING COMPANY

336 E 94th St (bet First and Second Ave), #1-E   212/427-5752
Mon-Fri: 9-5

If you need interior painting or wallpapering for your home, Gotham is a good resource. For over two decades they have done spray work, restoration, faux painting, and plastering. There are more than 50 full-time painters on staff, and all are fully licensed and bonded.

PARENTING RESOURCES

92ND STREET Y PARENTING CENTER

395 Lexington Ave (at 92nd St)   212/415-5611
Mon-Fri: 9-5 (office hours)   92y.org/parentingcenter

Just about everything the 92nd Street Y does is impressive, and its Parenting Center is no exception. It offers every kind of class you can imagine: a newborn-care class for expectant parents, prenatal yoga, boot camp for dads, a cooking class for preschoolers, a step-parenting class, and so on. Workshops and seminars are offered on a wide range of topics, from sleep problems to setting limits. They host drop-in sessions such as parent get-togethers. Perhaps most important, they act as a parenting resource and support center for members and the general public.

PARENTS LEAGUE

115 E 82nd St (bet Lexington and Park Ave)   212/737-7385
Mon-Thurs: 9-4; Fri: 9-noon   parentsleague.org

Celebrating 100 years in 2013, this nonprofit organization is a gold mine for parents in New York. They provide advisory services to families applying to preschools, private K-12 schools in the city, boarding schools, and for special-needs and summer camps and programs. In addition to putting together a calendar of events for parents of children of all ages, the Parents League maintains extensive files on summer camps, early-childhood programs, and private schools throughout the city. For a membership fee of $175 per academic year, you can access the online database of 1,500 resources, and attend workshops and other events.

Nannies at the Ready

If you need a nanny at the last minute, call **A Choice Nanny** (850 Seventh Ave, Suite 706, 212/246-5437, achoicenanny/nyc.com). Alan and Joan Friedman carefully screen personnel and offer several search options.

Another recommended source for nannies is **Pavillion Agency** (15 E 40th St, Suite 400, 212/889-6609), which is very reliable.

SOHO PARENTING
568 Broadway (at Prince St), Suite 402   212/334-3744
Mon-Fri: 8-8 (by appointment)   sohoparenting.com

Soho Parenting is dedicated to helping parents move through the changing stages of parenthood with support and guidance. It conducts workshops and group discussions for parents of newborns, toddlers, and older children. Individual therapy and couples counseling is available, too.

PARTY SERVICES

BUBBY GRAM
Mon-Thurs: 11-7; Fri: 11-5   212/353-3886
bubbygram.com

If creating fun and laughter is on your mind, then call this number. These folks have outrageous and humorous acts that run the gamut from simple singing telegrams to complete shows for gags, parties or business meetings. They'll provide celebrity impersonators, roasts, magicians, psychics, belly dancers, wedding officiants, and much more. Contact them after hours via their website.

ECLECTIC/ENCORE PROPS
620 W 26th St (at Eleventh Ave), 4th floor   212/645-8880
Mon-Fri: 9-5   eclecticprops.com

Their name says it all. Eclectic/Encore Props specializes in hard-to-find props for a theme party, a set for motion pictures or television, or a novel product announcement. They have been in business since 1986 and are known for an extensive collection of 18th-, 19th-, and 20th-century furniture and accessories. They have everything from an armoire to a zebra — even a rickshaw.

EXPRESSWAY MUSIC DJ
10 E 39th St (bet Fifth and Madison Ave)   212/953-9367
By appointment   expresswaymusic.com

Expressway Music DJ will furnish stylish DJs, karaoke services, and live music to your wedding, corporate party, or other special event. DJs and musicians are chosen according to your specifications for music style. All performers are professional and polished — soloists, trios, and specialty bands. Expressway will make sure your event is both unique and memorable.

LINDA KAYE'S PARTYMAKERS
23 E 69th St (bet Madison and Park Ave)   212/288-7112
Mon-Fri: 10-5:30 (parties available 7 days a week)   partymakers.com

Linda Kaye's Partymakers will handle every detail of your party, from invitation to cleanup. Themed children's birthday parties are offered at several locations. They also do safari-themed birthday parties, using the restaurant Serafina as a base camp and then moving on to the Central Park Zoo. Parties at the American Museum of Natural History have such themes as Dinosaur Discovery and Cosmic Blast Off. Partymakers also offers Linda Kaye's signature Bake-a-Cake party for ages four and up. The adult division of Partymakers specializes in corporate picnics and holiday parties, as well as grand openings. The website is a resource for birthday-party ideas, entertainers, and locations. Their blog, the Party Times, provides a steady stream of celebration ideas.

MARCY BLUM ASSOCIATES

55 Fifth Ave (bet 12th and 13th St), 19th floor   212/929-9814
By appointment   marcyblum.com

    Marcy Blum is a great lady, and she is so well organized that no matter what the event — wedding, reception, corporate event, birthday party, bar mitzvah, or dinner for the boss — she will execute it to perfection. As anyone knows, it's the details that count, and Marcy is superb at the nitty-gritty. Her events are beautiful, stylish, and somewhat surprising. Many celebrity weddings have been created by this talented "eventista."

PARTY POOPERS

By appointment   212/274-9955
                                                        partypoopers.com

    Established in 1991, Party Poopers is highly regarded in Manhattan's event-organizing world. This full-service party-planning company can handle a job as simple as booking entertainment all the way to designing and implementing an entire event. Party Poopers' roster of top entertainers, caterers, designers, DJs, and specialty acts will ensure that you have the best possible party. Although their niche is whimsical interactive kids' parties (Pirates on the Peking is a favorite!), they have launched an adult division called party-SWANK.

PEN REPAIR

FOUNTAIN PEN HOSPITAL

10 Warren St (bet Broadway and Church St)   212/964-0580, 800/253-7367
Mon-Fri: 8-5:30   fountainpenhospital.com

    Since 1946 this experienced establishment has been selling and repairing fountain pens of all types. A knowledgeable staff is at-the-ready with advice on an extensive parts and tools inventory for "do-it-yourselfers." Fountain Pen Hospital also carries one of the world's largest selections of modern and vintage writing tools.

Repair Services

Here is a listing of some special services to be found in Manhattan:

Ceramics: **Ceramic Restorations** (224 W 29th St, 12th floor, 212/564-8669; by appointment)

Chimney cleaning and repairs: **Homestead Chimney** (800/242-7668; Tues-Fri: 8-4; by appointment)

Clothing repairs: **Ban's Custom Tailor Shop** (1544 First Ave, 212/570-0444)

Glassware: **Glass Restorations** (1597 York Ave, 212/517-3287)

Leather: **Falotico Studio** (315 E 91st St, 212/369-1217)

Watch repair: **Master of Time** (15 W 47th St, Booth 8, 212/354-8463)

Woodwork restoration: **Traditional Line** (212/627-3555; by appointment)

Let's Dance!

When you need to learn how to gracefully hold your own on the dance floor, contact these studios. Most classes are geared for couples.

Dance Manhattan (39 W 19th St, 5th floor, 212/807-0802): group and private lessons, wedding-dance specialists

Dance with Me (466 Broome St, 212/840-3262): cofounded by dance professional Maksim Chmerkovskiy

DanceSport (22 W 34th St, 212/307-1111): group and private lessons, ballroom and Latin

Fred Astaire Dance Studios (201 E 34th St, 212/697-6535; 328 E 61st St, 212/209-2410; and 174 W 72nd St, 212/595-3200): private lessons; ballroom, Latin, swing, salsa, the Hustle

NY Wedding and Partner Dance (1261 Broadway, Suite 510, 646/742-1520): private lessons only, all genres of dance, three private rooms

PERSONAL SERVICES

ACK! ORGANIZING

646/831-9625
ackorganizing.com

Want to get and stay organized? Alison Kero is an expert in organization, time management, and productivity, whether it be for home or office. She will teach you the tools to get rid of unwanted clutter and move to a freer, organized future. Help is also available for relocations and home staging in preparation for a move. Pricing is by the hour with a three-hour minimum.

AL MARTINO DOMESTIC STAFFING

60 E 42nd St (bet Park and Madison Ave), Suite 2227   212/867-1910
Mon-Fri: 9:30-5:30   martinodom.com

The specialty at Al Martino Domestic Staffing is private chefs, but this agency has also been providing clientele with highly qualified butlers, housekeepers, nannies, estate managers, personal assistants, and chauffeurs since 1972. Look to Al Martino for party and seasonal help as well. Al Martino's fees are competitive and incorporate a long-term replacement service guarantee. They are completely licensed, bonded, and insured.

CELEBRITIES STAFFING SERVICES

20 Vesey St (bet Church St and Broadway), Suite 510   212/227-3877
Mon-Fri: 9-5   celebrities-staffing.com

Turn to Celebrities Staffing when you are looking to hire top-of-the-line baby nurses, governesses, nannies, "mannies" (male nannies), housekeepers, ladies' maids, butlers, housemen, chefs and cooks, couples, laundresses, house managers, estate managers, personal assistants, personal shoppers, chauffeurs, bodyguards, caregivers, companions, and other types of household personnel. Their services extend across the U.S. and internationally with clients who include royalty, celebrities, dignitaries, top executives, and families who are simply looking to hire the best.

CROSS IT OFF YOUR LIST

60 Madison Ave (at 27th St), Suite 1020   212/725-0122
Mon-Fri: 9-6   crossitoffyourlist.com

These folks will do virtually anything to help busy people manage their lives: organize closets and file cabinets, oversee a move, help with daily chores, pack bags, pick up or hold your mail, even provide on-call personal assistants. Cross It Off Your List can help you do just that!

FASHION UPDATE

82 Nassau St (bet John and Fulton St), Suite 318   718/897-0381, 888/447-2846
Mon-Fri: 9-5   fashionupdate.com

Sarah Gardner is the "Queen of Bargains." She started her business over 25 years ago by ferreting out substantial savings for clothing her family. She publishes *Fashion Update,* a quarterly publication that uncovers hundreds of bargains per season in women's, men's, and children's designer clothing, accessories, and jewelry. Furniture, home accessories, and spa services, too! She also leads shopping expeditions to designer showrooms and outlets at $175 per person for 2½ hours; group rates are available.   There's a bridal tour package as well.

FLATIRON CLEANING COMPANY

231 W 29th St (bet Seventh and Eighth Ave)   212/876-1000
Mon-Fri: 7-4   flatironcleaning.com

These people have cleaned many homes and apartments since opening in 1893. Expert services include residential house and window cleaning, installing, repairing, and refinishing wood floors, maid service, party help, laundry service, and carpet and upholstery cleaning. They can expertly clean crime scenes, too.

FLOOD'S CLOSET

By appointment   212/348-7257

Need some pampering! Barbara Flood will shop for clothes *for* you or *with* you. In her travels she collects what is pleasing and unique from flea markets, local artisans, and vintage shops. She will arrive at your home with armloads of

---

Learn to Drive

Whether your teen is preparing for his or her driver's license or you are mandated to attend driving classes, these schools provide instruction. Hours vary, as do the slate of services offered, which include defensive driving and parallel parking lessons, as well as instruction for obtaining special licenses.

Attila School of Driving (1690 Second Ave, 212/410-6363): private lessons

Driving Center of New York (1551 Second Ave, 212/396-1300): customized lessons; early and late appointments

Professional Driving School of the Americas (40 E 23rd St, 212/375-1111): prep for the written test

Magic Shop and Museum
Fantasma Magic (421 Seventh Ave, 2nd floor, 212/244-3633) is the largest manufacturer of magic kits in the world. The midtown shop includes two stages, flat screens, a 3D video display, magic props, and a Houdini museum with a huge collection of his original props. A secret VIP room can accommodate 250 to 300 guests for birthday parties and special events, or 75 seated guests for professional magic shows.

unique clothing, accessories, fabrics, and decor. Beyond the shopping, Flood can also help organize closets, as well as perform other time-consuming chores.

GLENN BRISTOW
212/243-0571

Glenn Bristow is a one-woman administrative staff proficient in bookkeeping, paralegal work, computer tasks, and human resources, who also acts as a liaison between clients and insurance companies. She'll work weekly, monthly, quarterly, or whenever you need her assistance (gbfc@panix.com).

INTREPID NEW YORKER
220 E 57th St (bet Second and Third Ave), Suite 2D   212/750-0400
Mon-Fri: 9-6   intrepidny.com

Beginning as a concierge service, Sylvia Ehrlich and her team provide one of the most complete relocation-consulting services in this area. They will help with your home search; arrange temporary housing, furniture rental, and storage; set up bank accounts; or whatever your needs. They maintain an ongoing hotline of resources.

LINDQUIST GROUP
708 Third Ave (at 44th St), Suite 3000   212/644-0990
Mon-Fri: 8:30-5   thelindquistgroup.com

With more than a hundred years experience, the Lindquist Group specializes in providing household staffing for an affluent clientele. You can be sure of highly-qualified butlers, cooks, housekeepers, chauffeurs, nannies, personal assistants, and estate couples. Temporary and permanent workers are available, many on a moment's notice. Employment references, criminal records, and drivers' licenses are checked independently.

MAID FOR YOU NEW YORK
718/433-1499
maidforyounewyork.com

Maid for You claims to be one of the largest residential and commercial cleaning services in New York. They offer free estimates and will customize a program for your specific needs — daily, weekly, monthly, or upon moving in or moving out. They do windows, floors and carpets; pick up dry cleaning; and remove and dispose of unwanted items (one room or an entire building). The highly-trained and uniformed employees provide quality "green" cleaning services at competitive rates. You can call their friendly customer-service line anytime to schedule an appointment.

NEW YORK'S LITTLE ELVES

151 First Ave (bet 8th and 9th St), Suite 204   212/673-5507
Mon-Fri: 8-6 (call for appointment)   nyelves.com

No need to worry about cleaning up! These folks will do the job, whether it is a normal dusting or cleaning up after a big party — even post-construction jobs. They can do window, chandelier, carpet, and upholstery cleaning. They provide free estimates, employ screened personnel, carry liability insurance, are fully bonded, and have an outstanding reputation.

PAVILLION AGENCY

15 E 40th St (bet Fifth and Madison Ave), Suite 400   212/889-6609
Mon-Fri: 9-5   pavillionagency.com

Pavillion has been a family business since 1962. If you are in need of nannies, baby nurses, housekeepers, laundresses, domestic couples, butlers, chefs, chauffeurs, caretakers, gardeners, property managers, or personal assistants, call and ask for Keith or Clifford Greenhouse. Applicants are screened by a private firm. They can also assist with payroll processing and on-site training.

TALK POWER, A PANIC CLINIC FOR PUBLIC SPEAKING

333 E 23rd St (bet First and Second Ave)   212/684-1711
By appointment   talkpowerinc.com

Need to speak to a group but experience intense anxiety? Talk Power will help you overcome the phobia. They are true professionals whose niche is training clients via a "panic clinic" for public speaking. Individual or group training as well as workshops are available.

UNAME IT ORGANIZERS

226 E 10th St (bet First and Second Ave), Suite 222   212/598-9868
By appointment   masterorganizers.com

Call uName It to do those tasks you've been putting off. They *can*, they *do*, and they *will*. This company has been freeing up time for people who can't get certain jobs done themselves. They perform over 200 services, including uncluttering, providing personal assistants or clergy, special editing, event planning, handling a traffic ticket, and even finding a soulmate. In the crowded field of organizers, uName It has been in business for over 15 years with many kudos from customers, so they must be doing something right.

WHITE GLOVE ELITE

39 W 32nd St (bet Fifth Ave and Broadway), Suite 504 212/684-4460
Mon-Fri: 9-6; Sat: 9-3 (cleaners available anytime)   whitegloveelite.org

Actors Sarah and Jim Ireland started this business as an adjunct to their stage careers. They provide trained cleaners for apartments in Manhattan, The Bronx, Brooklyn, and Queens. Many of their workers are also food servers. About half of their personnel are actors between jobs.

ZOE INTERNATIONAL HOMECARE

20 Vesey St (bet Church St and Broadway), Suite 510   212/227-3880
Mon-Fri: 9-5 (24-hour emergency service)   zoehomecare.com

Zoe International Homecare specializes in the placement of private-pay

Pawnbrokers

Looking for a short-term loan or to sell some of your goods for quick cash? Try these pawnshops:

Gem Pawnbrokers (3600 Broadway, 212/283-3333)

Lincoln Square Pawnbrokers (724 Amsterdam Ave, 212/865-8860)

New York Pawnbrokers (177 Rivington St, 212/228-7177)

caregivers — nurses and nurses' aides, home health- and personal-care aides, companions, and housekeepers to work for the elderly, sick, and chronically ill. The agency also has newborn specialists. They work closely with doctors, hospitals, health-care organizations, family members, friends, attorneys, estate planners, and others involved in a patient's life. Caregivers are available for live-in or live-out and they can work day or night shifts or provide 24-hour service. Specially priced packages are available for families on fixed incomes.

PHOTOGRAPHIC SERVICES

CLASSIC KIDS

1182 Lexington Ave (bet 80th and 81st St)	212/396-1160
395 Amsterdam Ave (at 79th St)	212/799-3730
Tues-Sat: 8:30-5:30 (by appointment)	classickidsphotography.com

Classic Kids is part of a consortium of child photographers who produce black-and-white and hand-tinted photographs of kids and families. No stuffy formal sittings are allowed; it's strictly fun for everyone involved. Belly laughs, mischievous grins, and playful poses are artistically captured to evoke treasured memories. The end products are heirloom pieces created the old-fashioned way: with film and handmade prints.

DEMETRIAD STUDIOS

1674 Broadway (at 52nd St), 4th floor	212/315-3400
Mon-Sat: 9-7	demetriad.com

Since 1985, this energetic, six-person team has parlayed their expertise into commercial portraiture and head-shot photography, as well as digital imaging and restoration of old and damaged photographs. They are pros at image retouching and high-end portrait and editorial photography. They also design individual and small-business websites.

HAND HELD FILMS

129 W 27th St (bet Ave of the Americas and Seventh Ave)	212/502-0900
Mon-Fri: 9-6	handheldfilms.com

Hand Held Films rents motion picture equipment for feature films, commercials, music videos, and documentaries, both for large and small productions. Digital high-definition cameras, lenses and accessories, and lighting are available. They have an impressive list of equipment — even a 20-foot truck to haul everything to your set.

PLUMBING AND HEATING

KAPNAG HEATING AND PLUMBING

150 W 28th St (at Seventh Ave), Suite 501   212/929-7111
24-hour emergency service   kapnagplumbing.com

In business since 1925, Kapnag reliably provides licensed heating and plumbing to New Yorkers. Two dozen professional workers handle plumbing repairs and renovations for kitchens and bathrooms, replace toilets, repair pipes and heating equipment, expertly diagnose plumbing system problems, install and repair sprinkler systems, and more.

RENTAL HOUSING AGENT

SHELLEY SAXTON

917/826-4195

Looking for an apartment in Manhattan? Call Shelley Saxton. Also known as the "Duchess of Rent," Shelley specializes in high-end leasing and sales. Her relentless energy and extensive relationships enable her to achieve outstanding results. She brokers with Brown Harris Stevens and is also a member of REBNY/RELO. Clients include international banks, multinational corporations, diplomats, and celebrities.

SCISSORS AND KNIFE SHARPENING

HENRY WESTPFAL & CO.

115 W 25th St (bet Ave of the Americas and Seventh Ave)   212/563-5990
Mon-Fri: 9:30-6   nysharpeningservice.com

The same family has been running Henry Westpfal since 1874. This premier knife-sharpening company does all kinds of sharpening and repair, from barber scissors and pruning shears to cuticle scissors; they'll also work on light tools. Cutlery, shears, scissors, and tools for leather workers are sold here. Even lefthanded scissors!

Online Travel Discounts

Several companies offer online discounts on airfare, car rental, and hotels. You can also call to find great deals in locations around the world.

Bookit.com (888/782-9722, bookit.com)

Expedia (800/397-3342, expedia.com)

Hotels.com (800/246-8357, hotels.com)

Hotwire (866/468-9473, hotwire.com)

Kayak (kayak.com): web only

Orbitz (888/656-4546, orbitz.com)

Priceline (800/658-1496, priceline.com)

Quickbook (800/789-9887, quickbook.com)

Travelocity (888/872-8356, travelocity.com)

Perhaps the best rates for Manhattan hotel rooms can often be obtained at **nycgo.com** (click on "Hotels"). Remember that prices change from day to day and even hour to hour.

Emergency Dentist

An evening or weekend dental emergency is both inconvenient and painful, especially if you are away from home. **Dr. Isaac Datikashvili, Emergency Dentist NYC** (8 Gramercy Park S, 212/486-9458, emergencydentistnyc.com) — Dr. Isaac, for short — will come to the rescue! He is available during normal business hours, weekends, evenings, and holidays to treat toothaches, perform emergency extractions and root canals, and re-cement crowns.

SHIPPING AND PACKAGING

UNITED SHIPPING & PACKAGING

200 E 10th St (at Second Ave)   212/475-2214
Mon-Fri: 10:30-8; Sat: 11-6

Known for their great service, United Shipping will send anything anywhere in the world! They also sell packaging supplies and boxes. Additional services include faxing, mailboxes, office supplies, and messenger services.

SHOE REPAIR

CESAR'S SHOE REPAIR

180 Seventh Ave (bet 20th and 21st St)   212/961-6119
Mon-Fri: 7:30-7; Sat: 9-6   cesarsshoerepair.com

Third-generation cobbler Edward Andrade and his skilled craftsmen implement the latest technologies to repair and refurbish shoes, boots, handbags, and other leather items. Besides the usual sole and heel repairs, Cesar's Shoe Repair can customize boots with calf extensions and stretching, zipper replacement, ankle tapering, and shortening the height of a boot.

JIM'S SHOE REPAIRING

50 E 59th St (bet Madison and Park Ave)   212/355-8259
Mon-Fri: 8-6; Sat: 9-4 (closed Sat in summer)   jimsshoerepair.com

This family operation has been offering first-rate shoe repair, shoeshines, and shoe supplies since 1932. The shoe-repair field has steadily been losing its craftsmen, and this is one of the few shops that upholds the tradition. Owner Jim Rocco specializes in orthopedic shoe and boot alterations. Bags and belts receive superior treatment, too.

LEATHER SPA

10 W 55th St (bet Fifth Ave and Ave of the Americas)   212/262-4823
Mon-Fri: 8-7; Sat: 10-6

Plaza Hotel Retail Boutiques
1 W 58th St (at Fifth Ave)   212/527-9944
Mon-Fri: 10-7; Sat: 10-6; Sun: noon-4

Grand Central Terminal (42nd St at Vanderbilt Ave), lower level   212/661-0307
Mon-Fri: 7-6:30; Sat: 10-5   leatherspa.com

Quality work is done here — shoe and handbag repair and reconditioning and custom work — and you will pay well for it. Notable luxury stores using their service include Manolo Blahnik, Jimmy Choo, and Gucci, to name a few. Leather Spa also offers delivery.

PAVLOS SHOE REPAIR

125 E 88th St (bet Lexington and Park Ave)   212/876-8569
Mon-Fri: 7-6; Sat: 8-5

Pavlos performs such customary tasks as repairing, cleaning, dyeing, and stretching shoes. They also shorten or lengthen heels or alter calf lengths on boots. Most leather items — boots, purses, luggage, jackets, and briefcases — can be rejuvenated here. A full range of shoe-care, shoe-fitting, and shoe-comfort products are for sale. Many repeat customers attest to the friendly and quality service at Pavlos, which has been around for almost four decades.

SILVERSMITHS

BRANDT & OPIS

46 W 46th St (bet Fifth Ave and Ave of the Americas), 5th floor   212/302-0294
Mon-Thurs: 8:30-5; Fri: 8:30-2

For anything silver, Roland Markowitz at Brandt & Opis can handle it. This includes silver repair and polishing, buying and selling estate silver, repairing and replating silver-plated items, and fixing silver tea and coffee services. They restore combs and brushes (dresser sets) and replace old knife blades. Other services include gold-plating, lamp restoration, and plating antique bath and door hardware. In short, Brandt & Opis is a complete metal-restoration specialist.

Psychic Services

In addition to his signature mix of tarot and astrology readings, **Joshua** (646/784-3628, psychicjoshua.com) does psychometry (reading photographs), handwriting analysis, and chakra readings. He also does readings for groups and entertains at parties.

THOME SILVERSMITH

49 W 37th St (bet Fifth Ave and Ave of the Americas), 4th floor
Wed, Thurs: 10-5   212/764-5426

Thome Silversmith has been cleaning, repairing, and replating silver since 1931. They also buy and sell magnificent silver pieces. They have a real appreciation for silver and other metal goods, and it shows in everything they do. They will restore antique silver and objets d'art; repair and polish brass and copper; and repair and clean pewter, gold, and bronze. Gold-plating, too!

STAINED-GLASS DESIGN AND RESTORATION

KELLY GLASS STUDIO AND GALLERY

368 E 8th St (bet Ave C and D)   212/677-9480
Call for appointment   kellyglassstudio.net

Patti Kelly, artist and founder of Kelly Glass Studio and Gallery, has over 25 years experience in stained-glass design, fabrication, and restoration. Within the studio, windows, skylights, and room dividers are created for churches, residences, and commercial properties. Patti imparts her knowledge of stained-glass design to small groups at eight-week sessions that cost $535. So if you want to introduce the warm beauty of stained glass to your space, do like top

Tailors

Bespoke (custom) tailoring is available from these folks. Most work by appointment only.

Alton Lane (11 W 25th St, 5th floor, 646/896-1212): a 3D body scanner records 300 measurements; 25 lining choices

Bespoke Tailors (509 Madison Ave, 212/888-6887)

Cameo Cleaners of Gramercy Park (284 Third Ave, 212/677-3949)

Domenico Vacca (781 Fifth Ave, 212/759-6333): He will do good things for your figure.

Dynasty Custom Tailors (6 E 38th St, 212/679-1075): dresses and wedding gowns

Fioravanti Bespoke Custom Tailors (45 W 57th St, Suite 402, 212/355-1540)

Ghost Tailor (153 W 27th St, 11th floor, 212/253-9727): dressmaker; one-of-a-kind wedding gowns and heirloom-dress reconstruction

Leonard Logsdail (9 E 53rd St, 212/752-5030)

Nino Corvato (420 Madison Ave, Suite 406, 212/980-4980)

architects and interior designers and seek her out. Selected finished pieces are on display and ready to purchase.

TAILORS

BHAMBI'S CUSTOM TAILORS

14 E 60th St (bet Madison and Fifth Ave), Suite 610   212/935-5379
By appointment   bhambis.com

At Bhambi's Custom Tailors you'll discover the incomparable luxury of a bespoke suit in the best British tradition at Bhambi's Custom Tailors. This longstanding family business combines style, quality, tradition, and skill to make suits, jackets, slacks, tuxedos, and shirts that will flatter the successful businessman or professional. A distinguished list of satisfied clients attests to Bhambi's superior merchandise and fair prices.

CEGO CUSTOM SHIRTMAKER

246 Fifth Ave (at 28th St), Suite 200   212/620-4512
Mon-Fri: 9:30-6; Sat: 10-3:30 (by appointment)   cego.com

For over two decades, service-oriented owner Carl Goldberg has been making quality shirts for both media types and regular people. Shirts are patterned, cut, and tailored by the experienced Goldberg team. Delivery usually takes two to three weeks. If time is important, shirts can produced in as little as two days. Prices start at $95 for Pima cotton broadcloth and go up to $400 for superb materials from Italy and Switzerland. The five-shirt minimum can be waived for weddings, gift certificates, and students.

MOHAN'S CUSTOM TAILORS

60 E 42nd St (bet Park and Madison Ave), Suite 1432   212/697-0050
Mon-Sat: 10-7:30; Sun   mohantailors.com

Mohan Ramchandani opened his doors in 1972 and has since created over 150,000 custom suits. In addition, Mohan's makes coats, sports jackets, slacks, shirts, and formal wear from over 10,000 fabric samples. To achieve the best-fitting suits, 25 measurements are taken. For one year after a piece is made, they offer free alterations if you lose or gain weight.

NELSON TAILOR SHOP

170 Rivington St (bet Attorney and Clinton St)   212/253-7071
Mon-Sat: 9-6

Magical work is done inside this unassuming tailoring shop, where dependable and reasonable are the bywords. Coats are relined, pants and skirts are shortened or lengthened, waistbands are let out or nipped in, necklines are reshaped, sleeves are made to fit, and whole garments are given an updated look at a fraction of the cost for a new item. Out-of-town customers have been known to pack their ill-fitting or damaged clothes, dropping them off at Nelson when they arrive and returning home with wearable, tailored attire.

PEPPINO TAILORS

138 E 61st St (at Lexington Ave), Suite 205   212/832-3844
Mon-Fri: 9-6:30; Sat: 9-3:30   peppinotailors.com

The fine craftsmen at Peppino Tailors have been tailoring clothes since 1973. All types of garments, including evening and bridal wear (for men and women), receive expert attention for alterations. Delivery is offered.

WINSTON TAILORS/CHIPP2

28 W 44th St (bet Fifth Ave and Ave of the Americas), lobby   212/687-0850
Mon-Fri: 7:15-4:30 (or by appointment)   chipp2.com

Paul Winston oversees the tailors at this family-owned business. The shop, also known as Chipp2, was started by Paul's father, who measured the likes of John and Robert Kennedy, among other famous clients. Known for turning out highly-coveted custom casual wear, Winston offers an array of brightly colored and unusual fabrics, including tussah silk. A big part of this business is making logo ties for companies, clubs, and groups. They also craft "dog" ties and canine-

---

Before Traveling Overseas

Overseas travelers can find valuable information and obtain immunizations at these places:

Travel Health Services (50 E 69th St, 212/734-3000; Mon-Fri, by appointment)

Traveler's Medical Service of New York (595 Madison Ave, Suite 1200, 212/230-1020; Mon-Fri: 9-4, by appointment)

Travelers' Wellness Center (952 Fifth Ave, Room 10, 212/737-1212; by appointment, hours vary)

> **Umbrella Repair**
>
> If your favorite umbrella has a broken rib, runner, tube, or stretcher, or if the fabric is ripped or worn, call umbrella repairman extraordinaire **Gilbert Center** (917/692-2078, gilcenter@aol.com). He takes great care to bring designer and vintage umbrellas back to life.

themed products for humans: ties, belts, suspenders, wallets, pillows, watches, and cuff links featuring a hundred different breeds. They will even apply your own pooch's happy face to a tie or some other item of your choosing!

TRANSLATION SERVICES
TRANSLINGUA
211 E 43rd St (bet Second and Third Ave), Suite 1404 212/697-2020
Mon-Fri: 9-5 translingua.com

Translingua is a total language solution by a team of business professionals. They provide a full complement of linguistic services in over 80 languages and dialects. Services include cultural consultation, translation, interpretation, website and software localization, desktop publishing, and audio and video production with subtitles and voiceovers.

TRAVEL SERVICES
PASSPORT PLUS
20 E 49th St (bet Fifth and Madison Ave), 3rd floor 212/759-5540
Mon-Fri: 9:30-5 passportplus.net

Getting a passport and the proper visas can be difficult and time-consuming. Passport Plus takes care of these chores by securing business and tourist travel documents; renewing and amending U.S. passports; obtaining duplicate marriage certificates; and obtaining international drivers' licenses. They work closely with the U.S. Passport Agency and foreign consulates and embassies. Passport Plus offers assistance in case of lost or stolen passports. These folks serve customers all over the country.

UNIFORM RENTAL
I. BUSS-ALLAN UNIFORM
121 E 24th St (bet Lexington and Park Ave), 7th floor 212/529-4655
Mon-Fri: 9-5 ibuss-allan.com

I. Buss-Allan Uniform has been renting and selling work apparel for several decades. Doormen, concierges, police and security personnel, firemen, maintenance and housekeeping staff, chefs, and others — all will find quality uniforms here.

WINDOW CLEANING
EXPERT WINDOW CLEANERS
212/831-1115
expertwindowcleaners.com

Yes, they do windows! Brent Weingard's window cleaning team assesses each job before they start. Different types of glass and grunge require various products and methods. Their expertise in window cleaning has led to a specialty in glass restoration, a process resulting in like-new condition at a fraction of the replacement cost. They also do building waterproofing and caulking.

FRANK'S WINDOW CLEANING COMPANY

212/288-4631

Are your windows, mirrors, or chandeliers dirty? If so, then call Frank's to put the sparkle and shine back on your glass surfaces. The experienced crew will also do general cleaning, floor waxing, and rug cleaning.

RED BALL WINDOW CLEANING

221 E 85th St (bet Second and Third Ave), Suite 4   212/861-7686
Mon-Sat: 7-5   redballwindowcleanersnyc.com

The people at Red Ball have cleaned a lot of windows since opening in 1928! Still a family business, they specialize in residential and commercial window cleaning. The higher the windows, the happier they are. The work is guaranteed; cash and checks only.

Chapter 6

WHERE TO
BUY IT

NEW YORK'S
BEST STORES

Absolutely anything you're looking for can be found in this great metropolis including extravagant luxuries at exorbitant prices, budget-friendly necessities at discount stores, and everything in between. Giant department stores offer huge selections for men, women, children, and the home. Specialty outlets feature every well-known or obscure item you might be seeking. There are more shopping options: street peddlers, marketplaces, e-commerce, and special events. How can one possibly make sense of it all? I suggest carefully reading this entire chapter for starters.

You will find all of the information you need for shopping in Manhattan, with the most useful and complete array of information available anywhere. Discovering a real treasure is still possible, so good luck and have fun!

GERRY'S
EXCLUSIVE
LIST

GERRY'S EXCLUSIVE LIST
THE BEST PLACES TO SHOP FOR SPECIFIC ITEMS IN NEW YORK

THINGS FOR THE PERSON (Men, Women, Children)

Accessories, fashion (vintage and contemporary) | **Eye Candy Store** (225 W 23rd St, 212/343-4275)

Accessories, women's | **Marc Jacobs** (385 Bleecker St, 212/924-6126)

Backpacks | **Bag House** (797 Broadway, 212/260-0940)

Briefcases | **Per Tutti** (49 Greenwich Ave, 212/675-0113)

Canes, walking | **Rain or Shine** (45 E 45th St, 212/741-9650)

Clothing, casual | **Mr. Joe** (500 Eighth Ave, 212/279-1090)

Clothing, children's (infants through teens) | **Lester's** (1534 Second Ave, 212/734-9292)

Clothing, children's French | **Catimini** (1125 Madison Ave, 212/987-0688) and **Jacadi** (1242 Madison Ave, 212/369-1616)

Clothing, children's (funky and fun) | **Space Kiddets** (26 E 22nd St, 212/420-9878)

Clothing, children's party dresses and suits | **Prince and Princess** (41 E 78th St, 212/879-8989)

Clothing, contemporary | **Theory** (40 Gansevoort St, 212/524-6790; flagship store)

Clothing, custom-made (good value) | **Saint Laurie Merchant Tailors** (22 W 32nd St, 5th floor, 212/643-1916; by appointment)

Clothing, designer (samples) | **Showroom Seven** (263 Eleventh Ave, 3rd floor, 212/643-4810)

Clothing, girls' (tweens) | **Berkley Girl** (410 Columbus Ave, 212/877-4770) and **Infinity** (1116 Madison Ave, 212/734-0077)

Clothing (good-quality) | **J. Crew** (91 Fifth Ave, 212/255-4848 and other locations)

Clothing, jeans, custom-finish | **Jean Shop** (435 W 14th St, 212/366-5326)

Clothing, jeans (discounted) | **Buffalo Exchange** (332 E 11th St, 212/260-9340 and 114 W 26th St, 212/675-3535), **OMG, The Jeans Store** (424 Broadway, 212/925-5190), and **Quiksilver** (3 Times Square, 212/840-8111; 587 Fifth Ave, 212/888-7526; and 519 Broadway, 212/226-1193)

Clothing, jeans (good quality) | **G-Star** (270 Lafayette St, 212/219-2744), **Lucky Brand Retail Store** (1151 Third Ave, 646/422-1192 and other locations), **Madewell** (115 Fifth Ave, 212/228-5172), **Paige Premium Denim** (869 Washington St, 212/807-1400; 245 Columbus Ave, 212/769-1500; and 71 Mercer St, 212/625-0800), and **Uniqlo** (666 Fifth Ave, 31 W 34th St, and 546 Broadway; 877/486-4756 for all locations)

Clothing, lingerie (discounted) | **Howard Sportswear** (69 Orchard St, 212/226-4307) and **Orchard Corset** (157 Orchard St, 212/674-0786)

Clothing, lingerie, fantasy | **Agent Provocateur** (133 Mercer St, 212/965-0229 and 675 Madison Ave, 212/840-2436)

Clothing, lingerie, fine | **Bra Smyth** (905 Madison Ave, 212/772-9400 and 2177 Broadway, 212/721-5111) and **Peress** (1006 Madison Ave, 212/861-6336)

Clothing, lingerie, post-breast surgery | **Underneath It All** (320 Fifth Ave, 10th floor; 212/717-1976; by appointment)

Clothing, men's boutique | **Odin** (199 Lafayette St, 212/966-0026 and 328 E 11th St, 212/475-0666)

Clothing, men's brand-name (discounted) | **Century 21** (22 Cortlandt St, 212/227-9092) and **L.S. Men's Clothing** (49 W 45th St, 3rd floor, 212/575-0933)

Clothing, men's classic | **FrankStella** (921 Seventh Ave, 212/957-1600 and 440 Columbus Ave, 212/877-5566) and **Peter Elliot** (997 Lexington Ave, 212/570-2301)

Clothing, men's contemporary | **Jay Kos** (55 Houston St, 212/319-2770)

Clothing, men's custom-made | **Alan Flusser** (3 E 48th St, 212/888-4500), **Ascot Chang** (110 Central Park S, 212/759-3333), and **Bhambi's Custom Tailors** (14 E 60th St, Suite 610, 212/935-5379)

Clothing, men's European suits | **Jodamo International** (321 Grand St, 212/219-1039)

Clothing, men's vintage | **Stock** (143 E 13th St, 212/505-2505)

Clothing, outdoor wear | **Eastern Mountain Sports** (530 Broadway, 212/966-8730 and 2152 Broadway, 212/873-4001)

Clothing, sportswear | **Atrium** (644 Broadway, 212/473-9200) and **Paul & Shark** (667 Madison Ave, 212/452-9868)

Clothing, vintage | **Reminiscence** (74 Fifth Ave, 212/243-2292) and **Resurrection** (217 Mott St, 212/625-1374)

Clothing, western | **Western Spirit** (395 Broadway, 212/343-1476)

Clothing, women's | **Juicy Couture** (650 Fifth Ave, 212/796-3360 and other locations)

Clothing, women's all-occasion dresses | **Huminska** (248 Mott St, 212/477-3458) and **Mint Julep** (173 Ludlow St, 212/533-9904)

Clothing, women's bridal and special-occasion | **Kleinfeld** (110 W 20th St, 646/633-4300), **Mary Adams The Dress** (31 E 32nd St, Room 604, 212/473-0237; by appointment), and **Reem Acra** (730 Fifth Ave, Suite 205, 212/308-8760; by appointment)

Clothing, women's bridal and special-occasion, custom-made | **Blue** (248 Mott St, 212/228-7744) and **Jane Wilson-Marquis** (42 E 76th St, 212/452-5335; by appointment)

Clothing, women's classic designer | **Nina McLemore** (135 E 55th St, 7th floor, 212/319-7700) and **Yigal Azrouël** (1011 Madison Ave, 212/929-7525)

Clothing, women's designer (resale) | **Ina** (101 Thompson St, 212/941-4757 and other locations) and **New & Almost New** (171 Mott St, 212/226-6677)

Clothing, women's imported | **Creatures of Comfort** (205 Mulberry St, 212/925-1005) and **Roberta Freymann** (958 Lexington Ave, 212/717-7373)

Clothing, women's maternity (consignment) | **Clementine** (39½ Washington Square S, 212/228-9333)

Clothing, women's pants | **Theory** (201 Columbus Ave, 212/362-3676)

Clothing, women's sportswear (good prices) | **Giselle** (143 Orchard St, 212/673-1900)

Clothing, women's tights | **Club Monaco** (121 Prince St, 212/533-8930)

Clothing and accessories, men's and women's | **Etro** (720 Madison Ave, 212/317-9096)

Clothing and accessories, women's | **Derek Lam** (764 Madison St, 212/966-1616) and **Design in Textiles by Mary Jaeger** (17 Laight St, Suite 21, 212/625-0081)

Cosmetics, men's and women's luxury | **Space NK** (99 Greene St, 212/941-4200)

Eyewear (elegant) | **Morgenthal-Frederics** (944 Madison Ave, 212/744-9444; 399 West Broadway, 212/966-0099; and 699 Madison Ave, 212/838-3090) and **Oliver Peoples** (812 Madison Ave, 212/585-3433 and 366 West Broadway, 212/925-5400)

Eyewear, vintage (discounted) | **Quality Optical** (169 E 92nd St, 212/289-2020)

Fabrics, designer | **B&J Fabrics** (525 Seventh Ave, 212/354-8150)

Fabrics and patterns | **P&S Fabrics and Crafts** (359 Broadway, 212/226-1534)

Fragrances | **Aedes de Venustas** (9 Christopher St, 212/206-8674)

Furs, fashion (best) | **G. Michael Hennessy Furs** (224 W 30th St, Suite 402, 212/695-7991)

Gloves, cashmere knit | **Meg Cohen Design Shop** (59 Thompson St, 212/966-3733)

Gloves, Italian | **Sermoneta Gloves** (609-611 Madison Ave, 212/319-5946)

Handbags, designer | **Lulu Guinness** (394 Bleecker St, 212/367-2120) and **Sigerson Morrison** (28 Prince St, 212/219-3893)

Handbags (magnificent, very expensive, exotic skins) | **Devi Kroell** (717 Madison Ave, 212/644-4499)

Handbags, men's and women's | **Club Monaco** (160 Fifth Ave, 212/352-0936) and **Longchamp** (132 Spring St, 212/343-7444 and 713 Madison Ave, 212/223-1500)

Handbags, vintage | **Sylvia Pines Uniquities** (1102 Lexington Ave, 212/744-5141)

Hats, custom-made fur | **Lenore Marshall** (231 W 29th St, 212/947-5945)

Hats, men's | **J.J. Hat Center** (310 Fifth Ave, 212/239-4368) and **Rod Keenan** (202 W 122nd St, 212/678-9275; by appointment)

Jewelry, charms | **Aaron Basha** (685 Madison Ave, 212/935-1960)

Jewelry, costume | **Lanciani** (992 Madison Ave, 212/717-2759; 826 Lexington Ave, 212/832-2092; and 510 Madison Ave, 212/759-4415) and **Lord & Taylor** (424 Fifth Ave, 212/391-3344)

Jewelry, cuff links | **Links of London** (402 West Broadway, 212/343-8024; 535 Madison Ave, 212/588-1177; and MetLife Building, 200 Park Ave, 212/867-0258) and **The Missing Link** (Showplace Antiques and Design Center, 40 W 25th St, Room 108, 212/645-6928)

Jewelry, cuff links, vintage | **Deco Jewels** (131 Thompson St, 212/253-1222)

Jewelry, custom-designed | **Karen Karch** (38 Gramercy Park N, 212/965-9699) and **Ted Muehling** (52 White St, 212/431-3825)

Jewelry, fine | **S.J. Shrubsole** (104 E 57th St, 212/753-8920) and **Stuart Moore** (411 West Broadway, 212/941-1023)

Jewelry, handmade | **Ten Thousand Things** (423 W 14th St, 212/352-1333) and **Wendy Mink Jewelry** (72 Orchard St, 212/260-5298)

Jewelry, vintage | **Deco Jewels** (131 Thompson St, 212/253-1222) and **Doyle & Doyle** (189 Orchard St, 212/677-9991)

Jewelry, wedding rings | **Wedding Ring Originals** (608 Fifth Ave, Suite 509, 212/751-3940; call ahead)

Leather goods | **Il Bisonte** (120 Sullivan St, 212/966-8773) and **M0851** (415 Broadway, 212/431-3069)

Massage oils | **Fragrance Shop** (65 E 4th St, 212/254-8950)

Millinery, vintage | **Ellen Christine** (99 Vandam St, Room 4E, 212/242-2457; by appointment)

Shaving products | **The Art of Shaving** (141 E 62nd St, 212/317-8436; 373 Madison Ave, 212/986-2905; and other locations) and **C.O. Bigelow Chemists** (414 Ave of the Americas, 212/533-2700)

Shoes (discounted) | **DSW** (40 E 14th St, 212/674-2146) and **Stapleton Shoe Company** (68 Trinity Pl, 212/964-6329)

Shoes, adult | **David Z** (556 Broadway, 212/431-5450; 384 Fifth Ave, 917/351-1484; and other locations), **Dr. Martens** (148 Spring St, 212/226-8500), and **Rag & Bone** (182 Columbus Ave, 212/362-7138; 100 Christopher St, 212/727-2999; and other locations)

Shoes, athletic | **JackRabbit** (42 W 14th St, 212/727-2980 and 1255 Lexington Ave, 212/727-2981)

Shoes, British brand | **Crockett and Jones** (7 W 56th St, 212/582-3800)

Shoes, children's (upscale) | **Harry's Shoes for Kids** (2315 Broadway, 212/874-2034) and **Shoofly** (42 Hudson St, 212/406-3270)

Shoes, men's and women's custom-made | **Eneslow** (470 Park Ave S, 212/477-2300 and 1504 Second Ave, 212/249-3800) and **Oberle Custom Shoes/ Mathias Bootmaker** (1502 First Ave, 212/717-4023)

Shoes, men's handmade | **E. Vogel** (19 Howard St, 212/925-2460)

Shoes, non-leather | **MooShoes** (78 Orchard St, 212/254-6512)

Shoes, sandals, handmade | **Jutta Neumann** (355 E 4th St, 212/982-7048)

Shoes, women's designer | **Sigerson Morrison** (28 Prince St, 212/219-3893) and **United Nude** (25 Bond St, 212/420-6000)

Shoes, women's casual | **Matt Bernson** (20 Harrison St, 212/941-7634)

Skiwear | **Bogner** (380 West Broadway, 212/219-2757; seasonal)

Soaps | **Fresh** (57 Spring St, 212/925-0099 and other locations)

Sunglasses, custom and vintage | **Fabulous Fanny's** (335 E 9th St, 212/533-0637)

Swimwear, men's and boys' | **Vilebrequin** (1007 Madison Ave, 212/650-0353 and 436 West Broadway, 212/431-0673)

Swimwear, women's | **Canyon Beachwear** (1136 Third Ave, 917/432-0732), **Malia Mills Swimwear** (199 Mulberry St, 212/625-2311; 1031 Lexington

Ave, 212/517-7485; and 220 Columbus Ave, 212/874-7200), and **Wolford** (619 Madison Ave, 212/688-4850 and other locations; seasonal)

Ties | **Andrew's Ties** (30 Rockefeller Center, 212/245-4563) and **Tie Coon** (400 Seventh Ave, 212/904-1433)

Ties, custom-made and limited-edition | **Seigo** (1248 Madison Ave, 212/987-0191)

Umbrellas | **Rain or Shine** (45 E 45th St, 212/741-9650)

Uniforms, medical and housekeeping | **Ja-Mil Uniform** (92 Orchard St, 212/677-8190)

Watchbands | **Central Watch** (Grand Central Terminal, 45th St passageway, 212/685-1689)

Watches | **Swatch** (640 Broadway, 212/777-1002; 1528 Broadway, 212/764-5541; and other locations)

Watches (discounted) | **Sandy Yaeger Watch** (578 Fifth Ave, 212/819-0088)

Watches, Swiss Army | **Victorinox Swiss Army Soho** (99 Wooster St, 212/431-4950)

Wedding bands | **Wedding Ring Originals** (608 Fifth Ave, Suite 509, 212/751-3940)

Zippers | **ZipperStop** (27 Allen St, 212/226-3964)

THINGS FOR THE HOME AND OFFICE

Air conditioners | **Elgot Sales** (937 Lexington Ave, 212/879-1200)

Appliances (discounted) | **Price Watchers** (800/336-6694)

Appliances, kitchen | **Gringer & Sons** (29 First Ave, 212/475-0600) and **Zabar's** (2245 Broadway, 212/787-2000)

Art, ancient Greek, Roman, Egyptian, and Near Eastern | **Royal Athena Galleries** (153 E 57th St, 212/355-2033)

Art, erotic | **Erotics Gallery** (41 Union Square W, Room 635, 212/633-2241; by appointment)

Art, 19th- and 20th-century Western | **J.N. Bartfield Fine & Rare Books** (30 W 57th St, 212/245-8890)

Art, 20th-century dadaist and surrealist | **Timothy Baum** (40 E 18th St, 212/879-4512; by appointment)

Art deco, French | **Maison Gérard** (53 E 10th St, 212/674-7611)

Baby equipment | **Schneider's** (41 W 25th St, 212/228-3540)

Baskets | **Bill's Flower Market** (816 Ave of the Americas, 212/889-8154)

Bath and bed items | **Bed Bath & Beyond** (620 Ave of the Americas, 212/255-3550; 410 E 61st St, 646/215-4702; 1932 Broadway, 917/441-9391; and 270 Greenwich St, 212/233-8450)

Bath fixtures (expensive) | **Boffi Soffi** (31½ Greene St, 212/431-8282)

Bedding and pillows | **Ankasa** (1200 Madison Ave, 212/996-5200 and 424 Broome St, 212/226-8002)

Beds (headboards and footboards) | **Charles P. Rogers** (26 W 17th St, 212/675-4400)

Beds, Murphy | **Murphy Bed Center** (113 W 25th St, 1st floor, 212/645-7079)

Beds, Swedish handmade | **Hästens** (75 Grand St, 212/219-8022; 876 Broadway, 212/505-8022; and 1100 Madison Ave, 212/628-8022)

Boxes, wooden | **An American Craftsman Galleries** (790 Seventh Ave, 212/399-2555)

Chandeliers | **Foundry Lighting** (225 E 58th St, 212/759-9332)

China (bargain pieces) | **Fishs Eddy** (889 Broadway, 212/420-9020)

China, English Imari | **Bardith, Ltd** (901 Madison Ave, 212/737-3775)

China, porcelain | **Porcelain Room** (13 Christopher St, 212/367-8206)

Christmas decor | **Christmas Cottage** (871 Seventh Ave, 212/333-7380) and **Matt McGhee** (174 Waverly Pl, 212/741-3138)

Christmas decorations (discounted) | **Kurt S. Adler Santa's World** (7 W 34th St, 212/924-0900; opens around Thanksgiving for sample sale)

Clocks, cuckoo | **Time Pieces, Inc.** (115 Greenwich Ave, 212/929-8011)

Cookbooks (used) | **Bonnie Slotnick Cookbooks** (163 W 10th St, 212/989-8962) and **Joanne Hendricks Cookbooks** (488 Greenwich St, 212/226-5731)

Decoupage items | **Kaas Glassworks** (117 Perry St, 212/366-0322) and **John Derian Company** (6 E 2nd St, 212/677-3917)

Dinnerware, Fiesta (individual pieces) | **Mood Indigo** (Showplace Antiques and Design Center, 40 W 25th St, Gallery 222, 212/254-1176)

Dinnerware, porcelain | **Bernardaud** (499 Park Ave, 212/371-4300)

Electronics, high-end | **Audioarts** (210 Fifth Ave, 212/260-2939; by appointment)

Electronics, vintage | **Waves** (Showplace Antiques and Design Center, 40 W 25th St, Gallery 107, 212/273-9616)

Fabrics, decorator (discounted) | **Zarin Fabrics** (314 Grand St, 212/925-6112)

FDNY merchandise | **FDNY Fire Zone** (34 W 51st St, 212/698-4529)

Flags and banners | **Art Flag Co.** (8 Jay St, 212/334-1890)

Floor coverings | **ABC Carpet & Home** (881 and 888 Broadway, 212/473-3000)

Floor coverings, vintage | **Doris Leslie Blau** (306 E 61st St, 212/586-5511; by appointment) and **Secondhand Rose** (230 Fifth Ave, 5th floor, 212/393-9002)

Floral designs | **L. Becker Flowers** (217 E 83rd St, 212/439-6001)

Flower bouquets | **Posies** (366 Amsterdam Ave, 212/721-2260)

Flowers, fresh-cut (from Europe) | **VSF** (204 W 10th St, 212/206-7236)

Flowers, orchids | **Judy's Plant World** (1410 Lexington Ave, 212/860-0055)

Flowers, silk | **Pany Silk Flowers** (146 W 28th St, 212/645-9526)

Foliage, live and artificial | **American Foliage & Design Group** (122 W 22nd St, 212/741-5555)

Frames, picture | **A.I. Friedman** (44 W 18th St, 212/243-9000) and **Framed on Madison** (976 Lexington Ave, 212/734-4680)

Furniture | **Design Within Reach** (903 Broadway, 212/475-0001; 408 W 14th St, 212/242-9449; and other locations)

Furniture and mattresses, foam | **Dixie Foam** (113 W 25th St, 212/645-8999)

Furniture, antique | **H.M. Luther Antiques** (35 E 76th St, 212/439-7919 and

61 E 11th St, 212/505-1485)

Furniture, classic hand-carved | **Devon Shops** (111 E 27th St, 212/686-1760)

Furniture, contemporary | **DwellStudio** (77 Wooster St, 646/442-6000)

Furniture, handcrafted (expensive) | **Thomas Moser Cabinetmakers** (699 Madison Ave, 2nd floor, 212/753-7005)

Furniture, handcrafted, 18th-century American reproductions | **Barton-Sharpe** (200 Lexington Ave, 646/935-1500)

Furniture, hardwood | **Pompanoosuc Mills** (124 Hudson St, 212/226-5960)

Furniture, home and office | **Knoll** (76 Ninth Ave, 11th floor, 212/343-4000)

Furniture, infants' | **Albee Baby** (715 Amsterdam Ave, 212/662-5740), **Kids' Supply Co.** (1343 Madison Ave, 212/426-1200), and **Schneider's** (41 W 25th St, 212/228-3540)

Furniture, modern-design (pricey) | **Cassina USA** (155 E 56th St, 212/245-2121)

Furniture, sofabeds | **Avery-Boardman** (Decoration & Design Building, 979 Third Ave, 4th floor, 212/688-6611)

Furniture, vintage | **Regeneration Furniture** (38 Renwick St, 212/741-2102)

Gadgets | **Brookstone** (18 Fulton St, 212/344-8108 and Rockefeller Center, 1230 Ave of the Americas, 212/262-3237)

Garden accessories | **Lexington Gardens** (1011 Lexington Ave, 212/861-4390)

Glass, Venetian | **End of History** (548½ Hudson St, 212/647-7598) and **Gardner & Barr** (305 E 61st St, 212/752-0555; by appointment)

Glassware, Steuben (used) | **Lillian Nassau** (220 E 57th St, 212/759-6062)

Glassware and accessories, vintage | **Mood Indigo** (Showplace Antiques and Design Center, 40 W 25th St, Gallery 222, 212/254-1176)

Glassware and tableware | **Avventura** (463 Amsterdam Ave, 212/769-2510)

Hardware, doorknobs | **Simon's Hardware & Bath** (421 Third Ave, 212/532-9220)

Hardware and accessories, brass | **The Brass Center** (248 E 58th St, 212/421-0090)

Home accessories | **Aedes de Venustas** (9 Christopher St, 212/206-8674) and **Scent Elate** (313 W 48th St, 212/258-3043)

Housewares | **Dinosaur Designs** (211 Elizabeth St, 212/680-3523) and **Gracious Home** (1201 and 1220 Third Ave, 212/517-6300 and 1992 Broadway, 212/231-7800)

Housewares (upscale) | **Lancelotti** (66 Ave A, 212/475-6851)

Kitchenware (best all-around store) | **Zabar's** (2245 Broadway, 212/787-2000)

Kitchenware, bakeware (discounted) | **Broadway Panhandler** (65 E 8th St, 212/966-3434)

Kitchenware, cookware | **Bed Bath & Beyond** (620 Ave of the Americas, 212/255-3550; 410 E 61st St, 646/215-4702; 1932 Broadway, 917/441-9391; and 270 Greenwich St, 212/233-8450), **Korin** (57 Warren St, 212/587-7021), and **Zabar's** (2245 Broadway, 212/787-2000)

Kitchenware, knives | **Roger & Sons** (268 Bowery, 212/226-4734)

Kitchenware, professional | **Hung Chong Imports** (14 Bowery, 212/349-3392) and **J.B. Prince** (36 E 31st St, 11th floor, 212/683-3553)

Lampshades | **Just Shades** (21 Spring St, 212/966-2757) and **Oriental Lampshade Co.** (223 W 79th St, 212/873-0812)

Lightbulbs | **Just Bulbs** (220 E 60th St, 212/228-7820)

Lighting, chandeliers | **The Lively Set** (33 Bedford St, 212/807-8417)

Lighting, custom-made and antique | **Lampworks** (New York Design Center, 200 Lexington Ave, Suite 903, 212/750-1500)

Lighting fixtures | **City Knickerbocker** (665 Eleventh Ave, 212/586-3939) and **Lighting by Gregory** (158 Bowery, 212/226-1276)

Lighting fixtures, antique | **Olde Good Things** (124 W 24th St, 212/989-8401; 5 E 16th St, 212/989-8814; 450 Columbus Ave, 212/362-8025; and other locations)

Lighting, photographic (purchase or rental) | **Flash Clinic** (164 W 25th St, 212/337-0447)

Linens | **Bed Bath & Beyond** (620 Ave of the Americas, 212/255-3550; 410 E 61st St, 646/215-4702; 1932 Broadway, 917/441-9391; and 270 Greenwich St, 212/233-8450), **Harris Levy** (98 Forsyth St, 212/226-3102), and **Layther's Linen & Home** (2270 Broadway, 212/724-0180 and 237 E 86th St, 212/996-4439)

Linens, vintage | **Geminola** (41 Perry St, 212/675-1994)

Mattresses (good value) | **Town Bedding & Upholstery** (203 Eighth Ave, 212/243-0426)

Office supplies, Muji | **Muji** (455 Broadway, 212/334-2002; 620 Eighth Ave, 212/382-2300; 16 W 19th St, 212/414-9024; and 52 Cooper Sq, 212/358-8693)

Perfume bottles, vintage | **Gallery 47** (1050 Second Ave, 212/888-0165)

Plumbing fixtures | **Blackman** (85 Fifth Ave, 2nd floor, 212/337-1000)

Porcelain items | **Lladro** (500 Madison Ave, 212/838-9356)

Portfolios, custom | **House of Portfolios** (133 W 25th St, 7th floor, 212/206-7323)

Posters, American and international movie | **Jerry Ohlinger's Movie Materials Store** (253 W 35th St, ground floor, 212/989-0869)

Posters, Broadway theater | **Triton Gallery** (630 Ninth Ave, 8th floor, 212/765-2472)

Posters, original, 1880 to present | **Philip Williams Posters** (122 Chambers St, 212/513-0313)

Posters, vintage | **La Belle Epoque Vintage Posters** (115-A Greenwich Ave, 212/362-1770) and **Ross Art Group** (532 Madison Ave, 4th floor, 212/223-1525)

Pottery, handmade | **Mugi Studio and Gallery** (993 Amsterdam Ave, 212/866-6202)

Prints, botanical | **W. Graham Arader** (29 E 72nd St, 212/628-3668 and 1016 Madison Ave, 212/628-7625)

Quilts | **Down and Quilt Shop** (527 Amsterdam Ave, 212/496-8980)

Rugs | **Rahmanan Antique & Decorative Rugs** (36 E 31st St, 9th floor, 212/683-0167)

GERRY'S EXCLUSIVE LIST

Safes | **Empire Safe** (6 E 39th St, 212/684-2255)

Screens, shoji | **Miya Shoji** (145 W 26th St, 212/243-6774)

Shower curtains | **Delphinium Home** (353 W 47th St, 212/333-7732)

Silver items, unusual | **Christofle** (846 Madison Ave, 212/308-9390) and **Jean's Silversmiths** (16 W 45th St, 212/575-0723)

Slipcovers | **Joe's Fabrics Warehouse** (102 Orchard St, 212/674-7089)

Tiles | **Mosaic House** (32 W 22nd St, 212/414-2525)

Tiles, ceramic and marble | **Complete Tile Collection** (42 W 15th St, 212/255-4450) and **Quarry Tiles, Marble & Granite** (132 Lexington Ave, 212/679-8889)

Trays | **Extraordinary** (247 E 57th St, 212/223-9151)

Typewriter ribbons | **Abalon Business Machines & Service** (60 E 42nd St, 212/682-1653)

Vacuum cleaners | **Desco** (131 W 14th St, 212/989-1800)

Wallpaper, vintage | **Secondhand Rose** (230 Fifth Ave, 5th floor, 212/393-9002)

Wrought-iron items | **Morgik Metal Design** (145 Hudson St, 212/463-0304)

THINGS FOR LEISURE TIME

Athletic gear | **Modell's Sporting Goods** (41 E 42nd St, 212/661-4242 and other locations)

Athletic gear, team | **New York Mets Clubhouse** (11 W 42nd St, 212/768-9534) and **Yankee Clubhouse** (110 E 59th St, 212/758-7844; 393 Fifth Ave, 212/685-4693; 245 W 42nd St, 212/768-9555; and 8 Fulton St, 212/514-7182)

Balloons | **Balloon Saloon** (133 West Broadway, 212/227-3838)

Beads | **Beads of Paradise** (16 E 17th St, 212/620-0642) and **Beads World** (1384 Broadway, 212/302-1199)

Bicycles | **Bicycle Habitat** (244 and 250 Lafayette St, 212/625-1347 and 228 Seventh Ave, 212/206-6949)

Bicycles, folding | **Frank's Bike Shop** (553 Grand St, 212/533-6332)

Binoculars | **Clairmont-Nichols** (1016 First Ave, 212/758-2346)

Books, African and African-American | **Jumel Terrace Books** (426 W 160th St, 212/928-9525; by appointment)

Books, children's, educators', and parents' | **Bank Street Bookstore** (2875 Broadway, 212/678-1654)

Books, comic | **Forbidden Planet NYC** (832 Broadway, 212/473-1576) and **Midtown Comics** (200 W 40th St, 459 Lexington Ave, and 64 Fulton St; 212/302-8192 for all locations)

Books, comic (vintage) | **Metropolis Collectibles** (873 Broadway, Suite 201, 212/260-4147; by appointment)

Books, exam-study and science-fiction | **Civil Service Book Shop** (38 Lispenard St, 212/226-9506)

Books, fashion design | **Fashion Design Bookstore** (250 W 27th St, 212/633-9646)

Books, metaphysical and religious | **Quest Bookshop** (240 E 53rd St, 212/758-5521)

Books, new, used, and review copies | **Strand Book Store** (828 Broadway, 212/473-1452)

Books, plates (lithographs) | **George Glazer Gallery** (28 E 72nd St, Room 3A, 212/535-5706)

Books, progressive political | **Revolution Books** (146 W 26th St, 212/691-3345)

Books, publications by artists | **Printed Matter** (195 Tenth Ave, 212/925-0325)

Books, rare | **Imperial Fine Books** (790 Madison Ave, 2nd floor, 212/861-6620), **Martayan Lan** (70 E 55th St, 6th floor, 212/308-0018), and **Strand Book Store** (828 Broadway, 212/473-1452)

Books, scholarly | **Book Culture** (536 W 112th St, 212/865-1588)

Camera, video | **AC Gears** (69 E 8th St, 212/260-2269)

Camping and outdoor equipment | **Tent and Trails** (21 Park Pl, 212/227-1761)

Cigarettes, luxury | **Nat Sherman** (12 E 42nd St, 212/764-5000)

Cigars | **Davidoff of Geneva** (515 Madison Ave, 212/751-9060), **DP Cigars** (265 W 30th St, 212/367-8949), and **Midtown Cigars** (562 Fifth Ave, 212/997-2227)

Compact discs, new and used | **Disc-O-Rama** (44 W 8th St, 212/206-8417)

Computers, Apple | **Apple Store** (103 Prince St, 212/226-3126; 767 Fifth Ave, 212/336-1440; 401 W 14th St, 212/444-3400; and 1981 Broadway, 212/209-3400)

Costumes and makeup | **New York Costumes/Halloween Adventure** (104 Fourth Ave, 212/673-4546)

Dance items | **World Tone Dance** (580 Eighth Ave, 2nd floor, 212/691-1934)

Dollhouses | **Tiny Doll House** (314 E 78th St, 212/744-3719)

Electronics, travel | **Tumi** (Rockefeller Center, 53 W 49th St, 212/245-7460; 520 Madison Ave, 212/813-0545; and other locations)

Embroidery, custom-designed | **Jonathan Embroidery Plus** (256 W 38th St, 212/398-3538)

Fishing tackle, fly | **Orvis** (522 Fifth Ave, 212/827-0698)

Games | **Compleat Strategist** (11 E 33rd St, 212/685-3880)

Games, chess sets | **Chess Forum** (219 Thompson St, 212/475-2369)

Games, video | **GameStop** (687 Broadway, 212/473-6571 and other locations)

Games (*Warhammer*) | **Games Workshop** (54 E 8th St, 212/982-6314)

Gifts | **Exit 9** (51 Ave A, 212/228-0145), **Greenwich Letterpress** (39 Christopher St, 212/989-7464), **House of Cards and Curiosities** (23 Eighth Ave, 212/675-6178), and **Pylones** (69 Spring St, 212/431-3244; 842 Lexington Ave, 212/317-9822; Grand Central Terminal, 42nd St at Vanderbilt Ave, 212/867-0969; and Rockefeller Center, 74 W 50th St, 212/227-9273)

Golf equipment (best selection) | **New York Golf Center** (131 W 35th St, 212/564-2255 and other locations)

Guns | **Beretta Gallery** (718 Madison Ave, 212/319-3235) and **Holland & Holland** (10 E 40th St, 19th floor, 212/752-7755)

Harley-Davidson gear | **Harley-Davidson of New York** (686 Lexington Ave, 212/355-3003)

Holographs | **Holographic Studio** (240 E 26th St, 212/686-9397)

Home-entertainment equipment and systems | **J&R Music & Computer World** (15 and 23 Park Row, 212/238-9000)

Horseback-riding equipment | **Manhattan Saddlery** (117 E 24th St, 212/673-1400)

Knitting | **Gotta Knit!** (14 E 34th St, 5th floor, 212/989-3030), **Knitty City** (208 W 79th St, 212/787-5896), **String** (33 E 65th St, 212/288-9276), and **The Yarn Company** (2274 Broadway, 212/787-7878)

Luggage and travel accessories | **Altman Luggage** (135 Orchard St, 212/254-7275), **Bag House** (797 Broadway, 212/260-0940), **Flight 001** (96 Greenwich Ave, 212/989-0001), **Pertutti** (49 Greenwich Ave, 212/675-0113), and **Tumi** (Rockefeller Center, 53 W 49th St, 212/245-7460; 520 Madison Ave, 212/813-0545; and other locations)

Magazines | **Eastern Newsstand** (many locations) and **Universal News** (977 Eighth Ave, 212/459-0932 and other locations)

Magic tricks | **Tannen's Magic** (45 W 34th St, 6th floor, 212/929-4500)

Maps and prints, antiquarian | **Argosy Book Store** (116 E 59th St, 212/753-4455)

Maps, globes, and atlases, antique | **George Glazer Gallery** (28 E 72nd St, Room 3A, 212/535-5706) and **Martayan Lan** (70 E 55th St, 6th floor, 212/308-0018)

Marine supplies | **West Marine** (12 W 37th St, 212/594-6065)

Memorabilia | **Firestore** (17 Greenwich Ave, 212/226-3142) and **Museum of the City of New York** (1220 Fifth Ave, 917/492-3330)

Musical instruments | **Music Inn World Instruments** (169 W 4th St, 212/243-5715), **Roberto's Winds** (333 W 34th St, 212/391-1315), **Rogue Music** (220 W 30th St, 212/629-5073), and **Universal Musical Instrument Co.** (732 Broadway, 212/254-6917)

Musical instruments, accordions | **Main Squeeze** (19 Essex St, 212/614-3109)

Musical instruments, guitars | **Carmine Street Guitars** (42 Carmine St, 212/691-8400), **Dan's Chelsea Guitars** (224 W 23rd St, 212/675-4993), **The Guitar Salon** (212/675-3236; by appointment), **Ludlow Guitars** (172 Ludlow St, 212/353-1775), and **Matt Umanov Guitars** (273 Bleecker St, 212/675-2157)

Novelties | **Gordon Novelty** (52 W 29th St, 212/696-9664)

Pens | **Arthur Brown & Brother** (2 W 45th St, 212/575-5555)

Pet supplies, discounted | **Petland Discounts** (314 W 23rd St, 212/366-0512 and other locations)

Pet supplies, holistic | **Spoiled Brats** (340 W 49th St, 212/459-1615)

Pets, dogs and cats | **Le Petit Puppy** (18 Christopher St, 212/727-8111) and **Pets-on-Lex** (1109 Lexington Ave, 212/426-0766)

Photographic equipment, rental and sales | **Calumet Photographic** (22 W 22nd St, 212/989-8500)

Pool tables | **Blatt Billiards** (809 Broadway, 212/674-8855)

Records, rare | **House of Oldies** (35 Carmine St, 212/243-0500)

Scuba-diving and snorkeling equipment | **Pan Aqua Diving** (460 W 43rd St,

212/736-3483) and **Scuba Network** (43 W 21st St, 212/243-2988)

Sewing and crafts, buttons, rare and unusual | **Tender Buttons** (143 E 62nd St, 212/758-7004)

Sewing and crafts, quilting supplies | **The City Quilter** (133 W 25th St, 212/807-0390)

Skateboards | **Supreme** (274 Lafayette St, 212/966-7799)

Skating equipment | **Blades** (156 W 72nd St, 212/787-3911 and 659 Broadway, 212/477-7350)

Snowboards | **Burton Snowboard Company** (106 Spring St, 212/966-8068)

Sports cards | **Alex's MVP Cards** (256 E 89th St, 212/831-2273)

Stationery | **Il Papiro** (1021 Lexington Ave, 212/288-9330), **Jam Paper & Envelope** (135 Third Ave, 212/473-6666; 1282 Third Ave, 212/737-0037; and 466 Lexington Ave, 212/687-6666), **Kate's Paperie** (435 Broome St, 212/941-9816), and **Paper Presentation** (23 W 18th St, 212/463-7035)

Tennis equipment | **Mason's Tennis** (56 E 53rd St, 212/755-5805)

Theatrical items | **One Shubert Alley** (1 Shubert Alley, 212/944-4133)

Toys (good selection) | **Kidding Around** (60 W 15th St, 212/645-6337 and 107 E 42nd St, 212/972-8697)

Toys, imported Japanese | **Image Anime** (242 W 30th St, 212/631-0966)

Toys, Lego | **LEGO Store** (Rockefeller Center, 620 Fifth Ave, 212/245-5973)

Toys, novelties and party supplies | **E.A.T. Gifts** (1062 Madison Ave, 212/861-2544)

Toys, young adult | **Kidrobot** (118 Prince St, 212/966-6688)

Videotapes, DVDs, and CDs, rare and foreign | **Kim's** (124 First Ave, 212/533-7390)

THINGS FROM FAR AWAY

African contemporary art | **Amaridian** (31 Howard St, 917/463-3719)

African clothing, custom-made | **Bébénoir** (2164 Frederick Douglass Blvd, 212/828-5775)

Buddhas | **Leekan Designs** (4 Rivington St, 212/226-7226)

Chinese dinnerware | **Wing On Wo & Co.** (26 Mott St, 212/962-3577)

Chinese goods | **Chinese American Trading Company** (91 Mulberry St, 212/267-5224), **Pearl River Mart** (477 Broadway, 212/431-4770), and **Ting's Gift Shop** (18 Doyer St, 212/962-1081)

European pottery (Italian, French, Portuguese) | **La Terrine** (1024 Lexington Ave, 212/988-3366)

French handmade pottery, chandeliers, furniture | **Le Fanion** (299 W 4th St, 212/463-8760)

Himalayan imports | **Himalayan Crafts** (2007 Broadway, 212/787-8500)

Indian imports | **Bharatiya Dress Shoppe** (83 Second Ave, 212/228-1463) and **Soigne K** (717 Madison Ave, 212/486-2890)

Indonesian home furnishings | **Andrianna Shamaris** (121 Greene St, 212/388-9898)

Italian clothing, men and women | **Moncler** (90 Prince St, 646/350-3620)

Italian shoes, exotic skins | **Cellini Uomo** (59 Orchard St, 212/219-8657)

Japanese clothing, high-end | **Uniqlo** (666 Fifth Ave, 31 W 34th St, and 546 Broadway; 877/486-4756 for all locations)

Korean art, traditional | **Kang Collection** (9 E 82nd St, 212/734-1490)

Mexican imports | **La Sirena** (27 E 3rd St, 212/780-9113) and **Pan American Phoenix** (857 Lexington Ave, 212/570-0300)

New Zealand clothing | **Icebreaker** (102 Wooster St, 646/861-2523; by appointment)

Scandinavian imports | **Just Scandinavian** (161 Hudson St, 212/334-2556)

Swedish outerwear | **Fjällräven** (262 Mott St, 212/226-7846)

Tibetan handicrafts | **Do Kham** (51 Prince St, 212/966-2404) and **Vajra** (146 Sullivan St, 212/529-4344)

Ukrainian clothing, newspapers, books, CDs, and tapes | **Surma — The Ukrainian Shop** (11 E 7th St, 212/477-0729)

NEW YORK STORES
THE BEST OF THE LOT

In this section you'll find dozens of descriptions for new stores; perennial favorites have been updated to reflect their efforts to bring shoppers the best possible deals and merchandise.

ANATOMICAL SUPPLIES
THE EVOLUTION STORE

120 Spring St (bet Greene St and Mercer St)   212/343-1114
Daily: 11-7   theevolutionstore.com

The Evolution Store is an authorized dealer selling unique science and natural-history collectibles, including insects, fossils, skulls and skeletons, medical models, minerals, posters, seashells, and decorative antique taxidermy. Unusual gifts and home furnishings are the norm here. Some merchandise is available for rental by the day, week, or month. Shopping is rarely this educational and fascinating, and kids will love the lollipops with edible bugs inside!

ANIMATION
ANIMAZING GALLERY SOHO

54 Greene St (at Broome St)   212/226-7374
Mon-Sat: 10-7; Sun: 11-6   animazing.com

A landmark in Soho since 1984, Animazing Gallery exhibits a unique collection of original and limited-edition animation and illustration artworks with color, playfulness, and beauty. Exclusive collections include art and sculpture by American illustrators like Maurice Sendak, Tim Burton, Theodor Geisel, and Charles M. Schulz. The gallery also showcases original vintage animation art and whimsical fine art, including *The PEANUTS Paintings*, by Tom

Everhart, and *Magical Realism*, by Daniel Merriam and Nicoletta Ceccoli in the AFA expansion. Check the website for current exhibitions, upcoming events, and opening receptions.

ANTIQUES

BOWERY

Lost City Arts (18 Cooper Square, 212/375-0500): midcentury furniture and fixtures

CHELSEA

David Stypmann Company (Showplace Antiques and Design Center, 40 W 25th St, Room 112, 212/226-5717): art pottery, art glass objects

EAST VILLAGE

Alan Moss (436 Lafayette St, 212/473-1310): 20th-century furniture, art, jewelry

FLATIRON DISTRICT

Secondhand Rose (230 Fifth Ave, 5th floor, 212/393-9002)

GREENWICH VILLAGE

End of History (548½ Hudson St, 212/647-7598): vintage hand-blown Venetian glass

Hyde Park Antiques (836 Broadway, 212/477-0033): 18th- and 19th-century English furniture

Karl Kemp & Associates (36 E 10th St, 212/254-1877): art deco and Beidermeier furniture

Kentshire Galleries (37 E 12th St, 212/673-6644): English antiques

La Belle Epoque Vintage Posters (115 Greenwich Ave, 212/362-1770): advertising posters

Le Fanion (299 W 4th St, 212/463-8760): French handmade pottery, chandeliers, furniture

Maison Gérard (53 E 10th St, 212/674-7611): French art deco

Ritter-Antik (35 E 10th St, 212/673-2213): early first-period Beidermeier

MIDTOWN

A la Vielle Russie (781 Fifth Ave, 212/752-1727): Russian art

Agostino Antiques, Ltd. (979 Third Ave, 15th floor, 212/421-8820): English and French 17th-to-19th-century furniture

Chameleon (223 E 59th St, 212/355-6300): lighting

Evergreen Antiques (200 Lexington Ave, 10th floor, 212/744-5664): European and Scandinavian furniture

George N. Antiques (227 E 59th St, 212/935-4005): mirrors, lighting, furniture, jewelry

Gotta Have It! (153 E 57th St, 212/750-7900): celebrity memorabilia

Gray & Davis (15 W 47th St, 212/719-4698): vintage engagement rings and other jewelry

J.J. Lally (41 E 57th St, 212/371-3380): Chinese art

James Robinson (480 Park Ave, 212/752-6166): silver flatware

Lars Bolander N.Y. (232 E 59th St, 3rd floor, 212/924-1000): 17th- and 18th-century Swedish and French antiques and reproductions

Leo Kaplan, Ltd. (114 E 57th St, 212/249-6766): ceramics and glass

Manhattan Art & Antiques Center (1050 Second Ave, 212/355-4400): 60 galleries

Martayan Lan (70 E 55th St, 6th floor, 212/308-0018): 16th- and 17th-century maps and books

Newel LLC (425 E 53rd St, 212/758-1970): all styles and periods

Philip Colleck (311 E 58th St, 212/486-7600): 18th- and early 19th-century English furniture

Ralph M. Chait Galleries (724 Fifth Ave, 10th floor, 212/758-0937): ancient Chinese art

S.J. Shrubsole (104 E 57th St, 212/753-8920): English silver and jewelry

Stephen Herdemian (78 W 47th St, 212/944-2534): antique and estate jewelry

NOHO/SOHO/TRIBECA

Donzella (17 White St, 212/965-8919): furnishings from the 1940s through the 1970s

Gill & Lagodich Gallery (108 Reade St, 212/619-0631; by appointment): period frames and restoration

Hostler Burrows Antik (51 E 10th St, mezzanine, 212/343-0471): midcentury Scandinavian, contemporary designs

Urban Archaeology (143 Franklin St, 212/431-4646): lighting, wash stands, accessories, reproductions

Wyeth (315 Spring St, 212/243-3661): early-to-mid-20th-century antiques and custom furniture from Denmark, Italy, and the U.S.

UPPER EAST SIDE

Antiquarium (948 Madison Ave, 212/734-9776): jewelry, classical Near Eastern and Egyptian antiquities

Arader Gallery (29 E 72nd St, 212/628-3668 and 1016 Madison Ave, 212/628-7625): rare prints and furniture

Art of the Past (1242 Madison Ave, 212/860-7070): South and Southeast Asia

Bernard & S. Dean Levy (24 E 84th St, 212/628-7088): American furniture and paintings

Bizarre Bazaar (130¼ E 65th St, 212/517-2100; appointment suggested): 20th-century industrial design

Cora Ginsburg (19 E 74th St, 3rd floor, 212/744-1352; by appointment): antique textiles

Dalva Brothers (53 E 77th St, 212/717-6600): 18th-century French furniture and porcelain

Didier Aaron (32 E 67th St, 212/988-5248): 18th- and 19th-century furniture; 17th-, 18th-, and 19th-century masters' paintings

Factory Outlet Malls in the Tri-State Region and Pennsylvania

Shop for deeply discounted merchandise at these outlet malls. Look for special events and coupon books to maximize your savings!

CONNECTICUT

Clinton Crossing Premium Outlets (20 Killingworth Turnpike, Clinton, CT; 860/664-0700, premiumoutlets.com): 70 upscale outlet stores

NEW JERSEY

Atlantic City Outlets (2014 Baltic Ave, Atlantic City, NJ; 609/344-0095): 100 Shops

Jackson Premium Outlets (537 Monmouth Rd, Jackson, NJ; 732/833-0503, premiumoutlets.com): 70 stores, top retailers

Jersey Gardens (651 Kapkowski Rd, Elizabeth, NJ; 908/354-5900, jerseygardens.com): over 200 stores, New Jersey's largest outlet center

Jersey Shore Premium Outlets (1 Premium Outlets Blvd, Tinton Falls, NJ; 732-918-1700, premiumoutlets.com): 120 stores, designer clothes and shoes

Liberty Village Premium Outlets (1 Church St, Flemington, NJ; 908/782-8550, premiumoutlets.com): 40 outlets, family shopping

NEW YORK

Tanger Outlet Center I & II (200 Tanger Mall Dr, Riverhead, NY; 631/369-2732, tangeroutlet.com): 165 shopping choices

Tanger Outlets at The Arches (152 The Arches Circle, Deer Park, NY; 631/667-0600, tangeroutlet.com): over 95 shops and services

Woodbury Common Premium Outlets (498 Red Apple Court, Central Valley, NY; 845/928-4000, premiumoutlets.com): 220 upscale outlet stores

PENNSYLVANIA

The Crossings Premium Outlets (1000 Premium Outlets Dr, Tannersville, PA; 570/629-4650, premiumoutlets.com): over 100 stores

Franklin Mills (1455 Franklin Mills Circle, Philadelphia, PA; 215/632-1500): nearly 200 manufacturers' and retail outlet stores

Closer to the city, an outlet mall is under construction in The Bronx.

Doris Leslie Blau (306 E 61st St, 212/586-5511; by appointment): rugs
Fanelli Antique Timepieces (790 Madison Ave, Suite 202, 212/517-2300): antique timepieces
Florian Papp (962 Madison Ave, 212/288-6770): European furniture
Friedman & Vallois (27 E 67th St, 212/517-3820): high-end French art deco furniture and lighting
Gardner & Barr (305 E 61st St, Suite 206, 212/752-0555; by appointment): vintage Murano glass
George Glazer Gallery (28 E 72nd St, Room 3A, 212/327-2598): maps, globes

Greene Street Interiors (210 E 60th St, 212/274-1076): Scandinavian and Beidermeier

Guild Antiques (1089 Madison Ave, 212/717-1810): English formal

Hayko Rugs (857 Lexington Ave, 212/717-5400): kilims

Karl Kemp & Associates (833 Madison Ave, 212/288-3838): art deco and Biedermeier furniture

Kentshire Antiques (700 Madison Ave, 212/421-1100): English antiques, jewelry

L'Antiquaire & the Connoisseur (36 E 73rd St, 212/517-9176): 18th-century French and Italian furniture

Linda Horn Antiques (1327 Madison Ave, 212/772-1122): late 19th- and 20th-century English and French

Macklowe Gallery (667 Madison Ave, 212/644-6400): Tiffany and art nouveau

Naga Antiques (145 E 61st St, 212/593-2788): antique Japanese screens, fine Asian and European furniture

Sotheby's (1334 York Ave, 212/606-7000): art

Sylvia Pines Uniquities (1102 Lexington Ave, 212/744-5141): jewelry and handbags

Ursus Books and Prints (699 Madison Ave, 212/772-8787): books

THE LIVELY SET

33 Bedford St (bet Carmine and Downing St)　　　　　212/807-8417
Mon-Fri: 11-7; Sat-Sun: 11-6

This diminutive West Village antique home and garden shop is chock-full of vintage furniture for living rooms and gardens and decorative accents for the entire home. The eclectic inventory, including lamps, chandeliers, sconces, accent tables, and Murano glass bowls changes frequently, adding to the store's allure.

MANTIQUES MODERN

146 W 22nd St (bet Ave of the Americas and Seventh Ave)　　212/206-1494
Mon-Fri: 10:30-6:30; Sat-Sun: 11-7　　　　　mantiquesmodern.com

No dainty antiques here! What an amazing collection of objects from the 18th, 19th, and 20th centuries. A journey through the crowded store might reveal luggage by Louis Vuitton, Goyard, and Hermes; mannequins; barware; a Gucci sculpture; industrial equipment suitable for home use; and an assortment of furniture, lighting, and wall decor. Be sure to look under, atop, and between all the items. Some of them may require a bit of imagination to fit into your scheme.

Joan Hamburg

When in the New York area, tune into WOR and take in **The Joan Hamburg Show**! This highly informed lady has been a fixture on the airwaves for dozens of years. For residents and visitors alike, Joan is a very knowledgeable authority on shopping, theater, travel, food, everyday activities, and information and celebrity interviews. Her show airs Monday through Friday from noon to 2 p.m. on WOR (710 AM).

Antiques Fun

The largest antiques center in New York is **Showplace Antiques and Design Center** (40 W 25th St, 212/633-6063, nyshowplace.com), with over 200 quality galleries on four floors selling jewelry, art glass, art nouveau, art deco, bronze, pottery, paintings, furniture, silver, and more. An eclectic selection of period pieces is showcased in designer rooms on the third floor. They are open from 10 to 6 on weekdays and 8:30 to 5:30 on weekends. A silversmith is on-premises every weekend.

ARCHITECTURAL ANTIQUES

DEMOLITION DEPOT & IRREPLACEABLE ARTIFACTS

216 E 125th St (bet Second and Third Ave)   212/860-1138
Mon-Fri: 10-6; Sat: 11-6   demolitiondepot.com

Look inside this shabby building and you'll be immersed in a treasure trove of interior and exterior vintage pieces. The idea is to preserve architectural history by reclaiming building elements. It may take a bit of imagination to come up with all the possibilities. There is a large assortment of fixtures, lighting pieces, doors, windows, bars, mantels, shutters, gates, railings, and even kitchen sinks, all in a variety of styles (art deco, French country, etc.). Services include demolition, reclamation, and on-site liquidation.

OLDE GOOD THINGS

5 E 16 St (bet Fifth Ave and Union Square W)   212/989-8814
Mon-Sat: 10-7; Sun: 11-7
302 Bowery (at Houston St)   212/498-9922
Mon-Thurs: 10-7; Fri: 10-8; Sat: 11-8; Sun: 11-7
149 Madison Ave (at 32nd St)   212/321-0770
Mon-Sat: 10-7; Sun: 11-7
124 W 24th St (bet Ave of the Americas and Seventh Ave)   212/989-8401
Daily: 10-7
450 Columbus Ave (bet 81st and 82nd St)   212/362-8025
Daily: 10-7   oldegoodthings.com

What a fascinating business this is! Olde Good Things salvages significant artifacts from old buildings, offering one of the largest showings of architectural antiques and salvaged items in the country. You'll find mantels, irons, doors, stone and terra cotta, hardware, garden items, tables and other furniture, tin pieces, floorings, mirrors, and an assortment of altered antiques.

ART SUPPLIES

LEE'S ART SHOP

220 W 57th St (bet Broadway and Seventh Ave)   212/247-0110
Mon-Fri: 9-7:30; Sat: 10-7; Sun: 11-6   leesartshop.com

Lee's Art Shop is a midtown landmark offering four stories of materials for amateur and professional artists and kids. There are architectural, drafting, and art supplies, as well as lamps, silk screens, paper goods, stationery, pens, cards, picture frames, calendars, crafts, gifts, and much more. Same-day on-premises framing is available.

NEW YORK CENTRAL ART SUPPLY

62 Third Ave (at 11th St)   212/473-7705
Mon-Sat: 8:30-6:15   nycentralart.com

Since 1905 artists have looked to this firm for fine-art materials, especially unique and custom-made items. There are two floors of fine-art papers, including one-of-a-kind decorative papers and over a thousand Oriental papers from Europe, Bhutan, India, and Nepal. Amateur and skilled artisans will find a full range of decorative paints and painting materials. Their brush selection is outstanding. This firm specializes in custom priming and stretching of artists' canvas. The canvas collection includes Belgian linens and cottons in widths from 54" to 144".

SAM FLAX

900 Third Ave (bet 54th and 55th St)   212/813-6666
Mon-Fri: 9:30-7; Sat: 10:30-6; Sun: noon-6   samflaxny.com

What started as a pushcart business, Sam Flax continues as one of the biggest and best art-supply houses in the business. The stock is enormous, the service special, and the prices competitive. They carry a full range of art and drafting supplies, organizational and archival storage items, gifts, pens, classic

---

Gerry's ABCs for Saving When Shopping

- **Approach clearance racks warily**—Be leery of a series of markdown prices, as the merchandise might be undesirable.
- **Avoid impulse buying**—You may regret it later.
- **Budget your dollars**—Know exactly what you can afford to spend and stick to it.
- **Buy off-season items**—Sales and markdowns can net you some real deals.
- **Check out frequent-shopper programs**—Good discounts for regular customers can be had.
- **Color-coordinate**—Buy outfits to mix and match.
- **Don't be afraid to haggle**—Believe it or not, haggling is still possible in many stores!
- **Frequent thrift shops**—Some excellent values can be found at resale stores.
- **Keep receipts**—Returns are much easier.
- **Look beyond brand names**—Many items without fancy labels are just as good.
- **Mention this book**—You might get a special discount!
- **Pay cash, if possible**—Better prices are often available, especially at smaller shops.
- **Price-check**—Know prices as much as possible before visiting a store.
- **Read ads carefully**—Sometimes the fine print is misleading.
- **Use coupons**—They can save you big bucks.

and modern furniture, home decor items, and photographic products. Framing services include custom design and creation of a display fit for your art or memorabilia.

AUTOGRAPHS

KENNETH W. RENDELL GALLERY

989 Madison Ave (at 77th St)   212/717-1776
Mon-Sat: 10-6 and by appointment   kwrendell.com

In the business for over 50 years, Keith Rendell offers an extensive collection of historical autographed material from famous figures in literature, arts, politics, and science. Rendell also shows autographed letters, manuscripts, documents, books, and photographs. All are authenticated, attractively presented, and priced according to rarity.

BARGAIN STORES

GABAY'S

225 First Ave (bet 13th and 14th St)   212/254-3180
Mon-Sat: 10-7; Sun: 11-7   gabaysoutlet.com

Gabay's sells designer overstocks. You'll find handbags, shoes, evening wear, suits, casual clothing, lingerie, and more at great prices. Goods come from some of Manhattan's best stores (like Bergdorf Goodman and Henri Bendel), with items for both men and women. Designer names include Chanel, Chloe, Jimmy Choo, Manolo Blahnik, Marc Jacobs, Oscar de la Renta, Yves St. Laurent, and Gucci.

JACK'S 99 CENT STORE/JACK'S WORLD

110 W 32nd St (bet Ave of the Americas and Seventh Ave)   212/268-9962

JACK'S WORLD

45 W 45th St (bet Ave of the Americas and Fifth Ave)   212/354-6888

JACK'S 99 CENT STORE

16 E 40th St (bet Madison and Fifth Ave)   212/696-5767
Hours vary by store   jacks99world.com

Yes, there really is a Jack! He is constantly working with manufacturers with excessive inventory or making packaging changes, and the amazing values are funneled to his customers. The results — inexpensive (99 cents!) paper goods, housewares, food, cleaning supplies, toiletries, and other everyday items. Jack's World has more of the same, plus electronics, domestics, gifts, toys, and goods of higher quality. You never know what will turn up at these discount stores!

SOIFFER HASKIN

317 W 33rd St (at Eighth Ave)   718/747-1656
Mon-Fri: 9-5 (closed July and August)   soifferhaskin.com

Since 1982, Soiffer Haskin has organized private sales of luxury goods at deep discounts that manufacturers and stores offer due to excess inventory. The varied stock includes clothing, silver, gifts, housewares, linens, shoes, and the like. It's a good idea to get on their mailing list for notification of private sale events.

Stores for Crafts

If you want to try your hand at a craft project, then check out these shops, where you'll likely find everything that's needed—and then some.

Beads of Paradise (16 E 17th St, 212/620-0642): beads and antiques

City Quilter (133 W 25th St, 212/807-0390): fabrics, patterns, supplies, quilting machines, notions, lessons

M&J Trimming (1008 Ave of the Americas, 800/965-8746): notions

Purl Soho (459 Broome St, 212/420-8796): yarns and notions, quilting supplies, needlework supplies and kits

Rita's Needlepoint (150 E 79th St, 212/737-8613): mainly needlepoint supplies; lessons by appointment

---

BATHROOM ACCESSORIES

A.F. SUPPLY CORPORATION

22 W 21st St (bet Fifth Ave and Ave of the Americas)　　212/243-5400
Mon-Fri: 8-5 and by appointment　　afsupply.com

A.F. Supply offers a great selection of mid- to high-end bath (some kitchen) products, fixtures, whirlpools, faucets, bath accessories, lighting, door and cabinet hardware, saunas, steam showers, shower doors, medicine cabinets, and spas from top architectural and decorative suppliers. Access to the showroom is by appointment only.

SHERLE WAGNER INTERNATIONAL

300 E 62nd St (at Second Ave)　　212/758-3300
Mon-Thurs: 9:30-5:30; Fri: 9:30-2　　sherlewagner.com

If you desire elegance and originality and price is no object, then come to Sherle Wagner for luxury hardware and accessories for the bathroom. The showroom displays all kinds of bed and bath items, plus furniture for your home. They've been around since 1945.

WATERWORKS

215 E 58th St (bet Second and Third Ave)　　212/371-9266
7 E 20th St (bet Fifth Ave and Broadway)　　212/254-6025
Mon-Fri: 8:30-5:30; Sat: 11-5 (closed Sat in summer)　　waterworks.com

If it is for the bathroom, then Waterworks will likely have it! You'll find faucets and shower heads, tubs, sinks, water closets; ceramic, glass, and stone surfacing; towels, rugs, mirrors, lighting, and a large stock of soaps, candles, and scents. There is also a selection of small furniture, including hampers, stools, etageres, and small tables.

BEADS

ELVEE ROSENBERG

11 W 37th St (bet Fifth Ave and Ave of the Americas)　　212/575-0767
Mon-Fri: 8:30-5　　elveerosenberg.com

Elvee Rosenberg imports beads, simulated pearls, and jewelry components and displays them floor-to-ceiling. You'll need some time to explore the showroom and four floors of wood, metal, crystal, Lucite, and vintage beads — over 25,000 bead styles. While single beads go for a dollar each at a department store one block away, this store sells them in bulk for a fraction of that price. Though they often deal with wholesalers, individual customers are treated courteously and wholesale prices are offered to all. Pearlized beads alone come in over 20 different styles and are used for everything from bathroom curtains to earrings and flowers. They stock needles, cords (in colors to match each bead), threads, chains, adhesives, jewelry tools, and costume-jewelry parts and pieces.

BOOKS

ANTIQUARIAN

COMPLETE TRAVELLER ANTIQUARIAN BOOKSTORE
199 Madison Ave (at 35th St)   212/685-9007
Mon-Fri: 9:30-6:30; Sat: 10-6; Sun: noon-5   ctrarebooks.com

Complete Traveller deals exclusively in rare, antiquarian, and out-of-print books pertaining to travel, and has the largest collection of Baedeker Handbooks. The 12,000-book collection includes volumes on polar expeditions, adventure travel, first editions, collectible children's classics, and 18th- and 19th-century maps. Fine literature, poetry, and books on New York are also available.

ART

PRINTED MATTER
195 Tenth Ave (bet 21st and 22nd St)   212/925-0325
Mon-Wed, Sat: 11-7; Thurs, Fri: 11-8   printedmatter.org

The name Printed Matter is a misnomer, since this store is devoted exclusively to artists' books — a trade term for portfolios of artwork in book form. They stock 15,000 titles by over 6,000 artists for viewing and purchase. The store is a nonprofit operation to promote public awareness of artists' projects and ideas. The idea is carried further with a selection of periodicals and audiotapes in a similar vein. Nearly all featured artists are contemporary (from 1960), so just browsing the store will bring you up-to-date on the art world.

CHILDREN'S

BANK STREET BOOKSTORE
2879 Broadway (at 112th St)   212/678-1654
Daily: 9 a.m.-9 p.m.   bankstreetbooks.com

This store has been a Manhattan icon for years and is a marvelous source of books for and about children, as well as books about education and parenting. Located adjacent to the Bank Street College of Education a progressive graduate school for teachers and a lab school for children — it also has a great selection of tapes, videos, and CDs. It's a treasure trove of educational toys, activity books, and teacher resources. While the two-floor store is a little cramped even when it isn't full of people, the staff really knows its stock and cares enormously about quality children's literature. Check the website for a schedule of readings and other special events for children.

BOOKS OF WONDER

18 W 18th St (bet Fifth Ave and Ave of the Americas)   212/989-3270
Mon-Sat: 10-7; Sun: 11-6   booksofwonder.com

   Books of Wonder is an enchanting spot with a special place in the hearts of New York children and parents alike. They specialize in old and new children's literature. In addition to their world-famous Oz section (as in *The Wizard of Oz*), this store is known for frequent "Meet the Author" events, beautiful used and often signed children's classics, and story hours for young children on Friday at 4 p.m. and Sunday at noon.

SCHOLASTIC STORE

557 Broadway (bet Prince and Spring St)   212/343-6166
Mon-Sat: 10-8; Sun: 11-6   scholastic.com/sohostore

   This bright, cheerful space is full of familiar titles and characters. In addition

---

Independent Bookstores

Independent bookstores offer personalized services, special events, and new, used, and sometimes rare editions.

Books of Wonder (18 W 18th St, 212/989-3270): children's

Complete Traveller Antiquarian Bookstore (199 Madison Ave, 212/685-9007): rare travel books

Crawford Doyle Booksellers (1082 Madison Ave, 212/288-6300): great neighborhood bookstore

Drama Book Shop (250 W 40th St, 212/944-0595): plays, musicals, theater; since 1917

Forbidden Planet NYC (832 Broadway, 212/473-1576): sci-fi, fantasy, Japanese animation, comics

McNally Jackson Books (52 Prince St, 212/274-1160): general bookstore with a cafe, too

Mysterious Bookshop (58 Warren St, 212/587-1011): thrillers and killers

Posman Books (Grand Central Terminal, 42nd St at Vanderbilt Ave, 212/983-1111; Chelsea Market, 75 Ninth Ave, 212/627-0304; and 30 Rockefeller Center, 212/489-9100): cookbooks at Chelsea Market location

Quest Bookshop (240 E 53rd St, 212/758-5521): spirituality and esoterica

St. Mark's Bookshop (31 Third Ave, 212/260-7853): eclectic stock with books on culture and foreign and domestic periodicals

Strand Book Store (828 Broadway, 212/473-1452): 18 miles of new and used books; something for everyone

Three Lives & Co. (154 W 10th St, 212/741-2069): specializes in literary fiction and nonfiction

to children's books, the Scholastic Store stocks a range of toys, puzzles, crafts, videos, and games. The life-size Magic School Bus houses science titles and kits. There is a tremendous selection of parent/teacher resource books on the second floor. Ask for a calendar of events, which lists readings, workshops, and performances.

COMICS

CHAMELEON COMICS & CARDS

3 Maiden Lane (at Broadway)   212/587-3411, 212/732-8525
Mon-Fri: 9-7; Sat: 10-5   chameleoncomics.com

   Chameleon Comics & Cards is a full-service collectibles store specializing in comic books, graphic novels, trading cards (sports and non-sports), and much more. You'll also find much more in this tiny shop: statues and busts of comic characters, comic-themed toys and action figures, and "japanime" (Japanese-American animation). New comics arrive every Wednesday. The staff is friendly and informed, and you can order books up to two months prior to publication from the preview catalog.

ST. MARK'S COMICS

11 St. Mark's Pl (bet Second and Third Ave)   212/598-9439
Mon-Tues: 10 a.m.-11 p.m.; Wed: 9 a.m.-1 a.m.; Thurs-Sat: 10 a.m.-1 a.m.;
Sun: 11 a.m.-11 p.m.   stmarkscomics.com

   This unique store carries mainstream and licensed products, as well as hard-to-find small-press and underground comics. They have a large selection of back issues and claim, "If it's published, we carry it." These service-oriented folks will even hold selections for you. Comic-related toys, T-shirts, statues, posters, and cards are stocked, and they also carry TV- and movie-related products.

COOKBOOKS

KITCHEN ARTS & LETTERS

1435 Lexington Ave (at 94th St)   212/876-5550
Mon: 1-6; Tues-Fri: 10-6:30; Sat: 11-6 (closed Sat in July and Aug)
          kitchenartsandletters.com

   Cookbooks are more popular than ever with all the interest in health, fitness, and natural foods. It should come as no surprise that Nachum Waxman's Kitchen Arts & Letters found immediate success as a store specializing in food- and wine-related books and literature, as well as domestic, imported, contemporary, and out-of-print material. A former cookbook editor, he identified a demand for out-of-print cookbooks. So while his cozy shop stocks more than 13,000 current titles, much of the business consists of finding a book "nobody else has;" the search service is free.

FOREIGN

KINOKUNIYA BOOKSTORE

1073 Ave of the Americas (bet 40th and 41st St)   212/869-1700
Mon-Sat: 10-8; Sun: 11-7:30   kinokuniya.com

   Japanese, English, and Chinese reading materials coexist in this bookstore, with the purpose of creating harmony between cultures. There are books,

CDs, DVDs, comics, hard-to-find magazines, beautiful stationery, and pictorial books; new stock arrives about three times a week. Subjects cover all aspects of Japanese culture: art, cooking, travel, language, literature, history, business, economics, martial arts, comic books, and more. The multilingual staff is a big plus.

GENERAL

BARNES & NOBLE

97 Warren St (at Greenwich Ave)	212/587-5389
555 Fifth Ave (at 46th St)	212/697-3048
2289 Broadway (at 82nd St)	212/362-8835

Numerous other locations
Hours vary by store   barnesandnoble.com

   Barnes & Noble stores continue to offer deep discounts on best sellers and other pop titles and are beloved by book buyers and browsers alike. Generations of New York students have purchased textbooks at the flagship store, 105 Fifth Avenue. Besides carrying an excellent selection of books (including bargain-priced remainders), they stock CDs, DVDs, audiobooks, videogames, toys, digital pocket dictionaries, e-book readers, magazines, and many gift items.

MCNALLY JACKSON BOOKS

52 Prince St (bet Lafayette and Mulberry St)   212/274-1160
Mon-Sat: 10-10; Sun: 10-9   mcnallyjackson.com

   McNally Jackson Books is a unique, independent bookstore, the inspiration of owner Sarah McNally. The store is chock-full of 8,300 titles in every category, organized by geographic area. Free Wi-Fi, comfortable sitting areas, a cafe, and personal, informed service are part of the big draw here. McNally has invested in a print-right-now "Espresso Book Machine," a machine that can download, bind, and trim a paperback in minutes. A cloud library of seven million titles is available for about the same price as a typical paperback. Budding authors can use it to print their own works; pretty amazing and gratifying to a new writer!

RIZZOLI BOOKSTORE

31 W 57th St (bet Fifth Ave and Ave of the Americas)   212/759-2424
Mon-Fri: 10-7:30; Sat: 10:30-7; Sun: 11-7   rizzoliusa.com

   Talk about class! Since 1964 and a move to this location in 1985, Rizzoli has maintained an elegant atmosphere that makes patrons feel as if they are browsing a European library rather than a midtown Manhattan bookstore. The emphasis is on art, architecture, foreign language, literature, photography, fashion, and interior design. There is a good selection of paperbacks, children's books, sports, and collectors' editions. You'll discover book finds in every nook and cranny on all three floors of this historic townhouse.

STRAND BOOK STORE

828 Broadway (at 12th St)   212/473-1452
Mon-Sat: 9:30 a.m.-10:30 p.m.; Sun: 11-10:30

STRAND BOOK KIOSK

Central Park, Fifth Ave at 60th St
10 a.m. – dusk, April-Dec (weather permitting)   strandbooks.com

Strand Book Store is the largest and best used bookstore in the world. Family-owned for over eight decades, it is a fascinating place to visit and shop. The store has over 2.5 million titles in stock — that's 18 miles of books — tagged at up to 85% off list prices. They sell secondhand, out-of-print, and rare books. Thousands of new books and quality remainders are sold at 50% off publisher's prices. An outstanding rare-book department is located on the third floor. You'll find 20th-century first editions, limited signed editions, fine bindings, and much more. Be sure to browse the famous dollar carts outside.

THREE LIVES & CO.
154 W 10th St (at Waverly Pl)   212/741-2069
Mon-Tues: noon-8; Wed-Sat: 11-8:30; Sun: noon-7   threelives.com

Three Lives is one of New York's top remaining independent bookstores. Founded in 1978, it specializes in literary fiction and nonfiction, with good sections on poetry, art, New York, cooking, and gardening. The staff is knowledgeable and helpful. Take note of their abbreviated hours.

UNOPPRESSIVE NON-IMPERIALIST BARGAIN BOOKS
34 Carmine St (bet Bedford and Bleecker St)   212/229-0079
Sun-Thurs: 11-10; Fri-Sat: 11 a.m.-midnight unoppressivebooks.blogspot.com

Beyond the intriguing name and teal awning are scads of books in all genres. The inventory at this family-owned store is constantly changing, as it is carefully chosen from publisher overstock. The shelves are overloaded with classics by authors like Chaucer and Hemingway, popular children's titles, art, travel, poetry, science fiction, politics, health, and food books. Tables flanking the front door are piled with the best deals, some books starting at $2. This is a great neighborhood spot with liberatingly low prices.

MUSIC

THE JUILLIARD STORE
144 W 66th St (bet Broadway and Amsterdam Ave)   212/799-5000, ext 237
Mon-Sat: 10-6; Sun: noon-5   thejuilliardstore.com

The Juilliard Store is one of the few remaining brick-and-mortar sheet music stores. With an extensive selection of sheet music and scores, and hard-to-find books on classical music, this bookstore claims to carry every classical-music book in print! You will also find general interest and specialty books, CDs, DVDs, musical accessories, and apparel and gifts. As a bonus, there are many talented classical musicians employed here, and they are ready to share their musical passions.

MYSTERY

MYSTERIOUS BOOKSHOP
58 Warren St (bet West Broadway and Church St)   212/587-1011
Mon-Sat: 11-7   mysteriousbookshop.com

One of the oldest mystery specialist bookstores in America, the shop stocks all types of new mystery books in hardcover and paperback. It is also filled from floor to ceiling with out-of-print, used, and rare books. Amazingly, the staff seems to know exactly what is in stock. If it is not on the shelves, they will order it. There is as much talk as business conducted here, and you can even converse with authors who sign their works from time to time. Mysterious carries thousands of autographed books, and over recent years has published some limited, signed editions by some of the most popular mystery authors.

NEW YORK

CITYSTORE

1 Centre St (at Chambers St), north plaza of Municipal Bldg	212/386-0007
Mon-Fri: 10-5	
141 Worth St (at Hamill Pl)	212/386-0007
Mon-Fri: 8:30-3:45	a856-citystore.nyc.gov

CityStore is the official store of the city of New York, the "museum store" for the city. It is the retail entity for gifts, collectibles, and research materials. From classic to fun, a variety of items includes authentic NYC memorabilia, sterling silver jewelry, City Seal silk ties and scarves, pins, taxi medallions, posters, and official merchandise for the NYPD, FDNY, DSNY, NYC Parks, NYC Taxi, NYC Subway, and more. Book topics include biking in NY, guides and maps, history, sports, and cookbooks. *The Green Book* is the official directory of the city of New York, listing phone numbers and addresses of more than 900 government agencies and 6,000 officials. It includes state, federal, and international listings, as well as courts and a section on licenses.

RARE AND OUT-OF-PRINT

ALABASTER BOOKSHOP

122 Fourth Ave (bet 12th and 13th St)	212/982-3550
Mon-Sat: 10-10; Sun: 11-10	abebooks.com

Alabaster Bookshop is the lone holdout on Fourth Avenue, once known as "Bookshop Row." Owner Steve Crowley offers a great selection of used and rare books in all categories while focusing on literature and the arts. Prices at this tiny outpost range from $2 paperbacks to a $1,000 first edition. Among the stacks of books, specialities include New York City, photography, and the arts, or check out bargains outside on the rolling carts on the sidewalk.

ARGOSY BOOK STORE

116 E 59th St (bet Park and Lexington Ave)	212/753-4455
Mon-Fri: 10-6; Sat: 10-5 (closed Sat in summer)	argosybooks.com

Since 1925 and now in its third generation of ownership, Argosy Book Store houses six stories of antiquarian and out-of-print items. They specialize in Americana, modern first editions, autographs, art, antique maps and prints, and the history of science and medicine. Beyond that, there are also thousands of books in other fields of interest. They offer a specialty service of finding unusual gifts.

BAUMAN RARE BOOKS

535 Madison Ave (bet 54th and 55th St)	212/751-0011
Mon-Sat: 10-6	baumanrarebooks.com

Bauman offers a fine collection of rare books and autographs, maps, and prints dating from the 15th through the 20th centuries. Included are works of literature, history, economics, law, science, medicine, nature, travel, and exploration. First editions and children's books are a specialty. Whether you are an advanced collector, novice, or just looking for a unique gift, Bauman is an excellent source with over 4,000 books and documents.

IMPERIAL FINE BOOKS

790 Madison Ave (bet 66th and 67th St), 2nd floor   212/861-6620
Mon-Fri: 10:30-6   imperialfinebooks.com

Imperial is the place to visit if you are in the market for books that look as great as they read. You will find fine leather, jeweled, and exhibition bindings, illustrated books, vintage children's books, unique first editions, and magnificent sets of prized volumes. Their inventory includes literary giants like Twain, Dickens, Brontë, and Shakespeare. An outstanding Oriental art gallery features Chinese ceramics and antiques. Services include complete restoration, binding, and cleaning of damaged or aged books, as well as custom bookbinding and library projects. A search office will locate titles and make appraisals.

J.N. BARTFIELD FINE & RARE BOOKS

30 W 57th St (bet Fifth Ave and Ave of the Americas), 5th floor 212/245-8890
Mon-Fri: 10-5; Sat: 10-3 (closed Sat in summer)   bartfield.com

In business since 1937, Bartfield buys and sells rare and fine books and manuscripts of every collecting category, including Americana. Selections are ever-changing as some pieces are accepted on consignment. Check online for recent acquisitions.

RELIGIOUS

J. LEVINE BOOKS & JUDAICA

5 W 30th St (bet Fifth Ave and Broadway)   212/695-6888
Mon-Wed: 9-6; Thurs: 9-7; Fri: 9-2; Sun: 10-5 (closed Sun in July)
                                                           levinejudaica.com

As one of the oldest Jewish bookstores in the city, Levine is a leader in the market. Over five generations, the store has likely achieved their goal of becoming the "Henri Bendel of Judaica." Though the emphasis is still on the written word, they also carry many gift items, tapes, coffee-table books, thousands of Judaica items, and one of the largest selections of Jewish marriage ketubahs. You can also shop and order online.

ST. PATRICK'S CATHEDRAL GIFT STORE

15 E 51st St (bet Fifth and Madison Ave)   212/355-2749, ext 820 or 825
Daily: 8:30-8   stpatscathedralgiftshop.com

With lovely music playing in the background, this store is an oasis of calm in midtown. You can browse books on Catholicism, displays of rosary beads, statues of saints, music, wall decor, medals, prayer cards, and children's and keepsake gifts. Proceeds benefit the cathedral and its upkeep.

THEATER

DRAMA BOOK SHOP
250 W 40th St (bet Seventh and Eighth Ave)　　　　212/944-0595
Mon-Sat: 11-7 (Thurs till 8); Sun: noon-6　　　　dramabookshop.com

　　Since 1917 this shop has been providing a valuable service to the performing-arts community. Its stock includes publications dealing with musical theater, TV, radio, film, Shakespeare, directing, writing, set design, and costumes. It is the premiere shop for screenplays and scripts, is well known for courteous and knowledgeable service.

RICHARD STODDARD — PERFORMING ARTS BOOKS
43 E 10th St (bet University Pl and Broadway), Room 6D　　212/598-9421
By appointment　　　　richardstoddard.com

　　Richard Stoddard runs a one-man operation dedicated to rare and out-of-print books, autographs, and to memorabilia relating to the performing arts. Equipped with a Ph.D. from Yale in Theater History and over three decades of experience as a dealer and appraiser of performing-arts materials, Stoddard offers a broad range of items. He has the largest collection of New York playbills (about 20,000) for sale in the U.S., as well as books, autographs, souvenir programs, and original stage designs, including hundreds of Broadway costume designs by Florence Klotz.

USED

HOUSING WORKS BOOKSTORE CAFE
126 Crosby St (bet Houston and Prince St)　　　　212/334-3324
Mon-Fri: 10-9; Sat, Sun: 10-5　　　　housingworks.org

　　All merchandise at Housing Works is donated. You'll find new and rare used books, collectibles, out-of-print titles, first editions, DVDs, CDs, vinyl records, and audiobooks. The cafe features baked goods, seasonal soups, sandwiches, salads, soft drinks, beer and wine, and catering services. Proceeds go to Housing Works, providing social services for homeless New Yorkers with HIV/AIDS.

BUTTONS

TENDER BUTTONS
143 E 62nd St (bet Lexington and Third Ave)　　　　212/758-7004
Mon-Fri: 10:30-6; Sat: 10:30-5:30　　　　tenderbuttons-nyc.com

　　Inside a tiny brick townhouse, Tender Buttons could be considered a lesson in the history of buttons. Diana Epstein and Millicent Safro show some of the most unusual examples discovered in their world travels in floor-to-ceiling displays. One antique wooden display cabinet shows off a selection of original buttons, many imported or made exclusively for the store. There are buttons of pearl, wood, horn, silver, leather, ceramic, bone, ivory, pewter, and semiprecious stones. Many are antiques. Some are as highly valued as artwork; a French enamel button, for instance, can cost almost as much as a painting! Unique pieces can be made into special cuff links — real conversation pieces for the lucky owner. Blazer buttons are a specialty. They also have a fine collection of antique and period cuff links and men's stud sets. I am a cuff link buff and have purchased some of my best pieces from this shop.

CHINA AND GLASSWARE

CRATE & BARREL

650 Madison Ave (at 59th St) — 212/308-0011
Mon-Fri: 10-8; Sat: 10-7; Sun: noon-6
611 Broadway (at Houston St) — 212/780-0004
Mon-Sat: 10-9; Sun: 11-7 — crateandbarrel.com

Named for their original display pieces, Crate & Barrel stores are loaded with attractive quality merchandise at sensible prices. Even if you aren't in the market for china, glassware, cookware, home accessories, bed and bath furnishings, storage pieces, or casual furniture, the creative displays will make shopping hard to resist. Quick, no-fuss checkout, too!

FISHS EDDY

889 Broadway (at 19th St) — 212/420-9020
Mon-Thurs: 9-9; Fri, Sat: 9 a.m.-10 p.m.; Sun: 10-8 — fishseddy.com

This shop is fun to browse for some of the most unusual and durable-strength china and glassware items available anywhere. Nearly everything at Fishs Eddy is made in America; the stock of dinnerware, flatware, glassware, and kitchenware changes regularly. Check out their own unique patterns including the New York Skyline, Brooklynese (buttah), and Dog Walker, or their random vintage pieces. This is a treasure trove for bargain hunters; you'll find interesting accessory selections of linens, T-shirts, coasters, and more.

CLOTHING AND ACCESSORIES

ANTIQUE AND VINTAGE

FAMILY JEWELS VINTAGE CLOTHING

130 W 23rd St (bet Ave of the Americas and Seventh Ave) — 212/633-6020
Sun-Tues: 11-7; Wed-Sat: 11-8 — familyjewelsnyc.com

Family Jewels is *the* place to go for American vintage clothing, shoes, accessories, and beautiful costume jewelry from the Victorian era through the 1980s. The men's and women's stock is well organized, the selections are huge, the service is excellent, and shopping is fun! Prices are reasonable, too. The decor is 1940s with retro background music. A costume and styling service is available.

LEGACY

109 Thompson St (between Prince and Spring St) — 212/966-4827
Daily: noon-7 — legacy-nyc.com

In keeping with their credo "it's in the mix," Legacy carries vintage women's fashions from the 1940s alongside original new designs, some made with vintage fabrics. Big-name designers like Gucci, Chanel, and Ungaro are represented in this eclectic Soho shop, which shows an assortment of suits, dresses, separates, outerwear, shoes, handbags, and accessories. Legacy's owner, Rita Brookoff, will help pair a vintage blouse with a current fashion suit or select the perfect black dress for a timelessly chic look.

REMINISCENCE

74 Fifth Ave (bet 13th and 14th St)   212/243-2292
Mon-Sat: 10-8; Sun: noon-7   reminiscence.com

At this hip emporium in Greenwich Village you will revisit the decades from
the 1960s through the 1980s. Founder Stewart Richer is a product of this era,
and his finds are unusual and wearable. Large selections of colorful vintage
clothing, attractive displays of jewelry, hats, gifts, and accessories are featured.
Richer's own brand of goods, although vintage in style, are inexpensive and
varied, with Hawaiian prints one of the most popular choices. The company
sells to outlets all over the world, and because of its vast distribution, Richer can
produce large quantities and sell at low prices.

SCREAMING MIMI'S

382 Lafayette St (bet 4th and Great Jones St)   212/677-6464
Mon-Sat: noon-8; Sun: 1-7   screamingmimis.com

Screaming Mimi's is a landmark vintage emporium founded in 1978. It is
known for its excellent selection of men's and women's clothing and accessories
from the 1950s through the 1990s. There is an excellent showing of handbags,
shoes, jewelry, sunglasses, and hats. One department also features high-end
vintage couture.

TRASH & VAUDEVILLE

4 St. Mark's Pl (bet Second and Third Ave)   212/982-3590
Mon-Thurs: noon-8; Fri: 11:30-8:30; Sat: 11:30-9; Sun: 1-7:30

trashandvaudeville.com

The stock at this energetic shop changes constantly and seems to have no
boundaries. Its inventory for men and women is geared toward outrageous rock,
punk, and goth clothing, footwear, and accessories. An excellent source for rock
and roll styles from the 1950s to the present; original designs, too.

ATHLETIC

LULULEMON ATHLETICA

481 Broadway (bet Broome and Grand St)	212/334-8276
15 Union Square W (bet 14th and 15th St)	212/675-5286
1928 Broadway (at 64th St)	212/712-1767
1127 Third Ave (at 66th St)	212/755-5019

Numerous other locations
Hours vary by store   lululemon.com

Founded in Canada, this yoga-inspired clothing store shows attractive and
offbeat wear for active people. You'll find clothing and gear for yoga, dancing,
running, and other athletic pursuits. Check out lululemon's in-store events,
including free yoga classes.

BRIDAL

HERE COMES THE BRIDESMAID

213 W 35th St (bet Seventh and Eighth Ave), Room 403   212/647-9686
Tues-Thurs: 11-8; Fri, Sat: 11-5   bridesmaids.com
By appointment

Apparel Bargains in New York!

Baby gear: **Buy Buy BABY** (270 Seventh Ave, 917/344-1555)

Clothing: **Old Navy** (150 W 34th St, 212/594-0115; 610 Ave of the Americas, 212/645-0663; 503-511 Broadway, 212/226-0838; and 300 W 125th St, 212/531-1544)

Clothing for the family: **H&M** (1328 Broadway, 646/473-1164 and other locations) and **Loehmann's** (101 Seventh Ave, 212/352-0856 and 2101 Broadway, 212/882-9990)

Clothing, men's and women's: **Zara** (101 Fifth Ave, 212/741-0555; 39 W 34th St, 212/868-6551; 500 Fifth Ave, 212/302-2551; 750 Lexington Ave, 212/754-1120; 580 Broadway, 212/343-1725; and 1963 Broadway, 212/362-4272)

Discount department store: **Century 21** (22 Cortlandt St, 212/227-9092 and 1972 Broadway, 212/518-2121)

Shoes: **DSW** (40 E 14th St, 212/674-2146; 213 W 34th St, 967-9703; and 2220 Broadway, 917/746-9422)

Shoes, running: **Super Runners Shop** (745 Seventh Ave, 212/398-2449 and other locations): apparel and accessories, too!

Shoes, athletic: **Sprint Sports** (2511 Broadway, 212/866-8077)

Now there's a store just for bridesmaids! Here Comes the Bridesmaid carries designer bridesmaid gowns available in every size from After Six, Bill Levkoff, Bari Jay, Lazaro, and others. Featured gowns can be hemmed and worn again to occasions other than weddings. Weekend hours make Here Comes the Bridesmaid especially convenient for working women.

KLEINFELD

110 W 20th St (bet Ave of the Americas and Seventh Ave) 646/633-4300
Tues, Thurs: 10:30-7; Fri: 11-5:30; Sat, Sun: 9:30-5:30 kleinfeldbridal.com
By appointment

From beginning to end, the Kleinfeld experience sets the standard for all brides-to-be. A 35,000-square-foot location features the most exclusive bridal- and evening-wear designs, including plus sizes. They are tops in the business, and the Manhattan salon is a wonder to experience. Brides will enjoy a private dressing room with an experienced consultant to review 1,500 styles of American and European designer bridal gowns (plus headpieces and accessories), including Amsale, Carol Hannah, Isaac Mizrahi, Pnina Tornai, and Temperley. The perfect Kleinfeld fit is achieved with an experienced team of professional stylists, bridal consultants, custom fitters, seamstresses, beaders, embroiderers, and pressers.

CHILDREN'S

Before describing what I consider to be the best children's clothing stores in New York, let me be clear about what I'm *not* including: big chains and the haughty "just so" boutiques that line Madison Avenue. That is not to say some of the chains don't have great stores here. GapKids and babyGap, The Children's

Place, and Gymboree all have good selections, as does the cavernous "big-box" buybuy BABY. But unlike the stores listed below, they sell very little that isn't available in any other city. As for the haughty boutiques, I see no reason to patronize these wildly overpriced and unwelcoming places.

BONNE NUIT
1193 Lexington Ave (at 81st St)   212/472-7300
Mon-Sat: 9-7; Sun: noon-5
    What a fun place to shop! You'll find mother-and-daughter pajamas, robes, and slippers; European children's wear for boys and girls (up to preteen sizes); old-fashioned children's books; wool and cashmere blankets; and baby gifts. Very personal service is another plus.

CLEMENTINE
39½ Washington Square S (bet Ave of the Americas and MacDougal St)
212/228-9333
Mon-Sat: 11-7; Sun: 11-5   clementineconsignment.com
    You can dress your little darlings at this adorable consignment shop, which specializes in infant and toddler fashions (up to size 4T) at exceptional prices. The mother-daughter owners select designer kids' brand names such as Bonpoint, Jacadi, Liz Lange, Oilily, and Isabella Oliver. There is an amazing selection of top-name maternity wear as well.

ESTELLA
27 W 20th St (bet Fifth Ave and Ave of the Americas)   212/255-3553
Mon-Fri: 9-5   estella-nyc.com
    Estella is a popular children's boutique created by the husband-and-wife team of Jean Polsky and Chike Chukwolozie. Clothing of unusual colors and fabrics includes such labels as Amelia, Bon Bon, Estella, Jellycat, Larucci, and Munster. Stock includes unique toys and gear, including the Bugaboo stroller line, and furniture. This is a great source for special and unusual gifts for youngsters six and under, and service is given with a smile.

GIGGLE
120 Wooster St (bet Spring and Prince St)   212/334-5817
Mon-Sat: 10-7; Sun: noon-6
1033 Lexington Ave (at 74th St)   212/249-4249
352 Amsterdam Ave (bet 76th and 77th St)   212/362-8680
Mon-Sat: 10-7; Sun: 11-6   giggle.com
    If you are a parent or about to become one, giggle is a godsend! You'll find most every baby item needed to take care of little ones, including furniture for the nursery. In addition, there are toys, books, music, bath and spa items, clothing, strollers, car seats, baby monitors, and information on keeping baby healthy and happy. Helpful personal shoppers and a baby registry are available.

LESTER'S
1534 Second Ave (at 80th St)   212/734-9292
Mon-Sat: 10-7 (Thurs till 8); Sun: 11-6   lesters.com
    If you're looking for stylish clothes, shoes, campwear, and/or accessories for

children and don't want to leave the East Side, Lester's is your best bet. It is large and inviting, including a downstairs section dedicated entirely to boys. In fact, you can clothe everyone from infants to teenagers — and even moms, with a selection of women's contemporary clothing. A good selection of shoes, too.

LUCKY WANG

799 Broadway (bet 10th and 11th St)	212/353-2850
1435 Lexington Ave (bet 93rd and 94th St)	212/360-6900
82 Seventh Ave (bet 15th and 16th St)	212/229-2900
Hours vary by location	luckywang.com

For something unusual or unique in children's wear, these sister stores showcase colorful contemporary kimonos and karate pants for babies and kids; they are as fashionable as they are practical. A few more labels are featured as well, as are pants, shoes, blankets, toys, and other items.

SPACE KIDDETS

26 E 22nd St (bet Park Ave S and Broadway)	212/420-9878
Mon-Sat: 10:30-6 (Wed, Thurs till 7); Sun: 11-5	spacekiddets.com

This cheerful store is overflowing with funky children's clothes, shoes, and accessories for newborns to tweens. The eclectic selection at Space Kiddets is always fresh and fun, with over 200 brands represented. Check out the vintage rock T-shirts from Angel Blue (Japanese) label. There is also a wide assortment of toys and playthings. Moreover, the sales staff is welcoming and helpful.

COSTUMES

ABRACADABRA

19 W 21st St (bet Fifth Ave and Ave of the Americas)	212/627-5194
Mon-Sat: 11-7; Sun: noon-5 (extended hours during Halloween season)	
	abracadabrasuperstore.com

Abracadabra is a gagster's heaven! They rent and sell costumes and costume accessories, magician's supplies, theatrical makeup, and props for magic tricks. You can be transformed into almost anything! Come to the free magic show on Sunday.

NEW YORK COSTUMES/HALLOWEEN ADVENTURE

104 Fourth Ave (bet 11th and 12th St)	212/673-4546
Mon-Sat: 11-8; Sun: noon-7 (extended hours during Halloween season and holidays)	
	newyorkcostumes.com

You and your family will be the talk of the neighborhood after a visit here. You'll find an extensive inventory of retail and rental costumes for adults, kids, and pets. Rave party gear and decor, wigs, hats, gags, magic items, props, and all manner of games and novelties are showcased. In addition, a professional makeup artist is on hand most of the time.

RICKY'S NYC

375 Broadway (bet Franklin and White St)	212/925-5490
111 Third Ave (bet 13th and 14th St)	212/674-9640
383 Fifth Ave (bet 35th and 36th St)	212/481-6701
Numerous other locations	
Hours vary by location (extended hours in Oct)	rickyshalloween.com

Ricky's may be best known for their Halloween paraphernalia: costumes and masks for the whole family, including pets, and every scary accessory under the full moon. With expanded locations throughout the city, they also stock crazy, funky, historical, and seasonal costumes for other holidays and events, plus everyday fashion accessories, cosmetics, and wigs.

FAMILY

FOREVER 21

1540 Broadway (bet 45th and 46th St)	212/302-0594
50 W 34th St (bet Broadway and Fifth Ave)	212/564-2346
40 E 14th St (bet University Pl and Broadway)	212/228-0598
Hours vary by store	forever21.com

Just follow the well-dressed younger crowd to this store. Merchandise is trendy, bright, fun, and moderately priced for men, women, and girls. Apparel choices include casual, business, occasion, maternity, and swimwear. There is also a line of good-looking plus-size clothing. Beauty products, shoes, and up-to-the minute accessories complete the look. The Times Square location (1540 Broadway) is open until 2 a.m.!

MARC JACOBS

163 Mercer St (bet Prince and Houston St), women's, men's	212/343-1490
298 W 4th St (at Bank St), Little Marc	212/206-6644
301 W 4th St (at Bank St), women's accessories	212/929-9455
382 Bleecker St (at Perry St), men's	212/929-0304
385 Bleecker St (at Perry St), men's and women's accessories	212/924-6126
400 Bleecker St (at 11th St), Bookmarc (books, stationery, and accessories)	
	212/620-4021
403-405 Bleecker St (at 11th St), women's	212/924-0026
Hours vary by store	marcjacobs.com

Walk around Bleecker Street and before long, you are sure to encounter a Marc Jacobs store! Each entity is a specialty shop, with offerings of very stylish ready-to-wear women's clothes and accessories, adorable children's togs, men's attire and accessories, eyeglasses, footwear, handbags, and books. This popular American designer has certainly made his mark in the West Village and Soho.

FURS AND LEATHER

BARBARA SHAUM

60 E 4th St (bet Bowery and Second Ave)	212/254-4250
Wed-Sat: 1-6	

Since 1963 Barbara Shaum has been doing magical things with leather. She's a wonder with sandals, bags, sterling-silver buckles, and belts (with handmade brass, nickel-silver, inlaid wood, and copper buckles). Everything is designed in the shop, and each item is meticulously crafted using only the finest materials.

G. MICHAEL HENNESSY FURS

224 W 30th St, Room 402	212/695-7991
Mon-Fri: 9:30-4:30; Sat: by appointment	

Hennessy furs and service are famous worldwide; the label assures you of superior pelts, great designs, and fair prices. Their showroom stocks hundreds of furs, ranging from highly-coveted minks and sables to sporty boutique furs and shearlings. You'll find all the newest fashion looks, colors, shapes, and techniques. If you already have a fur wardrobe, Rubye Hennessy can update it for an entirely new look. The firm's expertise in restyling is astonishing, in part due to Rubye's experience as a former fashion editor. Imagine a luxurious but outdated and oversized mink coat. Hennessy's workrooms can turn it into a flattering short-sheared mink garment that reverses to a raincoat or evening coat, depending on your choice of fabric. They can even remake your old mink coat into a bomber or motorcycle jacket, or create a shoulder shrug from leftover pieces; a good way to reinvest your fur. Services include storage; call for pickup in the Manhattan area.

Treasure & Bond

Northwest retailer Nordstrom has made a splash in Manhattan with its innovative **Treasure & Bond** (350 West Broadway, 646/669-9049). Not only does this store sell luxury home goods and clothing and accessories for men, women and children, but 100% of the net profits go back into the community to help local people in need. Nordstrom is planning a seven-story full-line store to be built at Broadway and 57th Street.

GOODMAN COUTURE
224 W 30th St, Room 402   212/244-7422
Mon-Fri: 9-5; Sat: by appointment

The Goodman family has been creating fine fur styles since 1918. Third-generation furrier David Goodman is famous for high-quality fur-lined and reversible fur coats and jackets. He carries a beautiful collection of the world's finest furs, including the latest fashions in minks, sheared minks, fine sables, and other unique furs, plus a luxurious selection of custom-made shearlings. Goodman is a trailblazer in restyling furs and restoring life to an out-of-style or unused fur coat. Another specialty is converting unused furs into fur-lined all-weather coats. Goodman's hottest new item is the "featherweight" fur-lined reversible coat — a "must-have" item and the perfect town-and-travel coat for women on the go.

HOSIERY

FOGAL
611 Madison Ave (at 58th St)   212/207-3080
785 Madison Ave (bet 66th and 67th St)   212/535-8510
155 Spring St (at West Broadway)   212/775-7400
Hours vary by store   fogal.com

If it's fashionable and different legwear you're after, Fogal has it. Plain hosiery comes in nearly a hundred hues. The elegant designs and patterns make the number of choices almost incalculable. Fogal also carries bodywear and fine knitwear.

MEN'S AND WOMEN'S — GENERAL

A BATHING APE

91 Greene St (bet Spring and Prince St)   212/925-0222
Mon-Fri: noon-7 (Fri till 8); Sat: 11-8; Sun: 11-7   us.bape.com

A Bathing Ape is a Japanese clothing label created by designer Nigo. This store is for lovers of urban streetwear. Offerings include digital printed T-shirts and unusual clothing (jackets, pants, and sweatshirts), shoes, and accessories (hats, belts, gloves, backpacks, and more). Fans of rock-star couture will be blown away.

BILLY REID

54 Bond St (at Bowery)   212/598-9355
Mon-Sat: 11-8; Sun: 11-7   billyreid.com

The style of clothes sold here might best be described as "Southern comfort." An Alabama gentleman, William "Billy" Reid designs tailored apparel in easy-to-wear moleskin, hopsack, tweeds, and plaids. Men and women will find outerwear, jackets, sweaters, pants, shirts, dresses, and tops. A custom-tailoring department will make you look extra sharp. It's worth a trip to Reid to see the decor, as recommissioned heirloom items from down South have taken on creative uses up North.

BLUE TREE

1283 Madison Ave (at 91st St)   212/369-2583
Mon-Fri: 10-6; Sat, Sun: 11-6   bluetreenyc.com

You never know what you might find at this unusual boutique! The street floor has gifts and trinkets for almost any occasion, while the second floor displays a rather exclusive collection of clothing and accessories for men and women. A number of big-name clothing designers are represented at Blue Tree. Eclectic music, home items, and fragrances can also be found.

CHRISTOPHER FISCHER

80 Wooster St (bet Broome and Spring St)   212/965-9009
1225 Madison Ave (bet 88th and 89th St)   212/831-8880
Mon-Sat: 10-6; Sun: noon-6   christopherfischer.com

Christopher Fischer is a home-style store that carries luxurious cashmere and leather goods for men, women, and children, including sweaters, blankets, shawls, scarves, bags, and cushions. There's even a cashmere line for babies.

Cuff Links

Links of London (MetLife Building, 200 Park Ave, 212/867-0258 and 535 Madison Ave, 212/588-1177)

The Missing Link (Showplace Antiques and Design Center, 40 W 25th St, Room 108, 212/645-6928): antique and new

Thomas Pink (520 Madison Ave, 212/838-1928; 1155 Ave of the Americas, 212/840-9663; Time Warner Center, 10 Columbus Circle, 212/823-9650; and 63 Wall St, 212/514-7683)

Plus-Sized Shopping

There's no need to forego fashionable styles if you wear larger sizes of clothing, especially if you buy from these shops:

Ashley Stewart (216W125th St, 212/531-0800 and 49 W 116th St, 917-492-3693)

HotSexyFit (35 W 125th St, 212/369-1979): Brazilian jeans

Imparali Custom Tailors (608 Fifth Ave, 212/245-5555): larger sizes at no additional charge, alterations

Marina Rinaldi (13 E 69th St, 212/734-4333): classy women's clothes, cashmere, boots, accessories

Monif C. Plus Sizes (325 W 38th St, Room 207, 212/842-1641): swimwear, cocktail dresses

Orchard Corset (157 Orchard St, 212/674-0786): sexy and affordable undergarments

Rochester Big & Tall (1301 Ave of the Americas, 212/247-7500): full selection of brand-name menswear

THE DRESSING ROOM BOUTIQUE & BAR

75-A Orchard St (bet Broome and Grand St)   212/966-7330
Tues-Wed: 1 p.m.-midnight; Thurs-Sat: 1 p.m.-2 a.m.; Sun: 1:30-8

thedressingroomnyc.com

Shoppers at this hybrid boutique are treated to a wide assortment of both new and consigned accessories, jewelry, and clothing, with emerging independent fashion and accessory designers being featured. The full-service bar on the first level is a welcome resting spot for the weary shopper — Wi-Fi, movies are shown on a large screen, and live DJ events are additional draws. On the lower level customers have the chance to shop or consign carefully selected vintage and secondhand items for cash or store credit.

GARGYLE

16-A Orchard St (bet Canal and Hester St)   917/470-9367
Daily: 11-7   gargyle.com

Leisure attire doesn't get any better than at Gargyle, purveyors of upscale country-club clothing, shoes, and classy accessories for men and women. They carry tops, bottoms, shoes, swimwear, and accessories from some of the world's best designers. Even if you're not part of the country-club set, you'll leave here dressed to impress.

H&M

150 E 86th St (at Lexington Ave)   855/466-7467 (all stores)
Shops at Columbus Circle
10 Columbus Circle, 2nd and 3rd floors
640 Fifth Ave (at 51st St)
1328 Broadway (at 34th St)

Numerous other locations
Hours vary by store   hm.com

Since its opening, H&M has been packing customers in, and it's no secret why! In a convivial atmosphere, up-to-date clothing and whimsical accessories for men, ladies, and children can be found at very reasonable prices. Don't come looking for pricey labels; what you will find are knockoffs of items that sell for much more at boutiques and department stores. The Swedes understand that American yuppies like to fill their closets with stylish, affordable clothing, and H&M is the place to get it. A nice collection of home items for bed, bath, and kitchen as well!

HARLEM UNDERGROUND
20 E 125th St (bet Fifth and Madison Ave)   212/987-9385
Mon-Thurs: 10-7; Fri, Sat: 10-8; Sun: noon-6

This is a great stop for comfortable, reasonably priced, and "cool" urban wear. Guys will like the Harlem-themed T-shirts. The merchandise has the feel of the historic neighborhood it represents. Personal or corporate embroidery is available for denim shirts and jackets, T-shirts, sweats, and caps.

JEAN SHOP
435 W 14th St (bet Ninth and Tenth Ave)   212/366-5326
Mon-Sat: 11-7; Sun: noon-6   worldjeanshop.com

These are not ordinary jeans. Each pair is created to a customer's specifications using high-quality Japanese selvedge denim (woven on projectile looms in Japan). Choose from classic and relaxed fit or rocker styles in short, medium, and long lengths, and show your personality with custom distressing and dyeing. Create a one-of-a-kind denim outfit from a selection of jackets, shirts, belts, and accessories; some leather clothing, too. These are quality goods, so expect to pay accordingly.

JEFFREY — NEW YORK
449 W 14th St (bet Ninth and Tenth Ave)   212/206-1272
Mon-Fri: 10-8 (Thurs till 9); Sat: 10-7; Sun: 12:30-6   jeffreynewyork.com

Jeffrey Kalinsky's store in the Meatpacking District offers chic and high-end men's and women's clothing. Besides ready-to-wear, there are innovative accessories, cosmetics, and an excellent selection of shoes. With fashion names like Prada, Gucci, Missoni, Nina Ricci, and Versace, expect matching price tags.

LOUIS VUITTON
1 E 57th St (at Fifth Ave)   212/758-8877
Mon-Wed: 10-7; Thurs-Sat: 10-8; Sun: 11-7
116 Greene St (bet Prince and Spring St)   212/274-9090
Mon-Thurs: noon-7; Fri, Sat: 11-7; Sun: noon-6   louisvuitton.com

In spectacular quarters, these shops have nearly everything you might expect with the Louis Vuitton name: a dramatic exterior, compelling windows, a tasteful assortment of merchandise, service with an attitude, and inflated prices. Classic leather goods and Marc Jacobs-designed apparel fill these exclusive spaces. If the LV signature is important to you, then this is the place to shop.

OPENING CEREMONY

35 Howard St (bet Broadway and Crosby St)   212/219-2688
Mon-Sat: 11-8; Sun: noon-7
Ace Hotel
1190-92 Broadway (bet 28th and 29th St)   646/695-5680
Daily: 11-9   openingceremony.us

Opening Ceremony is actually a multinational retail store, showroom, and gallery, all under one roof. Each year, men's and women's fashions by emerging designers and artists are added to the existing lines of brand-name designers and retailers. Many styles are avant-garde (don't expect bargain prices), and you'll find special lines from established brands like Pendleton, Rodarte, and Topshop. Since Opening Ceremony's startup more than a decade ago, fantastic lines from Brazil, Germany, the U.K., Sweden, and Japan have been introduced, sometimes springboarding a designer into the American retail market.

RALPH LAUREN

888 Madison Ave (bet 71st and 72nd St), women's and home flagship
                                                              212/434-8000
878 Madison Ave (bet 71st and 72nd St), children's store   212/606-3376
872 Madison Ave (bet 71st and 72nd St), baby store   212/434-8083
867 Madison Ave (at 71st St), men's flagship   212/606-2100
811 Madison Ave (bet 67th and 68th St), eyewear   212/988-4620
109 Prince St (at Greene St), men's, women's   212/625-1660

RRL

31 Prince St (at Mott St), men's   212/343-0841
381 Bleecker St (at Perry St), men's   212/462-4390
383 Bleecker St (bet Charles and Perry St), men's   212/645-5513
379 West Broadway (bet Spring and Broome St), men and women's
                                                              212/625-3480

DENIM & SUPPLY

99 University Pl (bet 11th and 12th St), denim store   212/677-1895
Hours vary by store   ralphlauren.com

Ralph Lauren's life story is the epitome of the American dream, and in the past decades he has only furthered the image with an outstanding collection of clothing for men, women, and children, plus a top-flight line of home goods and accessories. His merchandise is available in the outlets listed above. Department stores, particularly Macy's, show a great collection of Lauren and associated labels. Be sure to visit the men's and children's store in the fabulous Rhinelander Mansion (867 Madison Avenue). The label's largest women's store is across the street (888 Madison Avenue) in a beautiful mansion with expanded lingerie and fine jewelry lines and a complete home store, too. **RRL** and **Denim & Supply** are extensions of the brand and feature rugged, cowboy-influenced clothing and a denim line of clothing and accessories. If you are label-conscious, you can't do better than Ralph Lauren. If price is a major consideration, you might want to shop around a bit more!

STEVEN ALAN

230 Elizabeth St (bet Prince and Houston St)	212/343/7974
103 Franklin St (bet Church St and West Broadway)	212/343-0692
465 Amsterdam Ave (bet 82nd and 83rd St)	212/595-8451
158 Franklin St (bet Varick and Hudson St), home store	646/402-9661

Numerous other locations
Hours vary by store   stevenalan.com

Steven Alan has gathered an eclectic group of more than 20 emerging designers and showcases their creations in his stores. You'll find men's and women's casual essentials, outerwear, handbags, accessories, and toiletries — all unique. A home shop was recently added which features an assortment of bed, bath, and tabletop items; books; food items; and even a line of bicycles.

TOPSHOP/TOPMAN SOHO

478 Broadway (bet Broome and Grand St)   212/966-9555
Mon-Sat: 10-9; Sun: 11-8   topshop.com, topman.com

Housed within the same building, these Soho stores are the only U.S. affiliates of these trendy British retail chains. Topshop offers three floors of the latest style-setting apparel for ladies (sizes zero to 12); accessories and shoes, too. Guys will find plenty of modern shirts, pants, sweaters, coats, and hoodies for their wardrobes at Topman. Personal stylists are on hand to help customers pull together the right look. The experience is spread over four floors, and new merchandise is constantly arriving.

UNIQLO

546 Broadway (at Spring St)   877/386-4756 (all stores)
31 W 34th St (bet Fifth Ave and Ave of the Americas)
666 Fifth Ave (at 53rd St)
Mon-Sat: 10-9; Sun: 11-8   uniqlo.com

These Uniqlo locations are branches of one of Japan's largest retailers, started in 1984 in Hiroshima, Japan. Their motto is "made for all." You'll find high-quality casual wear for men, women, and children in a wide range of fabrics and prices. Denim and cashmere items with matching accessories are featured. The ultra-modern midtown location has over 100 dressing rooms in the 89,000-square-foot space.

MEN'S FORMAL WEAR

CUSTOM MEN

140 W 57th St (bet Ave of the Americas and Seventh Ave), Suite 4C
                                                                 212/767-0545
Mon-Fri: 10-8; Sat: 10-5; Sun: by appointment   custommen.com

The choices at Custom Men are almost limitless! Men's suits, sport coats, slacks, tuxedos, topcoats, and shirts are individually tailored. There are about 15,000 fabrics to peruse, including Wain Shiell, Holland & Sherry, and Ermenegildo Zegna for suits; French pique, Italian tessitura, and pinpoint Oxford shirtings; and a wide variety of linings. Choose from double- or single-breasted jackets. Pants can be made in any style to fit all shapes and sizes. There are dozens of shirt-collar, cuff, and front- and back-style combination options. Prices are competitive (especially sale prices), free alterations are offered within one

Wigs, Hairpieces, and Extensions

Wigs may be a necessity for some men and women and a convenience for others. Before you shell out big bucks for a new head of hair, research all the options and work with a reputable wig salon.

Design by Flora (248 E 78th St, 212/510-8805): top quality European hair wigs, extensions, falls

Helena Collection (120 W 31st St, 212/967-9945): men's and women's ready-made and custom hair pieces

Joseph Fleischer Company (276 Fifth Ave, 212/686-7701): custom made for men and women

Karen's Wigs (1776 Broadway, Suite 1708; 212/977-2555): ready-made pieces

Wigbar (431 W 54th St, 212/233-0908): European or synthetic hair

year of purchase, and home or office appointments are available. The company is family-owned and -operated, and all articles are crafted by experienced, skilled tailors.

DANTE ZELLER TUXEDO & MENSWEAR

459 Lexington Ave (at 45th St), 3rd floor   212/286-9786
Tues-Fri: 9-7; Sat: 10-6   dantezeller.com

Dante Zeller is Manhattan's largest locally owned formal wear specialist, with over 75 years of experience. Their wide selection includes the newest styles and colors from Calvin Klein, Joseph Abboud, Ralph Lauren, and others. Along with tuxedos and suits are vast selections of contemporary and traditional vests, shirts, shoes, and accessories. Rentals, too!

MEN'S — GENERAL

BILLIONAIRE BOYS CLUB & ICECREAM

456 West Broadway (at Houston St)   212/777-2225
Mon-Sat: noon-7; Sun: noon-6   bbcicecream.com

At Billionaire Boys Club & Icecream the young-at-heart will find a novel collection of men's clothing with equally unique branding. The vision of musician Pharrell Williams and Japanese designer Nigo resulted in two floors of edgy clothing and shoes. Lots of colors and patterns; unique shirts, T-shirts, jackets, pants, shorts, and accessories are yours for a pretty price. By the way, Icecream is a brand, not the frozen treat!

CAMOUFLAGE

141 Eighth Ave (at 17th St)   212/741-9118
139 Eighth Ave (bet 16th and 17th St)   212/691-1750
Mon-Sat: noon-6:45; Sun: noon-5

In a rather minimalist space, Camouflage can attire customers with a dignified but unique look. You'll find men's upscale sportswear and outerwear, plus private-label trousers, shirts, ties, and accessories — Burberry and Helmut

Lang to name a few. Considering some of the designers represented, prices are reasonable.

DAVE'S NEW YORK

581 Ave of the Americas (bet 16th and 17th St)   212/989-6444
Mon-Fri: 9-7; Sat: 10-6; Sun: 11-5   davesnewyork.com

Dave's New York is family-run and has been in business since 1963. Branded "Americana" work clothes and military wear fill these shelves. Reasonably priced clothing and boots (such as Dickies, Levi's, Carhartt, Columbia, Woolrich, Alpha Industries, and Red Wing) are neatly arranged. These clothes have stood the test of time and are favorites of construction workers and those looking for solid, long-wearing apparel.

EISENBERG AND EISENBERG

16 W 17th St (bet Fifth Ave and Ave of the Americas)   212/627-1290
Mon, Wed, Fri: 9-5:45; Tues: 9-5:30; Thurs: 9-6:45; Sat: 9-5

eisenbergandeisenberg.com

Eisenberg and Eisenberg continues to offer great men's dress attire and matching service, as it has since 1898. Their main business is the sale and rental of designer tuxedos, dinner jackets, and elegant accessories. Featured designers include Baroni, Ralph Lauren, Joseph Abboud, and Andrew Fezza.

ETIQUETA NEGRA

273 Lafayette St (bet Prince and Houston St)   212/219-4015
Mon-Wed: 11-7; Thurs-Sat: 11-8; Sun: noon-7   etiquetanegra.us

The inventory at this upscale shop is made up of comfortable yet stylish men's clothes from mostly South American designers. Fashion-forward gents like the selection of casual and dress shirts, Argentine leather jackets, blazers, sweaters, slacks, and denims. The ambience is definitely masculine. It's a great place to build a "black label" (translation of the shop's name) wardrobe.

FAÇONNABLE

636 Fifth Ave (at 51st St)   212/319-0111
Mon-Sat: 10-8; Sun: 11-6   faconnable.com

Frenchmaker Façonnable has made a name for itself in the fashion world with tailored Euro-clothes that appeal to conservative dressers. Their New York store carries a good showing of men's and women's sportswear, tailored clothing, suits, and shoes, all rich in style and color. You'll find that your tab can add up quickly here.

FREEMANS SPORTING CLUB

Freeman Alley
8 Rivington St (bet Bowery and Chrystie St)   212/673-3209
343 Bleecker St (bet 10th and Christopher St)   212/255-5509
Mon-Fri: 11-8; Sat: 11-7; Sun: noon-6   freemanssportingclub.com

Here's a good source for classic work shirts, custom suiting, and high-quality outerwear. The majority of their products are made within ten miles of their shop, that kind of local sourcing of clothing is pretty much unheard of these days! The entire F.S.C. brand is built around the vanishing trade of handmade

Notable Consignment and Thrift Shops in Manhattan

CHELSEA

Angel Street Thrift Shop (118 W 17th St, 212/229-0546)

Fisch for the Hip (90 Seventh Ave, 212/633-6965): high-end consignment

Goodwill (103 W 25th St, 646/638-1725)

Housing Works Thrift Shop (143 W 17th St, 718/838-5050): additional locations

New York Vintage (117 W 25th St, 212/647-1107): women's designer evening wear

Second Time Around (94 Seventh Ave, 212/255-9455)

Shareen Vintage (13 W 17th St, 2nd floor, 212/206-1644)

EAST 20s

City Opera Thrift Shop (222 E 23rd St, 212/684-5344)

Goodwill (220 E 23rd St, 212/447-7270)

Salvation Army Thrift Shop (208 E 23rd St, 212/532-8115)

Vintage Thrift (286 Third Ave, 212/871-0777)

EAST VILLAGE

Jane's Exchange (191 E 3rd St, 212/677-0380): children's, maternity fashions

Tokio 7 (83 E 7th St, 212/353-8443)

GREENWICH VILLAGE

Fisch for the Hip (33 Greenwich Ave), 212/633-9053)

NOLITA

Second Time Around (262 Mott St, 212/965-8415)

SOHO

A Second Chance Designer Resale (155 Prince St, 212/673-6155): trendy clothing

Ina (101 Thompson St, 212/941-4757)

Second Time Around (111 Thompson St, 212/925-3919)

V.I.A. Vintage Intelligence Agency (611 Broadway, Suite 534, 212/673-0703): women's clothing and accessories; by appointment only

UPPER EAST SIDE

A Second Chance Designer Resale (1109 Lexington Ave, 2nd floor, 212/744-6041): designer handbags

Arthritis Foundation Thrift Shop (1430 Third Ave, 212/772-8816)

Bis Designer Resale (1134 Madison Ave, 2nd floor, 212/396-2760)

Cancer Care Thrift Shop (1480 Third Ave, 212/879-9868)

Council Thrift Shop (246 E 84th St, 212/439-8373)

Memorial Sloan-Kettering Thrift Shop (1440 Third Ave, 212/535-1250)

Michael's, The Consignment Shop for Women (1041 Madison Ave, 212/737-7273)

Second Time Around (1040 Lexington Ave, 212/628-0980)

UPPER WEST SIDE

Off Broadway Boutique (139 W 72nd St, 212/724-6713)

clothing for stylish guys; pieces are durable and meant to be worn day in and day out. Next to the Freeman Alley location, F.S.C. Barber is an old-school barbershop to keep men looking ruggedly handsome.

J. PRESS

380 Madison Ave (at 47th St)   212/687-7642
Mon-Fri: 8:30-7; Sat: 9-7; Sun: noon-6   jpressonline.com

Since its beginning in 1902, J. Press has been one of New York's classic conservative men's stores. Its salespeople, customers, and attitude have changed little from the time of the founder. The Ivy League styles are impeccable and distinguished; blazers are blue, and shirts are button-down and straight. For distinguished made-to-measure menswear, a visit here will not disappoint.

JOHN VARVATOS

122 Spring St (at Greene St)   212/965-0700
Mon-Sat: 11-7; Sun: noon-6
315 Bowery (at Bleecker St)   212/358-0315
Mon-Sat: 11-8; Sun: noon-6   johnvarvatos.com

The John Varvatos brand offers refined tailoring with a modern edge. The outstanding menswear collection shows off leather and shearling outerwear, sportswear, footwear, belts and other accessories, and fragrance items. Men of all ages will feel comfortable with the Old World detailing of a line that exudes class. The Bowery location shows an edgier mixture of retro clothing and accessories, as well as audio equipment and vintage records (Varvatos is a music buff). The stores reek of atmosphere, and the salespeople couldn't be more helpful.

> **Shopping in Chinatown**
> **Pearl River Mart** (477 Broadway, 212/966-1010): steps away from Chinatown; large selection
> **Ting's Gift Shop** (18 Doyers St, 212/962-1081): novelties
> **Yunhong Chopsticks Shop** (50 Mott St, 212/566-8828): chopsticks boutique

L.S. MEN'S CLOTHING

49 W 45th St (bet Fifth Ave and Ave
of the Americas), 3rd floor   212/575-0933
Mon-Thurs: 9-6:30; Fri: 9-3; Sun: 10-4   lsmensclothing.com

L.S. Men's is known for discounting American-made, high-end custom suits. The main attraction, though, is the tremendous selection of executive-class styles. Within that category, a man could outfit himself almost entirely at L.S. Men's. Natural soft-shoulder suits by name designers are available in all sizes. The custom-order department stocks an amazing number of Italian and English fabrics. Custom-made suits take two to four weeks and sell from $645 to $1,295. Ready-made shirts, pants, sport coats, and an extensive size range of ready-to-wear (sizes from 36 short to 60 extra long) are available at a 40% to 60% savings. Ask for Izzy!

PAUL STUART

Madison Ave at 45th St   212/682-0320
Mon-Fri: 8-6:30 (Thurs till 7); Sat: 9-6   paulstuart.com

Paul Stuart has been supplying luxury menswear since 1938. Preppy made-to-measure and bespoke menswear are of the utmost quality; worth the price! A great selection of sweaters, ties (bow ties, too!), socks, shirts, and more is shown, with a small offering of ready-to-wear for women, too.

ROTHMAN'S
222 Park Ave S (at 18th St)   212/777-7400
Mon-Fri: 10-7 (Thurs till 8); Sat: 9:30-6; Sun: noon-6   rothmansny.com

One of the last family-run clothing stores in Manhattan, Rothman's moved to an expanded, lofty space in 2012. Harry Rothman's grandsons, Ken and Jim Giddon, made the physical move and a conscious decision to move away from the "discount store" mantra. "Clothes for real men" is their tag today, with their goal to find the best designer names, in a range of $695 to $795. Classic suits, coats, and accessories fill the modern, 11,000-square-foot space. Let the family help you find exactly what you're looking for!

SAINT LAURIE MERCHANT TAILORS
22 W 32nd St (bet Fifth Ave and Ave of the Americas), 5th floor 212/643-1916
Mon-Fri: 9-6; Sat: 9-4 (closed Sat in summer)   saintlaurie.com

With a long history of creating many items for Broadway shows, TV, and movies, you know these folks must be good! For four generations Saint Laurie has provided quality made-to-order handmade clothing including tuxedos, suits, and shirts for men (and women) at rack prices; they buy fabric directly from weavers, resulting in price savings for customers. Their showroom and manufacturing facility occupy the same location. A fine selection of accessories is also offered; check out the Mimi Fong neckwear!

SEIZE SUR VINGT
78 Greene St (bet Spring and Broome St)   212/625-1620
Mon-Sat: 11-7; Sun: noon-6   16sur20.com

Everything about this store is first-class: the elegant materials; the quality craftsmanship and styles; and the faultless fit. The translation of their name, seize sur vingt, is "16 out of 20," as in a test score. Ready-made shirts, suits, and sportswear are proportioned for the lean, well-toned man or woman. If you want to splurge, order a bespoke suit of the finest imported wool, linen, or cashmere. Shirts, sportswear, and accessories are also custom-made. Be sure to check out the colorful buck shoes!

MEN'S HATS

J.J. HAT CENTER
310 Fifth Ave (at 32nd St)   212/239-4368
Mon-Fri: 9-6; Sat: 9:30-5:30   jjhatcenter.com

This renowned hat shop stocks thousands of brand-name hats and caps (to size 8), from black-tie fedoras to Greek fisherman caps. Founded in 1911, it is New York's oldest hat shop. Special services include free brush-up, hat stretching, or tightening. A satellite location called **Pork Pie Hatters** is located in the East Village (440 E 9th Street, 212/260-0408).

WORTH & WORTH
45 W 57th St (bet Fifth Ave and Ave of the Americas), 6th floor 212/265-2887
Mon, Tues: 10-6; Wed-Sat: 10-7   hatshop.com

Worth & Worth has specialized in men's hats since 1922; all hats are made on-site. You'll find a good selection of fedoras, panamas, felts, caps, and berets at reasonable prices. Custom orders can be ready in two to three weeks. There are a few choices for women, too.

MEN'S SHIRTS

NEPENTHES
307 W 38th St (bet Eighth and Ninth Ave)   212/643-9540
Mon-Sat: noon-7; Sun: noon-5   nepenthesenewyork.com

Forego boring white button-down oxford shirts in favor of Nepenthes' vibrant and unique patterned shirts. This men's store has great looking jackets, vests, wraps, backpacks and other bags, accessories, and boat shoes.

SHIRT STORE
51 E 44th St (bet Vanderbilt and Madison Ave)   212/557-8040
Mon-Fri: 9-6:30; Sat: 10-6   justwhiteshirts.com

The appeal of the Shirt Store is that you're buying directly from the manufacturer, so there's no middle man to hike prices. The Shirt Store offers 100% cotton dress shirts for men in sizes from 14½x32 to 18½x37; sports shirts and accessories have been added. Although the ready-made stock is great, they also do custom work for men and women. An office visit with swatches is not unusual. Additional services include mail order, alterations, and monogramming.

MEN'S TIES

ANDREW'S TIES
30 Rockefeller Plaza (bet 48th and 49th St), concourse level   212/245-4563
Mon-Fri: 8:30-7; Sat: 10-5; Sun: noon-5   andrewstiesusa.com

There are very few really good tie stores left in New York. It's certainly not like it used to be, when one could find great selections and bargains on the Lower East Side. But Andrew's Ties has some classic handmade Italian ties made of silk and cashmere, along with some trendier options. Also displayed are ascots, bow ties, pocket squares, cuff links, belts, shirts, men's and women's scarves, and the like. Prices are reasonable.

RESALE CLOTHING

ALLAN & SUZI
237 Centre St (bet Grand and Broome St)   212/724-7445
Daily: 12:30-6:30   allanandsuzi.net

Allan & Suzi's "retro clothing store" is quite an operation. Under one roof you'll find a real mix of both new clothing from current designers and vintage clothing for men and women, along with old and new shoes and accessories. There are big names like Gaultier, Gucci, Prada, Roberto Cavalli, Versace, and newer cutting-edge labels. Some outfits are discounted. They dress a number of Hollywood and TV personalities. Ask for Allan Pollack or Suzi Kandel.

DESIGNER RESALE

324 E 81st St (bet First and Second Ave)   212/734-3639
Mon-Fri: 11-7 (Thurs till 8); Sat: 10-6; Sun: noon-5

designerresaleconsignment.com

Designer Resale offers previously-owned ladies' designer clothing, shoes, and accessories at moderate prices. The shop carries one of the largest collections of American and European designer brands in the area. You might find Chanel, Armani, Donna Karan, Gucci, Hermes, Prada, Louis Vuitton, and hundreds of others. Prices on many items are marked down 20% to 50% at the first of each month. Call Myrna Skoller to inquire about the latest bargains or possible consignment of your own items. Just next door is the companion store, Gentlemen's Resale (see write-up below).

ENCORE

1132 Madison Ave (bet 84th and 85th St), upstairs   212/879-2850
Mon-Sat: 10:30-6:30 (Thurs till 7:30); Sun: noon-6   encoreresale.com

Since 1954 Encore has offered new and almost new clothing of designer/couture quality. It is a consignment boutique, not a charity thrift shop. Its donors receive a portion of the sales price, and many of them are socialites and other luminaries who don't want to be seen in the same outfit twice. The fashions are up to date and sold at 50% to 70% off original retail prices. There are over 6,000 items in stock, including a small selection for men. Prices range from reasonable to astronomical—but just think about the amounts on the original tags!

GENTLEMEN'S RESALE

322 E 81st St (bet First and Second Ave)   212/734-2739
Mon-Fri: 11-7; Sat: 10-6; Sun: noon-5   gentlemensresaleclothing.com

Gentlemen interested in top-quality exclusive designer suits, jackets, sportswear, shoes, and accessories can save a bundle at this resale operation. Gentlemen's Resale is the men's version of Designer Resale (see full write-up above). Shopping here is like a treasure hunt, and that is half the fun. Imagine picking up a $1,000 Armani suit for $200! Call Gary Scheiner to learn about earning some extra bucks by consigning items from your own wardrobe.

INA

101 Thompson St (bet Prince and Spring St), women	212/941-4757
19 Prince St (bet Mott and Elizabeth St), men	212/334-2210
21 Prince St (bet Mott and Elizabeth St), women	212/334-9048
15 Bleecker St (bet Lafayette St and Bowery), men and women	212/228-8511
207 W 18th St (bet Seventh and Eighth Ave)	212/334-6572
Hours vary by store	inanyc.com

INA offers the latest designer clothing, shoes, handbags, and accessories (plus selected vintage) at a fraction of the original cost. These consignment shops routinely carry Gucci, Halston, Louis Vuitton, and Vera Wang couture for both men and women. Some items are new and have been creatively acquired through networking with stylists, models, and manufacturers; others have been gently worn. Get a heads up on special sales and fashion trends by checking their online blogs, and contact them about consigning your still-stylish fashions, as they are always looking for more great merchandise.

MICHAEL'S, THE CONSIGNMENT SHOP FOR WOMEN

1041 Madison Ave (at 79th St), 2nd floor   212/737-7273
Mon-Sat: 9:30-6 (Thurs till 8)   michaelsconsignment.com

Since 1954, Michael's has been *the* source for pieces from top designers. If you are dying to own one of those fabulous designer gowns you have seen in the magazines or on TV, visit this family-run consignment store. Blahnik; Chanel; Gucci; Hermes; Prada; YSL; all amazing labels! Along with evening wear you'll also find pantsuits, skirts, suits, bags, shoes, and more. Personal attention is assured, and prices are right.

ROUNDABOUT

31 E 72nd St (bet Madison and Park Ave), ground floor   646/755-8009
Mon-Sat: 10-6; Sun: noon-6
115 Mercer St (at Prince St)   212/966-9166
Mon-Sat: 11-7; Sun: noon-6

This new and resale women's clothing boutique offers high-end clothing, shoes, handbags, and accessories. The owners started their business in Connecticut and successfully branched out to Manhattan. Some of the items bear brand names like Pucci, Prada, Gucci, Hermes, and Chanel, with savings up to 70% off retail. You can add a little green to your wallet by consigning your designer couture with Roundabout.

TATIANA DESIGNER RESALE

767 Lexington Ave (bet 60th and 61st St), 2nd floor   212/755-7744
Mon-Fri: 11-7; Sat: noon-6   tatianaresale.com

High fashion at low cost! Since 1998, famous models and high-society trendsetters have consigned their barely used *haute couture* garments at Tatiana Designer Resale. The shop also has samples from Italy, showroom pieces, and a vintage collection of designer couture. Designers represented include Chanel, Dior, Hermes, Gucci, Prada, and Fendi. You'll find top label clothing, shoes, jewelry, and handbags at amazing markdowns.

SHOES — CHILDREN'S

HARRY'S SHOES FOR KIDS

2315 Broadway (bet 83rd and 84th St)   212/874-2034
Mon, Thurs: 10-7:45; Tues, Wed, Fri, Sat: 10-6:45; Sun: 11-6 harrys-shoes.com

This popular Upper West Side shoe store is not fancy and is often wildly busy, but the terrific inventory makes a visit worthwhile. Every single person working here knows how to fit shoes. There are lots of big-name brands, and prices are often more reasonable than at other Manhattan shoe stores. Just bring along some patience, particularly on weekends and in summer. Down the street, **Harry's Shoes** (2299 Broadway, 212/874-2035) offers quality footwear for the rest of the family.

LITTLE ERIC

1118 Madison Ave (bet 83rd and 84th St)   212/717-1513
Mon-Sat: 10-6; Sun: noon-6

Little Eric is not just a shoe store; they are foremost an Italian shoemaker.

Christopher Street Businesses

Greenwich Village has an ever-expanding selection of intriguing places to shop and dine. Christopher Street, in the West Village, offers several notable choices.

Christopher 19 (19 Christopher St, 212/627-9159): jewelry and accessory boutique

I Sodi (105 Christopher St, 212/414-5774): Tuscan cuisine

The Jane (113 Jane St, 212/924-6700): inexpensive accommodations; shared bathrooms

Leffot (10 Christopher St, 212/989-4577): luxury shoes for men

Le Petit Puppy (18 Christopher St, 212/727-8111): boutique specializing in small-breed dogs

McNulty's Tea & Coffee Company (109 Christopher St, 212/242-5351): great service; custom blends

Rag & Bone (100 Christopher St, 212/727-2999): tailored menswear; women's collection two doors down at 104 Christopher Street

Village Cigar (110 Seventh Ave, 212/242-3872): West Village landmark since the 1900s

Everything in this shop is designed and manufactured by them for their private label. Little Eric's knowledgeable staff will fit children's fast-growing feet with beautiful Italian-made shoes in a multitude of colors. They specialize in dressy and casual shoes, boots, and sandals for infants and children. They also indulge adults with women's and men's sizes to 12. Parents will love the welcoming family atmosphere and outstanding customer service.

SHOOFLY
42 Hudson St (bet Duane and Thomas St)   212/406-3270
Mon-Sat: 10-7; Sun: noon-6   shooflynyc.com

Shoofly can take care of your children's shoewear needs with styles that are both classic and funky. Attractive and reasonably-priced European shoes for infants to 14-year-olds are displayed. Women with tiny feet will appreciate the chic selection of footwear, as well. Amazing colors and detailing adorn most styles, and the selection of tights, socks, and accessories are impressive, too.

SHOES — FAMILY

E. VOGEL
19 Howard St (one block north of Canal St, bet Broadway and Lafayette St)
    212/925-2460
Mon-Fri: 8-4:30; Sat: 8-2 (closed Sat in summer)   vogelboots.com

In operation since 1879, Jack and Hank Vogel and Jack Lynch are the third- and fourth-generation family members to join this business. They will happily fit and supply made-to-measure boots for everyone and shoes for men. Once your pattern is on record, they can make new shoes without a personal visit. Howard is one of those streets that even native New Yorkers don't know exists; yet, many beat a path to Vogel for top-quality shoes and boots (including equestrian boots). While not inexpensive, prices are reasonable for the fine craftsmanship and materials involved. There are more than 500 Vogel dealers throughout the world, but this is the original store and the people here are super.

KENNETH COLE

595 Broadway (at Houston St)	212/965-0283
95 Fifth Ave (at 17th St)	212/675-2550
107 E 42nd St (bet Vanderbilt and Park Ave)	212/949-8079
130 E 57th St (at Lexington Ave)	212/688-1670
Hours vary by store	kennethcole.com

American clothing designer Kenneth Cole started selling shoes from a production trailer on Avenue of the Americas. Now four outposts offer his quality shoes at sensible prices. Other trendy staples include belts, handbags, scarves, watches, sportswear, outerwear, and accessories for men and women.

T.O. DEY CUSTOM MADE SHOES

151 W 46th St (bet Ave of the Americas and Seventh Ave)	212/683-6300
Mon-Fri: 9-6	todeyshoes.com

Needing a pair of comfortable shoes? Visit this midtown shop for a pair of custom-made shoes. T.O. Dey welcomes a wide spectrum of customers, from individuals to Broadway shows. Choose from finished samples, bring a style to copy, or confer with staff to design your own footwear. Whether you need orthopedic shoes or simply want a comfortable, perfect fit for fashion, dancing, running, walking, or whatever, this experienced team of shoemakers can help.

SHOES — MEN'S

CHURCH'S SHOES

689 Madison Ave (at 62nd St)	212/758-5200
Mon-Sat: 10-6 (Thurs till 7); Sun: noon-5	churchs-footwear.com

Anglophiles will feel right at home here, not only because of the *veddy* English atmosphere but also for the pure artistry and "Englishness" of the shoes. Church's has been selling durable dress shoes for men since 1873 and is known for classic styles, superior workmanship, and fine leathers. A small collection of women's shoes is available, too. The styles basically remain unchanged year after year, although new designs are occasionally added as a concession to fashion. All shoes are custom-fitted, and if a style or size does not feel right, they will special order a pair that does.

STAPLETON SHOE COMPANY

68 Trinity Pl (at Rector St)	212/964-6329
1 Rector St (bet Broadway and Trinity Pl)	212/425-5260
Mon-Thurs: 8:30-5; Fri: 8:30-4	

For over 60 years Stapleton Shoe Company has provided "better shoes for less," but there is much more to this superlative operation. Gentlemen, these closely located stores offer Bally, Alden, Allen-Edmonds, Cole Haan, Timberland, Rockport, Johnston & Murphy, and a slew of other top names at discount. There isn't a better source for quality shoes. They are size specialists, carrying expanded men's sizes from 5 to 17 in widths A to EEE.

Women's Luxury Shoes (and other goods)

Charlotte Olympia (22 E 65th St, 212/744-1842): whimsical touches

Christian Louboutin (59 Horatio St, 212/255-1910 and 965 Madison Ave, 212/396-1884): red-soled Parisian women's shoes

Coach (595 Madison Ave, 212/754-0041)

Diane von Furstenberg (440 Washington St, 646/486-4800)

Fratelli Rossetti (625 Madison Ave, 212/888-5107): classic Italian beauties

Jimmy Choo (645 Fifth Ave, 211/593-0800; 716 Madison Ave, 212/759-7078; and 407 Bleecker St, 212/366-1305)

Louis Vuitton (1 E 57th St, 212/758-8877 and 116 Greene St, 212/274-9090)

Macy's (151 W 34th St, 212/695-4400): The largest selection in the city!

Manolo Blahnik (31 W 54th St, 212/582-3007): sexy shoes

Nicholas Kirkwood (807 Washington St, 646/559-5239): architectural heels

Pierre Hardy (30 Jane St, 646/449-0070): color-blocked

Prada (575 Broadway, 212/334-8888; 724 Fifth Ave, 212/664-0010; 45 E 57th St, 212/308-2332; and 841 Madison Ave, 212/327-4200)

Salvatore Ferragamo (655 Fifth Ave, 212/759-3822)

Steve Madden (41 W 34th St, 212/736-3283; 720 Lexington Ave, 212/888-5919; 861 Broadway, 212/206-1682; and other locations)

Stuart Weitzman (625 Madison Ave, 212/750-2555 and other locations)

Versace (647 Fifth Ave, 212/317-0224 and 160 Mercer St, 212/966-8111)

SPORTSWEAR

FOOTACTION USA

225 W 34th St (bet Seventh and Eighth Ave)   646/473-1945
Daily: 9 a.m.-10 p.m.   footaction.com

Athletic footwear, apparel, and accessories can be found here. Men, women, and children will find a nice selection of athletic shoes at fair prices — Nike, Reebok, Jordan, and Adidas. Big-name clothing brands include Jordan, Levi's, Rocksmith, Nike, and Timberland.

NIKE RUNNING

156 Fifth Ave (at 20th St)   212/243-8560

NIKE SPORTSWEAR

21 Mercer St (at Grand St)   212/226-5433

NIKETOWN NEW YORK

6 E 57th St (bet Fifth and Madison Ave)   212/891-6453
Hours vary by location   nike.com

Within these three entities Nike showcases the creative product innovation and sports heritage by which their empire is known. Cutting-edge athletic and workout apparel, including a zillion footwear choices, fill these flashy spaces. You'll find colorful sports-specific clothing in the newest designs and materials for basketball, baseball, football, soccer, running, and training; exactly what you'd expect from Nike. Check out hot new tech-lab products like the Nike FuelBand which can track your daily movement.

PATAGONIA

101 Wooster St (bet Prince and Spring St)	212/343-1776
426 Columbus Ave (bet 80th and 81st St)	917/441-0011
414 W 14th St (bet Ninth Ave and Washington St)	212/929-6512
Mon-Sat: 11-7; Sun: 11-6	patagonia.com

You'll often hear the name Patagonia if you ask outdoors enthusiasts about their favorite brand of attire for hiking, climbing, surfing, or skiing. This green-minded company designs family clothing, packs and totes, blankets, and books. They make wetsuits from organic cotton and sturdy man-made fabrics. The company takes pains to assure that their clothing allows freedom of movement, is durable, and looks and feels good. Even those who don't spend much time in the great outdoors appreciate Patagonia attire.

SURPLUS

KAUFMAN'S ARMY & NAVY

319 W 42nd St (bet Eighth and Ninth Ave)	212/757-5670
Mon-Fri: 11-6 (Thurs till 7); Sat: noon-6	

Kaufman's has long been a favorite destination for its extensive selection of genuine military surplus from around the globe. Since 1938 they have outfitted dozens of Broadway and TV shows and supplied a number of major movie productions with military garb. The store is a treasure trove of military collectibles, hats, helmets, uniforms, and insignias. You'll also find peacoats, parkas, outdoor gear, bags, and maps. The inventory is constantly in flux; great bargains are just waiting to be discovered.

UNCLE SAM'S ARMY NAVY OUTFITTERS

37 W 8th St (bet Fifth Ave and Ave of the Americas)	212/674-2222
Mon-Wed: 10-8; Thurs-Sat: 10-9; Sun: 11-8	armynavydeals.com

Uncle Sam's lays claim as the only army-navy surplus outlet in the city that gets its stock straight from military branches. Authentic apparel and products from 26 countries around the world are randomly displayed. You'll find an excellent selection of pants, shirts, flight jackets, watches, flags, pins, patches, and more.

SWIMWEAR

CANYON BEACHWEAR

1136 Third Ave (bet 66th and 67th St)	917/432-0732
Mon-Fri: 10-8; Sat: 10-7; Sun: 11-6	canyonbeachwear.com

Come to this store before you dive into a pool, visit a beach, or take a cruise. Canyon Beachwear is the ultimate in swim, sun, and vacation wear. You'll find over a thousand swimsuits, with most major manufacturers represented; cover-ups and accessories, too. Great salespeople, also!

Shopping Abbreviations

Be sure to read the fine print in sales ads and in-store promotions. Some are sprinkled with abbreviations. Here are a few common ones:

AR: after rebate   **MIR**: mail-in rebate
BOGO: buy one, get one   **RTW**: ready-to-wear
CPN: coupon   **S&H**: shipping and handling

PARKE & RONEN
176 Ninth Ave (at 21st St)   212/989-4245
Mon-Sat: noon-8; Sun: 1-6   parkeandronen.com

For men's swimsuits, come to Parke & Ronen. Styles include bikinis, briefs, and trunks (two-, four-, six-, and eight-inch lengths). All are folded neatly in an array of stripes, plaids, and paisley patterns. Designers Ronen Jehezkel and Parke Lutter feature their unique creations in this store, although Parke & Ronen designs are also sold in other retailers. You will also find shirts, T-shirts, tanks, jeans, and trousers, all with refined details, quality fabrics, and exquisite fit.

UNIFORMS

JA-MIL UNIFORM
92 Orchard St (bet Delancey and Broome St)   212/677-8190
Mon-Thurs: 10-5 (or by appointment)

Ja-Mil is *the* bargain spot for those who must wear uniforms for work but do not want to spend a fortune on them. There are outfits for doctors, nurses, and technicians, as well as the finest domestic uniforms and chef's apparel. Clogs, Nurse Mates, and SAS shoes are available in white and colors. Note the store's limited hours.

WESTERN WEAR

WESTERN SPIRIT
395 Broadway (at Walker St)   212/343-1476
Mon-Fri: 10:30-7:30; Sat, Sun: 11-8

Yes, you can find authentic Western fashions in Manhattan. At Western Spirit there are cowboy hats, shirts, jeans, jackets, and stylish boots. Colorful selections of Native American jewelry, leather belts, and silver belt buckles are interspersed among the clothing and leather saddles. Western furniture and artistic home-decor items befitting a bunkhouse, kid's room, or your own home on the range complete the stock.

WOMEN'S ACCESSORIES

ARTBAG
1130 Madison Ave (at 84th St)   212/744-2720
Mon-Fri: 9:30-5; Sat: 10-4   artbag.com

At Artbag, European-trained artisans craft purses, wallets, belts, accessory cases, briefcases, and even pet accessories from a large selection of exotic skins, leathers, and fine fabrics. Choose from ready-made, beautifully beaded bags and handsome wallets, or supply your own quality materials for a unique accessory. They also clean and repair all types of umbrellas, luggage, and handbags, from minor stitching to total renovations.

DESIGN IN TEXTILES BY MARY JAEGER
17 Laight St (bet Varick St and Ave of the Americas), 2nd floor   212/625-0081
By appointment   maryjaeger.com

Mary Jaeger is located in a gallery adjacent to her Tribeca design studio. Handcrafted women's textile items include scarves, capes, shawls, limited-edition Shibori T-shirts, and 3D textured wool wraps. You'll also find such custom accessories as pillows and some gift items. Call Mary for custom interior design expertise or for a list of her other products.

FOLLI FOLLIE
575 Madison Ave (bet 56th and 57th St)   212/421-3155
133 Prince St (bet Wooster St and West Broadway)   212/780-5555
Mon-Fri: 10-7; Sat: 10-6; Sun: noon-5   follifollie.com

Fun, glam, and bling! Quality accessories at Folli Follie feature jewelry, watches, and handbags. The handbags are colorful and stylish. The trendy jewelry collections include necklaces, bracelets, rings, earrings, and pendants. Each piece is sold individually. The chic watches also make a fashion statement. Guys will find a nice assortment of fashion and sport watches, too. It may look expensive, but shopping here won't break the bank.

JIMMY CHOO
716 Madison Ave (bet 63rd and 64th St)   212/759-7078
645 Fifth Ave (at 51st St)   212/593-0800
407 Bleecker St (at 11th St)   212/366-1305
Hours vary by store   jimmychoo.com

Just follow the celebrities to a Jimmy Choo boutique, where you can find classic boots, daytime and evening bags, small leather goods, scarves, belts, fabulous designer footwear, jeweled sandals, and fragrances. The designs are ultra-chic, but bring your "goldest" credit card!

MZ WALLACE NEW YORK
93 Crosby St (bet Prince and Spring St)   212/431-8252
98 Christopher St (at Bleecker St)   212/206-1192
Mon-Sat: 11-7; Sun: noon-6
993 Lexington Ave (bet 71st and 72nd St)   212/737-0347
Mon-Sat: 10-6; Sun: noon-5   mzwallace.com

The enterprising ladies behind this company have developed a quality line of designer handbags in a variety of sizes for different purposes. Plain or fancy, they are primarily made of Bedford nylon, with Italian leather trim and custom hardware. The boutiques are reminiscent of galleries, with merchandise meticulously shown in uncluttered displays.

RAIN OR SHINE
45 E 45th St (bet Madison and Vanderbilt Ave)   212/741-9650
Mon-Sat: 10-6:30 (Thurs till 7); Sun: only when raining   rainorshine.biz

---

Guided Shopping in the Big Apple

With so many choices, shopping in New York can be a bit intimidating, especially on a first visit. **ZTrend** (917/945-2418, ztrend.com) could be a helpful solution. Affordable guided walking-shopping experiences (private, custom, or group) are highlighted with stops at independent high-end shops. Understand that this is for the "serious" shopper; it is not just a tour. Sample sales, vintage and designer resale, and little known unique boutiques are some of the options. ZTrend works with designer labels, artisans, and independent boutiques, many of which produce one-of-a-kind items locally. What a great idea for women's groups and international shoppers alike! If you prefer to take your time and shop at your own pace, made-to-order self-guided shopping maps can be purchased as well. Happy shopping!

There are run-of-the-mill unisex umbrellas, and then there are umbrellas and parasols which make a stylish statement — open or closed. Enter Rain or Shine under the umbrella-shaped awning to peruse a full array of bumbershoots for men and women in myriad shapes, sizes, colors, designs, and accouterments, including hard-to-find styles and brands. The selection of walking canes is impressive: plain to fancy; ergonomic, telescopic, and folding; and with handsome decorative handles of wood, marble, sterling silver, and other materials. Conveniently, they will repair umbrellas purchased here.

SUAREZ

5 W 56th St (bet Fifth Ave and Ave of the Americas)   212/315-3870
Mon-Sat: 10-6; Sun: noon-5 (closed Sun in summer)   suarezny.com

Since 1938 Suarez has been cultivating a reputation for quality merchandise, good service, excellent selection, and luxury prices. Women-in-the-know look to them as a resource for fine leather goods. A great selection of city chic, luxury trends, and exotics are offered in a variety of colors, some hand-painted.

WOMEN'S — GENERAL

ANNELORE

636 Hudson St (at Horatio St)   212/255-5574
18 Jay St (bet Greenwich and Hudson St)   212/775-0077
Mon-Sat: 11-7; Sun: 11-6   annelorenyc.com

Timeless fashion defines the clothes at Annelore, which explains why the shops have become somewhat of a celebrity magnet. The well-edited collection of Juliana Cho is inspired by and made in New York City. These shops also highlight locally-crafted one-of-a-kind jewelry and accessories.

BOUTIQUE OFF BROADWAY

139 W 72nd St (bet Amsterdam and Columbus Ave)   212/724-6713
Mon-Fri: 10:30-8; Sat: 10:30-7; Sun: 1-7   boutiqueoffbroadway.com

It really is hard to say what sparkles more: the vast array of stylish jewelry or vivacious owner Lynn Dell. She travels the world to acquire clothing and accessories for her customers. There's a little bit of everything to appeal to women of varying sizes and age. New merchandise is in the front with day and evening wear, sportswear, and exciting hats and accessories. Vintage and consigned items are in the back; all are dramatic and new or gently worn. Alterations can be done in-house.

CALYPSO

900 Madison Ave (bet 72nd and 73rd St)	212/535-4100
280 Mott St (bet Prince and Houston St)	212/965-0990
137 West Broadway (bet Duane and Thomas St)	212/608-2222
407 Broome St (at Lafayette St), home	212/925-6200
Numerous other locations	
Hours vary by store	calypso-celle.com

This chain of upscale stores features casual resort-like flirty women's attire and accessories that are trendy and colorful. You will understand the bohemian-chic merchandise when you realize that the store started in the West Indies and the designer was born in the south of France. High-end home decor in both modern and vintage styles features earthy, natural fabrics. Shopping the amazing sales may help keep your budget on track.

EILEEN FISHER

314 E 9th St (bet First and Second Ave)	212/529-5715
521 Madison Ave (bet 53rd and 54th St)	212/759-9888
341 Columbus Ave (bet 76th and 77th St)	212/362-3000
166 Fifth Ave (bet 21st and 22nd St)	212/924-4777
Numerous other locations	
Hours vary by store	eileenfisher.com

From a small start in the East Village to outlets scattered throughout Manhattan, Eileen Fisher has assembled a collection of easy-care, mostly washable natural-fiber outfits in earthy colors. This talented designer's clothes are cool, loose, and casual; they travel well; and are admired for their simple and attractive lines. Accessories, sleepwear, outerwear, and shoes will round out your wardrobe.

ELIZABETH CHARLES

639½ Hudson St (bet Gansevoort and Horatio St)	212/243-3201
Mon-Sat: 11-7; Sun: noon-6	elizabeth-charles.com

An ever-changing mix of original clothes for all occasions, from domestic

---

Yoga Style!

These shops sell yoga wear endorsed by professionals:

Jivamukti Yoga School (841 Broadway, 2nd floor, 212/353-0214)

lululemon athletica (15 Union Square W, 212/675-5286; 1127 Third Ave, 212/755-5019; 481 Broadway, 212/334-8276; 2139 West Broadway, 212/362-5294; 1146 Madison Ave, 212/452-1909; and 1928 Broadway, 212/712-1767): good variety, high quality

YogaWorks (459 Broadway, 212/965-0801 and other locations)

and international designers, makes this a very special shop. The stylish, high-end fashions include designer clothing, shoes, handbags, jewelry, belts, sunglasses, and perfume from Carven, Isabel Marant, Preen, Lady Grey, and Bantu. This is a great choice for a shopping party with your friends.

GEMINOLA

41 Perry St (bet Seventh Ave and 4th St)   212/675-1994
Mon-Wed: noon-7; Thurs-Sat: noon-8; Sun: 11-7   geminola.com

This unique store shows an eclectic assortment of handmade and one-of-a-kind dresses, skirts, and tops for women. The pricey clothing is made from vintage (pre 1950) fabrics, ribbons, and lace. Home items include unusual curtains, napkins, and bed linens. Geminola also has a few selections for girls.

GISELLE

143 Orchard St (bet Delancey and Rivington St)   212/673-1900
Sun-Thurs: 9-6; Fri: 9-5 (Fri till 3 in winter)   giselleny.com

Giselle is one of the more popular shopping boutiques on the Lower East Side. They offer women's top European designers, current-season goods, a large selection (sizes 4 to 20), and discount prices. Etro, Basler, Bianca, and Laurel are just a few of the coveted names. All merchandise is first-quality. Factor in excellent service and four floors of merchandise, and Giselle is well worth a trip.

KIRNA ZABÊTE

477 Broome St (bet Greene and Wooster St)   212/941-9656
Mon-Sat: 11-7; Sun: noon-6   kirnazabete.com

Two friends (nicknamed Kirna and Zabete) brainstormed this unique shop. All manner of women's clothing, from swimwear to casual to evening wear is shown, with well over 60 designers represented. Celine, Erdem, Misela, and Sacai are a sampling. And there is a mixture of other quality items — jewelry, shoes, bags, and more — with *color* and *imagination* the bywords.

LANVIN

815 Madison Ave (bet 68th and 69th St)   646/439-0381
Mon-Sat: 10-6   lanvin.com

This women's couture and ready-to-wear boutique is nestled in a glamorous, renovated five-story townhouse on the Upper East Side. Steep prices come with the famous name. Seasonal collections, shoes, handbags, fragrances, and accessories are lavishly displayed. When you venture into the store, browse the display of vintage photos of Lanvin models.

PIXIE MARKET

100 Stanton St (bet Ludlow and Orchard St)   212/387-7871
Mon-Sat: noon-8; Sun: noon-7   pixiemarket.com

Young, fun, and *funky* describe Pixie Market's clothing and accessories. Only a few of the cute women's separates and dresses are stocked in each size, and most are priced under $100. Artsy handbags and hats will flatter your newest outfit. Be sure to check out the owner's private Italian-leather shoe label, Maud.

PRADA

575 Broadway (at Prince St)	212/334-8888
841 Madison Ave (at 70th St)	212/327-4200
45 E 57th St (bet Park and Madison Ave)	212/308-2332
724 Fifth Ave (bet 56th and 57th St)	212/664-0010
611 Fifth Ave (bet 49th and 50th St)	212/319-3062
Hours vary by store	prada.com

Prada locations are glamorous destinations that attract well-heeled fashionistas as well as tourists. The distinctive, coveted label embellishes chic clothing, knockout shoes, and trendy leather goods and accessories (including fragrances) for men and women. Many ladies consider a Prada handbag an essential fashion statement, and there is certainly an ample assortment of sizes, shapes, and colors. Be sure to mark your calendar for the July and December end-of-season sales.

REALLY GREAT THINGS

284 Columbus Ave (bet 73rd and 74th St)	212/787-5354
300 Columbus Ave (at 74th St)	212/787-5868
Tues-Sat: 11-7; Sun: 1-6	

These Upper West Side stores are unique! The store at 284 Columbus Avenue is filled with high couture merchandise, while the one at 300 Columbus Avenue has a more casual feel and lower prices. Both are indeed full of really great things: clothing, bags, shoes, and accessories from the hottest European designers. Copies of some internationally-known designers are also available.

REBECCA TAYLOR

34 Gansevoort St (bet Greenwich and Hudson St)	212/243-2600
260 Mott St (bet Houston and Prince St)	212/966-0406
980 Madison Ave (bet 76th and 77th St)	646/560-2515
Hours vary by store	rebeccataylor.com

Rebecca Taylor designs clothing, shoes, handbags, hosiery, jewelry, and accessories. This is a popular stop for the young (and young-at-heart) who are looking for whimsical merchandise. Lots of unconventional color combinations and prints show off this very feminine fashion.

ROBERTA FREYMANN

958 Lexington Ave (at 70th St)	212/717-7373
Mon-Sat: 10-6; Sun: noon-5	robertafreymann.com

The vibrant clothing and accessories at this shop are inspired by Roberta Freymann's world travels. Further north on Lexington is Roberta's home store, **Roberta Roller Rabbit** (1019 Lexington Ave, 212/772-7200), where a sea of colorful prints permeates the home furnishings, unique furniture, linens, gift items, and beach and resort wear. Visiting these shops is like going to an international bazaar!

SAN FRANCISCO CLOTHING

975 Lexington Ave (at 71st St)	212/472-8740
Mon-Sat: 11-6	sanfranciscoclothing.com

The women's items at San Francisco Clothing are perfect for a casual

Shopping Sample Sales

As I've said elsewhere, shopping in New York can be expensive. However, with a little legwork, dressing fashionably or outfitting your home with designer goods does not necessarily mean paying full retail prices. Designer sample sales are held in retail stores and temporary locations on a regular basis with deep discounts.

Here are a few tips:

- Know your size, as dressing rooms are not always available.
- Bring cash, since checks and plastic are not always accepted.
- Scrutinize your intended purchases, as all sales are final.
- Be prepared for disarray; many locations are temporary sales rooms located up several flights of stairs.
- Scout out sample-sale shopping websites such as **Daily Candy** (dailycandy.com/new-york), shopping sections of *New York* and *Time Out New York*, or be on the lookout for flyers and billboards.

weekend. The mature woman will find an interesting collection that is comfortable, colorful, and classy. A full selection of white shirtings is their specialty, but there are also great pieces of classic outerwear.

WOMEN'S — MATERNITY

BELLY DANCE MATERNITY

548 Hudson St (bet Charles and Perry St)   212/645-3640
Mon-Thurs: 11-7; Fri, Sat: 11-6; Sun: noon-5   bellydancematernity.com

Hip and fashionable moms-to-be need to know about Belly Dance Maternity, a bright and funky store that's taken the West Village by storm. This is a great source for affordable jeans, T-shirts, lingerie, swimsuits, and cool dresses — even ultra-cool diaper bags. Both classic and up-and-coming designs are available in a wide range of price points.

WOMEN'S MILLINERY

BARBARA FEINMAN MILLINERY

66 E 7th St (bet First and Second Ave)   212/358-7092
Tues-Sat: 12:30-8; Sun: 12:30-7   barbarafeinmanmillinery.com

The big draw in this tiny, romantic space is the couture hats, made on-premises from original designs. If you are looking for something really funky or, by contrast, very classy, try this spot first. Costume jewelry is also a specialty and custom orders are welcome.

THE HAT SHOP

120 Thompson St (at Prince St)   212/219-1445
Mon-Sat: noon-7; Sun: 1-6 (closed Mon in summer)   thehatshopnyc.com

The owner at the Hat Shop, Linda Pagan, has quite a background. She was formerly a Wall Street broker, bartender, and world traveler. The stock reflects her diverse history, with showings from 30 local milliners. Sewn, knit, and blocked hats are available in many colors and trims. Special orders are accepted.

SUZANNE COUTURE MILLINERY

136 E 61st St (bet Park and Lexington Ave)   212/593-3232
Mon-Fri: 10-6; Sat: 11-6   suzannehats.com

For over 25 years Suzanne and her talented staff have been creating stunning bridal headpieces and high-fashion hats. Exotic feathers, Austrian crystals, gleaming pearls, and quality trims embellish classic and contemporary hat shapes resulting in one-of-a-kind designs. A Suzanne bridal headpiece is a work of art, be it a simple tiara or a long, flowing veil with a fresh-flower band. No matter the occasion, visit Suzanne for the perfect ready-to-wear or custom-order hat. Customers include overseas royalty!

WOMEN'S UNDERGARMENTS

A.W. KAUFMAN

73 Orchard St (bet Broome and Grand St)   212/226-1629
Sun-Thurs: 11-5; Fri: 11-3:30   awkaufman.com

A.W. Kaufman has combined excellent merchandise with quality customer service for three generations. They specialize in European designer lingerie for women and men. Among the wonderful labels you will find are Bonsoir, Hanro, Chantell, Wolford, LaPerla, Zimmerli, and Pluto. Items include bras, panties, pantyhose, bodywear, camisoles, nightgowns, pajamas, robes, and more.

HOWARD SPORTSWEAR

69 Orchard St (at Grand St)   212/226-4307
Sun-Fri: 9-5

Located on the Lower East Side, Howard Sportswear is a fashionable boutique with bargain prices. They carry an excellent selection of women's underwear, including top names like Bali, Danskin, Warners, Wacoal, Olga, Lilyette, and Jockey. Prices are routinely 20% to 30% off retail.

LA PETITE COQUETTE

51 University Pl (bet 9th and 10th St)   212/473-2478
Mon-Sat: 11-7 (Thurs till 8); Sun: noon-6   thelittleflirt.com

La Petite Coquette offers a large, eclectic mix of sexy lingerie from around the world in a diverse price range. The atmosphere is described as: "Flirtatious!" You'll find everything from classic La Perla to edgy designers like Aubade. There are also old standbys like Cosabella, Hanky Panky, Mary Green, On Gossamer, and Eberjey.

LINDA'S BRA SALON

828 Lexington Ave (bet 63rd and 64th St)   212/751-2727
Mon-Sat: 10-8; Sun: noon-7
552 Third Ave (bet 36th and 37th St)   646/736-1949
Mon, Tues: 10-8; Wed-Fri: 10-9; Sat: 10-8; Sun: 11-7   lindasonline.com

Linda's carries dozens of brands and hundreds of sizes of bras for petite to full-figured gals, nursing mothers, post-surgery, and athletes. Though not required, reservations are suggested for a fitting consultation with trained experts. They

The Shops at Columbus Circle

Time Warner Center (10 Columbus Circle, 212/823-6300) is a vertical mall in a dramatic setting on the corner of Central Park West and Central Park South. **The Shops at Columbus Circle** is a mall that compares with the very best in America. Assembled under one roof are bebe, Bose, Coach, Cole Haan, Davidoff of Geneva, Equinox Fitness Club, Godiva Chocolatier, L'Occitane, Microsoft, Montmartre, Stuart Weitzman, Swarovski, Thomas Pink, Whole Foods Market, Williams-Sonoma, and more. The magnificent Mandarin Oriental New York (see Services) is among the city's most luxurious hotels.

are sensitive to clients' needs and give the same attention to customers whether buying mastectomy bras, shapewear, or swimwear.

ONLY HEARTS

386 Columbus Ave (bet 78th and 79th St)   212/724-5608
Mon-Sat: 11-7:30; Sun: 11-6:30
230 Mott St (bet Prince and Spring St)   212/431-3694
Mon-Sat: 11:30-7:30; Sun: 11:30-6:30   onlyhearts.com

Helena Stuart offers romantics a beguiling array of "inner outwear," all designed and sewn in the Garment District of Manhattan. Feminine bras, panties, camis, tanks, slips, leggings, skirts, and slip dresses are all stylishly sexy. And along with the store's heart-themed name, you'll find an extraordinary collection of European designer accessories, jewelry, posh scents, soaps, and candles, most are accented with a heart. The store on Columbus has a larger selection of the gift items.

TOWN SHOP

2270 Broadway (bet 81st and 82nd St)   212/724-8160
Mon-Fri: 10-7; Sat: 9:30-6; Sun: 11-5   townshop.com

This Upper West Side store has earned a reputation for superior customer service, over 60 designer brands of intimate apparel, and expert bra-fitting. Merchandise includes activewear, sleepwear, shapewear, slips, hosiery, bras, and panties. Specialties include bridal and sexy lingerie, maternity and nursing bras, and mastectomy bras and breast prostheses.

UNDERNEATH IT ALL

320 Fifth Ave (bet 32nd and 33rd St), 10th floor   212/717-1976
Mon-Thurs: 9:30-4:30
By appointment   underneathitallnyc.com

The staff at Underneath It All work hard to give attentive, informed, and personal service to women who have had breast surgery. The store carries a large selection of breast forms in light and dark skin tones and in a variety of shapes, sizes, and contours. They specialize in breast equalizers and enhancers to create body symmetry. There is a complete line of mastectomy and brand-name bras; mastectomy and designer swimwear; sleepwear, loungewear, and body suits; and wigs and fashionable head accessories.

COINS, STAMPS

STACK'S BOWERS GALLERIES

123 W 57th St (at Ave of the Americas)   212/582-2580
Mon-Fri: 10-5; Sat: 10-3   stacksbowers.com

Specializing in coins, medals, bullion, and paper money of interest to collectors, Stack's Bowers has a solid reputation for individual service, integrity, and knowledge of the numismatic field. In addition to walk-in business, about ten or so public auctions are conducted each year. Visit the gallery to add to your collection, sell items outright, or consign for auction.

COSMETICS, DRUGS, AND PERFUMES

C.O. BIGELOW CHEMISTS

414 Ave of the Americas (bet 8th and 9th St)   212/533-2700
Mon-Fri: 7:30 a.m.-9 p.m.; Sat: 8:30-7; Sun: 8:30-5:30   bigelowchemists.com

Bigelow touts itself as the oldest apothecary in America, and the old-school approach to customer service helps explain its longevity. The selection of signature Bigelow products and other brand names is vast, with treatments for almost any condition from acne to sleeplessness. Cruise the aisles for beauty and health-care products, plus carefully selected gifts and fragrances. They are open 365 days a year.

KIEHL'S

109 Third Ave (bet 13th and 14th St)   212/677-3171
154 Columbus Ave (bet 66th and 67th St)   212/799-3438
841 Lexington Ave (at 64th St)   917/432-2511
Numerous other locations
Hours vary by store   kiehls.com

Kiehl's has been a New York institution since 1851. Their special treatments and preparations are made by hand. Natural ingredients are used in their lines of cleansers, toners, moisturizers, bath and shower products, shampoos, conditioners, and other treatments. Express an interest in a particular product and you'll receive a decent-size sample and advice about using it.

MIN NEW YORK

117 Crosby St (bet Prince and Houston St)   212/206-6366
Sun, Mon: noon-6; Tues-Sat: 11-7   minnewyork.com

Beauty and grooming products and fragrances from around the world for men and women are attractively displayed in this relaxing Soho shop. Testing and smelling the personal indulgences is encouraged. MiN New York stocks many luxury brands, such as Amouage, Ibitara, and Sospiros. Equally luxurious gifts and home accessories fill this Crosby Street charmer.

CRAFTS

ALLCRAFT JEWELRY & ENAMELING CENTER

135 W 29th St (bet Ave of the Americas and Seventh Ave), Room 205
                                                          212/279-7077
Mon-Fri: 9:15-5:30 (open late some evenings)   allcraftusa.com

Allcraft is *the* jewelry-making supply store. Their catalog includes a complete line of tools and supplies for jewelry making, silver- and metal-smithing, lost-wax casting, and much more. Crafters shouldn't miss the opportunity to visit this gleaming cornucopia.

THE CITY QUILTER
133 W 25th St (bet Ave of the Americas and Seventh Ave)   212/807-0390
Tues-Fri: 11-7; Sat: 10-6; Sun: 11-5   cityquilter.com

The City Quilter is the only shop in Manhattan that's completely devoted to quilting. They serve everyone from beginners to professionals with classes, books, notions, thread, gifts, New York-themed fabrics, patterns and kits, and more than 3,000 bolts of all-cotton fabrics, felt, felted wool, and silk. Classes include hand- and machine-quilting, embroidery, photo transfers, and much more.

CLAYWORKS POTTERY
332 E 9th St (bet First and Second Ave)   212/677-8311
Tues: 3:30-7; Wed: 2-7; Thurs: 2-8:30; Fri: 3:30-8:30; Sat, Sun: 1:30-8:30;
    Mon: by appointment   clayworkspottery.com

If you are interested in stoneware and fine porcelain, then you will love Clayworks, run by talented Helaine Sorgen since 1974. It has a wide range of items for tabletop and home decor. All of Clayworks' pottery is lead-free and dishwasher- and microwave-safe. Everything is individually produced, from teapots to casseroles, mugs, and sake sets. One-of-a-kind decorative pieces include honey pots, garlic jars, pitchers, cream and sugar sets, butter and cheese domes, oil bottles, vases, candleholders, goblets, platters, and bowls. Small classes in wheel-throwing are given for adults.

GOTTA KNIT!
14 E 34th St (bet Fifth and Madison Ave), 5th floor   212/989-3030
Mon-Wed: noon-6; Thurs: noon-7; Sun: 11-4   gottaknit.net

At Gotta Knit! you'll find luxury hand-dyed cashmere and specialty yarns for hand-knitting and crocheting. Custom pattern-writing for unique garments is available. Browse the equally fine selection of buttons, accessories, and books. Individual instruction and knitting classes are offered, too.

KNITTY CITY
208 W 79th St (bet Broadway and Amsterdam Ave)   212/787-5896
Mon, Tues, Fri, Sat: 11-6; Wed, Thurs: 11-8; Sun: noon-5   knittycity.com

Knitty City stocks a fine selection of beautiful yarn for knitting and crocheting, and an assortment of free patterns. There are also needle art books and magazines, notions, patterns, classes for every level, and a sampling of finished items.

THE YARN COMPANY
2274 Broadway (bet 81st and 82nd St), 2nd floor   212/787-7878
Mon: 11-6; Tues: 11-8; Wed, Thurs: 11-7; Fri, Sat, Sun: 11-6   theyarnco.com

A brother-sister team head up The Yarn Company which is said to have the largest selection of high-end knitting yarns in the city. You'll find cashmeres, merino wools, silks, linens, rayons, and more. There are many samples to look at, and these folks are up to date on new fibers, textures, and color combinations. Guest workshops and classes in knitting, crocheting, tatting, and hand-sewing will teach you to purl, cast-on, and bind-off.

DANCE ITEMS

CAPEZIO DANCE THEATRE SHOPS

1650 Broadway (at 51st St), 2nd floor	212/245-2130
201 Amsterdam Ave (at 69th St)	212/586-5140
1651 Third Ave (bet 92nd and 93rd St), 3rd floor	212/348-7210
126 E 13th (bet Third and Fourth Ave)	212/388-0876
Hours vary by store	capeziodance.com

Capezio Dance Theatre Shops offer one-stop shopping for all of your dance, theater, and fitness needs. These dance emporiums stock the Capezio brand's full line, including sections for men, flamenco, and a variety of shoes and accessories. The 7,000-square-foot flagship store on Broadway overlooks the Theatre District. You don't have to be a performer to appreciate the wares. Note that the Third Avenue location carries only children's goods.

ON STAGE DANCEWEAR

197 Madison Ave (bet 34th and 35th St)	212/725-1174
Mon-Sat: 11-7; Mon-Fri: 10-6:30; Sat: 11-6	onstagedancewear.com

On Stage serves professional ballet and theater companies across the world, including the New York City Ballet. Individuals are welcome, too! You'll find everything in dancewear for ballet, tap, flamenco, and ballroom. They specialize in discount dancewear and are an authorized dealer for Capezio. This is also a good source for bodywear for yoga and cheerleading, skate wear, and warm-ups.

DEPARTMENT STORE SCENE IN MANHATTAN

The trend away from crowded and yuppie suburban malls has been a plus for New York department stores. Although some of the great names of the past live no longer, the current scene is quite healthy. At the top of the scale (price-wise) is Bergdorf Goodman (both the men's and women's stores); at the bottom end with some good values are the two Century 21 stores. In between, while Lord & Taylor and Saks Fifth Avenue have had some uneven spells, Macy's and Bloomingdales are doing very well. Smart shoppers watch the advertised (and mailed) sales events, particularly at the end of each season. Soon Nordstrom will open on West 57th Street.

BARNEYS CO-OP (116 Wooster St, bet Spring and Prince St, 212/965-9964; barneys.com): This store appeals to younger shoppers who live and shop downtown; price points are somewhat lower, and the selection of clothing for work and play is really quite good.

BARNEYS NEW YORK (660 Madison Ave, at 61st St, 212/826-8900 and 2151 Broadway, at 75th St, 646/335-0978; barneys.com): Barneys still has a loyal following of folks who remember when that label really spelled "class."

Nowadays the store is a skeleton of its former self, with merchandise presented in a manner that smart shoppers find unappealing. Combine that with service that can be haughty and the aisles are quite empty; although the stores are very busy at sales times.

BERGDORF GOODMAN (754 Fifth Ave, at 57th St, 212/753-7300; bergdorfgoodman.com): One cannot get more upscale than at this stylish emporium, where practically every top label can be found in their many clothing departments. The store is noted for its personalized service. If the salespeople know you, there is nothing they won't do to be of service. If you are the casual looker/shopper, it is a very different story. BGs windows are always avant-garde; check them out when you stroll down Fifth Avenue. Several convenient restaurants are available, as well as some very interesting gift sections. Bring along as gold a credit card as you can find.

BERGDORF GOODMAN MEN (745 Fifth Ave, at 58th St, 212/753-7300; bergdorfgoodman.com): The male members of your family who like to shop, and who are very fashion-savvy, love this store, where (like the sister store for women) nearly every world-famous label in men's furnishings and clothing is featured. Of course, you pay the price, but you probably will not see the same suit on your friends at the country club. Custom-made suits are a specialty, as well as the latest in formal wear. As some of the longtime salespeople retire, younger replacements seem happier to assist the overwhelmed shopper. I find the sportswear sections particularly well stocked.

BLOOMINGDALE'S (1000 Third Ave, at 59th St, 212/705-2000 and 504 Broadway, at Broome St, 212/729-4900; bloomingdales.com): The Upper East Side shopper can find a tremendous selection of better merchandise at this famous store; its cosmetic department must be among the largest in the world. A fine selection of women's clothing and home furnishings, gifts, luggage, and china and glassware also are featured. The men's clothing section is not great, nor is the furniture department. (Remember those creative model rooms of former years? No more.) A number of handy refreshment stops are located throughout the store; I particularly like the delicious frozen yogurt at **40 Carrots** on the seventh floor. Very good burgers are available at **Flip** on the lower level. Service is vastly improved, and the store is spending millions on the modernization of various departments. One could happily spend full days and much cash going from one floor to another in this well-merchandised store. Now when are they going to get some modern looking nameplates above the entrances on Lexington Avenue? The downtown Bloomies is a convenient place for young-nesters to shop, but this smaller store does not carry the vast assortments of its uptown sister store.

CENTURY 21 (22 Cortlandt St, at Church St, 212/227-9092 and 1972 Broadway at 66th St, 212/518-2121; c21stores.com): For decades lower Manhattan shoppers have found great bargains at this mainly discount department store. Now Upper West Siders can enjoy some of the great finds at the newer Lincoln Square location. One should not expect to find fancy fixtures or big dressing rooms, but they will find good selections of moderately-priced clothing for the family, especially for the youngsters. Shoes are another specialty. For those men working in lower Manhattan, this is a very good place to find clothing and furnishings for work or play at good prices.

HENRI BENDEL (712 Fifth Ave, at 56th St, 212/247-1100; henribendel. com): With a great Fifth Avenue location, this specialty store was once *the* place for working girls to shop. It has not kept up with the times, but does still offer some good selections of women's clothing, accessories, and cosmetics. Make sure you look at the great Lalique art glass windows on the upper floors.

LORD & TAYLOR (424 Fifth Ave, at 38th St, 212/391-3344; lordandtaylor. com): Now operated by Canada's Hudson's Bay Company, Lord & Taylor is finally getting around to modernizing its departments, making shopping here easier and certainly more attractive. In recent years, Lord & Taylor has lost much of its traffic to nearby Macy's, but still does a very good job of featuring American fashion labels. At one time, New York matrons swore by this store; that was in the days of legendary CEO Dorothy Shaver, a top merchandiser. Perhaps with renewed energy and big bucks, the glory days may return. Two things you will still find at L&T: good food and great window displays (especially at holiday time). Personnel are especially helpful and well trained.

MACY'S (151 W 34th St, at Herald Square, 212/695-4400; macys.com): Of all the Manhattan department stores that have become famous, Macy's now stands out in first place. Under the dynamic leadership of Terry Lundgren, considered the number one retail executive in the country, the store has clearly become the leader in innovation in the industry. In addition, merchandise assortments have been broadened, customer service vastly improved, and a record $400 million is being spent over four years in modernization of the sprawling buildings that have been combined to become the world's largest store (Herald Square). Interspersed throughout the building are a number of convenient eating venues, including the new Italian **Stella 34 Trattoria** (see restaurant section). In addition to almost daily full page ads heralding frequent sales event, Macy's is the sponsor of the spectacular 4th of July fireworks event and the Thanksgiving Day parade. Outstanding departments in this huge emporium include home furnishings and women's accessories. No shopping experience in Manhattan is complete without a visit to this great store with over 300,000 pairs of women's shoes!

SAKS FIFTH AVENUE (611 Fifth Ave, at 49th St, 212/753-4000; saksfifthavenue.com): Once the grand lady of upper Fifth Avenue, Saks has recently seen a number of reincarnations in an attempt to decide where this venerable store fits into the retail picture. Not all have been successful, although now management has seemed to settle on featuring mainly top grade merchandise in a series of special name boutiques (primarily on the first floor). Recently, the store was purchased by Canada's Hudson's Bay Company. Shoppers will find excellent women's fashion departments and outstanding men's furnishings and clothing sections. For in-store dining, the eighth floor restaurant is excellent. Hopefully the musical chairs in management and merchandise direction will settle down, and this fine store can once again enjoy the prestige it enjoyed for so many decades. Shoppers should keep a close lookout for sales; some great bargains on top quality merchandise can be found here.

DOMESTIC GOODS

BED BATH & BEYOND

620 Ave of the Americas (bet 18th and 19th St)	212/255-3550
410 E 61st St (at First Ave)	646/215-4702

1932 Broadway (at 65th St)   917/441-9391
270 Greenwich St (bet Warren and Murray St)   212/233-8450
Hours vary by store   bedbathandbeyond.com

The name says it all! At Bed Bath & Beyond you'll find most everything you could need for your home, in every possible category. The selection is huge. The quality is unquestioned. The service is prompt and informed. Prices are discounted. The store on Avenue of the Americas has over 103,000 square feet stuffed floor to ceiling with sheets, blankets, rugs, kitchen gadgets, towels, dinnerware, hampers, window treatments, furniture, cookware, kid's items, pillows, paper goods, and appliances. The fine-china and giftware department is superb. Several locations now have health and beauty departments. Unique seasonal items and a wedding/baby registry are added bonuses at Bed Bath & Beyond.

BOUTIQUE D. PORTHAULT

470 Park Ave (at 58th St)   212/688-1660
Mon-Sat: 10-6 (closed Sat in August)   dporthault.com

Wherever the name Porthault appears — for instance, on linens at some fancy hotels — you know you're at a top-notch operation. Their printed sheets seem to last forever and are handed down from one generation to another. Custom-made linens are available in a wide range of designs, scores of colors, and weaves of luxurious density. Porthault can handle custom work of an intricate nature for odd-sized beds, baths, and showers. Specialties include signature prints (hearts, clovers, stars, and *mille fleurs*), printed terry towels, children's special-occasion clothing, and unique gift items. The Porthault brand is available at Bergdorf Goodman as well.

HARRIS LEVY

98 Forsyth St (bet Grand and Broome St)   212/226-3102
Mon-Fri: 9-5:45; Sun: 10-5:45; Sat: by appointment   harrislevy.com

Founded in 1894, this fourth-generation business sports the finest in bed linens, table linens, towels, robes, down comforters, pillows, cashmere blankets, and wool and cotton blankets. The list goes on: imported soaps and body products, room fragrances, laundry and lingerie wash, giftware, throw pillows, trays, coasters, metal and wood beds, mattresses, paper goods, and more. Quality and customer service are first-rate, but prices are downtown. Custom monogramming is available.

PRATESI

829 Madison Ave (at 69th St)   212/288-2315
Mon-Sat: 10-6   pratesi.com

Since 1906 families have been proudly handing down Pratesi bed and bath linens to the next generation. This three-level store has a garden that sets a mood for perusing luxurious bed and bath linens. Pratesi staff will help you coordinate linens to decor and create a custom look. Towels are made in Italy exclusively for Pratesi and are of a quality and thickness that must be felt to be believed. Bathrobes are plush and quietly understated. Cashmere pillows, throws, and blankets are available, and baby boutique items can be special ordered. Plan your visit to the arrival of new collections in spring and fall.

ELECTRONICS AND APPLIANCES

AC GEARS
69 E 8th St (bet Broadway and Mercer St)   212/260-2269
Mon-Sat: 11-8; Sun: noon-7   acgears.com

   Attention gadget lovers! AC Gears features Japanese and European electronic design and ingenuity at its best. The latest electronic products, such as audio gear, computer mice, and diminutive digital video cameras, are displayed in a gallery-like setting. There is an impressive selection of headphones from Audio-Technica, Beyerdynamic, and HiFiMan. The array of iPod speakers (including cute ones shaped to depict miniature musicians) have great sound.

DALE PRO AUDIO
22 W 19th St (bet Fifth Ave and Ave of the Americas), 2nd floor 212/475-1124
Mon-Fri: 9:30-5:30   daleproaudio.com

   Visit Dale Pro Audio for the largest selection of audio merchandise for recording, broadcast, DJ, and sound contracting in the country, including hundreds of brands from A Designs to Zoom. Dale has been a family business for over a half century, offering superior technical expertise. Top-notch demo rooms are available; prices are competitive.

GRINGER & SONS
29 First Ave (at 2nd St)   212/475-0600
Mon-Fri: 8:30-5:30; Sat: 8:30-4:30   gringerandsons.com

   Come to family-owned Gringer & Sons for brand-name major appliances (and some you may have never heard of), all at discount prices. Bosch; Frigidaire; Kitchen Aid; Maytag; Whirlpool; and others. Gringer's informed personnel sell refrigerators, microwaves, ranges, and other appliances to both residential and commercial customers. If it plugs in for cooking or cleaning, they likely sell it!

J&R MUSIC & COMPUTER WORLD
23 Park Row (across from City Hall Park)   212/238-9000
Mon-Wed: 10-7; Thurs, Fri: 10-7:30; Sat, Sun: 11-7   jr.com

   J&R is one of the nation's most complete electronics and home-entertainment department stores. The vast expanse of merchandise will make you dizzy. They carry cameras, printers and other photo accessories; iPods and other personal music players; TVs and home-theater components; one of New York's largest selections of music and movies; and home-office gear, including telephones, smartphones, PDAs, faxes, multifunction printers, and desktop and laptop computers (both PCs and Macs). The place is well organized, though it can get rather hectic at times. Prices are competitive and merchandise is guaranteed.

P.C. RICHARD & SON
120 E 14th St (bet Third and Fourth Ave)   212/979-2600
53 W 23rd St (bet Fifth Ave and Ave of the Americas)   212/924-0200
205 E 86th St (bet Second and Third Ave)   212/289-1700
2372 Broadway (at 86th St)   212/579-5200
Mon-Fri: 9 a.m.-9:30 p.m.; Sat: 9-9; Sun: 10-7   pcrichard.com

   P.C. Richard started as a hardware business, and the dedication to personalized service has successfully been passed down from one generation to

Apple Source

No outfit is better at merchandising than Apple! One of New York's most exciting shopping destinations is the **Apple Store** (767 Fifth Ave, 212/336-1440). Located in a unique setting just off Central Park, the place never closes and is always crowded. Just look for the General Motors building and the magnificent illuminated glass cube in front. Other Apple Stores can be found around town (401 West 14th St, 212/444-3400; 1981 Broadway, 212/209-3400; 45 Grand Central Terminal, 212/284-1800; and 103 Prince St, 212/226-3126), but only the flagship Fifth Avenue location is open 24/7.

the next. They also get high marks for friendliness. Since 1909 this family-owned and -operated store has been selling appliances, electronics, TVs, cameras, car audio, and computers. They offer a large inventory, good prices, delivery seven days a week, and in-house repair service.

SONY STORE
Sony Plaza
550 Madison Ave (bet 55th and 56th St) 212/833-8800
Mon-Sat: 10-7; Sun: 11-6 sony.com

Inside Sony's expansive flagship store you'll find the latest computers, cameras, TV and home theater equipment, portable electronics, iPods, PlayStations and games, and all types of accessories. Be forewarned that these items are tagged to fetch top dollar. This mecca appeals to technophiles of all ages. The adjacent **Sony Wonder Technology Lab** (212/833-8000) offers special events, workshops, and interactive exhibits; it's open Tuesday through Saturday and is free.

STEREO EXCHANGE
627 Broadway (bet Bleecker and Houston St) 212/505-1111
Mon-Fri: 11-7:30; Sat: 10:30-7; Sun: noon-7 stereoexchange.com

For high-end audio-video products, visit this outfit! Since 1984 Stereo Exchange has been carrying top names like Integra, McIntosh, and B&W. Trained, certified engineers will work with architects and designers on home installations. Before you make your decision, check out the sound quality in one of their listening rooms. They also buy and sell previously-loved high-end audio equipment.

WAVES
Showplace Antiques and Design Center
40 W 25th St (bet Fifth Ave and Ave of the Americas), basement 212/273-9616
Wed-Sun: 11-5 wavesllc.com

Searching for a vintage radio or record player? At Waves, Bruce and Charlotte Mager allow the past to live on with their collection of vintage record players, radios, receivers, and televisions. They favor the age of radio over the high-tech present; the shop is a virtual shrine to the 1930s and before. At Waves you'll find the earliest radios (still operative!) and artifacts. There are promotional pieces, such as a radio-shaped cigarette lighter, gramophones, and virtually anything dealing with the radio age. Waves will rent phonographs, telephones, and neon clocks, and they also repair and appraise items.

EYEWEAR AND ACCESSORIES

20/20 EYEWEAR
57 E 8th St (bet Broadway and University Pl)   212/228-2192
Mon-Fri: 10-7:30; Sat: 10-6

Whether you see glasses as a simple necessity, a statement of style, or both, the large selection at 20/20 will likely suit your needs. For over 35 years 20/20 has offered trendsetting eyewear in a wide range of price points. They provide eye exams, prescription fulfillment, and overnight delivery.

THE EYE MAN
2264 Broadway (bet 81st and 82nd St)   212/873-4114
Mon, Wed: 10-7; Tues: 10-7:30; Thurs: 10-8; Fri, Sat: 10-6   eyeman.com

Dozens of stores in Manhattan carry eyeglasses, but few take special care with children. Family-owned and -operated, The Eye Man carries a great selection of frames for young people, as well as specialty eyewear and contact lenses. They have been providing eye exams since 1976.

FABULOUS FANNY'S
335 E 9th St (bet First and Second Ave)   212/533-0637
Daily: noon-8   fabulousfannys.com

"If you have to wear them, make it fun!" That is the slogan of Fabulous Fanny's. What they are referring to are glasses. This store has the largest and best selection of antique and vintage eyewear in the country. Both men and women will be dazzled by the stock which includes modern and avante-garde frames.

ILORI
138 Spring St (bet Greene and Wooster St)   212/226-8276
Mon-Sat: 10-8; Sun: 11-7   iloristyle.com

Ilori displays hundreds of luxury eyeglass frames and sunglasses from well-known companies and in limited-edition designs. Chrome Hearts, Dolce & Gabbana, Gucci, Maui Jim, and Tiffany & Co. are just a few. All are temptingly displayed in this Soho gallery-style boutique. The staff can recommend the ideal shape and color of shades to best play up your facial features. You may want to spring for a couple of unusual pairs to change your persona.

J.F. REY EYEWEAR DESIGN
448 West Broadway (at Prince St)   212/777-5888
Mon-Sat: 11-7:30; Sun: noon-6   jfreyusa.com

Owner Joël Nommick and a crew of professionals stock some of the most fashionable, contemporary specs in town. While you won't find other brand names here, the selection is good whether you are looking for frames for prescription glasses, readers, or sunglasses. They have a reputation for superior service. Vision exams are not offered, so bring your optical prescription.

MORGENTHAL-FREDERICS

699 Madison Ave (bet 62nd and 63rd St)	212/838-3090
944 Madison Ave (bet 74th and 75th St)	212/744-9444
399 West Broadway (at Spring St)	212/966-0099
Shops at Columbus Circle	
10 Columbus Circle	212/956-6402
Hours vary by store	morgenthalfrederics.com

Put Morgenthal-Frederics high on your list if you're looking for unique eyewear and accessories. They display high-end innovative styles and exclusive designs of eyewear and sunglasses. With their various locations and attentive staff, clients are truly well serviced. The Soho location (on West Broadway) offers eye exams on certain days.

OPTYX

599 Lexington Ave (bet 52nd and 53rd St)	212/688-3580
1076 Third Ave (bet 63rd and 64th St)	212/751-6177
1225 Lexington Ave (bet 82nd and 83rd St)	212/628-2493
2384 Broadway (at 87th St)	212/724-0850
Numerous other locations	
Hours vary by store	optyx.com

Optyx enjoys a reputation for excellent service. They carry a superb selection of specialty eyewear: sunglasses, theater glasses, sports spectacles, and party eyewear. Ask about emergency fittings and one-day turnaround.

FABRICS AND TRIMMINGS

B&J FABRICS

525 Seventh Ave (at 38th St), 2nd floor	212/354-8150
Mon-Fri: 8-5:45; Sat: 9-4:45	bandjfabrics.com

Appropriately located in the Garment District, B&J started its fabric business in 1940. In this well-organized space, they carry high-quality fashion fabrics, many imported directly from Europe. Specialties of the house: natural fibers, designer fabrics, bridal fabrics, ultra-suede, Liberty of London, and silk prints (over a thousand in stock!). Swatches are sent free of charge by specific request. You will also find a wonderful selection of hand-dyed batiks, brocades, tweeds, and faux furs.

BECKENSTEIN FABRIC AND INTERIORS

32 W 20th St (bet Fifth Ave and Ave of the Americas)	212/366-5142
Mon-Sat: 10-6 (Thurs till 8)	beckensteinfabrics.com

Beckenstein has a rich history as purveyors of fine fabrics for window treatments, bedding, pillows, and home accessories. There is a wallpaper department and select finished furniture pieces are displayed. Custom upholstery work is their specialty — restoration, restyling, or reupholstering to spruce up a new decor. Impressive selections, reliable service, and excellent workmanship have kept them in business since 1918.

HYMAN HENDLER AND SONS

21 W 38th St (bet Fifth Ave and Ave of the Americas)	212/840-8393
Mon-Fri: 9-5	hymanhendler.com

The time-honored store that Hyman Hendler began is now proudly run by his capable son-in-law. In the trimmings world, it is one of the oldest businesses (established in 1900) and the crown head of the ribbon field. Used by dressmakers, milliners, and crafters alike, Hyman Hendler manufactures, retails, imports, and acts as a wholesaler for every kind of ribbon: basic, vintage, and novelty ribbon. It's hard to believe the many variations that are jammed into this store.

JOE'S FABRICS WAREHOUSE

102 Orchard St (at Delancey St)   212/674-7089
Sun-Thurs: 9-6; Fri: 9-4:30   joesfabrics.com

Enter this Orchard Street establishment and you'll find an extensive assortment of top-quality European and Asian upholstery fabrics — velvet, damask, linen, silk, lace, and other opulent fabrics and trims. Decorating professionals, Broadway set designers, and do-it-yourselfers are welcome to select from the thousands of choices. There is no minimum order. The experienced custom-upholstery department will transform pieces that have seen better days into good-as-new furniture. They also excel with slipcovers and window coverings.

LES TOILES DU SOLEIL

261 W 19th St (bet Seventh and Eighth Ave)   212/229-4730
Mon-Fri: noon-8; Sun: noon-6   lestoilesdusoleilnyc.com

Walking into this sunny boutique will brighten any day! Fabulous striped cotton fabrics associated with the French Riviera are available as throw pillows, computer cases, tote bags, aprons, deck chairs, espadrilles, and other useful items. These French-made fabrics are woven on traditional looms and most are sun-, stain-, and water-resistant. This makes them ideal for outdoor use and as custom-made goods (window or shower curtains, cushions, etc.). Accessories are made in the store. The translation of the store name — the "cloth of the sun" — sums up their product line!

LIBRA LEATHER

259 W 30th St (bet Seventh and Eighth Ave), 6th floor   212/695-3114
Mon-Fri: 9-5   libraleather.com

Libra Leather has been a popular source for fashionable fur and leather skins. Proclaiming himself the "Leather King," Mitch Alfus has become an iconic figure in the leather business. His pioneering leather processes and finishes bring out the beauty and natural character of luxurious and exotic skins from Italy, France, and Spain. You'll find leather, suede, and shearling skins displayed in the showroom, as well as some novelty items and accessories for the home.

M. SCHWARTZ & GETTINGER FEATHER

16 W 36th St (bet Fifth Ave and Ave of the Americas), Suite 802 212/695-9470
Mon-Thurs: 9-5; Fri: 9-4   mschwartzfeather.com

The Schwartz and Gettinger families have been in the feather business since 1910. With fewer and fewer family-owned businesses left, and almost no other sources for fine quality feathers, this is a find! Decorative and fancy feathers abound: peacock, pheasant, rooster, goose, and turkey, as well as feather boas and hatbands. Natural or brilliantly-dyed feathers are all beautiful and of the highest quality.

M&J TRIMMING

1008 Ave of the Americas (bet 37th and 38th St)   212/391-6200
Mon-Fri: 9-8; Sat: 10-6; Sun: 11-6   mjtrim.com

M&J Trimming claims to have the largest selection of high-quality trims at one location, and I'm inclined to believe them! You will find everything from imported trims, buckles, buttons, and decorator trims to various fashion accessories. One area specializes in clothing and fashion trims, like sequins, bridal beading and Swarovski crystals, and rhinestone appliqués; another features interior decor trim.

PARON FABRICS

257 W 39th St (bet Seventh and Eighth Ave)   212/768-3266
Mon-Thurs: 8:30-7; Fri: 8:30-6; Sat: 9-5; Sun: 11-4   paronfabrics.com

Paron Fabrics carries an excellent selection of contemporary designer fabrics suitable for clothing, home decor, theatrical set design, and costumes, all at discount prices. Many of the goods are available only in this store. A full line of patterns is also stocked. This is a family operation, so personal attention is assured.

ROSEN & CHADICK FABRICS

561 Seventh Ave (at 40th St), 2nd and 3rd floors   212/869-0142
Mon-Fri: 8:30-5:45; Sat: 9-4:30   rosenandchadickfabrics.com

For over a half-century this family-owned business has been offering customers (including the theatrical trade) a huge selection of designer fabrics: silks, wools, cashmeres, linens, cottons, laces, velvets, brocades, and more. The selection of cashmere is particularly impressive. You can be assured of personal, attentive service at this two-floor showroom. Ask for David Chadick, the hands-on owner.

SPANDEX HOUSE, INC.

263 W 38th St (bet Seventh and Eighth Ave)   212/354-6711
Mon-Fri: 9-6; Sat: 10-5   spandexhouse.com

This firm claims to have the largest selection of Spandex and Lycra in the world. The assortment is amazing, including animal prints, meshs, lamés, laces, metallics, velvets, and mattes. You can buy it plain or embellished with glitter, beads, and sequins. These fabrics are widely used by costume designers for ice- and figure-skaters; gymnasts, dancers, wrestlers, and other athletes; and circus performers. They're also perfect for anyone who just wants really comfortable clothes that move easily with you. The minimum for wholesale or retail orders is $20 and one yard of material.

TOHO SHOJI

990 Ave of the Americas (bet 36th and 37th St)   212/868-7465
Mon-Fri: 9-7; Sat: 10-6; Sun: 10-5   tohoshoji-ny.com

Only in New York will you find an establishment like Toho Shoji, which stocks all manner of items for designing and making custom jewelry: earring parts, metal findings, chains, and every type of jewelry component. Beads are made of ceramic, shell, CZ (cubic zirconia), wood, glass, and more. Items are well displayed for easy selection at this "bead supermarket."

ZARIN FABRICS

72 Allen St (bet Broome and Grand St), 2nd floor   212/925-6112
Mon-Fri: 9-6; Sun: 9-5   zarinfabrics.com

Founded in 1936, Zarin is the largest and oldest drapery and upholstery fabric warehouse in Manhattan. This "fabric heaven" stocks thousands of designer fabrics and trims at below wholesale prices. It is a favorite source for decorators, set designers, and celebrity clientele. Zarin carries some of the finest ready-made collections of window panels, lamps and custom lampshades, and other home furnishings. Select trimmings, fringe, tassels, tiebacks, and drapery and upholstery hardware are also shown.

ZIPPERSTOP

27 Allen St (bet Hester and Canal St)   212/226-3964
Mon-Fri: 9-4:30; Sun: 9-3   zipperstop.com

One could say that Eddie Feibusch's business has literally been going up and down since 1941! He's the man behind ZipperStop, which sells YKK zippers of every color and description imaginable: rainbow-colored teeth, leather tapes, and studded with Swarovski crystals. There are zippers for every purpose, including handbags, clothing, sleeping bags, upholstery, tents, and even hot-air balloons. Numerous other sewing essentials, including cleaning fluid and lubricating wax for zippers, fill three floors.

FIREPLACE ACCESSORIES

WILLIAM H. JACKSON COMPANY

18 E 17th St (bet Fifth Ave and Broadway)   212/753-9400
Mon-Thurs: 9:30-4:45; Fri: 9:30-4   wmhjacksoncompany.com

Wood-burning fireplaces are hugely popular in New York. In business since 1827, William H. Jackson is familiar with the various types of fireplaces in the city; in fact, they originally installed many of those fireplaces. Jackson has hundreds of mantels on display in its showroom. They range from antiques and reproductions (in wood or marble combinations) to starkly modern pieces. There are also beautiful andirons, fire tools, and screens. Jackson does repair work (removing and installing mantels is a specialty) but they're better known for selling custom fireplace accessories.

FLAGS

ACE BANNER FLAG AND GRAPHICS

107 W 27th St (at Ave of the Americas)   212/620-9111
Mon-Fri: 8-4   acebanner.com

If you need a flag, Ace is the place. Established in 1916, Ace prides itself on carrying the flags of every nation, as well as New York City and New York State flags in all sizes. Custom flags can be made to order. They range in size from small desk flags to bridge-spanning banners. Ace also manufactures custom banners, from podium to building size. Portable trade-show graphics and large-format digital prints are available on a quick turnaround. They will ship anywhere. Ask for owner Carl Calo.

Bargain Sources for Home and Office

Asian goods: **Pearl River Mart** (477 Broadway, 212/431-4770)

Electronics: **J&R Music & Computer World** (23 Park Row, 212/238-9000)

Flowers, cut: **Wholesale Flower Market** (29th St bet Ave of the Americas and Seventh Ave) — retail and wholesale

Furniture: **Room & Board** (105 Wooster St, 212/334-4343)

Home furnishings: **Bed Bath & Beyond** (270 Greenwich St, 212/233-8450; 410 E 61st St, 646/215-4702; 620 Ave of the Americas, 212/255-3550; and 1932 Broadway, 917/441-9391)

Kitchenware: **Broadway Panhandler** (65 E 8th St, 212/966-3434)

Photo equipment & supplies: **B&H Photo Video Pro Audio** (420 Ninth Ave, 212/444-6615)

Sewing and upholstering notions: **M&J Trimming** (1008 Ave of the Americas, 212/391-9072)

Stationery and office products: **Jam Paper & Envelope** (135 Third Ave, 212/473-6666)

FLOOR COVERINGS

COUNTRY FLOORS

15 E 16th St (bet Fifth Ave and Union Square W)   212/627-8300
Mon-Fri: 9-6 (Thurs till 7); Sat: 10-5   countryfloors.com

Country Floors began in 1964 in a tiny, cramped basement under the owner's photography studio. It has grown to include huge stores in New York, Los Angeles, and San Francisco. The finest floor and wall tiles made of stone, glass, porcelain, mosaics, and terra cotta are shown. Sources include artisans from all over the world. A visit (or at least a look at their website) is necessary to appreciate the quality and intricacy of each design. Even the simplest solid-color tiles are exquisite.

ELIZABETH EAKINS

654 Madison Ave (bet 60th and 61st St), 14th floor   212/628-1950
Mon-Fri: 10-5:30   elizabetheakins.com

Elizabeth Eakins is a first-class source for custom, high-end wool, cotton, and linen rugs. Elizabeth designs and makes hand-woven and hand-hooked natural fiber rugs in standard and hand-dyed colors. The designs are amazing! Since this is a small shop, it is best to call ahead for an appointment.

JANOS P. SPITZER FLOORING COMPANY

131 W 24th St (bet Ave of the Americas and Seventh Ave)   212/627-1818
Mon-Fri: 8:30-4:30   janosspitzerflooring.com

This top-notch hardwood flooring company features installation of high-end (read: pricey) wooden floors in residences, as well as expert restoration and repair. You'll find many unusual finishes, as they source wood from around the world: domestic, imported, and exotic tree species. The selection ranges from simple to elegant, with unique borders and parquets. With 50 years of experience, Janos Spitzer brings the best in craftsmanship and service.

PASARGAD CARPETS

180 Madison Ave (bet 33rd and 34th St)   212/684-4477
Mon-Fri: 9-6; Sat: 11-5; Sun: by appointment   pasargadcarpets.com

Pasargad is a fifth-generation family business established in 1904. They have one of the largest collections of new and antique decorative rugs in the country. Persian and Oriental rugs are their specialty, showing traditional, tribal, antique, silk, and more. In-house cleaning and restoration is available. Pasargad will also buy or trade quality antique rugs.

FLOWERS, PLANTS, AND GARDENING ITEMS

BELLE FLEUR

134 Fifth Ave (bet 18th and 19th St), 4th floor   212/254-8703
Mon-Fri: 9-6   bellefleurny.com

This mother-daughter team's floral style is refined, abundant, and luxurious. (I would add "expensive" to that description.) Their gift bouquets and wedding/event displays are absolutely gorgeous works of art, using exotic blooms from around the globe. If you'd like to make your own floral arrangement, hands-on private classes and workshops are scheduled.

BLOOM FLOWERS

255 Murray St (at Vesey St)   212/832-8094
Mon-Fri: 10-8; Sat: 10-6; Sun: noon-6   bloomflowers.com

When price is no object, you can do no better in the floral department than Bloom. Come here for a superb bouquet or arrangement when you have a special occasion to celebrate. If you're fortunate enough to have an outdoor space, their landscape-architecture experts do wonders with rooftop gardens, poolside areas, and country estates.

CASEYS FLOWER STUDIO

1 Greenwich Ave (bet Ave of the Americas and 8th St)   212/243-0906
Mon-Fri: 9-7:30; Sat, Sun: 9-7   caseysflowerstudio.com

Caseys specializes in orchids and fresh florals for all occasions: weddings, parties, and large and small special events. Their shipments arrive from Holland to ensure the largest blooms and best quality.

CHELSEA GARDEN CENTER HOME

580 Eleventh Ave (at 44th St)   212/727-7100
Mon-Sat: 9-6; Sun: 10-6   chelseagardencenter.com

For the urban gardener this place is a dream, offering a wide selection of indoor and outdoor plants and flowers, as well as other garden items from fertilizers to fountains. The knowledgeable crew can give gardening and landscaping advice or can expertly complete your next outdoor project. You'll find other items at the garden center like candles, holiday decor, garden books, and more.

FLORISITY

I W 19th St (bet Fifth Ave and Ave of the Americas)	212/366-0891
Mon-Fri: 9-5; Sat: 10-2	florisity.com

Each exotic arrangement and centerpiece is custom-designed and made especially for the recipient. Expect to pay handsomely for the breathtaking blooms. Some of the creative artists were formerly with Takashimaya Floral. If you are looking for a special vase, Florisity has a great selection, some antique.

JAMALI GARDEN SUPPLIES

149 W 28th St (bet Ave of the Americas and Seventh Ave)	212/244-4025
Mon-Sat: 6:30-5	jamaligarden.com

This store in the Flower Market carries just about everything *except* live plants and fresh flowers. The stock includes colorful accouterments to create stunning arrangements for any occasion. Creative event planners, brides, and floral designers shop here for party lights, candles and holders, plant fertilizers, tabletop items, curtains, pillows, baskets, ribbons, floral picks, and all sorts of other objects.

JONATHAN COUTURE

224 W 29th St (bet Seventh and Eighth Ave)	212/586-8414
Mon-Sat: 9-6	jonathancouture.com

Jonathan's boasts one of the most beautiful Christmas floral displays in the city. The designers use top-quality, exotic fresh flowers and gifts and accessories from private collections to create one-of-a-kind artistic arrangements. Birthdays, weddings, anniversaries, and other occasions are more spectacular and memorable with florals from Jonathan. Major events with distinctive themes and elegant styles are a specialty.

ROSA ROSA

831-A Lexington Ave (bet 63rd and 64th St)	212/935-4706
Mon-Fri: 8-8; Sat: 9-7; Sun: 11-5	rosarosaflowers.com

Rosa Rosa specializes in high-quality roses at low prices. The fragrant beauties arrive daily from Ecuador in a rainbow of colors and variety of sizes. Other specialties are fresh-daily seasonal Dutch flowers and orchid plants. All are used in classic bouquets and dramatic floral arrangements for every occasion, as well as budget-pleasing daily specials. Same-day local delivery is offered weekdays, and overnight delivery of roses and tulips is available nationally.

SIMPSON & CO. FLORISTS

457 W 56th St (at Tenth Ave), 2nd floor	212/765-6929
Mon-Fri: 9-6	simpsonflowerstudio.com

This flower shop specializes in cut flowers, plants, and orchids. Baskets of wicker and wrought-iron and a good selection of fine glass containers are available for their flower creations. They will decorate for gatherings of all sizes, and their prices are very competitive. Affable George Simpson is a delight to work with!

TREILLAGE

418 E 75th St (at York Ave)	212/535-2288
Mon-Thurs: 10-6; Fri: 10-5	treillageonline.com

New Yorkers have gardens, too, although they are necessarily small. Many times they are just patio blooms, but still they add special charm to city living. Treillage can help make an ordinary outside space into something special. They carry furniture and accessories for indoors and out, with a great selection of unusual pieces to set your place apart, and many one-of-a-kind antiques and textiles. They sell everything *except* plants and flowers! Prices are not inexpensive, but why not splurge to enhance your little corner of the world?

VSF
204 W 10th St (at Bleecker St)   212/206-7236
Mon-Fri: 10-5; Sat: 11-4   vsfnyc.com

Colorful; voluptuous; unique. When it comes to fresh-cut flowers and dried or silk creations, you'll be happy with VSF. Unusual fresh flowers are shipped in daily from flower markets around the world. Their top-drawer list of clients attests to their talents for weddings and other special events. Ask for owners Jack Follmer or Todd Rigby.

ZEZÉ FLOWERS
938 First Ave (at 52nd St)   212/753-7767
Mon-Sat: 8-6 (closed Sat in summer)   zezeflowers.com

With roots in Rio de Janeiro, Zezé came to New York bringing a bit of drama to Manhattan's flower business. Zezé's romantic windows reflect his unique talent. The exotic orchid selection is outstanding. You'll find premium fresh-cut flowers, topiaries, ceramics and glassware, furniture, gift items, and antiques. They offer the ultimate in personalized service, including same-day delivery and special requests. A small, skylit venue space around the corner on 52nd Street is a delightful setting for a small catered affair.

FRAMES

HOUSE OF HEYDENRYK
601 W 26th St (bet Eleventh and Twelfth Ave), Suite 305   212/206-9611
Mon-Fri: 10-6; Sat: by appointment   heydenryk.com

House of Heydenryk has been doing frame reproductions of the highest quality since 1845 in Amsterdam; and since 1936 in Manhattan. In this showroom/factory they stock reproductions, contemporary moldings, and an extensive collection of European and American antique frames dating from the 15th through the 20th centuries. They also feature exclusive original frame designs

---

Furniture Consignment Store

Furnish your home or apartment with high-end furniture and accessories from **Décor NYC** (159 W 25th St, 212/488-4977) and it won't cost you an arm and a leg. The goods are consigned by decorators, customers, and showrooms to bring you sizable savings. One day you may find a dining room table and chairs to seat all your Thanksgiving dinner guests and another day you may come across the perfect sculpture to place on the buffet. The unpredictable merchandise mix may include antiques and uniques, fine art, sculptures, lighting, rugs, and more for every room in your home — large or small.

created over the years for such artists as Picasso, Dali, Hopper, O'Keeffe, and Wyeth. A team of master finishers, gilders, carvers, and carpenters continue to carry on this art of frame-making.

FURNITURE

GENERAL

CHARLES P. ROGERS

26 W 17th St (bet Fifth Ave and Ave of the Americas)   212/675-4400
Mon-Fri: 9-8; Sat: 10-7; Sun: noon-6   charlesprogers.com

Rogers has been making comfortable, handcrafted beds since 1885! Their brass beds are made from heavy-gauge brass tubing with solid brass castings. Iron beds are hand-forged, rendering them exceptionally heavy and sturdy. Wooden, leather, and upholstered beds are available, too. Rogers stocks bed linens made from the finest materials, including European linen.

COVE LANDING

1065 Lexington Ave (bet 75th and 76th St)   212/288-7597
By appointment

Cove Landing is a collector's paradise! This miniature jewel shows carefully selected pieces of 18th- and 19th-century English and continental furniture. Tasteful Chinese art objects, beautiful artwork, and fine accessories from the same period are also displayed.

FLOU

42 Greene St (bet Broome and Grand St)   212/941-9101
Mon-Sat: 11-7; Sun: noon-5   flou.it

In its U.S. flagship store, the Italian retailer Flou shows everything for the bedroom, from designer beds, mattresses, and furniture to bed linens. This outfit is well known in Europe and Japan, where they tout the brand as promoting "the art of sleeping." The furniture designs are sleek and minimal and include beds, dressers, and wardrobes.

GRANGE

New York Design Center Building
200 Lexington Ave (at 32nd St), 2nd floor   212/685-9057
Mon-Fri: 9-6   grange.fr

French furniture and accessories fill this stylish showroom. Pieces range from classic period designs to exotic and contemporary styles. All of them emphasize form, function, and comfort. Dozens of finishes and levels of antiquing are available on most furniture pieces.

KENTSHIRE GALLERIES

37 E 12th St (bet University Pl and Broadway)   212/673-6644
Mon-Thurs: 9-5; Fri: 9-2:30; Sat: by appointment
700 Madison Ave (bet 62nd and 63rd St)   212/421-1100
Mon-Fri: 10:30-6; Sat: 11-5 (closed Sat in July and Aug)   kentshire.com

Kentshire presents eight floors of English fine antique furniture, accessories, and jewelry circa 1690 to 1870, with a particular emphasis on the Georgian and Regency periods. This gallery has an excellent international reputation, and the displays are a delight to see, even if prices are a bit high. A Kentshire boutique at Bergdorf Goodman features antique and estate jewelry.

LOST CITY ARTS

18 Cooper Square (Bowery at 5th St)   212/375-0500
Mon-Fri: 10-6; Sat, Sun: noon-6 (closed Sun in summer)   lostcityarts.com

Established in 1982, Lost City Arts shows mostly mid-20th-century (1950s to 1970s) modern furniture, lighting fixtures, and accessories. Owner James Elkind travels the world in search of unique pieces. You'll also find some of the company's own production pieces in the same style.

OFFICE FURNITURE HEAVEN

22 W 19th St (bet Fifth Ave and Ave of the Americas), 4th floor 212/989-8600
Mon-Fri: 9-6   officefurnitureheaven.com

Visit Office Furniture Heaven if you are setting up an office or upgrading one. There are great bargains in first-quality contemporary pieces; some are new, while others are manufacturers' close-outs and discontinued or used items that have been refurbished to look almost new. You'll find a large showroom display of refurbished Knoll and Haworth furniture and new ones by Global and OFS. There are conference tables, chairs, bookcases, file cabinets, accessories, and much more.

RESOURCE FURNITURE

969 Third Ave (at 58th St), 4th floor   212/753-2039
Mon-Fri: 9:30-6; Sat: noon-5   resourcefurniture.com

It is possible to squeeze great looking furniture into a wee Manhattan apartment. Resource Furniture is known for its contemporary, space-saving European furniture. Of course, there are wall beds modeled after the familiar

---

Designer Showrooms

It used to be that only those holding designer's cards were admitted to some trade buildings. These days, a number of design outfits will take care of individual customers, even if the signs on their doors say "Trade Only." Listed below are some of the trade buildings worth checking out. Each has a multitude of shops where you can find just about anything you need to fix up an apartment or home.

Architects & Designers Building (150 E 58th St, 212/644-2766; Mon-Fri: 9-5): 35 showrooms

Decoration & Design Building (979 Third Ave, 212/759-5408; Mon-Fri: 8:30-5:30): 18 floors

Manhattan Art & Antiques Center (1050 Second Ave, 212/355-4400; Mon-Sat: 10:30-6; Sun: noon-6): over 130 galleries

NY Design Center (200 Lexington Ave, 212/679-9500; Mon-Fri: 9-5): 90 showrooms

Shopping for Vintage

Every weekend thousands of New Yorkers and visitors head to the **Hell's Kitchen Flea Market** (39th Street at Ninth Ave and other locations). This popular outdoor market has been around since 1996. As you might imagine, the selection is vintage and eclectic: clothing, home furnishings, bric-a-brac, jewelry, silver, ethnic attire and accessories, decorative arts, antiques, and collectibles. You'll find more merchandise at their **West 25th Street Market** (25th St bet Broadway and Ave of the Americas). Nearby is the **Antiques Garage** (112 W 25th St), a destination since 1994 for vintage and antique merchandise. Arrive at the 9 a.m. opening for the best selection at the markets, which close by 6 p.m. Check out the website (hellskitchenfleamarket.com) for more information.

Murphy beds. What's really impressive is a sofa that transforms into a bunk-bed set. Beautiful fabrics and quality structural materials combine good looks with functionality. Resource also stocks tables, seating, lighting, rugs, and executive office pieces to complete the look.

INFANTS AND CHILDREN

ALBEE BABY
715 Amsterdam Ave (at 95th St)   212/662-7337
Mon-Fri: 10-7; Sat: 10-6; Sun: 11-6   albeebaby.com

Albee has one of the city's best selections of basics for infants and toddlers. This longtime family-owned and -operated store has everything from strollers and car seats to cribs and rocking chairs. Furniture for baby's room includes cribs, changing tables, dressers, and gliders, and moves up to bunk and twin beds. If you can't find what you need, check in with the helpful staff.

SCHNEIDER'S
41 W 25th St (bet Broadway and Ave of the Americas)   212/228-3540
Mon-Sat: 10-6 (Tues till 8)   schneidersbaby.com

This Chelsea store is a find for those interested in children's furniture at comfortable prices. Bedroom suites are fit for a princess or young gent. You'll also find car seats, strollers, diaper bags, bedding, backpacks, and much more for infants through teens.

GAMES

COMPLEAT STRATEGIST
11 E 33rd St (at Fifth Ave)   212/685-3880
Mon, Tues, Thurs: 11-7; Wed, Fri: 11-9, Sat: 10-6; Sun: noon-6
                                        thecompleatstrategist.com

The Compleat Strategist touts itself as the "true gamers strategic choice." Established over a quarter century ago, it began as an armory of sorts for military games and equipment. As time went on, the store branched into science fiction, fantasy, and murder-mystery games, as well as adventure games, DVDs, and books. The stock is more than ample, and the personnel are knowledgeable and friendly. They now have chess and backgammon sets, Monopoly, other older games, and cards!

GIFTS AND ACCESSORIES

BIZARRE BAZAAR

130¼ E 65th St (bet Lexington and Park Ave)   212/517-2100
Mon-Fri: by appointment   bzrbzr.com

For the discerning and serious collector, Bizarre Bazaar offers antique toys, aviation and automotive memorabilia, industrial-inspired curiosities, vintage Louis Vuitton luggage, enamel glassware, French perfume bottles, Lalique pieces, artists' mannequins, architectural miniatures, jewelry, and much more — all of high quality.

DE VERA

1 Crosby St (at Howard St)   212/625-0838
26 E 81st St (at Madison Ave)   212/288-2288
Tues-Sat: 11-7   deveraobjects.com

As he travels the world, Federico de Vera purchases whatever catches his eye. The result is a unique operation, with decorative arts, antiques, Japanese lacquerware, Venetian glass, ivory carvings, and other unusual items. There's an emphasis on jewelry (vintage, one-of-a-kind, and some even designed by Federico). Both a craftsman and a merchant, he does wonders with the most unusual vintage elements.

DELPHINIUM HOME

353 W 47th St (bet Eighth and Ninth Ave)   212/333-7732
Mon-Sat: 11-8; Sun: noon-7   delphiniumhome.com

Whimsical and *practical* would describe many of the gift items sold here. Kitchen-scrubber holders in animal shapes, timers that look like mini-blenders, shower curtains printed with a map of the New York subway system, and a metal cow that serves as a watering can are some favorites. Less quirky decor and accessories for the kitchen, bath, and home are attractively displayed. The kids' line features similarly whimsical items, including books and bath toys. You'll also find cards, candles, jewelry, clocks, wine caddies, all unique in design, and perfect for that surprise gift.

DOMUS

413 W 44th St (at Ninth Ave)   212/581-8099
Tues-Sat: noon-8; Sun: noon-6   domusnewyork.com

Shopping at this eclectic Hell's Kitchen housewares store is fun! Luisa Cerutti

---

Sales Alert!

Top Button is a web-based company (topbutton.com) that informs consumers about sample, warehouse, outlet, clearance, and promotional sales. Categories include apparel, housewares, accessories, food, beauty, and many more. Information can be accessed by company name, product type, and date. It's a great resource, and the service is free.

and Nicki Lindheimer have excellent taste. On their travels they have picked out one-of-a-kind European and Asian imports (many handcrafted), including jewelry, pottery, tabletop, vintage glassware, linens, china, furniture, and unusual, eye-catching pieces. By working directly with international artisans, they are able to trim costs by eliminating middle men. Domus (which is Latin for *home*) is a super place to shop for wedding gifts. Free gift wrapping and same-day delivery in Manhattan are available.

EXTRAORDINARY

247 E 57th St (bet Second and Third Ave)   212/223-9151
Daily: 11-10   extraordinaryny.com

An international gift selection is the draw at Extraordinary. Owner J.R. Sanders has a background in museum exhibition design, and it shows. You'll find hand-painted boxes, hand-carved bowls, lacquered trays, metal candle holders, unique lamps, jewelry, and other items for the home. The round-the-world theme includes merchandise from the Philippines, Japan, Thailand, China, Vietnam, India, Morocco, Ghana, Peru, and other stops; local artists are also featured. No matter your budget, you'll have no trouble finding something "extraordinary" from a wide range of price points.

GLOBAL TABLE

107 Sullivan St (bet Prince and Spring St)   212/431-5839
471 Amsterdam Ave (bet 82nd and 83rd St)   646/657-0318
Mon-Sat: noon-7; Sun: noon-6   globaltable.com

Looking for a thoughtful surprise for mom or a hostess gift for a dinner party? Make a stop at Global Table. The carefully edited inventory at this crowded tabletop and accessory store is affordable, different, fun, and worldwide in scope. Scan the one-of-a-kind pottery, ceramic, wood, and plastic items from around the world; most with simple lines and vivid colors. Sure to please!

MICHAEL C. FINA

500 Park Ave (at 59th St)   212/557-2500
Mon-Thurs: 10-8; Fri, Sat: 10-6; Sun: noon-6   michaelcfina.com

Michael C. Fina has been a New York tradition since 1935. This popular bridal-gift registry firm has an extensive selection (over 200 brand names) of sterling silver, china, crystal, barware, and home decor. Frames, vases, bowls, decorative accents, and vintage silver are all of superior quality. It is renowned for an exquisite selection of wedding and engagement rings; designers include Mark Patterson, Christofle, Penny Preville, and Tacori. Prices are attractive, quality is top-notch, and the store is well organized.

RANDOM ACCESSORIES

77 E 4th St (bet Bowery and Second Ave)   212/358-0650
Mon: noon-6; Tues: noon-7; Wed-Sat: noon-8; Sun: noon-7

At this small East Village shop, an amazing assortment of lighthearted, must-have merchandise fills the shelves. *Cute* and *frivolous* best describe the mix of baby gifts, books, kitchen gadgets, frames, vases, decor items, personal accessories, and cards. There are also cuff links and other jewelry. It is a great place to shop for an "off-the-wall" gift that will raise a smile.

SUSTAINABLE NYC

139 Ave A (bet St. Mark's Pl and 9th St)   212/254-5400
Mon-Fri: 8 a.m.-9 p.m.; Sat, Sun: 9-9

In trying to be a responsible steward of our planet, this store offers local, organic, recycled, fair-trade, repurposed, and biodegradable products and gifts. The shop itself is built from reclaimed 300-year-old lumber from New York City buildings. Even the sign is solar-powered. There is a variety of books, cards, paper, jewelry, clothing, shoes, bags, beauty products, and solar-powered gadget chargers. You'll want to take a break from your shopping at the in-store cafe/coffee shop.

WORKS GALLERY

1250 Madison Ave (bet 89th and 90th St)   212/996-0300
Mon-Thurs: 10-6:30; Fri, Sat: 10-6   worksgallery.com

At Works Gallery you will find one-of-a-kind jewelry, art-glass items, and wall art handmade by talented artists. The gallery presents 30 studio jewelers, glassmakers, woodworkers, and fine artists. You can also have a personal piece made from your own stones, or have an item redesigned, repaired or resized. They have been in business for over two decades.

GREETING CARDS

UNICEF CARDS & GIFT SHOP

3 United Nations Plaza (44th St bet First and Second Ave)   212/326-7054
Mon-Fri: 10-6   unicefusa.org/shop

The United Nations Children's Emergency Fund (UNICEF) has been improving the lives of the world's children for over 60 years. One way this tremendous organization raises money for its lifesaving projects and programs is through the sale of cards and gifts. If you've never seen UNICEF products before, then you're in for a treat at this well-planned and friendly store, which carries fabulous calendars, greeting cards, stationery, books and puzzles for children, home decor, jewelry, scarves, bags, and other accessories — all for a good cause.

HOBBIES

JAN'S HOBBY SHOP

1435 Lexington Ave (bet 93rd and 94th St)   212/987-4765
Mon-Sat: 10-6:30; Sun: 11-5

Jan's stocks everything a serious model builder could possibly want. The store has a superb stock of plastic scale models, model war games, and all kinds of model cars, trains, planes, remote-controlled helicopters, ships, and tanks. Jan's also carries remote-controlled planes and boats. Owner Fred Hutchins can be found some mornings at the 72nd Street Model Boat Pond in Central Park showing off some of his remote-controlled boats.

HOME FURNISHINGS

ABC CARPET & HOME

881 and 888 Broadway (at 19th St)   212/473-3000
Mon-Sat: 10-7 (Thurs till 8); Sun: noon-6   abchome.com

If you can visit only one home-furnishings store in Manhattan, ABC should

Restaurant-Supply Companies

The Bowery was previously known as the place where restaurateurs shopped for dishware, cookware, kitchen appliances, cutlery, specialized tools, equipment, and other essentials to set up a working kitchen and dining room. Formerly only those in the restaurant business could shop for chefs' preferred brands and gadgets at supply stores on The Bowery. Celebrity chefs have introduced folks to complicated recipes and techniques, many of which require special tools, gadgets, and paraphernalia. As a result, these restaurant suppliers are now treasure troves for professional chefs and novice cooks alike.

Bari Restaurant Equipment (240 Bowery, 212/925-3845): restaurant and pizza equipment

Bowery Restaurant Supply (183 Bowery, 212/254-9720): restaurant and bar essentials

Daroma Restaurant Equipment (180 Bowery, 212/260-2463): knives

Roger & Sons (268 Bowery, 212/226-4734): everything for a deli or restaurant

be it! Starting in 1897 as a pushcart business, ABC expanded into one of the city's most unique, exciting, and well-merchandised emporiums. (It's actually two buildings, located across the street from each other.) ABC is the Bergdorf Goodman of home furnishings. There are floors of great-looking furniture, dinnerware, linens, gifts, home accessories, and antiques. You will see many one-of-a-kind pieces as you explore corner after corner. There is an entire floor of fabrics by the yard and an extensive selection of carpets and rugs at reasonable prices. Don't miss their restaurant, **ABC Kitchen** (38 E 19th St, 212/475-5829), a class operation from Jean-Georges Vongerichten that serves brunch, lunch, and dinner.

ADELAIDE

702 Greenwich St (at 10th St)   212/627-0508
Wed-Sun: noon-7   adelaideny.com

The elegant interior of this shop belies its former life as a trucking garage. Exceptional furniture, rugs, lighting, interesting decor pieces, and artwork from the 1930s to the 1960s are attractively displayed. Classy vignettes incorporate gleaming aluminum, glass, brass tables, and interesting accessories alongside upholstered chairs, settees, and sofas. The stock changes frequently.

CALYPSO SOHO

407 Broome St (at Lafayette St)   212/925-6200
Mon-Sat: 11-7; Sun: noon-6   calypsostbarth.com

Bedrooms will look casual and breezy with high-end merchandise from Calypso. This outfit specializes in beautiful pillows, throws, textiles, furniture, rugs, lighting, and other home items, including some designer originals, most from earthy, natural fibers. Many items are loungey, but there is a mix of modern and coastal decor.

MACKENZIE-CHILDS

20 W 57th St (bet Fifth Ave and Ave of the Americas)   212/570-6050
Mon-Sat: 10-6 (Thurs till 7); Sun: 11-5   mackenzie-childs.com

   With a 2012 move just a few doors up on 57th Street, landscape murals, greenhouse door partitions, and red brick paving make this boutique an exciting and inviting space. And it is all about style, color, and quality. Stripes, checks, plaids, florals, and black-and-white patterns adorn the handcrafted and hand-painted tableware, kitchen accessories, gifts, home decor, lighting, unique furniture pieces, garden furniture and outdoor decor, and stunning accessories. This same theme carries over to the selection of apparel and holiday items. Check out the whimsical bathroom sinks! A visit to free-spirited MacKenzie-Childs will brighten any day.

RESTORATION HARDWARE

935 Broadway (at 22nd St)   212/260-9479
Mon-Sat: 10-8; Sun: 11-7   restorationhardware.com

   Restoration Hardware is a luxury brand that represents more than its name would indicate. Part home furnishings and part hardware, you'll find a large selection of furniture, bed and bath items, home decor, drapery, outdoor and garden, lighting, bathware, cabinets, and retro hardware. There's also a good selection of cleaning and maintenance supplies. With the belief that old things can be chic, Restoration proudly reproduces an antique look in many of its products; it is among the best in its field.

SURPRISE! SURPRISE!

91 Third Ave (bet 12th and 13th St)   212/777-0990
Mon-Sat: 10-7; Sun: 11-6   surprisesurprise.com

   At Surprise! Surprise! you'll find a complete line of reasonably priced items for the home. With all their inventory and know-how, you can stock and furnish your apartment in no time. Choose from a large selection of kitchenware, bath accessories, wall decor, dressers, wardrobes, bookshelves, chairs, tables, desks, and lamps.

A British Toast!

Alexander McQueen (417 W 14th St, 212/645-1797): fashion designer

Asprey (835 Madison Ave, 212/688-1811): designer accessories

Carry On Tea & Sympathy (108-110 Greenwich Ave, 212/807-8329): British groceries, teapots, Christmas crackers, gifts

Lulu Guinness (394 Bleecker St, 212/367-2120): handbags

Reiss (309-313 Bleecker St, 212/488-2411; 197-199 Columbus Ave, 212/799-5560; and 387 West Broadway, 212/925-5707): men's and women's clothing and accessories

> **Hardware for Kitchen and Bath**
>
> For bathroom and kitchen fix-ups, these firms stand out:
>
> **Krup's Kitchen & Bath** (11 W 18th St, 212/243-5787): good source for appliances; custom cabinetry and countertops, too
>
> **Simon's Hardware & Bath** (421 Third Ave, 212/532-9220): everything for the bathroom and kitchen; fixtures, hardware, even towels

WEST ELM

112 W 18th St (bet Ave of the Americas and Seventh Ave)	212/929-4464
1870 Broadway (at 62nd St)	212/247-8077
Mon-Sat: 10-9; Sun: 11-7	westelm.com

West Elm is like a slightly less expensive Crate & Barrel. You'll find minimalist modern furniture, shelving, mirrors, lamps, quilts, bedding, shower curtains, bath accessories, towels, kitchen tools, clocks, room accents, rugs, dinnerware, glassware, and flatware. The stores are attractive and merchandise is well-displayed.

HOUSEWARES AND HARDWARE

BASICS PLUS

2315 Broadway (bet 84th and 83rd St)	212/873-7837
845 Second Ave (at 45th St)	212/682-6311
194 Third Ave (at 18th St)	212/432-2230
386 Canal St (at West Broadway)	212/219-7601
Numerous other locations	
Mon-Fri: 8 a.m.-10 p.m.; Sat: 9 a.m.-10 p.m.; Sun: 10-10	basicsplusny.com

After starting his first locksmith company on the Upper East Side, Zvi Cohen realized he needed merchandise on the shelves. He asked his customers what they would buy, and the rest is history. Every Basics Plus location has a New York Locksmith service counter, as well as hardware-store essentials like tools, cleaning supplies, repair items, housewares, paint, fasteners, and automotive basics. Oh, and let's not forget the locks!

BROADWAY PANHANDLER

65 E 8th St (bet Broadway and University Pl)	212/966-3434
Mon-Sat: 11-7 (Thurs till 8); Sun: 11-6	broadwaypanhandler.com

Broadway Panhandler maintains a tradition of great assortments and low prices. Family-owned and operated since 1976, the folks here are a pleasure to deal with. Thousands of cutlery, bakeware, tabletop items, and cookware pieces are available at sizable savings. Guest chefs make periodic appearances, and a fine selection of professional items is offered to walk-in customers and restaurant and hotel buyers.

DICK'S CUT-RATE HARDWARE

9 Gold St (at Maiden Lane)	212/425-1070
Mon-Fri: 7:30-6:30; Sat: 9-6; Sun: 10-5	dickshardwarenyc.com

Hardware stores like Dick's are a great convenience for shoppers. In a

Lower Manhattan location where there are few such stores, Dick's provides good prices and informed service. You will find great selections of electrical and plumbing supplies, tools, cleaning and gardening supplies, housewares, plus much more. They also cut duplicate keys.

GARBER HARDWARE

710 Greenwich St (bet 10th and Charles St)   212/242-9807
Mon-Thurs: 8-8; Fri, Sat: 8-5; Sun: 10-4   garberhardware.com

This unique family business has become a New York institution. The Garbers have been operating their old-style hardware store since 1884 with this appealing motto: "Either we have it or we can get it for you." You will find a complete inventory of paints; hardware; home and garden; plumbing and electrical supplies; locks; tools; and building materials. Making custom window shades, key-cutting, and pipe-cutting are among the many handy services offered.

GEORGE TAYLOR SPECIALTIES

76 Franklin St (bet Church St and Broadway)   212/226-5369
Mon-Thurs: 7:30-5; Fri: 7:30-4

Porcelain and chrome abounds here! Antique-style towel bars, tubs, toilets, pedestal sinks, and bath accessories are among Taylor's specialties. They offer hard-to-find vintage items and custom designs of fittings for unique installations. Founded in 1869, Taylor remains a friendly, family-run operation. Ask for father Chris, daughter Valerie, or son John.

GRACIOUS HOME

1201 and 1220 Third Ave (bet 70th and 71st St)   212/517-6300
1992 Broadway (at 67th St)   212/231-7800
45 W 25th St (at Ave of the Americas)   212/414-5710
Hours vary by store   gracioushome.com

Savvy New Yorkers love Gracious Home! These stores are must-visits for anyone interested in fixing up their home, establishing a new one, looking for gifts, or just browsing stores that typify the New York lifestyle. The quality, expertise, and service are outstanding. You'll find appliances, wall coverings, paint, gifts, hardware, decorative bath accessories, lighting, china, casual furniture, bedding, shelving, pots and pans, and heaven knows what else! They install window coverings and large appliances, offer tool rental and repair services, create custom lampshades, and provide a gift registry and special-order department. The location in Chelsea (W 25th Street) is a design center limited to decorative and architectural hardware and plumbing supplies.

MANHATTAN WARDROBE SUPPLY

245 W 29th St, 8th floor (bet Seventh and Eighth Ave)   212/268-9993
Mon–Fri: 9–6:30; Sat: noon–6   wardrobesupplies.com

I've never seen a shop like this! Manhattan Wardrobe Supply has all sorts of items having to do with making, storing, cleaning, and displaying clothes for the home or theater; theatrical makeup and hair and wig accessories; jewelry maintenance and storage; and miscellaneous bits and pieces, like location-set bags, fabric dyes, and distressing kits. If you're a wardrober, you'll definitely want

---

Sources for Lumber

Remodelers and builders, take note! For lumber, plywood, Masonite, bricks, cork, paint, and more, try these stores:

Chinatown Lumber (140 East Broadway, 212/608-2055)

City Lumber (550 W 37th St, 212/244-3743)

Metropolitan Lumber and Hardware (175 Spring St, 212/966-3466)

Prince Lumber (404 W 15th St, 212/777-1150)

---

to shop here. If not, you'll learn the secrets of the professionals to maintain your attire in tiptop condition. (Note: clothes are not sold here.)

P.E. GUERIN

23 Jane St (bet Greenwich and Eighth Ave)   212/243-5270
Mon-Fri: 9-5:30 (by appointment)   peguerin.com

Andrew Ward is the fourth generation to run the oldest decorative hardware firm in the country and the only remaining foundry in the city. The company began in 1857 and has been on Jane Street since 1892. In that time, the firm has grown into an impressive worldwide operation. Under this same roof they manufacture and/or import decorative hardware and bath accessories. Artisans craft intricate metalwork in brass, nickel, pewter, verde, or bronze, and the foundry can make virtually anything from those materials, including copies and reproductions. They stock 25,000 beautiful items. No job is too small for Guerin, which operates like the hometown firm it still believes itself to be. They offer free estimates and can help with any hardware problem.

S. FELDMAN HOUSEWARES

1304 Madison Ave (at 92nd St)   212/289-3961
Mon-Sat: 9-6; Sun: 11-5   sfeldmanhousewares.com

Sam Feldman opened this store, originally a five-and-dime store, during the Depression. Over the years it has changed dramatically, but it is still family-owned and -operated. Customer service is a top priority; they even provide free espresso for shoppers. With over 12,000 items to choose from, this is truly a one-stop shopping spot. You'll find housewares, cookware, home decor, gifts, tabletop items, appliances, toys, gift items, and more. They repair vacuum cleaners and offer free delivery in New York City. What more could they do?

SAIFEE HARDWARE

114 First Ave (at 7th St)   212/979-6396
Mon-Thurs: 8:30-7:30; Fri, Sat: 8:30-8; Sun: 10-7:15   saifeehardware.com

This is your neighborhood hardware store, that is, if you live in the East Village. Saifee has the usual supplies for plumbing, electrical, gardening, and small building projects, as well as housewares, decorative items, tools, and other gadgets. Although prices are not as low as at big-box stores, the personal attention and expertise you'll find make it worth the stop.

SIMON'S HARDWARE & BATH
421 Third Ave (bet 29th and 30th St)   212/532-9220
Mon-Fri: 8-5:30 (Thurs till 7); Sat: 10-5   simonsny.com

Simon's is really a hardware supermarket, offering one of the city's finest selections of quality decorative hardware items, bath and kitchen fixtures, and accessories. Woodworkers and plumbers will find myriad tools, supplies, and materials. The personnel are patient and helpful, even if you just need something to fix a broken handle on a door or chest of drawers.

SUR LA TABLE
75 Spring St (at Crosby St)   212/966-3375
1320 Third Ave (bet 75th and 76th St)   646/843-7984
306 W 57th St (at Eighth Ave)   212/574-8334
Hours vary by store   surlatable.com

Whether you are outfitting a tiny kitchenette or a sprawling kitchen and dining room, this is *the* place to shop. You'll find a large and colorful assortment of essentials for cooking and entertaining, with name brands such as Epicurean, Le Creuset, and Zoku, not to mention Sur la Table's own quality merchandise. Foodies love the frequent cooking demos!

WILLIAMS-SONOMA
1175 Madison Ave (at 86th St)   212/289-6832
110 Seventh Ave (at 17th St)   212/633-2203
121 E 59 St (bet Park and Lexington Ave)   917/369-1131
10 Columbus Circle (Time Warner Center)   212/581-1146
Hours vary by store   williams-sonoma.com

Williams-Sonoma came from humble beginnings in the wine country of Sonoma County, California. It has since expanded across the nation and is referred to as the "Tiffany of cookware stores." The serious cook will find a vast display of quality gourmet cookware, bakeware, cutlery, kitchen linens, specialty foods, cookbooks, small appliances, kitchen furniture, glassware, and tableware. Only the Columbus Circle location carries a home-furniture collection. The stores also offer a gift and bridal registry, cooking demonstrations, free recipes, gift baskets, and shopping assistance for corporations or individuals. Especially at holiday time, the candy assortment is first-class. Call customer service (877/812-6235) or access William-Sonoma's website to request their attractive catalog, which includes a number of excellent recipes.

IMPORTS

AFGHAN

NUSRATY AFGHAN IMPORTS
85 Christopher St (bet Bleecker and 4th St)   212/691-1012
Tues-Sun: noon-8   nusratyafghanimports.com

This shop is jam-packed with colorful textiles, carpets and rugs, and antique silver and jewelry. Abdul Nusraty has an unerring eye for things unique and of high quality. Many items are from Afghanistan, Egypt, and Morocco. There are magnificently embroidered native dresses and shirts displayed alongside semiprecious stones mounted in jewelry. Be sure to look up to see the beautiful wall hangings and silk paintings anchored from the ceiling.

AUSTRALIAN

R. M. WILLIAMS

46 E 59th St (bet Park and Madison Ave)   212/308-1808
Mon-Fri: 10-6; Sat: 11-5   rmwilliams.com

A visit to this bush outfitter is akin go going "down under" without leaving the city! High-quality Australian jeans, belts, and boots are specialties and denim goods are like no other you have seen or felt. Merchandise is geared toward gents; there is only a very small selection for ladies. Items are not bargain priced, this place is for the discerning shopper.

CHINESE

CHINESE PORCELAIN COMPANY

475 Park Ave (at 58th St)   212/838-7744
Mon-Fri: 10-6; Sat: 11-5   chineseporcelainco.com

The Chinese Porcelain Company has been offering Asian and European works of art and fine furniture since 1984. Their specialty is Chinese ceramics, but there are also beautiful creations in wood, stone, lacquer, jade, glass, enamel, and ivory. Chinese, Tibetan, Indian, Khymer, and Vietnamese sculptures are represented, along with French and continental furniture.

CQ ASIAN FURNITURE

37 W 20th St (at Ave of the Americas)   212/366-1888
Daily: 10:30-7:30   cqasianantiquefurniture.com

Whether you decorate with an Asian theme or need the perfect accent piece, check out the vast selection at CQ. Antiques, reproduction furniture, and accessory collections (like vases, ginger jars, and bronze carvings) have been imported from Korea, Mongolia, Tibet, and Beijing. Choose from a variety of table styles, armoires, buffets, chairs, and desks. Talk to store personnel if you don't find exactly what you're looking for, as they have a huge warehouse and take custom orders.

PEARL RIVER MART

477 Broadway (bet Broome and Grand St)   212/431-4770
Daily: 10-7:20   pearlriver.com

Pearl River Mart is a true Chinese department store, presenting items imported from China and other Asian countries. The store is busy, well-organized, and well-stocked with clothing and accessories, home furnishings, kitchenware, arts and crafts, Chinese brocade, and more, most at low prices. A furniture department is located on the upper level.

WING-ON TRADING

145 Essex St (bet Delancey and Houston St)   212/477-1450
Mon-Fri: 9:30-6; Sat: 10-5

There's no need to go to the Orient to get your Chinese porcelain or earthenware. Wing-On has a complete and well-organized stock of household goods. One of their specialties is Chinese teas at low prices.

YUNHONG CHOPSTICKS SHOP

50 Mott St (bet Bayard and Pell St)   212/566-8828
Daily: 10:30-8:30   happychopsticks.com

The name is truly descriptive of the merchandise here. Chopsticks in all manner of materials: plastic, steel, ceramic, porcelain, and various woods. Some are elaborately embellished; some are themed. All are priced accordingly, from a couple of dollars to $1,000 for boxed sets. For the chopstick-challenged (like me), there are "training sticks" for kids. Associated mealtime merchandise rounds out the selection: spoons, bowls, and, of course, chopstick stands. Presenting chopsticks as a gift is considered giving someone happiness.

ESKIMO/NATIVE AMERICAN

ALASKA ON MADISON

1065 Madison Ave (bet 80th and 81st St), 2nd floor   212/879-1782
Tues-Sat: 1:30-6:30   alaskaonmadison.com

This gallery is New York's most complete collection of Inuit and Northwest Coast ceremonial artifacts and sculptures and objects from the Old Bering Sea cultures. It is run by collectors for collectors. Periodic shows highlight aspects of these cultures. A number of contemporary artists whose works have been shown here have gained international acclaim.

GENERAL

KATINKA

303 E 9th St (at Second Ave)   212/677-7897
Tues-Sat: 4-7 (call ahead; hours can vary)

This closet-sized shop is an import paradise, with jewelry, natural-fiber clothing, shoes, scarves, belts, hats, musical instruments, incense, and artifacts from India, Thailand, Pakistan, Afghanistan, and South America. The most popular items are colorful shoes and embroidered silk skirts from India. Jane Williams and Billy Lyles make customers feel like they have embarked on a worldwide shopping safari! Prices are reasonable.

SHEHERAZADE HOME

121 Orchard St (bet Delancey and Rivington St)   212/539-1771
Mon, Wed-Fri: 11-7; Sat: noon-7; Sun: noon-6   sheherazadehome.com

Sheherazade features handcrafted home decor imported from a number of countries. You'll find home furnishings from North Africa, the Middle East, and Asia, including antique and contemporary furniture, carpets, tapestries, chandeliers, textiles, glassware, lanterns, jewelry, and gifts. Islamic art and Oriental decorative furnishings are also featured. Owner Rachid works with native artisans to bring exotic pieces that are exclusive to his store.

JAPANESE

MUJI

620 Eighth Ave (at 40th St)   212/382-2300
455 Broadway (bet Grand and Canal St)   212/334-2002

52 Cooper Square (near Astor Place)   212/358-8693
Mon-Sat: 11-9; Sun: 11-8

16 W 19th St (bet Fifth Ave and Ave of the Americas)   212/414-9024
Mon-Sat: 11-8; Sun: 11-6:30   muji.us

    This Johnny-come-lately Japanese department store stocks eye-catching and unique desk, office, and stationery items as part of their no-name generic line. They also carry personal accessories, housewares and home accessories, and books — even furniture and lighting! Shoppers appreciate the quality goods at low prices.

SARA JAPANESE POTTERY

950 Lexington Ave (bet 69th and 70th St)   212/772-3243
Mon-Fri: 11-7; Sat: noon-6   saranyc.com

    If you're looking for something with a Japanese flair, Sara is the place to go for modern Japanese ceramics, glassware, tableware, cast iron, and gifts. Check out the colorful lacquerware, textiles, bamboo products, and even iron sculptures. Artist exhibitions and Japanese tea ceremonies are occasionally held at Sara; check the website or call for a schedule of events.

THINGS JAPANESE

800 Lexington Ave (bet 61st and 62nd St), 2nd floor   212/371-4665
Mon-Sat: 11-5   thingsjapanese.com

    This gallery specializes in original 18th- to 20th-century Japanese woodblock prints for collectors, decorators, and gift-givers. Each piece is accompanied by a certificate of authenticity. The staff knows the field well and will help collectors establish a grouping or assist decorators in finding pieces to round out decor. There are also porcelains, baskets, chests, lacquers, and books. Things Japanese will help you appreciate both the subject matter and the artistry in the works it sells.

MEXICAN

PAN AMERICAN PHOENIX

857 Lexington Ave (bet 64th and 65th St)   212/570-0300
Mon-Fri: 10:30-6:30; Sat: 11-6 (closed Sat in Aug); Sun: noon-5 (Dec only)
                                                   panamphoenix.com

    Colorful items made of gleaming silver, vibrant glass, pottery, and fabrics from Mexico and Latin American have adorned this East Side locale for over 50 years. Some items are wearable, including jewelry for men and women and traditional clothing (such as *huipiles*). Decorative and useful home items with a Latin American flair are also sold: textiles, tabletop and holloware, mirrors, rugs, pillows, lanterns, figurines, and holiday goods.

MIDDLE EASTERN

PERSIAN SHOP

534 Madison Ave (bet 54th and 55th St)   212/355-4643
Mon-Sat: 10-6 (call ahead Sat in summer)

    The Persian Shop features unusual Middle Eastern items: end tables, chairs, frames, mirrors, and brocades sold by the yard or made into magnificent neckties. The jewelry selection is especially noteworthy. You'll find precious and semiprecious items, silver and gold cuff links, rings, earrings, bracelets, necklaces, and heirloom pieces. A purchase here will add a touch of the exotic.

UKRAINIAN

SURMA — THE UKRAINIAN SHOP

11 E 7th St (at Third Ave)	212/477-0729
Mon-Fri: 11-6; Sat: 11-4	surmastore.com

Surma has functioned as the "general store of the Slavic community in New York City" since 1918. This bastion of Ukrainism makes it difficult to believe you're still in New York. The clothing is pure ethnic opulence: dresses, vests, shirts, blouses, and accessories. All are hand-embroidered with authentic detailing. Home items include colorful, hand-woven kilims, porcelains, ceramics, woodcrafts, hand-embroidered linens, hand-painted *pysanky* (Easter eggs), and Surma's own Ukrainian-style honey (different and very good). Above all, Surma is known for its educational tapes and books. Pay particular attention to the artwork and stationery, which depict ancient Ukrainian glass paintings. A visit here is like a walk through the old country.

JEWELRY

ALEXIS BITTAR

1100 Madison Ave (bet 82nd and 83rd St)	212/249-3581
353 Bleecker St (bet 10th and Charles St)	212/727-1093
465 Broome St (bet Mercer and Greene St)	212/625-8340
410 Columbus Ave (at 80th St)	646/590-4142
Hours vary by store	alexisbittar.com

Designer Alex Bittar is known for his chic, handcrafted Lucite jewelry. Each colorful pin, ring, bracelet, necklace, and earring is hand-carved and hand-painted; some are embellished with a sprinkling of semiprecious stones; others are brass with a rhodium or gold coating. Whatever you choose is certain to draw attention!

CATWALK

100 Park Ave (bet 40th and 41st St), 34th floor	212/249-5066
By appointment	catwalk10021.com

Want to make a bold statement with your accessories? Catwalk offers one of the largest selections of couture costume jewelry in the city. Featured designers include Chanel, Laquoix, YSL, and more. Check the website for current "runway" items. If you don't see what you want, contact them and they will try to locate it!

CHRISTOPHER 19

19 Christopher St (bet Ave of the Americas and Seventh Ave)	212/627-9159
Daily: 11:30-7 (Thurs, Fri till 8)	christopher19.com

Artist and designer William Felder handcrafts fashion jewelry in Greenwich Village and sells the collection at Christopher 19. A select group of local and international designers also sell their jewelry and men's and women's accessories at this attractive boutique. You'll find jewelry made of metal, wood, beads, crystals, glass, and many types of stones. The price range is as varied as the selection of merchandise.

CHROME HEARTS
870 Madison Ave (bet 70th and 71st St)   212/794-3100
Mon-Sat: 10-6   chromehearts.com

If you're looking for rocker-type accessories, Chrome Hearts is the place to go! They show a broad selection of handmade jewelry (with lots of attitude and studs) in sterling silver, 22-karat gold, platinum, and precious stones. Inventory is across the board with clothing in leather and fabric; gadgets for people who think they have everything; handcrafted furniture in exotic woods; great-looking eyewear; and much more. Be sure to bring your biggest wallet.

DOYLE & DOYLE
189 Orchard St (bet Houston and Stanton St)   212/677-9991
Tues-Sun: 1-7 (Thurs till 8)   doyledoyle.com

Two creative sisters operate this shop, which specializes in antique and estate jewelry, with an emphasis on treasured engagement rings. You'll find Georgian, Victorian, Edwardian, art deco, art nouveau, and retro pieces. The Doyles also show their own design collection. This is a great source for men's vintage cuff links and rings.

FRAGMENTS
116 Prince St (bet Greene and Wooster St)   212/334-9588
Mon-Sat: 11-7; Sun: noon-6   fragments.com

Fragments showcases the latest fine and fashion jewelry from some of the country's top designers. You'll find Anna Alex, Gurhan, Elizabeth Cole, Mizuki, and others among their unique selection. Much of the credit for the success of this highly curated designer boutique goes to Janet Goldman, its founder and CEO. Constantly discovering new artists, Goldman believes that there is always a fresh perspective, a worthwhile new assortment of original designs, and something for everyone.

JENNIFER MILLER JEWELRY
972 Lexington Ave (bet 70th and 71st St)   212/734-8199
Mon-Sat: 10:30-6   jennifermillerjewelry.com

Jennifer Miller is the ultimate jewelry store, and therefore a great place to build on your jewelry wardrobe! Miller specializes in contemporary, classic, and estate jewelry, both fine and faux. The varied selection changes daily. A wide choice of classically chic earrings, necklaces, bracelets, rings, and watches   in yellow or white gold, with man-made or genuine stones come in a wide range of prices. Handbags, shoes, and decorative home items round out the mix.

PIPPIN VINTAGE JEWELRY
112 W 17th St (bet Ave of the Americas and Seventh Ave)   212/505-5159
Mon-Sat: 11-7; Sun: noon-6   pippinvintage.com

Get ready for a treasure hunt! At Pippin Vintage Jewelry value-priced rhinestone, Bakelite, crystal, silver, plastic, and ceramic vintage baubles are neatly spread out, begging to be tried on. The colorful pieces include such names as Sarah Coventry, Coro, and Trifari. But there's more! A display case full of fine jewelry holds baubles of gold, platinum, diamonds, and other genuine stones, from the Victoria age to the 1980s. Continue through the shop to **Pippin**

Vintage Home (212/206-0008), where you'll find fine vintage furniture and home furnishings. By the way, Pippin is the friendly resident guard dog.

LADDERS

PUTNAM ROLLING LADDER COMPANY
32 Howard St (bet Lafayette St and Broadway)   212/226-5147
Mon-Fri: 8:30-4   putnamrollingladder.com

This is certainly an esoteric shop! And why, you might ask, would anyone in New York need those magnificent rolling ladders traditionally used in formal libraries? Could there possibly be enough business to keep a place like this "rolling" since 1905? The answer is that clever New Yorkers turn to Putnam to improve access to their lofts (especially sleeping lofts) and display shelves. Ladders come in a dozen woods and 15 hardware finishes and range from rolling ladders (custom-made, if necessary) to folding library ladders.

LIGHTING FIXTURES AND ACCESSORIES

CITY KNICKERBOCKER
665 Eleventh Ave (at 48th St), 2nd floor   212/586-3939
Mon-Fri: 8:30-5   cityknickerbocker.com

The fourth generation of the Liroff family operates this outfit, which has been in business since 1906. These folks are reliable when it comes to all aspects of lighting, including quality antique reproductions, glassware, and first-rate repairs and restoration. The large sales inventory includes contemporary art-glass lamps; table and floor lamps; ceiling and wall fixtures; and shades and globes in a multitude of colors, shapes, and sizes from top manufacturers.

JUST BULBS
220 E 60th St (bet Second and Third Ave)   212/888-5707
Mon-Sat: 10-7; Sun: noon-6   justbulbsnyc.com

Just Bulbs stocks almost 25,000 types of bulbs, including some that can be found nowhere else. Incandescent, halogen, fluorescent, mercury, sodium, metal halide, you'll find it all. The shop looks like an oversized dressing-room mirror. Everywhere you turn, bulbs are connected to switches that can be flicked on and off. Besides standard sizes, there are light bulbs for use in old fixtures. They will also make repairs and "refresh" light fixtures, changing bulbs and cleaning fixtures at your home or office.

JUST SHADES
21 Spring St (at Elizabeth St)   212/966-2757
Tues-Fri: 9:30-6 (Thurs till 8); Sat: 9:30-5; Sun: 11-5   justshadesny.com

Just Shades has specialized in custom and ready-made lampshades for over

---

For the Dogs
Are you ready to get a dog? If it is a purebred you want, call the **American Kennel Club** (919/233-9767) and tell them the breed you have in mind. Another good bet is **Bide-a-Wee** (410 E 38th St, 212/532-4455). If you need to train your dog, try **Follow My Lead** (212/873-5511).

40 years. They are experts at matching shades to lamps and willingly share their knowledge with retail customers. They have lampshades of silk, hide, parchment, mica, and other intriguing materials. You'll also find a large selection of finials. No job, residential or commercial, is too large or small.

LAMPWORKS
New York Design Center
200 Lexington Ave (bet 32nd and 33rd St), 9th floor   212/750-1500
Mon-Fri: 9-5   lampworksinc.com
    Lampworks' specialty is custom fabrication of lighting and shades. The showroom offers an extensive selection of table lamps, floor lamps, sconces, chandeliers, exterior fixtures, and stock shades; over 45 lines are represented. Beautiful antique lighting, all restored and rewired, are definitely worth a look.

LIGHTING BY GREGORY
158 Bowery (bet Delancey and Broome St)   212/226-1276
Mon-Fri: 8:30-6; Sat, Sun: 10-6   lightingbygregory.com
    Celebrities, museums, and film companies are among the satisfied customers at this full-service designer lighting store. It is the largest contemporary and traditional lighting and ceiling-fan distributor in America. They are major dealers of Lightolier, Tech Lighting, Monte Carlo, Artemide, and Murray Feiss. They are packed with a fantastic selection of lamps, sconces, ceiling lights, and outdoor lighting, and are also experts in track lighting.

LIGHTING PLUS
680 Broadway (bet Great Jones and Bond St)   212/979-2000
Mon-Sat: 10-6:30; Sun: 11-6:30
    Lighting Plus is a very handy neighborhood lighting store, featuring floor and table lamps, all manner of bulbs, and extension cords. There are dimmers, sockets, electrical cord by the yard, party lights, work lights, and more. Prices and service are good, but the selection is even better.

SCHOOLHOUSE ELECTRIC
27 Vestry St (at Hudson St)   212/226-6113
Tues-Sat: 10:30-6   schoolhouseelectric.com
    At Schoolhouse Electric you'll find period lighting fixtures and glass shades, all hand-blown in authentic antique molds. They replicate more than a hundred light fixtures from the early 1900s to the late 1940s. Handcrafted solid brass lighting fixtures, historically accurate and made to order in many finishes, are also available.

LUGGAGE AND OTHER LEATHER GOODS
DEAN LEATHER
822 Third Ave (at 50th St)   212/583-0461
Mon-Fri: 8:30-7:30; Sat: 9-7:30; Sun: 9-6
877 Seventh Ave (bet 55th and 56th St)   212/581-5228
Daily: 9-8
    If it is leather, you can probably find it at Dean Leather: briefcases, wallets, luggage, watchbands, and gift items. The prices are right on many top names like Hartmann, Swiss Army, Samsonite, Briggs & Riley, Bosca, Tumi, and more.

LEXINGTON LUGGAGE

793 Lexington Ave (bet 61st and 62nd St)   800/822-0404
Mon-Sat: 9-6; Sun: 11-5   lexingtonluggage.com

Stop here if you are in the market for luggage. Lexington Luggage has been family-owned and -operated for over 30 years. They carry nearly every major brand: Samsonite, Delsey, Travelpro, Kipling, A. Saks, Rimowa, and Briggs & Riley — at deep discounts. Most luggage and handbag repairs can be done the same day. Other pluses: free same-day delivery, free monograms, and friendly personnel. You'll also find attaché cases and backpacks.

T. ANTHONY

445 Park Ave (at 56th St)   212/750-9797
Mon-Fri: 9:30-6; Sat: 10-6   tanthony.com

T. Anthony handles luxurious, handcrafted luggage of distinction. Anything purchased here will stand out in a crowd. Luggage ranges from small overnight bags to massive steamer trunks. Their briefcases, jewelry boxes, desk sets, albums, key cases, and wallets make terrific gifts, individually or in matched sets. While you won't find discount prices, T. Anthony's high quality and courteous service are established New York traditions. Engraving and repair service on their products are available.

MAGIC

ENCHANTMENTS

424 E 9th St (bet First Ave and Ave A)   212/228-4394
Wed-Mon: 1-9   enchantmentsincnyc.com

Enchantments claims to be the largest and oldest occult store in the city, and one best not argue with them! There is a great selection of essential and fragrance oils, lotions, potions, herbs, resins, and incense; many of these items are custom-blended. Hundreds of magical formulas can be mixed upon request. Ask for guidance when purchasing magical candles, talismans, and charms with a desired outcome in mind.

TANNEN'S MAGIC

45 W 34th St (bet Fifth Ave and Ave of the Americas), Suite 608   212/929-4500
Mon-Fri: 11-6; Sat, Sun: 10-4   tannens.com

Stocking more than 8,000 magic tricks, books, and DVDs, Tannen is one of the world's largest suppliers of magicians' items. It has been patronized by the most accomplished magicians, as well as novices, since 1925. The floor demonstrators are some of the best in the business — always friendly, helpful, and eager to share their knowledge of "effects." Tannen also runs a "Magic Summer Camp" for budding magicians age 11 to 20, spawning some of today's greatest working magicians. Be sure to check the website for upcoming workshops and lectures by some of the best in the magic field.

MEMORABILIA

FIRESTORE

17 Greenwich Ave (bet Christopher and 10th St)   212/226-3142
Mon-Thurs: 11-7; Fri, Sat: 11-8; Sun: noon-6   nyfirestore.com

Firefighters, police, and families and fans of these first responders can find

New York City Souvenirs

CityStore (Manhattan Municipal Building, 1 Centre St, 212/386-0007): official City of New York merchandise

FDNY Fire Zone (34 W 51st St, 212/698-4520): officially licensed FDNY products

Harlem Underground (20 E 125th St, 212/987-9385): mugs and T-shirts with Harlem logos and uptown attitude

Macy's Herald Square Arcade (151 W 34th St, 212/695-4400): unique and classy items

The Metropolitan Museum of Art (1000 Fifth Ave, 212/535-7710): posters of recent art exhibits

Museum of the City of New York (1220 Fifth Ave, 212/534-1672): ties, scarves, and umbrellas with New York-themed designs

New York Gifts (729 Seventh Ave, lobby, 212/391-7570)

New-York Historical Society (170 Central Park W, 212/873-3400): posters, prints, and holiday cards featuring scenes of old New York

Statue of Liberty Gift Shop (Liberty and Ellis Islands, 212/363-3180): mini statues, books, postcards, glassware, and holiday ornaments

everything under the sun relating to them. Patches, pins, T-shirts, sweatshirts, turnout coats, caps, work shirts, FDNY memorial shirts, firefighter jackets, jewelry, calendars, and toys are available at this fascinating shop!

GOTTA HAVE IT!

153 E 57th St (bet Lexington and Third Ave)   212/750-7900
Mon-Fri: 10:30-6; Sat: 11-5 (call ahead on Sat)   gottahaveit.com

Do you have a favorite sports star, Hollywood personality, musical entertainer, or political figure? Since 1994, Gotta Have It! has been a pop-culture time capsule. The shop features original and unique top-quality collectibles in these categories. There are signed photos, musical instruments, baseball bats, used sports uniforms, documents, and movie props. All items are fully authenticated and guaranteed.

NBC EXPERIENCE STORE

30 Rockefeller Plaza (49th St bet Fifth Ave and Ave of the Americas)
    212/664-7174
Mon-Sat: 8-7; Sun: 9-6   rockefellercenter.com/shop-and-eat

The NBC Experience Store is a 20,000-square-foot facility located directly across from Studio 1A, home of *The Today Show*. It stocks games, DVDs, T-shirts, mugs, key chains, and other merchandise with the NBC logo or images from such popular TV shows as *The Biggest Loser, Friday Night Lights,* and *Saturday Night Live.* The shop offers walking tours that go behind the scenes of NBC's studios and around Rockefeller Center, one of New York's most recognizable landmarks.

MOVIES
VIDEOROOM
1403 Third Ave (bet 79th and 80th St)   212/879-5333
Mon-Thurs: 10-10; Fri, Sat: 10 a.m.-11 p.m.; Sun: noon-10   videoroom.net

As the largest and oldest independent video store in New York City, VideoRoom stocks over 12,000 VHS and DVD titles. They specialize in foreign, classic, and hard-to-find films, but there is also an in-depth selection of new releases. The highly competent staff are students of film, motivating them to help inquiring customers. Gold and platinum memberships offer such privileges as advance reservations and free delivery.

MUSEUM AND LIBRARY SHOPS

For one-of-a-kind gifts that are classy, artistic, and well-made, I especially recommend shopping in the following unique and large museums. In most cases, at least some of the wares relate directly to current and past exhibits or the museum's permanent collection. Even at museums that charge an admission fee, you need not pay if you just want to shop. However, you might save money with a museum membership, which generally offers store discounts.

AMERICAN FOLK ART MUSEUM
2 Lincoln Square (Columbus Ave at 66th St)   646/783-5985
Tues-Sat: noon-7:30; Sun: noon-6   folkartmuseum.org

Located across from Lincoln Center, the American Folk Art Museum runs an excellent gift shop. Stock includes items such as stationery, jewelry, toys, books and media, clothing and accessories, and home decor. Most items are handcrafted in folk tradition. This is a great source for finding quirky and original gifts in a wide range of prices.

AMERICAN MUSEUM OF NATURAL HISTORY
Central Park W at 79th St   212/769-5100
Daily: 10-5:45   amnh.org

This museum's amazing three-level store features a wide selection of unusual merchandise related to the natural world, diverse cultures, and exploration and discovery. There is the Space Shop, with items like meteorite specimens, gems, books, movies, and iconic museum apparel and memorabilia; the Science Shop, with science kits, toys and games, posters, postcards, and more; and the Dinosaur Shop, which features dinosaur-themed games, puzzles, fossil replicas and models, books, posters, and apparel. Smaller satellite shops featuring products related to special exhibitions are located near each exhibition's exit doors.

ASIASTORE
725 Park Ave (at 70th St)   212/327-9217
Tues-Sun: 11-6 (Fri till 9, Sept through June)   asiasociety.org

The Asia Society and Museum's fabulous AsiaStore showcases the best in Asian design. Offerings include hundreds of unique items from Asia and Asian-American artists: jewelry, apparel and accessories, home accents, stationery, music, and gifts. A selection of books includes scores of titles on Asian art, culture, politics, religion, and philosophy.

EL MUSEO DEL BARRIO
1230 Fifth Ave (at 104th St)   212/660-7191
Wed-Sat: 11-6   elmuseo.org

La Tienda is the charming museum gift shop at El Museo del Barrio. It is a great source for unique jewelry and handicrafts; art from Latin America, the Caribbean, and local artists; children's books in Spanish and English; and books for adults about the history, art, and culture of Latin America, the Caribbean, and immigrants from these regions.

FRICK COLLECTION
1 E 70th St (at Fifth Ave)   212/547-6848
Tues-Sat: 10-5:45; Sun: 11-4:45   frick.org

The Frick's gift shop makes the most of its small space by concentrating on exquisite cards, stationery, prints, posters, and art books. You will also find a small collection of paperweights, scarves, and other quality museum-inspired gifts. Note that the shop closes 15 minutes before the museum.

INTERNATIONAL CENTER OF PHOTOGRAPHY
1133 Ave of the Americas (at 43rd St)   212/857-0000
Tues-Sun: 10-6 (Fri till 8)   store.icp.org

If you're shopping for a photography buff, this store is definitely worth a look. It has an excellent collection of books about the history and technology of photography and photojournalism, plus coffee-table books of collected works by photographers. Prints, picture frames, unusual postcards, toy cameras, home accessories, and monographs round out the choices.

THE JEWISH MUSEUM
1109 Fifth Ave (at 92nd St)   212/423-3211
Sun-Tues: 11-5:45; Wed: 11-3; Thurs: 11-8; Fri: 11-5:45   thejewishmuseum.org

This relatively large store is an excellent source for Jewish literature, decorative art, and Judaica. Its selection of menorahs is among the classiest in the city. The store also sells cards, coffee-table books, and numerous children's books with Jewish themes and characters. **Celebrations** (1 E 92nd St, 212/423-3260), the Jewish Museum's design shop, is housed in an adjacent brownstone. It is worth a look if you're interested in high-quality ceremonial objects.

MET OPERA SHOP
Metropolitan Opera House
Lincoln Center (Columbus Ave at 65th St)   212/580-4090
Mon-Sat: 10-8; Sun: noon-6   metoperashop.org

Opera lovers will be in heaven at the Metropolitan Opera Shop. In addition to operas and ballet on CD and DVD, you'll find opera glasses, books, umbrellas, totes, cards, journals, T-shirts, jewelry, and wall art for the opera buff. And if you're looking for posters and prints from various seasons, visit The Gallery on the lower concourse.

THE METROPOLITAN MUSEUM OF ART

1000 Fifth Ave (bet 80th and 84th St)	212/570-3894

Rockefeller Center

15 W 49th St (bet Fifth Ave and Ave of the Americas)	212/332-1360

The Cloisters

799 Fort Washington Ave (Fort Tryon Park)	212/650-2277
Hours vary by store	store.metmuseum.org

The two-floor store inside the Metropolitan Museum of Art is the grandfather of all museum gift shops. It specializes in reproductions of paintings and other pieces in The Met's incredible collection, as well as from museum collections around the world. (For limited-edition prints, go to the mezzanine gallery or call 212/650-2910.) You can find jewelry, statues, vases, scarves, ties, porcelains, prints, rugs, and scores of other beautiful gift items. They also carry books relating to special exhibits, as well as umbrellas, tote bags, and other items with the Metropolitan name on them. Prices are reasonable and the salespeople are generally patient and helpful. Smaller "remote" shops can be found throughout the museum, and satellite shops are located at LaGuardia and Kennedy airports, as well as the locations in Manhattan listed above. Both the main Met store (2nd floor) and the satellite shop in Rockefeller Center have particularly good children's sections.

MOMA DESIGN AND BOOK STORE

11 W 53rd St (bet Fifth Ave and Ave of the Americas)	212/708-9700

MOMA DESIGN STORE/MUJI AT MOMA

44 W 53rd St (bet Fifth Ave and Ave of the Americas)	212/767-1050
Daily: 9:30-6:30 (Fri till 9)	

MOMA DESIGN STORE, SOHO/MUJI AT MOMA

81 Spring St (at Crosby St)	646/613-1367
Mon-Sat: 10-8; Sun: 11-7	momastore.org

These magnificent stores are dedicated to what the curators consider the very best in modern design. Furniture, textiles, books, vases, kitchen gadgets, silverware, frames, watches, lamps, and toys and books for children are among the things you'll find. The addition of Muji brings an extensive collection of architectural and design books. These items are not cheap, but the selection is truly exceptional.

NATIONAL MUSEUM OF THE AMERICAN INDIAN

1 Bowling Green (foot of Broadway)	212/514-3767
Daily: 10-5 (Thurs till 8)	nmai.si.edu

Like everything else about the National Museum of the American Indian, the Gallery Store is a classy operation. There is a wide selection of weavings, pottery, jewelry, and other handicrafts by skilled Native artisans. You'll also find children's books, DVDs, toys, and craft kits, along with T-shirts and cards at the second-level shop. Because the museum is part of the Smithsonian Institution, associate members receive a discount on every purchase.

NEUE GALERIE BOOK STORE AND DESIGN SHOP

1048 Fifth Ave (at 86th St)	212/994-9492
Thurs-Mon: 11-6	neuegalerie.org

The Neue Galerie Book Store is clearly *the* source for books on fine art, architecture, and decorative arts in Germany, Austria, and Central Europe in the 19th and 20th centuries; posters, calendars, and postcards, too. The Design Shop has a small but smart selection of beautiful high-end jewelry, tableware, textiles, and other decorative arts based on modern German and Austrian designers like Biedermeier. Most merchandise is related to past or current exhibits.

NEW YORK PUBLIC LIBRARY SHOP

476 Fifth Ave (bet 41st and 42nd St), Room 116   212/930-0641
Mon, Thurs-Sat: 10-6; Tues, Wed: 10-8   nypl.org

This is the perfect gift shop for book lovers. Located just off the main lobby of the New York Public Library's main branch, it features a high-quality selection of unusual merchandise. You'll find books about New York and the library's history, catalogs of past library shows, fine stationery and writing tools, jewelry, and whimsical totes and T-shirts.. There are children's books with themed dolls and puppets, puzzles, and slippers. The staff is particularly pleasant and helpful.

NEW YORK TRANSIT MUSEUM STORE

Grand Central Terminal (42nd St at Vanderbilt Ave)   212/878-0106
Mon-Fri: 8-8; Sat, Sun: 10-6   transitmuseumstore.com

Train and subway buffs love this little shop and gallery. Items for sale include books about Grand Central Terminal, clever T-shirts, replicas of trains and old station signs, banks for children in the shape of city buses, jewelry made from old tokens, token collections, and mosaic and photo tiles. Bus and subway maps, as well as other MTA information, are also available. Note that this shop is a branch of the much larger main store at the **New York Transit Museum** in Brooklyn Heights (Boerum Place at Schermerhorn Street, 718/694-1600).

PICKMAN MUSEUM SHOP OF THE
MUSEUM OF JEWISH HERITAGE

36 Battery Pl (in Battery Park City)   646/437-4213
Sun-Thurs: 10-5:45 (Wed till 8); Fri: 10-3   mjhnyc.org

This shop is a fitting companion to the museum in its celebration of Jewish art, crafts, and culture. The selection is diverse, and many items are related to the museum's collection. Everything is high quality; some is quite unusual. One section includes carefully chosen books and gifts for children of various ages. Elegant jewelry, DVDs, music, holiday items, and Judaica are also shown. The prices are extremely good. Note that the store and the museum are closed on all major Jewish holidays.

THE SHOP AT SCANDINAVIA HOUSE:
THE NORDIC CENTER IN AMERICA

58 Park Ave (at 38th St)   212/847-9737
Mon-Sat: noon-6 (Wed till 7)   scandinaviahouse.org

This lifestyle shop is nestled in Scandinavia House: the Nordic Center in America. It showcases leading modern designers alongside the legends of Nordic culture. Luxurious home-design items, tableware, art glass, textiles, fashion, jewelry, and accessories range from trendy to classic.

SOLOMON R. GUGGENHEIM MUSEUM STORE
1071 Fifth Ave (at 89th St)   212/423-3615
Sun-Wed, Fri: 9:30-6:15;Thurs: 11-6; Sat: 9:30-8:30   guggenheimstore.org
Although much for sale here is typical gift shop fare (including scarves,T-shirts, prints and posters, tote bags, note cards and stationery, jewelry, and children's toys), the design and craftsmanship are anything but ordinary. If you're looking for an unusual clock, a great wedding present, or just the right pair of earrings, try this store. Do be aware, however, that prices are often through the roof. Of course, the store also carries books on modern art and exhibition catalogs. Unlike many other museum stores, this one is actually open before and after the museum itself closes. It is also open on Thursday, when the museum is closed.

THE STORE AT MUSEUM OF ARTS AND DESIGN
2 Columbus Circle (at Eighth Ave)   212/299-7700
Mon-Sat: 10-7 (Thurs, Fri till 9); Sun: 10-6   thestore.madmuseum.org
With its Columbus Circle address, this is one of the most attractive museum stores in town. Works by exceptional artisans from around the globe are displayed. Choose from a constantly changing collection of beautifully designed jewelry, glassware, textiles, home accessories, and more.

THE STUDIO MUSEUM IN HARLEM
144 W 125th St (bet Malcolm X and Adam Clayton Powell, Jr. Blvd)
                                                       212/864-4500, ext. 237
Sun, Wed: noon-6;Thurs: noon-7; Fri: noon-9; Sat: 10-6   studiomuseum.org
Located just inside the museum's entrance on the right, this store sells a wide and generally high-quality selection of jewelry, textiles, crafts, note cards, limited-edition prints, and calendars created by African-Americans and artists of African descent. It also carries an unusually broad selection of cookbooks, fiction, biographies, children's books by and about Africans and African-Americans, catalogs of art by artists of African descent, museum logo merchandise, and the usual tourist gift items.

THE UKRAINIAN MUSEUM
222 E 6th St (bet Second and Third Ave)   212/228-0110
Wed-Sun: 11:30-5   ukrainianmuseum.org
Fabulous *pysanka* Ukrainian Easter eggs (premade eggs or kits for do-it-yourselfers) lure customers to this store. Art books, exhibition catalogs, music, cards, posters, toys, jewelry, embroidery, and other handicrafts are also waiting to be discovered.

UN BOOKSHOP/UN GIFT SHOP
United Nations Visitor Centre
First Ave at 42nd St   212/963-7680
Mon-Fri: 9-5:30   visit.un.org
The UN Bookshop is located within the new United Nations Visitor Centre. The store carries the latest titles published by the UN and other international publishers, children's books, posters, and small souvenirs like UN emblem items (lapel pins, window decals, and magnets). Walk over to the UN Gift Shop for traditional handicrafts, gifts, accessories (jewelry and scarves),

flags of member nations, and N.Y.C. souvenirs.

MUSIC

ACADEMY RECORDS & CDS

12 W 18th St (bet Fifth Ave and Ave of the Americas)   212/242-3000
Daily: 11-7   academy-records.com

Academy Records & CDs has Manhattan's largest stock of used, out-of-print, and rare classical LPs, CDs, and DVDs. They emphasize opera, contemporary classical, and early music (through the Baroque period), but jazz and rock can be found as well. Academy boasts an international reputation and a knowledgeable staff.

FRANK MUSIC

244 W 54th St (bet Broadway and Eighth Ave), 10th floor   212/582-1999
Mon-Fri: 11-5 (hours can vary in summer)   frankmusiccompany.com

Owner Heidi Rogers tends to an enormous volume of classical sheet music, all wrapped in brown folders and piled high on metal shelves. There are aisles for voice, violin, piano, and so on; music is bundled by composer. Rogers' knowledge of the "heavy longhair" business is encyclopedic. Warning: don't come here looking for band music.

JAZZ RECORD CENTER

236 W 26th St (bet Seventh and Eighth Ave), Room 804   212/675-4480
Mon-Sat: 10-6   jazzrecordcenter.com

Jazz Record Center is run by Fred Cohen, a charming guy who really knows his business. It is the only jazz specialty store in the city. They deal in rare, out-of-print, and new jazz records (some blues), CDs, videos, books, posters, photos, concert programs, periodicals, postcards, and T-shirts. The store buys collections, fills online orders, and offers appraisals. They auction jazz rarities on eBay, too.

OTHER MUSIC

15 E 4th St (bet Broadway and Lafayette St)   212/477-8150
Mon-Fri: 11-9; Sat: noon-8; Sun: noon-7   othermusic.com

Other Music is an independent music store specializing in rare, indie, and imported music. They have an excellent stock of CDs and vinyl and hard-to-find releases. Ask about getting cash or store credit for your used CDs and records. Other Music frequently hosts in-store performances and readings.

WESTSIDER RECORDS

233 W 72nd St (at Broadway)   212/874-1588
Mon-Thurs: 11-7; Fri, Sat: 11-9; Sun: noon-6   westsiderbooks.com

Westsider remains one of the few stores specializing in rare and out-of-print LPs. CDs have been added to the stock of 30,000 LPs. You'll also find printed music and books on the performing arts. There are all genres: classical, jazz, rock, pop, blues, country, folk, and spoken word. Turntables (new and used) are sold as well. A short walk away is their sister store, **Westsider Rare & Used Books** (2246 Broadway, 212/362-0706). These places buy, sell, and trade records and books, respectively.

MUSICAL INSTRUMENTS
THE GUITAR SALON

212/675-3236
By appointment   theguitarsalon.com

The Guitar Salon is known for its outstanding collection of classical and flamenco guitars. Beverly Maher's unique one-person operation is located in a historic brownstone in Greenwich Village. She is an expert in 19th- and 20th-century vintage instruments and offers beautiful, handmade classical and flamenco guitars for students, professionals, and collectors. Appraisals are available, and lessons are given on all styles of guitars. Celebrity customers who have shopped here include Keith Richards, Paul Simon, and the Rolling Stones!

SAM ASH
333 W 34th St (bet Eighth and Ninth Ave)   212/719-22991
Mon-Sat: 10-8; Sun: 11-7   samashmusic.com

Sam Ash offers a full selection of quality musical instruments — guitars, drums, keyboards, wind, and string instruments. In addition, there's recording equipment and software, lighting, sheet music, music books, amplifiers, DJ gear, and more. Sam Ash has just about anything that a band, orchestra, or solo musician might need.

PETS AND ACCESSORIES
BARKING ZOO
172 Ninth Ave (bet 20th and 21st St)   212/255-0658
Mon-Fri: 11-8; Sat: 10-6; Sun: noon-5   barkingzoo.com

Barking Zoo offers quality items for your favorite canine. They stock plenty of healthy, organic food options for dogs (and cats); also toys, beds, clothes, bowls, and other accessories for your barking family member. Read their in-store and online posts for valuable information on the care of dogs and cats and a list of dog runs.

DOGGYSTYLE, NYC
46 University Pl (bet 9th and 10th St)   212/228-5824
Mon-Wed: 10-7; Thurs-Sat: 10-8; Sun: 11-6   doggystylenyc.com

Shop here for practical items for your pet at sensible prices. DoggyStyle features boutique-quality collars, leashes, coats, messenger bags, and feeding bowls, plus handy products for traveling with a pet. Dog and cat grooming is available.

Tobacconist

Gentlemen, are you tired of searching for a place where cigar smoking is not only allowed, but encouraged? At **De La Concha** (1390 Ave of the Americas, 212/757-3167), you can enjoy your stogie and good conversation, or make use of their Wi-Fi. High quality, imported and domestic cigars, cigarillos, pipes, tobacco, humidors, and leather goods are carried here.

Piano Row
Faust Harrison Pianos (207 W 58th St, 212/489-3600) is a prestigious source for the most sought-after brands of pianos (new, used, and rebuilt). Additionally, the showroom has a performance area for student recitals and concerts. Fewer shops now make up the famed Piano Row which was once considered the destination for a perfect piano.

LE PETIT PUPPY
18 Christopher St (bet Waverly Pl and Gay St)   212/727-8111
Mon-Sat: 10:30-8; Sun: 10:30-7   lepetitpuppynyc.com

This upscale puppy boutique displays some of its small breeds in the storefront "puppy window." Choose from small breed, toy, and teacup puppies: Dachshunds, Poodles, Shih Tzus, Chihuahuas, Pugs, Maltese, and Terriers. Adoptions include pet health guarantees and ongoing hotline support. Everything needed to care for and pamper a new puppy is here as well: food and treats, apparel, accessories, beds, grooming (cats, too), day care, training, and boarding.

PACIFIC AQUARIUM & PET
46 Delancey St (bet Forsyth and Eldridge St)   212/995-5895
Daily: 10-7   pacificnyc.com

Goldfish are their specialty! Pacific Aquarium & Pet also carries all types of freshwater and saltwater fish, aquatic plants, dozens of species of fancy goldfish, and every kind of aquarium and related supply you could imagine. Custom-made tanks (up to 500 gallons) are installed in homes, businesses and restaurants. Tank maintenance packages are available.

PHOTOGRAPHIC EQUIPMENT AND SUPPLIES
ADORAMA CAMERA
42 W 18th St (bet Fifth Ave and Ave of the Americas)   212/741-0063
Mon-Thurs: 9-8; Fri: 9-5; Sun: 9:30-5   adorama.com

Adorama carries a huge stock of photographic equipment and supplies, new and used, and for amateurs to pros. They also showcase astronomy equipment, iPods and cell phones, stockroom accessories, frames and albums, and video paraphernalia, all sold at discount. Workshops for all skill levels are frequently offered, and they have an array of rental equipment.

B&H PHOTO VIDEO PRO AUDIO
420 Ninth Ave (at 34th St)   212/444-6615
Mon-Thurs: 9-7; Fri: 9-2; Sun: 10-6   bhphotovideo.com

B&H is a superstore in more ways than one! You'll find departments for photo, video, and pro audio, as well as a wide array of home entertainment equipment, computers, and accessories. The store has been in operation since 1974 and is staffed by informed personnel. Inventory levels are high (about 235,000 products), prices are reasonable, and hands-on demo areas make browsing easy. Trade-ins are considered; quality used equipment is sometimes available.

CALUMET PHOTOGRAPHIC

22 W 22nd St (bet Fifth Ave and Ave of the Americas)   212/989-8500
Mon-Fri: 8:30-6; Sat: 9-5:30   calumetphoto.com

In business for over 70 years, this firm provides start-to-finish photographic services. Professional camera equipment (digital, video, and traditional); film and accessories; computers, printers, and scanners; and lighting equipment, are all available at good prices. Service-oriented repair technicians are factory-trained. Ask about equipment rental.

WILLOUGHBY'S IMAGING CENTER

298 Fifth Ave (at 31st St)   212/564-1600
Mon-Fri: 9-7; Sat: 9-6; Sun: 10-7   willoughbys.com

Willoughby's is New York's oldest camera store. With a huge stock they have built an extensive clientele and a solid reputation. Cameras and photo equipment for every budget and skill level fill the shelves, plus camcorders, binoculars and telescopes, and other high-tech equipment. They service cameras, supply photographic equipment, and recycle used items; used cameras are bought and sold.

PICTURES, POSTERS, AND PRINTS

JERRY OHLINGER'S MOVIE MATERIALS STORE

253 W 35th St (bet Seventh and Eighth Ave)   212/989-0869
Mon-Sat: 11-7   moviematerials.com

A perfect stop for movie buffs! Jerry Ohlinger stocks a huge selection of movie posters (from the 1930s to the present) and photographs from film and TV. Lobby cards and press books are also part of the collection. Jerry researches these items and will gladly provide a catalog.

OLD PRINT SHOP

150 Lexington Ave (bet 29th and 30th St   212/683-3950
Tues-Fri: 9-5; Sat: 9-4 (closed Sat in summer)   oldprintshop.com

The Old Print Shop exudes old-fashioned charm, and its stock only reinforces the impression of timelessness. Kenneth M. Newman specializes in Americana, including original prints, town views, Currier & Ives prints, atlases, and original maps that reflect America's yesteryear. Many of the nostalgic pictures that have adorned calendars and stationery were copies of prints found here. Amateur and professional historians have a field day in this shop. Newman also does "correct period framing." Everything bought and sold here is original; Newman purchases estate and single items.

PHILIP WILLIAMS POSTERS

122 Chambers St (bet Church St and West Broadway)   212/513-0313
Tues-Sat: 11-7   postermuseum.com

This is perhaps the largest vintage poster gallery in the world, with over 50,000 original posters, from 1870 to the present. Philip Williams features prints in a variety of categories, including travel, food, dance, trains, sports, magic, political, and films. Vintage maps and books about posters are carried; custom framing and poster restoration are also available.

PHYLLIS LUCAS GALLERY — OLD PRINT CENTER

235 E 60th St (bet Second and Third Ave)   212/755-1516
Mon-Fri: 10-5; Sat: 2-5; Sun: by appointment   phyllislucasgallery.com

Inside Phyllis Lucas Gallery — Old Print Center is a treasure trove of antiquarian prints, antique maps, and illustrations. Modern engravings, photographs, original paintings, and a large selection of New York City scenes are displayed. The Gallery is known for its superior custom framing services.

TRITON GALLERY

630 Ninth Ave (at 44th St), 8th floor   212/765-2472
Mon-Fri: 10-6; Sat: noon-6   tritongallery.com

No one presents theater posters like Triton. Posters of current Broadway and Off-Broadway shows join a stock of rare and highly-collectible show posters. Posters range in size from 23" x 46" to 42" x 84" and, as you would expect, are priced according to rarity, age, and demand. Window cards for all shows are archived for historical preservation. Triton also does custom framing.

RUBBER GOODS

CANAL RUBBER SUPPLY COMPANY

329 Canal St (at Greene St)   212/226-7339
Mon-Fri: 9-4:45; Sat: 9-3:45   canalrubber.com

The motto at this wholesale-retail operation is "If it's made of rubber, we have it." Canal Rubber has occupied the same location since 1954. There are foam mattresses, bolsters, cushions, dock bumpers, pads cut to size, hydraulic hoses, rubber tubing, vacuum hoses, floor matting, tiles, stair treads, and sheet-rubber products. Looking for rubber boots? They have those, too.

SAFES

EMPIRE SAFE

6 E 39th St (bet Fifth and Madison Ave)   212/684-2255
Mon-Fri: 9-5 or by appointment   empiresafe.com

Empire shows the city's largest and most complete selection of high-security safes and vault rooms for residences and businesses. They also offer specialized burglary-protection safes with jewelry and watch drawers. Whether you want to protect jewelry and valuables at home or documents in an office building, you can rely on these folks. Delivery and installation are available.

TRAUM SAFE

946 Madison Ave (at 74th St)   212/452-2565
Mon-Sat: 10-6   traumsafe.com

Traum Safe designs and constructs luxury vaults to protect your collection, no matter what that might be. Safes come in contemporary or classic styles, bold or subdued, and include interior lighting and electronic locks. From consultation to installation, Traum can analyze your needs and recommend the right size and finish to match your decor. There is even a safe with custom-made drawers that wind your watches!

SECURITY EQUIPMENT

SPY TEC

252 W 38th St (bet Seventh and Eighth Ave), 6th floor　　212/957-7400
Mon-Fri: 9:30-6　　　　　　　　　　　　　　　　　　　spytecinc.com

　　If you're looking for security or surveillance equipment, then look no further than Spy Tec. This outfit offers video surveillance and counter surveillance items, network cameras, digital and analog recorders, nanny cams, wireless camera detection and location, metal detectors, GPS trackers, infrared sensors, and more. All items are available for residential or commercial installation and Spy Tec's trained personnel will discreetly take care of any need.

SIGNS

LET THERE BE NEON

38 White St (bet Broadway and Church St)　　　　　212/226-4883
Mon-Fri: 9-5　　　　　　　　　　　　　　　　　letherebeneon.com

　　Flashing neon signs have become the ultimate urban cliché, but here they are rendered as fine art. Let There Be Neon operates as a gallery with a variety of sizes, shapes, functions, and designs to entice the browser. Almost all their sales are custom pieces; some vintage and others stock. Even a rough sketch is enough for them to create a literal or abstract neon sculpture. You can view their current projects when you visit.

SILVER

JEAN'S SILVERSMITHS

16 W 45th St (at Fifth Ave)　　　　　　　　　　　212/575-0723
Mon-Fri: 9-4:45　　　　　　　　　　　　　　　jeanssilversmiths.com

　　Want to replace a fork that went down the disposal? Proceed directly to Jean's Silversmiths, where you will find more than 2,000 discontinued, obsolete, and current flatware patterns. A card catalog keeps track of items — new, estate, and used — from mass market to high end. Unusual pieces include duck shears, marrow scoops, and oyster ladles. Jean's will restore, engrave, and polish your prized silver for you.

TIFFANY & CO.

727 Fifth Ave (at 57th St)　　　　　　　　　　　212/755-8000
Mon-Sat: 10-7; Sun: noon-6
97 Greene St (bet Prince and Spring St)　　　　　212/226-6136
Mon-Sat: 11-7 (Thurs till 8); Sun: 11-6　　　　　　tiffany.com

　　The Tiffany legacy began in 1837 as a small "fancy goods" store. With the growing reputation of Tiffany as the "King of Diamonds," it soon became a magnet for the rich and famous. Yes, there really is a Tiffany diamond; a yellow diamond that can be viewed on the first floor of the flagship Fifth Avenue location. That floor also houses the watch and jewelry departments. The stores are famous for exquisite diamonds, but they carry much more: silver jewelry, sterling silver items, bar accessories, small leather goods, fragrances, china, crystal, glassware, flatware, and gift items. The real surprise is that Tiffany carries an excellent selection of reasonably priced items. Many are emblazoned with the Tiffany name and wrapped in the signature blue box. Tourists and residents alike enjoy walking by the beautiful displays in the store's magical windows.

SPORTING GOODS

BICYCLES AND ACCESSORIES

ADELINE ADELINE

147 Reade St (bet Greenwich and Hudson St)   212/227-1150
Daily: 11:30-6:30   adelineadeline.com

European two-wheelers are the top sellers at this bicycle boutique. These are not just ordinary bicycles, but vehicles designed especially for relaxed, comfortable rides. Notable models include the traditional English Pashley, the Italian Bella Ciao, folding bikes, and attention-getting front-load cargo bikes. Outfit yourself and your bike with stylish grips, lights, racks, gloves, helmets, bags, baskets, and other accessories. Be sure to take a test drive before buying. The shop is conveniently located by a designated bike lane.

BICYCLE HABITAT

244 and 250 Lafayette St (bet Spring and Prince St)   212/431-3315
Mon-Sat: 10-7 (Thurs, Fri till 8); Sun: 10-6
228 Seventh Ave (bet 23rd and 24th St)   212/206-6949
Mon-Sat: 11-8 (Sat till 7); Sun: 11-6   bicyclehabitat.com

These customer-oriented folks are "geared" toward cycling buffs and they really want to get more people interested in biking! There's something for everyone at Bicycle Habitat — tricycles for the little ones, urban commuter bikes, very expensive racing bikes, and all the accessories for riding, transporting, and storing bikes. If you don't find what you want, they will special order it or have a bike custom-built to your specifications. Attend one of their bike maintenance classes, including one on roadside emergencies.

BICYCLE RENAISSANCE

430 Columbus Ave (at 81st St)   212/724-2350
Mon-Fri: 10:30-7; Sat, Sun: 10-5   bicyclerenaissance.com

Biking is a way of life at Bicycle Renaissance. They carry commuter, road, racing, mountain bikes, and kids' bikes by Cannondale, Felt, Kuota, Jamis, and Specialized, as well as custom frames for Guru and Calfee Designs. Services include custom-building bikes and bicycle repair. Mechanics aim for same-day service on all makes and models. Prices are on par with so-called discount shops.

CITY BICYCLES

315 W 38th St (bet Eighth and Ninth Ave)   212/563-3373
Mon-Fri: 9-6:30; Sat: 10-5   citybicyclesnyc.com

City Bicycles carry a huge selection of bicycles and also design and construct custom bikes for the ultimate ride. They have commuter, road, mountain, and BMX models from manufacturers such as Bianchi, Schwinn, Jamis, and Haro. The informed staff will help you decide which kind of bike is best for your needs — classic, suspension, or hybrid. See them for bike rentals and repairs.

BILLIARDS

BLATT BILLIARDS
809 Broadway (bet 11th and 12th St)   212/674-8855
Mon-Fri: 9-6:30; Sat: 10-5   blattbilliards.com

Blatt's six floors are outfitted from top to bottom with everything for billiards. Both factory and showroom, this is where skilled craftsmen design, carve, build, and polish each detailed table. The variety inside this shop is amazing: custom and antique billiard tables, jukeboxes, an art gallery, arcade games, table games, bars and accessories, and other items. They also carry everything else you need to play these games and furnish your game room.

EXERCISE EQUIPMENT

GYM SOURCE
40 E 52nd St (bet Park and Madison Ave)   212/688-4222
Mon-Fri: 9-7; Sat: 10-6   gymsource.com

The largest exercise equipment dealer in the Northeast, Gym Source carries new and pre-owned treadmills, ellipticals, exercise bikes, stair-steppers, weight machines, rowers, and fitness gear. Top brands are available at good prices, and Gym Source's skilled technicians provide competent servicing. They rent equipment and will deliver items for use in Manhattan hotel rooms.

FISHING

CAPITOL FISHING TACKLE COMPANY
132 W 36th St (bet Seventh Ave and Broadway)   212/929-6132
Mon-Fri: 10-7; Sat: 10-5   capitolfishing.com

Right in the heart of Manhattan, anglers will find the store of their dreams! Established in 1897, Capitol Fishing is the oldest surviving fishing-tackle store in the U.S. These folks carry a full line of fishing gear from names like Penn, Shimano, Fenwick, Power Pro, and Storm.

URBAN ANGLER
381 Fifth Ave (bet 35th and 36th St)   212/689-6400
Mon-Fri: 10-6 (Wed till 7); Sat: 10-5   urbanangler.com

Urban Angler is your Manhattan source for anything that's fly fishing. You'll find fly-fishing tackle, high-end spin and surf tackle, and travel clothing. Manufacturers include Sage, Simms, Tibor, Hatch, and more. They offer casting and fly-tying lessons and will organize fishing trips to anywhere you want to go.

GENERAL

EASTERN MOUNTAIN SPORTS (EMS)
530 Broadway (bet Prince and Spring St)   212/966-8730
Mon-Fri: 10-9:30; Sat: 10-9; Sun: 11-8
2152 Broadway (bet 75th and 76th St)   212/873-4001
Mon-Sat: 10-9; Sun: 11-8   ems.com

Active and adventurous people look to EMS as a great place for outdoor clothing and gear. Although prices can be bettered elsewhere, it is an excellent source for one-stop shopping, and the merchandise is top-quality. EMS covers virtually all outdoor sports, including mountain climbing, backpacking, skiing, hiking, kayaking, and camping.

G&S SPORTING GOODS

43 Essex St (at Grand St)   646/213-1100
Mon-Sat: 9-6; Sun: 11-6 (closed Sun in summer)   gandssportinggoods.com

Looking to buy a birthday or Christmas gift for a sports buff? I recommend G&S. They have a large selection of brand-name sneakers, in-line skates, boxing equipment, balls, gloves, toys, games, sports clothing, and accessory items. Prices reflect a 20% to 25% discount.

MODELL'S SPORTING GOODS

607 Ave of the Americas (bet 17th and 18th St)   212/989-1110
1293 Broadway (at 34th St)   212/244-4544
51 E 42nd St (bet Madison and Vanderbilt Ave)   212/661-4242
1535 Third Ave (bet 86th and 87th St)   212/996-3800
Numerous other Manhattan locations
Hours vary by store   modells.com

You can't beat this popular chain for quality and value! Founded in 1889, Modell's is America's oldest family-owned sporting-goods chain, with a total of 11 stores in Manhattan. They carry a large selection of footwear and apparel for men, women, and children, including team apparel. Competitor's coupons are generally accepted.

PARAGON SPORTS

867 Broadway (at 18th St)   212/255-8889
Mon-Sat: 10-8:30 (Sat till 8); Sun: 11-7   paragonsports.com

Paragon is truly a sporting-goods mecca, with over 100,000 square feet of specialty shops devoted to all kinds of sports and fitness equipment and apparel. There are departments for team equipment, athletic footwear, skateboards, ice skates, in-line skates, racquet sports, aerobics, swimming, golf, skiing and snowboarding, hiking, camping, diving, biking, watersports, and anything else that can be done in the great outdoors — all top brands.

GOLF

NEW YORK GOLF CENTER

131 W 35th St (bet Seventh Ave and Broadway)   212/564-2255
Chelsea Piers, Pier 59 (West Side Hwy at 18th St)   212/242-8899
100 Park Ave (at 40th St)   212/564-0078
Hours vary by store   nygolfcenter.com

Golfers will find the latest equipment and styles at New York Golf Center. There are clubs, bags, clothing, shoes, accessories, and novelties — everything except one's own hard-won golfing expertise. They carry pro-line equipment by such names as Callaway, TaylorMade, Cleveland, Titleist, Odyssey, Tour Edge, and Nike. Employees couldn't be more helpful in finding the correct product and fit.

GUNS

JOHN JOVINO GUN SHOP

183 Grand St (at Mulberry St)   212/925-4881
Mon-Sat: 10-6; Sun: 2-6

John Jovino Gun Shop has been in business since 1911. They carry all major brands of handguns, rifles, and shotguns, as well as ammunition, holsters, bulletproof vests, knives, and scopes. Major brands include Smith & Wesson, Colt, Ruger, Beretta, Browning, Remington, Walther, Glock, Winchester, and Sig Sauer. Jovino is an authorized warranty repair station for gun manufacturers.

MARINE

WEST MARINE

12 W 37th St (bet Fifth Ave and Ave of the Americas)   212/594-6065
Mon-Fri: 10-7; Sat. Sun: 10-4   westmarine.com

Somewhat surprising, West sells marine supplies as if it were situated in the middle of a New England seaport rather than the heart of Manhattan. They carry marine electronics, sailboat fittings, gamefish tackle, lifesaving gear, ropes, anchors, compasses, clothing, clocks, and barometers. You'll also find foul-weather suits and a line of clothing for yachters.

OUTDOOR EQUIPMENT

TENT AND TRAILS

21 Park Pl (bet Broadway and Church St)   212/227-1761
Mon-Sat: 9:30-6 (Thurs, Fri till 7); Sun: noon-6   tenttrails.com

Before leaving town on that weekend camping trip, head to Tent and Trails. In the urban canyons near City Hall, this 6,000-square-foot store is devoted to camping. The staff is experienced and knowledgeable. There are boots from Asolo, Lowa, Merrell, Hi-Tec, and Scarpa Footwear. They carry camping gear from top makers like Patagonia, Big Agnes, Canada Goose, and Osprey. You'll find backpacks, sleeping bags, tents, down clothing, and much more. Tent and Trails also rents camping equipment.

RUNNING

SUPER RUNNERS SHOP

2543 Broadway (at 95th St)   646/756-5058
1337 Lexington Ave (at 89th St)   212/369-6010
821 Third Ave (bet 50th and 51st St)   212/421-4444
745 Seventh Ave (at 49th St)   212/398-2449
Hours vary by store   superrunnersshop.com

Co-owner Gary Muhrcke's passion for running became his livelihood; that was over 33 years ago. Incidentally, Gary won the first New York City Marathon in 1970. The stock at Super Runners Shop includes a superb selection of state-of-the-art men's and women's running and racing shoes, as well as performance running clothes. The informed staff, themselves runners, know firsthand the importance of proper fit and size. Check with them for details on upcoming races.

BLADES

156 W 72nd St (bet Broadway and Columbus Ave)   212/787-3911
Mon-Sat: 10-8; Sun: 10-7
659 Broadway (at Bleecker St)   212/477-7350
Mon-Sat: 10-9; Sun: 11-7   blades.com

Blades embraces the skate/snow/surf lifestyle. The store has a great selection of equipment for snowboarding, skateboarding, and in-line skating; a good stock of men's and women's apparel, footwear, and accessories; enthusiastic, informed service; and a 30-day price guarantee.

TENNIS

MASON'S TENNIS

56 E 53rd St (bet Park and Madison Ave)   212/755-5805
Mon-Fri: 10-7; Sat: 10-6; Sun: noon-6   masonstennis.com

Mason's is the oldest tennis specialty store in Manhattan. Mark Mason offers a superb collection of clothing by Adidas, Fila, Polo, Nike, Ralph Lauren, Lucky in Love, Spanx, and more. U.S. Open products are carried from May to December. You will also find ball machines, bags, and other tennis paraphernalia. They sell racquets and shoes at the minimum prices allowed by the manufacturers and will special order any tennis product. Same-day stringing is offered. A yearly half-price clothing sale takes place in mid-January.

STATIONERY

JAM PAPER & ENVELOPE

135 Third Ave (bet 14th and 15th St)   212/473-6666
Mon-Fri: 8:30-8 (Fri till 7); Sat, Sun: 10-6   jampaper.com

At 7,000 square feet, Jam Paper is the largest paper and envelope store in the city and perhaps the world! They stock over 150 kinds of paper, with matching card stock and envelopes. You will find a vast selection of presentation folders, plastic portfolios, plastic envelopes and folders, cello sleeves, translucents, bags, tissue, and raffia — all in matching colors. Close-outs and discounted items provide excellent bargains.

PAPER PRESENTATION

23 W 18th St (bet Fifth Ave and Ave of the Americas) 212/463-7035
Mon-Fri: 9-7:30; Sat, Sun: 11-6   paperpresentation.com

Come here for a huge selection of quality paper goods. Business cards, writing paper, invitations, post cards, place cards, envelopes, folders and portfolios, bags, gift wrap, labels, and more. Select from a rainbow of colors and a multitude of textures and finishes: matte, metallic, parchment, transparent, and linen included.

TILES

BISAZZA

43 Greene St (bet Broome and Grand St)   212/334-7130
Mon-Sat: 10-6   bisazzausa.com

Bisazza claims to be the world's leader in glass mosaic. Whether that is true, there is no disputing that the Italian mosaic designs are beautiful and colorful.

They have large stocks of glass mosaic tiles, custom mosaics, and tiles for indoor and outdoor use — for kitchens, bathrooms, pool areas, or wherever.

COMPLETE TILE COLLECTION
42 W 15th St (bet Fifth Ave and Ave of the Americas)   212/255-4450
Mon-Fri: 10-6:30; Sat: 11-6   completetile.com

If you are shopping for quality tiles, come to Complete Tile Collection. They carry American art tiles; glass, ceramic, concrete, metal, slate, granite, and molded tiles; marble and limestone mosaics; and a large assortment of handmade tiles. Design services are available, and the selection, including 800 varieties of natural stone and 500 colors of ceramic tile, is tops. They fabricate stone countertops, too!

IDEAL TILE
405 E 51st St (at First Ave)   212/759-2339
Mon-Fri: 9-5; Sat: 10-3   idealtile.com

Ideal Tile imports porcelain, granite, and natural stone from Italy, Spain, and Brazil. Installation of tiles by skilled craftsmen is guaranteed. They also offer marble and granite fabrication for fireplaces, countertops, window sills, and tables.

TOBACCO AND SMOKING ACCESSORIES

BARCLAY-REX
75 Broad St (bet Beaver and William St)   212/962-3355
70 E 42nd St (bet Madison and Park Ave)   212/692-9680
570 Lexington Ave (at 51st St)   212/888-1015
Hours vary by store   barclayrex.com

The Barclay-Rex shop is the product of three generations of the Nastri family. From 1910 they have catered to devotees of fine cigars, pipes, tobaccos, plus smoking-related gifts and accessories. Their shops are stocked with more than 200 brands of imported and domestic tobaccos. The finest tobaccos from all over the world are hand-blended and packaged under the Barclay-Rex label. Custom blending is one of their specialties. Cigars are housed in walk-in humidors at controlled temperatures. Their signature line of pipes are made from beautiful natural woods.

MIDTOWN CIGARS
562 Fifth Ave (at 46th St)   212/997-2227
Mon-Fri: 9-8; Sat: 10-6; Sun: 11-5   midtowncigar.com

Midtown Cigars showcases over 200 brands of domestic and handmade imported cigars, plus quality humidors and cigar accessories. They claim to have Manhattan's lowest prices. Manager Marie Jeune suggests checking their website for special cigar-sampling events.

OK CIGARS
383-A West Broadway (bet Spring and Broome St)   212/965-9065
Daily: noon-8   okcigars.com

Looking for a really good cigar? Len Brunson carries some of the best in a pleasant atmosphere. Unique accessories are available, including some of the finest and most peculiar antique tobacciana to be found.

TOYS AND CHILDREN'S ITEMS

GENERAL

DINOSAUR HILL

306 E 9th St (bet First and Second Ave)   212/473-5850
Daily: 11-7   dinosaurhill.com

    Dinosaur Hill stocks diverse and consistently high-quality merchandise. There are brightly colored toys, solid wood blocks, and a wonderful assortment of games, hats, music boxes, stuffed toy animals, puppets, and musical instruments. In addition, there is handmade clothing, quilts, bibs, and T-shirts in natural-fiber fabrics, some made locally.

F.A.O. SCHWARZ

767 Fifth Ave (at 58th St)   212/644-9400
Sun-Thurs: 10-8; Fri, Sat: 10-9   fao.com

    You know you're in for an experience when you are greeted by a toy soldier! This New York institution offers merchandise that is over the top and that is not readily available elsewhere; pricey, too. The mere fact that your purchase came from F.A.O. Schwarz makes it special for many youngsters (and adults).

KIDDING AROUND

60 W 15th St (bet Fifth Ave and Ave of the Americas)   212/645-6337
Mon-Sat: 10-7; Sun: 11-6

Grand Central Terminal
107 E 42nd St (at Vanderbilt Ave)   212/972-8697
Mon-Fri: 8-8; Sat: 10-8; Sun: 11-6   kiddingaround.us

    These independent toy emporiums are arguably the city's best toy stores. Books, toys, puzzles, balls, games, craft supplies, and birthday party favors are colorful, great finds. In addition to a wide selection of Playmobil, Brio, and Corolle dolls, Kidding Around stocks an amazing assortment of quality wooden toys for riding, building, and just having fun. The clothing section is small but well chosen, and the dress-up clothes are great, too. It's impressive how much fun is crammed into these neighborhood shops!

MARY ARNOLD TOYS

1010 Lexington Ave (at 72nd St)   212/744-8510
Mon-Fri: 9-6; Sat, Sun: 10-5 (closed Sun in summer)   maryarnoldtoys.com

    Mary Arnold Toys is a spacious, well-organized, and well-stocked source for the basics. There are separate sections for games, early-development toys, puzzles, books, videos, dolls, stuffed animals, and craft kits and supplies. The dress-up collection deserves a close look.

TOYS "R" US

1514 Broadway (at 44th St)   646/366-8800
Sun-Fri: 10 a.m.-11 p.m.; Sat: 9 a.m.-11 p.m.   toysrus.com

    No family trip to Manhattan is complete without a visit to this Toys "R" Us in Times Square. This marketing marvel features a huge stage set with a giant animatronic T-Rex dinosaur and a 60-foot-tall ferris wheel. Each car of the ferris wheel models a different toy. A Barbie life-size dollhouse displays two floors of the latest toys and fashions. A huge plasma screen showcases the latest electronic games. Every square inch of this busy store is filled with kid-pleasing merchandise. **Babies "R" Us** (24-30 Union Square E, 212/798-9905) is a one-stop baby-supply destination: clothing, toys, baby equipment, and other necessities.

SPECIALTY AND NOVELTY

ALPHABETS

115 Ave A (bet 7th and 8th St)	212/475-7250
64 Ave A (bet 4th and 5th St)	212/353-2201
Daily: noon-8	alphabetsnyc.com

In what is a combination toy store and novelty shop, you might find funky items like a Gumby and Pokey piggybank, kitschy ceramics, and a Beatles T-shirt. Alphabets is *the* place to visit for baby boomers wanting to relive their childhood or to purchase the perfect retro gift.

AMERICAN GIRL PLACE

609 Fifth Ave (at 49th St)	877/247-5223
Mon-Thurs: 10-7; Fri: 10-9; Sun: 9-7	americangirl.com

If you have a young girl in your life, you are probably aware of the American Girl doll phenomenon! This store is a restaurant, retail store, and giant credit-card bill all wrapped up into one. A whole-day dream package starts at $260 for one child over six and an accompanying adult. Birthday-party packages run from $37 to $59 per child. In addition to dolls and doll clothes, there is doll furniture, accessories for dolls, or choose from matching doll-girl outfits. Enjoy a break from shopping at the American Girl Cafe which serves brunch, lunch, afternoon tea, and dinner. A doll hospital, doll hair salon, doll ear piercing, exhibits, and plenty of special events will complete your visit.

DISNEY STORE

1540 Broadway (bet 45th and 46th St)	212/626-2910
Daily: 10 a.m.-1 a.m.	disneystore.com

This three-floor maze of merchandise in Times Square is filled with Disney-themed items: Mickey Mouse, Winnie the Pooh, Buzz Lightyear, Disney princesses, and the most recent characters from *Planes*. Besides the expected toys, games, movies, and books, you will find clothing, luggage, backpacks, and accessories; just about anything that can be emblazoned with Disney logos, characters, and creations. For collectors, their gallery offers authentic pieces of Disney art from past and present. The staff really knows the stock and they are personable as well. Call or check online for frequent in-store events.

FORBIDDEN PLANET NYC

832 Broadway (bet 13th and 14th St)	212/473-1576
Sun-Tues: 9 a.m.-10 p.m.; Wed-Sat: 9 a.m.-12 a.m.	fpnyc.com

This unique shop is a shrine for science-fiction artifacts. Forbidden Planet stocks fantasy related toys and games, including anime figures, military figures and vehicles, model kits, and plush and vinyl toys. There are sci-fi comic books and publications, videos, posters, T-shirts, and cards.

Stores for Fine Watches

Here are several stores for fine watches:

Cellini Fine Jewelry (509 Madison Ave, 212/888-0505 and Waldorf Astoria New York, 301 Park Ave, 212/751-9824)

Kenjo (40 W 57th St, 212/333-7220)

Tourneau (510 Madison Ave, 212/758-5830; 12 E 57th St, 212/758-7300; and Time Warner Center, 10 Columbus Circle, 212/823-9425)

Wempe Jewelers (700 Fifth Ave, 212/397-9000)

IMAGE ANIME

242 W 30th St (bet Seventh and Eighth Ave)   212/631-0966
Mon-Fri: 11-7; Sat, Sun: noon-6   imageanime.com

Image Anime specializes in imported Japanese toys, models, and collectibles. If that category interests you — and a great many children and adults are fanatically devoted to it — then this packed little store will thrill you. Lines include Gundam, Pokémon, Transformers, Robotech, Zoids, and nearly every other popular Japanese line.

LEGO STORE

Rockefeller Center
620 Fifth Avenue (at 50th St)   212/245-5973
Mon-Sat: 10-8; Sun: 11-7   stores.lego.com

A corner of Rockefeller Center is home to the incredible LEGO Store, featuring the famous colorful plastic bricks from Denmark. The selection is vast: there are sets to fabricate farms and villages, vehicles, landmarks, and collectible kits with action-movie and character themes. Large Lego sculptures, play areas, and computer design stations are sure to stimulate the imagination and challenge the dexterity of folks of all ages.

THE RED CABOOSE

23 W 45th St (bet Fifth Ave and Ave of the Americas), basement 212/575-0155
Mon-Fri: 11-7; Sat: 11-5   theredcaboose.com

Owner-operator Allan J. Spitz says that 99% of his customers are not wide-eyed children, but sharp-eyed adults who are dead serious about model railroads. The Red Caboose claims to have 100,000 items on hand, including a line of 300 hand-finished, imported brass locomotives; New York subway cars, too. The five basic sizes (1:22, 1:48, 1:87, 1:161, and 1:220 in a ratio of scale to actual size) allow model railroaders to build layouts sized to fit everything from a desk drawer to an entire room. They stock an extensive line of track, plastic kits, paints, tools, model supplies, and related books. Red Caboose also carries die-cast airplanes and vehicles (military and commercial), autos, trucks, and ships.

TOY TOKYO

91 Second Ave (at 5th St)   212/673-5424
Sun-Thurs: 1 p.m.-9 p.m.; Fri, Sat: 1p.m.-10 p.m.   toytokyo.com

This store is another great example of why I love New York! Since 2000,

Toy Tokyo has been selling toys and collectibles from every genre, including wonderful Japanese anime figures, *Star Wars* collectibles, and hard-to-find classics. The pop culture stock changes a bit every week, and many items come straight from Hong Kong, Japan, and other points east. If you're a collector or just a curious browser, put this overflowing shop on your list. You must see it to believe it!

TRAVEL ITEMS
FLIGHT 001
96 Greenwich Ave (bet Jane and 12th St)   212/989-0001
Mon-Sat: 11-8; Sun: noon-6   flight001.com

An in-flight brainstorm by two businessmen was the beginning of this helpful travel store. Their mission: to procure and develop the best travel products. You will find novel and useful travel aids, including luggage, luggage tags, passport holders, spacepaks, wallets, TSA travel bottles; and all manner of bags — clear cosmetics bags, lingerie bags, shoe bags, laundry bags, and "stuff" bags. Jetsetters love this place!

WATCHES
SANDY YAEGER WATCH
578 Fifth Ave (at 47th St), Space 54   212/819-0088
Mon-Fri: 10-5   yaegerwatch.com

Sandy Yaeger Watch carries over 2,000 discounted watches. Choose from the latest styles and classics in name brands retailing from $100 to $150,000. If you don't find what you want, Yaeger will begin a search for you. Watch repair and warranties are offered, and prices are quoted over the phone. The store has been owned by the same family since 1973.

TEMPVS FVGIT
Showplace Antiques and Design Center
40 W 25th St (bet Ave of the Americas and Broadway)   212/633-6063
Thurs-Sun: 10-5   tempvsfvgit.com

This could be the place if you are looking for a vintage Rolex! They also carry other collectibles and top brand watches, plus quality watchbands — all at considerable savings. Watch repair and restoration are among the services offered. Before you make the trip, you can view many of the watches at the Tempvs website.

Chapter 7

WHERE TO
"EXTRAS"

T his chapter contains a dozen or so subjects not found elsewhere in this edition. Here you'll find where to purchase tickets, attend music and sporting events, take kids, spend a romantic evening, and host a party or special event.

ANNUAL EVENTS

While stores, museums, restaurants, and the like are open all year, some special events are held only during certain seasons or once a year. Keep in mind that since some of these events are seasonal, dates and venues frequently change.

JANUARY
Polar Bear Club New Year's Dip (Coney Island)
Ice skating (Rockefeller Center, Central Park, and Bryant Park)
Winter Antiques Show (Park Avenue Armory)
Chinese New Year (January or February)
New York National Boat Show (Jacob K. Javits Convention Center)

FEBRUARY
Westminster Kennel Club Dog Show (Madison Square Garden)
Empire State Building Run-Up (Empire State Building)
Valentine's Day wedding ceremony (Empire State Building)
Outsider Art Fair (Chelsea)

MARCH

St. Patrick's Day Parade (Fifth Ave)
Big East and NIT college basketball tournaments (Madison Square Garden)
Macy's Spring Flower Show
Artexpo New York (Pier 94 on the Hudson River)

APRIL

Major League Baseball season opens (Yankees and Mets)
New York Antiquarian Book Fair (Park Avenue Armory)
New York International Auto Show (Jacob K. Javits Convention Center)
Tribeca Film Festival

MAY

Ninth Avenue International Food Festival (Ninth Ave)
Ukrainian Festival (7th St in the East Village)
Fleet Week for the U.S. Navy and Coast Guard (week before Memorial Day)
River to River Festival (Lower Manhattan)
Washington Square Outdoor Art Exhibit (University Pl)

JUNE

Salute to Israel Parade (Fifth Ave)
Free concerts and performances (Central Park and other city parks)
Lesbian and Gay Pride Week and Parade
Museum Mile Festival (Fifth Ave bet 82nd and 105th St)

JULY

Free concerts and performances (Central Park and other city parks)
Free movies (Bryant Park and other locations)
Fourth of July fireworks (East River and other locations)
Mostly Mozart Festival (Avery Fisher Hall, Lincoln Center)
Midsummer Night Swing (Lincoln Center)

AUGUST

Free concerts and performances (Central Park and other city parks)
Free movies (Bryant Park and other locations)
New York City Triathlon
Lincoln Center Out-of-Doors Festival (Lincoln Center)
New York International Latino Film Festival
U.S. Open tennis tournament begins (USTA Billie Jean King National Tennis
    Center in Flushing Meadows, Queens)
Harlem Week

SEPTEMBER

Washington Square Outdoor Art Exhibit (University Pl)
National Football League season opens (Giants and Jets)
Feast of San Gennaro (Little Italy)
New York Film Festival (Lincoln Center)

OCTOBER

Columbus Day Parade
National Basketball Association season opens (Knicks and Liberty)
National Hockey League season opens (Rangers and Islanders)
Union Square Autumn Fair (Broadway at 23rd St)
Halloween Parade (Greenwich Village)
The ING New York City Marathon (late October or early November)

NOVEMBER

New York Comedy Festival
Margaret Mead Film Festival (American Museum of Natural History)
Macy's Thanksgiving Day Parade
Christmas tree lighting (Rockefeller Plaza)
New York Chocolate Show

DECEMBER

Christmas windows (Saks Fifth Avenue, Macy's, Lord & Taylor, and other locations)
Messiah Sing-In (Avery Fisher Hall, Lincoln Center)
Radio City Christmas Show (Radio City Music Hall)
Holiday bazaar (Grand Central Terminal)
Christmas Day walking tour (Big Onion Walking Tours)
New Year's Eve celebrations (Times Square and other locations)
First Night celebrations (Grand Central Terminal, Central Park, and other locations)

WHERE TO PLAY

FILMS

Like any city, New York has a multitude of theaters for first-run movies. Indeed, most movies debut in New York and Los Angeles before opening anywhere else. (Depending on the size of the crowds they draw, some never do open elsewhere.) Call 212/777-FILM (3456) for information about what movies are showing at virtually every theater in Manhattan and to purchase tickets by credit card at many of those theaters. If you're online, go to moviefone.com.

If you're looking for an old movie, a foreign film, an unusual documentary, a 3D movie, or something out of the ordinary, try calling one of the following theaters. Most numbers connect you with a recording that lists current movies and times, ticket costs (some places accept cash only), and directions.

American Museum of Natural History's IMAX Theater (Central Park W at 79th St, 212/769-5100)
Angelika Film Center and Cafe (18 W Houston St, 212/995-2570)
Anthology Film Archives (32 Second Ave, 212/505-5181)
Asia Society and Museum (725 Park Ave, 212/288-6400)
Austrian Cultural Forum (11 E 52nd St, 212/319-5300)
Film Forum (209 W Houston St, 212/727-8110)

Florence Gould Hall at the French Institute (55 E 59th St, 212/355-6160)
Japan Society Gallery (333 E 47th St, 212/715-1258)
Lincoln Plaza Cinema (1886 Broadway, 212/757-2280)
Paley Center for Media (25 W 52nd St, 212/621-6800)
Quad Cinema (34 W 13th St, 212/255-8800)
Symphony Space (2537 Broadway, 212/864-5400)
Walter Reade Theater at Lincoln Center (165 W 65th St, 212/875-5600)
Whitney Museum of American Art (945 Madison Ave, 212/570-3676)

Like everything else, the price of movie tickets in New York tends to be higher than elsewhere in the country. Second-run theaters, film societies, and museums usually charge a little less, and Bryant Park, Central Park, and other parks throughout the city host free movies in summer.

Of course, New York is home to dozens of popular film festivals. The best known is the Film Society of Lincoln Center's **New York Film Festival**, held in late September and early October. This annual event showcases top international films and special events and gets more popular every year. Call the Walter Reade Theater box office, 212/875-5601, for more information.

> **Party On!**
> There's lots of dancing and singles action at **bOb Bar** (235 Eldridge St, 212/529-1807). DJs keep the music going all evening, but the party really kicks into high gear around midnight Tuesday through Sunday. Call for bOb Bar's roster of guest DJs and cover charges.

NIGHTLIFE

Whether you want an evening of elegant dining and dancing, rocking and rolling till the wee hours, dropping in on a set of jazz, or catching some stand-up comedy, New York's club scene offers endless choices. I've listed several popular places in each category to get you started. Most levy a cover charge, many offer at least a light menu, and a very few require reservations (dress codes may apply). As with so many other things, it is wise to call in advance.

CABARET ROOMS
54 Below (254 W 54th St, 646/476-3551): dinner shows
Cafe Carlyle, The Carlyle (35 E 76th St, 212/744-1600): closed in summer months
Don't Tell Mama (343 W 46th St, 212/757-0788)
The Duplex (61 Christopher St, 212/255-5438)
Metropolitan Room (34 W 22nd St, 212/206-0440)

COMEDY CLUBS
Caroline's on Broadway (1626 Broadway, 212/757-4100)
Comedy Cellar (117 MacDougal St, 212/254-3480)
Dangerfield's (1118 First Ave, 212/593-1650)
Gotham Comedy Club (208 W 23rd St, 212/367-9000)

Up Late and Looking for Something to Do?
Bowlmor Lanes (222 W 44th St, 212/680-0012): Friday and Saturday until 2 a.m.
Bowlmor Lanes and Greenwich Village Country Club (110 University Pl, 212/255-8188): Friday and Saturday until 2 a.m.
Cafeteria (119 Seventh Ave, 212/414-1717): American classics served 24/7
Crunch Fitness Club (404 Lafayette St, 212/614-0120): 24/7
The Dressing Room Boutique & Bar (75-A Orchard St, 212/966-7330): Thursday through Saturday until 2 a.m.
Forever 21 (1540 Broadway, 212/302-0594): shop until 1 a.m.
Slate Billiards (54 W 21st St, 212/989-0096): Friday and Saturday until 4 a.m.

Greenwich Village Comedy Club (99 MacDougal St, 212/777-5233)
Stand-Up New York (236 W 78th St, 212/595-0850)
Tribeca Comedy Lounge (22 Warren St, 646/504-5653): lower level of Brick NYC; great pizza and more
Upright Citizens Brigade Theatre (307 W 26th St, 212/366-9176 and 153 E 3rd St, 212/366-9231): inexpensive; also classes in improvisation and sketch comedy

DANCING

Cielo (18 Little W 12th St, 212/645-5700)
Greenhouse (150 Varick St, 212/807-7000)
Pacha (618 W 46th St, 212/209-7500)
Pianos (158 Ludlow St, 212/505-3733): in the Upstairs Lounge
SOB (204 Varick St, 212/243-4940)
Sullivan Room (218 Sullivan St, 212/252-2151)

GAY AND LESBIAN CLUBS

Boiler Room (86 E 4th St, 212/254-7536): gay
G Lounge (225 W 19th St, 212/929-1085): gay
Henrietta Hudson (438 Hudson St, 212/924-3347): lesbian
Posh (405 W 51st St, 212/957-2222)
Stonewall Inn (53 Christopher St, 212/488-2705): historic bar

JAZZ CLUBS

Arthur's Tavern (57 Grove St, 212/675-6879): The Grove Street Stompers play every Monday night.
Bill's Place (148 W 133rd St, 212/281-0777): Bill Saxton's Jazz Club and Speakeasy; BYOB
Birdland (315 W 44th St, 212/581-3080)
Blue Note (131 W 3rd St, 212/475-8592)
Iridium Jazz Club (1650 Broadway, 212/582-2121)
Jazz Standard (116 E 27th St, 212/576-2232): Blue Smoke restaurant is upstairs.

Showman's Jazz Club (375 W 125th St, 212/864-8941)
Smoke Jazz and Supper Club (2751 Broadway, 212/864-6662)
Swing 46 (349 W 46th St, 212/262-9554): live bands nightly
Village Vanguard (178 Seventh Ave S, 212/255-4037)

ROCK, FOLK, AND BLUES CLUBS

A Happy Ending (302 Broome St, 212/334-9676): two floors of music, drinks, and partygoers; Wednesday through Saturday
B.B. King's Blues Club and Lucille's Grill (237 W 42nd St, 212/997-4144)
Bitter End (147 Bleecker St, 212/673-7030): one of the original Greenwich Village folk clubs, with rock and blues as well
Bowery Ballroom (6 Delancey St, 212/533-2111): the city's premier rock (with a bit of everything else) showcase venue

MUSIC IN THE MUSEUMS

Brooklyn Museum (200 Eastern Parkway, Brooklyn, 718/638-5000): free music and entertainment from 5 to 11 on the first Saturday of every month
The Cloisters Museum and Gardens (Fort Tryon Park, 99 Margaret Corbin Drive, 212/923-3700): winter and spring concerts
Frick Collection (1 E 70th St, 212/288-8700): concerts on some Sundays at 5

> ### For Jazz Lovers
> Keep the **Garage Restaurant & Cafe** (99 Seventh Ave S, 212/645-0600) in mind if you're looking for live jazz. You can hear jazz seven days a week: over a relaxing brunch on the weekends, nightly during dinner, and on into the wee morning hours. If you're a people watcher, opt for a table on the balcony or a sidewalk cafe table in the summer.

The Metropolitan Museum of Art (1000 Fifth Ave St, 212/535-7710): classical music on Friday and Saturday from 4 to 8:30 in the Great Hall Balcony Bar
The Morgan Library and Museum (225 Madison Ave, 212/685-0008): lots of concerts, mostly classical; tickets required

RECREATION

People who live in Manhattan know that you can do just about anything in New York that can be done anywhere else; and then some! Whether it's batting cages, tennis courts, or bocce ball, chances are that New York has it. You just have to know where to look.

BADMINTON

New York Badminton Club (646/271-3228)

BASEBALL

Baseball Center NYC (202 W 74th St, 212/362-0344)
Central Park (212/628-1036): 26 ball fields throughout the park
Field House at Chelsea Piers (23rd St at Hudson River, 212/336-6500)

> **Jazz at Lincoln Center**
> **Jazz at Lincoln Center** is actually at the Time Warner Center (10 Columbus Circle; take the JAZZ elevator). The managing and artistic director is none other than jazz trumpeter Wynton Marsalis. He and his orchestra are featured regularly; other nights might bring a surprise guest appearance or up and coming musicians. **Dizzy's Club Coca-Cola** (212/258-9595) is the venue for it all, with great food to accompany the great music.

BASKETBALL
BasketBall City (Pier 36 at South St, 212/233-5050)
Field House at Chelsea Piers (23rd St at Hudson River, 212/336-6500)

BILLIARDS
Amsterdam Billiards and Bar (110 E 11th St, 212/995-0333)
Slate Billiards (54 W 21st St, 212/989-0096)

BOCCE BALL
Bryant Park (Ave of the Americas bet 40th and 42nd St)
Il Vagabondo (351 E 62nd St, 212/832-9221)
Saggio (829 W 181st St, 212/795-3080)

BOWLING
300 New York (Chelsea Piers, 23rd St at Hudson River, 212/835-2695)
Bowlmor Lanes and Greenwich Village Country Club (110 University Pl, 212/255-8188): indoor mini-golf
Bowlmor Lanes (222 W 44th St, 212/680-0012): carnival; Boomer Esiason's Stadium Grill
Frames (Port Authority Bus Terminal, 550 Ninth Ave, 212/268-6909): plus billiards, games, and dance clubs

CHESS, CHECKERS, AND BACKGAMMON
Bryant Park (Ave of the Americas bet 40th and 42nd St)
Chess NYC (82 W 3rd St, 212/475-8130): chess instruction for all ages
Washington Square Park (foot of Fifth Ave, below 8th St)

CLIMBING
Field House at Chelsea Piers (23rd St at Hudson River, 212/336-6500)

GOLF
Golf Club at Chelsea Piers (Pier 59, 23rd St at Hudson River, 212/336-6400)

ICE SKATING
Citi Pond at Bryant Park (Ave of the Americas at 42nd St, 212/661-6640)
Riverbank State Park (679 Riverside Dr, 212/694-3642): state-of-the-art facilities; summer roller skating

Rockefeller Center (Fifth Ave bet 49th and 50th St, 212/632-3975)

Sky Rink at Chelsea Piers (Pier 61, 23rd St at Hudson River, 212/336-6100): year round

Trump Lasker Rink (Central Park at E 107th St, 917/492-3856)

Trump Wollman Rink (Central Park, 59th St at Ave of the Americas, 212/439-6900)

SLEDDING

Central Park, Pilgrim Hill (Fifth Ave at 72nd St) and **Cedar Hill** (Fifth Ave bet 76th and 79th St)

Morningside Park (115th St at Morningside Dr)

Riverside Park (91st St at Riverside Dr)

SOCCER

Field House at Chelsea Piers (23rd St at Hudson River, 212/336-6500)

SWIMMING

Asphalt Green Aqua Center (1750 York Ave, 212/369-8890)

Tony Dapolito Recreation Center (1 Clarkson St, 212/242-5418): indoor and outdoor pools

Vanderbilt YMCA (224 E 47th St, 212/912-2500)

TENNIS

Central Park Tennis Center (Central Park W, bet 94th and 96th St, 212/280-0205)

Midtown Tennis Club (341 Eighth Ave, 212/989-8572)

Riverside Tennis Association (96th St and Riverside Dr, 212/978-0277): ten red clay courts

Sutton East Tennis Center (488 E 60th St, 212/751-3452): closed in summer

USTA Billie Jean King National Tennis Center (Flushing Meadows, Queens, 718/760-6200)

Vanderbilt Tennis and Fitness Club (Grand Central Terminal, 42nd St at Vanderbilt Ave, 212/599-6500): one indoor court

Yorkville Tennis Club (1725 York Ave, 212/987-0301)

SPECTATOR SPORTS

Some people associate New York with fine food and expensive stores, while

---

Sports Activities

If you have a child who wants to climb a wall, take batting practice, or kick a soccer ball, then go to the **Field House at Chelsea Piers**. Located on the far west side of Manhattan, between 17th and 23rd streets, this is a remarkable complex. Call 212/336-6500 or go to chelseapiers.com for more information. They offer camps, scholarships, and plenty of sports programs for adults, too.

A Walk in the Park

Nothing can compare to Central Park in size or attractions, but here are several other relaxing spots throughout the city:

Greenacre Park (51st St bet Second and Third Ave): A beautiful waterfall is surrounded by lush greenery.

High Line Park (parallels Tenth Ave bet Gansevoort and 34th St): built along a 1.45-mile-long elevated defunct rail line.

Hudson River Park (Battery Park City to 59th St): biking, skating, rock climbing, water sports

Jefferson Market Garden (Greenwich Ave bet 10th St and Ave of the Americas): best viewed from May to October; one-third acre

Paley Park (53rd St bet Fifth and Madison Ave): The former site of the legendary Stork Club with a 20-foot-tall section of the Berlin Wall and an enticing waterfall.

Sutton Place Park (57th St at East River): comprised of five tiny parks with a wild boar statue, kids' sandbox, and view of the Queensboro Bridge

Teardrop Park (Battery Park City, River Terrace between Murray and Warren St): lots of rocks for sitting, walking, and climbing.

West Side Community Garden (89th St bet Amsterdam and Columbus Ave): floral amphitheater, massive spring tulip display

---

others link the city with the Yankees, the Mets, the Knicks, the Rangers, and other professional sports teams. The New York area is home to more than half a dozen professional sports teams; although only basketball's Knicks and hockey's Rangers actually play in Manhattan. Home field for the city's two pro football teams, the Jets and the Giants, is across the river in New Jersey, while pro baseball's Yankees and Mets play in the New York City boroughs of The Bronx and Queens, respectively.

If you want tickets to a professional sporting event, plan as far in advance as possible. Each team's website has detailed information about schedules, tickets, and how to get there.

A word of warning: New York fans are like no others. They are loud, rude, and typically very knowledgeable about their teams and sports in general. If you're cheering against the home team, keep your voice down; and your head, too!

BASEBALL

New York Mets (Citi Field, Flushing Meadows, Queens, newyork.mets.mlb.com)

New York Yankees (Yankee Stadium, 1 E 161st St, The Bronx, newyork.yankees.mlb.com)

BASKETBALL

New York Knicks (Madison Square Garden, nba.com/knicks)

New York Liberty (Prudential Center, Newark, NJ, wnba.com/liberty)

FOOTBALL

The Giants and the Jets share a state-of-the-art sports facility across the Hudson River.

New York Giants (MetLife Stadium, East Rutherford, NJ, giants.com)

New York Jets (MetLife Stadium, East Rutherford, NJ, newyorkjets.com)

HOCKEY

New York Rangers (Madison Square Garden, rangers.nhl.com)

WHERE TO GO

GREAT VIEWS, PHOTO OPS

There are thousands of great views and photo opportunities in every part of New York. If you're a photographer or just want a memorable "only in New York" photo, then here are some favorite views and backdrops worth checking out.

Battery Park Esplanade (length of Battery Park City along the Hudson River)

Brooklyn Bridge (anywhere along its length)

Central Park rock outcrops (just inside the park's southwest corner)

The Cloisters Museum and Gardens (Fort Tryon Park)

LOVE Sculpture (Ave of the Americas at 55th St)

Morris-Jumel Mansion grounds (65 Jumel Terrace, in Harlem Heights)

New York Harbor (particularly from the Staten Island Ferry)

Patience and Fortitude (lion statues in front of New York Public Library, 455 Fifth Ave)

Prometheus Statue (Rockefeller Plaza, west of Fifth Ave bet 49th and 50th St)

Roosevelt Island (anywhere on the west side, particularly Lighthouse Park)

Statue of Liberty (off Battery Park in New York Harbor)

Wall Street Bull (bronze sculpture, Broadway at Bowling Green)

Washington Arch (Washington Square Park, foot of Fifth Ave in Greenwich Village)

IN THE MIDDLE OF THE NIGHT

New York bills itself as "the city that never sleeps," and many who live here are night people. They include not only actors and artists, but also those who clean and maintain the huge office buildings, put together morning newspapers

---

New York City Recreation Center Memberships

For $100 to $150 a year (just $25 for senior citizens over 62 and free for children under 18), you can use the city's wonderful recreation centers, including indoor pools and excellent facilities, and sign up for all sorts of classes. Go to nycgovparks.org and click on "Facilities" and "Recreation Centers" for descriptions of each center and its offerings.

> ## Running
>
> Central Park may come to mind first if you're looking for a running trail in New York City. There are many other routes, ask your concierge or check at a sporting goods store for suggestions and definitely don't overlook the Brooklyn Bridge.
>
> **City Running Tours** (877/415-0058, cityrunningtours.com) organizes group runs throughout the borough and a monthly Brooklyn Brewery run
>
> **Fun on Foot** (funonfoot.com) maintains a list of running clubs and groups

and newscasts, and work the night shift at hospitals and other businesses that never close.

In general, stores and restaurants in Soho, Tribeca, and Greenwich Village stay open later than those in the rest of the city. The restaurants and mom-and-pop operations along Broadway on the Upper West Side and on Lexington and Third avenues on the Upper East Side also tend to keep late hours. As with everything else, call before setting out.

WITH KIDS

Remember that New York can be totally overwhelming for children. (The same is true for adults!) Don't push too hard and plan to retreat to quiet spaces from time to time. Remember, too, that New York can be a wonderland for all ages, if you know where to go. Look inside toy stores and bookstores for seasonal calendars, and obtain a copy of *New York Metro Parents* (nymetroparents.com) or one of the other free parenting magazines published in New York. Some good websites for families and children in New York:

gocitykids.parentsconnect.com
ny.com/kids

I've suggested things to do with kids in several categories: entertainment, museums, and sights; restaurants; and toy stores and bookstores. In many cases, these places are described in detail in other parts of this book. Of course, children's interests can vary dramatically, so I've inevitably included places that one child will love and another might find boring. I'll let you be the judge of that! I also recommend looking at the Children's Books, Children's Clothing Stores, and Toy Stores sections in Chapter VI.

ENTERTAINMENT, MUSEUMS, AND SIGHTS

BUSY LITTLE ONES

92nd Street Y (Parenting Center, 1395 Lexington Ave, 212/415-5611)

Central Park Zoo and Tisch Children's Zoo (behind The Arsenal in Central Park at E 64th St, 212/439-6500)

Children's Museum of the Arts (103 Charlton St, 212/274-0986)

Field Station Dinosaurs (One Dinosaur Way, Secaucus, NJ, 855/999-9010)

Friedsam Memorial Carousel (behind The Arsenal in Central Park at E 64th St)

The Heimbold Family Children's Playing and Learning Center (Scandinavia House: The Nordic Center in America, 58 Park Ave, 212/879-9779)

Le Carrousel (Bryant Park, Ave of the Americas at 42nd St)

LEGO Store (Rockefeller Center, 620 Fifth Ave, 212/245-5973)

Pier 62 Carousel (Hudson River Park at 23rd St, 212/627-2020): 33 hand-carved animals

MUSEUMS WITH A FAMILY FOCUS

American Museum of Natural History (Central Park W at 79th St, 212/769-5100)

Children's Museum of Manhattan (212 W 83rd St, 212/721-1223)

Dyckman Farmhouse Museum (4881 Broadway, 212/304-9422)

Fraunces Tavern Museum (54 Pearl St, 212/425-1778)

Liberty Science Center (Liberty State Park, Jersey City, NJ, 201/200-1000)

Lower East Side Tenement Museum (108 Orchard St, 212/431-0233)

Madame Tussauds (234 W 42nd St, 212/512-9600)

Museum of the City of New York (1220 Fifth Ave, 212/534-1672)

New York City Fire Museum (278 Spring St, 212/691-1303)

New-York Historical Society, DiMenna Children's History Museum (170 Central Park W, 212/873-3400)

Seaport Museum (12 Fulton St, 212/748-8786)

Sony Wonder Technology Lab (550 Madison Ave, 212/833-8100)

FOR TWEENS AND TEENS

Dylan's Candy Bar (1011 Third Ave, 646/735-0078)

Field House at Chelsea Piers (23rd St at Hudson River, 212/336-6500)

Frames (Port Authority Bus Terminal, 550 Ninth Ave, 212/268-6909): bowling, games

Madame Tussauds (234 W 42nd St, 212/512-9600)

Museum of Comic and Cartoon Art (128 E 63rd St, 212/838-2560)

On Location Tours (212/683-2027)

The Shark (South Street Seaport, 212/742-1969): speedboat harbor ride

Sony Wonder Technology Lab (550 Madison Ave, 212/833-8100)

NEW YORK CLASSICS

Bronx Zoo (2300 Southern Blvd, The Bronx, 718/367-1010)

Sailing

Enjoy the waters around Manhattan without having to share the ride with hundreds of others on the 82-foot *Shearwater*, a restored 1929 schooner that holds up to 48 passengers. Scheduled trips and charters begin and end at North Cove Marina.

Kids will enjoy the 158-foot topsail schooner *Clipper City*. This 150 passenger tall ship departs from Pier 17 at the South Street Seaport. Make reservations for either boat at manhattanbysail.com or call 212/619-0885.

Join the Circus!

If you'd like to fly through the air with the greatest of ease, like the famed daring young man on the flying trapeze, you can make it happen at **Circus Warehouse** (53-21 Vernon Blvd, Long Island City, NY; 212/751-2174). It is the only professional training facility in the New York area for aspiring circus stars. Weekend and evening professional and recreational classes are taught by pros from Cirque du Soleil and Ringling Brothers; Circus Warehouse also takes their shows on the road to private parties and events.

Empire State Building (350 Fifth Ave, 212/736-3100)
New York Hall of Science (47-01 111th St, Queens, 718/699-0005)
Statue of Liberty and Ellis Island (New York Harbor, 212/363-3200)
United Nations (First Ave bet 42nd and 47th St, 212/963-4440)
Yankee Stadium (1 E 161st St, The Bronx, 212/926-5337)

PLAYS, MOVIES, AND TV

American Museum of Natural History IMAX Theater (Central Park W at 79th St, 212/769-5100)
The Lion King (Minskoff Theater, 1515 Broadway)
NBC Studio Tour (30 Rockefeller Plaza, 49th St bet Fifth Ave and Ave of the Americas, 212/664-3700)
Paley Center for Media (25 W 52nd St, 212/621-6800)

BOATS AND OTHER TRANSPORTATION

Circle Line Sightseeing Tours (Pier 83, 42nd St at Hudson River, 212/563-3200)
New York Transit Museum (Boerum Pl at Schermerhorn St, Brooklyn, 718/694-1600)
Roosevelt Island Tram (Second Ave bet 59th and 60th St): inexpensive
Staten Island Ferry (Whitehall Ferry Terminal, south end of Manhattan): free

RESTAURANTS

Cercle Rouge (241 West Broadway, 212/226-6174): weekend brunch and magic show
Peels (325 Bowery, 646/602-7015)
Shake Shack (Madison Square Park, Madison Ave at 23rd St; 366 Columbus Ave; 154 E 86th St; 691 Eighth Ave; and 215 Murray St)
Union Square Cafe (21 E 16th St, 212/243-4020)

GREAT BASICS

EJ's Luncheonette (1271 Third Ave, 212/472-0600)
Jackson Hole Burgers (232 E 64th St, 212/371-7187; 521 Third Ave, 212/679-3264; 1611 Second Ave, 212/737-8788; 1270 Madison Ave, 212/427-2820; and 517 Columbus Ave, 212/362-5177)

John's Pizzeria (260 W 44th St, 212/391-7560 and other locations)
Lombardi's (32 Spring St, 212/941-7994)
Two Boots (42 Ave A, 212/254-1919 and other locations)

GREAT DESSERTS

Bubby's (120 Hudson St, 212/219-0666)
Cafe Lalo (201 W 83rd St, 212/496-6031)
ChikaLicious (203 E 10th St, 212/995-9511)
Peanut Butter & Co. (240 Sullivan St, 212/677-3995)
Serendipity 3 (225 E 60th St, 212/838-3531)
Veniero's (342 E 11th St, 212/674-7070)

THEME RESTAURANTS

Barking Dog Luncheonette (1678 Third Ave, 212/831-1800 and other locations)
Brooklyn Diner USA (212 W 57th St, 212/977-1957 and 155 W 43rd St, 212/265-5400)
Hard Rock Cafe (1501 Broadway, 212/489-6565)
Jekyll and Hyde (91 Seventh Ave, 212/989-7701)
Ninja New York (25 Hudson St, 212/274-8500)

BOOKSTORES

Bank Street Bookstore (2875 Broadway, 212/678-1654)
Scholastic Store (557 Broadway, 212/343-6166)

TOY STORES

Boomerang Toys (119 West Broadway, 212/226-7650 and 1 North End Ave, 212/227-7271)
E.A.T. Gifts (1062 Madison Ave, 212/861-2544)
F.A.O. Schwarz (767 Fifth Ave, 212/644-9400)
Kidding Around (60 W 15th St, 212/645-6337 and Grand Central Terminal, 42nd St at Vanderbilt Ave, 212/972-8697)
Toy Tokyo (91 Second Ave, 212/673-5424)
Toys "R" Us (Times Square, 1514 Broadway, 646/366-8800)
West Side Kids (498 Amsterdam Ave, 212/496-7282)

Just as some things are fun to do with kids, there are other activities that you should *not* do with them. Check your destination's age requirement before bringing

---

Father Duffy Square

The focal point of Father Duffy Square is the glowing ruby-red stairs, which are built mostly of structural-strength glass. The 27 wide steps seat 1,500 (if everyone gets cozy) and offer a commanding view down Broadway. It's a great place to meet friends or come solo. Don't forget your latte or lunch, as eating and drinking are welcome here. LED lights bring the stairs to life at night, and an innovative heating system keeps them snow- and ice-free.

Roller-Skating Rink

Looking for a roller-skating rink in Manhattan? You'll need to look a little further. The last of the hardwood rinks has closed, but head over to Staten Island to **RollerJam USA** (236 Richmond Valley Rd, 718/605-6600) which includes an entertainment center and arcade. Check the schedule for sessions and classes. DJs keep the pace moving with lively tunes. For special events, book the party room, which serves beer and wine to legal-age adults.

---

the kids. If you're going shopping at a perpetually crowded place like Zabar's or Fairway, don't take kids, or keep a firm grip on their hands if you do. The latter holds true just about everywhere in New York; it's easy for a young one to get lost in a crowd! And remember that kids tire more quickly than adults. Chances are you'll do a lot of walking, and they're taking two or three steps for every one of yours! As the *New York Times* once put it, "Baby miles are like dog years."

Finally, it's a challenge to tote an infant or toddler in New York. While hundreds of thousands of children are born and raised in the city, visitors who are accustomed to carting children through malls in strollers and around town in car seats may have trouble here. Many places, including the subway system, are not exactly stroller-accessible. Taxis with functioning seatbelts have become much easier to find in recent years, but ones with children's car seats are a rarity. Taxi drivers must allow passengers to install car seats.

FOR FREE

Even the most frugal and resourceful visitors often feel as if they're bleeding money. ("Didn't we just get $200 out of the ATM!?") Still, you can find some good deals and do a lot of sightseeing for free.

MUSEUMS AND SIGHTS

The Museum of Modern Art reached the $25 ceiling for adult admission and other museums' rates are climbing. Still, you can find some free or reduced price museums and sights in New York; and remember, most have days and times with pay-what-you-wish or free admission. They include:

American Folk Art Museum (2 Lincoln Square)

American Numismatic Society (75 Varick St, 11th floor)

Cathedral Church of Saint John the Divine (1047 Amsterdam Ave)

Drawing Center (36 Wooster St)

Federal Hall National Memorial (26 Wall St)

Federal Reserve Bank (33 Liberty St)

Forbes Magazine Galleries (62 Fifth Ave)

General Grant National Monument (Riverside Park)

Hispanic Society of America (613 W 155th St)

Museum at FIT (Seventh Ave at 27th St) .

Museum of American Illustration and Museum of Comic and Cartoon Art (128 E 63rd St)

National Museum of the American Indian (Alexander Hamilton U.S. Custom House)

New York Public Library (455 Fifth Ave)
New York Transit Museum Gallery Annex (Grand Central Terminal, 42nd St at Vanderbilt Ave)
Sony Wonder Technology Lab (550 Madison Ave)
Staten Island Ferry (Whitehall Ferry Terminal)
Theodore Roosevelt Birthplace (28 E 20th St)
Tibet House (22 W 15th St)
Trinity Church (74 Trinity Pl)

Many places admit children under 12 for free. Active-duty military personnel in uniform are admitted free to the Empire State Building, and Smithsonian Institution members are admitted free to the Cooper-Hewitt, National Design Museum. Although it definitely isn't free, you can tour both The Cloisters Museum and Gardens and The Metropolitan Museum of Art on the same day for one admission price. You can also get a discount on admission to the Jewish Museum if you show a ticket stub from the Museum of Jewish Heritage (and vice versa). You will find addresses, phone numbers, and more information on these and other museums in Chapter III.

FOR TICKETS

Nowhere else in the world will you find such a wealth of performing arts. And no trip to New York is complete without taking in at least one play, musical, ballet, concert, or opera.

The trick, of course, is getting tickets. People have written entire books about how and where to get tickets, while others have made lucrative careers out of procuring them for out-of-towners. I've provided a variety of approaches for getting theater tickets and to find out about other performances. Keep your eye out for student and other discounts, but be aware that good deals for the best shows and performances are few and far between.

BROADWAY

People often have different things in mind when they say they want to see a show. Some may have their hearts set on great seats at a Saturday night performance of the hottest show on Broadway, while others are willing to sit anywhere and see anything. A lot of people fall somewhere between those extremes. In addition, some are willing to pay whatever it takes to see the show

---

Theater Tickets

I'm often asked about reliable ticket brokers. **Americana Tickets** (800/833-3121, 212/581-6660, americanatickets.com) has been recognized for setting the standard. The third generation of the Radler family is outstanding to deal with! Americana offers availability of the specific theater, sports, and concert tickets you want at all price points and discounts available for current, next day, and later dates. Americana's new retail store is located in Times Square (Broadway at 47th St) and their main headquarters is in the New York Marriott Marquis (Broadway at 46th St). In Times Square, look for Americana's Street Team wearing black shirts printed with the word "tickets."

they want, while others just won't go if they can't pay less than full price. If the main purpose of your visit to the city is to see a particular show (or shows), make sure you have the tickets you want before leaving home so you're not disappointed.

Box Offices and Phone Orders—If you want to save money and pick your seat, go directly to the theater's box office with cash or a major credit card. Ask to see a diagram of the theater if it isn't posted, although most theaters are small enough to ensure that every seat has a good view. The best time to try is midweek. You can also ask the box office if day-of-performance cancellations or rush tickets will be released. (See "Hot Deals" box below.)

If you're willing to spend a little extra money and let a computer pick the "best available" seat, call the number or go to the website listed and have your credit card ready. Most numbers will be for **Telecharge** (212/239-6200 or 800/432-7250, telecharge.com) or **TicketMaster** (800/745-3000, ticketmaster.com). Both charge a handling fee in addition to the ticket price.

Be forewarned: full-price tickets to Broadway shows typically cost $100 and sometimes fetch well over $300. Moreover, if the play or musical you want to see is hot, it may be sold out the entire time you're in New York. In fact, a few really hot shows may be sold out months in advance.

Care-Tix—If you have your heart set on a particular show and cost is no obstacle, **Broadway Cares/Equity Fights AIDS** sells house seats for sold-out Broadway and off-Broadway shows for twice the box-office price. The extra money goes to a good cause and is a tax-deductible contribution. Call 212/840-0770 and ask for Care-Tix or visit broadwaycares.org.

Hot Deals

Every theater does things differently, so you really need to get accurate, up-to-date information if you want to secure in-demand tickets at lower prices. Some theaters have lotteries a couple of hours before each performance for seats in the first few rows. Some offer Standing Room Only (SRO) tickets. Some give discount tickets only to students, while others have so-called rush tickets available for certain performances. To make sense of it all, go to talkinbroadway.com and click on "All That Chat," then "Rush." Be sure to bring lots of patience, a student ID, and enough cash to cover whatever tickets you might wind up buying.

TKTS Outlets—If you want to see a Broadway show, are flexible, and have some free time, go to one of the TKTS outlets in Manhattan. Operated by the not-for-profit Theatre Development Fund, these outlets sell whatever tickets happen to be left for various shows on the day of performance for half price or less (plus a $4 per-ticket charge). The most popular TKTS outlet is easily located as a result of some snazzy construction. Look for the ruby-red glass stairs at Father Duffy Square (47th St and Broadway) where 12 ticket windows are tucked underneath the steps.

For matinee performances, tickets are sold Wednesday and Saturday from 10 to 2 and Sundays from 11 to 3. For evening performances, tickets are sold Monday through Saturday from 3 to 8 (from 2 on Tuesday) and Sunday from 3 until an hour before the latest curtain time for show tickets being sold that day. A less crowded TKTS outlet is located in Lower Manhattan at the intersection of Front and John streets, just below South Street Seaport's main plaza. It's open Monday through Saturday from 11 to 6, and Sunday in summer months from 11 to 4. Matinee tickets at this location go on sale the day *before* a performance. To see what shows are available at the TKTS locations, you can download their free app which shows in real time what shows are available or see the same information online at tdf.org/tktslive. Tickets may be purchased with major credit cards as well as cash.

Bring the Kids!

It used to be that everyone dressed up for the theater and nobody would think of bringing a young child. Now the pre-teen set is seen in almost every Broadway theater, especially at performances of *The Lion King; Annie; Spider-Man, Turn Off the Dark;* and *Newsies.* Some theaters thoughtfully provide booster seats! Here's some advice from this adult: choose productions your child will appreciate, and leave promptly if your little one behaves disruptively. I know you paid a lot for that ticket, but so did the rest of us!

The Theatre Development Fund also offers extremely good deals to its members on tickets to theater and other performances. If you're a student, member of the clergy or armed forces (serving or retired), teacher, union member, or performing artist, go to the Fund's website for more information. TDF acquires a small number of deeply discounted tickets for people in wheelchairs and their companion or attendant. Call the theater box office directly for more information.

Off-Broadway and off-off-Broadway—In part because staging a Broadway production has become almost prohibitively expensive, off-Broadway and off-off-Broadway theaters have really taken *off.* Thanks to a glut of talented actors and actresses in New York, such theater is typically excellent and often innovative. Tickets for off-Broadway and off-off-Broadway productions tend to be significantly less expensive.

OPERA AND CLASSICAL MUSIC

No other city in the world has as many musical events to choose from as New York! Contact the **92nd Street Y** (212/415-5500, 92y.org) if you're interested in chamber music or recitals by top performers. Otherwise, here's how to find schedule and ticket information at New York's top venues:

Carnegie Hall—Individual musicians, out-of-town orchestras, and chamber-music ensembles perform at Carnegie Hall all year. For detailed information about performances, rush tickets, same-day student, senior, and partial-view ticket discounts, call 212/247-7800 or go to carnegiehall.org. A limited number of partial-view seats are available for $10 on the day of each performance.

Metropolitan Opera—The season for the internationally renowned Met runs from fall through spring, and ticket sales are broken into three periods. Try the box office (212/362-6000, metoperafamily.org) at Lincoln Center from 10 to 8 (noon to 6 on Sunday). Be aware that choice seats can cost as much as

---

Online Tickets

Here are some better-known websites for event tickets in the city (and sometimes elsewhere). Check for discount programs associated with Costco, AAA, and other membership cards. Compare prices from a couple of sites to make sure you are getting the best deal.

Broadway.org (information on all New York shows)

BroadwayBox.com (discounted theater, sports events, and concerts)

High5tix.org ($5 tickets for teens from 13 to 18 to music, dance, theater, and visual-arts events)

Kidsnightonbroadway.com (For one week each spring, kids from 6-18 attend free with a full-paying adult at participating shows.)

StubHub.com (Buy or sell any tickets to any event, anywhere.)

$375! If you have a little time on your hands, there are bargains to be had for members, subscribers, and students. Standing Room Only (SRO) tickets are often available the day of the performance.

New York City Opera—The season for this exceptional but often overshadowed opera runs September through April. For schedule, tickets, and venue information, visit the opera's website (nycopera.com) or call 212/870-5600.

New York Philharmonic—The Philharmonic's season runs from September through June at Avery Fisher Hall in Lincoln Center. For schedule and ticket information, go to the Philharmonic's website (nyphil.org) or call 212/875-5656. If you would rather attend a performance during the day and save a bit, ask about reduced-price tickets to open rehearsals. Rush tickets may also be available.

DANCE AND BALLET

New York is home to several world-class companies and a great many smaller ones. They include:

Alvin Ailey American Dance Theater (212/405-9000, alvinailey.org): The Alvin Ailey American Dance Theater is at the **Joan Weill Center for Dance** (405 W 55th St).

American Ballet Theater (212/477-3030, abt.org)

Dance Theatre of Harlem (212/690-2800, dancetheatreofharlem.org)

New York City Ballet (212/870-5656, nycballet.com)

New York Live Arts (212/691-6500, newyorklivearts.org)

Paul Taylor Dance Company (212/431-5562, ptdc.org)

A number of major companies perform at the **New York City Center** (131 W 55th Street). Contact **CityTix** (212/581-1212, nycitycenter.org), or visit an individual dance company's website for information about tickets and upcoming performances.

TELEVISION SHOW TAPINGS

There is one kind of ticket almost everybody wants to get in New York: one that allows you to become part of the studio audience for one of the many TV talk shows filmed here. I've listed some of the most popular shows with a brief description for obtaining tickets; *Dr. Oz, Live! With Kelly and Michael*, and other shows have similar policies. Check their websites for particulars.

The Daily Show with Jon Stewart —These tickets must be ordered well in advance. Simply go to thedailyshow.com and complete the online reservation form. The website for **The Colbert Report** is colbertnation.com, and the method is the same, although tickets are not easy to acquire. Standby tickets are sometimes available, so check when you are online. Bring identification, as audience members must be at least 18 years of age.

Late Show with David Letterman —These remain among the hottest tickets in town, and you must be at least 18 to qualify. You can apply by filling out a form at cbs.com/lateshow or go in person to the Ed Sullivan Theater box office (1697 Broadway, bet 53rd and 54th St) between 9:30 and 12:30 on weekdays or 10 to 6 on weekends. Expect to wait at least six to eight months and probably longer. Standby tickets are sometimes distributed at 11 on the morning of a show

Saturday Night Live —Year in and year out, these are the hardest tickets of all to get. A lottery is held every August from emails collected during the preceding 12 months, and each winner gets two tickets. If you want to be included in the lottery, send an email to snltickets@nbcuni.com. Standby tickets for the 8 p.m. dress rehearsal and the 11:30 p.m. live show are available at 7 a.m. on the day of the show at the 49th Street entrance to 30 Rockefeller Plaza.

The View —This women's gabfest is taped Monday through Thursday at ABC Studios on Manhattan's Upper West Side (320 W 66th St). Go to abc.go.com/daytime/theview/tickets to request tickets for a specific date at least three months in advance. If you're in town and feel lucky, go by the studio between 8 and 9 on a morning when they're taping and pick up a standby number. You must be at least 16 years old to attend.

FOR A ROMANTIC INTERLUDE

Whether you're falling in love for the first time or celebrating a wedding anniversary, New York can be one of the most romantic places in the world to celebrate. If you're in the mood for love or want to create a mood that's just right for romance, try the following:

Join the Audience!

Look for NBC's **Today Show** crowd on the sidewalk along 49th Street between Fifth Avenue and Avenue of the Americas. People show up before dawn, although cameras don't start rolling until 7 a.m. ABC's **Good Morning America** welcomes audiences Monday through Friday for their 7 to 9 a.m. live show. See their website (abcnews.go.com/gma) for ticket information. A standby line forms outside the Times Square studio (44th St and Broadway), alongside those with tickets. Fans of CBS's **The Early Show** may stop by the Early Show plaza (Fifth Ave and 59th St) before 7:15 a.m. to join the audience. Backstage tours of the studio are conducted after the show. No tickets are needed.

Puppet Show

The **Swedish Cottage Marionette Theatre** is a whimsical structure in Central Park (79th St at West Dr, 212/988-9093) that serves as a puppeteer's venue for kids' performances. The charming theater seats 100 and a party room accommodates 30 special guests. Reservations are required and show times vary. The cottage has an interesting past. It was imported in 1876 as Sweden's exhibit for the Centennial Exposition in Philadelphia and brought to Central Park a year later. It has served as a tool shed, comfort station, and entomological lab. The current use is by far its best role!

- Drinks by the fireplace followed by dinner at **One if by Land, Two if by Sea** (17 Barrow St)
- A summertime dinner in the garden at **Barbetta** (321 W 46th St)
- Dinner at the discreet and classy **Le Périgord** (405 E 52nd St)
- Drinks at **Campbell Apartment**, an elegant spot tucked away in a corner of Grand Central Terminal (just east of Vanderbilt Ave)
- A late-night visit to the **Empire State Building Observation Deck** (Fifth Ave between 33rd and 34th St)
- A walk across the Brooklyn Bridge is a must!
- Watching the sun rise from the **Brooklyn Bridge**, the **Battery Park Esplanade**, **Lighthouse Park** on Roosevelt Island, or the deck of the **Staten Island Ferry**
- A visit to the **Winter Garden** (World Financial Center)
- A picnic lunch overlooking the Hudson River from **The Cloisters Museum and Gardens**
- A stroll through the splendid lobby of the **Waldorf Astoria New York**
- An early evening spent listening to classical music from the balcony of the **The Metropolitan Museum of Art**'s Great Hall
- A rowboat or gondola ride on **Central Park Lake** or a nighttime sail around Manhattan
- An evening carriage ride through **Central Park**, especially after a fresh snow has fallen, or a springtime stroll on some of its less traveled paths

FOR PARTIES AND SPECIAL EVENTS

If you're looking for the perfect place to hold a wedding reception, bar mitzvah, or gala event for thousands, New York inevitably has the right place ... and the people to put it together. The trick, of course, is finding them. The other trick is paying for the event!

If you want to throw a party at your favorite museum, restaurant, hotel, or bar, by all means ask. Many museum spaces, including the **Mount Vernon Hotel Museum and Garden**; the **Cooper-Hewitt, National Design Museum**; and the Theodore Roosevelt Rotunda at the **American Museum of Natural History** (complete with its dinosaur display) can be rented for parties and other events. Many restaurants have spaces allocated for private parties, as do most hotels.

Some of my favorite private party rooms in New York are at **Barbetta** (321 W 46th St), **FireBird** (365 W 46th St), **Four Seasons** (99 E 52nd St), **Gramercy Tavern** (42 E 20th St), **Le Périgord** (405 E 52nd St), **One if by Land, Two if by Sea** (17 Barrow St), **Serendipity 3** (225 E 60th St), and **Tribeca Grill** (375 Greenwich St).

Some venues available for special events take care of all the catering, while others simply provide the space. This list should give you an idea of the breadth of spaces available: **New York Public Library** (455 Fifth Ave), **Studio 450** (450 W 31st St), **Astra** (979 Third Ave), **The Loeb Boathouse** (in Central Park), **Pier 60** (at Chelsea Piers), and **91** (Upper Crust, 91 Horatio St). Catering is optional at the **New York Botanical Garden** (in The Bronx) and the **Pratt Mansions** (1027 Fifth Ave).

Information, Please!

311 is New York City's all-purpose information number. If you need to know how to rent a baseball field in Central Park, how to sign up for a Gracie Mansion tour, how to pay a parking fine, or anything related to New York City (including loud music and noise complaints), operators are standing by. Outside of the local area, call 212/639-9675. Dial 911 for emergencies.

Before forging ahead with planning a party in New York, be aware that it's going to cost a great deal of money. I'm talking *really* big bucks. You can save money by avoiding Saturday evening, holding your numbers down, and throwing your party in the off months of July and August or between January and early April. Some venues and caterers may negotiate on price, but don't expect any great or even particularly good deals. Make your reservations at least two months and as far as two years in advance.

FOR RESTROOMS

Nothing's more bothersome than not being able to find a bathroom when one is needed. By law, public buildings are required to have public restrooms.

Seasonal Activities

Some things can only be done in New York if you're in town at the right time.

■ If you are planning a trip in spring or summer, get tickets to a baseball game at **Yankee Stadium** (newyork.yankees.mlb.com) or **Citi Field**, home of the Mets (newyork.mets.mlb.com).

■ If you're in town during the summer, find out what's going on in **Central Park** (centralparknyc.org).

■ In the fall, get tickets to the **Metropolitan Opera** (metoperafamily.org).

■ If you're in town around Christmas, take the family to see the Christmas Spectacular at **Radio City Music Hall** (radiocity.com).

Sailing Lessons

Have you always wanted to learn how to sail? Strap on a life jacket and head to **Manhattan Sailing School** (385 South End Ave, Room 7-G, 212/786-0400). Programs, including hands-on experience, include basics, coastal cruising, racing, and jib sailing. Sailing school grads are eligible to join the Manhattan Sailing Club with access to two seasonal floating clubhouses.

They are not, however, required to be clean and safe.

Following is a list of bathrooms that meet at least minimal standards of safety and cleanliness. You may need to ask for directions or a key, but all are free to the public. As a general rule, try hotel lobbies, department stores, schools, theaters, municipal government buildings, churches, libraries, and even hospitals. **Starbucks** and other coffee house locations throughout the city are also good bets. Of course, if you have small children in tow, just about any store or restaurant will likely take pity.

Wherever you end up, be sure to follow a few safety tips. Leaving anything on the floor in a public restroom is a mistake, as purses and packages have a bad habit of disappearing while you're occupied! The same is true of items left hanging on the back of a stall door. Avoid deserted bathrooms, as well as those in parks (unless listed below) and most subway stations.

BELOW 14TH STREET

Castle Clinton National Monument (inside Battery Park)
National Museum of the American Indian (1 Bowling Green)
Trinity Church (Broadway at Wall St)
Federal Hall National Memorial (26 Wall St, at Broad St)
South Street Seaport (Fulton St at Water St)
Hotel on Rivington (107 Rivington St, bet Essex and Ludlow St)
Essex Street Market (120 Essex St, at Delancey St)
New York City Fire Museum (278 Spring St, bet Hudson and Varick St)
Strand Book Store (828 Broadway, at 12th St)

BETWEEN 14TH AND 42ND STREETS

Loehmann's (101 Seventh Ave, at 17th St)
ABC Carpet & Home (888 Broadway, at 19th St)
Macy's (Herald Square, 151 W 34th St, at Broadway)
Science, Industry, and Business Library (188 Madison Ave, at 34th St)
New York Public Library (455 Fifth Ave, bet 40th and 42nd St)
Bryant Park (40 W 40th St, at Ave of the Americas)
Grand Hyatt New York (109 E 42nd St, bet Park and Lexington Ave)
Grand Central Terminal (42nd St at Vanderbilt Ave)

MIDTOWN

United Nations (First Ave bet 42nd and 47th St)
Waldorf Astoria New York (301 Park Ave, at 50th St)

Saks Fifth Avenue (611 Fifth Ave, bet 49th and 50th St)

Rockefeller Center (concourse level, bet Fifth Ave and Ave of the Americas from 49th to 51st St)

Fendi (677 Fifth Ave, bet 53rd and 54th St)

Park Avenue Plaza (55 E 52nd St, at Madison Ave)

Henri Bendel (712 Fifth Ave, at 56th St)

Park Central New York (870 Seventh Ave, at 56th St)

Sony Wonder Technology Lab (550 Madison Ave, at 56th St)

UPPER EAST SIDE

McDonald's (1499 Third Ave, bet 57th and 58th St)

Bloomingdale's (1000 Third Ave, at 59th St)

Asia Society and Museum (725 Park Ave, at 70th St)

Ralph Lauren (867 Madison Ave, at 72nd St)

Marimekko (1262 Third Ave, at 73rd St)

Niketown New York (6 E 57th St, at Madison Ave)

92nd Street Y (1395 Lexington Ave, at 92nd St)

Charles A. Dana Discovery Center (in Central Park, Fifth Ave at 110th St)

UPPER WEST SIDE

Avery Fisher Hall (Lincoln Center, 65th St at Columbus Ave)

New York Public Library for the Performing Arts (Lincoln Center, 65th St at Broadway)

Cathedral Church of Saint John the Divine (1047 Amsterdam Ave, at 112th St)

FOR VISITORS WITH SPECIAL NEEDS

If you're coming to New York with a physical challenge, you ought to know about a couple of resources. First, get a copy of an exceptional guide to the city's cultural institutions that describes in detail facilities for people in wheelchairs, as well as the blind and deaf. This invaluable guide is available from **Hospital Audiences, Inc.** (hainyc.org); this organization also runs a hotline (212/575-7676) on weekdays. Second, the **Metropolitan Transportation Authority** has a very informative website (mta.info/accessibility). The **Mayor's Office for People with Disabilities** (212/788-2830, nyc.gov/html/mopd) is also a great resource. Finally, many Broadway theaters offer deeply discounted tickets for people in wheelchairs and their companions. Call individual theaters for more information.

INDEX

The index is in word-by-word alphabetical order. Business names that begin with a number precede the alphabetical list. All-cap entries indicate a main write-up or review for that listing. The main write-up is on the bold page number.

NOTES

NOTES

NOTES

NOTES

NOTES

NOTES